THE NONVIOLENT MESSIAH

THE NONVIOLENT MESSIAH

JESUS, Q, AND THE ENOCHIC TRADITION

SIMON J. JOSEPH

Fortress Press
Minneapolis

THE NONVIOLENT MESSIAH

Jesus, Q, and the Enochic Tradition

Cover image: Riviere, Briton (1840-1920). The Temptation in the Wilderness, 1898 Guildhall Art Gallery, London, Great Britain, Art Resources

Cover design: Erica Rieck

Library of Congress Cataloging-in-Publication Data

Print ISBN: 978-1-4514-7219-6

eBook ISBN: 978-1-4514-8443-4

The paper used in this publication meets the minimum requirements of American National Standard for Information Sciences — Permanence of Paper for Printed Library Materials, ANSI Z329.48-1984.

Manufactured in the U.S.A.

This book was produced using PressBooks.com, and PDF rendering was done by PrinceXML.

For Jennifer

Μακάριός ἐστιν ὅς ἐὰν μὴ σκανδαλισθῇ ἐν ἐμοί.

"Blessed Is Whoever Is Not Offended By Me" (Q 7:23)

CONTENTS

Preface xi

Part I.

1. Jesus, Q, and the Gospels 3
2. The Nonviolent Jesus 23
3. The God of War 51
   Divine Violence in the Hebrew Bible
4. The Apocalyptic Jesus 71
   Divine Violence in the New Testament

Part II.

5. Jesus Christos 93
6. The Christologies of Q 111
7. The Messianic Secret of the Son of Man 125
8. The Enochic Son of Man 145
9. The Enochic Adam 167

Part III.

10. The Kingdom, the Son, and the Gospel 197
11. Conclusion 229

Bibliography 233
Index of Names 317
Index of Ancient Sources 333

PREFACE

This study draws together the research results from a number of publications and earlier studies in Early Judaism and Christianity. My first book, *Jesus, Q, and the Dead Sea Scrolls: A Judaic Approach to Q* (WUNT 2/333), critically compared several major themes in Q 3–7 with relevant texts from the Dead Sea Scrolls. The results of this study suggested that Q is an ethnically Judean text with a distinctive compositional profile, social history, and Christology. Q is a remarkably coherent text in its appeal to certain themes: the role of John the Baptist, the kingdom of God, Jesus as the son of man, the coming judgment on "this generation." Its eschatological wisdom traditions are distinctive, as is its apparent lack of interest in Davidic messianism. Q 7:22, in particular, shares a number of Isaianic motifs with 4Q521, and this literary correspondence suggests some kind of relationship between the two faith-communities, as both shared similar messianic expectations. At the end of my book I noted that further work needed to be done on the Christology of Q and the Enoch traditions. Over the last few years I have published a number of articles on the identity, role, function, and influence of the mysterious Adamic figure who appears at the end of the *Animal Apocalypse* and the diverse ways in which Adamic traditions appear in Early Judaism and Christianity. It is my present conviction that these traditions represent an important key to unlocking some of the most obscure aspects of early Christianity.

Q is not, of course, a perfect solution to the Synoptic Problem, nor is it a simple cipher for "Jesus." Nonetheless, Q is a *useful* hypothesis (or corollary of the Two Document Hypothesis) and makes good historical sense of the data. I suspect that it is precisely because it is widely understood to be an *early* Palestinian *Jewish* text containing some of Jesus' most distinctive ethical teachings that it continues to hold the allegiance of most biblical scholars. We should not lose sight of the fact that Q also represents and reflects our best understanding of how the Jesus movement actually originated and developed: as a Jewish renewal movement in Judea and Galilee that subsequently expanded to greater Syria and the wider Roman Empire. Q is a useful tool because it anchors its traditions in Jesus' Palestinian Jewish movement and does not reflect or represent the mostly Gentile network of communities founded by Paul.

The present study draws together several streams of research into a new approach to historical Jesus study. It might seem like the height of *hubris* to presume that one could offer anything new in Jesus Research—it is not so fashionable to do old-fashioned historical study today and many regard the Quest for the historical Jesus as little more than a fool's errand—but it is my contention that Jesus' identity, role, teaching, and practice have still not been fully understood in their original Jewish contexts. What does it mean to call Jesus "messiah" or "Christ" when he does not appear to fulfill the role many Jews of his day seem to have anticipated a messianic figure to perform? What does it mean to describe Jesus as "nonviolent" when the New Testament calls for God's eschatological vengeance? The tensions between the historical Jesus' apparent nonviolence and the violence attributed to Davidic messianism—not to mention the violence of apocalyptic eschatology—reveal deep, even fundamental paradoxes and ambiguities in the biblical tradition.

Like many, I grew up with the Bible and, like many, I have long been disturbed by the "dark side" of the Bible. The problems are legion. This study represents my own attempt to wrestle with these questions. A few words, therefore, about its structure are in order.

The study is divided into three parts. The first part, chapters 1-4, is a series of extended methodological essays addressing definitional issues regarding Jesus, Q, the Gospel(s), and the relationship between the historical Jesus and violence. These essays are framed within broader conversations about religion and violence in the Hebrew Bible and the New Testament. The second part, chapters 5-9, represents a chronological reevaluation of Jewish messianism and the case for a "messianic Jesus." There is an incredible variety of messianic texts and templates in Second Temple Judaism—ranging from Davidic to prophetic, apocalyptic, sectarian, Enochic, son of man, new Adam, and Suffering Servant—and the historical Jesus' own particular "messianic" identity must be located (if it is to be located at all) on this spectrum. Accordingly, this study reexamines the Gospel accounts of Jesus' crucifixion and *titulus*, Paul's use of *Christos*, Q's apparent lack of messianic language, and the so-called "messianic secret" in the Gospel of Mark, in an attempt to determine whether these traditions might shed light on how and why Jesus first came to be understood as "messiah." What emerges from this study, largely as a result of renewed specialist interest in Enoch traditions, is that the *Parables*' "son of man" tradition and the *Animal Apocalypse*'s Adamic figure represent the two most relevant messianic models or templates for Jesus research. The third part of this study, chapter 10, tests and demonstrates this proposal by analyzing some of the most distinctive and historically reliable texts and themes in Q.

I do not presume to think that this study represents any last words on these subjects. Given the range and scope of the project, I am more than likely to have missed some pertinent publications. Such omissions were unintentional, and I hope to be able to remedy any such deficiencies in the future. I also realize that this study does not adequately address the full complexity of Jesus' relationship to the Torah and Temple, subjects I also intend to explore further in the near future. I am indebted here to far too many scholars to name, but I would like to acknowledge two who have been more than supportive with their time, kindness, and consideration. James A. Sanders has been exceptionally kind in his support of my work and his expert guidance on the Jubilee tradition. James M. Robinson, as always, has been encouraging at every step along the way, and remains an ever-gracious mentor and friend. I would also like to thank Neil Elliott for recommending this book for publication with Fortress Press and Lisa Gruenisen for her assistance with the project's efficient production.

I am very grateful to Kathy Horneck, Interlibrary Loan Coordinator *extraordinaire* at California Lutheran University's Pearson Library, for so cheerfully facilitating numerous requests. My thanks also go to Julia Fogg and the Department of Religion for the warm and welcoming academic environment within which I have conducted some of this research.

Some sections of the present work are based on my earlier published work and are reproduced here with permission from the publishers. I would also like to thank John Barclay, John Muddiman, Katherine Southwood, Andrzej Gieniusz, Gabriele Boccaccini, Loren Stuckenbruck, James C. VanderKam, David Bossman, and Eibert Tigchelaar for their editorial assistance with these publications, as well as the anonymous reviewers who helped me improve them.

Chapter 6, "The Christologies of Q," grew out of a paper presented in the Q Section of the Society of Biblical Literature's Annual Meeting on November 18, 2006 in Washington, DC, and was subsequently published as "Blessed is Whoever is Not Offended by Me: The Subversive Appropriation of (Royal) Messianic Ideology in Q 3–7," *New Testament Studies* 57, no. 3 (2011): 307–24.

A small section of chapter 7, "The Messianic Secret of the Son of Man," originated as a paper presented in the Society of Biblical Literature's International Meeting on July 2, 2009 in Rome, Italy, entitled "A Social Identity Approach to the Rhetoric of Apocalyptic Violence in the Sayings Gospel Q."

A section of chapter 8, "The Enochic Son of Man," first appeared in "'Seventh from Adam' (Jude 1:14-15): Re-examining Enoch Traditions and the Christology of Jude," *Journal of Theological Studies* 64, no. 2 (2013): 463–81.

Some of the material in chapter 9, "The Enochic Adam," was first published in "'His Wisdom Will Reach All Peoples': "4Q534-36, Q 17:26-27, 30, and *1 En.* 65.1-67.3, 90," *Dead Sea Discoveries* 19, no. 1 (2012): 71–105, and "The Eschatological 'Adam' of the *Animal Apocalypse* (*1 En.* 90) and Paul's 'Last Adam': Excavating a Trajectory in Jewish Christianity," *Henoch* 34, no. 1 (2012): 144–70.

Parts of chapter 10, "The Kingdom, the Son, and the Gospel of Nonviolence," were first published as "'Seek His Kingdom': Q 12,22b-31, God's Providence, and Adamic Wisdom," *Biblica* 92, no. 3 (2011): 392–410; "'Love Your Enemies': The Adamic Wisdom of Q 6:27-28, 35c-d," *Biblical Theology Bulletin* 43, no. 1 (2013): 29–41; and "Why Do You Call Me 'Master'? Q 6:46, the Inaugural Sermon, and the Demands of Discipleship," *Journal of Biblical Literature* 132, no. 4 (2013): 953-69.

Santa Monica, CA
August 2013

PART I

1

Jesus, Q, and the Gospels

The quest for the historical Jesus continues to be a site of vigorous debate in the contemporary study of Christian origins.[1] The most distinctive feature of this quest,[2] particularly in the last thirty years, has been its emphasis on the *Jewishness* of Jesus,[3] although there is still no consensus on what *kind* of Jew Jesus was.[4] The Gospels portray Jesus as challenging Jewish ethnic

1. For the widely accepted "facts," see E. P. Sanders, *Jesus and Judaism* (Philadelphia: Fortress Press, 1985), 11; idem, *The Historical Figure of Jesus* (London: Penguin, 1993), 10–11; Craig A. Evans, "Authenticating the Activities of Jesus," in *Authenticating the Activities of Jesus*, ed. Bruce D. Chilton and Craig A. Evans (NTTS 28/2; Leiden: Brill, 1999), 3–29.

2. N. T. Wright, *Jesus and the Victory of God*, vol. 2, *Christian Origins and the Question of God<f/i> (Minneapolis: Fortress Press, 1996), xiv–xv, coined the term "The Third Quest." See also Stephen Neill and N. T. Wright, The Interpretation of the New Testament 1861–1986 (2d ed.; Oxford: Oxford University Press, 1988). But see Fernando Bermejo Rubio, "The Fiction of the 'Three Quests': An Argument for Dismantling a Dubious Historiographical Paradigm," JSHJ 7 (2009): 211–53; Dale C. Allison, Jr., Resurrecting Jesus: The Earliest Christian Tradition and Its Interpreters (New York: T&T Clark, 2005), 1–18; Stanley E. Porter, The Criteria for Authenticity in Historical-Jesus Research: Previous Discussion and New Proposals (JSNTSup 191; Sheffield: Sheffield Academic Press, 2000), 28–59.*

3. See Gerd Theissen and Annette Merz, *Der historische Jesus* (Göttingen: Vandenhoeck & Ruprecht, 1996), 29; Wright, *Jesus and the Victory of God*, 119–20; Tom Holmén, "The Jewishness of Jesus in the 'Third Quest,'" in *Jesus, Mark and Q: The Teaching of Jesus and its Earliest Records* (JSNT Sup 214; Sheffield: Sheffield Academic Press, 2001), 143–62; idem, ed., *Jesus from Judaism to Christianity: Continuum Approaches to the Historical Jesus* (London: T&T Clark, 2007).

4. The rabbinical literature—late, negative, and polemical—is not particularly reliable. See, for example, *b. Sanh.* 43a, where Jesus/*Yeshu* is hanged because "he practiced sorcery and enticed Israel to apostasy." See also *b. Sanh.* 107b; *b. Gittin* 56b; 57a. For Jesus as the son of "Pantera/Pandera," see *Qohelet Rabbah* 1:8(3); *Tosefta Hullin* 2:22f; *Toledot Yeshu*. See also Peter Schäfer, *Jesus in the Talmud* (Princeton: Princeton University Press, 2007); Hermann Strack, *Jesus, die Häretiker und die Christen nach den ältesten jüdischen Angaben* (Leipzig: J. C. Hinrichs'sche Buchhandlung, 1910); Morris Goldstein, *Jesus in the Jewish Tradition* (New York: Macmillan, 1950); Jacob Z. Lauterbach, "Jesus in the Talmud," in idem, *Rabbinic Essays* (Cincinnati: Hebrew Union College, 1951); Johann Maier, *Jesus von Nazareth in der talmudischen*

boundaries and in conflict with some of his contemporaries, but these conflicts were *Jewish* conflicts *within* Judaism. Moreover, despite the fact that Jesus can be relatively easily understood as a Jewish teacher, healer, and prophet, our models sometimes seem to function in mutually exclusive ways and fail to encompass the full range of Jesus' personality, sayings, and deeds.[5] Our sources do not conform to our desires to extract and secure reliable information from them.[6] The utility and reliability of the traditional criteria of authenticity have also recently come under fire.[7] Different scholars apply the same criteria to the same sources and attain different results. Our criteria are not sufficient in and of themselves to differentiate the authentic from the inauthentic. The criterion of multiple attestation depends on contested judgments regarding which sources are actually independent.[8] The criterion of dissimilarity, in particular, has been rightly criticized for its historical, theological, and methodological inadequacies.[9] Intended to identify what was distinctive about Jesus,[10] the criterion misses much of what was culturally continuous between Jesus and his

Überlieferung (Darmstadt: Wissenschaftliche Buchgesellschaft, 1978); Jacob Neusner, *Judaism in the Matrix of Christianity* (Philadelphia: Fortress Press, 1986). But see Joseph Klausner, *Jesus of Nazareth* (Boston: Beacon Press, 1925).

5. Mahlon H. Smith, "Israel's Prodigal Son: Reflections on Reimaging Jesus," in *Profiles of Jesus*, ed. Roy W. Hoover (Santa Rosa: Polebridge, 2002), 87–113, esp. 93; Ben Witherington III, *The Christology of Jesus* (Minneapolis: Fortress Press, 1990), 267; Marcus J. Borg, "Con: Jesus was not an Apocalyptic Prophet," in *The Apocalyptic Jesus: A Debate*, ed. Robert J. Miller (Santa Rosa: Polebridge, 2001), 35; John P. Meier, *A Marginal Jew: Rethinking the Historical Jesus*, Vol. 2, *Mentor, Message and Miracles* (New York: Doubleday, 1994), 407.

6. Rafael Rodriguez, "Authenticating Criteria: The Use and Misuse of a Critical Method," *JSHJ* 7 (2009): 152–67, at 167, calls them "*vehicles of subjectivity*."

7. See *Jesus, Criteria, and the Demise of Authenticity: The 2012 Lincoln Christian University Conference*, ed. Chris Keith and Anthony Le Donne (New York: T&T Clark International, 2012). For reservations, see James D. G. Dunn, *Jesus Remembered* (Grand Rapids: Eerdmans, 2003), 92–97, 191–92; Rodriguez, "Authenticating Criteria"; Dale C. Allison, Jr., "How to Marginalize the Traditional Criteria of Authenticity," in *Handbook for the Study of the Historical Jesus*, ed. Tom Holmén and Stanley E. Porter (4 vols.; Leiden: Brill, 2011), 3–30. On the criteria, see also D. G. A. Calvert, "Examination of the Criteria for Distinguishing the Authentic Words of Jesus," *NTS* 18 (1972): 209–19, at 211; M. Eugene Boring, "Criteria of Authenticity: The Beatitudes as a Test Case," in *Foundations and Facets Forum I* (1985): 3–38, at 3.

8. E. P. Sanders and Margaret Davies, *Studying the Synoptic Gospels* (London: SCM, 1989), 323–30, esp. 323; Dennis Polkow, "Method and Criteria for Historical Jesus Research," ed. Kent H. Richards, *Society of Biblical Literature 1987 Seminar Papers* (Atlanta: Scholars Press, 1987), 336–56, at 350–51; John P. Meier, *A Marginal Jew: Rethinking the Historical Jesus*, I, *The Roots of the Problem and the Person* (New York: Doubleday, 1991), 174–75; Allison, *Resurrecting Jesus*, 75. See also Jens Schröter, "The Historical Jesus and the Sayings Tradition: Comments on Current Research," *Neot* 30 (1996): 151–68, at 158.

Jewish environment and risks misrepresenting Jesus by making him different from Judaism.[11] We simply do not have enough information about Second Temple Judaism(s) or early Christianity to determine precisely how Jesus was dissimilar from either. Moreover, the criterion may only tell us what was distinctive, not necessarily what was characteristic of Jesus.[12] The criterion of embarrassment, while useful in certain cases,[13] founders on conflicting interpretations of what Jesus' early followers might have found embarrassing. The criterion of coherence only confirms the authenticity of sayings or deeds by comparing them to material already determined to be authentic.[14] Recent interest in social memory theory may provide alternative approaches to our sources, assuming that the Synoptic Gospels contain oral retellings of the same events,[15] but memory is fallible, reproductive, and ideologically invested.[16]

9. See Morna D. Hooker, "On Using the Wrong Tool," *Th* 75 (1972): 570–81; David L. Mealand, "The Dissimilarity Test," *SJT* 31 (1978): 41–50; Sanders, *Jesus and Judaism*, 16–17, 252–55; R. T. Osborn, "The Christian Blasphemy: A Non-Jewish Jesus," in *Jews and Christians: Exploring the Past, Present, and Future*, ed. James H. Charlesworth (New York: Crossroad, 1990), 211–38; Tom Holmén, "Doubts about Double Dissimilarity: Restructuring the Main Criterion of Jesus-of-History Research," in *Authenticating the Words of Jesus*, 47–80; Richard B. Hays, "The Corrected Jesus," *First Things* 43 (1994): 43–48, at 45. For responses to Hooker, see Reginald H. Fuller, "The Criterion of Dissimilarity: The Wrong Tool?" in *Christological Perspectives*, ed. Robert F. Berkey and Sarah A. Edwards (New York: Pilgrim, 1982), 42–48; Craig A. Evans, "Jesus' Dissimilarity from Second Temple Judaism and the Early Church," in *Memories of Jesus: A Critical Appraisal of James D. G. Dunn's Jesus Remembered*, ed. Robert B. Stewart and Gary R. Habermas (Nashville: B & H Academic, 2010), 145–58. N. T. Wright suggests the corrective "double dissimilarity": Jesus must both fit *within* Judaism *and* stand out from within it.

10. See Norman Perrin, *Rediscovering the Teaching of Jesus* (New York: Harper & Row, 1967), 39; idem, *The New Testament: An Introduction: Proclamation and Parenesis, Myth and History* (New York: Harcourt Brace Jovanovich, 1974), 281; Ernst Käsemann, "The Problem of the Historical Jesus," in idem, *Essays on New Testament Themes* (SBT 41; London: SCM, 1964), 15–47, at 37; Sanders and Davies, *Studying the Synoptic Gospels*, 316; Gerd Theissen and Dagmar Winter, *The Quest for the Plausible Jesus: The Question of Criteria*, trans. M. Eugene Boring (Louisville: Westminster John Knox, 2002).

11. Susannah Heschel, *The Aryan Jesus* (Princeton: Princeton University Press, 2008).

12. Dale C. Allison, Jr., *Jesus of Nazareth: Millenarian Prophet* (Minneapolis: Fortress Press, 1999), 4.

13. Meier, *A Marginal Jew* 1:168.

14. Jack T. Sanders, "The Criterion of Coherence and the Randomness of Charisma: Poring Through Some Aporias in the Jesus Tradition," *NTS* (1998): 1–25; Charles E. Carlston, "A Positive Criterion of Authenticity," *BR* 7 (1962): 33–44; Polkow, 'Method and Criteria for Historical Jesus," 350; Meier, *A Marginal Jew* 1:174–75; Robert W. Funk, *Honest to Jesus: Jesus for a New Millennium* (New York: Harper San Francisco, 1996), 138. See also Gerd Theissen and Annette Merz, "The Delay of the Parousia as a Test Case for the Criterion of Coherence," *LS* 32 (2007): 49–66; Theissen and Winter, *The Quest for the Plausible Jesus*, 17.

15. Dunn, *Jesus Remembered*, 212.

The historical Jesus will always be a *constructed* Jesus.[17] Historical Jesus traditions may be accessible in and through the impact Jesus made on his followers, but social memory theory does not work primarily on the level of reconstructing "what happened" *in the actual past*; rather, it attempts to reconstruct how Jesus-memories were transmitted and communicated. Social memory theory is therefore less useful in providing access to Jesus than it is in providing access to Jesus' followers and biographers. Critics of this new methodology have accused its advocates of covertly trying to reinscribe (the social memories found in) the Gospels as historically reliable,[18] but social memory theory—*as theory*—fails to establish either the reliability or unreliability of the Gospels; it is simply a theoretical tool useful in understanding how groups *process* their memories. We still have to determine *whose* memories we are reconstructing. The challenge, in other words, still remains one of applying the best methods *and criteria* in identifying what is reliably authentic Jesus tradition.

Like the criteria of authenticity, the historical-critical method has also been subject to critical scrutiny,[19] particularly its tendency to produce hierarchical, patriarchal, and Eurocentric readings.[20] It has been charged with a lack of

16. For the application of social memory to the Jesus tradition, see Jens Schröter, *Erinnerung an Jesu Worte. Studien zur Rezeption der Logienüberlieferung in Markus, Q und Thomas* (WMANT 76; Neukirchen-Vluyn: Neukirchener Verlag, 1997); Alan Kirk, "Memory Theory and Jesus Research," in *Handbook for the Study of the Historical Jesus*, 1:809–42; Dale C. Allison Jr., *Constructing Jesus: Memory, Imagination, and History* (Grand Rapids: Baker Academic, 2010), esp. 1–30; Richard Bauckham, *Jesus and the Eyewitnesses: The Gospels as Eyewitness Testimony* (Grand Rapids: Eerdmans, 2006); Dunn, *Jesus Remembered*; Anthony Le Donne, *The Historiographical Jesus: Memory, Typology, and the Son of David* (Waco: Baylor University Press, 2009); Rafael Rodriguez, *Structuring Early Christian Memory: Jesus in Tradition, Performance, and Text* (LNTS; London: T&T Clark, 2010). For criticism, see Gerd Häfner, "Das Ende der Kriterien? Jesusforschung angesichts der geschichtstheoretischen Diskussion," in *Historiographie und fiktionales Erzählen: Zur Konstruktivität in Geschichtstheorie und Exegese* (BThSt 86; Neukirchen-Vluyn: Neukirchener Verlag, 2007) 102–14; Alexander J. M. Wedderburn, *Jesus and the Historians* (WUNT 269; Tübingen: Mohr Siebeck, 2010), 222–23; Paul Foster, "Memory, Orality, and the Fourth Gospel: Three Dead-Ends in Historical Jesus Research," *JSHJ* 10, no. 3 (2012): 191–227.

17. William E. Arnal, *The Symbolic Jesus: Historical Scholarship, Judaism, and the Construction of Contemporary Identity* (RC; London: Equinox, 2005). On the near-impossibility of questing for a pre-interpreted Jesus, see Jens Schröter, "Die Frage nach dem historischen Jesus und der Charakter historischer Erkenntnis," in *The Sayings Source Q and the Historical Jesus*, ed. A. Lindemann (Leuven: Leuven University Press, 2001), 207-254

18. Zeba A. Crook, "Collective Memory Distortion and the Quest for the Historical Jesus," *JSHJ* 11 (2013): 53-76; Foster, "Memory," 193.

19. See, e.g., Dale B. Martin, *Pedagogy of the Bible: An Analysis and Proposal* (Louisville: Westminster John Knox, 2008); David R. Law, *The Historical-Critical Method: A Guide for the Perplexed* (London/New York: Bloomsbury T & T Clark, 2012).

critical self-reflexivity, an interest solely in the past, the exclusion of other traditions of interpretation, and a naively idealistic Romantic quest for mythic origins. Destabilizing grand narratives, however, is not the same thing as constructing plausible accounts of the past. Postmodern approaches may engage in discourses no less mythic than those they deconstruct.[21] What is needed, in other words, is a critical postmodern historiography that can still self-reflexively (re)construct plausible accounts of the past or, in this case, an historical person.

Jesus and Q

Since the mid-1980s historical Jesus scholars have increasingly been basing their research on Q, the so-called Synoptic "Sayings Source" or "Gospel." Q is the single most important source for reconstructing the teachings of the historical Jesus.[22] This does not mean that the historical Jesus can be *conflated* with the Jesus of Q.[23] The Jesus of Q is "a literary character, constructed from a network of sayings, stories, and editorial comments,"[24] and the dominant focus in Q studies has long been on its redactional profile, compositional history,

20. Fernando F. Segovia, *Decolonizing Biblical Studies: A View from the Margins* (Maryknoll: Orbis Books, 200), 3-33, esp. 15. See also Elisabeth Schüssler Fiorenza, "The Ethics of Biblical Interpretation: Decentering Biblical Scholarship," *JBL* 107 (1988): 3-17.

21. See George Aichele, Peter Miscall, and Richard Walsh, "An Elephant in the Room: Historical-Critical and Postmodern Interpretation of the Bible," *JBL* 128.2 (2009): 383-404; John Van Seters, "A Response to G. Aichele, P. Miscall and R. Walsh, An Elephant in the Room: Historical-Criticism and the Postmodern Interpretation of the Bible," *JHS* 9.26 (2009): 2-13.

22. Gerd Theissen and Annette Merz, *The Historical Jesus: A Comprehensive Guide*, trans. John Bowden (Minneapolis: Fortress Press, 1998), 29. On Q and the historical Jesus, see James M. Robinson, "The Jesus of the Sayings Gospel Q" (OPIAC 28; Claremont: Claremont Graduate School, 1993); idem, "The Critical Edition of Q and the Study of Jesus," in *The Sayings Source Q and the Historical Jesus*, ed. Andreas Lindemann (BETL 158; Leuven: Peeters, 2001), 27–52; Daniel Kosch, "Q und Jesus," *BZ NF* 36 (1992): 30–58; Dieter Lührmann, "Die Logienquelle und die Frage nach dem historischen Jesu," paper presented at the fall meeting at Westar Institute, Edmonton, Alberta, Oct 24–27, 1991; Jens Schröter, "Markus, Q und der historische Jesus: Methodologische und exegetische Erwägungen zu den Anfängen der Rezeption der Verkündigung Jesu," *ZNW* 89 (1998): 173–200; John S. Kloppenborg, "The Sayings Gospel Q and the Quest of the Historical Jesus," *HTR* 89, no. 4 (1996): 307–44; idem, "Discursive Practices in the Sayings Gospel Q and the Quest of the Historical Jesus," in *The Sayings Source Q and the Historical Jesus*, 149–90; Richard A. Horsley, "Q and Jesus: Assumptions, Approaches, and Analyses," *Semeia* 55 (1991): 175–209; Dale C. Allison Jr., *The Jesus Tradition in Q* (Harrisburg, PA: Trinity Press International, 1997), 60–61.

23. Dennis Ingolfsland, "Kloppenborg's Stratification of Q and its Significance for Historical Jesus Studies," *JETS* 46, no. 2 (2003): 217–32.

24. Kloppenborg, "Discursive Practices," 161–62.

provenance, and social setting. Nonetheless, the study of Q has significant implications for Jesus research[25] and is inevitably linked to the quest.[26] Q is our earliest source of authentic Jesus tradition,[27] and while the move from Q to Jesus may be "fraught with enormous methodological difficulties,"[28] Q also takes us "nearer to Jesus than anywhere else on the pages of history."[29] This so-called "first Gospel" is "older than the traditional Gospels, older than the Christian church itself . . . More than any other document, this text holds the answer to the mysteries surrounding Jesus."[30]

The existence of Q continues to be doubted in some circles,[31] but the Two-Document Hypothesis (2DH) of Markan Priority and Q (*Quelle*) remains the dominant consensus solution to the Synoptic Problem in contemporary New Testament scholarship. Nonetheless, Q's existence should not be taken for granted, and something should be said at the outset in its defense, especially as the Farrer-Goulder-Goodacre hypothesis (FGGH) also affirms Markan priority, but posits that Luke reworked Matthean material to suit his own literary and theological purposes.[32] The FGGH attempts to resolve the minor agreements,[33]

25. Kloppenborg, "The Sayings Gospel Q and the Quest for the Historical Jesus," 315–19; Ron Cameron, "The Sayings Gospel Q and the Quest for the Historical Jesus: A Response to John S. Kloppenborg," *HTR* 89, no. 4 (1996): 351–54; Helmut Koester, "The Sayings Gospel Q and the Quest for the Historical Jesus: A Response to John S. Kloppenborg," *HTR* 89, no. 4 (1996): 345–49.

26. James M. Robinson, "Theological Autobiography," in *The Sayings Gospel Q*, 3–34, at 24–25.

27. See Kloppenborg, "The Sayings Gospel Q and the Quest for the Historical Jesus," 334–43, for the methodological principles to be applied in utilizing Q in Jesus studies.

28. Christopher M. Tuckett, "The Son of Man and Daniel 7: Q and Jesus," in *The Sayings Source Q*, 371–94, at 389.

29. Robinson, *The Sayings Gospel Q*, 180, 183.

30. Marcus J. Borg, *The Lost Gospel Q: The Original Sayings of Jesus*, consulting ed. Marcus Borg; ed. Mark Powelson and Ray Riegert (Berkeley: Ulysses, 1999), 25.

31. See especially Austin Farrer, "On Dispensing with Q," in *Studies in the Gospels: Essays in Memory of R. H. Lightfoot*, ed. Dennis E. Nineham (Oxford: Blackwell, 1955), 55–88; Michael Goulder, "On Putting Q to the Test," *NTS* 24 (1978): 218–34; "Is Q a Juggernaut?" *JBL* 115 (1996): 667–81; Mark S. Goodacre, *The Case Against Q: Studies in Markan Priority and the Synoptic Problem* (Harrisburg, PA: Trinity Press International, 2002). For the existence of Q see Joseph A. Fitzmyer, "The Priority of Mark and the 'Q' Source in Luke," in *Jesus and Man's Hope* (Pittsburgh: Pittsburgh Theological Seminary, 1970), 131–70; Charles E. Carlston and Dennis A. Norlan, "Once More—Statistics and Q," *HTR* 64 (1971): 59–78; Petros Vassiliadis, ΛΟΓΟΙ ΙΗΣΟΥ*: Studies in Q* (Atlanta: Scholars Press, 1999), 1–38; Christopher M. Tuckett, "The Existence of Q," in *Q and the History of Early Christianity: Studies on Q* (Peabody, MA: Hendrickson, 1996), 1–39; David R. Catchpole, "Did Q Exist?" in *The Quest for Q* (Edinburgh: T & T Clark, 1993), 1–59; Harry Fledderman, *Q: A Reconstruction and Commentary* (BTS 1; Leuven: Peeters, 2005), 41–68. John S. Kloppenborg Verbin, *Excavating Q: The History and Setting of the Sayings Gospel* (Edinburgh: T & T Clark, 2000).

Mark–Q overlaps, and double tradition without positing Q, and so its primary appeal is its apparent methodological economy. The FGGH also affirms, with the 2DH, that Luke used a number of sources.[34] The main problem with the FGGH is that it does not easily explain why Luke changed virtually every detail in Matthew's infancy narrative, resurrection narrative,[35] and Sermon on the Mount.[36] The amount of textual surgery that Luke would have had to perform on these Matthean sections is formidable.[37] The claim that Luke contains Matthean vocabulary is undermined by Matthew's use of *Lukan* vocabulary.[38] There are instances in which Luke seems to retain a more primitive form of a saying in Matthew. Luke also seems to follow the original order of the double tradition more faithfully than Matthew. The minor agreements *are* a problem for the 2DH, but there are also a number of ways to explain them.[39] The FGGH does not easily, let alone compellingly, explain

32. See J. H. Ropes, *The Synoptic Gospels* (Cambridge: Harvard University Press, 1934), 66–73; Morton S. Enslin, *Christian Beginnings* (New York: Harper & Brothers, 1938), 426–36; Goulder, "On Putting Q to the Test," 218–34; "Is Q a Juggernaut?," 667–81; Mark S. Goodacre, *Goulder and the Gospels: An Examination of a New Paradigm* (JSNTSup 133; Sheffield: Sheffield University Press, 1996); Goodacre, *The Case Against Q*; idem, "A Monopoly on Marcan Priority? Fallacies at the Heart of Q," *Society of Biblical Literature Seminar Papers 2000* (Atlanta: Society of Biblical Literature, 2000), 538–622. On the Griesbach hypothesis, see Allan J. McNicol, et al., *Beyond the Q Impasse—Luke's Use of Matthew: A Demonstration by the Research Team of the Internacional Institute for Gospel Studies* (Valley Forge, PA: Trinity Press International, 1996); Mark A. Matson, "Luke's Rewriting of the Sermon on the Mount," *Society of Biblical Literature Seminar Papers 2000* (SBL Seminar Paper Series 39; Atlanta: Society of Biblical Literature, 2000), 623–50; Edward C. Hobbs, "A Quarter Century Without Q," *PSTJ* 33, no. 4 (1980): 10–19; E. P. Sanders and Margaret Davies, *Studying the Synoptic Gospels* (London: SCM, 1989), 117.

33. See *Minor Agreements: Symposium Göttingen 1991*, ed. Georg Strecker (Göttingen: Vandenhoeck & Ruprecht, 1993); Frans Neirynck, *The Minor Agreements of Matthew and Luke against Mark with a Cumulative List* (BETL 37; Leuven: Leuven University Press, 1974).

34. Luke 1:1-3.

35. See B. H. Streeter, *The Four Gospels: A Study of Origins* (London: Macmillan, 1924), 183.

36. Matson, "Luke's Rewriting of the Sermon on the Mount," 623–50.

37. See Christopher M. Tuckett, review of *The Case Against Q*, *NovT* 46, no. 4 (2004): 401–3. Raymond E. Brown, *The Death of the Messiah: From Gethsemane to the Grave: A Commentary on the Passion Narratives in the Four Gospels* (2 vols.; New York: Doubleday, 1994), 1: 42: "it takes immense imagination stretched to the point of utter implausibility to contend that Luke wrote knowing Matt's infancy narrative."

38. John S. Kloppenborg, "Goulder and the New Paradigm: A Critical Appreciation of Michael Goulder on the Synoptic Problem," in *The Gospels according to Michael Goulder: A North American Response*, ed. Chris A. Rollston (Harrisburg, PA: Trinity Press International, 2002), 58.

39. Simon J. Joseph, *Jesus, Q, and the Dead Sea Scrolls: A Judaic Approach to Q* (WUNT 2d ser. 333; Tübingen: Mohr Siebeck, 2012), 34–38.

Luke's redactional activity, or the distinctive and coherent themes found in Q,[40] including its identification of Jesus as "the One Who Is To Come," its Deuteronomistic theology, prominent interest in Wisdom, repeated use of the rejected prophets motif, and its notable non-use of the term *Christos*.

It is, of course, theoretically possible that Luke knew *of* or *about* Matthew's structural modifications to Mark (that is, Matthew's Davidic genealogy, infancy narrative, post-resurrection appearances) without having a physical copy of Matthew at hand, which could explain some of the similarities between the two Gospels, maintain the *relative* independence of the two authors (and thus Q) without appealing to the close re-working required of the FGGH, but Luke's alleged use of Matthew can only "dispense" with Q in so far as it adequately explains how and why Luke used Matthew. The FGGH does not address, let alone explain, where *Matthew* got these traditions from. The FGGH simply increases—to a significant degree—the amount of special "M" material available to Matthew, essentially *renaming* "Q" "M." But whether we call this material "Q," "M," a pre-Matthean "sayings collection,"[41] or "double tradition," much of Q, especially its instructional material, is arguably coherent, authoritative, dominical, canonical, and authentic Jesus tradition. There is, in other words, and for our present purposes, no "dispensing" with "Q." A rose by any other name would smell as sweet.

Q and Christian Origins

Following the founding of the Jesus Seminar in 1985, John Kloppenborg's *Formation of Q* proposed that Q developed as a collection of six sapiential speech-clusters conforming to the instructional genre. Kloppenborg's proposal

40. On Q's distinctiveness, see Catchpole, *The Quest for Q*, 7; Kloppenborg, "Introduction," in *The Shape of Q: Signal Essays on The Sayings Gospel*, ed. John S. Kloppenborg (Minneapolis: Fortress Press, 1994), 2; Kloppenborg Verbin, *Excavating Q*, 163–64. Goodacre, *The Case Against Q*, 66–75, explains Q's apparent distinctiveness as Matthean passages "displeasing" to Luke.

41. Francis Watson, *Gospel Writing: A Canonical Perspective* (Grand Rapids: Eerdmans, 2013), 118, affirms Markan priority and posits Matthean use of a "sayings source" or "collection," arguing that Luke *interpreted* Matthew, thus "dispensing" with Q, an hypothesis that "entails a radical reconstruction of Christian origins" (118). For Watson, Q—as *Urevangelium*—represents a model within which the "fourfold canonical" Gospels "decline into untruth and illusion" (113) and where Q and the historical Jesus are "set *in opposition to* the canonical gospels, Paul, and the mainstream church" (118). See now also John C. Poirer and Jeffrey Peterson, eds., *Marcan Priority without Q: Explorations in the Farrer Hypothesis* (LNTS; London/New York: T & T Clark International, 2014).

became a working hypothesis for many North American scholars and directly influenced Burton Mack and John Dominic Crossan, both of whom appropriated Kloppenborg's stratification theory in their work on Jesus. Mack found a Galilean Cynic-like Jesus in Q,[42] whereas Crossan found a radical Galilean "Jewish peasant Cynic."[43] Responding in part to the methodological confusion elicited by (mis)applications and (mis)representations of his proposal, Kloppenborg published a study on the methodological challenges involved in using Q as a source for the historical Jesus.[44] He argued that interpreters must (1) acknowledge Q as literary "invention" and "arrangement,"[45] (2) carefully interpret Q's "silence" (that is, its notable lack of a passion and resurrection narrative),[46] and (3) recognize Q's essential "conservatism and continuity" with its inherited traditions. For Kloppenborg the redaction of Q is neither the result of an editor introducing "previously unknown materials" nor a "massive change from a 'noneschatological' to an 'apocalyptic' document."[47] Rather, the redaction of Q signifies a "fundamental change" in "rhetorical posture," so that "one must presume a basic continuity in eschatological outlook between Q1 and Q2."[48]

In July 2000, the forty-ninth Colloquium Biblicum Lovaniense was held in Leuven, Belgium, and focused on the study of Q and the historical Jesus. William Arnal acknowledges this impressive "wealth of scholarship," but holds that the Colloquium's collected papers also testify "to the impasse Q scholarship appears to have reached,"[49] "a field in serious danger of stagnation." For Arnal, "Q scholarship remains too invested in, and charged by, its (putative) implications for reconstructing the historical Jesus."[50] For Arnal the golden age

42. Burton L. Mack, *A Myth of Innocence: Mark and Christian Origins* (Philadelphia: Fortress Press, 1988), 53–77; *The Lost Gospel: The Book of Q & Christian Origins* (San Francisco: HarperSanFrancisco, 1993).

43. John Dominic Crossan, *The Historical Jesus: The Life of a Mediterranean Jewish Peasant* (San Francisco: Harper and Row, 1991). See also Jeffrey Carlson and Robert A. Ludwig, eds., *Jesus and Faith: A Conversation on the work of John Dominic Crossan* (Maryknoll, NY: Orbis Books, 1994).

44. Kloppenborg, "The Sayings Gospel Q and the Quest of the Historical Jesus."

45. Ibid., 326.

46. Ibid., 329.

47. Ibid., 336.

48. Ibid., 337.

49. William E. Arnal, review of *The Sayings Source Q and the Historical Jesus*, *CBQ* 69, no. 3 (2007): 627–29, at 629.

50. Ibid., 629.

of Q studies began with Kloppenborg's work,[51] but this breakthrough has not yet been developed or extended to "other areas of Christian origins."

In 2004, the Society of Biblical Literature's Seminar on Ancient Myths and Modern Theories of Christian Origins published *Redescribing Christian Origins*, a collection of papers that attempt to identify a number of viable alternative methodological approaches to the canonical narrative of early Christianity.[52] The volume focuses on three projects: (1) the social formation of the Q community; (2) the early Jerusalem community; and (3) the messianic and titular interpretation of Paul's use of *Christos*. Taking Q and the *Gospel of Thomas* as "alternative points of departure to the typical assumption of the apocalyptic and kerygmatic orientation of the first followers of Jesus,"[53] and presupposing Kloppenborg's stratification of Q, Willi Braun and William Arnal see the Q community as a kind of philosophical school, a "Galilean Jesus Association" or collective of deracinated "village scribes."[54] At the same time, Dennis Smith, Burton Mack, and Luther Martin question the historical existence of a Jerusalem community as a product of early Christian "mythmaking,"[55] challenging Paul's references to a "Jerusalem community" (Paul's "churches of Judea")[56] comprised of the "pillars" Peter, James, and the "brothers of the Lord," not to mention the Twelve and the five hundred.[57] Merrill P. Miller further argues that Jesus research fails to explain the relationships between Jesus' teaching, his "messianic" death, and a "messianic" Jerusalem community that "survived relatively unmolested for more than a generation."[58] He concludes that "it is unlikely that either the death of Jesus or the identity of the group of followers in Jerusalem revolved around messianic

51. Ibid., 628–29.

52. Ron Cameron and Merrill P. Miller, eds., *Redescribing Christian Origins* (SBL SS 28; Atlanta: Society of Biblical Literature, 2004). See also now *Redescribing Paul and the Corinthians*, ed. Ron Cameron and Merrill P. Miller (Atlanta: Society of Biblical Literature, 2011).

53. Merrill P. Miller, "Introduction to the Papers from the Third Year of the Consultation," in *Redescribing Christian Origins*, 33–41, at 33.

54. Willi Braun, "The Schooling of a Galilean Jesus Association (The Sayings Gospel Q)," in *Redescribing Christian Origins*, 43–66; William E. Arnal, "Why Q Failed: From Ideological Project to Group Formation," ibid., 67–88.

55. Dennis E. Smith, "What Do We Really Know about the Jerusalem Church? Christian Origins in Jerusalem according to Acts and Paul," in *Redescribing Christian Origins*, 237–52; Burton L. Mack, "A Jewish Jesus School in Jerusalem," ibid., 253–62; Luther H. Martin, "History, Historiography, and Christian Origins: The Jerusalem Community," ibid., 263–75.

56. Gal. 1:22.

57. 1 Cor. 15:6. Merrill P. Miller, "'Beginning from Jerusalem . . .': Re-examining Canon and Consensus," *JHC* 2, no. 1 (1995): 3–30.

confrontations, claims, or titles."[59] The appeal to Jerusalem thus has more to do with early Christian "mythmaking and social history" than with historical fact.[60] Merrill Miller and Barry Crawford also pursue Burton Mack's thesis that the Christ-*kerygma*-cult was created by pre-Pauline Hellenistic groups, and that Paul's use of *Christos* is non-messianic and may even have originated as a kind of "nickname."[61]

Since Q does not use the term *Christos*, several members of the Seminar argue "against the common assumption of the emergence of Christianity as a messianic sect."[62] They suggest that the use of *christos* as a messianic title first appears not in Paul's letters, but "only later in the narrative tradition of the canonical Gospels."[63] The Seminar concedes that Paul did not *introduce* the term and that its near-ubiquitous presence in his letters demonstrates that both he and his readers were intimately familiar with it,[64] but holds that its original referent and significance "cannot be derived from what is to be found in the Gospels and Acts."[65] Miller's proposal, for example—that "pre-Pauline usages of *christos* did not presuppose the usages of the term in the Gospels"—attempts to reverse "the usual assumptions about the provenance and significance of the term in its earliest usage."[66] The open agenda of the Seminar, in other words, is to deny any historical "appeal to a messianic conception of Jesus" and to any pre-Pauline messianic Jewish Palestinian Jesus movement.[67] The earliest use of the term *christos* was "not titular, not royal, not eschatological, and not martyrological": the identification of Jesus as *Christos* reflects (Hellenistic) "mythmaking," not Palestinian Jewish messianism.[68]

58. Ron Cameron, "Proposal for the First Year of the Seminar," in *Redescribing Christian Origins*, 141–50, at 141.

59. Miller, "Beginning from Jerusalem," 30.

60. Ibid., 27–28.

61. Merrill P. Miller, "The Problem of the Origins of a Messianic Conception of Jesus," in *Redescribing Christian Origins*, 301–36; Barry S. Crawford, "*Christos* as Nickname," ibid., 337–48; Merrill P. Miller, "The Anointed Jesus," ibid., 375–416.

62. Cameron, "Proposal for the Second Year of the Seminar," in *Redescribing Christian Origins*, 285–92, at 288.

63. Ibid.

64. Cameron, "Introduction to the Papers from the Second Year of the Seminar," in *Redescribing Christian Origins*, 293–300, at 296 (emphases added).

65. Cameron, "Proposal for the Second Year of the Seminar," 288.

66. Ibid., 287.

67. However, see Ron Cameron and Merrill P. Miller, "Issues and Commentary," in *Redescribing Christian Origins*, 443–57, at 454.

The Seminar's attempt to "reinvent" the term *Christos* does have the virtue of recognizing that the messianic identification of Jesus has long been a puzzle in modern critical scholarship,[69] but it is problematic to limit the range of scholarly responses to this problem to two models: *either* Jesus was "a political revolutionary who failed" *or* the messianic identification of Jesus is "a stunning reinterpretation" of "Jewish messianic hopes,"[70] with the latter model basically recapitulating "the canonical paradigm of Christian origins." In seeking to find "a more plausible reading of beginnings," the Seminar's greatest concern is exposed: "if messianic beginnings are a point of departure, then the Jesus movements as we have understood and redescribed them [Q and *Thomas*] will be lost, absorbed by the dominant (canonical) paradigm of Christian origins."[71] In conclusion, the Seminar claims that they have "successfully problematized . . . the picture of messianic beginnings" and "achieved . . . a more reasonable explanation for the emergence of the designation *christos*."

This confidence is not echoed widely outside the Seminar's relatively small circle of contributors.[72] Cameron and Miller may reject the "Gospel story" because "Jesus did not fit the expectation of a Messiah,"[73] but even if we were to bracket the diversity of first-century messianism for a moment, what are we to make of the Seminar's claim that *they* have sought to "resolve" this "anomaly" while *most* other scholars simply seek to "retain" it?

The Seminar provides us with a welcome set of experiments attempting to determine *whether* a non-messianic paradigm of Christian origins can be sustained. The question is whether their proposals have sufficient explanatory power to compel a non-messianic reading of the early Jesus tradition. They do not. Despite the theoretical validity of a sociological redescription of the data, the Seminar is unable to explain away Paul's 270 references to Jesus as *Christos*, unable to divorce the term from its titular associations, and unable to explain why the title originated, if not from an early messianic identification of Jesus, a man crucified as "*king* of the Jews." The Redescribing Christian Origins project is an extreme example of the Quest for an alternative ideological narrative—a tradition that can be traced back to the dawn of the Enlightenment—but

68. Burton L. Mack, "Why *Christos*? The Social Reasons," in *Redescribing Christian Origins*, 365–74, at 365.

69. Ron Cameron, "Introduction to the Papers from the Second Year of the Seminar," 293.

70. Ibid.

71. Ibid., 296.

72. See especially James D. G. Dunn, review of *Redescribing Christian Origins*, *JBL* 124, no. 4 (2005): 760–64, and John Parrish, review, *MTSR* 20, no. 3 (2008): 291–95.

73. Cameron and Miller, "Issues and Commentary," 446.

its claims fail to convince, with the end result being a further polarizing of the field. We see this most clearly in ongoing debates about wisdom and apocalypticism,[74] where our terms have become "so freighted with misconceptions, ambivalences, and ideological concerns that they have ceased to function as good descriptive categories."[75] In Q and Jesus studies these terms have been deployed to construct oppositional paradigms to the question of whether or not Jesus "proclaimed an empirical cosmic transformation in the imminent future."[76] The real "impasse" in Q studies, in other words, may not be the conservative leanings of a guild unwilling to accept any particular leap forward in research, but rather the exaggerated claims attending the appropriation of Q in ideological redescriptions of Christian origins, claims that have turned out to be easily countered, easily refuted, and easily dismissed, taking with them many of the more reliable results in recent Q studies.

For example, many historical Jesus scholars have appealed to the stratigraphy of Q in order to reconstruct Jesus as a non-messianic Galilean peasant. It is debatable, however, whether Q is really non-messianic or represents a low Christology.[77] It is also debatable whether the provenance of Q should be located in a rural Galilean setting. Simplistic descriptions of Q's sapiential/instructional material have led to ideological and polemical caricatures of Jesus as a "teacher of wisdom" when this proposal is clearly undermined by the pervasive eschatology contained throughout Q. We clearly need to revisit the social, cultural, and theological matrices of Q in Second Temple Judaism if we are going to use Q more responsibly in Jesus research.

Q is an ethnically and geographically Palestinian Judean text.[78] Compositionally, Q is a composite text, a collection of Jesus' sayings arranged into discursive structures containing disparate voices from different forms of social experience. The Inaugural Sermon (Q 6:20-49), for example, is framed by the Temptation and Centurion narratives. This Sermon is not worldly wisdom by any common standard, nor is its guarantor a mere teacher of wisdom. The Jesus of Q is the "Son of God" who defeats Satan and can work signs and wonders at will. The Inaugural Sermon also begs the question: what was the original "good news" or message of Jesus? And should that original message or "good news" also be designated as a "Gospel?"

74. Kloppenborg, "The Sayings Gospel Q," 339–43.

75. Ibid., 339.

76. Ibid., 340.

77. Simon J. Joseph, "'Blessed is Whoever is Not Offended by Me': The Subversive Appropriation of (Royal) Messianic Ideology in Q 3–7," *NTS* 57, no. 3 (2011): 307–24.

78. Joseph, *Jesus, Q, and the Dead Sea Scrolls*, 45-93.

Q and the Gospels

Q does not so much provide us with new *information* about Jesus as it allows for a different perspective on the origins and development of the earliest Jesus traditions.[79] There has been some discussion about whether Q qualifies as a "Gospel" as opposed to a theoretical literary "source," but that discussion is more than academic. If Q is a Gospel, perhaps even the *earliest* Gospel, then its theological authority must also be reckoned with. Q "makes a difference."[80] If the term Gospel is limited to the Pauline interpretation of Jesus' life and death, then maybe Q is not a Gospel.[81] But if what we mean by "Gospel" is a literary-theological narrative representation of Jesus, then Q certainly seems to qualify. Finally, if Q represents our best access to the "good news" proclaimed by Jesus, then what *was* that "good news" all about?

The word "Gospel" is an English translation of the Greek word εὐαγγέλιον, which means "good news." The term εὐαγγέλιον was used in imperial Roman inscriptions to celebrate the blessings of peace and prosperity brought about by Caesar Augustus,[82] but our earliest evidence for the use of the term in the New Testament is found in Paul's first letter to the Corinthians, where Paul refers to "*the* good news" (τὸ εὐαγγέλιον) through which "you are saved" (σῴζεσθε).[83] Paul's "Gospel," which he claims to have "received" from the Lord,[84] focuses on the death and resurrection of Jesus Christ.

79. Philip Jenkins, *Hidden Gospels: How the Search for Jesus Lost Its Way* (New York: Oxford University Press, 2002).

80. John S. Kloppenborg, *Q, The Earliest Gospel: An Introduction to the Original Stories and Sayings of Jesus* (Louisville: Westminster John Knox, 2008), 61. See also James M. Robinson, *The Gospel of Jesus: In Search of the Original Good News* (New York: HarperSanFrancisco, 2005); Arland Jacobson, *The First Gospel: An Introduction to Q* (FF; Sonoma, CA: Polebridge, 1992).

81. See Frans Neirynck, "Q: From Source to Gospel," *ETL* 71, no. 4 (1995): 421–30; Jean-Paul Michaud, "Quelle(s) communauté(s) derrière la Source Q," in *The Sayings Source Q and the Historical Jesus*, 577–606; idem, "Effervescence in Q Studies," in *Studien zum Neuen Testament und seiner Umwelt* 30 (2005): 61–103; "De quelques présents débats dans la troisième quête," in *De Jésus à Jésus-Christ. I. Le Jésus de l'histoire* (Paris: Mame-Desclée, 2010), 189–214.

82. Koester, *Ancient Christian Gospels*, 3–4.

83. 1 Cor. 15:1-2. For alternative views see Martin Hengel, "The Titles of the Gospels and the Gospel of Mark," in *Studies in the Gospel of Mark*, ed. idem (London: SCM, 1985), 64–84; idem, *The Four Gospels and the One Gospel of Jesus Christ: An Investigation of the Collection and Origin of the Canonical Gospels* (London: SCM, 2000); Graham Stanton, "The Fourfold Gospel," *NTS* 43 (1997): 317–46. Lawrence M. Wills, *The Quest for the Historical Gospel: Mark, John and the Origins of the Gospel Genre* (London: Routledge, 1997), argues that the "gospel" genre originated in the narratives of the (dead) hero cult.

Today the semantic range of the word "Gospel" seems to include a wide variety of possible meanings. According to Darrell Bock, for example, the "gospel" is "the good news of God's love and initiative . . . to bring us into a healthy relationship with Himself" and "save us from hell."[85] Jesus delivered the "good news" that "God's promised rule" had arrived, although the gospel should not be understood simply as "a transaction—the removal of a debt," as this does not sound like very "good news."[86] For Bock, the cross is "the hub of the gospel, but Jesus' dying for sin is *not* the entire gospel."[87] Here the term "gospel" has essentially become a cipher for the entirety of the Christian faith. Similarly, Scot McKnight notes the dissociation between Jesus and the cross-centered "Gospel" of contemporary Evangelical Christianity and argues that the Jesus story can only be understood in relation to the larger "story of Israel" and God's "plan of salvation."[88] First Corinthians 15 is the "true gospel of the church's tradition."[89] For McKnight "the 'gospel' is the Story of Jesus that fulfills, completes, and resolves Israel's Story."[90] Paul's gospel "was the same as Jesus' and—in fact—the same as everyone's in the first century,"[91] and since Jesus claimed "*Israel's story was fulfilled in himself*," this means that Jesus also "*preached the gospel*!"

The word "Gospel" did not initially signify a particular literary *genre*, but rather a story, preaching, or proclamation (κήρυγμα) *about* Jesus.[92] The Gospels appear to be theological "biographies" (βίοι) of Jesus,[93] but there is no denying a certain degree of ambiguity in the use of the term, both in contemporary usage and in the Gospels. The Gospel of Mark, for example, opens with the

84. See Klaus Wegenast, *Das Verständnis der Tradition bei Paulus und in den Deuteropaulinen* (WMANT 8; Neukirchen: Neukirchener Verlag, 1962), 57–70.

85. Darrell L. Bock, *Recovering the Real Lost Gospel: Reclaiming the Gospel as Good News* (Nashville: B & H Academic, 2010), 9.

86. Bock, *Recovering the Real Lost Gospel*, 10–11.

87. Ibid., 12–13.

88. Scot McKnight, *The King Jesus Gospel: The Original Good News Revisited* (Grand Rapids: Zondervan, 2011).

89. Ibid., 47, or "the *apostolic gospel tradition*" (p. 46).

90. Ibid., 51.

91. Ibid., 78.

92. Craig A. Evans and James A. Sanders, "Gospels and Midrash: An Introduction to Luke and Scripture," in *Luke and Scripture: The Function of Sacred Tradition in Luke-Acts* (Minneapolis: Fortress Press, 1993), 2.

93. On the Gospels as ancient biographies (βίοι), see Richard A. Burridge, *What Are the Gospels?: A Comparison with Graeco-Roman Biography* (SNTSMS 70; Cambridge: Cambridge University Press, 1992). Garry Wills, *What the Gospels Meant* (New York: Penguin, 2008), 7, defines a Gospel as "a meditation on the meaning of Jesus in the light of Sacred History as recorded in the Sacred Writings."

"good news *of* Jesus Christ,"[94] but Jesus has not taught anything yet, so it seems that what Mark had in mind was something like Paul's gospel of Jesus' death and resurrection.[95] Mark's Jesus also preaches the "good news of [the *kingdom* of] God" (τὸ εὐαγγέλιον τοῦ θεοῦ).[96] The Gospel of Matthew portrays Jesus as preaching "the good news of the *kingdom*" (τὸ εὐαγγέλιον τῆς βασιλείας). It would seem, therefore, that Jesus' proclamation of the kingdom, his "good news to the poor,"[97] can also be called a "Gospel."[98] It is no accident that Luke portrays Jesus as announcing his mission by citing Isaiah 61:1:

> The spirit of the Lord God is upon me . . .
> the Lord has anointed me (משח/ἔχρισέ)
> to proclaim good news to the poor (εὐαγγελίσασθαι πτωχοῖς).[99]

Isa. 52:7 also envisions a coming age of peace and salvation as "good news" to be inaugurated by a divinely authorized "messenger":[100]

> How beautiful upon the mountains are the feet of the messenger
> who announces peace (שלום/εἰρήνης),
> who brings good news (εὐαγγελιζομένου),
> who announces salvation (ישועה/σωτηρίαν),
> who says to Zion, 'Your God reigns' (βασιλεύσει σου ὁ Θεός).

In his response to John the Baptist's inquiry, the Jesus of Q 7:22 cites a number of Isaianic passages in order to confirm his identity as "the One Who Is To Come," explicitly referring to the eschatological "good news" being proclaimed to the poor:

> "the blind see, and the lame walk, the lepers are cleansed,

94. Mark 1:1.

95. Stuhlmacher, *Das paulinische Evangelium*, 234–38.

96. Mark 1:14. Some manuscript witnesses read "of the kingdom."

97. Q 7:22; Luke 4:18.

98. Matt. 4:23; 9:25; 24:14.

99. Isa. 61:1; cf. Luke 4. See also Isa. 40:9; 52:7. Isaiah 61 is generally dated to c. 530 B.C.E..

100. Peter Stuhlmacher, "The Theme: The Gospel and the Gospels," in *The Gospel and the Gospels*, ed. idem; trans. John Vriend (Grand Rapids: Eerdmans, 1991), 1–25; William Horbury, "'Gospel' in Herodian Judaea," in *The Written Gospel*, ed. Markus Bockmuehl and Donald Hagner (Cambridge: Cambridge University Press, 2005), 7–30; Hubert Frankemölle, "Jesus als deuterojesajanische Freudenbote? Zur Rezeption von Jes 52,7 und 61,1 im Neuen Testament, durch Jesus und in den Targumim," in *Vom Christentum zu Jesus. Festschrift für Joachim Gnilka*, ed. Hubert Frankemölle (Freiberg: Herder, 1989), 34–67.

> and the deaf hear, and the dead are raised,
> and the poor have *good news* preached to them (καὶ πτωχοὶ εὐαγγελίζονται)."

The literary and theological relationships between Jesus, Q, Luke, and Isaiah 61 are significant, not least because Isaiah 61 served as an exegetical key for Early Jewish groups and provided a Judaic semantic root and anchor for the Greek gospel genre (LXX: εὐαγγελίσασθαι). Q 7:22 contains a series of clauses reflecting passages from Isa. 29:18, 35:5-6, and 61:1.[101] Isaiah 61 "is used to inform and delineate the teaching of Jesus . . . and his own interpretation of his work."[102] Q 7:22 provides an organizing principle for the first major section of Q 3–7.[103]

The publication of 4Q521 in 1992 provided a remarkably similar description of what God would perform when "his messiah" (משיחו) arrived:[104]

> . . . liberating the captives, giving sight to the blind,
> straightening the bent . . .
> For he will heal the wounded, revive the dead,
> and proclaim *good news* to the poor.

4Q521 refers to a messianic figure and a series of eschatological blessings described in Isaiah, including an explicit reference to the resurrection of the dead. Jesus' "good news" was part of an exegetical tradition in which Isaiah

101. Christopher Tuckett, "Scripture and Q," in *The Scriptures in the Gospels*, ed. idem (BETL 131; Leuven: Leuven University Press, 1997), 21.

102. Tuckett, "Scripture and Q," 21.

103. Robinson, "Building Blocks in the Social History of Q," in *Reimagining Christian Origins: A Colloquium Honoring Burton Mack*, ed. Elizabeth A. Castelli and Hal Taussig (Valley Forge, PA: Trinity Press International, 1996), 87–112, in Robinson, *The Sayings Gospel Q*, 500, notes the "pervasive dependence of the Q trajectory on Isaiah 61:1."

104. 4Q521 2 ii 8, 12. Joseph A. Fitzmyer, *The Dead Sea Scrolls and Christian Origins* (Grand Rapids: Eerdmans, 2000), 37. For the original publication, see Émile Puech, "Une Apocalypse Messianique (4Q521)," *RevQ* 15 (1992): 475–519; *Discoveries of the Judaean Desert XXV: Qumran Grotte 4 XVIII: Textes Hebreux (4Q521–4Q528, 4Q576–4Q579)* (Oxford: Clarendon Press, 1998), 1–38; Robert Eisenman, "A Messianic Vision," *BAR* 17, no. 6 (1991): 65; Robert Eisenman and Michael O. Wise, *The Dead Sea Scrolls Uncovered* (Shaftesbury: Element, 1992), 19–23; James D. Tabor and Michael O. Wise, "4Q521 'On Resurrection' and the Synoptic Gospel Tradition: A Preliminary Study," in *Qumran Questions*, ed. James H. Charlesworth (Sheffield: Sheffield Academic Press, 1995); Geza Vermes, "Qumran Forum Miscellanea I," *JJS* 43 (1992): 299–305; Lawrence H. Schiffman, *Reclaiming the Dead Sea Scrolls: The History of Judaism, the Background of Christianity, the Lost Library of Qumran* (Philadelphia: Jewish Publication Society, 1994), 347–50; John J. Collins, "The Works of the Messiah," *DSD* 1 (1994): 98–112.

61 was understood as heralding an eschatological new age of peace, salvation, healing, and debt-forgiveness: the Jubilee year.[105]

According to Leviticus 25 and Deuteronomy 15, God commanded that a Jubilee year be held every forty-nine years for the release of slaves, the remission of debts, and the restoration of property.[106] The Jubilee year was a "day" of physical and spiritual release and restoration.[107] The socio-economic difficulties associated with the Jubilee motivated the Pharisees to invent a legal compromise (the *Prosbul*) in order to avoid implementing the Jubilee. The authority to proclaim the Jubilee was ultimately shifted from the king to the priests to God and the eschatological age. The Dead Sea Scrolls illustrate that the Qumran community was well aware of the Jubilee tradition of liberty to the captives and release from debt, slavery, and sin.[108]

11QMelchizedek, a *pesher* (scriptural interpretation) drawing from Leviticus, Deuteronomy, Isaiah, and the Psalms, announces the arrival of an *eschatological* Jubilee. Melchizedek appears as a heavenly figure inaugurating the liberation of the "captives"[109] and ushering in the "day of [peace]" (יום ה[שלום). This text, drawing directly from Isa. 61:1-2,[110] may have been "the first *messianic*

105. James A. Sanders, "From Isaiah 61 to Luke 4," in *Christianity, Judaism and Other Greco-Roman Cults: Studies for Morton Smith at Sixty*, ed. Jacob Neusner (Leiden: Brill, 1975), 1:75–106; idem, "Isaiah in Luke," in *Interpreting the Prophets*, ed. James L. Mays and Paul J. Achtemeier (Philadelphia: Fortress Press, 1987), 75–85; idem, "Sins, Debts, and Jubilee Release," in *Luke and Scripture*, 84–92.

106. Deuteronomy 15; Lev. 25:10.

107. John Sietze Bergsma, *The Jubilee from Leviticus to Qumran: A History of Interpretation* (VTSup 115; Leiden: Brill, 2007), 20. See also James C. VanderKam, "Sabbatical Chronologies in the Dead Sea Scrolls and Related Literature," in *The Dead Sea Scrolls in Their Historical Context*, ed. Timothy H. Lim (Edinburgh: T & T Clark, 2000), 159–78. See also Robert G. North, *Sociology of the Biblical Jubilee* (AnBib 4; Rome: Pontificio Instituto Biblico, 1954); Jean-François Lefebvre, *Le jubilé biblique: Lv 25—exégèse et théologie* (OBO 194; Göttingen: Vandenhoeck & Ruprecht, 2003).

108. For bibliography, see Adam S. van der Woude, "Melchisedek als himmlische Erlösergestalt in den neugefundenen eschatologischen Midraschim aus Qumran Höhle XI," *Oudtestamentische Studien* 14 (1965): 354–73; idem, "11QMelchizedek and the New Testament," *NTS* 12 (1966): 301–26; Joseph A. Fitzmyer, "Further Light on Melchizedek from Qumran Cave 11," *JBL* 86 (1967): 25–41; David Flusser, "Melchizedek and the Son of Man," *Christian News from Israel* 17 (1966): 23–29; Yigael Yadin, "A Note on Melchizedek and Qumran," *IEJ* 15 (1965): 152–54; Merrill P. Miller, "The Function of Isa 61:1-2 in 11QMelchizedek," *JBL* 88, no. 4 (1969): 467–69; Daniel F. Miner, "A Suggested Reading for 11QMelchizedek 17," *JSJ* 2 (1971): 144–48; J. T. Milik, "Milkî-Sedeq et Milkî-Reš' dans les anciens écrits juifs et chrétiens," *JJS* 23 (1972): 95–112, 124–26; James A. Sanders, "The Old Testament in 11QMelchizedek," *Janes* 5 (1973): 373–82; Émile Puech, "Notes sur le manuscrit de XIMelkîsédeq," *RevQ* 12 (1987): 483–513.

109. See Isa. 61:1.

110. 11QMelch 2.4, 6, 9, 13.

re-interpretation of the jubilee,"[111] conflating Isa. 52:7 and Isa. 61:1-2 in its depiction of the coming "messenger . . . anointed of the spirit" (משיח הרוח המבשר הואה), who will announce "salvation."[112] 4Q521 and 11QMelchizedek illustrate that the Jubilee tradition was developed by the Qumran community, for whom eschatological redemption and salvation—the time when the poor, oppressed, and imprisoned would hear the "good news" of God's favor and release—was an imminent reality. The Jesus of Q 6:20, Q 7:22, and Luke 4 takes a special interest in Isaiah 61: Jesus announces his ministry as the arrival of the Jubilee year.[113] The Lord's Prayer in Q explicitly refers to the cancelling of debts:

> *Forgive our debts* (ἄφες ἡμῖν τὰ ὀφειλήματα ἡμῶν) for us,
> as we too have cancelled for those in debt to us.[114]

Jesus' instruction to repeatedly forgive interpersonal sin is also found in Q 17:3-4:

> "If your brother *sins* (ἁμαρτήσῃ) . . . *forgive* him (ἄφες αὐτῷ).
> And if seven times a day he sins against you,
> also seven times shall you *forgive* him."

As James Sanders notes, such an announcement—the eschatological release of debts and the forgiveness of sins—would have transformed the social, economic, and political landscape of first-century Judea.[115] Whether or not Jesus believed

111. Bergsma, *The Jubilee from Leviticus to Qumran*, 202.

112. 11QMelch 2.18-19. "Salvation" translates ישועה. Bruce D. Chilton and Craig A. Evans, "Jesus and Israel's Scriptures," in Chilton and Evans, eds., *Studying the Historical Jesus: Evaluations of the State of Current Research* (NTTS 19; Leiden: Brill, 1994), 283–335, at 325. Bergsma, *The Jubilee from Leviticus to Qumran*, 294, concludes that the figure of Melchizedek takes on the roles of the "anointed of the spirit" (Isa. 61:1-2), "anointed prince" (Dan. 9:25-26), and "messenger" (Isa. 52:7).

113. Robert B. Sloan Jr., *The Favorable Year of the Lord: A Study of Jubilary Theology in the Gospel of Luke* (Austin: Schola Press, 1977); Sharon H. Ringe, "The Jubilee Proclamation in the Ministry and Teachings of Jesus: A Tradition-Critical Study in the Synoptic Gospels and Acts," (unpublished) Ph. D. diss., Union Theological Seminary, 1981; Donald W. Blosser, "Jesus and the Jubilee (Luke 4:16-30): The Year of Jubilee and Its Significance in the Gospel of Luke," Ph. D. diss., St. Andrew's University, 1979.

114. Q 11:4.

115. Sanders, "Isaiah in Luke," 81; idem, "Sins, Debts, and Jubilee Release," 87–88. John Howard Yoder proposed that Jesus embraced a politics of nonviolence based on the Jubilee tradition (*The Politics of Jesus: Vicit Agnus Noster* [Grand Rapids: Eerdmans, 1972], 39). See also his *Nonviolence: A Brief History: The Warsaw Lectures*, ed. Paul H. Martens, Matthew Porter, and Myles Werntz (Waco: Baylor University Press, 2010); *Nevertheless: The Varieties and Shortcomings of Religious Pacifism* (Scottdale, PA: Herald Press,

that the Jubilee year's provisions should have been implemented literally—and is not simply Luke's symbolic representation of Jesus' eschatological significance—it seems safe to conclude that Jesus' central message was not an announcement of his own imminent death, but rather the proclamation of God's restorative work occurring in and through his own life and ministry, that is, the kingdom of God.

Jesus proclaimed the "good news" of the kingdom of God, but after Jesus' death the Gospel of Jesus became the Gospel of Christ crucified:[116] "*The proclaimer became the proclaimed.*"[117] It is not likely, however, that Jesus intended his teachings to be ignored, compromised, or superseded. Jesus' teachings may be idealistic and inconvenient, but they are not irrelevant. If the ultimate goal of Jesus Research is to accurately reconstruct the social, economic, political, and theological contexts of Jesus' life and teachings, and if the requirements of Christian discipleship—that is, "following Jesus"—have anything to do with the historical figure of Jesus' life and teachings, then careful historical and theological reexaminations of the historical Jesus are clearly still in order.

1992); *The Original Revolution: Essays on Christian Pacifism* (Scottdale, PA: Herald Press, 1972); *The War of the Lamb: The Ethics of Nonviolence and Peacemaking* (Grand Rapids: Brazos, 2009). See also Stanley Hauerwas, *The Peaceable Kingdom: A Primer in Christian Ethics* (Notre Dame, IN: University of Notre Dame Press, 1983).

116. Acts 5:42; 8:4-5, 35; 11:20; 17:18; Rom. 1:1-4; 10:8-17; 15:19-20; 2 Cor. 4:4-6; 11:4; Gal. 1:16; Eph. 3:8; Phil. 1:15-18; 2 Tim. 2:8. On the *one* Gospel, see Rom. 1:11-17; 2 Thess. 2:13-14; Gal. 1:7; 2:7-9. On the problem between Paul's "Gospel" and Jesus' Gospel of the kingdom, see Robert A. Guelich, "What Is the Gospel?" *Theology, News, and Notes* 51 (2004): 4–7.

117. Rudolf Bultmann, *Theology of the New Testament*, trans. Kendrick Grobel (2 vols.; New York: Scribners, 1955), 33. Koester, *Ancient Christian Gospels*, 13.

2

The Nonviolent Jesus

Did the historical Jesus have a hidden violent streak?[1] Did Jesus come "not to bring peace, but a sword?"[2] Did Jesus entertain the idea of a military revolt against Rome? Did Jesus instruct his disciples to buy swords? Did Jesus use a "whip of cords" during the Temple incident? Was the incident itself an example of Jesus' "revolutionary activity?"[3] Was Judas Iscariot one of the *sicarii*? Were

1. On Jesus as a political revolutionary, see Robert Eisler, *ΙΗΣΟΥΣ ΒΑΣΙΛΕΥΣ ΟΥ ΒΑΣΙΛΕΥΣΑΣ: Die messianische Unabhängigkeitsbewegung vom Auftreten Johannes des Täufers bis zum Untergang Jakobs des Gerechten nach der Neuerschlossenen Eroberung von Jerusalem des Flavius Josephus und den Christlichen Quellen* (RB 9; Heidelberg: Carl Winters Universitätsbuchhandlung; vol. 1, 1929; vol. 2, 1930); ET: *The Messiah Jesus and John the Baptist, trans. Alexander Haggerty Krappe* (London: Methuen, 1931); S. G. F. Brandon, *Jesus and the Zealots: A Study of the Political Factor in Primitive Christianity* (New York: Scribner, 1967), 331–36; Hyam Maccoby, *Revolution in Judaea: Jesus and the Jewish Resistance* (London: Orbach and Chambers, 1973); Charles H. Talbert, ed., *Reimarus: Fragments*, trans. R. S. Fraser (LJS; Philadelphia: Fortress Press, 1970), 146–50; George Aichele, "Jesus' Violence," in *Violence, Utopia and the Kingdom of God: Fantasy and Ideology in the Bible*, ed. George Aichele and Tina Pippin (London: Routledge, 1998), 72–91. See now also Rabbi Schmuley Boteach, *Kosher Jesus* (Jerusalem: Gefen, 2012); Reza Aslan, *Zealot: The Life and Times of Jesus of Nazareth* (New York: Random House, 2013). Jennifer A. Glancy, "Violence as Sign in the Fourth Gospel," *Biblical Interpretation* 17 (2009): 100-117, esp. 109-110, sees Jesus as a man "with some familiarity with a whip." J. Harold Ellens, "The Violent Jesus," in *The Destructive Power of Religion: Violence in Judaism, Christianity, and Islam*; Vol. 3, *Models and Cases of Violence in Religion* (ed. J. Harold Ellens; Westport: Praeger, 2004), 15-37, esp. 16-17, sees Jesus as having various "fits of violence." But see Ernst Bammel, "The Revolution Theory from Reimarus to Brandon," in *Jesus and the Politics of His Day*, ed. Ernst Bammel and C. F. D. Moule (Cambridge: Cambridge University Press, 1984), 11–68; Oscar Cullmann, *Jesus and the Revolutionaries* (New York: Harper & Row, 1970); Richard B. Hays, *The Moral Vision of the New Testament: Community, Cross, New Creation: A Contemporary Introduction to New Testament Ethics* (San Francisco: HarperSanFrancisco, 1996), 332–36; G. H. C. Macgregor, "Does the New Testament Sanction War?" in *A Peace Reader*, ed. E. Morris Sider and Luke L. Keefer Jr. (Nappanee: Evangel, 2002), 49–57; Victor P. Furnish, "War and Peace in the New Testament," *Int* 38 (1984): 369–71; I. Howard Marshall, "New Testament Perspectives on War," *EvQ* 57 (1985): 115–32.

2. Q 12:51, citing Mic. 7:5-6, which refers to family conflicts.

John and James Zebedee named "Sons of Thunder" because they were rebels?[4] Was Simon the Zealot a revolutionary?[5] Did Jesus really stage a messianic and militaristic "triumphal entry?" Is the pacifistic Jesus of the early Christian tradition—the "Prince of Peace"—a complete fabrication?

The Gospels seem to portray Jesus as both violent and nonviolent.[6] At first sight, therefore, these questions might seem to require affirmative answers: Jesus had a violent side. The idea that the historical Jesus lived, taught, and practiced a way of nonviolence seems to be undermined, even contradicted, by a number of passages in the Gospels that seem to portray Jesus in less idealistic terms. It is important, therefore, to review these passages in their literary, historical, and theological contexts before affirming this allegedly dark and violent side of Jesus. Let us begin, however, by first clarifying our use of terms. Violence, nonviolence, pacifism, and passivity are notoriously slippery words. For our purposes, *violence* can be defined as the *intentional* use of force in order to hurt, damage, or kill another person or group.[7] Violent force, however, takes multiple forms and expressions: personal, physical, sexual, psychological, emotional, interpersonal, socio-political, military, systemic, and structural. As we will see, the relationship between religion and violence has come under increased discussion in biblical scholarship.

Nonviolence is, of course, a modern English term and category that cannot be found as such in the biblical tradition, which instead emphasizes the language and vocabulary of peace. Nonetheless, nonviolence can be defined as a religious, philosophical, and theological ethic of abstention from violence and a pragmatic strategy of political resistance oriented toward social change, including nonviolent acts of protest, persuasion, noncooperation, and intervention.[8]

3. Ernst Bammel, "The Poor and the Zealots," in *Jesus and the Politics of His Day*, 109–28, at 124. See also Brandon, *Jesus and the Zealots*, 333.

4. Mark 3:17.

5. Luke 6:15; Mark 3:18; Matt. 10:4.

6. Michel Desjardins, *Peace, Violence and the New Testament* (Sheffield: Sheffield Academic Press, 1997), 62–110, esp. 72–78, 111. See also Albert Curry Winn, *Ain't Gonna Study War No More: Biblical Ambiguity and the Abolition of War* (Louisville: Westminster John Knox, 1993).

7. On structural violence, see Johan Galtrung, "Violence, Peace and Peace Research," *Journal of Peace Research* 6/3 (1969): 167-91; "Cultural Violence," *Journal of Peace Research* 27/3 (1990): 291-305. On violence as "violation of personhood," see Robert MacAfee Brown, *Religion and Violence* (2d edn.; Philadelphia: Westminster [1973] 1987), 7.

8. For different theoretical approaches see John Howard Yoder, *Nonviolence: A Brief History: The Warsaw Lectures*, ed. Paul Martens, Matthew Porter, and Myles Werntz (Waco: Baylor University Press, 2010); Reinhold Niebuhr, *An Interpretation of Christian Ethics* (New York: Seabury, 1979); idem, "Why the Church is Not Pacifist," in his *Christianity and Power Politics* (New York: Scribner's, 1940; repr. North

Theories and theologies of nonviolence have been developed and enacted in contemporary times in resistance movements led by Mahatma Gandhi and Martin Luther King Jr., implemented in terms of socio-economic justice by Dorothy Day and the Catholic Worker, deployed as rhetorical weapons in critiquing the Church's support of Just War theory, and used as effective strategies in peaceful political revolutions and conscientious objections to military service,[9] although ethical philosophies of nonviolence date back far beyond the first century C.E.[10]

Pacifism, like nonviolence, is a modern term,[11] representing a variety of views ranging from the complete rejection of physical violence under any circumstances to the allowance of limited expressions of violence in situations of self-defense. Pacifism is also to be differentiated from passivity, which involves

Haven, CT: Archon, 1969); Hannah Arendt, *On Violence* (New York: Harcourt, Brace, and World, 1969); Thomas Merton, *Faith and Violence: Christian Teaching and Christian Practice* (Notre Dame, IN: University of Notre Dame Press, 1968); Joan V. Bondurant, *Conflict: Violence and Non-Violence* (Chicago: Aldine-Atherton, 1971); eadem, *The Conquest of Violence: The Gandhian Philosophy of Conflict* (Princeton: Princeton University Press, 1988); Charles McCollough, *The Non-Violent Radical: Seeing and Living the Wisdom of Jesus* (Eugene, OR: Wipf & Stock, 2012); Keith Akers, *The Lost Religion of Jesus: Simple Living and Nonviolence in Early Christianity* (New York: Lantern, 2000).

9. See Henry David Thoreau, "Civil Disobedience," in *Walden and Civil Disobedience* (Boston: Houghton Mifflin, 1960) and numerous editions; Mahatma Gandhi, *Nonviolent Resistance* (New York: Schocken, 1961); Richard Attenborough, *The Words of Gandhi* (New York: Newmarket Press, 1982); William Borman, *Gandhi and Nonviolence* (Albany: SUNY Press, 1986); Martin Luther King Jr., *Strength to Love* (New York: Harper and Row, 1963); idem, *Where Do We Go From Here: Chaos or Community?* (New York: Harper and Row, 1967); idem, *A Testament of Hope: The Essential Writings and Speeches of Martin Luther King, Jr.*, ed. James M. Washington (San Francisco: Harper and Row, 1986); John Dear, *The God of Peace: Toward a Theology of Nonviolence* (Maryknoll, NY: Orbis Books, 1994); idem, *Put Down Your Sword: Answering the Gospel Call to Creative Nonviolence* (Grand Rapids: Eerdmans, 2008); Eugene Sharp, *The Politics of Nonviolent Action,* Vol. 1: *Power and Struggle*; Vol. 3: *The Pole Dynamics of Nonviolent Action* (Boston: Porter Sargent, 1973); Robert Cooney and Helen Michalowski, *Power of the People: Active Nonviolence in The United States* (Philadelphia: New Society, 1987); *Nonviolence in Theory and Practice*, ed. R. L. Holmes (California: Wadsworth, 1990).

10. For nonviolence in Jainism, see Christopher Chapple, *Nonviolence to Animals, Earth, and Self in Asian Traditions* (Albany: SUNY Press, 1993).

11. Keith Robbins, *The Abolition of War: The Peace Movement in Britain, 1914-1919* (University of Wales Press, 1976), 10, claims that the term was coined by Émile Arnaud and adopted at the Universal Peace Congress in Glasgow in 1901. See also Peter Brock and Paul Socknat, *Challenge to Mars: Essays on Pacifism from 1918 to 1945* (Toronto: University of Toronto Press, 1999), ix; Jenny Teichman, *Pacifism and the Just War: A Study in Applied Philosophy* (New York: Basil Blackwell, 1986). On Christian pacifism, see Theron F. Schlabach and Richard T. Hughes, *Proclaim Peace: Christian Pacifism from Unexpected Quarters* (Urbana: University of Illinois, 1997).

doing nothing whereas pacifism advocates doing the least harm in any given situation. Nonviolence and pacifism are thus both philosophies of action useful in ethical and political programs of social change.

"I Have Come Not To Bring Peace": Jesus and the Sword(s)

According to Q 12:51, Jesus did not come "to bring peace, but a sword (μάχαιραν)."[12] This is one of Jesus' most enigmatic and misrepresented sayings.[13] Most scholars rightly regard this saying as symbolic or metaphorical, referring either to the familial division that allegiance to Jesus precipitated,[14] or the persecution faced by the disciples. In other words, Jesus is not referring to a *literal* physical sword of revolutionary violence but rather to the conflict and division that loyalty to his movement would provoke, specifically in a familial context. Jesus' use of "sword" language should not be taken literally.[15] The Jesus of Q 12:51/Matt. 10:34 does not use the "sword" to endorse violence.[16] The saying's clear allusion to the book of Micah (7:5-6; cf. Matt 10:36) also suggests that this saying reflects an eschatological "day of the Lord," a day when

> the son treats the father with contempt, the daughter rises up
> against her mother, the daughter-in-law against her mother-in-law;
> [and] a man's enemies are the men of his own house.

12. Matt. 10:34. See Stephen J. Patterson, "Fire and Dissension: *Ipsissima Vox Jesu* in Q 12:49, 51-53?" *Forum* 5 (1989): 121–39.

13. John P. Meier, *A Marginal Jew: Rethinking the Historical Jesus,* vol. 3: *Companions and Competitors* (ABRL; New York: Doubleday, 2001), 68-69, 111; Dunn, *Jesus Remembered*, 804; Dale C. Allison, "Q 12:51-53 and Mark 9:11-13 and the Messianic Woes," in Authenticating the Words of Jesus, ed. Bruce D. Chilton and Craig A. Evans (Leiden: Brill, 1999), 289-310; Christoph Heil, "Die Rezeption von Micah 7,6 in Q und Lukas," *ZNW* 88 (1997): 211-22; Wright, *Jesus and the Victory of God*, 401-402; Stephen J. Patterson, "Ipsissima Vox Jesu in Q 12:49, 51-53?," *Forum* 5 (1989): 121-39; Matthew Black, "Uncomfortable Words III. The Violent Word," *ExpT* 81 (1970): 115-18;

14. Aslan, *Zealot*, 120, insists that Jesus "was certainly no pacifist," citing Matt. 10:34 (Q 12:51) as evidence.

15. Luke 22:35-38. Dale C. Allison Jr., *Jesus of Nazareth: Millenarian Prophet* (Minneapolis: Fortress Press, 1998), 146; idem, "Q 12:51-53 and Mk 9:11-13 and the Messianic Woes," in *Authenticating the Words of Jesus*, ed. Craig A. Evans and Bruce Chilton (Leiden: Brill, 1998), 289–310; idem, *Jesus of Nazareth*, 145–46. See also Perrin, *Jesus and the Language of the Kingdom*, 46.

16. Allison, *Jesus of Nazareth*, 146.

Many scholars affirm the saying's authenticity.[17] Jesus almost certainly inspired familial divisions during his ministry in Judea and Galilee. The Church would probably not have created a saying in which Jesus denied that he had come to bring peace.[18] On the other hand, this saying could easily represent the social strain on early Christian families throughout the first-century.[19] Jesus may have alluded to Micah; the allusion could also be a Christian proof-text.[20] The fact that good arguments can be raised both to affirm and deny the saying's authenticity symbolizes our interpretive challenge: the early Jesus tradition contains both eschatological judgment *and* salvation sayings. The time of salvation *and* judgment has arrived.

According to Q 16:16, another difficult saying, the kingdom suffers violence. But *who* is *inflicting* this violence? Historically, Jesus suffered *political violence* at the hands of the Romans, but theologically, Jesus either suffers *divine violence* in order to atone for human sin or suffers *demonic violence* at the hands of the "powers" he thereby defeats.[21] Many Jewish apocalyptic texts envision the end-time as an era of great violence,[22] but Jesus does not *engage* in physical, interpersonal violence. Jesus' consistent response to this kind of violence is nonviolence.

According to the author of the Gospel of Luke, Jesus instructed his disciples to buy swords. This would seem to suggest that Jesus, although programmatically nonviolent during his ministry, may have changed his mind shortly before his arrest:[23]

17. Meier, *A Marginal Jew*, 3:68-69; Ehrman, *Jesus*, 170-171; Allison, "Q 12:51-53," 300-306; Wright, *Jesus and the Victory of God*, 401-402; Crossan, *The Historical Jesus*, xvi, 439; Meyer, *The Aims of Jesus*, 213.

18. Jesus' birth inaugurates an era of "peace" (Luke 2:14). He instructs his disciples to declare "peace" during their missions (Q 10:5-6). He laments Jerusalem's refusal to recognize the "things that make for peace" (Luke 19:42) and the risen Jesus greets his disciples by saying "peace be with you" (Luke 24:36; John 20:19, 21, 26).

19. So Lüdemann, *Jesus After 2000 Years*, 350; Bultmann, *History of the Synoptic Tradition*, 155.

20. Funk, et al, *The Five Gospels*, 174.

21. For the idea that the kingdom suffers violence at the hands of demonic "powers" (*Geistermächte*), see Martin Dibelius, *Die urchristliche Überlieferung von Johannes dem Täufer* (FRLANT 15; Göttingen: Vandenhoeck & Ruprecht, 1911), 23-29, esp. 26. See also Norman Perrin, *Jesus and the Language of the Kingdom: Symbol and Metaphor in New Testament Interpretation* (NTL; London: SCM, 1976), 46.

22. *1 En.* 91.11; 91.6-7; 103.15; 104.9; 4Q171 2.14-15, 18-19; 1QHa 10.20-22. On the theme of eschatological violence at Qumran and in Q 16:16, see Allison, *The End of the Ages Has Come*, 123.

23. T. C. Butler, *Luke* (HBC; Nashville: Abingdon, 2000), 371.

> "When I sent you out without a purse, bag, or sandals, did you lack anything?"
>
> They said, "No, not a thing." He said to them, "but now, the one who has a purse must take it, and likewise a bag; and the one who has no sword must sell his cloak and buy one. For I tell you, this scripture must be fulfilled in me:
>
> 'And he was numbered among the lawless,' and indeed what is written about me is being fulfilled." They said, "See, Lord, here are two swords."
>
> "It is enough," he replied.[24]

Did Jesus suddenly change his mind during his last hours? Was this the Lukan Jesus' way of telling his disciples that violence was permitted in certain extreme cases of self-defense? What does Jesus mean by "It is enough" (Ἱκανόν ἐστιν)? "Enough" for what? Two swords were most definitely not "enough" to mount a revolt against the Roman Empire, nor were they even "enough" to resist arrest—if Jesus had wanted to do so. But Luke denies that Jesus resisted arrest; in fact, when a disciple (Peter in John) uses his sword to cut off the ear of Malchus, the servant of the high priest, Jesus *rebukes* the disciples ("No more of this!") and heals the servant.[25] Jesus also rebukes the guards: "Have you come out with swords and clubs as if I were a bandit (λῃστὴν)?"[26] Why does the Lukan Jesus tell his disciples to buy swords and then tell them not to use them? A literal reading of Luke does not allow much time for his disciples to sell their cloaks and buy swords. It does not seem likely that Jesus was testing his disciples to see if they would resort to violence, nor does it seem likely that Jesus' cry of "enough" is exasperation.[27] Perhaps we should simply take the saying metaphorically.

Alternatively, is the two-swords saying Luke's way of contrasting the providential care enjoyed by the disciples during their early mission with the

24. Luke 22:35-38. NRSV.

25. Luke 22:49-51.

26. Luke 22:52.

27. See also Jeremy Thomson, "Jesus and the Two Swords: Did Jesus Endorse Violence?" *Anabaptism Today* 33 (June 2003): 10–16. As protection, see Guy F. Herschberger, *War, Peace, and Nonresistance* (Scottdale, PA: Herald Press, 1969), 302–3. As a test, see John K. Stoner, "The Two Swords Passage: A Command or a Question? Nonviolence in Luke 22," in *Within the Perfection of Christ*, ed. T. L. Brensinger and E. M. Sider (Nappanee: Evangel Press, 1990), 67–80. As exasperation, see Richard B. Hays, *The Moral Vision of the New Testament: Community, Cross, New Creation: A Contemporary Introduction to New Testament Ethics* (New York: Harper Collins, 1966), 333. As irony, see I. Howard Marshall, *The Gospel of Luke* (NIGCT; Exeter: Paternoster, 1978), 823.

hostility of the political and religious opposition toward Jesus in Jerusalem? Or do Luke's two swords refer to the "two eras" of the church?[28] Has God's providential care been "abrogated" by Jesus' death? Is life without Jesus going to be dangerous and unsupported? Is Jesus reversing the mission instructions in Q 10:1-12, Matt. 10:5-14, and Mark 6:7-13? Or is this just Luke's way of explaining why there actually were swords among the disciples at Jesus' arrest—a retroverted instruction to provide authority for the embarrassing historical fact that a disciple used violence against the servant of the high priest? Why does Jesus accept the presence of swords and then forbid their use? The most compelling explanation—and the one Luke himself provides—is that the two swords were "enough" for Jesus to *fulfill the scripture*: Jesus needed to be "numbered among the lawless" in order to fulfill Isa. 53:12:[29]

> he poured out himself to death, and was numbered with the transgressors.
> Yet he bore the sin of many, and made intercession for the transgressors.

Criminals were known for being armed; the two swords, therefore, serve a *symbolic* function: not to justify violence but to fulfill scripture:[30] Jesus would be found among "outlaws" and arrested as a criminal. Jesus does not endorse the use of violence. Given Jesus' rebuke of Peter's use of the sword, the Temple guards,[31] Jesus' healing act in Luke,[32] his nonresistance to arrest, his instruction to "love enemies" and "turn the other cheek," Jesus' kingdom not being "of this world,"[33] and his disciples' nonresistance, there is no compelling reason here to conclude that Jesus endorsed or used violence.

28. Hans Conzelmann, *The Theology of St. Luke*, trans. Geoffrey Buswell (New York: Harper, 1960).

29. Jean Lasserre, *War and the Gospel*, trans. Oliver Coburn (Scottdale, PA: Herald Press, 1962), 37–45; Willard M. Swartley, *Covenant of Peace: The Missing Peace in New Testament Theology and Ethics* (Grand Rapids: Eerdmans, 2006), 131.

30. Jeremy Schipper, *Disability and Isaiah's Suffering Servant* (BR; New York: Oxford University Press, 2011), 75. See also Kevin L. Moore, "Why Two Swords Were Enough: Israelite Tradition History Behind Luke 22:35-38," Ph. D. dissertation, University of Denver, 2009.

31. Luke 22:36; Matt. 26:52; John 18:11.

32. Luke 22:51.

33. John 18:36.

Jesus and Caesar

The Gospel of Mark follows the triumphal entry scene with Jesus being questioned about the Roman tribute. The saying is widely regarded as authentic.[34] It has also long been used as a scriptural warrant for the separation of Church and State, relegating politics and religion to two separate spheres of authority. It is important, therefore, to read this text in its literary and historical contexts. The narrative setting involves Jesus being trapped by "some Pharisees and some Herodians." They ask him the politically loaded question:

> "Is it lawful (ἔξεστιν) to pay taxes (κῆνσον) to the emperor, or not?[35] Should we (δῶμεν) pay them, or should we not?" But knowing their hypocrisy, he said to them, "Why are you putting me to the test? Bring me a *denarius* (δηνάριον) and let me see it." And they brought one. Then he said to them, "Whose head (εἰκὼν) is this, and whose title (ἡ ἐπιγραφή)?" They answered, "The emperor's" (Καίσαρος). Jesus said to them, "Give (ἀπόδοτε) to the emperor the things that are the emperor's, and to God the things that are God's."[36]

Authorities weigh in on different sides. On one hand, there are those who claim that Jesus is commanding people to respect the state's authority and pay the taxes demanded of them. This is the traditional view,[37] and it is supported by Paul. In his letter to the Romans, Paul advises paying taxes because the earthly authorities were introduced by God:

34. Bultmann, *History of the Synoptic Tradition*, 26; Roy W. Hoover and The Jesus Seminar, *The Five Gospels: The Search for the Authentic Words of Jesus* (New York: Maxwell Macmillan International, 1993), 102. For further bibliography see J. Spencer Kennard Jr., *Render to God: A Study of the Tribute Passage* (New York: Oxford, 1950); Richard J. Cassidy, *Christian and Roman Rule in the New Testament* (New York: Crossroad, 2001); John R. Donahue, "A Neglected Factor in the Theology of Mark," *JBL* 101 (1982): 563–94; Paul C. Finney, "The Rabbi and the Coin Portrait (Mark 12:15b, 16): Rigorism Manqué," *JBL* 112 (1993): 629–44; Charles Homer Giblin, "The 'Things of God' in the Question Concerning Tribute to Caesar (Lk 20:25; Mk 12:17; Mt 22:21)," *CBQ* 33 (1971): 510–27; William R. Herzog, "Dissembling, a Weapon of the Weak: The Case of Christ and Caesar in Mark 12:13-17 and Romans 13:1-7," *Perspectives in Religious Studies* 21 (1994): 339–60; Richard A. Horsley, *Jesus and the Spiral of Violence: Popular Jewish Resistance in Roman Palestine* (San Francisco: Harper & Row, 1987), 306–17.

35. For ἔξεστιν as referring to the Mosaic law, see Mark 2:24, 26; 3:4; 6:18; 10:2.

36. Mark 12:13-18 (Matt. 22:15-22; Luke 20:20-26). NRSV. See also *Thomas* L. 100; Papyrus Egerton 2.

37. Justin, *Apology* 1.17.

> Let every person be subject to the governing authorities; for there is no authority (ἐξουσία) except from God, and those authorities that exist have been instituted by God.[38]

The prophetic tradition also envisions God as using foreign nations to serve his purposes, which is why Isaiah can call Cyrus "the Lord's Anointed."[39] One might also recall Josephus's idealized description of the Essenes, who, he claims, swear "constant loyalty to all, but above all to those in power; for authority never falls to a man without the will of God."[40]

It is not uncommon to find the Jewish apocalyptic vision depending entirely on God for deliverance and not appealing to military action.[41] We might also recall that Matthew's Jesus advises Peter to pay the Temple tax for the two of them in order to avoid offending the authorities.[42] What all of this seems to amount to is that Jesus' response "allows for a limited realm in which Roman rule is legitimate, but keeps Jewish practice inviolate from that realm."[43] A plain reading of "Give back to Caesar" seems to suggest that Jesus recommended paying the Roman tribute. But are things really this simple? Some think that Jesus is openly defying Roman authority by advocating tax resistance.[44] If this were true, it would suggest that Jesus was covertly advocating militant resistance against Rome.[45] After all, in the trial scene before Pilate the charge is repeated that Jesus "opposes payment of taxes to Caesar *and* claims to be messiah, a king."[46] Was Jesus advocating the non-payment of the Roman tribute, a position that would certainly have justified the charge of sedition?

38. Rom. 13:1. See also 1 Pet. 2:13-14. But see Horsley, *Jesus and the Spiral of Violence*, 311.

39. Isa 45:1.

40. *War* 2.139-140.

41. Paula Fredriksen, *Jesus of Nazareth, King of the Jews* (New York: Alfred A. Knopf, 1999), 243.

42. Matt. 17:24-27.

43. Amy-Jill Levine and Marc Zvi Brettler, *The Jewish Annotated New Testament: New Revised Standard Version Bible Translation* (New York: Oxford University Press, 2011), 85.

44. M. K. Gandhi, "Render Unto Caesar," *Young India* (1930): 43.

45. Aslan, *Zealot*, 250–51, translates βιάζεται in the middle voice to read "the Kingdom of Heaven has been coming violently" as the "original form of the verse." The International Q Project interprets Q 16:16 to refer to violence done *to* the kingdom, preferring the passive, which appears to be more consistent with the next clause: "and violent men (βιασταὶ) plunder it." This seems plausible, given that John the Baptist died a violent death. The saying has nothing to do with advocating violence or revolutionary activity against Rome. For the saying's tradition history, see Stephen Llewelyn, "The *Traditionsgeschichte* of Matt. 11:12-13, Par. Luke 16:16," *NovT* 36, no. 4 (1994): 330–49; Peter Scott Cameron, *Violence and the Kingdom: The Interpretation of Matthew 11:12* (ANTJ 5; New York: Peter Lang, 1988).

46. Luke 23:1-4.

First-century Jews paid several types of taxes: the Temple tax, customs taxes, and land-taxes. But the question posed to Jesus is not about "taxes" in general. It is a question about *Roman* tribute. The question is one that deeply divided Jews and should be seen within the larger historical context of tax resistance in first-century Judea. In 6 C.E. the institution of a new poll tax led to a revolt by Judas of Gamala in Galilee.[47] Judas taught that this taxation was no better than an induction into slavery and that God alone was king of Israel. This ideology ultimately led to military revolt and Judas's sons became leaders in what would become the Zealot resistance movement. The Roman tribute was thus a central symbol of Jewish resistance and provoked the controversial question: who was the *true* King—God or Caesar?

The Synoptics locate this scene immediately after Jesus' "triumphal entry." Jesus has just been proclaimed "king." He has been claiming the authority to interpret the Law. The Pharisees and the Herodians try to trap him with a question he cannot answer. If he says it is permissible to pay the tribute, then he is a collaborator and will receive the scorn of his fellow Jews. What kind of a messianic candidate would approve of Roman occupation? If he says it is not permissible to pay the tribute, he is guilty of sedition. There is apparently no way out of this trap. No matter what he says, he will be in trouble.

What does he do? He refuses to answer the question. Instead, he asks for a *denarius*, the coin that bears the "image" (εἰκὼν) of Caesar, the coin that "belongs" to Caesar. The irony does not escape Mark. Here is the true Son of God and Prince of Peace examining the coin that bears the image of another Son of God and Priest of the Roman *Pax Romana*.

> *TI CAESAR DIVI AUG F AUGUSTUS*
> Caesar Augustus Tiberius, son of the god Augustus

The Greek word for "inscription" (ἐπιγραφή) occurs only one other time in Mark, to describe the "inscription" (ἐπιγραφὴ) of the charge against Jesus, which read Ὁ βασιλεὺς τῶν Ἰουδαίων, "the *king* of the Jews."[48] The *denarius*, the "image," and the "inscription" all "belong" to Caesar, so they can be "given back" to Caesar. What, then, "belongs" to God? The text does not tell us exactly what Jesus means. On the one hand, *everything* belongs to God: "The earth is the Lord's, and everything in it, the world, and all who live in it."[49] And yet the Romans are claiming that everything belongs to them. Jesus' reference to

47. Acts 5:37; *War* 2.117-18; *Ant.* 18.4-10.

48. Mark 15:26.

49. Ps. 24:1.

the "image" inscribed on the coin may be a clue. According to Gen. 1:26-27, humanity (Adam) is made in the "image" of God. What would it mean, then, for the things that "belong" to God to be returned?[50]

Here we need to recall the cosmic *dualism* of the early Jesus tradition.[51] This is not a dualism of Church and State. Jewish apocalypticism generally recognized two distinct domains of authority: worldly authority and divine authority. Jesus claimed to have derived his charismatic authority from the divine, which is why he could say that his kingdom was "*not* of/from this world" (οὐκ ἔστιν ἐκ τοῦ κόσμου τούτου).[52] This is also why he could reject Satan's offer of "all the kingdoms *of this world*," according to Q's Temptation narrative. It is the devil who exercises authority over "this world."[53] The kingdom of God was breaking *into* this world. The world of wealth—Caesar's *denarius*—was part of the domain of Mammon and Satan. One cannot serve God *and* Mammon.[54] But the two worlds, the two "kingdoms," *coexist*.[55]

Jesus turns a potentially explosive political challenge back on his challengers without advocating violent action against Rome. If his challengers expected him to reject the tribute so they could entrap him, they were confounded by his response. Jesus does not advocate a militant, revolutionary, let alone violent response to Roman rule. If anything, he challenges such an attitude by implying that Caesar should be "given back" what "belongs" to him. On the other hand, Jesus' enigmatic response could also be interpreted—by his fellow Jews—to mean that he did indeed defy Roman rule because everything really "belonged" to God. This may be why the charge was (unsuccessfully) repeated at Jesus' trial in the Gospel of Luke.[56]

In the Johannine trial scene Jesus tells Pilate that his kingdom "is *not* of this world."[57] This enigmatic confession, in conjunction with the tribute saying, has often been taken to mean that Jesus was not interested in political rule and that his messianic identity did not involve military action. There is good reason for such a view. In Q's Temptation narrative Jesus explicitly rejects "all

50. Gregory A. Boyd, *The Myth of a Christian Religion: Losing Your Religion for the Beauty of a Revolution* (Grand Rapids: Zondervan, 2009), 26.

51. As recognized by Ched Myers, *Binding the Strong Man: A Political Reading of Mark's Story of Jesus* (Maryknoll, NY: Orbis Books, 1990), 312.

52. John 18:36.

53. 1 John 5:18-19; John 12:31; 14:30; 16:11; Eph. 2:2; 2 Cor 4:4.

54. Matt. 6:24; Luke 16:13.

55. John Howard Yoder, *The Politics of Jesus: Vicit Agnus Noster* (Grand Rapids: Eerdmans, 1972), 53.

56. Luke 23:2.

57. John 18:36.

the kingdoms of this world," kingdoms under the authority of Satan.[58] When we transfer Jesus' cosmic dualism into the politico-religious arena of the tribute passage—and recall that Jesus exorcised the demon called "Legion" by casting it/them into the sea, another ironic aside not missed by Mark—we find that Jesus' reference to what "belongs" to God suggests that God is "reclaiming" what belongs to him. This is why so many of the "kingdom" sayings suggest the *presence* and/or the arrival of the kingdom.

Jesus may not answer the question posed to him—a question framed so as to entrap him in sedition—and his response may have been purposefully ambiguous, so as to accommodate both nationalists and collaborators, but his rhetorical evasion cannot be interpreted to suggest that Jesus in any way advocated or endorsed armed military resistance against Rome.

Jesus the Revolutionary

The idea that Jesus was a political revolutionary or "Zealot" has recently been popularized with some notoriety by Reza Aslan,[59] but there is little to commend it. There is nothing new here under the sun.[60] The Revolutionary Jesus is as old

58. Q 4.

59. See, for example, Craig A. Evans, "Reza Aslan Tells an Old Story about Jesus," *Christianity Today*, http://www.christianitytoday.com/ct/2013/august-web-only/zealot-reza-aslan-tells-same-old-story-about-jesus.html, August 9, 2013 [accessed Dec. 13, 2013]; Elizabeth Castelli, "Reza Aslan—Historian?," *The Nation*, http://www.thenation.com/article/175688/reza-aslan-historian, August 9, 2013 [accessed Dec. 13, 2013); Dale B. Martin, "Still a Firebrand, 2,000 Years Later," *The New York Times*, August 5, 2013, http://www.nytimes.com/2013/08/06/books/reza-aslans-zealot-the-life-and-times-of-jesus-of-nazareth.html?_r=0, [accessed Dec. 13, 2013]; Stephen Prothero, "Book Review: 'Zealot: The Life and Times of Jesus of Nazareth,'" *The Washington Post*, August 2, 2013, http://www.washingtonpost.com/opinions/book-review-zealot-the-life-and-times-of-jesus-of-nazareth-by-reza-aslan/2013/08/02/029f6088-f087-11e2-bed3-b9b6fe264871_story.html, [accessed Dec. 13, 2013]; Allan Nadler, "What Jesus Wasn't: *Zealot*," *Jewish Review of Books*, August 11, 2013, http://jewishreviewofbooks.com/articles/449/reza-aslan-what-jesus-wasnt/, [accessed Dec. 13, 2013]. Nadler's review is especially scathing: "The only novelty in Aslan's book is his relentlessly reductionist, simplistic, one-sided and often harshly polemical portrayal of Jesus as a radical, zeaously nationalistic, and purely political figure." Nadler also notes that "The crucial distinction that Aslan fails to acknowledge is that what clearly sets Jesus so radically apart from all of these figures is his adamant rejection of violence . . . which Aslan willfully misconstrues." See also Robert Gundry, "Jesus as a Jewish Jihadist," *Books & Culture* 19 (Dec. 2013): 14: "the reconstruction is riddled with factual errors."

60. Aslan bases his portrait of Jesus on Brandon's earlier work. One of the more telltale signs of this debt is how Aslan describes the Temple incident as an attack on Rome itself. According to Brandon, *Jesus and the Zealots*, 332: "This attack on the Temple trading system constituted, therefore, a most radical challenge to the authority of the sacerdotal aristocracy, and it was also a truly revolutionary act, for the

as Reimarus. Nonetheless, Aslan claims that Jesus was a "zealous revolutionary" who "promoted violence."[61] The Zealots, of course, did not even exist until decades *after* Jesus' death, but no matter. Tellingly, Aslan uses Matt. 10:34 (Q 12:51), the sword-saying, as his epigraph, clearly suggesting that this single saying is representative of his Jesus. The problem is that this saying, again, has *nothing* to do with physical violence. It uses the sword as a metaphor to signify how loyalty to Jesus *divides* families, separating brothers, sisters, mothers, and fathers. For Aslan, "The common depiction of Jesus as an inveterate peacemaker . . . (is) a complete fabrication . . . Jesus was "no pacifist . . . Jesus was not a fool."[62] Aslan admits that there is "no evidence that Jesus himself openly advocated violent actions,"[63] but he still asserts that Jesus called for "revolution, plain and simple." The "Kingdom of God" was synonymous with "revolt" and wouldn't "happen without the annihilation of the present leaders."[64] Jesus' "revolution" would not be "free of violence and bloodshed."[65] This is not Islamic propaganda. This is just bad history.

A far more robust version of this proposal was already made long ago by S. G. F. Brandon. In a 1951 study focused on how the destruction of Jerusalem affected the early (Jewish) Christian church,[66] Brandon referred to the "two swords" passage in Luke as one example of Jesus' movement having a "sufficient semblance of sedition to cause the Roman authorities to regard him as a possible revolutionary." Brandon emphasizes how Jesus' disciples were "armed," the Roman or Jewish guards "heavily armed," and how "armed resistance" was offered by the disciples, attesting "the presence of a political aspect of some kind."[67] Brandon then turns to the Temple incident, suggesting that "the excitability and fierce passions of an oriental people" may have resulted in

high priest held his office and authority from the Romans, and was thus an essential factor of the Roman government in Judaea. To challenge the rule of the high priest was thus, in effect, to challenge the Roman rule." As for crucifixion being reserved solely for violent "insurrection," ba nditry, and murder, this is simply not true. The Romans also crucified people for defamation of the emperor (Seutonius, *Domitian* 10.1; Quintillian, *Institutio Oratoria* 9.2.65), "stirring up the people" (Paulus, *Sententiae* 5.22.1), and military desertion (Livy, *Ab urbe condita* 30.43.13). Josephus also reports the Romans crucifying Jews for no apparent reason at all during the Revolt (*War* 5.447–49).

61. Aslan, *Zealot*, xxiv.

62. Ibid., 122.

63. Ibid., 120.

64. Ibid., xxix, 119.

65. Ibid., 120.

66. S. G. F. Brandon, *The Fall of Jerusalem and the Christian Church: A Study of the Effects of the Jewish Overthrow of A. D. 70 on Christianity* (London: SPCK, 1957 [1951]), esp. 102–09.

67. Ibid., 103.

"violent action" by Jesus' followers. He then refers to Simon "the Zealot" as evidence that "a member of the extreme nationalist party of contemporary Jewish life was a close supporter of Jesus."[68] For Brandon, this is "the one surviving piece of evidence about his true attitude towards its members and their ideals,"[69] leaping to the conclusion that "Palestinian Christianity . . . was closely associated with the nationalist aspirations of Israel . . . the profession of Zealotism was not incompatible with allegiance to Jesus."[70]

Brandon claims that the origin of the concept of "the Pacific Christ" is to be found in the Markan (mis)representation of Jesus as an apolitical, innocent target of Jewish hatred who cautiously endorsed the Jewish tribute to Rome.[71] For Brandon, this apologetic portrait was designed to domesticate Jesus for early pro-Roman Gentile religious consumption as a universal savior uninterested in Jewish politics. It only worked because the early Jewish Christian community was decimated by the Revolt. Brandon argues that Matthew and Luke further transformed the Markan Jesus into that of the pacific Christ.[72] Matthew developed Mark's portrait "of a Jesus who endorsed the Roman rule in Judaea into that of a Christ who eschewed all resort to arms."[73] This distanced Gentile Christians from Jewish nationalism and reassured the Roman authorities that they were pacifistic.[74]

While Brandon is certainly correct in arguing that the Gospels are tendentious in their representation of Pilate's innocence in Jesus' death, he does not consider the possibility that Jesus ended up on a Roman cross based on a charge originating within a *Jewish* cultural context of royal messianic expectations.[75] Brandon does not make much of Jesus' apparent failure to fulfill any militaristic expectations, his public record of rejecting militaristic solutions to social injustice,[76] and his movement's complete lack of a violent,

68. Ibid., 105.

69. Ibid., 106.

70. Ibid., 109. Cf. Brandon, *Jesus and the Zealots*, 355.

71. Brandon, *Jesus and the Zealots*, 283–321.

72. Ibid., 285.

73. Ibid., 306.

74. Ibid., 316.

75. Brandon, *Jesus and the Zealots*, 336, 342, simply concludes that "Jesus' execution by the Romans resulted not from any overt and direct revolutionary act against them, but from his attack on the authority of the Jewish sacerdotal aristocracy . . . This attack was motivated by Jesus' desire to prepare Israel spiritually for the advent of the kingdom of God."

76. For criticism, see Martin Hengel, Review of *Jesus and the Zealots*, *Journal of Semitic Studies* 14 (1969): 231–40; Walter Wink, "Jesus and Revolution: Reflections on S. G. F. Brandon's Jesus and the Zealots," *Union Seminary Quarterly Review* 25 (1969): 37–59; William Klassen, "Jesus and the Zealot

nationalistic, or militaristic reputation.[77] The alleged evidence for a nationalistic, violence-prone, Revolutionary Jesus—the Temple incident (as an alleged act of insurrection); the (two) swords; the possible presence of a "Zealot" in Jesus' entourage; and Jesus' execution for sedition—simply do not support the thesis. The nationalistic-revolutionary hypothesis almost completely misrepresents the historical Jesus.

While the Gospels do identify a "Zealot," an "Iscariot," and two "Sons of Thunder" in Jesus' entourage, there is no particular reason to associate "Simon the Zealot" (Ζηλωτὴν) with the Zealots of the 60s described by Josephus.[78] Similarly, Judas "Iscariot" ('Ισκαριώθ) is more plausibly understood as Simon "of Kerioth" than an early initiate of the *sicarii*. The appellation "Sons of Thunder" does not require us to read violent revolutionary tendencies into these disciples when it may only refer to their heated tempers. There is no good evidence to suggest that Jesus' disciples constituted a small militia or army, let alone a revolutionary band intent on overthrowing Rome.

The so-called "triumphal entry" into Jerusalem may be multiply attested,[79] embarrassing, and inconsistent with the idea that Jesus distanced himself from the role and title of "king,"[80] but even if the scene contains an historical kernel–an assumption not all scholars are willing to make[81]—it would not tell us very much about Jesus' alleged tendency towards politico-military violence. The Davidic tradition may have envisioned the future king riding into Jerusalem to overthrow Israel's enemies and liberate the people, but Jesus'

Option," *Canadian Journal of Theology* 16 (1970): 12-21. Raymond E. Brown, *The Death of the Messiah: From Gethsemane to the Grave: A Commentary on the Passion Narratives in the Four Gospels* (2 vols.; New York: Doubleday, 1994), 1: 680, sees the theory as suffering "from imprecision and/or unrestrained imagination in reading the evidence of Josephus." Brandon's response to his critics in "Jesus and the Zealots: Aftermath," *Bulletin of the John Rylands Library* 54 (1971): 47-66, here 57, was unrepentant: "my hypothesis provides a reasonable explanation of how the Christian movement began."

77. The fact that Jesus—but not his disciples—was arrested by the Temple guards, and that Jesus—but none of his disciples—were executed by Pilate has rightly been recognized as a major argument *against* seeing Jesus or his movement as nationalistic, violent, or militaristic.

78. Børge Salomonsen, "Some Remarks on the Zealots with Special Regard to the Term 'Qannaim' in Rabbinic Literature," *NTS* 13 (1966): 164–76, at 175; Brandon, *Jesus and the Zealots*, 355. See idem, "Jesus and the Zealots: A Correction," *NTS* 17 (1971): 453.

79. Mark 11:1-10; Matt. 21:1-11; Luke 19:28-40; John 12:12-15.

80. Contra Rudolf Bultmann, *History of the Synoptic Tradition*, trans. John Marsh (New York: Harper, 1963), 122.

81. David R. Catchpole, "The 'Triumphal' Entry," in *Jesus and the Politics of His Day*, ed. Ernst Bammel and C. F. D. Moule (Cambridge: Cambridge University Press, 1984), 319–34. See also Bultmann, *History of the Synoptic Tradition*, 122.

arrival was not a military campaign. He did not attack the Romans, nor did he encourage his followers to do so. He did not liberate Jerusalem or restore Israel's independence. If anything, Jesus' "triumphal entry" sets the Markan stage for a *non*-military interpretation of Jewish messianism.

Alternatively, some regard the Temple incident as evidence that Jesus used violence.[82] After all, the Gospel of John does describe Jesus using a "whip of cords":

> Making a whip of cords (φραγέλλιον ἐκ σχοινίων), he drove (ἐξέβαλεν) all of them out of the Temple, both the sheep and the cattle.[83]

The fact that this reference to a "whip of cords" is found *only* in John should urge caution. In addition, John does *not* tell us that Jesus used it to *strike* anyone, not even the "sheep and the cattle." Jesus "found" the sellers and the moneychangers, but he "threw *all* of them," that is, *the sheep and cattle*, out of the Temple.[84] Surely a "whip of cords" could also be used just to make a striking sound rather than to inflict a bodily blow. Although Jesus is reported to have overturned tables, this use of physical *force* in the Temple does not seem to have been an act of *violent contact* against animals *or* human beings. It sounds more like a spontaneous attempt to move a group of animals by "shooing" them away without ever striking anyone.[85] Consequently, those who read John's account as evidence that Jesus used a "whip" to beat others are reading this into the text. The Temple incident is very shaky ground indeed upon which to build the case for a violence-prone Jesus.

The Nonviolent Jesus

There is no unambiguous evidence that Jesus ever used or advocated violence against another person. Jesus lived, taught, and practiced a way of nonviolence. This disciplined principled practice of nonviolence is distinctive *and*

82. John 2:14–15; Matt. 21:12–13; Mark 11:15–17; Luke 19:45–46. See the discussion in Mark R. Bredin, "John's Account of Jesus' Demonstration in the Temple: Violent or Nonviolent?" *BTB* 33 (2003): 44–50.

83. John 2:13.

84. Jostein Ådna, "Jesus and the Temple," in *Handbook for the Study of the Historical Jesus*, ed. Tom Holmén and Stanley E. Porter (4 vols.; Leiden: Brill, 2011), 3:2635–75, esp. 2644 n. 24.

85. Thomas R. Yoder Neufeld, *Killing Enmity: Violence and the New Testament* (Grand Rapids: Baker Academic, 2011), 15.

characteristic of the historical Jesus.[86] This conclusion is supported by multiple attestation, the instructional content of Q, Jesus' nonresistance during his arrest, and the indisputably historical tradition of early Christian pacifism.[87] Indeed, the evidence for Jesus' nonviolence is so strong that E. P. Sanders could write that "It is now virtually universally recognized that there is not a shred of evidence which would allow us to think that Jesus had military/political ambitions."[88] Jesus was not perceived by the Roman authorities as a serious politico-military threat.[89] The "Kingdom Jesus preached would be brought about by an act of God, not by human effort or force of arms."[90] Jesus was not a revolutionary "engaged in political revolution." Jesus did not attempt to physically overthrow Roman rule with armed, violent warfare and be crowned as the new "king of the Jews." Jesus did not form an army to overthrow a powerful empire through violence, nor did he behave like a military leader, and neither did his disciples. The Synoptic parable tradition refers to the kingdom with similes and metaphors because it was *not* like the political kingdoms of this world. Jesus' revolution was the announcement of a different *kind* of kingdom, one that would certainly affect, challenge, change, and subvert the political authorities' temporal rule and order, and so would indeed be "revolutionary," but this would be a "*nonviolent* revolution."[91] It is not incorrect to attribute political and revolutionary aims and goals to Jesus, but there is no evidence that Jesus ever advocated violence to fulfill them. On the contrary, "the rejection of violence

86. Gerd Theissen and Dagmar Winter, *The Quest for the Plausible Jesus: The Question of Criteria*, trans. M. Eugene Boring (Louisville: Westminster John Knox Press, 2002), 210–11. Craig A. Evans, "Authenticity Criteria in Life of Jesus Research," *CSR* 19 (1989): 6–31, at 6; Dagmar Winter, "Saving the Quest for Authenticity from the Criterion of Dissimilarity: History and Plausibility," in Chris Keith and Anthony Le Donne, eds., *Jesus, Criteria, and the Demise of Authenticity*, 113-31, here 125. James Dunn, *A New Perspective on Jesus: What the Quest for the Historical Jesus Missed* (Grand Rapids: Baker Academic, 2005), 69, refers to "the characteristic Jesus"; so also in his "Remembering Jesus: How the Quest of the Historical Jesus Lost Its Way," in *Handbook for the Study of the Historical Jesus*, 1:183–205, at 203. See now also Preston Sprinkle, *Fight: A Christian Case for Non-Violence* (Colorado Springs: David C. Cook, 2013).

87. Justin, *Dialogue with Trypho* 110; Clement of Alexandria, *Protrepticus* 10–11; Tertullian, *On Idolatry* 19; *On the Crown* 11; Origen, *Against Celsus* 8.73. On the practice of "enemy love" by Christian martyrs, see Walter Bauer, "Das Gebot der Feindesliebe und die alten Christen," *ZTK* (1917): 37–54.

88. E. P. Sanders, *Jesus and Judaism* (Philadelphia: Fortress Press, 1985), 231. See also Ben Witherington III, *The Christology of Jesus* (Minneapolis: Fortress Press, 1990), 103.

89. Fredriksen, *Jesus of Nazareth, King of the Jews*, 242–43.

90. Ibid., 244.

91. See, for example, John Dominic Crossan, *Jesus: A Revolutionary Biography* (San Francisco: HarperSanFrancisco, 1994).

of any kind is the theme of New Testament proclamation from beginning to end."[92]

This does not mean that Jesus' nonviolence is easily engaged, embraced, or adopted. As John L. McKenzie, a former president of the Society of Biblical Literature, noted: "The statement of the renunciation of violence as a means of dealing with other people is clear enough; Christians have never questioned either that Jesus said it or that it admits no qualification. Christians . . . have simply decided they cannot live according to these sayings of Jesus. To put it more accurately, they have decided that they do not wish to live according to these sayings."[93] Similarly, Father Emmanuel Charles McCarthy, a Catholic priest and Nobel Peace Prize nominee, has promoted a radical vision of Jesus' nonviolence for over forty years: "The issue of whether Jesus teaches by word and deed a way of nonviolent love of friends and enemies is settled. He does! All attempts today to justify violence from the life of Jesus or His teachings are devoid of spiritual and intellectual merit. That is not opinion, that is fact."[94] It is the Church's "calculated inattentiveness" and "evasion" that prevents Jesus' nonviolence from getting "a hearing." Why? Because Jesus' nonviolence is a "non-thought" or is casually dismissed as "fatuous, fanciful, utopian, idealist, silly, impractical."[95] Jesus' teachings are "theologically unsophisticated, rationally absurd, pragmatically impossible and spiritually unsubstantial." Our default position is to assume that "for all practical purposes, Jesus needs . . . correction because He does not understand very well the realities of violence."[96] McCarthy's critique contains provocative implications for interfaith dialogue,[97] Just War theory, and capital punishment, for he asserts that if Christian authorities are "under a divine mandate to teach what He taught on the subject of violence,"[98] then to do anything less is to betray Jesus.[99]

While the social, political, economic, and theological consequences of Jesus' nonviolence are largely marginalized in mainstream society, the subject

92. Yoder, *The Politics of Jesus*, 250.

93. John L. McKenzie, *The Civilization of Christianity* (Chicago: Thomas More Press, 1986), 158–59; see also 136–37.

94. Emmanuel Charles McCarthy, *All things flee thee for thou fleest Me: A Cry to the Churches and Their Leaders to Stop Running from the Nonviolent Jesus and His Nonviolent Way* (Wilmington: Center for Christian Nonviolence, 2003), 1.1; idem, *Christian Just War Theory: The Logic of Deceit* (Wilmington: Center for Christian Nonviolence, 2003).

95. Ibid., 3.9.

96. Ibid., 9.6.

97. Ibid., 3.2.

98. Ibid., 1.7, 8.

99. Ibid., 6.6.

is also remarkably underrepresented in historical Jesus research. For example, in the recently published encyclopedic *Handbook for the Study of the Historical Jesus* there are no entries directly addressing this most characteristic aspect of Jesus' sayings and deeds.[100] This is not to say that our theme has been entirely ignored. Marcus Borg has long argued that Jesus' nonviolence was not based simply on a political strategy, but rather "grounded in his perception of God's character . . . God's character is nonviolent; therefore be nonviolent."[101] Gerd Theissen and Dagmar Winter also readily acknowledge that Jesus' kingdom was nonviolent: "the people of the kingdom are nonviolent and are committed to nonviolence."[102] Similarly, N. T. Wright argues that Jesus critiqued violence within his Jewish context.[103] For Wright, Jesus articulated "*a new way of understanding the fulfilment of Israel's hope*. He radicalized the tradition."[104] This "redefinition of the kingdom" asserted that the Jews "had misread the signs of their own vocation and were claiming divine backing for a perversion of it."[105] The Jewish nation needed to repent of its revolutionary desire for war.[106] The "real enemy" was not Rome, but Satan, and the "true battle" and "victory" would be won in Jesus' blood sacrifice and God's violent judgment. Wright concludes that Jesus' message was vindicated with Jerusalem's destruction,[107] but this only affirms the theologically problematic violence of Jesus' oracles of eschatological judgment. Was Jesus really a prophet of eschatological violence?[108] While Wright's Jesus critiques his Jewish *contemporaries* as Satanic,

100. James H. Charlesworth, "The Historical Jesus: How to Ask Questions and Remain Inquisitive," in *Handbook for the Study of the Historical Jesus*, 1:104–9, esp. 107, affirms that "Scholars are almost all now convinced . . . that Jesus . . . did not strive to lead a rebellion against Rome or support such a revolt." John Dominic Crossan, "Context and Text in Historical Jesus Methodology," in ibid., 1:159–81, at 181, briefly refers to the "absolute and programmatic non-violence" of the early Q tradition.

101. Marcus J. Borg, *Jesus: Uncovering the Life, Teachings, and Relevance of a Religious Revolutionary* (New York: HarperSanFrancisco, 2006), 250–51. See also now J. Denny Weaver, *The Nonviolent God* (Grand Rapids: Eerdmans, 2013).

102. Theissen and Winter, *Quest for the Plausible Jesus*, 248.

103. N. T. Wright, *Jesus and the Victory of God*, Vol. 2, *Christian Origins and the Question of God* (Minneapolis: Fortress Press, 1996).

104. Ibid., 176.

105. Ibid., 274, 446–50.

106. Ibid., 317.

107. Ibid., 324.

108. The Markan narrative tales of Jesus "killing" a herd of demon-possessed swine (Mark 5:1-20; Matt. 8:28-34; Luke 8:26-39), "cursing" a fig tree to death (Mark 11:12-14, 20-25; Matt. 21:18-22), or keeping a "Zealot" in his entourage (Luke 6:15; Acts 1:13) are not particularly persuasive evidentiary examples of violence. On the mistranslation of "Zealot," see John P. Meier, *A Marginal Jew: Rethinking the Historical Jesus*, Vol. 3, *Companions and Competitors* (New York: Doubleday, 2001), 132–35.

Wright ignores the very real possibility that Jesus rejected significant elements of the tradition itself, particularly the vengeful, wrathful portrayal of God found in many biblical passages, the same God who would punish his own people by using a foreign power (Rome) as his chosen vehicle of judgment.[109]

Richard Horsley focuses on the "spiral of violence" in first-century Judea[110] and the Jesus movement's socio-political response to Roman occupation.[111] Horsley correctly outlines the structural violence of imperial Rome, and it is difficult to find fault with the idea that economic injustice, religious ideals, and apocalyptic eschatology could inspire nonviolent resistance to oppression and provide hope for a renewed social order. Josephus reports that first-century Jews often turned to nonviolent resistance against imperial Rome.[112] Many of these acts of resistance centered on religious issues. For example, Josephus describes an instance when Pilate brought Roman military standards with the embossed image of Caesar to Jerusalem.[113] An angry mob of Jews asked Pilate to remove the standards and when he refused, they "fell prone all around his house and remained motionless for five days and nights." Pilate was prepared to kill them, but when the Jews defied him by offering him their necks—"shouting that they were ready to be killed rather than transgress the law"—Pilate acquiesced and ordered the standards removed. On another occasion, Philo reports that Pilate set up "gilded shields" in Herod's palace in Jerusalem. The Jews asked him to remove them but Pilate—"a man of inflexible, stubborn, and cruel disposition, obstinately refused"—to which the Jews responded with threats that they would send an embassy or delegates directly to Tiberius, after which Tiberius ordered the shields removed.[114] Josephus also tells us that Pilate took Temple funds

109. For an attempt to work out a nonviolent theology of atonement, see J. Denny Weaver, *The Nonviolent Atonement* (Grand Rapids: Eerdmans, 2001). For a feminist critique, see Joan Carlson Brown and Rebecca Parker, "For God So Loved the World?" in *Christianity, Patriarchy, and Abuse: A Feminist Critique*, ed. J. C. Brown and C. R. Bohn (New York: Pilgrim, 1989), 1–30.

110. See Helder Cámara, *Spiral of Violence* (London: Sheed and Ward, 1971), 30.

111. Horsley, *Jesus and the Spiral of Violence*. See most recently his *Jesus and Empire: The Kingdom of God and the New World Disorder* (Minneapolis: Fortress Press, 2003).

112. David M. Rhoads, *Israel in Revolution 6–74 C. E— A Political History Based on the Writings of Josephus* (Philadelphia: Fortress Press, 1976). See also E. Mary Smallwood, *The Jews Under Roman Rule from Pompey to Diocletian* (Leiden: Brill, 1981); Paul L. Maier, "The Episode of the Golden Shields at Jerusalem," *HTR* 62 (1969): 109–21; Daniel R. Schwartz, "Josephus and Philo on Pontius Pilate," *The Jerusalem Cathedra* 3 (1983): 26–45; Per Bilde, "The Roman Emperor Gaius (Caligula)'s Attempt to Erect his Statue in the Temple of Jerusalem," *Studia Theologica* 32, no. 1 (1978): 67–93; Carl H. Kraeling, "The Episode of the Roman Standards at Jerusalem," *HTR* 35, no. 4 (1942): 263–89.

113. *War* 2.169-174; *Ant.* 18.55-59.

114. Philo, *Legatio ad Gaium*, 38.299-305.

to build a new aqueduct in Jerusalem, and when the Jews objected, Pilate had many of them killed.[115] Finally, Josephus reports that Caligula ordered a statue of himself to be erected in the Temple in Jerusalem c. 39 C.E.[116] Thousands of Jews nonviolently objected, willing to die before they allowed this to occur. These examples demonstrate that first-century Jews were willing to use nonviolent means to political and religious ends, whether these included direct personal appeals to authority, organized group demonstrations, or willingness to endure physical danger or even death for their religious convictions.

Jesus' program was intended as a renewal of Israelite society.[117] Horsley claims, however, that "nonviolence was not a principal theme in his preaching and practice," and that "we have no evidence that he ever directly or explicitly addressed the issue of violence."[118] Horsley admits that "there is no evidence that Jesus advocated violence." He also asserts that Jesus "actively opposed violence."[119] There seems to be something of a paradox in Horsley's logic: he concedes that (1) there is no evidence that Jesus committed violent acts; that (2) Jesus did not advocate violence; that (3) Jesus opposed violence; and that (4) Jesus taught an unqualified "love of enemies," yet he says that (5) Jesus did *not* "advocate" nonviolence. Horsley's Jesus is a political provocateur, a prophet of judgment and destruction, and a would-be popular king "engaged not simply in resistance but in a more serious revolt of some sort against the established order in Palestine."[120] For Horsley, portrayals of Jesus as an advocate of nonviolence depend on the Zealots as "a foil for Jesus' position" and Matt. 5:38-48, but if the Zealot movement did not exist until the Revolt (66–73 C.E.),[121] and Q 6:27-28 refers "to local enemies and not to foreign political enemies,"[122] then these portrayals are incorrect.

115. *War* 2.175-177; *Ant.* 18.60-62. See also the episode in Luke 13:1.

116. *War* 2.184-203; *Ant.* 18.261-309; Philo, *Legatio ad Gaium*, 29–43. However, see Tacitus, *Historiae*, 5.9.2.

117. Richard A. Horsley, *The Prophet Jesus and the Renewal of Israel: Moving Beyond A Diversionary Debate* (Grand Rapids: Eerdmans, 2012).

118. Horsley, *Jesus and the Spiral of Violence*, 318.

119. Ibid., 319. See also 326: Jesus "actively opposed violence" but was not a pacifist; he was a "revolutionary" but not a "violent political revolutionary."

120. Ibid., 321.

121. Rhoads, *Israel in Revolution*.

122. *Contra* much of the literature. See also his "Ethics and Exegesis: 'Love Your Enemies' and the Doctrine of Non-Violence," *JAAR* 54 (1986): 3–31, esp. 23. For the traditional view of the passage as referring to enemies in the broadest sense, see O. J. F. Seitz, "Love Your Enemies," *NTS* 16 (1969): 43–44, 46, 48, 50, 52; Robert J. Daly, "The New Testament and Early Church," in *Non-Violence, Central*

God, it seems, would put an end to the spiral of violence "violently," with even *greater* violence.[123] The problem is that it is precisely within this violent context that we should be looking for Jesus' distinctive response to the "spiral of violence," which Horsley calls the "direct manifestations of God's kingdom in his practice and teaching." Horsley's overarching interest in deconstructing the Zealot hypothesis and the "apolitical Jesus" by reconstructing Jesus in light of sociological critiques of systemic and structural violence ultimately loses sight of Jesus' critique of violence *within* the Jewish tradition itself.[124]

Walter Wink proposes that Jesus advocated a "third way" of nonviolent resistance.[125] Jesus was the one who first "revealed to the world . . . God's domination-free order of nonviolent love."[126] This set the stage for Jesus' radical critique of the family, the law, purity, holiness, ethnicity, sacrifice, violence, and discrimination against women. It is no surprise that the "domination system" killed him. Wink's reconstruction of Jesus' nonviolence is based on Q 6:27-28.[127] He argues that Matt. 5:39 ("Do not resist an evildoer") is better understood as nonviolent resistance and μὴ ἀντιστῆναι is better translated "Do not resist *violently*," appealing to its use as a military term suggesting "counteractive aggression," as in "withstanding" violence.[128] This reading would then conform to Matt. 26:52 ("those who live by the sword").[129] But

to Christian Spirituality: Perspectives from Scripture to the Present, ed. Joseph T. Culliton (TST; Toronto: Edwin Mellen, 1982), 33–62, at 41, 52; Martin Hengel, *Victory over Violence* (Philadelphia: Fortress Press, 1973); Luise Schottroff, "Non-Violence and the Love of One's Enemies," in *Essays on the Love Commandment*, ed. idem, et al. (Philadelphia: Fortress Press, 1978), 9–39; Wolfgang Schrage, *The Ethics of the New Testament* (Philadelphia: Fortress Press, 1988).

123. Horsley, *Jesus and the Spiral of Violence*, 326.

124. For the study and redefinitions of violence in light of liberation theology, see Robert McAfee Brown, *Religion and Violence* (Philadelphia: Westminster Press, 1987).

125. Walter Wink, *Jesus and Nonviolence: A Third Way* (Minneapolis: Fortress Press, 2003). See also idem, *Engaging the Powers: Discernment and Resistance in a World of Domination* (Minneapolis: Fortress Press, 1992); *Unmasking the Powers: The Invisible forces That Determine Human Existence* (Philadelphia: Fortress Press, 1986); *Naming the Powers: The Language of Power in the New Testament* (Philadelphia: Fortress Press, 1984). On the myth of sacred violence, see René Girard, *Things Hidden Since the Foundation of the World* (Stanford: Stanford University Press, 1987), 4–47.

126. Wink, *Engaging the Powers*, 45.

127. Wink, *Jesus and Nonviolence*, 59.

128. Eph. 6:1. See also Mark 15:7; Luke 23:19, 25; Acts 19:40, 23:10.

129. For its historical plausibility in relation to Josephus's account of Pilate's response to Jewish nonviolent resistance (*War* 2.169; *Ant.* 18.35) see Gerd Theissen, "Gewaltverzicht und Feindesliebe (Mt 5,38-48/Lk 6,27-38) und deren sozialgeschichtlicher Hintergrund," in his *Studien zur Soziologie des Urchristentums* (WUNT 19; 3d ed.; Tübingen: Mohr Siebeck, 1989), 191; English: *Social Reality and the Early Christians*, trans. Margaret Kohl (Minneapolis: Fortress Press, 1992), 150–51.

does turning the other cheek always rob the "oppressor" of "power," or does it simply invite a second blow? Does the one who also gives up his or her coat really shame the creditor and "unmask" a system of oppression, or does he or she just end up naked and humiliated? Is not the one going the "second mile" still following orders? Nonviolent action may expose violence for what it is, but Wink's use of Q results in an abstract analysis of honor/shame dynamics that hardly "unmasks" the oppressive system.[130] Wink also fails to critique the biblical tradition and Christianity as complicit in violence and the "domination system." Horsley has criticized Wink for constructing an abstract ethical system of nonviolence that had little to do with social protest in first-century Judea,[131] but both scholars reconstruct Jesus in light of their own interests in postcolonial and liberation-theological critiques of systemic oppression and structural violence. These investments sometimes seem to undermine the realized-eschatological structure of Jesus' renewal program in lieu of a contemporary interest in social justice.

David J. Neville suggests that it is in his nonviolence that "the voice of Jesus breaks through the strata of later traditions with sufficient clarity" and "should be heeded."[132] Violence is "a derivative distortion" of God's will.[133] Consequently, the "moral stance of Jesus as a historical figure should be juxtaposed alongside later developments so as to allow for the possibility of critique."[134] The Gospel of Matthew, for example, contains some of the most violent and ethically problematic language in the New Testament.[135] Neville also focuses on the book of Acts and the book of Revelation in an attempt to develop a "peaceable" (as opposed to a "retributive") eschatology and "hermeneutic of *shalom*."[136] He correctly identifies what he calls "a discrepancy

130. Swartley, *Covenant of Peace*, 64.

131. Horsley, "Ethics and Exegesis," 13–14. See also Richard A. Horsley, "Response to Walter Wink: Neither Passivity nor Violence: Jesus' 'Third Way,'" in *The Love of Enemy and Nonretaliation in the New Testament*, ed. Willard M. Swartley (Louisville: Westminster John Knox, 1992), 131–32. But see also Walter Wink, "Counterresponse to Richard Horsley," 133-36, in the same volume, esp. 134.

132. David J. Neville, *A Peaceable Hope: Contesting Violent Eschatology in New Testament Narratives* (Grand Rapids: Baker Academic, 2013), 44.

133. John Milbank, *Theology and Social Theory: Beyond Secular Reason* (Oxford: Blackwell, 1990).

134. David J. Neville, "Toward a Teleology of Peace: Contesting Matthew's Violent Eschatology," *JSNT* 30, no. 2 (1997): 131–61, at 158.

135. Ibid., 155. See also "Faithful, True and Violent? Christology and 'Divine Vengeance' in the Revelation to John," in *Compassionate Eschatology: The Future as Friend*, ed. Ted Grimsrud and Michael Hardin (Eugene, OR: Cascade Books, 2011), 56–84; "Justice and Divine Judgment: Scriptural Perspectives for Public Theology," *IJPT* 2, no. 3 (2009): 339–56.

136. Neville, *A Peaceable Hope*.

at the heart of the New Testament": the Gospels' portrayal of Jesus as "an advocate of peace and practitioner of nonretaliation" alongside other texts that anticipate the future arrival of Jesus "in the guise of a violent avenger."[137] Neville qualifies this provocative conclusion, however, by noting that his work is "*not* concerned with Jesus as a *historical* figure but with a select number of *texts*."[138] Neville also affirms "divine judgment as biblically and theologically meaningful,"[139] not least because it appeals to our need for divine justice. This relatively narrow focus on the *literary* representations of Jesus is ultimately unsatisfying, despite the fact that Neville correctly identifies competing literary tensions in the tradition. He admits that these tensions are "disorienting" and "perplexing,"[140] but does not attempt to resolve the historical problem that produces the tension. Neville does not make use of Q, privilege any particular solution to the Synoptic Problem, or engage in source-critical isssues.[141] This decision not to engage historical Jesus research or Q studies thus limits his ability to address this particular elephant in the room. Still, it is a step in the right direction.

In a similar vein, Robert Beck has developed a narrative analysis approach to the nonviolent Jesus traditions in the Gospels of Mark and Matthew.[142] Beck sees Matthew's post-70 C.E. provenance as a key to understanding why Jesus' message of nonviolence "had become even less credible" than before:[143] Matthew's greater emphasis on God's eschatological violence is a response to God's apparent "impotence" in saving the Temple.[144] Beck argues that Matthew's God "scandalizes us" not because he will execute an eschatological judgment but because Jesus commands nonviolence.[145] Matthew's passion narrative highlights the dissonance: the Temple incident is "a deliberate prophetic action that is nondestructive and nonviolent," but leads to Jesus'

137. Ibid., 1.

138. Ibid., 1 n. 2 (emphases added).

139. Ibid., 9.

140. Ibid., 2.

141. See David J. Neville, *Arguments from Order in Synoptic Source Criticism: A History and Critique* (Macon, GA: Mercer University Press, 1994), for his balanced approach.

142. Robert R. Beck, *Banished Messiah: Violence and Nonviolence in Matthew's Story of Jesus* (Eugene, OR: Wipf & Stock, 2010); idem, *Nonviolent Story: Narrative Conflict Resolution in the Gospel of Mark* (Maryknoll, NY: Orbis Books, 1996); Barbara Reid, "Violent Endings in Matthew's Parables and Christian Nonviolence," *CBQ* 66 (2004): 237–55; Warren Carter, "Constructions of Violence and Identity in Matthew's Gospel," in *Violence in the New Testament*, 81–108, esp. 98–99.

143. Beck, *Banished Messiah*, x.

144. Ibid., 152.

145. Ibid., 161.

nonretaliatory surrender and defenselessness.[146] Jesus' "temptation" in the Garden of Gethsemane is linked to his temptation in the desert (Q 4) to highlight his rejection of "violent methods of resistance."[147] Jesus' arrest in the Garden is "a form of nonviolent resistance, a position between violent resistance and nonresistance."[148] Jesus "absorbs" violence "so that it stops there,"[149] introducing the theme of forgiveness, which "interrupts a strand of violent reprisals by refusing to pay it back." Beck sees Jesus' message as signifying a "shift from judgment to healing," a "clear break with the policy of retribution."[150]

Despite these studies' noteworthy goals in identifying and problematizing the themes of violence and nonviolence in the Gospel narratives, Jesus' position on violence and nonviolence is not merely a literary or historical triviality but directly affects how contemporary Christian theology understands and represents Jesus, God, eschatology, and humanity. John Dominic Crossan insists that "our very humanity demands that we reject definitively the lure of a violent ultimacy, a violent transcendence, or a violent God."[151] The relationship between Jesus, God, and eschatology requires us to reconsider whether "the judgment which Jesus will bring" is consistent with "the ethic which he teaches."[152] If the New Testament "perceived in Jesus the measure of God,"[153] and Jesus' rejection of violence is incompatible with the nature of God, then perhaps Jesus' nonviolence should be theologically "privileged."[154]

146. Ibid., 48.

147. Ibid., 147.

148. Ibid., 176.

149. Ibid., 187.

150. Ibid., 150.

151. John Dominic Crossan, "Eschatology, Apocalypticism, and the Historical Jesus," in *Jesus Then and Now: Images of Jesus in History and Christology*, ed. Marvin W. Meyer and Charles Hughes (Harrisburg, PA: Trinity Press International, 2001), 91–112, esp. 97–98; idem, *The Birth of Christianity: Discovering what happened in the years immediately after the execution of Jesus* (San Francisco: HarperSanFrancisco, 1998), 283; John Dominic Crossan and Jonathan L. Reed, *Excavating Jesus: Beneath the Stones, Behind the Texts* (New York: HarperSanFrancisco, 2001), 274, refer to Jesus' "programmatically nonviolent resistance . . . confronting present economic, social, and political realities."

152. John Riches, *Conflicting Mythologies: Identity Formation in the Gospels of Mark and Matthew* (Edinburgh: T & T Clark, 2000), 287.

153. Crossan, *Birth of Christianity*, 155–56.

154. Neville, "Toward a Teleology of Peace," esp. 156, 158. See also idem, "The Second Testament as a Covenant of Peace," *BTB* 37, no. 1 (2007): 27–35; idem, "Violating Faith via Eschatological Violence: Reviewing Matthew's Eschatology," in *Validating Violence—Violating Faith? Interfaith Perspectives on Religious Violence*, ed. William W. Emilsen and John T. Squires (Adelaide: ATF Press, 2008), 95–110. See

What if we were to emphasize the positive value of peace, in contradistinction to the negative theme of *non*violence, where the discourse itself is defined by violence, as a major theme in the New Testament?[155] In *Covenant of Peace*, Willard Swartley argues that the New Testament not only supports nonviolence but *advocates* active peace-*making*—an enterprise involving "inclusion of the outsider, the overcoming of enmity, and the extension of the kingdom of God to all people"[156]—as "the core component of proclaiming the gospel of Jesus Christ."[157] The Gospel of Luke, in particular, affirms the "good news" as peace, framing the beginning, middle, and end of the Gospel:

> Luke 1:79: to guide our feet into the way of *peace*.
> Luke 2:14: Glory to God in the highest heaven, and on earth *peace*....
> Luke 7:50: [Jesus] said to the woman, "Your faith has saved you; go in *peace*."
> Luke/Q 10:5-6: Whatever house you enter, first say, "*Peace* to this house!"
> Luke 19:38: *Peace* in heaven, and glory in the highest heaven! . . .
> Luke 19:42: [Jesus] wept over it, saying, "If you, even you, had only recognized on this day the things that make for *peace*!
> Luke 24:36: Jesus . . . said to them, "*Peace* be with you."[158]

Swartley's contribution is an impressive remedy to a notable deficiency in our field, but it is also problematic insofar as Jesus' peace-teaching is set within "the longer biblical theology perspective on war and peace." According to this view of biblical theology, God is both "Peacemaker" *and* "Divine Warrior fighting against evil to establish and maintain peace and justice."[159] Swartley's canonical approach to Scripture thus affirms the tradition of "Holy War" as "motivated by God's judgment on idolatry and God's jealousy for Israel" perpetuated in

also the essays in *Coping with Violence in the New Testament*, ed. Pieter G. R. de Villiers and Jan Willem van Henten (STR 16; Leiden: Brill, 2012).

155. Swartley, *Covenant of Peace*. Jeremy Gabrielson, *Paul's Non-Violent Gospel: The Theological Politics of Peace in Paul's Life and Letters* (Eugene: Pickwick, 2013), 2: "adoption of a politics of non-violence was, for Paul and the communities he established, a constitutive part of the gospel of Jesus Christ."

156. Ibid., 15.

157. Ibid., 12.

158. Ibid., 123–28; idem, "Politics and Peace (Eirēnē) in Luke's Gospel," in *Political Issues in Luke-Acts*, ed. Richard J. Cassidy and Philip J. Scharper (Maryknoll, NY: Orbis Books, 1983), 18–37, at 26–29.

159. Swartley, *Covenant of Peace*, 51.

Jesus' identification as a "divine warrior" whose mission is to defeat the powers of evil. Swartley can only reconcile violent portrayals of God by differentiating between *human violence* and *divine vengeance*.[160] In absolving God of violence, one makes God an agent of divine *judgment*: God's divine violence is not *really* violence.[161]

It is not clear, however, whether simply renaming or redescribing violence solves the problem. What does one do with God's commands to *commit* violence in the Torah? What about God's commands to launch holy wars of ethnic cleansing? Does Jesus teach love of enemies because *God* loves enemies—or not? According to Matthew and Paul, loving one's enemies only seems to be the proper protocol because "vengeance" belongs to the Lord.[162] Is this what the historical Jesus had in mind? If Jesus is the "Son," and truly represents the Father, then how can Jesus (and Jesus' disciples) imitate God (or Jesus) if God judges, punishes, and condemns—and Jesus does not?[163]

Our scriptures seem to contain inconsistent and apparently contradictory descriptions of Jesus and God. How do we know that our interpretations are accurate when we encounter two apparently opposing ideas? One solution is to ignore the contradictions. Another is to accept them as unintended and irreconcilable literary-scribal errors. Yet another is to attempt to hold contradictory ideas in tension, perhaps by appealing to the inscrutable mystery of God. Still yet another solution is to appeal to our contemporary ethical conscience. In a Christian context, the challenge involves rediscovering the original criterion for assessing ethical Christian belief and practice: the nonviolent Jesus.

160. See especially Millard Lind, *Yahweh Is A Warrior* (Scottdale, PA: Herald Press, 1980); Miroslav Volf, *Exclusion and Embrace: A Theological Explanation of Identity, Otherness, and Reconciliation* (Nashville: Abingdon, 1996), 301, 304: "the practice of nonviolence requires a belief in divine vengeance." Scott Holland, "The Gospel of Peace and the Violence of God," in *Seeking Cultures of Peace: A Peace Church Conversation*, ed. Fernando Enns, Scott Holland, and Ann Riggs (Scottdale, PA: Herald Press, 2004), 132–46, at 142; Terence E. Fretheim, "Theological Reflections on the Wrath of God in the Old Testament," *HBT* 24 (2002): 1–26.

161. Swartley, *Covenant of Peace*, 384. See also Christopher D. Marshall, *Beyond Retribution: A New Testament Vision for Justice, Crime, and Punishment* (Grand Rapids: Eerdmans, 2001).

162. Rom. 12:19-20. Luise Schottroff, "Give to Caesar What Belongs to Caesar and to God What Belongs to God: A Theological Response of the Early Christian Church to Its Social and Political Environment," in *Love of Enemy and Nonretaliation*, ed. Willard M. Swartley (Louisville: Westminster John Knox, 1992), 223–57, at 232.

163. Michael Hardin, "'All We Are Saying Is Give Peace A Chance': An Appraisal of Willard Swartley's *Covenant of Peace*," paper presented to the Colloquium on Violence and Religion, Washington, DC, November 2006.

It is the contention of this study that the historical and theological implications of an *historically* nonviolent Jesus have not yet been adequately integrated into the discipline. There are many historical, social, theological, and political reasons for this, but the end result is that while we tend to *acknowledge* Jesus' nonviolence, we do not generally apply it as a criterion of authenticity to the Jesus tradition as a whole nor to Jesus' response to the Jewish matrix within which he lived. The result is predictable: we continue to be largely unable to differentiate betweeen authentic and inauthentic traditions. A rigorous application of this criterion would require approaching any counter or contrary data with a hermeneutic of suspicion: that is, if Jesus was *consistently* nonviolent, then violent Jesus traditions would have little to no claim to being authentic. Jesus' nonviolence would thus provide us with a key to authenticating Jesus traditions.[164]

164. Jerome F. D. Creach, *Violence in Scripture* (Interpretation: Resources for the Use of Scripture in the Church; Louisville: Westminster John Knox Press, 2013), refers to this as the "organizing center" or "guide to understanding the whole" of the Bible and advocates reading the Bible "with Christ as its center." This method "highlights particular aspects of the Bible as central or normative," so that Jesus, "for Christians," presents "an authoritative *interpretation* of the Old Testament, not a repudiation of it."

3

The God of War

Divine Violence in the Hebrew Bible

Since September 11, 2001, the relationship between religion and violence has become one of the most pressing concerns in contemporary society and has led to a renewed interest in the role of violence in the biblical tradition. The editors of a recent collection of papers on "the biblical heritage" of violence identify this as "the most pressing issue facing biblical scholarship today,"[1] a heritage that continues to be reinscribed in Western culture.[2] The origin, phenomenology,

1. David A. Bernat and Jonathan Klawans, "Preface," in *Religion and Violence: The Biblical Heritage: Proceedings of a Conference held at Wellesley College and Boston University, February 19-20, 2006* (eds. D. A. Bernat and J. Klawans; RRBS 2; Sheffield: Sheffield Phoenix Press, 2007).

2. On biblical violence see Ra'anan Boustan, *Violence, Scripture, and Textual Practice in Early Judaism and Christianity* (Leiden: Brill, 2010); Eric Seibert, *Disturbing Divine Behavior: Troubling Old Testament Images of God* (Philadelphia: Fortress Press, 2009); *Encountering Violence in the Bible*, ed. Markus Zehnder and Hallvard Hagelia (Bible in the Modern World 55; Sheffield: Sheffield Phoenix Press, 2013); *Sanctified Aggression: Legacies of Biblical and Post-Biblical Vocabularies of Violence*, ed. Yvonne Sherwood and Jonneke Bekkenkamp (London/New York: T & T Clark, 2003); David Penchansky, *What Rough Beast? Images of God in the Hebrew Bible* (Louisville: Westminster John Knox, 1999), 82–86; Regina M. Schwartz, *The Curse of Cain: The Violent Legacy of Monotheism* (Chicago: University of Chicago Press, 1997); Phyllis Trible, *Texts of Terror: Literary-Feminist Readings of Biblical Narratives* (Philadelphia: Fortress Press, 1984); Walter Wink, *The Powers That Be: Theology for a New Millennium* (New York: Doubleday, 1998), 84; Adrian Thatcher, *The Savage Text: The Use and Abuse of the Bible* (Chichester: Wiley-Blackwell, 2008); Mark G. Brett, *Decolonizing God: The Bible in the Tides of Empire* (Sheffield: Sheffield Phoenix Press, 2008); Randal Rauser, "Let Nothing that Breathes Remain Alive: On the Problem of Divinely Commanded Genocide," *Philosophia Christi* 11, no. 1 (2009): 27–41; Gareth Lloyd Jones, "Sacred Violence: The Dark Side of God," *JBV* 20 (1999): 184–99. For pacifist perspectives on the biblical tradition of "holy war," see Patrick D. Miller Jr., "God the Warrior: A Problem in Biblical Interpretation and Apologetics," *Int* 19 (1965): 39–46; Waldemar Janzen, "War in the Old Testament," *Mennonite Quarterly Review* 46 (1972): 155–66; Jacob J. Enz, *The Christian and Warfare: The Roots of*

and function of violence has also recently drawn the attention of scholars from many different disciplines.[3] Ultimately, our examination of violence in the biblical tradition is part of a much larger sociological, psychological, social-psychological, and anthropological conversation in the academy and the public arena on the origins of violence and human nature. Theories of *religious* violence have focused on a number of interrelated factors, including religious particularism,[4] modern threats to religious identity,[5] ideological differences,[6] the role of religious dogma,[7] the exclusivity of monotheism in collective identity formation,[8] reactions against secularism,[9] territoriality and humiliation as motivating factors in modern acts of religious-based terrorism,[10] and "scarce-resource theory."[11] The most influential theorist of violence, René Girard,

Pacifism in the Old Testament (Scottdale, PA: Herald Press, 1972); Vernard Eller, *War and Peace from Genesis to Revelation* (Scottdale, PA: Herald Press, 1981); Millard Lind, *Yahweh Is a Warrior: The Theology of Warfare in Ancient Israel* (Scottdale, PA: Herald Press, 1980).

3. For an anthropological view see David Riches, "The Phenomenon of Violence," in *The Anthropology of Violence*, ed. idem (Oxford: Blackwell, 1986), 1–7. On the biological origins of aggression see Konrad Lorenz, *On Aggression*, trans. M. K. Wilson (New York: Bantam Books, 1966); Luigi Valzelli, *Psychobiology of Aggression and Violence* (New York: Raven, 1981). For psychological interpretations see Leonard Berkowitz, *Aggression: Its Causes, Consequences, and Control* (Philadelphia: Temple University Press, 1993). On sociological theories of aggression and violence see *Aggression and Violence: Social Interactionist Perspectives*, ed. Richard B. Felson and James T. Tedeschi (Washington, DC: American Psychological Association, 1993); Robert Ardrey, *The Territorial Imperative: A Personal Inquiry into the Origins of Property and Nations* (New York: Atheneum, 1966).

4. Charles Y. Glock and Rodney Stark, *Christian Belief and Anti-Semitism* (New York: Harper and Row, 1966).

5. Martin Marty and R. Scott Appleby, *The Fundamentalism Project* (5 vols.; Chicago: University of Chicago Press, 1991–1995).

6. Phil Zuckerman, *Strife in the Sanctuary: Religious Schism in a Jewish Community* (Walnut Creek, CA: AltaMira Press, 1999).

7. Timothy Gorringe, *God's Just Vengeance: Crime, Violence, and the Rhetoric of Salvation* (Cambridge: Cambridge University Press, 1996); Walter Stephens, *Demon Lovers: Witchcraft, Sex, and the Crisis of Belief* (Chicago: University of Chicago Press, 2002).

8. Schwartz, *The Curse of Cain*.

9. Mark Juergensmeyer, *Terror in the Mind of God: The Global Rise of Religious Violence* (Berkeley/Los Angeles: University of California Press, 2000).

10. Jessica Stern, *Terror in the Name of God: Why Religious Militants Kill* (New York: Harper Collins, 2003). See also the essays in *The Destructive Power of Religion: Violence in Judaism, Christianity and Islam*, ed. J. Harold Ellens (4 vols.; Westport, CT: Praeger, 2004). See also Marc Gopin, *Holy War, Holy Peace: How Religion Can Bring Peace to the Middle East* (New York: Oxford University Press, 2002); Charles Kimball, *When Religion Becomes Evil* (San Francisco: HarperSanFrancisco, 2002).

11. Hector Avalos, *Fighting Words: The Origins of Religious Violence* (Amherst, MA: Prometheus, 2005), 18.

locates the origins of human violence in "mimetic desire."[12] According to his theory, an object is desired because another desires it, and since rivalry is part of human nature, and desire leads to violence, human beings transfer their violent desires to surrogates, giving birth to systems of sacrifice, ritual, and religion. Vengeance, or "reciprocal violence,"[13] becomes an act of "unanimous violence,"[14] the murder that lies behind sacrificial practice.[15] This transferred violence breeds reenactment and domesticates the cycle of violence. The "innocent" victim's murder establishes peace and sanctifies the victim. This "scapegoating mechanism" is the key to the (Girardian) origins of religion: human culture is founded on an act of sacrificial violence. Girard identifies Jesus' death as a classic mythic account of an innocent victim murdered and commemorated in perpetual ritual reenactment. In the Gospels, Jesus' innocence symbolizes the destruction of the sacrificial system because it reveals the foundation of the social order on murder.[16] Girard's approach has been adopted in some circles, but its oversimplification of the complexity of human culture and society too easily facilitates Christian supersessionist readings of the early Jesus tradition.[17]

While the relationship between religion and violence continues to be explored,[18] it is important for us to recognize that the way we understand the

12. René Girard, *Violence and the Sacred* (Baltimore: Johns Hopkins University Press, 1977); idem, *Things Hidden Since the Foundation of the World* (Stanford, CA: Stanford University Press, 1987). For an overview of Girard's theory see Leo D. Lefebure, *Revelation, the Religious, and Violence* (Maryknoll, NY: Orbis Books, 2000), 20–23, 29–31. For an application of Girard's theory to the Bible see James G. Williams, *The Bible, Violence, and the Sacred: Liberation from the Myth of Sanctioned Violence* (San Francisco: HarperSanFrancisco, 1991). See also Raymund Schwager, *Must There Be Scapegoats? Violence and Redemption in the Bible* (San Francisco: Harper and Row, 1987); Bradley McLean, "The Absence of an Atoning Sacrifice in Paul's Soteriology," *NTS* 38 (1992): 531–53. See also Anthony Bartlett, *Cross Purposes: The Violent Grammar of Christian Atonement* (Harrisburg, PA: Trinity Press International, 2001).

13. Girard, *Violence and the Sacred*, 27, 55.

14. Ibid., 85, 93.

15. Ibid., 19, 93.

16. Girard, *Things Hidden*, 180. See Robert Hamerton-Kelly, *Sacred Violence: Paul's Hermeneutic of the Cross* (Minneapolis: Fortress Press, 1992).

17. For criticism see Richard D. Hecht, "Studies on Sacrifice," *RelSRev* 8, no. 3 (1982): 253–59, esp. 257–58; Luc de Heusch, *Sacrifice in Africa: A Structuralist Approach*, trans. Linda O'Brian and Alice Morton (Bloomington: Indiana University Press, 1985), 15–17; Ninian Smart, "Review of *Violence and the Sacred*," *RelSRev* 6, no. 3 (1980): 173–77; Ivan Strenski, *Religion in Relation: Method, Application, and Moral Location* (Columbia, SC: University of South Carolina Press, 1993), 202–16; Bruce D. Chilton, *The Temple of Jesus: His Sacrificial Program within a Cultural History of Sacrifice* (University Park, PA: Pennsylvania State University Press, 1992), 3–42, 163–80. For further criticism see *Violence and Truth: On the Work of René Girard*, ed. Paul Dumouchel (Stanford, CA: Stanford University Press, 1988).

nature, origin, and meaning of violence directly affects how we understand human nature, the biblical tradition, the value and relevance of Jesus' ethical instructions, and the character of God. It is not easy to accept that "violence lies at the heart of scripture."[19] It is not easy to find violence inscribed in images, words, actions, religious figures, and the very "centre of God's being." Scriptural violence, however, not only needs to be openly acknowledged, but problematized, insofar as faith communities "desire, or demand, to have a scriptural text speak with a holy voice."[20] A "reality check" is needed to identify where violent ideas are present and violent actions "commanded" and condoned.[21] The interpretative process, therefore, requires not only the acknowledgment of ethically problematic texts but responsible (re)evaluation as well. After all, it is not only those Jews, Christians, or Muslims "who justify acts of violence by reference to scripture [who] are distorting or hijacking their sacred texts for illegitimate ends."[22] The Torah, the New Testament, and the *Qur'an* each contain "a violent dimension" within them.

Fortunately, there is more to religion than violence, and each tradition represents a broad spectrum of perspectives on human and divine violence.[23] Nor is violence, or the internal critique of violence, limited to the Abrahamic faiths. William Emilsen points out that the principle of nonviolence served as the central criterion by which Gandhi assessed scripture.[24] The nonviolent Jesus serves a similar function in relationship to the Jesus tradition and the *Christian* scriptures. The problem is that the historical Jesus must first be understood and reconstructed within first-century Judaism, although Jesus and Judaism are notoriously difficult to reconstruct. We must begin, nonetheless, by reexamining the relationship(s) between religion, scripture, and violence in Judaism.

18. See *Sacrifice, Scripture, and Substitution: Readings in Ancient Judaism and Christianity*, ed. Ann W. Astell and Sandor Goodhart (Notre Dame, IN: University of Notre Dame Press, 2011), and Douglas Hedley, *Sacrifice Imagined: Violence, Atonement, and the Sacred* (New York: Continuum, 2011).

19. William W. Emilsen and John T. Squires, "Introduction," in *Validating Violence—Violating Faith? Religion, Scripture and Violence*, ed. William W. Emilsen and John T. Squires (Adelaide: ATF Press, 2008), xiii.

20. Emilsen and Squires, "Conclusion," in ibid., 219.

21. Ibid., 220, referring to how the "holy text endorses the violent action."

22. Christopher D. Stanley, "Words of Death: Scripture and Violence in Judaism, Christianity and Islam," in ibid., 17–37, at 36.

23. Christopher D. Stanley, "Words of Life: Scripture and Non-violence in Judaism, Christianity and Islam," in ibid., 39–56.

24. William W. Emilsen, "Gandhi, Scripture and Non-violence," in ibid., 127–42.

What would the Torah look like without divine violence? An inventory of its historical narratives provides us with a deeply troubling legacy.[25] There are literally hundreds of passages of explicit violence in the Bible, hundreds of verses where God uses violence in punishing Israel and dozens of passages in which God commands others to kill people. In far too many passages to ignore or discount, God acts unethically and immorally, killing indiscriminately and punishing inconsistently.[26]

The Torah sanctions polygamy,[27] slavery, and the death penalty in cases of dishonoring parents,[28] sexual deviancy,[29] idolatry,[30] blasphemy,[31] and Sabbath violations.[32] The great religious figures of ancient Israel are portrayed as behaving in ways that we today find ethically problematic. Abram lies.[33] Jacob cheats.[34] Moses murders.[35] David commits adultery.[36] God himself acts in morally questionable ways. He favors Abel's offerings over Cain's,[37] kills every first-born Egyptian,[38] and drowns the entire Egyptian army.[39] God gets angry,[40] hates,[41] deceives,[42] and leads other nations astray.[43] Above all, God punishes[44] and commits good and evil acts.[45] God is a divine Warrior.[46] He commands

25. For illustrative examples, see Gen. 6:5-7; 7:21-23; 12:17; 15:9; 19:24; Exod. 4:24-26; 12:12; 14:4-28; 21:15; 21:17; 22:18-21; 22:23; 31:14; 32:27-28; 35:2-3; Lev. 20:9-10; 20:13; 20:27; 24:16-17; Num. 3:4; 11:1-2; 14:12; 14:36-37; 15:32-36; 16:31-33; 21:34-35; 25:1-5; 25:6-9; 31:1-54; Deut. 2:33-36; 4:3; 6:15; 7:1-2; 7:16; 13:12-16; 18:20; 19:18-19; 21:18-21.

26. David R. Blumenthal, *Facing the Abusive God: A Theology of Protest* (Louisville: Westminster John Knox, 1993), allows for the existence of divine injustice and "abuse."

27. Judg. 8:30; 2 Sam. 5:13; 1 Kgs. 11:3.

28. Exod. 21:15, 17.

29. Lev. 20:12; 20:13, 20:11, 20:15-16; 18:22.

30. Deut. 13:6-11.

31. Lev. 24:14.

32. Num. 15:32-36.

33. Gen. 12:10-20; 20:1-18.

34. Gen. 27:1-29.

35. Exod. 2:11-15.

36. 2 Samuel 11.

37. Gen. 4:3-5.

38. Exod. 12:29.

39. Exod. 14.

40. Jer. 4:8.

41. Mic. 1:2-3.

42. Jer. 4:10.

43. Isa. 30:27-28.

44. Isa. 9:13-17; 24:1-6.

45. Isa. 45:7; Amos 3:6.

46. Exod. 15:3; Num. 21:14; 1 Sam. 18:17; 25:28; 30:26; Isa. 34:2-3; 63:1-6.

genocidal slaughter.[47] During the conquest the Israelites repeatedly "devoted the city to the LORD and destroyed with the sword every living thing in it—men and women, young and old, cattle, sheep, and donkeys."[48] It is possible, of course, to simply assert that we are not in any position to adjudicate God's will as portrayed in the Bible; God has his reasons.[49] God may also allow bad things to happen without directly causing them or being responsible for them,[50] but the problem is that it is *God* who commands the wholesale slaughter of the Canaanites in Joshua 6–11. The biblical narratives repeatedly ascribe to God the power and agency of genocidal actions.

The Bible has troubled us from the very beginning. From Marcion to Origen to Jefferson, problematic biblical passages have been excised, typologized, allegorized,[51] and/or eliminated in order to construct a more ethically palatable collection of texts. These passages make most of us uncomfortable. They represent an ethical system that is no longer acceptable in contemporary Western culture because it is based on tribal traditions affirming a tribal God, a tribal law code endorsing slavery and genocide, tribal narratives of violent regional conquest, tribal theodicy, and tribal vengeance. The results of historical-critical scholarship on the problem of divine violence may be taken seriously by some conservative Christian apologists,[52] but New Atheists like

47. Josh. 10:40.

48. Josh. 6:21.

49. Seibert, *Disturbing Divine Behavior*, 71–73.

50. Guy F. Hershberger, *War, Peace, and Nonresistance* (3d ed.; Scottdale, PA: Herald Press, 1981), 25–27. See also Kenton Sparks, *Sacred Word, Broken Word: Biblical Authority and the Dark Side of Scripture* (Grand Rapids: Eerdmans, 2012). Sparks locates the blame in the "fallen" state of the Bible's human authors, not in God.

51. Origen identified the difficult passages as allegorical: the extermination of enemies represents the destruction of wrath and lust (*Homilies on Joshua* 15.3; *De Principiis* 4.1.8). See also Joseph H. Lynch, "The First Crusade: Some Theological and Historical Context," in *Must Christianity Be Violent? Reflections on History, Practice, and Theology*, ed. Kenneth R. Chase and Alan Jacobs (Grand Rapids: Brazos, 2003), 23–36, esp. 30. On Marcion see Robert Smith Wilson, *Marcion* (London: James Clarke, 1933); Edwin C. Blackman, *Marcion and His Influence* (New York: AMS Press, 1978 [1948]). On Jefferson's Bible, see Thomas Jefferson, *The Jefferson Bible* (Boston: Beacon, 1989).

52. For example, Jerome F. D. Creach, *Violence in Scripture* (Interpretation: Resources for the Use of Scripture in the Church; Louisville: Westminster John Knox Press, 2013). Richard B. Hays, *The Moral Vision of the New Testament*, 336, argues that "If irreconcilable tensions exist between the moral vision of the New Testament and that of particular Old Testament texts, the New Testament vision trumps the Old Testament." See also William Lane Craig and Joseph E. Gorra, *A Reasonable Response: Answers to Tough Questions on God, Christianity, and the Bible* (Chicago: Moody Publishers, 2013); Paul Copan, *Is God a Moral Monster?: Making Sense of the Old Testament God* (Grand Rapids: Baker Books, 2011); David T. Lamb, *God Behaving Badly: Is the God of the Old Testament Angry, Sexist and Racist* (Downers Grove:

Richard Dawkins, Christopher Hitchens, and Sam Harris regularly appeal to the Achilles heel of the Bible—the problem of divine violence—in their manifestos. Dawkins infamously describes the God of the Old Testament as

> "the most unpleasant character in all fiction: jealous and proud of it; a petty, unjust, unforgiving control-freak; a vindictive, bloodthirsty ethnic cleanser; a misogynistic, homophobic, racist, infanticidal, genocidal, filicidal, pestilential, megalomaniacal, sadomasochistic, capriciously malevolent bully."[53]

Dawkins' unflattering portrait may be a one-sided hyperbolic caricature of the biblical God, but it also strikes a sensitive nerve: the scriptural representation of God offends modern sensibilities. The "dark side" of the Bible is no less troubling for us today than it was to the earliest Christians who commented on and (re)interpreted these passages.[54] Indeed, a small but significant academic industry has developed on this very topic. This growing industry indicates an increasing discomfort with the implications of biblical violence and an intensifying awareness of the dis-ease it represents for contemporary ethics and religiosity.

Does the Bible justify violence?[55] Conceding that it "appears to endorse and bless the recourse to violence,"[56] and that God's power in war "was a major consideration in early Israelite worship,"[57] John Collins has examined the biblical ban (חרם)[58]—the ritual destruction of the cities and peoples of Canaan—its military function, "ritualistic character,"[59] the history of human

InterVarsity, 2011); Christopher J. H. Wright, *The God I Don't Understand: Reflections on Tough Questions of Faith* (Grand Rapids: Zondervan, 2008).

53. Richard Dawkins, *The God Delusion* (New York: Bantam Books, 2006), 51.

54. See Gerd Lüdemann, *The Unholy in Holy Scriptures: The Dark Side of the Bible*, trans. John Bowden (Louisville: Westminster John Knox, 1997).

55. John J. Collins, *Does the Bible Justify Violence?* (Facets; Minneapolis: Fortress Press, 2004); originally published as "The Zeal of Phineas: The Bible and the Legitimization of Violence," *JBL* 122 (2003): 3–21. For violence in the Old Testament/Hebrew Bible see also Susan Niditch, *War in the Hebrew Bible: A Study in the Ethics of Violence* (New York: Oxford University Press, 1993). See also K. Lawson Younger, *Ancient Conquest Accounts: A Study in Ancient Near Eastern and Biblical History Writing* (Sheffield: JSOT, 1990).

56. Collins, *Does the Bible Justify Violence?* 2.

57. Ibid., 4.

58. Philip D. Stern, *The Biblical Ḥerem: A Window on Israel's Religious Experience* (BJS 211; Atlanta: Scholars Press, 1991). See also J. A. Naude, "חרם," *NIDOTTE* 2:275–76.

59. Collins, *Does the Bible Justify Violence?* 7.

sacrifice in early Israel, as well as the "irony" of Deuteronomy's ethical principles and Exodus's tale of "liberation."[60] Collins suggests that the Bible justifies its violence by appealing to Israel as God's chosen, covenantal people,[61] but "hopes" that most *scholars* have learned that these texts "tell us more about the purposes of their human authors than about the purposes of God."[62] The Bible is "no infallible guide on ethical matters,"[63] Collins concedes, but "not all violence is necessarily to be condemned":[64] the portrayals of God as a divine Warrior and eschatological Judge "have often given hope to the oppressed." On the other hand, this cannot "negate the force of the biblical endorsements of violence." Collins thus finds the "power" of the Bible in its inconsistency:[65] it gives us "an unvarnished picture of human nature." Isaiah's messianic vision of peace is forever set in the "*utopian* future."[66]

While many scholars now doubt the historicity of the conquest narratives of Joshua 6–11,[67] the ethics of divinely mandated genocide are inescapably problematic.[68] There is simply no denying that the Torah's narratives of genocide, whether historical or rhetorical, have justified further acts of violence. We cannot avoid wrestling with these texts, for to do so ultimately becomes, even if only by default, an act of ethical evasion.

In response, biblical scholars have developed a number of exegetical and interpretative reading strategies in order to come to terms with these texts.[69] Eryl Davies identifies five distinct approaches: (1) evolutionary, (2) cultural

60. Ibid., 11–12.

61. Ibid., 11.

62. Ibid., 13 (emphasis added).

63. Ibid., 32.

64. Ibid., 28.

65. Ibid., 31.

66. Ibid. (emphasis added).

67. Lori L. Rowlett, *Joshua and the Rhetoric of Violence: A New Historicist Analysis* (JSOTSup 226: Sheffield: Sheffield Academic Press, 1996); Richard S. Hess and Elmer A. Martens, *War in the Bible and Terrorism in the Twenty-First Century* (Winona Lake: Eisenbrauns, 2008). David A. Bernat and Jonathan Klawans, *Religion and Violence: The Biblical Heritage* (Sheffield: Sheffield Phoenix Press, 2007), 9, suggest that the genocidal slaughter of the Canaanites described in the Torah is nothing more than "a complete fantasy." See also Douglas S. Earl, *The Joshua Delusion: Rethinking Genocide in the Bible* (Eugene, OR: Cascade/Wipf & Stock, 2010). Walter Brueggemann, *Divine Presence amid Violence: Contextualizing the Book of Joshua* (Eugene, OR: Cascade, 2009), 62, does not provide any method of approach to the problematic nature of the violence in these passages.

68. Avalos, *Fighting Words*, 381–82, 360–61, 371. See also "The Letter Killeth: A Plea for Decanonizing Violent Biblical Texts," *Journal of Religion, Conflict, and Peace* 1 (2007): 16. See now also *Holy War in the Bible: Christian Morality and an Old Testament Problem*, ed. Heath A. Thomas, Jeremy Evans, and Paul Copan (Downer's Grove: InterVarsity, 2013).

relativism, (3) canonical, (4) paradigmatic, and (5) reader-response criticism. The evolutionary approach holds that biblical ethics develops in stages over time, with Israel "progressing" in its moral perception.[70] Based on a neo-Darwinian and Hegelian view of history and a nineteenth-century ideal of progress, which tends to assume development from primitive tribalism to ethical monotheism,[71] this approach holds that Israelite morality improved over time: the ethically problematic passages represent the most primitive stages in Israel's moral development. This approach has the advantage of providing a historical framework of development that appeals to scientific theories of progress and evolution. Advocates of this approach often seek to ground the final stages of Israel's ethical development in the person and teachings of Jesus.[72] The problem with this approach is not only its covert supersessionism but the more pressing fact that the "image of God as divine warrior extends throughout the Hebrew Bible," as it does in the New Testament.[73]

Alternatively, the cultural relativist's approach maintains that customs, beliefs, and practices vary across culture and must be understood within their particular socio-historical contexts.[74] Since the biblical writers lived in an "agrarian, slave-based, patriarchal, polygamous society,"[75] we simply cannot hold them accountable to contemporary ethical standards.[76] The problem with this approach is that once we dissociate biblical ethics from contemporary

69. Eryl W. Davies, *The Immoral Bible: Approaches to Biblical Ethics* (New York: T&T Clark, 2010), 1; idem, "The Morally Dubious Passages of the Hebrew Bible: An Examination of Some Proposed Solutions," *CBR* 3, no. 2 (2005): 196–228.

70. Ibid., 22–42.

71. A. B. Davidson, *The Theology of the Old Testament* (Edinburgh: T&T Clark, 1904); H. G. Mitchell, *The Ethics of the Old Testament* (Chicago: University of Chicago Press, 1912); J. M. P. Smith, *The Moral Life of the Hebrews* (Chicago: University of Chicago Press, 1923); Harry Emerson Fosdick, *A Guide to Understanding the Bible: The Development of Ideas Within the Old and New Testaments* (London: Harper and Brothers, 1938); W. S. Bruce, *The Ethics of the Old Testament* (Edinburgh: T&T Clark, 1909).

72. C. H. Dodd, *The Authority of the Bible* (rev. ed.; London: Nisbet, [1938] 1983), 255; Julius Wellhausen, *Prolegomena to the History of Israel*, trans. J. Sutherland Black and Alan Menzies (Edinburgh: A&C Black, 1885).

73. Davies, *The Immoral Bible*, 40. For further criticism see Walther Eichrodt, *Theology of the Old Testament*, trans. J. A. Baker (2 vols.; London: SCM Press, 1961, 1967); William F. Albright, *From the Stone Age to Christianity: Monotheism and the Historical Process* (Baltimore: Johns Hopkins University Press, 1940).

74. Ibid., 43–62.

75. Ibid., 44.

76. Dennis Nineham, *The Use and Abuse of the Bible: A Study of the Bible in an Age of Rapid Cultural Change* (London: Macmillan, 1976); Cyril Rodd, *Glimpses of a Strange Land: Studies in Old Testament Ethics* (Edinburgh: T&T Clark, 2001).

ethics, how can the Bible continue to guide contemporary faith-communities?[77] If the Bible is the product of a particular time and place, a series of "time-conditioned, situational statements that cannot easily be applied to contemporary concerns," then isn't it already "outmoded, obsolete and irrelevant"?[78]

A third method, the canon-within-the canon approach, encourages readers to pick and choose the texts they find useful for their ethical guidance.[79] Liberation theologians privilege the book of Exodus and the prophets who called for defense of the poor and social justice.[80] Feminist biblical critics emphasize those that view the female role in a more positive light.[81] This approach, while it avoids endorsing offensive biblical texts, creates a chaos of individual "canons" that is highly eclectic, selective, and idiosyncratic. While Exodus' liberating message may be inspiring for African Americans, many Native Americans and Palestinians identify more with the dispossessed Canaanites who suffered genocide at the hands of those who invented "manifest destiny."[82] This method is often criticized as the exegetical equivalent of conveniently "cherry-picking" scripture, especially when it does not appeal to critical controls or authoritative criteria.

More conservatively, the canonical approach rejects the idea that you can single out some texts and reject others. Brevard Childs argues that the Bible can only be theologically and ethically appreciated when the *entire* canonical corpus is taken into account.[83] Childs privileges the final, fixed form of the canon as a way of lessening the negative effects of ethically problematic passages by locating them in the larger context of the canon as a whole. The method can thus be used to juxtapose offensive texts with less offensive ones and thereby decrease the offense. This approach, however, has been criticized as "a crude attempt to return to a pre-critical era of biblical interpretation."[84] Why should

77. Davies, *The Immoral Bible*, 48.

78. Ibid., 54, 56.

79. Ibid., 63–100.

80. Isa. 1:16-17; Amos 5:10-12. Anthony C. Thiselton, *New Horizons in Hermeneutics: The Theory and Practice of Transforming Biblical Reading* (Grand Rapids: Zondervan, 1992), 416; Gustavo Gutiérrez, *A Theology of Liberation* (London: SCM, 1974).

81. For example, Prov. 8; 31:10-31; Num. 27:1-11; Song of Solomon.

82. See the classic essay by Robert Allen Warrior, "A Native American Perspective: Canaanites, Cowboys, and Indians," in *Voices from the Margin: Interpreting the Bible in the Third World*, ed. R. S. Sugirtharajah (Maryknoll, NY: Orbis Books, 1995), 289–92.

83. Brevard S. Childs, *Biblical Theology in Crisis* (Philadelphia: Westminster, 1970); idem, *Biblical Theology of the Old and New Testaments: Theological Reflection on the Christian Bible* (London: SCM, 1992); idem, *Old Testament Theology in a Canonical Context* (London: SCM, 1985).

we privilege the fourth century's Catholic canon as opposed to the Protestant, the Greek Orthodox, or the Ethiopian?[85] Besides, the Bible is not coherent and cannot be harmonized without violating its particular and distinctive ethical perspectives.

The paradigmatic approach attempts to distill the "underlying principles" of the Bible as opposed to what is now perceived to be the outdated *letter* of the law.[86] The goal is to identify and apply what is still ethically relevant from the biblical text to contemporary society, but, like other approaches that blunt the edge of the Bible's divine violence, this approach also "tends to produce skewed readings" of the text and "principles" that reflect "the interpreter's own preconceived value judgments."[87] Finally, reader-response criticism explores different ways the implied, ideal, actual, or "resisting" reader can engage problematic texts,[88] The "resisting reader" interacts with the text, challenging assumptions, questioning insights, and discrediting dubious claims.

How do these different reading strategies work in practice? In *Show Them No Mercy*, four biblical scholars focus their efforts on the slaughter of the Canaanites as one of the major obstacles to understanding the "abiding message" of the Old Testament.[89] They set themselves the Herculean task of reconciling the God who commands the "indiscriminate slaughter" of an entire

84. Davies, *The Immoral Bible*, 85. For criticism see Douglas A. Knight, "Canon and the History of Tradition: A Critique of Brevard S. Childs' *Introduction to the Old Testament as Scripture*," *HBT* 2 (1980): 127–49, esp. 146.

85. Ibid., 91.

86. Christopher J. H. Wright, *Living as the People of God: The Relevance of Old Testament Ethics* (Leicester: InterVarsity, 1983); idem, *Walking in the Ways of the Lord: The Ethical Authority of the Old Testament* (Leicester: Apollos, 1995); idem, *Old Testament Ethics for the People of God* (Leicester: InterVarsity, 2004).

87. Davies, *The Immoral Bible*, 107.

88. For the "implied reader," see Wolfgang Iser, *The Implied Reader: Patterns of Communication in Prose Fiction from Bunyan to Beckett* (Baltimore: Johns Hopkins University Press, 1974); Wayne C. Booth, *The Company We Keep: An Ethics of Fiction* (Berkeley: University of California Press, 1988). For the "model reader," see Umberto Eco, *The Role of the Reader: Explorations in the Semiotics of Texts* (London: Hutchinson, 1981). For the "ideal reader," see Jonathan D. Culler, *On Deconstruction: Theory and Criticism after Structuralism* (London: Routledge & Kegan Paul, 1983). For the "informed reader," see Stanley E. Fish, *Is There a Text in This Class? The Authority of Interpretive Communities* (Cambridge, MA: Harvard University Press, 1980). For the "actual reader," see Hans Robert Jauss, *Toward an Aesthetic of Reception*, trans. Timothy Bahti (Minneapolis: University of Minnesota Press, 1982). For the "resisting reader," see Judith Fetterley, *The Resisting Reader: A Feminist Approach to American Fiction* (Bloomington and London: Indiana University Press, 1978); for discussion on feminist biblical use of reader-response criticism, see Eryl W. Davies, *The Dissenting Reader: Feminist Approaches to the Hebrew Bible* (Aldershot: Ashgate, 2003).

people with Jesus' commandment to love enemies while still affirming the "authority and inspiration" of the Bible.

Daniel Gard approaches the biblical text as "God-breathed"[90] and holds that "the word of Moses is as much the word of God as the recorded word of Jesus,"[91] just as the "God in the Old Testament is precisely the same God in the New Testament." Gard does not question the historical veracity of the Bible's narratives of genocide,[92] but rather takes these accounts (and the genocidal acts themselves) as genuine historical revelations of God.[93] His case for an "eschatological continuity" between the Old and New Testaments posits a trajectory from the early biblical narratives through Chronicles, the Intertestamental apocalypses, and the book of Revelation. Consequently, he views the "images of Old Testament genocide" as "types of an eschatological event," asserting that "the Chronicler foresaw a new David coming," a prophecy fulfilled in the person of Jesus, the "new and final David," with the "present Davidic age . . . to be succeeded in history by a new Solomonic era."[94] Gard also envisions a future Christian חרם, a "total destruction of the entire earth," as described in 2 Pet. 4:7, 10, 13, the book of Revelation, and Matthew's eschatological parables,[95] where Jesus returns "in glory and power . . . as the righteous Judge who speaks the final word of judgment,"[96] the "Lamb and Judge" who "bore the full wrath of God's justice in the place of the entire human race," and will come back to destroy his enemies.[97] Gard admits that there is as much violence in the *New* Testament as in the Old, yet insists that "Such images are not to be understood as paradigms for implementation by any

89. Stan Gundry, "Introduction," in C. S. Cowles, et al., *Show Them No Mercy: 4 Views on God and Canaanite Genocide* (Grand Rapids: Zondervan, 2003), 7–9, at 7.

90. Daniel L. Gard, "A Response to C. S. Cowles," 53–56, at 53.

91. Ibid., 55.

92. *Contra* Patrick D. Miller Jr., *The Divine Warrior in Early Israel* (HSM 5; Cambridge, MA: Harvard University Press, 1973).

93. Gard, "The Case for Eschatological Continuity," *Show Them No Mercy*, 111–44, at 119, citing Fritz Stolz, *Jahwes und Israels Kriege: Kriegstheorien und Kriegserfahrungen im Glaube des alten Israels* (Zürich: Theologischer Verlag, 1972); Roland de Vaux, *Ancient Israel* (2 vols.; New York: McGraw-Hill, 1965) 1:213–66; Rudolf Smend, *Yahweh War and Tribal Confederation: Reflections upon Israel's Earliest History*, trans. Max Gray Rogers (Nashville: Abingdon, 1970); Edgar W. Conrad, *Fear Not Warrior: A Study of 'al tira' Pericopes in the Hebrew Scriptures* (BJS 74; Chico: Scholars Press, 1985); T. R. Hobbs, *A Time for War: A Study of Warfare in the Old Testament* (Wilmington, DE: Michael Glazier, 1989).

94. Gard, "The Case for Eschatological Continuity," 132–33.

95. Matt. 13:40–43; 25:41. See Gard, "The Case for Eschatological Continuity," 135.

96. Gard, "A Response to C. S. Cowles," 56.

97. Gard, "The Case for Eschatological Continuity," 140.

modern nation."[98] Yahweh's violence is *exceptional*, and "what appears to the human mind as 'evil' acts of God . . . are in fact not 'evil' acts at all since they come from the Lord himself."[99]

Like Gard, Tremper Longman argues for "spiritual continuity" between the Testaments, although in Jesus there is "a radical transformation, intensification, and progression of revelation."[100] Nonetheless, Longman also admits that the "revelation of Jesus in the New Testament is no less violent than the revelation of God in the Old Testament."[101] The New Testament simply "builds on the revelation of the Old Testament" and is "equally as bloody as the Old Testament."[102] For Longman, therefore, "warfare is worship. The battlefield is sacred space. To be involved in warfare is a holy activity analogous to going to the temple."[103] God is "ontologically violent."[104] Jesus is the "divine warrior" of the book of Revelation.[105]

Eugene Merrill, on the other hand, proposes a "moderate discontinuity" between the Testaments in which "Yahweh war" is seen as "distinct from war in general."[106] Since Yahweh was the "owner of the land," he needed to "undertake measures to destroy and/or expel the illegitimate inhabitants."[107] Recognizing that Yahweh war passages have "their own set of technical terms and unique form-critical characteristics,"[108] Merrill emphasizes the ritual or cultic aspects of worshiping a God of war,[109] and affirms that war was "necessary to Israel's escape from Egypt" and "her conquest and settlement of Canaan."[110]

98. Ibid., 136.

99. Ibid., 127.

100. Tremper Longman III, "A Response to C. S. Cowles," in *Show Them No Mercy*, 57– 60, at 60.

101. Ibid., 58–59.

102. Longman, "The Case for Spiritual Continuity," 163.

103. Ibid., 164.

104. Cowles, "A Response to Tremper Longman III," 192.

105. Longman, "The Case for Spiritual Continuity," 183.

106. Eugene H. Merrill, "The Case for Moderate Discontinuity," in *Show Them No Mercy,* 63–94, at 65. On "Yahweh war," see Gwilym H. Jones, "'Holy War' or 'Yahweh War'?" *VT* 25 (1965): 654–58; Smend, *Yahweh War and Tribal Confederation*, 36–37; Manfred Weippert, "'Heiliger Krieg' in Israel und Assyrien: Kritische Anmerkungen zu Gerhard von Rads Konzept des 'Heiligen Kriegs im alten Israel," *ZAW* 84 (1972): 460–93.

107. Ibid., 67.

108. See Gerhard von Rad, *Holy War in Ancient Israel*, trans. and ed. Marva J. Dawn (Grand Rapids: Eerdmans, 1991), 41–51; idem, "Deuteronomy and the Holy War," in *Studies in Deuteronomy*, trans. Davis Stalker (London: SCM, 1953), 45–59, at 50–51. See also Gwilym H. Jones, "The Concept of Holy War," in *The World of Ancient Israel: Sociological, Anthropological, and Political Perspectives*, ed. Ronald E. Clements, 299–321, at 309; Norman K. Gottwald, "'Holy War' in Deuteronomy: Analysis and Critique," *RevExp* 61, no. 4 (1964): 296–310, at 299.

Merrill does not seem to find the idea that "such war was conceived by God, commanded by him, executed by him, and brought by him alone to successful conclusion" problematic.[111] Yahweh's use of genocide transcends good and evil because it is *exceptional*: "The issue then cannot be whether or not genocide is intrinsically good or evil—its sanction by a holy God settles that question."[112] God "can accomplish his purpose in any way that pleases him."[113] Like Job, who are we to question God?[114] Yahweh war was necessary in biblical times: the Canaanites needed to be eliminated because of the "irremediable hardness" of their hearts, to "protect Israel against spiritual corruption,"[115] to destroy idolatry, and to educate Israel on the "character" of God.[116]

C. S. Cowles, in contrast, makes a case for "radical discontinuity" between the Old and New Testament portrayals of God. He proposes that Jesus introduces "the shocking, unprecedented, and utterly incomprehensible news that God is nonviolent."[117] Jesus revealed a God who "never has been and never will be party to genocide of any sort."[118] Appealing to John Wesley's "Christological hermeneutic,"[119] with its appeal to Jesus as the criterion for evaluating scripture, Cowles seeks to transcend the "tension between the texts."[120] He argues that the "earliest Christians were so sure of the nonviolent nature of God as revealed in Christ that they renounced all forms of violence, including military service. . . ."[121] Jesus himself "renounced the use of violence"[122] and introduced "an entirely new way of looking at God."

109. The biblical חרם refers to the "utter destruction" and/or (ritual) "devotion/separation" of entire cities, including men, women, children, and livestock. See Deut. 20:1-20; 13:12-18; Josh. 6:1-27; 8:1-29; 10–11; 1 Sam. 15:1-23.

110. Merrill, "The Case for Moderate Discontinuity," 77.

111. Ibid., 80–81.

112. Ibid., 93.

113. Ibid., 85.

114. Ibid., 94.

115. Seibert, *Disturbing Divine Behavior*, 77–80, at 77. See also Gleason L. Archer, *New International Encyclopedia of Bible Difficulties: Based on the NIV and the NASB* (Grand Rapids: Zondervan, 1982), 158; Terence E. Fretheim, "God and Violence in the Old Testament," *Word and World* 24 (2004): 18–28, esp. 24–25; idem, "'I Was Only a Little Angry': Divine Violence in the Prophets," *Interpretation* 58 (2004): 365–75.

116. Merrill, "The Case for Moderate Discontinuity," 85. Seibert, *Disturbing Divine Behavior*, 74–77.

117. C. S. Cowles, "The Case for Radical Discontinuity," in *Show Them No Mercy*, 11–46, at 24.

118. Ibid., 26.

119. Ibid., 35.

120. Ibid., 33.

121. Ibid., 28. See also Roland Bainton, *Christian Attitudes Toward War and Peace: A Historical Survey and Critical Re-evaluation* (New York: Abingdon, 1960), 73, 76.

Consequently, if our God is made in the image of Christ, then God "is not a destroyer . . . God does not engage in punitive, redemptive, or sacred violence."[123] This means that "Moses and Joshua misunderstood the will and purpose of God."[124] The Bible, at least in part, misrepresents God.

Gard, Longman, and Merrill each criticize Cowles for *selectively* choosing the Jesus traditions "which he finds acceptable" and avoiding the "divine warrior" passages in the book of Revelation,[125] where Jesus "judges and makes war . . . dressed in a robe dipped in blood."[126] The problem with appealing to the book of Revelation, however, is that it does *not* represent the teachings or person of the historical Jesus. Moreover, the eschatological kingdom and victory over evil occur *nonviolently* in Revelation.[127] The rider's robe is "dipped in blood *before* the supposed battle" and his name is "The Word of God." The "armies of the kings of the earth are defeated by the sword that extends from the rider's mouth." It is the *word* of God, not violence, that defeats evil.

Was the Jesus who taught "love your enemies" simply mistaken, hypocritical, or deceptive when he grounded this ethic in the unconditionally loving and forgiving character of God? Is the historical Jesus guilty—by association—of divine violence? If Yahweh war was necessary in order to eliminate the exceptionally wicked Canaanites, or to protect Israel from corruption and idolatry, or to educate Israel in God's character, it surely did not succeed. The Canaanites were *not* destroyed, idolatry was *not* abolished, and the Israelites were *not* protected from moral and spiritual corruption. What are we to make of all of this? Should biblical scholars even be engaged in critiquing the Bible?[128] Or are we to remain silent, professional apologists for the ethically reprehensible?

The Old Testament portrayal of God is ethically problematic. This raises troubling questions about the nature of God in the biblical tradition, especially

122. Cowles, "The Case for Radical Discontinuity," 29.

123. Ibid., 30.

124. Ibid., 41.

125. Longman, "A Response to C. S. Cowles," 59.

126. Rev. 19:11-15.

127. See J. Denny Weaver, "Narrative *Christus Victor*: The Answer to Anselmian Atonement Violence," in *Atonement and Violence: A Theological Conversation*, ed. John Sanders (Nashville: Abingdon, 2006), 1–32, esp. 17–20; here at 20.

128. D. J. A. Clines, *The Bible and the Modern World* (BS 51; Sheffield: Sheffield Academic Press, 1997), 23. For further need of an "ethical analysis" of the biblical texts see Michael Prior, *The Bible and Colonialism: A Moral Critique* (Sheffield: Sheffield Academic Press, 1997), 13, 291. Elisabeth Schüssler Fiorenza, *Rhetoric and Ethic: The Politics of Biblical Studies* (Minneapolis: Fortress Press, 1999), 51, calls for "a hermeneutics of ethical and theological evaluation."

because this portrayal stands in contrast to key elements in the Jesus tradition. One can either deny that the Old Testament accurately portrays God (thus safeguarding God from malicious slander) or apologetically defend God's honor and the Old Testament's authority by justifying God's command to commit genocide. To endorse both is simply to make Jesus' entire ministry a peaceful intermission or interlude, a calm before the storm of eschatological judgment and violence. To do so is also to make Jesus' peaceful teachings irrelevant, secondary to the Grand Narrative of God's "justice." Biblical scholars understandably do not want to assume responsibility for perpetuating a legacy of violence, and they generally deny that the biblical tradition should be used as a warrant for ethnic cleansing or genocide, but one cannot help but wonder if this politically and ethically correct stance is reconcilable with the idea that the biblical text is historically, ethically, and theologically accurate in its representation of God.

The Marcionite heresy casts a long, dark shadow across the pages of history. Marcion posited a radical discontinuity between the God of the Old Testament and the God revealed by Jesus, resolving this tension by positing *two* Gods,[129] rejecting the God of the Old Testament as evil.[130] In response, early Church Fathers compiled a list of canonical books in an attempt to create a *coherent* account of divine revelation.[131] Today the charge of "Marcionism" is often brought against those who suggest that the ethically problematic passages in the Bible are fundamentally *inconsistent* with the teachings of Jesus, but the charge is unwarranted. The identification of ethically problematic passages in the Bible does not require positing a second God. On the contrary, it is the presupposition of *one* God that reveals the tension *within* the Testaments, sometimes within the same *text*. Simplistic dichotomies between the Old and

129. Marcion constructed a dualistic system that set the good God revealed by Jesus against and in opposition to the evil God who created the (evil) world of matter, gave the Law (which led to the knowledge of sin), and lusted after war. For Marcion, the God of the Old Testament was inconsistent, fallible, and lacked omniscience.

130. Tertullian, *Against Marcion* 1.6; 2.12.1; 1.15.5; Justin, *1 Apol.* 26.5; 58.1; Irenaeus, *Adv. Haer.* 3.12.12; 1.27.2; Hippolytus, *Ref.* 7.29–31; Origen, *De Principiis* 2.5; Clement of Alexandria, *Stromata* 2.39.1; Epiphanius, *Pan.* 42.3.1–2. See also Sebastian Moll, *The Arch-Heretic Marcion* (WUNT 250; Tübingen: Mohr Siebeck, 2010); Adolf von Harnack, *Marcion: Das Evangelium vom fremden Gott* (Darmstadt: Wissenschaftliche Buchgesellschaft, 1996 [1921]). See now also Jason D. BeDuhn, *The First New Testament: Marcion's Scriptural Canon* (Salem: Polebridge, 2013).

131. Moll, *The Arch-Heretic Marcion*, 150, notes that the "crucial difference" between Marcion and Justin is that "Both men see Christ in opposition to the Old Testament Law . . . but for Marcion this antithesis consists in a permanent fight between two Gods . . . whereas Justin believes that the antithetical new law has simply replaced the old one."

New Testaments simply do not do justice to the complex, diverse, and multifaceted representations of the divine in these texts. Similarly, the presupposition that the Old and New Testaments represent a seamless historical and theological narrative and ideological continuity undermines Jesus' own distinctive interpretation of the Jewish tradition. Theological discontinuities between Jesus and the Old Testament are not to be ignored or projected onto supersessionistic debates between Judaism and Christianity,[132] but problematized as tensions within a first-century Jewish context, that is, tensions *within* Judaism.

Philip Jenkins, a prolific scholar of religion, has recently attempted to bring the discussion of these problematic passages—these Deuteronomistic "death verses"—into the public forum.[133] Jenkins calls for Judaism, Christianity, and Islam to "grow past their bloody origins" and "selective amnesia."[134] His goal is to find new ways of reading disturbing passages in order to "show how they can be absorbed, comprehended, and freely discussed," *and* whether these texts "might legitimately be rejected."[135] He notes that "We have to read such texts in context, holistically, and we have to know the history."[136] This calls for "a process of truth and reconciliation" so that believers can "discuss or even preach" on these difficult passages "without compromise or apology."[137] It is one thing, of course, to *identify* problematic passages; it is quite another to critically *engage* them. Jenkins traces the terrifying ways in which these passages have been used and calls for "public or liturgical readings" of the darkest texts where they can be read in context with other passages that "frame and expound their meaning."[138]

132. For attempts to affirm the continuity between the Testaments by reading Jesus in(to) the Old Testament, see, for example, D. A. Carson, ed., *The Scriptures Testify About Me: Jesus and the Gospel in the Old Testament* (Wheaton: Crossway, 2013); Iain M. Duguid, *Is Jesus in the Old Testament? Basics of the Faith* (Philipsburg: P & R Publishing, 2013); Michael J. Williams, *How to Read the Bible Through the Jesus Lens: A Guide to Christ-Focused Reading of Scripture* (Grand Rapids: Zondervan, 2012); Nancy Guthrie, *The Son of David: Seeing Jesus in the Historical Books* (Wheaton: Crossway, 2013); David Murray, *Jesus on Every Page: 10 Simple Ways to Seek and Find Christ in the Old Testament* (Nashville: Thomas Nelson, 2013). For a more careful approach, see Herbert Bateman IV, Gordon Johnston, and Darrell Bock, *Jesus the Messiah: Tracing the Promises, Expectations, and Coming of Israel's King* (Grand Rapids: Kregel, 2012).

133. Philip Jenkins, *Laying Down the Sword: Why We Can't Ignore the Bible's Violent Verses* (New York: HarperOne, 2011), 30. See now also Ramon Martínez de Pisón, *From Violence to Peace: Dismantling the Manipulation of Religion* (Conflict, Ethics, and Spirituality 1; Leuven: Peeters, 2013).

134. Ibid., 23, 16.

135. Ibid., 24.

136. Ibid., 25.

137. Ibid., 26.

138. Ibid., 241.

In a similar vein, the controversial Episcopal bishop and author John Shelby Spong has also sought "to expose and challenge" the "sins of scripture," to "lay bare the evil done by these texts in the name of God."[139] As a "committed Christian," Spong asserts from that perspective that the Bible's "hurtful texts" have left "a trail of pain, horror, blood and death" but this "fact is not often allowed to rise to consciousness."[140] He asks whether these texts, "the source of so much evil," can be "turned around and brought to an end" or whether the Bible is "too stained?"[141] Spong is not the first to point out the Bible's problematic passages on homosexuality, women, or Jews, but he does so with vehemence, setting out "to deconstruct the Bible's horror stories,"[142] and arguing that these scriptures should be "either jettisoned or reinterpreted."[143] Any text that "uses, violates or diminishes . . . must be called evil,"[144] while those used "to justify our hostility toward the Jews need to be banished forever."[145] Spong insists "on filtering the biblical stories through the crucible of contemporary knowledge,"[146] which essentially means affirming scientific rationalism and a God based on "our experience." It is not difficult to see why so many find Spong's suggestions offensive.

There is no consensus on what to do with the divine violence inscribed in the Bible. Some scholars shy away from the problem. Others seek to defend biblical genocide. Still others appropriate the texts that serve their own special interests, while some attempt to deconstruct the texts, resurrecting the heretical specters of Marcion and Jefferson. Others suggest that the Bible's violent passages can help us redirect how we think about God.[147] If the Bible is historically and theologically accurate, then the Canaanite genocide was an act of justified violence commanded by God. On the other hand, the portrayal of God as one who initiates, commands, and performs violence may not accurately reflect God's true nature.[148] Here Eric Seibert correctly identifies the problematic "control belief" that many exegetes (and believers) assume—an

139. John Shelby Spong, *The Sins of Scripture: Exposing the Bible's Texts of Hate to Reveal the God of Love* (New York: HarperOne, 2006), xiii.

140. Ibid., 4.

141. Ibid., 5.

142. Ibid., 24.

143. Ibid., 100.

144. Ibid., 142.

145. Ibid., 209.

146. Ibid., xi.

147. Seibert, *Disturbing Divine Behavior*; idem, *The Violence of Scripture: Overcoming the Old Testament's Troubling Legacy* (Minneapolis: Fortress Press, 2012).

148. Ibid., 242.

assumption that has led to enormous expenditures of apologetic ingenuity—namely, that "God actually said and did what the Old Testament claims."[149] The question, of course, is what if God did *not* actually say or do some of the things attributed to him in the Bible? This would certainly protect God's reputation from accusations of genocide, but it would also undermine the historical and theological reliability of the Bible, as well as highlight the ethically disturbing fact that the biblical authors portrayed God as a violent, vengeful, and judgmental deity. But if God is not like the way he is described in the exodus and conquest narratives, then what *is* he like? And why did the biblical authors portray him that way? Moreover, is it even *possible* to perform a "salvage operation" on these problematic biblical texts within a biblical and scriptural worldview?

Seibert proposes a "Christocentric hermeneutic" as the primary criterion for testing the authenticity of the Bible's portrayal of God.[150] He affirms Jesus' revelation of God and suggests that any portrayal of God inconsistent with the portrayal of God found in Jesus' life and teachings can be categorically rejected: "If a biblical concept corresponds to what we know of God in Christ, it is acceptable, if not, it is invalid."[151] The God that Jesus reveals should be the "standard" by which all other portrayals of God are evaluated, the basis for making distinctions between the *textual* and the *actual* God.[152] A crucial element of Seibert's proposal is that God is coherent and consistent; this allows him to invalidate certain contradictory portrayals of God in the Hebrew Bible.

The problem with this approach is that Jesus is the primary causal agent for the threat of eschatological violence and destruction in the New Testament.[153]

149. Ibid., 86.

150. See also Jack B. Rogers and Donald K. McKim, *The Authority and Interpretation of the Bible* (San Francisco: Harper and Row, 1979), 77. On Jesus as ethical model see also Ted Grimsrud, *Embodying the Way of Jesus: Anabaptist Convictions for the Twenty-First Century* (Eugene: Wipf & Stock, 2007). See now also *The Message of Jesus: John Dominic Crossan and Ben Witherington III in Dialogue*, ed. Robert B. Stewart (Minneapolis: Fortress Press, 2013), where Crossan remarks on p. 64: "I can't find the violent God in Jesus. I see Christianity working zealously to get a violent God back into Jesus. But I don't find such a God revealed in Jesus . . . Jesus is the norm for the Christian Bible."

151. Seibert, *Disturbing Divine Behavior*, 183. See also Cowles, "The Case for Radical Discontinuity," in *Show Them No Mercy*, 13–44. See also Jack Nelson-Pallmeyer, *Jesus Against Christianity: Reclaiming the Missing Jesus* (Harrisburg: Trinity Press International, 2001).

152. Ibid., 12, following Terence E. Fretheim and Karlfried Froehlich, *The Bible as Word of God: In a Postmodern Age* (Minneapolis: Fortress Press, 1998), 116–17.

153. John Anderson, "Review of *Disturbing Divine Behavior*," *RBL* 03/2011, at http://www.bookreviews.org (2011). Creach, *Violence in Scripture*, 48, finds Seibert's proposal (to "separate the presentation of God as a warrior in the text from the *real* God") theologically "unhelpful"

The New Testament contains a great deal that is "overtly violent."[154] So if Jesus is going to be our *ethical ideal*, we must first identify what Jesus taught. We cannot simply pay lip service to Jesus' "nonviolence." There is much more to Jesus than Q 6:27's programmatic admonition to love enemies. Like the Hebrew Bible, the New Testament also contains passages that legitimize slavery, condemn homosexual acts, oppress women, and anticipate a violent eschatological judgment. Marcus Borg and N. T. Wright suggest that Jesus' judgment sayings should be read in the context of his criticism of "*this* generation," that is, his own contemporaries, not as eternal threats of damnation for everyone in every age. In this light, Jerusalem's destruction in 70 C.E. was the fulfillment of Jesus' prediction of divine judgment. This may be a persuasive suggestion for those passages that can plausibly be identified as predictive—it is indeed highly likely that Jesus issued warnings to his contemporaries and predicted the possible results of their actions—but there are also passages that portray Jesus as clearly threatening a bleak future of divine violence. We cannot simply contrast a nonviolent Jesus with the violent God inscribed in the Torah. To do so is not only simplistic and potentially supersessionistic; it also undermines the fact that Jesus was Jewish. The historical Jesus' critiques of Jewish individuals, traditions, and institutions were complex Jewish critiques *within* Judaism. Jesus' internal cultural criticism must be used to understand Jesus in his original early first-century Jewish context. In order to do this, we must reevaluate the vexing problem of the "apocalyptic Jesus."

and "misguided." According to Creach, Seibert's approach "overlooks the potentially positive role this image plays in Scripture and in Christian theology," i.e., the role of God as a Warrior who corrects oppression and injustice, a God who stands "against violence." The purpose of this image is to "comfort those oppressed by the evil forces of the world" (71).

154. Michel Desjardins, *Peace, Violence and the New Testament* (Sheffield: Sheffield Academic Press, 1997), 83–92. For challenges to the Marcionite dichotomy, see Shelly Matthews and E. Leigh Gibson, *Violence in the New Testament* (London: T&T Clark International, 2005).

4

The Apocalyptic Jesus

Divine Violence in the New Testament

A dominant school of thought in biblical scholarship holds that Jesus was an apocalyptic *and* eschatological figure.[1] It is not difficult to find textual support for this claim.[2] The Jesus of Q explicitly condemns the Galilean villages of Chorazin, Bethsaida, and Capernaum because they have not repented and refers to an imminent catastrophe with the arrival of the son of man, "the one who delivers judgment on God's behalf."[3] Q represents Jesus issuing numerous predictions of eschatological judgment (κρίσις).[4]

1. Dale C. Allison Jr., *The End of the Ages Has Come: An Early Interpretation of the Passion and Resurrection of Jesus* (Philadelphia: Fortress Press, 1985); idem, "A Plea for Thoroughgoing Eschatology," *JBL* 114 (1994): 664–67; idem, *Jesus of Nazareth: Millenarian Prophet* (Minneapolis: Fortress Press, 1998); idem, "The Eschatology of Jesus," in *The Encyclopedia of Apocalypticism*, Vol. 1: *The Origins of Apocalypticism in Judaism and Christianity*, ed. John J. Collins (New York: Continuum, 2000), 267–302. See also Bart D. Ehrman, *Jesus: Apocalyptic Prophet of the New Millennium* (New York: Oxford University Press, 1999); Ben Witherington III, *Jesus, Paul, and the End of the World: A Comparative Study in New Testament Eschatology* (Downer's Grove: InterVarsity, 1992); Arland Hultgren, "Eschatology in the New Testament: The Current Debate," in *The Last Things: Biblical and Theological Perspectives on Eschatology*, ed. Carl E. Braaten and Robert W. Jenson (Grand Rapids: Eerdmans, 2002), 67–89, esp. 84–89; N. T. Wright, *Jesus and the Victory of God*, Vol. 2, *Christian Origins and the Question of God* (Minneapolis: Fortress Press, 1996). On the debate see especially *The Apocalyptic Jesus: A Debate*, ed. Robert J. Miller (Santa Rosa: Polebridge, 2001); Stephen J. Patterson, "The End of Apocalypse," *TT* 52 (1995): 29–58; Marcus J. Borg, *Conflict, Holiness & Politics in the Teaching of Jesus* (New York: Edwin Mellen, 1984), 201–27; idem, "A Temperate Case for a Non-Eschatological Jesus," *Forum* 2, no. 3 (1986): 81–103; idem, *Jesus in Contemporary Scholarship* (Valley Forge, PA: Trinity Press International, 1994), 26–27, 86–90; idem, "Jesus and Eschatology: A Reassessment," in *Images of Jesus Today*, ed. James H. Charlesworth and Walter P. Weaver (Valley Forge, PA: Trinity Press International, 1994), 42–67.

2. For example, Mark 9:1, 13:30; Matt. 10:23; *Thom* 111:1; Q 11:49-51, 12:40, 17:26-27; Luke 18:7-8, 21:34-36; Matt. 25:13.

What is the historical relationship between Jesus' teaching about the kingdom and what appear to be these multiply attested threats of an imminent violent judgment? Our earliest evidence seems fairly consistent: the wrath of God is coming on "this generation" and it is one's loyalty to Jesus that plays a central, if not defining role in escaping this judgment. But what are Jesus' *terms* in offering salvation and/or judgment? I do not wish to imply here that Jesus did not seek to improve ethical behavior, failed to take advantage of teaching opportunities that could lead to repentance, or was reluctant to instruct others on the consequences of their actions. That is clearly not the case. I also do not wish to suggest that Jesus did not have the gift of foresight. It is perfectly reasonable to think that Jesus anticipated his own death (considering what had happened to John the Baptist) and could see how Judean politico-military resistance to Rome would end. The prophets had frequently warned Israel of impending disasters at the hands of foreign powers. But Jesus' warning of politico-military disaster would be very different from saying that God was going to inflict judgment on Israel for not listening to him (that is, Jesus) or not accepting his offer of salvation. It is the difference between a predictive warning and a vindictive threat. Jesus is recorded as proclaiming the *reversal* of worldly judgments, overturning ideas about how God judges the unjust.[5] We should be careful in critically analyzing the historical Jesus' terms of salvation and judgment.

Gerd Theissen and Annette Merz recognize this as a major problem in Jesus research. They argue that there is a close connection between Jesus' preaching of the kingdom and his preaching of judgment, claiming to find this connection in Judaism, where "God's eschatological action *always* has an aspect of judgment and an aspect of salvation."[6] Jesus shares this "dialectical connection between salvation and disaster," although he "puts the announcement of

3. As, for example, in Q 17:26. Gerd Theissen and Annette Merz, *The Historical Jesus: A Comprehensive Guide*, trans. John Bowden (Minneapolis: Fortress Press, 1998), 267.

4. Q 10:12, 13, 14, 15; 11:29, 32, 50–51; 13:28, 34–35; 17:26; 22:28–30.

5. Q 6:35c–d.

6. Theissen and Merz, *The Historical Jesus*, 264 (emphasis added). Petr Pokorný, "Demoniac and Drunkard: John the Baptist and Jesus According to Q 7:33-34," in *Jesus Research: An International Perspective: The Proceedings of the Biennial Princeton-Prague Symposium on the Current State of Studies on the Historical Jesus*, ed. James H. Charlesworth and Petr Pokorný (Grand Rapids: Eerdmans, 2009), 170–82, proposes that Jesus and John the Baptist parted ways on interpreting the final judgment of God. See also James H. Charlesworth, *Jesus within Judaism: New Light from Exciting Archaeological Discoveries* (New York: Doubleday, 1988), 38: "The apocalyptists tend to be vengeful, often calling upon God to destroy Jews' enemies. Jesus was more concerned with inward dispositions and an attitude of compassion and outgoing love."

salvation at the centre of his preaching,"[7] while "the aspect of judgment remarkably fades into the background." Nonetheless, it is not "completely absent" as "those who do not accept the salvation he offers in words and deeds incur the judgment." In other words, "Jesus proclaims salvation, but in the background threatens with judgment."[8] The arrival of the kingdom is intended to produce "repentance" (μετάνοια), and those who accept Jesus receive "protection in the judgment." Judgment is thus "self-chosen or deserved exclusion."[9] It is "the self-exclusion of those who do not repent."[10] Jesus did *not* offer *unconditional* love, grace, or salvation; it was contingent on accepting his offer of salvation—or else.

Theissen and Merz admit that Q's threats of judgment against "this generation" may be "reactions to negative experiences of the mission to Israel,"[11] but they conclude that "on the whole the *attacks* on 'this generation' probably go back to Jesus."[12] Jesus simply continues John's preaching of judgment, even if "now and again sayings of John the Baptist have found their way into the sayings of Jesus." This conflation is problematic, for not only is there reason to suspect that compositional motifs have been added to Q, but John does not even seem to recognize Jesus as "the One Who Is To Come."[13] Jesus' kingdom is *inclusive* and brings "a revaluation of stigmatized groups within Israel," including groups with social, physical, and moral "defects."[14] Theissen and Merz's attempt to forge a theological unity out of Jesus' offer of salvation and judgment concludes with the disturbing realization that Jesus "knows the dark side of God" and "brings it out in a threatening way":[15] Jesus preaches God's "punitive energy," his power to "punish sinners." God's "blazing fire of ethical energy" becomes "the devastating fire of hell for those who exclude themselves from salvation."[16]

Similarly, Marius Reiser challenges the tendency in North American scholarship to eschew the eschatological components of the Jesus tradition and points to what he calls "a remarkable silence regarding Jesus' proclamation of judgment."[17] He argues that with few exceptions[18] scholars are reluctant to

7. Ibid., 265.
8. Ibid., 275.
9. Ibid., 265.
10. Ibid., 267.
11. Ibid., 268.
12. Ibid., 268 (emphasis added).
13. Q 7:22-23.
14. Theissen and Merz, *The Historical Jesus*, 270–71.
15. Ibid., 273.
16. Ibid., 274.

broach the subject, citing the Jesus Seminar's explanation that "The vindictive tone of these sayings is uncharacteristic of Jesus."[19] In contrast, Reiser locates Jesus firmly within "the reality of early Jewish eschatology," which he describes as "the expectation of a definitive change to be wrought by God in the direction of historical events and the course of world history, and followed by an enduring time of salvation in which the righteous need no longer suffer at the hands of sinners."[20] For Reiser, apocalypticism is a more developed form of prophetic eschatology, the "principal feature" of which is "the eschatological judgment."[21] He constructs a classificatory system of eschatological ideas,[22] with the end-time as "the final reversal in the history of Israel and the nations,"[23] "a great action of punishment and destruction" in which "God creates justice where human beings have been unable or unwilling to bring it about." The true purpose of judgment, therefore, is not the punishment of the wicked, but "the salvation of the righteous." Judgment is justice.[24]

Jesus' proclamation of judgment is thus a necessary corollary, a prerequisite to his proclamation of salvation.[25] For Reiser, Jesus' eschatology is the culmination of the entire Jewish eschatological tradition that can be traced back through prophetic references to the Day of Yhwh,[26] Isaiah 65–66, the Psalms, the book of Daniel, *1 Enoch*, the Qumran library, the Assumption of Moses, the Testaments of the Twelve Patriarchs, the Sibylline Oracles, and *4 Ezra*—a formidable corpus of texts that clearly and repeatedly refer to a violent end-time judgment. Assembling the evidence in this way gives one the impression that Judaism was an essentially eschatological religious system perpetually awaiting God's judgment.[27] The problem is that this is also an abstract, artificial construct

17. Marius Reiser, *Jesus and Judgment: The Eschatological Proclamation in Its Jewish Context*, trans. Linda M. Maloney (Minneapolis: Fortress Press, 1997), 1–2.

18. Notably Hans Conzelmann, "Jesus Christus," *RGG* 3 (1959): 619–53; Joachim Gnilka, *Jesus von Nazareth. Botschaft und Geschichte* (HThKSup 3; Freiburg: Herder, 1990), 157–65.

19. Citing Robert Funk, Roy W. Hoover, and The Jesus Seminar, *The Five Gospels: The Search for the Authentic Words of Jesus* (New York: Maxwell Macmillan International, 1993), 188.

20. Reiser, *Jesus and Judgment*, 20.

21. Ibid., 23.

22. See also Egon Brandenburger, "Gerichtskonzeption im Urchristentum und ihre Voraussetzungen. Eine Problemstudie," *SNTU* 16 (1991): 5–54.

23. Reiser, *Jesus and Judgment*, 6.

24. Ibid., 145.

25. Ibid., 4.

26. Isa. 13:13; 34:8; Jer. 46:10; Ezek. 7:19; Zeph. 1:15, 18; 2:2, 3; Ezek. 34:12; Joel 2:2; Mal. 3:2.

27. Reiser, *Jesus and Judgment*, 144. See also Wilhelm Bousset and Hugo Gressmann, *Die Religion des Judentums im späthellenistischen Zeitalter* (HNT 21; 4th ed.; Tübingen: Mohr Siebeck, 1966), 202; David S.

of an essentialist normative eschatology, a monolithic system compiled from different texts composed over a seven-hundred year period of time.[28]

While Reiser correctly identifies two "*unresolved sets of problems*" in Jesus' sayings about judgment—the relationship between judgment and the kingdom and the relationship between judgment and the son of man[29]—Reiser's methodology *presumes* the authenticity of Jesus' judgment sayings.[30] This is problematic, not only because it presumes what should be established by evidence and argument, but more so because the Jesus tradition is composite, representing disparate streams of tradition that can be identified as sapiential, prophetic, eschatological, and apocalyptic. Jesus' judgment sayings, for example, appeal to and derive from prophetic traditions of social critique. The prophet is "a mediator who claims to receive messages direct from a divinity . . . and communicates these messages to recipients."[31] The prophets were often involved in conflicts with the ruling authorities and so it is not surprising that Jesus was regarded as a prophet in his own lifetime:[32] one of the prophet's classic functions was to evaluate the current state of the covenantal relationship with God. According to William Herzog, Jesus combined the "good news" of the kingdom with the warning of what would happen to an unrepentant Israel.[33] But while few would contest the idea that Jesus appeared as a prophet to his contemporaries, Jesus' prophecy of an end-time judgment on "this generation" seems to have been not only merciless but an utter failure.

Ben Witherington suggests that Jesus simply wasn't *sure* if the end was imminent: "Jesus did not proclaim that the end was *necessarily* imminent. At most he could only have spoken of its possible imminence, something which

Russell, *The Method and Message of Jewish Apocalyptic: 200 BC–A.D. 100* (Philadelphia: Westminster, 1964), 380.

28. Similar problems beset Brian Han Gregg, *The Historical Jesus and the Final Judgment Sayings in Q* (WUNT 2d ser. 207; Tübingen: Mohr Siebeck, 2006).

29. Reiser, *Jesus and Judgment*, 203.

30. Ibid., 204.

31. Lester L. Grabbe, *Priests, Prophets, Diviners, Sages: A Socio-Historical Study of Religious Specialists in Ancient Israel* (Valley Forge, PA: Trinity Press International, 1995), 107, 116.

32. So also Gerd Lüdemann, *Jesus After 2000 Years: What He Really Said and Did*, trans. John Bowden (London: SCM, 2000), 689; John P. Meier, *A Marginal Jew: Rethinking the Historical Jesus*, Vol. 2, *Mentor, Message and Miracles* (New York: Doubleday, 1994), 1046, proposes that Jesus presented himself as one "who could even tell Israelites what they should or should not observe in the Law." See also William R. Herzog II, *Prophet and Teacher: An Introduction to the Historical Jesus* (Louisville: Westminster John Knox, 2005), 12.

33. William R. Herzog II, *Jesus, Justice, and the Reign of God* (Louisville: Westminster John Knox, 2000), ch. 3.

I believe he did do."[34] The suggestion that Jesus wasn't *sure* whether the end-time was imminent not only makes Jesus indecisive; it also ignores passages like Mark 13:30, where Jesus explicitly claims that the end *is* imminent. The price one pays in reconstructing Jesus as an apocalyptic prophet sometimes comes at the cost of dominical error. Bart Ehrman's Jesus, for example, is a *failed* prophet posthumously deified by his disciples who saw in him the future coming son of man.[35] If Jesus really expected an "imminent . . . cosmic act of destruction," it would seem that he was quite wrong. As James Dunn puts it, Jesus' hopes "were not fulfilled. There were 'final' elements in his expectation which were not realized. Putting it bluntly, Jesus was proved wrong by the course of events."[36] If "this generation" would not "pass away until all these things have happened," then why did Jesus also say that "concerning that day or that hour, no one knows"?[37] Was Jesus wrong about the time of judgment but right about the time of salvation?

Paula Fredriksen proposes that what is truly distinctive about Jesus is his *timing*: "what distinguished Jesus' prophetic message from those of others was primarily its timetable, not its content . . . Jesus had stepped up the Kingdom's timetable from *soon* to *now*."[38] We can call this "realized eschatology,"[39] "inaugurated eschatology,"[40] "actualized eschatology,"[41] or "sapiential eschatology," but the common element is the conviction that the kingdom is a

34. Ben Witherington III, *The Jesus Quest: The Third Search for the Jew from Nazareth* (Downers Grove: InterVarsity, 1995), 96.

35. Ehrman, *Jesus: Apocalyptic Prophet of the New Millennium*, 160.

36. James D. G. Dunn, *Jesus Remembered* (Grand Rapids: Eerdmans, 2003), 479.

37. Mark 13:30, 13:32. For the authenticity of this saying see Witherington, *The Jesus Quest*, 96. For its inauthenticity see Robert Miller, *The Jesus Seminar and Its Critics* (Santa Rosa: Polebridge, 1999), 115.

38. Paula Fredriksen, *Jesus of Nazareth, King of the Jews* (New York: Knopf, 1999), 266–67.

39. C. H. Dodd, *The Parables of the Kingdom* (London: Nisbet, 1935; rev. ed. 1961); idem, "The Eschatological Element in the New Testament and Its Permanent Significance," *Int* 20 (1923): 17–21; "The This-Worldly Kingdom of God in Our Lord's Teaching," *Theology* 14 (1927): 258–60, at 259. See also Henry Burton Sharman, *The Teaching of Jesus about the Future According to the Synoptic Gospels* (Chicago: University of Chicago Press, 1909); Gerhard Kittel, "The This-Worldly Kingdom of God in Our Lord's Teaching," *Theology* 14 (1927): 260–62, at 261; E. F. Scott, "The Place of Apocalyptical Conceptions in the Mind of Jesus," *JBL* 41 (1922): 137–42; William Manson, *Christ's View of the Kingdom of God* (London: James Clarke, 1918); Rudolf Otto, *The Kingdom of God and the Son of Man: A Study in the History of Religion*, trans. Floyd V. Filson and Bertram L. Woolf (Grand Rapids: Zondervan, 1938). But see Clayton Sullivan, *Rethinking Realized Eschatology* (Macon, GA: Mercer University Press, 1988), for a critique of Dodd's "realized eschatology."

40. George Eldon Ladd, *A Theology of the New Testament* (Grand Rapids: Eerdmans, 1993 [1974]).

41. Stephen J. Patterson, *The Gospel of Thomas and Jesus* (FF; Sonoma: Polebridge, 1993), 210–11.

present reality: "Apocalyptic eschatology is world-negation stressing imminent divine intervention: we wait for God to act; sapiential eschatology is world-negation emphasizing immediate divine imitation: God waits for us to act."[42] For John Dominic Crossan, sapiential eschatology is relatively synonymous with John Kloppenborg's "radical wisdom of the kingdom,"[43] a lifestyle of discipleship based on the "imitation of the merciful and generous God . . . and as 'following' or 'listening to' or 'coming to' Jesus."[44] Is this Jesus of realized eschatology the real Jesus? We have here two competing schools of thought: sapiential wisdom and apocalypticism: one focuses on the present, the other on the future; one on salvation, the other on judgment. Is there a way beyond this simplistic dichotomy?

Q, our earliest evidence for John the Baptist, portrays John as a prophet of repentance (μετάνοια) predicting God's imminent wrath (μέλλουσης ὀργῆς), and the arrival of "One Who Is To Come" and perform judgment.[45] Q 3 parallels "Holy Spirit *and* fire" (πνεύματι ἁγίῳ καὶ πυρί), combining eschatological salvation and judgment.[46] Josephus, on the other hand, describes John's ministry but emphasizes his *ethical* teachings of "virtue," "justice to one another," and "piety towards God."[47] Josephus says nothing about John's preaching of judgment. This may be because Josephus downplays the theme; it may also be that Q overplays it. Josephus tells us that John's baptism was *not* for the "forgiveness of sins" but rather for the cleansing of the body, in contrast to Mark, where it is "a baptism of repentance *for* the forgiveness of sins" (βάπτισμα μετανοίας εἰς ἄφεσιν ἁμαρτιῶν).[48] Did Jesus replace John's threat of imminent judgment with the present kingdom?[49] There is evidence that Jesus saw his healings and exorcisms as signs of victory over Satan. Did he abandon the idea that God's judgment would result in eschatological violence?[50]

Jesus is remembered, at least in Q 6:37, as commanding his disciples *not* to "pass judgment." This prohibition is generally understood as referring to

42. John Dominic Crossan, *The Essential Jesus: Original Sayings and Earliest Images* ([1998] Eugene, OR: Wipf & Stock, 2008), 8.

43. John S. Kloppenborg, *The Formation of Q: Trajectories in Ancient Wisdom Collections* (Philadelphia: Fortress Press, 1987), 189, 242, 318.

44. Ibid., 241.

45. Q 3:12.

46. Q 3:16b.

47. Josephus, *Ant.* 18.116–119.

48. Mark 1:4.

49. Theissen and Merz, *The Historical Jesus*, 210–211.

50. John K. Riches, *Jesus and the Transformation of Judaism* (London: Darton, Longman, and Todd, 1980).

criticizing others,[51] but what makes the saying significant is that it is almost universally recognized as authentic. There are "no genuine Jewish parallels for this radical prohibition on judging."[52] The biblical tradition does contain examples of reciprocity between humanity and God[53] so Jesus may be developing "an original variation of a common Jewish principle,"[54] but the finality of the prohibition establishes the conditions within which eschatological judgment would be an impossibility and foregrounds the nature of God as fundamentally merciful and forgiving. Jesus' prohibition "*not* to judge" could be interpreted as relegating that task solely to God or to self-inflicted judgment, but there is a major difference between concerned warnings of consequences for one's actions and the vehement condemnation we find in many apocalyptic texts in the Second Temple period. In other words, there is a wide spectrum in the rhetorical use of judgment-language ranging from concerned *warnings* to *prophecies*, *threats*, and *condemnations*. We must fit Jesus within this spectrum and not conflate either the different phases of the Jesus movement's engagement with Israel or its later voices speaking on Jesus' behalf.

It is difficult to conceive of a just God who does *not* punish the mass murderers of this world. The concept of hell satisfies our thirst for justice, which is so often denied. Heaven and hell not only serve as deterrents to unethical behavior; they also appeal to us as just rewards for our loyalty toward God. On the other hand, the idea of hell has also been used to judge enemies, coerce conversion, and sell salvation to sinners. Some may even find a kind of pathological pleasure in imagining the future sufferings of others. Many of us, however, would like to think that some day this world might be turned around. This also seems to be what Jesus envisioned: a restoration of this world according to God's will. To be clear, then, I am denying neither the *justice* nor the *judgment* of God.[55] What I *am* denying is that God's justice or judgment

51. Heinz Schürmann, *Das Lukasevangelium Erster Teil. (Kommentar zu Kap. 1,1–9,50)* (HThK 3; 3d ed.; Freiburg: Herder, 1984), 1:361; I. Howard Marshall, *The Gospel of Luke: A Commentary on the Greek Text* (Exeter: Paternoster, 1978), 265–66; Siegfried Schulz, *Q: Spruchquelle der Evangelisten* (Zürich: Theologischer Verlag, 1972), 148; Joseph A. Fitzmyer, *The Gospel according to Luke: Introduction, Translation, and Notes* (2 vols.; AB 28–28A; New York: Doubleday, 1983–1985), 1:641; Adolf Schlatter, *Der Evangelist Matthäus. Seine Sprache, sein Ziel, seine Selbständigkeit* (Stuttgart: Calwer Verlag, 1929; 7th ed., 1982), 240.

52. Reiser, *Jesus and Judgment*, 265. See *m.'Abot* 2.4: "Judge not your fellow man until you have reached his place."

53. Mal. 3:7; 1 Sam. 2:30; 2 Chr. 24:20; Sir. 28:2; Ezek. 7:27.

54. Reiser, *Jesus and Judgment*, 266.

55. Thomas R. Yoder Neufeld, *Killing Enmity: Violence and the New Testament* (Grand Rapids: Baker Academic, 2011), 52: "there is simply too much evidence that Jesus shared with those who tell us of him,

necessarily looks *anything* like the divine judgment imagined by imperfect human beings experiencing rejection, persecution, and disappointment and inscribing a vision of hell, punishment, revenge, torture, and annihilation in the name of God. We have simply confused God's justice and judgment with (human) violence and vengeance.

It is not unreasonable to hold that our tradition contains both faithful transmissions of Jesus' original teachings and new materials composed in response to the social pressures experienced by Jesus' disciples as they interacted with their fellow Jews. These social interactions often involved social conflicts, which introduced a wide range of psychological responses and reactions to the tradition, including sentiments of hurt, hostility, anger, betrayal, rejection, and the desire for revenge and divine vindication. The appeal to eschatological violence as a means of insuring future justice must have been attractive, given that apocalyptic judgment-language was ready at hand in Second Temple Judaism. The introduction of eschatological violence as a rhetorical weapon, while theologically useful in resolving an apparent lack of justice in the world, would simultaneously have distorted the tradition by introducing an apparent lack of feeling for the eschatological fate of the judged, and this seems incongruous with Jesus' well-attested compassion for others.

There would have been nothing offensive about Jesus promising God's forgiveness and salvation to those who *repented*; in fact, "he would have been a national hero."[56] And yet Jesus offended. Why? Is it because Jesus offered forgiveness "*before* requiring reformation"?[57] Or was Jesus offensive because he was promising salvation to sinners without repentance? E. P. Sanders suggests that Jesus "may have offered them inclusion in the kingdom not only *while they were still sinners* but also *without* requiring repentance as normally understood."[58] Jesus thus seems to have changed the admission rules into the kingdom: "some of the traditional practices of Judaism may be foregone by those who follow Jesus . . . Jesus put 'following' him above observing the law."[59] Jesus was not so much a preacher of repentance[60] or conditional forgiveness, but a preacher

whether evangelists or apostles, the conviction that God is judge." The *nature* of that "judgment," however, is what is open to interpretation. For an attempt to develop a new system of "restorative punishment" based on the New Testament, see Christopher D. Marshall, *Beyond Retribution: A New Testament Vision for Justice, Crime, and Punishment* (SPS; Grand Rapids: Eerdmans, 2001).

56. E. P. Sanders, *Jesus and Judaism* (Philadelphia: Fortress Press, 1985), 203.

57. Ibid., 204.

58. Ibid., 206.

59. Ibid., 207.

60. Ibid., 203.

of "*good* news," although his provocatively open call was not continued by the early church,[61] which did not share Jesus' apparently "high tolerance" for sinners.

Presupposing the historicity of Jesus' prophetic threats of destruction against Jerusalem, N. T. Wright proposes that Jesus took "upon himself the fate, the exile, of Israel."[62] Jesus decided to enact the "suffering and exile . . . to undergo the fate he had announced in symbol and word for Jerusalem as a whole."[63] Here the theme of "eschatological restoration" is again used to catalogue a variety of "messianic woes," "birth pangs," and "great tribulation(s)" in order to affirm the possibility that Jesus understood his own death in salvific terms. Wright argues that Jesus believed he needed to undergo the tribulation himself in order to inaugurate the kingdom,[64] but this interpretation does "not arise naturally from the study of the texts . . . [it] seems to be imposed upon them."[65] This pan-eschatological approach not only conflates different texts and traditions from different times and contexts, it also tends to ignore the fact that the "messianic woes" were supposed to *precede* the coming of the messiah and salvation whereas Jesus' ministry (and the *kingdom*) arrived *before* (or during) the "messianic woes" and he *himself* allegedly suffered the "messianic woes," an idea that runs counter to traditional messianic ideas of military victory and national restoration. These objections can justifiably be countered by suggesting that Jesus himself was radically innovative in interpreting his own role in the eschatological timetable (and that many Second Temple Jews and early Christians were not deterred from adjusting this timetable), but the fact remains that our earliest Christian texts were composed in a cultural context that anticipated, participated in, witnessed, and suffered a series of very real social, political, and military crises; it is only natural that our texts reflect these contexts and "remember" the historical Jesus through these lenses. The problem with Wright's proposal, therefore, is that there are no pre-Christian Jewish traditions of a "suffering and dying messiah" (hence Jesus' innovation). An additional concern is that this interpretation simply transfers God's divine violence and judgment from Jerusalem to *Jesus*. Was Jesus' God a God of mercy and compassion or a God of implacable, unforgiving wrath who can only be

61. Ibid., 211, 174.

62. Wright, *Jesus and the Victory of God*, 593.

63. Ibid., 594.

64. Ibid., 591-603, esp. 591. See also Dunn, *Jesus Remembered*, 824. See now also Brant Pitre, *Jesus, the Tribulation, and the End of the Exile: Restoration Eschatology and the Origin of the Atonement* (Tübingen: Mohr Siebeck; Grand Rapids: Baker Academic, 2005).

65. Sanders, *Jesus and Judaism*, 23.

appeased, and forgive, through Jesus' blood sacrifice? How are we to resolve this disturbing theological tension inscribed within the tradition?

Dale Allison has long and cogently argued that apocalypticism is the most appropriate interpretive lens through which to view the Jesus tradition prior to and "apart from detailed evaluation" of the tradition.[66] This presupposition rests on three main premises: (1) apocalyptic continuity between Jesus, John the Baptist, and the Jesus movement;[67] (2) Jesus' resurrection as an eschatological event, a herald of the general resurrection; and (3) the idea that prophetic eschatology was common in the Roman and Jewish worlds of Jesus' day.[68] Allison suggests, however, that the eschatological "consummation" is to be understood *literally*: Jesus and his followers longed for a new, better world, "a revolutionary change."[69] They took the apocalyptic prophecies of the end "at more or less face value,"[70] and the threat of eschatological violence is a pervasive and *authentic* component of the Jesus tradition. How compelling is this particular approach?

The judgment sayings do *seem* to indicate a significant apocalyptic continuity between the Jesus tradition, John the Baptist, and the Jesus movement. But there is also good reason for Jesus' followers to have adopted the expectation of an imminent judgment on Israel *after* Jesus' death: its religious leaders had just conspired in executing Jesus. Jesus' violent death, the movement's perceived rejection by its fellow Jews, and the internal conflicts precipitated by a rapid influx of law-free Gentile converts in Pauline communities led to numerous unresolved tensions in the tradition. It is reasonable to conclude that the theme of apocalyptic judgment significantly *increased* between 30 and 70 c.e. with the murders of John the Baptist, Jesus, and James, as well as Stephen, Peter, and Paul, not to mention the catastrophic Jewish Revolt against Rome.[71] There is no question that Jesus' message of a loving, providential God stands in tension with the Baptist's rhetoric of apocalyptic judgment.[72] Jesus' resurrection, while it undoubtedly had a profound effect on the early Jesus movement, was also associated with the

66. Allison, *Jesus of Nazareth*, 45.

67. Dale C. Allison Jr., "John and Jesus: Continuity and Discontinuity," *JSHJ* 1, no. 1 (2002): 6–27.

68. Allison, *Jesus of Nazareth*, 44.

69. Ibid., 155. Crossan, "The Historical Jesus and Early Christianity," in Miller, ed., *The Apocalyptic Jesus*, at 138.

70. Allison, *Jesus of Nazareth*, 169.

71. Philip Vielhauer and Georg Strecker, "Apocalyptic in Early Christianity," in *New Testament Apocrypha*, ed. Edgar Hennecke, Wilhelm Schneemelcher, and Robert McL. Wilson (2 vols.; Cambridge: James Clarke; Louisville: Westminster John Knox, 1992), 2:569–602, at 571.

idea of an imminent *general* resurrection. This caused confusion in Paul's communities simply because it did not happen (see 1 Thessalonians; 1 Corinthians). Similarly, the Roman world of Jesus' day may have been "dominated by prophetic eschatology,"[73] but the nearly ubiquitous presence of eschatological thought in the Jesus tradition does not require cataclysmic interpretations in each instance. Ancient eschatological thought comes in many forms, not just Jewish apocalypticism of the catastrophic kind.[74]

This brings us to a significant methodological concern: that of *definition*.[75] While eschatology refers to the study of "last things" and apocalyptic(ism) (ἀποκάλυψις) to something "revealed," biblical scholars have come to use the term *apocalypticism* in a variety of ways to signify "a cluster of themes and expectations—cataclysmic signs and suffering, resurrection of the dead, universal judgment, heavenly redeemer figures, a divine utopia . . . typically in association with belief in a near end."[76] The problem involved in constructing a research program with the sheer volume and variety of this catalogue of apocalyptic data should be obvious: how do we determine which *particular* aspects of this monolithic apocalypticism actually apply to *Jesus* and which apply to his followers or their cultural matrices?[77] And why is apocalypticism

72. John Dominic Crossan, *The Birth of Christianity: Discovering What Really Happened in the Years Immediately After the Execution of Jesus* (San Francisco: HarperSanFrancisco, 1998), 287.

73. The phrase is from Helmut Koester, "Jesus the Victim," *JBL* 111 (1992): 3–15, at 10–11.

74. Dale C. Allison Jr., *Constructing Jesus: Memory, Imagination, and History* (Grand Rapids: Baker Academic, 2010), 157.

75. Ron Cameron, "The Anatomy of a Discourse: On 'Eschatology' as a Category for Explaining Christian Origins," *MTSR* 8 (1996): 231–45.

76. Dale C. Allison Jr., "Apocalyptic, Polemic, Apologetics," in *Resurrecting Jesus: The Earliest Christian Tradition and Its Interpreters* (New York: T&T Clark, 2005), 111–48, esp. 112 n. 1. For the common working generic definition see John J. Collins, *The Apocalyptic Imagination: An Introduction to Jewish Apocalyptic Literature* (2d rev. ed.; Grand Rapids: Eerdmans, 1998), 13; idem, "Introduction: Towards the Morphology of a Genre," in *Apocalypse: The Morphology of a Genre*, ed. John J. Collins (Semeia 14; Missoula: Scholars Press, 1979), 1–20, esp. 9. For criticism see Crispin Fletcher-Louis, "Jewish Apocalyptic and Apocalypticism," in *Handbook for the Study of the Historical Jesus*, ed. Tom Holmén and Stanley E. Porter (4 vols.; Leiden: Brill, 2011), 2:1569–1607; idem, "Jesus and Apocalypticism," *Handbook* 3:2877–2909. See also Lester Grabbe, "Introduction and Overview," in *Knowing the End from the Beginning: The Prophetic, the Apocalyptic and their Relationships*, ed. Lester L. Grabbe and Robert D. Haak (London: T&T Clark, 2003), 2–43; Christopher C. Rowland, *The Open Heaven: A Study of Apocalyptic in Judaism and Christianity* (New York: Crossroad, 1982), 70–71.

77. Crossan, "Jesus and Early Christianity," 139, refers to this as "mono-apocalypticism." See also Elisabeth Schüssler Fiorenza, "Critical Feminist Historical-Jesus Research," in *Handbook for the Study of the Historical Jesus* 1:–509–48, esp. 544.

defined as virtually synonymous with "catastrophe?" The term simply signifies a "revelation" or "unveiling" of some kind; it does not necessarily presuppose eschatological *violence*.[78]

Here we come to the crossroads in Jesus Research. The Jesus tradition contains internal tensions and contradictions, many of which are not inconsequential, but rather central to Jesus' understanding of the nature of God. Did the historical Jesus share John the Baptist's apparently future-oriented apocalyptic eschatology *and/or* stress the "immediate nearness of God?"[79] Is the kingdom a violent shattering of the time-space continuum *and/or* Jesus' visionary perception of the divine presence here and now? Did Jesus alternately command "love of enemies"' *and* condemn them to hell?[80] In other words, was Jesus inconsistent?[81] We all may have our own cognitive and emotional inconsistencies, but I am not referring to personal psychology here. The Jesus tradition's composite portrait of Jesus—and our reluctance to parse its antithetical components—is not bringing us any closer to the historical Jesus. Reinscribing our conflicting sources' elision and conflation of Jesus' eschatological blessings *and* woes may in fact be a rather perilous course. The Inaugural Sermon in Q, an ethical instruction on love and nonviolence, may serve to control our confusion. The alternative is simply to affirm Jesus' theological *inconsistency*: Jesus taught "love your enemies" to his disciples *and* simultaneously condemned them to oblivion.[82] The idea that Jesus' vision of God was primarily if not entirely providential and positive (as in Q 12:22-31) may be subject to the criticism of *selective* reading, but all readings are selective. Jesus' eschatological vision was, presumably, "*good* news." Uncritically

78. Crossan, "Jesus and Contemporary Faith," in *The Apocalyptic Jesus*, 160, highlights the stakes: "we can struggle non-violently with a violent world only if we are grounded in transcendent non-violence."

79. Hans Conzelmann, "Present and Future in the Synoptic Tradition," in *God and Christ: Existence and Province*, ed. Robert T. Funk (JTC 5; New York: Harper & Row, 1968), 26–44; Ernst Käsemann, "The Beginnings of Christian Theology," in *New Testament Questions for Today* (Philadelphia: Fortress Press, 1969), 82–107.

80. Allison, "The Problem of Gehenna," in *Resurrecting Jesus*, 56–110, at 84, 88.

81. Dale C. Allison Jr., "The Problem of Audience," in *Resurrecting Jesus*, 27–55, at 48–50; Allison, *Jesus of Nazareth*, 105 n. 38; Joel Marcus, "Modern and Ancient Jewish Apocalypticism," *JR* 76 (1996): 18–23. But see Emmanuel Charles McCarthy, *All things flee thee for thou fleest Me: A Cry to the Churches and Their Leaders to Stop Running from the Nonviolent Jesus and His Nonviolent Way* (Wilmington: Center for Christian Nonviolence, 2003), 2.1–2.

82. Neufeld, *Killing Enmity*, 27-35. Neufeld seees mercy and love, not nonviolence, as that which "informs enemy love" (32) because "mercy is unintelligible apart from judgement." See also Thomas R. Yoder Neufeld, "Resistance and Nonresistance: The Two Legs of a Biblical Peace Stance," *Conrad Grebel Review* 21 (2003): 56-81.

acquiescing to the theological inconsistencies of the tradition risks far more than we may realize. Rejecting the nonviolent Jesus affirms, if only by default, a violent and inconsistent Jesus.

Stephen Patterson has recently suggested that Jesus simply did not have enough time to make up his mind about these things before his death: the contradictions within the tradition reflect Jesus' own un-made-up mind.[83] This indecisive Jesus may not have been overly concerned about or aware of how things were turning out. Perhaps he was simply unsure of himself, or unclear about his own ideas.[84] Was the kingdom here and now, as in Q 17:21, or a "cosmic battle between the forces of good and evil?"[85] Patterson recognizes that the "Christian tradition harbors a great utopian vision,"[86] but he argues that "the texts are themselves divided" on the issue,[87] and this inconsistency cannot be resolved "into a simple both/and, the 'already, not yet' of the neo-orthodox theologians."[88] For Patterson, Jesus was an admirer of John the Baptist, and John preached an apocalyptic message. When John died, Jesus became "disillusioned" and repudiated John's message.[89] Jesus needed to "think things over" and may have had "second thoughts," but he simply ran out of time.

Some of us, however, would like to think that Jesus knew what he was doing. This is not to say that Jesus need be granted supernatural powers of divine foreknowledge, only that he maintain a certain consistency of thought and action. If *consistency* is "the property of holding together and retaining shape," it would certainly seem that different results in Jesus Research may ultimately come down to different levels of comfort that different scholars have with their perceptions of the consistency and coherence of the early Jesus tradition. Ralph Waldo Emerson may have said, in an apparent attack on the idea of ethical or intellectual consistency,[90] that "a foolish consistency is the hobgoblin of little minds," but a closer inspection of the original context of this famous passage indicates that he was simply advocating nonconformity in

83. Stephen J. Patterson, "An Unanswered Question: Apocalyptic Expectation and Jesus' *Basileia* Proclamation," *JSHJ* 8, no. 1 (2010): 67–79.

84. Ibid., 7.

85. Ibid., 67.

86. Ibid., 79.

87. Ibid., 68.

88. Ibid., 69.

89. Ibid., 76. As an "ideological shift," see Anthony Le Donne, *Historical Jesus: What Can We Know and How Can We Know It?* (Grand Rapids: Eerdmans, 2011), 86.

90. See also Aldous Huxley, "Wordsworth in the Tropics," in *Do What You Will: Essays by Aldous Huxley* (London: Chatto and Windus, 1929), chapter 6; F. Scott Fitzgerald, "The Crack-Up," in *Esquire* (February, March, April 1936).

order for individuals to follow their own instincts and ideas.[91] It is a "*foolish* consistency" or conformity to social norms that corrupts. Jesus was certainly a "self-reliant" non-conformist guided by his own sense of the correct response to each individual situation.

Ultimately it comes down to coherence. Nonviolent sayings and acts *cohere*; violent sayings, nonviolent sayings, and nonviolent acts do not. This dissonance is manifest in the tradition and requires explanation: did Jesus say "both sorts of things,"[92] that is, proclaim both salvation and judgment ("good news" *and* "bad news")? Or did he emphasize salvation but keep judgment in the background ("good news" now/"bad news" later)? Or did he proclaim salvation without judgment (only "good news")?

The threat of eschatological judgment either reflects Jesus' view of God or it does not.[93] There are only so many interpretive options to choose from. Perhaps Jesus' teachings are "less violent than they appear?"[94] Maybe Jesus only predicted a *future* judgment when God would "utterly destroy the wicked in an act of final and irreversible punishment?"[95] If such were the case, we might still be able to absolve Jesus of violence and affirm the Gospels' scriptural authority. Unfortunately, this position is contingent on the assumption that Jesus *actually* pronounced judgment on his contemporaries—an assumption that not all are willing to make—as it essentially reinscribes a punishing God and a violent future judgment. Alternatively, perhaps eschatological judgment does *not* reflect Jesus' view of God. Perhaps "Jesus'" teachings on eschatological judgment did not originate with Jesus. If the general expectation in Second Temple Jewish apocalypticism was that salvation and judgment were two sides of the same coin, does Jesus conform to this allegedly "normative" pattern or break from it?

The thematic and theological tension between a loving, forgiving God and a punishing, vengeful God is clearly present in Q. It is not difficult to find evidence in Q that Jesus' God is non-judgmental, merciful, unconditionally loving, healing, forgiving, and inclusive:

91. Ralph Waldo Emerson, "Self-Reliance," in *The American Scholar. Self Reliance. Compensation* (New York: American, 1893 [1841]).

92. Sanders, *Jesus and Judaism*.

93. Eric Siebert, *Disturbing Divine Behavior: Troubling Old Testament Images of God* (Philadelphia: Fortress Press, 2009), 248–52.

94. Ibid., 251.

95. Ibid., 261.

Q 6:20	The Kingdom is for the Poor
Q 6:27, 28, 35c-d	Love Your Enemies
Q 6:31	The Golden Rule
Q 6:32-34	Unconditional Love
Q 6:36	Be Merciful, Like Your Father
Q 7:22	Healing the Blind, the Lame, the Leper
Q 14:16-18, 21, 23	Invitation to the Banquet
Q 15:4-5a, 7	The Lost Sheep
Q 15:8-10	The Lost Coin
Q 17:3-4	Forgive Your Brother

Jesus' instruction to "love enemies" is based on God's unconditional love.[96] The instruction to be merciful is warranted because God is merciful. The lost sheep is worth more than the ninety-nine. Brothers are to be forgiven; judgment is to be renounced. The theme of radical inclusion is continued in the Synoptics. In Luke's Parable of the Prodigal Son the father refuses to treat the lost and wayward son as less deserving than the loyal older brother.[97] In Matthew, the householder who hires day laborers pays the same wage to all his workers.[98] The Good Samaritan does not discriminate against the Jew/Judean, although the priest and Levite do,[99] radically redefining who the good neighbor is. Jesus' challenge to his Jewish contemporaries was not simply questioning social boundaries and the assumption of ethnic election (Q 3:8); it also redescribed and redefined the nature of God as a loving Father. On the other hand, it is not difficult to find sayings in Q threatening an imminent divine judgment, with salvation dependent on one's immediate response to Jesus.[100] Here God seems to be envisioned as judgmental, vengeful, conditionally loving, punishing, and exclusive. Is God somehow inscrutably both forgiving and unforgiving, judgmental and non-judgmental, inclusive and exclusive?

We have now identified the earliest textual vestiges of a theological crisis at the very heart of the Jesus tradition. If Jesus taught that God loved *everyone*—and there is no good reason to doubt this, based on Q 6:20-49—this radical vision not only subverted traditional claims of Israel's special election but also undermined the social, political, religious, and economic hierarchical structure of Jewish society. It is time for us to put to rest the supposedly irreconcilable

96. Q 6:27-28, 35c-d.

97. Luke 15:11-32.

98. Matt. 20:1-15.

99. Luke 10:30-35.

100. Q 12:8-9.

differences of a nonviolent Jesus and a violent God and rethink how we identify and describe Jesus as an "eschatological" figure.

The *language* and *vocabulary* of eschatology may have been pervasive in Early Judaism, but this does not always mean that they should always be taken literally. George Caird's suggestion that modern readers sometimes find literal meaning where they should find metaphor remains cogent. Biblical texts are mythopoeic and often make use of symbol, simile, and metaphor to convey spiritual realities. The recognition of metaphorical language in the Jesus tradition is not an attempt to "exclude Jesus from the error of imminent eschatological expectation by excising large portions from the tradition."[101] A non-literal interpretation is simply "sometimes unavoidable."[102] The Qumran War Scroll (1QM), for example, is not "a prophecy of a real eschatological battle complete with fighting angels."[103] It is *not* a description of a physical battle. Some scholars appeal to 1QM as evidence of militancy.[104] After all, 1QM narrates a final conflict between the forces of good and evil, and describes military equipment, army formations, battle plans, trumpets, standards, shields, and soldiers. It depicts an angelic host leading the battle. But 1QM is an idealized depiction of an eschatological war.[105] The phases of battle are predetermined, as is the outcome. 1QM is not a training manual for holy war.[106] Some eschatological texts are metaphorical and symbolic.[107]

101. Allison, *Jesus of Nazareth*, 152, citing C. H. Dodd, *The Parables of the Kingdom* (New York: Scribner, 1961); G. B. Caird, *The Language and Imagery of the Bible* (Philadelphia: Westminster, 1980), 243-71, 153; N. T. Wright, *The New Testament and the People of God* (Minneapolis: Fortress Press, 1992), 280-338; idem, *Jesus and the Victory of God*, 320-68.

102. Contra Allison, *Jesus of Nazareth*, 157.

103. Ibid., 157.

104. Jean Duhaime, "War Scroll," in *The Dead Sea Scrolls: Hebrew, Aramaic, and Greek Texts with English Translations*, Vol. 2: *Damascus Document, War Scroll, and Related Documents*, ed. James H. Charlesworth (PTSDSSP 2; Tübingen: Mohr Siebeck, 1995), 80–203, at 84; Geza Vermes, *The Complete Dead Sea Scrolls in English* (New York: Penguin, 1997), 163; Lester Grabbe, "Warfare," in *The Encyclopedia of the Dead Sea Scrolls*, ed. James C. VanderKam and Lawrence H. Schiffman (2 vols.; New York: Oxford University Press, 2000), 2:963–965, at 965; Hans Bardtke, "Die Kriegsrolle v. Qumran übersetzt," *TLZ* 80 (1955): 401–20; Leonard Rost, "Zum Buch der Kriege der Söhne des Lichtes gegen die Söhne der Finsternis," *TLZ* 80 (1955): 205–8.

105. Collins, *Apocalypticism in the Dead Sea Scrolls*, 127.

106. Helmer Ringgren, *The Faith of Qumran: Theology of the Dead Sea Scrolls*, trans. Emilie T. Sander (Philadelphia: Fortress Press, 1963), 18–19; Willis S. Barnstone, *The Other Bible* (New York: Harper San Francisco, 1984), 235–36.

107. *2 Bar.* 29:5; 36-37.

The apocalyptic Jesus was *wrong* about the end-time, wrong about his return as the son of man, and wrong about the *final* judgment on "this generation."[108] The apocalyptic Jesus "did in fact *erroneously* hail the end as near."[109] Was Jesus really a tragically misguided messiah broken on the wheel of history?[110] Or is Jesus' apparent "failure" to accurately predict an era of eschatological violence on "this generation" actually the failure of the Jesus tradition to represent Jesus accurately? The apocalyptic Jesus has had a long and successful career.[111] It may be time to put him to rest. This retirement of the apocalyptic Jesus, however, does not require abandoning the concept and the cultural, historical, and theological matrix of *restorative eschatology*.[112] The historical Jesus is an *eschatological* Jesus, not an "apocalyptic Jesus."[113]

The apocalyptic Jesus model cannot reconcile the troubling fact that while Jesus lived and taught the way of nonviolence, there are dark traditions of divine violence in both the Old and New Testaments. Surely this is a theological riddle worth unravelling. Here we have the paradox of the Savior who cannot save

108. Philip Vielhauer, "Gottesreich und Menschensohn in der Verkündigung Jesu," in *Festschrift für Günther Dehn, zum 75. Geburtstag am 18. April 1957* (Neukirchen: Kreis Moers, Verlag der Buchhandlung Erziehungsvereins, 1957), 51–79.

109. Allison, *Jesus of Nazareth*, 166 (emphasis added); Markus Bockmuehl, review of *Jesus of Nazareth*, *JTS* 51, no. 2 (2000): 637–41, at 640, describes Allison's Jesus as "a poor idealistic blighter whose misguided religious zeal got the better of him."

110. Albert Schweitzer, *The Quest of the Historical Jesus: A Critical Study of its Progress from Reimarus to Wrede*, trans. William Montgomery (New York: Macmillan, 1910), 370–71.

111. See Jörg Frey, "Die Apokalyptik als Herausforderung der neutestamentlichen Wissenschaft. Zum Problem: Jesus und die Apokalyptik," *in Apokalyptik als Herausforderung neutestamentlicher Theologie*, ed. Michael Becker and Markus Öhler (WUNT 2/214; Tübingen: Mohr Siebeck, 2006), 23–94.

112. Sanders, *Jesus and Judaism*, 72, notes that although the conclusion that "Jesus intended Jewish restoration" is secure, "One must still ask in what sense he did so" (116). He proposes that "the expectation that Israel would be restored points to the hope for a fundamental renewal, a new creation accomplised by God" (230). Sanders sees Q 16:18 as signifying "a serious decree for a new age and a new order" (234). Q 16:18 indicates that God's original intention was central, not incidental, to Jesus' particular program of eschatological restoration.

113. John Dominic Crossan, *In Parables: The Challenge of the Historical Jesus* (New York: Harper and Row, 1973), 25–27; idem, *The Birth of Christianity*, 257–87. John S. Kloppenborg, "Symbolic Eschatology and the Apocalypticism of Q," *HTR* 80 (1987): 287–306, at 291, 304–5, argues that Q uses apocalyptic language "to dramatize the transfiguration of the present . . . characterized by nonviolence." Allison's insistence that "our choice is not between an apocalyptic Jesus and some other Jesus; it is between an apocalyptic Jesus and no Jesus at all" (*Constructing Jesus*, 46–47) seems to presuppose a monolithic idea of "apocalypticism." In *Resurrecting Jesus*, 129, he dismisses objections as little more than a "theological gripe." But see David J. Neville, "Toward a Teleology of Peace: Contesting Matthew's Violent Eschatology." *JSNT* 30, no. 2 (1997): 131–61, at 153.

us from a violent God and a violent eschatological judgment, just as he could not save himself from the wrath of his Jewish contemporaries, Roman overlords, Satanic "powers," or Father-God. Despite assertions to the contrary, this Jesus does not seem to save us from violence, redeem human nature, or fulfill a messianic vocation of peace. Instead, he becomes the human face of an angry, threatening, punishing, vengeful, violent Deity. And herein lies our problem: divine violence is inscribed in our traditions, and this legacy is killing us. Did Jesus endorse narratives of genocide and threaten eternal damnation? Or did he live in tension with—even radical opposition to—these ideas and suffer the fate of that opposition?

Should we accept the Bible at face value as the divine revelation of a violent God? Or should we regard it as an ancient theological tradition compromised to reflect inconsistent and contradictory portraits of both Jesus and God? If the historical Jesus is consistently nonviolent, then it is time to reexamine the early Jesus tradition and resolve this age-old theological dilemma of divine violence. Let us begin by starting to unravel the riddle of the nonviolent messiah.

PART II

5

Jesus Christos

The proclamation of Jesus as messiah is a central tenet of the Christian faith,[1] yet Jesus did not seem to fulfill what many Jews appear to have expected of a Davidic king: he did not mount a political throne and defeat Israel's enemies. He did not "destroy the power particularly of Rome . . . inaugurate a dynasty of the proper line . . . spur and enable the exiles to return to Palestine . . . (and) usher in the long-awaited final judgment of God."[2] He did not gather in the exiles,[3] put an end to evil, sin,[4] disease, and death,[5] or inaugurate a new age of peace, harmony,[6] fertility, or abundance.[7]

1. See Martin Hengel, *Studies in Early Christology* (Edinburgh: T & T Clark, 2004); Ragnar Leivestad, "Jesus-Messias-Menschensohn: Die jüdischen Heilandserwartungen zur Zeit der ersten römischen Kaiser und die Frage nach dem messianischen Selbstbewusstsein Jesu," *ANRW* II 25.1 (1982): 220–64; idem, *Jesus in His own Perspective: An Examination of His Sayings, Actions, and Eschatological Titles*, trans. David E. Aune (Minneapolis: Augsburg, 1987), 176; Douglas R. A. Hare, *The Son of Man Tradition* (Minneapolis: Fortress Press, 1990), 278; Graham Stanton, *Gospel Truth? New Light on Jesus and the Gospels* (Valley Forge, PA: Trinity Press International, 1995), 180, 190; Edward P. Meadors, *Jesus the Messianic Herald of Salvation* (WUNT 72; Tübingen: Mohr Siebeck, 1995); idem, "The Messianic Implications of the Q Material," *JBL* 118 (1999): 253–77; Gerd Theissen and Annette Merz, *The Historical Jesus: A Comprehensive Guide* (London: SCM, 1998), 538–39; Ben F. Meyer, "Appointed Deed, Appointed Doer: Jesus and the Scriptures," in *Authenticating the Activities of Jesus*, ed. Bruce Chilton and Craig A. Evans (NTTS 28.2; Leiden: Brill, 1999), 155–76, at 174; James D. G. Dunn, *Unity and Diversity in the New Testament: An Inquiry into the Character of Earliest Christianity* (Philadelphia: Westminster, 1977), 41–42.

2. Samuel Sandmel, *We Jews and Jesus* (New York: Oxford University Press, 1965), 32–33. Jacob Immanuel Schochet, *Mashiach: The Principle of Mashiach and the Messianic Era in Jewish Law and Tradition* (New York: S. I. E., 1992), 17.

3. Isa. 11:11-12, 16; *Bereshit Rabba* 98:9; *Midrash Hagadol* on Gen. 49:11.

4. Ezek. 37:23; Zeph. 3:13; 13:2; Mal. 3:19; Isa. 60:21; Jer. 50:20; *Sukkah* 52a; *Eliyahu Rabba* 4; *Ber. Rabba* 48.11; *Pesiq. Rabati* 33.4; *Yal. Shimoni* 1.133.

5. *Ber. Rabba* 20:5; Isa. 35:5-6; 25:8.

6. Isa. 2:4; Mic. 4:3; Hos. 2:20; Zech. 9:10; Isa. 11:6-9; 65:25.

Nonetheless, a considerable number of ancient Jews evidently found Jesus' "messianic" credentials more than acceptable.[8] So why was Jesus first identified as "messiah?"[9] Some scholars hold that Jesus himself never claimed to be a messiah: the early Church did it for him.[10] Some have argued that Paul's use of Χριστός can be explained as more of a proper name or nickname than a title.[11]

7. Lev. 26:5; Joel 4:18; *Lev. Rabba* 17:4; *Pesiq. deR. Kahana* 8.

8. Sandmel, *We Jews and Jesus*, 44.

9. Michael F. Bird, *Are You the One who is to Come? The Historical Jesus and the Messianic Question* (Grand Rapids: Baker, 2009), 27–28.

10. William Wrede, *The Messianic Secret*, trans. J. C. G. Greig (Cambridge: James Clark, 1971); Reginald H. Fuller, *The Mission and Achievement of Jesus* (SBT 12; London: SCM, 1954), 108, 116; Oscar Cullmann, *The Christology of the New Testament*, trans. Shirley C. Guthrie and Charles A. M. Hall (Philadelphia: Westminster, 1959), 133–36; Albert Schweitzer, *The Quest of the Historical Jesus: A Critical Study of its Progress from Reimarus to Wrede*, trans. William Montgomery (New York: Macmillan, 1910), 13–15, 70–71; Burton L. Mack, "The Christ and Jewish Wisdom," in *The Messiah: Developments in Earliest Judaism and Christianity: The First Princeton Symposium on Judaism and Christian Origins*, ed. James H. Charlesworth, et al. (Minneapolis: Fortress Press, 1992), 192–221, at 217; Robert W. Funk, Roy W. Hoover, and the Jesus Seminar, *The Five Gospels: The Search for the Authentic Words of Jesus: New Translation and Commentary* (New York: Macmillan, 1993); E. P. Sanders, *Jesus and Judaism* (Philadelphia: Fortress Press, 1985), 307–8; H. J. de Jonge, "The Historical Jesus' View of Himself and of His Mission," in *From Jesus to John: Essays on Jesus and New Testament Christology in Honour of Marinus de Jonge*, ed. Martinus C. de Boer (Sheffield: JSOT, 1993), 21–37; Jürgen Becker, *Jesus of Nazareth* (New York: de Gruyter, 1998), 197; Marcus J. Borg, *Conflict, Holiness, and Politics in the Teachings of Jesus* (Harrisburg, PA: Trinity Press International, 1998), 17–18; Gerbern S. Oegema, "Messiah/Christ," in *Encyclopedia of the Historical Jesus*, ed. Craig A. Evans (New York: Routledge, 2008), 399-404, at 399.

11. Merrill P. Miller, "How Jesus Became Christ: Probing a Thesis," *Cont* 2, nos. 2-3 (1993): 243–70; idem, "The Problem of the Origins of a Messianic Conception of Jesus," in *Redescribing Christian Origins*, ed. Ron Cameron and Merrill P. Miller (SBL SS 28; Atlanta: Society of Biblical Literature, 2004), 301–35; A. E. Harvey, *Jesus and the Constraints of History* (Philadelphia: Westminster, 1982), 80–82. See also Nils A. Dahl, "The Messiahship of Jesus in Paul," in idem, *The Crucified Messiah, and Other Essays* (Minneapolis: Augsburg, 1974), 37–47; idem, "Die Messianität Jesus bei Paulus," in *Studia Paulina in honorem Johannis de Zwaan septuagenarii* (Haarlem: Bohn, 1953), 83–95; Douglas R. A. Hare, "When Did 'Messiah' Become a Proper Name?" *ExpT* 121 (2009): 70–73; George MacRae, "Messiah and Gospel," in *Judaisms and Their Messiahs at the Turn of the Christian Era*, ed. Jacob Neusner, William Scott Green, and Ernest S. Frerichs (Cambridge: Cambridge University Press, 1987), 169–86, at 170–72; Andrew Chester, "Messianism, Mediators, and Pauline Christology," in *Messiah and Exaltation* (WUNT 207; Tübingen: Mohr Siebeck, 2007), 329–96; Werner Georg Kümmel, *The Theology of the New Testament according to Its Major Witnesses: Jesus-Paul-John*, trans. John E. Steely (Nashville: Abingdon, 1973), 154; Marinus de Jonge, "The Earliest Christian Use of *Christos*: Some Suggestions," *NTS* 32 (1986): 321–43, at 321–22; Paula Fredriksen, *From Jesus to Christ: The Origins of the New Testament Images of Christ* (New Haven: Yale University Press, 2000), 56; Larry Hurtado, "Paul's Christology," in *Cambridge Companion to St. Paul*, ed. James D. G. Dunn (Cambridge: Cambridge University Press, 2003), 185–98, at 191.

Some are reluctant even to use the term "messiah" for Jesus.[12] Some argue that the Jewish *crowds* proclaimed Jesus as messiah, but that he rejected the title.[13] Others claim that Jesus neither claimed nor rejected the title.[14] Still others argue that Jesus revised the *meaning* of the role.[15]

12. Burton L. Mack, *The Lost Gospel: The Book of Q and Christian Origins* (San Francisco: HarperSanFrancisco, 1993), 4; idem, *The Christian Myth: Origins, Logic, and Legacy* (New York: Continuum, 2001), 114.

13. Günther Bornkamm, *Jesus of Nazareth* (London: Hodder & Stoughton, 1973), 172; Geza Vermes, *The Religion of Jesus the Jew* (London: SCM, 1973), 154; Dahl, "Messiahship of Jesus in Paul," 42–43; Raymond E. Brown, *The Death of the Messiah: From Gethsemane to the Grave: A Commentary on the Passion Narratives in the Four Gospels* (2 vols.; ABRL; New York: Doubleday, 1994), 1: 478–79; Paula Fredriksen, *Jesus of Nazareth, King of the Jews* (New York: Vintage, 1999), 234, 244–59; James D. G. Dunn, *Jesus Remembered* (Grand Rapids: Eerdmans, 2003), 653–54.

14. Dahl, "Messiahship of Jesus in Paul," 43–44; C. K. Barrett, *Jesus and the Gospel Tradition* (London: SPCK, 1967), 19–24; Erich Dinkler, "Peter's Confession and the Satan Saying: The Problem of Jesus' Messiahship," in *The Future of Our Religious Past: Essays in Honour of Rudolf Bultmann*, ed. James M. Robinson (New York: Harper & Row, 1971), 169–202, at 169–72; Brown, *Death of the Messiah*, 1:479–80; C. H. Dodd, *The Founder of Christianity* (London: Collins, 1971), 103; Joseph A. Fitzmyer, *The One Who Is To Come* (Grand Rapids: Eerdmans, 2007), 140–41; Christopher M. Tuckett, *Christology and the New Testament: Jesus and His Earliest Followers* (Louisville: Westminster John Knox, 2001), 212–13; Martin Hengel, "Jesus, the Messiah of Israel," in idem, *Studies in Early Christology* (London: T & T Clark International, 2004), 1–72, at 58, 69.

15. Johannes Weiss, *Jesus' Proclamation of the Kingdom of God*, trans. and ed. Richard H. Hiers and D. Larrimore Holland (1971 repr., Chico: Scholars Press, 1985), 127–28; Schweitzer, *Quest of the Historical Jesus*, 316–19; Adolf Schlatter, *The History of the Christ: The Foundation of New Testament Theology* (Grand Rapids: Baker Academic, 1997), 109, 124–26, 280, 283–85; Cecil J. Cadoux, *The Historic Mission of Jesus: A Constructive Re-examination of the Eschatological Teaching in the Synoptic Gospels* (London: Lutterworth, 1941), 51–60; William Manson, *Jesus the Messiah* (London: Hodder & Stoughton, 1943); Otto Betz, "Die Frage nach dem messianischen Bewusstsein Jesu," *NovT* 6 (1963): 24–37; T. W. Manson, *The Servant Messiah* (Cambridge: Cambridge University Press, 1961); Joachim Jeremias, *New Testament Theology* (London: SCM, 1971), 254–55; C. F. D. Moule, *The Origin of Christology* (Cambridge: Cambridge University Press, 1977), 31–35; Hengel, "Messiah of Israel," 1–72; Christopher Rowland, *Christian Origins* (London: SCM, 1985), 182; Peter Stuhlmacher, *Jesus of Nazareth, Christ of Faith* (Peabody, MA: Hendrickson, 1988), 22–29; Howard Clark Kee, *What Can We Know about Jesus?* (New York: Cambridge University Press, 1990), 111; Markus Bockmuehl, *This Jesus: Martyr, Lord, Messiah* (Edinburgh: T&T Clark, 1994), 51–58; Ben Witherington III, *The Christology of Jesus* (Minneapolis: Fortress Press, 1990), 115–16, 118, 263–77; W. D. Davies and Dale C. Allison Jr., *The Gospel According to Saint Matthew* (ICC; Edinburgh: T&T Clark, 1991), 2:595–601; Craig A. Evans, *Jesus and His Contemporaries: Comparative Studies* (AGJU 25; Leiden: Brill, 1995), 437–56; N. T. Wright, *Jesus and the Victory of God*, Vol. 2, *Christian Origins and the Question of God* (Minneapolis: Fortress Press, 1996), 477–539; Robert Stein, *Jesus the Messiah* (Downers Grove: InterVarsity, 1996), 147–49, 248; Marinus de Jonge, *Jesus, the Servant-Messiah* (New Haven: Yale University Press, 1991), 68–72; Dale C. Allison Jr.,

The idea that Jesus avoided the term "messiah" because of its politico-military connotations is accepted by many as an historically plausible explanation within the context of first-century Judaism.[16] E. P. Sanders, for example, identifies Jesus as a prophet but claims that he saw himself as God's eschatological "viceroy," the "head of the judges of Israel, subordinate only to God himself,"[17] although he had neither political nor military ambitions. Nonetheless, Jesus had an exalted self-conception, which can be seen by Jesus' arrival in Jerusalem on a donkey, presumably in fulfillment of Zechariah's "messianic" prophecy: a "'king,' yes, of a sort; military conqueror no."[18] Similarly, Ben Witherington concludes that Jesus thought of himself as having a unique relationship with God as his Son "anointed" with the Spirit,[19] but cautions that the term "messiah" is "not wholly adequate to express how Jesus viewed himself . . . the possibility of misunderstanding was indeed great, especially in view of the nationalistic expectations that existed in Jesus' day."[20]

Jesus of Nazareth: Millenarian Prophet (Minneapolis: Fortress Press, 1998), 67–68 n. 251; Scot McKnight, *A New Vision for Israel: The Teachings of Jesus in National Context* (Grand Rapids: Eerdmans, 1999), 6; Jonathan Knight, *Jesus: An Historical and Theological Introduction* (UBW; London: T&T Clark, 2004), 145; Theissen and Merz, *The Historical Jesus*, 538; Giorgio Jossa, *Jews or Christians?* (WUNT 202; Tübingen: Mohr Siebeck, 2006), 54–63; Andrew Chester, *Messiah and Exaltation: Jewish Messianic and Visionary Traditions and New Testament Christology* (WUNT 207; Tübingen: Mohr Siebeck, 2007), 307–24.

16. Christopher M. Tuckett, *The Messianic Secret*, ed. Christopher M. Tuckett (Philadelphia: Fortress Press, 1983), 1; John P. Meier, "From Elijah-like Prophet to Royal Davidic Messiah," in *Jesus: A Colloquium in the Holy Land*, ed. D. Donnelly (New York: Continuum, 2001), 45–83, at 63, 71; Witherington, *The Christology of Jesus*, 143; idem, *The Gospel of Mark: A Socio-Rhetorical Commentary* (Grand Rapids: Eerdmans, 2001), 41; R. T. France, *The Gospel of Mark: A Commentary on the Greek Text* (Grand Rapids: Eerdmans, 2002), 31; Vincent Taylor, *The Gospel According to St. Mark: The Greek Text with Introduction, Notes, and Indexes* (Grand Rapids: Baker Book House, 1981), 377; Manson, *The Servant-Messiah*, 71–72; Peter Stuhlmacher, *Jesus of Nazareth—Christ of Faith* (Peabody, MA: Hendrickson, 1993), 6–7; James D. G. Dunn, "Messianic Ideas and Their Influence on the Jesus of History," in Charlesworth, ed., *The Messiah*, 365–81; Bockmuehl, *This Jesus*; I. Howard Marshall, *The Origins of New Testament Christology* (Downers Grove: InterVarsity, 1976), 63–96; Otto Betz, *Jesus: Der Messias Israels: Aufsätze zur biblischen Theologie* (Tübingen: Mohr Siebeck, 1987); Peter Pokorný, *The Genesis of Christology* (Edinburgh: T&T Clark, 1987).

17. E. P. Sanders, *The Historical Figure of Jesus* (London: Penguin, 1993), 239, 242; idem, *Jesus and Judaism*, 235.

18. Ibid., 241–42.

19. Witherington, *The Christology of Jesus*; idem, *The Jesus Quest: The Third Search for the Jew of Nazareth* (Downers Grove: InterVarsity, 1995), 213–32.

20. *Christology of Jesus*, 143.

The problem with many scholarly reconstructions of Jesus' messianic identity is that various messianic roles and functions are uncritically conflated in order to construct a composite portrait of Jewish messianism. For example, Marinus de Jonge rightly notes that "Jesus is at the center of all early (and later) Christology. This presupposes some degree of continuity between what he said and did and people's reactions."[21] So far, so good. De Jonge is on secure ground when he finds evidence for Jesus as a prophet sent by God but rejected by Israel, but he then asserts that Jesus "believed himself to have been sent as God's final envoy, as the inaugurator of God's rule on earth,"[22] that Jesus saw himself as "the suffering righteous Servant" whose death had "redemptive" power, and that Jesus proclaimed himself both messiah and son of man, a "cryptic self-designation" which "implied obscurity, homelessness and rejection, humility, service, suffering, and ultimately death."[23] In a similar vein, N. T. Wright affirms Jesus' Davidic messianic identity and concedes that while there was no pre-Christian expectation for a Jewish messiah to suffer, this was Jesus' distinctive innovation. Clearly, the challenge of properly assessing Jesus' "messianic" self-understanding is not a new one.

In the following chapters we will reassess the historical and literary evidence for the messianic identification of Jesus. This topic is problematic for several reasons: first, because the uncritical conflation of various messianic roles, functions, and attributes into a single title projected onto Jesus collapses the complex phenomenon of first-century Jewish messianism and fails to isolate the distinctive ways in which "messiah-language" might accurately describe Jesus; second, because the historical problem of Jesus' identity continues to be framed in dichotomous terms, that is, Jesus either was "*the* messiah" (with the definite article) or he was not. The problem with this framing is that there is no such thing as "*the* messiah." Second Temple Judaism produced a plurality of messianic ideas, expectations, typologies, titles, attributes, motifs, traditions, and prospective candidates, and any attempt to pronounce a definitive, exclusive identification of Jesus as "the messiah" is more at home in religious and theologically apologetic debates than in historical Jesus studies. A third problem associated with this complex topic is that Jewish messianism itself was a developing tradition. In some cases rabbinical messianic traditions developed

21. Marinus de Jonge, *Christology in Context: The Earliest Christian Response to Jesus* (Philadelphia: Westminster, 1988), 21. See also idem, *God's Final Envoy: Early Christianity and Jesus' Own View of His Mission* (SHJ; Grand Rapids: Eerdmans, 1998); *Jesus the Servant Messiah* (New Haven: Yale University Press, 1991); *From Jesus to John*, ed. Martinus C. De Boer (JSNTS 84; Sheffield: JSOT, 1993).

22. De Jonge, *God's Final Envoy*, 145.

23. De Jonge, Ibid., 88.

in order to counter Christian claims about the legitimacy of Jesus' messianic identity.[24] It is not methodologically appropriate, therefore, to appeal to post-70 C.E. rabbinical Jewish messianic traditions to prove or disprove Jesus' early first-century messianic identity. Christianity began as a *Jewish* messianic movement, not a Christian movement rejected by Jews. We will proceed, therefore, by first establishing the historical and theological origins of first-century Jewish messianism.

There are numerous methodological problems associated with the study of ancient Jewish messianism.[25] The word *messiah* is derived from the Hebrew משיח ("anointed") or Aramaic משיחא, and can be used adjectivally and/or as a noun or title, to refer to a king, priest, or prophet divinely appointed to fulfill a particular task.[26] The term is also used to refer to figures not explicitly identified as "messiahs."[27] One can be "anointed" without actually being identified as a "messiah" in a titular sense.[28] "The messiah" as a proper title and role does not

24. See especially Daniel Boyarin, *Border Lines: The Partition of Judaeo-Christianity* (Divinations; Philadelphia: University of Pennsylvania Press, 2004).

25. Neusner, et al., *Judaisms and Their Messiahs at the Turn of the Christian Era*; John J. Collins, *The Scepter and the Star: The Messiahs of the Dead Sea Scrolls and Other Ancient Literature* (New York: Doubleday, 1995); Kenneth Pomykala, *The Davidic Dynasty Tradition in Early Judaism: Its History and Significance for Messianism* (Atlanta: Scholars Press, 1995); Antti Laato, *A Star is Rising: The Historical Development of the Old Testament Royal Ideology and the Rise of the Jewish Messianic Expectations* (Atlanta: Scholars Press, 1997); Dan Cohn-Sherbok, *The Jewish Messiah* (Edinburgh: T&T Clark, 1997); Gerbern S. Oegema, *The Anointed and His People: Messianic Expectations from the Maccabees to Bar Kochba* (JSPSup 27; Sheffield: Sheffield Academic Press, 1998); William Horbury, *Jewish Messianism and the Cult of Christ* (London: SCM, 1998); *King and Messiah in Israel and the Ancient Near East*, ed. John Day (JSOTSup 270; Sheffield: Sheffield Academic Press, 1998); *Israel's Messiah in the Bible and the Dead Sea Scrolls*, ed. Richard S. Hess and M. Daniel Carroll R. (Grand Rapids: Baker Academic, 2003); *Redemption and Resistance: The Messianic Hopes of Jews and Christians in Antiquity*, ed. Markus Bockmuehl and James Carleton Paget (London: T&T Clark, 2007); *The Messiah: In Early Judaism and Christianity*, ed. Magnus Zetterholm (Minneapolis: Fortress Press, 2007); Richard A. Horsley and John S. Hanson, *Bandits, Prophets, and Messiahs: Popular Movements in the Time of Jesus* (Minneapolis: Winston, 1985); Sigmund Mowinckel, *He That Cometh*, trans. G. W. Anderson (Nashville: Abingdon, 1954); Joseph Klausner, *The Messianic Idea in Israel from Its Beginning to the Completion of the Mishnah* (New York: Macmillan, 1955).

26. Mowinckel, *He That Cometh*; Nils Alstrup Dahl, "Messianic Ideas and the Crucifixion of Jesus," in Charlesworth, ed., *The Messiah*, 382–403, at 389; David E. Aune, "Christian Prophecy and the Messianic Status of Jesus," in Charlesworth, ed., *The Messiah*, 404–22, at 411; Horbury, *Jewish Messianism and the Cult of Christ*, 25; Joseph A. Fitzmyer, *The Dead Sea Scrolls and Christian Origins* (Grand Rapids: Eerdmans, 2000), 76, 78.

27. Fitzmyer, *Dead Sea Scrolls and Christian Origins*, 73, 82. Collins, *The Scepter and the Star*, 145–64, uses the term to refer to "an agent of God in the end-time who is said . . . to be anointed, but who is not necessarily called 'messiah' in every passage."

even occur in the Hebrew Bible.[29] When eschatological messianism does begin to appear (c. 200 B.C.E.) it does not take the form of a coherent theology. Rather, "messiahs" appear as nebulous figures in different texts with conflicting portraits. Moreover, the emergence of eschatological messianism in the second century B.C.E. follows the post-exilic period: messianism seems to be a relatively late development in post-exilic Judaism,[30] even if the origins of the "messianic idea" have their roots in the royal ideology of kingship in the ancient Near East, where the king was often regarded as the living embodiment of the human and the divine.[31]

The covenant with David took the form of an eternal loyalty to the house and line of David: his dynasty would endure forever.[32] Each king was heralded as receiving his kingship from God and celebrated in the royal psalms (Pss. 2, 72, 110) composed in honor of the king. These psalms describe the king as God's son,[33] an eternal priest and "king of righteousness"[34] given universal dominion.[35] The ideal king judges "with righteousness" and defends "the cause of the poor."[36] The anointed king was consecrated to God.[37] This noble ideal was never realized in the historical kings of Israel. As a result, Israel's misfortunes were seen to reflect this less-than-ideal realization of the king's role and royal

28. Lev. 4:3, 5, 16; 16:15; 1 Kgs. 19:16). See also Ps. 105:15; 1 Cor. 16:22; 1 Kgs. 19:16; Isa. 61:1-12; Joel 3:1; 1 Sam. 24:6, 10; 26:16; 2 Sam. 1:14, 16.

29. See Lev. 4:3, 5, 16; 6:15; 1 Sam. 2:10, 35; 12:3, 5; 16:6; 24:7, 11; 26:9, 11, 16, 23; 2 Sam. 1:14, 16; 19:22; 22:51; 23:1; Isa. 45:1; Hab. 3:13; Ps. 2:2; 18:51; 20:7; 28:8; 84:10; 89:39, 52; 105:15; 132:10, 17; Lam. 4:20; Dan. 9:25, 26: 1 Chron. 16:22; 2 Chron. 6:42. See also J. J. M. Roberts, "The Old Testament's Contribution to Messianic Expectations," in Charlesworth, ed., *The Messiah*, 39–51, at 51.

30. Collins, *The Scepter and the Star*, 33.

31. Mowinckel, *He That Cometh*. On the problematic essentialist presuppositions of such an "idea" see Matthew V. Novenson, *Christ Among the Messiahs: Christ Language in Paul and Messiah Language in Ancient Judaism* (New York: Oxford University Press, 2012), 35–41. As examples see James Scott, "Historical Development of the Messianic Idea," *OTS* 7 (1888): 176–80; Julius H. Greenstone, *The Messiah Idea in Jewish History* (Philadelphia: Jewish Publication Society, 1906); W. O. E. Oesterley, *The Evolution of the Messianic Idea: A Study in Comparative Religion* (New York: Dutton, 1908); Klausner, *The Messianic Idea in Israel*; Gershom Scholem, *The Messianic Idea in Judaism and Other Essays on Jewish Spirituality* (New York: Schocken, 1971). On Jesus' messianism as the fulfillment of ancient royal Israelite enthronement festivals, see Shirley Lucass, *The Concept of the Messiah in the Scriptures of Judaism and Christianity* (LSTS 78; London: T & T Clark, 2011).

32. 2 Sam. 7:11-16 and Ps. 89:20-38.

33. Ps. 2:7.

34. Ps. 110:4.

35. Ps. 72:8.

36. Ps. 72:2-14; Gen. 49:10; Num. 24:17; Isa. 10:34–11:5.

37. Dahl, "Messianic Ideas and the Crucifixion of Jesus," 384.

ideology came to have a predominantly future idealization: the present king may be wicked, but the *future* king will restore the Davidic kingdom to its former glory.[38] The hopes that had once been placed on individual Davidic kings were now projected onto a future anointed figure who would fulfill them *someday*. The royal king ultimately became an eschatological agent of divine redemption and salvation.

John J. Collins has identified four major messianic paradigms: that of anointed "king, priest, prophet, and heavenly messiah."[39] Collins also holds that there was a common popular "expectation," that of the royal warrior-king who would restore the kingdom of Israel, overthrow Israel's enemies, unite the twelve tribes, and bring universal peace.[40] While there certainly was diversity in how messianic ideas were expressed, the most common understanding of the term seems to draw on and appeal to the idea of divine kingship. So there is both diversity and a certain qualified unity of concept.[41] The classic "messianic" texts of the Hebrew Bible refer to the Davidic king:

> The scepter will not depart from Judah,
> nor the ruler's staff from between his feet.[42]
>
> A star will go forth from Jacob,
> and a scepter will rise from Israel;
> it will shatter the borders of Moab
> and tear down all the sons of Sheth.[43]
>
> I will establish the throne of his kingdom forever.
> I will be a *father* to him,
> and he will be a *son* (בן/υἱόν) to me.[44]

These texts do not refer to a "messiah"*per se*, but rather to a future Jewish king. Isaiah 11:1-4, a royal *Davidic* text ("the stump of Jesse"), imbues the future king, that is, the "branch" (נצר) with a number of divine qualities:

38. Mowinckel, *He That Cometh*, 99.

39. Collins, *The Scepter and the Star*, 12.

40. Ibid., 67. Dunn, *Jesus Remembered*, 622.

41. Amy-Jill Levine, *The Misunderstood Jew: The Church and the Scandal of the Jewish Jesus* (New York: Harper San Francisco, 2006), 128–29.

42. Gen. 49:10.

43. Num. 24:17.

44. 2 Sam. 7:13/14.

The spirit of the Lord will rest on him,
the spirit of wisdom and understanding,
the spirit of counsel and might,
the spirit of knowledge and the fear of the Lord.
He will not judge by what his eyes see,
or decide by what his ears hear,
but with righteousness he will judge the poor,
and decide with equity for the meek of the earth;
he will strike the earth with the rod of his mouth,
and with the breath of his lips he will kill the wicked.

Note here how the divine characteristics of the future king—the "spirit of the Lord," "wisdom," "understanding," "counsel," "might," and "knowledge"—are conflated with his military role: to "strike the earth" and "kill the wicked." Isaiah 11:6-9 continues with a utopian/paradisial vision of a restored, peaceful, and vegetarian creation:

The wolf will live with the lamb,
the leopard will lie down with the kid,
the calf and the lion and the fatling together,
and a little child will lead them . . .
and the lion will eat straw like the ox . . .
They will not hurt or destroy on all my holy mountain;
for the earth will be full of the knowledge of the Lord
as the waters cover the sea.

The "root of Jesse" will "stand as a signal to the peoples: the nations will inquire of him."[45] The future king will "assemble the outcasts of Israel, and gather the dispersed of Judah from the four corners of the earth."[46] Isaiah 45:1 identifies King Cyrus as the "Lord's anointed" (משיחו/χριστῷ), which indicates that "messianic" language was far more flexible in ancient Israel than a narrowly drawn exclusive definition of a single eschatological figure. The prophetic figure of Isa. 61:1 is also described as "anointed":

The spirit of the Lord God is upon me,
because the Lord has *anointed* me (משׁח/ἔχρισε);

45. Isa. 11:10.
46. Isa. 11:12.

> he has sent me to bring good news (εὐαγγελίσασθαι)
> to the oppressed,
> to bind up the brokenhearted,
> to proclaim liberty to the captives,
> and release to the prisoners;
> to proclaim the year of the Lord's favor,
> and the day of vengeance of our God.

Note here how Isaiah conflates the messianic "good news" of liberty and the year of "the Lord's favor" with the "day of vengeance." The utopian or paradisial elements stand in considerable tension with the politico-military role envisioned for the king.

The book of Daniel contains two references to "an anointed (one)," yet the lack of a definite article in Dan. 9:25-26 requires the translation: "*an* anointed" figure(s), not "*the* anointed (one)." Daniel describes a time of tribulation "until an anointed one, a prince (עד משיח נגיד)." Daniel 9:26 marks another transitional period, predicting that "after threescore and two weeks an anointed one will be cut off, and will have nothing" (ירכת משיח ואין לו). The author of Daniel refers to Cyrus's proclamation of support for the rebuilding of the Temple.[47] The "anointed" who is "cut off" seems to be a reference to Onias III, the anointed high priest murdered during the reign of Antiochus IV in 171 B.C.E., the "destruction" of the city to an invasion of Jerusalem in 168 B.C.E. by Antiochus,[48] and the "abomination that causes desolation" to an altar of Zeus that Antiochus installed in the Temple. Daniel 9 is not a *royal* or Davidic prophecy.

The Qumran corpus also attests to a considerable variety of messianic texts. Attempts have been made to delineate historical development,[49] but the evidence does not support such efforts, although various motifs do reoccur.[50] The Qumran community anticipated the arrival of *two* messiahs, and the offices of the priestly and royal messiah were conceived as two distinct roles.[51] These figures were expected to appear at the same time.[52] According to 1QS 9.11, the community was to live by the original laws in which it was first instructed "until

47. Isa. 44:29; 45:13; Zech. 1:16; Ezra 6:14.

48. 1 Macc. 1:29-39.

49. Jean Starcky, "Les quatres étapes du messianisme à Qumran," *RB* 70 (1963): 481–505.

50. Collins, *The Scepter and the Star*, 12.

51. Craig A. Evans, "Qumran's Messiah: How Important Is He?" in Collins and Kugler, eds., *Religion in the Dead Sea Scrolls*, 135–49, at 147; Shermaryahu Talmon, "The Concepts of *Mashiah* and Messianism in Early Judaism," in Charlesworth, ed., *The Messiah*, 79–115, at 112.

the coming of the prophet and the messiahs of Aaron and Israel."[53] 1QS and CD refer to a time when the "messiah(s) of Aaron and Israel" will appear.[54] 1QSa is a rule for all "the congregation of Israel" in the last days, when the messiah of Israel (משיח ישראל) will be born (יו[לי]ד).[55] The royal messiah is the "son of God." 1QSa 11–12 refers to the time "when God begets the messiah."[56] This idea seems to be derived from Ps. 2:7, where God declares "You are my son; today I have begotten you." In 4Q252 (4QPatrBles 5.1–7), a *pesher* on the star prophecy of Gen. 49:10 dated to the first half of the first century B.C.E., the "messiah of righteousness" (משיח הצדק) will appear at the End of Days. He will observe "the law with the men of the community."[57] 11QMelch refers to the "herald" of Daniel as the "messiah of the spirit" (משיח הרוח).[58] The *Psalms of Solomon* also refer to a "king, the son of David," who will

> drive out the sinners from the inheritance . . .
> with a rod of iron to break all their substance,
> to destroy the lawless nations by the word of his mouth . . .

52. David Flusser, *The Spiritual History of the Dead Sea Sect*, trans. Carol Glucker (Tel Aviv: MOD, 1989), 85.

53. עד בוא נביא ומשיחו אהרון וישראל

54. John F. Priest, "The Messiah and the Meal in 1QSa," *JBL* 82 (1963): 95–100; Lawrence H. Schiffman, *The Eschatological Community of the Dead Sea Scrolls: A Study of the Rule of the Congregation* (SBLMS 38; Atlanta: Scholars, 1989); H. Neil Richardson, "Some Notes on 1QSa," *JBL* 76 (1957): 108–22; Robert Gordis, "The 'Begotten' Messiah in the Qumran Scrolls," *VT* 7 (1957): 191–94; Philip Sigal, "Further Reflections on the 'Begotten' Messiah," *HAR* 7 (1983): 221–33.

55. Geza Vermes, *The Complete Dead Sea Scrolls in English* (New York: Allen Lane/Penguin, 1997), 157, dates the text to the mid-first century B.C.E..

56. See Talmon, "The Concepts of *Mashiah*," 110 n. 73; Frank Moore Cross, *The Ancient Library of Qumran* (3d ed.; Minneapolis: Fortress Press, 1995), 87; Schiffman, *The Eschatological Community*, 53–54. But see also Richardson, "Some Notes on 1QSa"; Joseph A. Fitzmyer, *Essays on the Semitic Background of the New Testament* (London: Chapman, 1971), 153 n. 27; John J. Collins, "The *Son of God* Text," in *From Jesus to John*, 65–82, at 78–79; Martin Hengel, *The Son of God* (Philadelphia: Fortress Press, 1976), 44; Robert Gordis, "The 'Begotten' Messiah in the Qumran Scrolls," *VT* 7 (1957): 191–94; Morton Smith, "'God's Begetting the Messiah' in 1QSa," *NTS* 5 (1959): 218–24; Philip Sigal, "Further Reflections on the 'Begotten' Messiah." *HAR* 7 (1983): 221–33. This reading is consistent with the notions of God's begetting of the king in Ps. 2:2, 7 and 2 Sam. 7:11-16. Vermes, *The Complete Dead Sea Scrolls*, 159 n. 1.

57. Gerbern S. Oegema, "Messianic Expectations in the Qumran Writings: Theses on their Development," in *Qumran Messianism: Studies on the Messianic Expectations in the Dead Sea Scrolls*, ed. James H. Charlesworth, et al. (Tübingen: Mohr Siebeck, 1998), 53–82, at 73; Vermes, *Complete Dead Sea Scrolls*, 462–63; Fitzmyer, *The Dead Sea Scrolls and Christian Origins*, 87–88.

58. 11QMelch 2.18. Lawrence H. Schiffman, "Messianic Figures and Ideas in the Qumran Scrolls," in Charlesworth, ed., *The Messiah*, 116-–99; Oegema, *Anointed and His People*, 302–3.

For they shall all be holy,
and their king shall be the lord messiah (χριστός κύριος).[59]

Given the diversity of messianic texts and traditions in Second Temple Judaism, there does not seem to have been any unified Jewish messianic expectation at the time of Jesus,[60] nor any single, identifiable role for a messiah to fulfill.[61] First-century Judaism was not uniform.[62] There was substantial diversity in how Jews regarded the Torah, viewed the Temple, practiced *halakhah*, and assimilated to or resisted Greco-Roman culture. We cannot impose a normative view of Jewish messianism on all first-century Jews. This diversity suggests that first-century Jews would be amenable to diverse fulfillments of "anointed" figures, whether through conventional warfare (royal-political), predictions of prophetic deliverance (prophetic), or charismatic powers or alternatives to the Temple (priestly). That is, some "anointed" figures could conceivably issue challenges to the traditions that other first-century Jews held dear. Naturally, this would result in sectarian conflict.

Josephus describes a number of charismatic prophetic movements linked with political revolution in the years leading up to and during the Jewish Revolt of 66–73 C.E. Some of these movements were led by figures recognizably characteristic of "prophets." Others are more adequately designated as popularly acclaimed "kings."[63] For example, during the Revolt, Simon bar Giora, the

59. *Pss. Sol* 17:21-32.

60. Fitzmyer, *The Dead Sea Scrolls and Christian Origins*, 78; Charlesworth, *The Messiah*, 5; Oegema, *Anointed and his People*, 303; Kenneth E. Pomykala, *The Davidic Dynasty Tradition in Early Judaism: Its History and Significance for Messianism* (EJ 7; Atlanta: Scholars Press, 1995), 271; Martin Karrer, *Der Gesalbte. Die Grundlagen des Christustitels* (FRLANT 151; Göttingen: Vandenhoeck & Ruprecht, 1990), 243; Marinus de Jonge, "The Use of the Word 'Anointed' in the Time of Jesus," *NovT* 8 (1966): 132–48; Neusner, et al., *Judaisms and Their Messiahs*; Richard A. Horsley, "'Messianic' Figures and Movements in First-Century Palestine," in Charlesworth, ed., *The Messiah*, 276–95.

61. Charlesworth, *The Messiah*, 5; Sanders, *The Historical Figure of Jesus*, 240–41; Morton Smith, "What is Implied by the Variety of Messianic Figures?" *JBL* 78 (1959): 66–72. See also Albert I. Baumgarten, *The Flourishing of Jewish Sects in the Maccabean Era: An Interpretation* (JSJ Sup 55; Leiden: Brill, 1997), 153–54; Neusner et al., *Judaisms and their Messiahs*; Collins, *The Scepter and the Star*.

62. Neusner, *Judaisms and their Messiahs*; *Messiah and Christos: Studies in the Jewish Origins of Christianity, Presented to David Flusser on the Occasion of his Seventy-Fifth Birthday*, ed. Ithamar Gruenwald, et al. (Tübingen: Mohr Siebeck, 1992); Charlesworth, *The Messiah*; *Messias-Vorstellungen bei Juden und Christen*, ed. Ekkehard Stegemann (Stuttgart: Kohlhammer, 1993). Collins, *The Scepter and the Star*, 189: "we should think of a spectrum of messianic expectation."

63. For prophetic figures see Josephus on Jesus, son of Hananiah, "Theudas" (*Ant.* 20.97-98) and the "Egyptian" (*War* 2.261-62; *Ant.* 20.169-71). For (would-be) "kings," see Josephus on Athronges (*War* 2.57, 60; *Ant.* 17.273, 278-85), Simon, and Judas the son of Hezekiah (*War* 2.56; *Ant.* 17.271-72).

military commander in Jerusalem, entered Jerusalem as a Davidic king and was executed by Rome as "king of the Jews."[64] Josephus also mentions Menahem, who broke into Herod's arsenal and "returned like a king to Jerusalem."[65] It is reported that when R. Akiba saw Simon bar Kochba, he said: "This is the king messiah (דין הוא מלכא משיחא).[66] Josephus states that his fellow Jews were incited by "an ambiguous oracle" (χρησμὸς ἀμφίβολος) found in scripture describing how one of their countrymen would become the "ruler of the world" (ἄρξει τῆς οἰκουμένης).[67] The idea of a "messianic" ruler who would bring the whole world under his rule may have been a common Jewish hope.[68]

The alleged identification of "the messiah" as a fixed theological concept in first-century Judaism has been over-determined. There were multiple ways in which various individuals proposed to fulfill divinely appointed tasks, and prospective kings, prophets, and priests could be regarded as "anointed." At the same time, first-century Judaism could presuppose a common royal ideology based on scriptural tradition, Davidic legend, and nationalistic biblical (and extra-biblical) narratives. The tension between this common royal ideology and the remarkable diversity on the ground characterizes the complexity of first-century Jewish messianism. Yet it is within this cultural complexity that the historical Jesus must be located and identified.

Jesus was crucified as "King of the Jews."[69] This expression was used as the *titulus*, or inscription, fixed to the cross (*Iesus Nazarenus Rex Iudaeorum*).[70] The motif is located firmly in many different sources and was embarrassing for the early church. It was not used by Jews or Christians as a title for Jesus.[71] Jesus

64. *War* 7.29-31, 36, 153-54; 4.507-534.

65. *War* 2.433-34.

66. *y. Ta'an* 4.8/17.

67. *War* 6.312. Josephus, of course, interpreted the oracle unambiguously as referring to Vespasian.

68. Tacitus, *Hist.* 5.13; Suetonius, *Vesp.* 4.5.

69. On crucifixion see Josephus, *War* 5.11.1; Martin Hengel, *Crucifixion in the Ancient World and the Folly of the Message of the Cross*, trans. John Bowden (Philadelphia: Fortress Press, 1977); James H. Charlesworth, "Jesus and Jehohanan," *ExpT* 84 (1973): 147–50; Joseph Zias and Eliezer Sekeles, "The Crucified Man from Giv'at ha-Mivtar: a Reappraisal," *IEJ* 35 (1985): 22–27; Frederick T. Zugibe, "Two Questions about Crucifixion: Does the Victim Die of Asphyxiation; Would Nails in the Hand Hold the Weight of the Body?" *BRev* 5 (1989): 35–43; James H. Charlesworth and J. Zias, "Crucifixion," in *Jesus and the Dead Sea Scrolls*, ed. James H. Charlesworth (New York: Doubleday, 1992), 273–89; David W. Chapman, "Perceptions of Crucifixion Among Jews and Christians in the Ancient World," Ph. D. dissertation, Cambridge University, 1999.

70. Mark 15:26; Nils Alstrup Dahl, *Jesus the Christ: The Historical Origins of Christological Doctrine* (Minneapolis: Fortress Press, 1991), 58. See also Ferdinand Hahn, *The Titles of Jesus in Christology* (London: Lutterworth, 1969), 172–89.

was crucified as *king*, not Χριστός. It is highly unlikely that Jesus' followers "introduced this title into the narrative since it was otherwise used in clearly political contexts."[72] The title appears in Pilate's speech,[73] the Barabbas scene,[74] and Jesus' mock salute by Roman soldiers. The authenticity of the *titulus* is virtually certain.[75] Our earliest and most reliable source of information about Jesus' messianic identification is his Roman crucifixion.

Jesus was crucified as "an alleged royal Messiah."[76] It is not Jesus' resurrection that introduced his messianic identification: there were no traditions of a resurrected messiah.[77] Jesus' movement was *not* a military uprising. The idea of a crucified messiah was virtually unthinkable in pre-Christian Judaism.[78] While various accusations may have been leveled against Jesus, including leading people "astray,"[79] violating the Torah or traditional

71. Dahl, *Jesus the Christ*, 36–37; Fitzmyer, *The One Who Is To Come*, 141; Hengel, "Messiah of Israel," 46; Rudolf Pesch, *Das Markusevangelium* (2 vols.; HTKNT; Freiburg: Herder, 1976–77), 2:484; Dunn, *Jesus Remembered*, 628; Brown, *Death of the Messiah*, 1:476; Wright, *Jesus and the Victory of God*, 486–89; Collins, *The Scepter and the Star*, 205; Theissen and Merz, *Historical Jesus*, 458–59; Becker, *Jesus of Nazareth*, 353–54; Gerd Lüdemann, *Jesus After Two Thousand Years: What He Really Said and Did*, trans. John Bowden (London: SCM, 2000), 108.

72. Dahl, "Messianic Ideas and the Crucifixion of Jesus," 383.

73. Mark 15:2.

74. Mark 15:9, 12.

75. See also Ernst Bammel, "The Titulus," in *Jesus and the Politics of His Day*, ed. Ernst Bammel and C. F. D. Moule (Cambridge: Cambridge University Press, 1984), 353–64; Joachim Gnilka, *Jesus of Nazareth: Message and History*, trans. Siegfried S. Schatzmann (Peabody, MA: Hendrickson, 1997), 304; Ferdinand Hahn, *Christologische Hoheitstitel: Ihre Geschichte im frühen Christentum* (5th ed.; Göttingen: Vandenhoeck & Ruprecht, 1995), 178. For a skeptical view see Wolfgang Reinhold, *Der Prozess Jesu* (BTSc 28; Göttingen: Vandenhoeck & Ruprecht, 2006), 91–95; David Catchpole, "The 'Triumphal' Entry," in *Jesus and the Politics of His Day*, 319–34, at 328–30; Adela Yarbro Collins, *Mark: A Commentary* (Hermeneia; Minneapolis: Fortress Press, 2007), 747–48.

76. Dahl, "Messianic Ideas and the Crucifixion of Jesus," 383.

77. In Rom 1:4, Paul describes Jesus as "descended from David according to the flesh" and "declared to be Son of God with power according to the spirit of holiness by resurrection from the dead," but the messianic identification of Jesus—and the royal messianic charge of Jewish "kingship"—*preceded* the resurrection.

78. Joel B. Green, *The Death of Jesus* (WUNT 2d ser. 33; Tübingen: Mohr Siebeck, 1988), 164–69. See also Donald J. Juel, *Messianic Exegesis* (Philadelphia: Fortress Press, 1988), 89–133; Morna D. Hooker, *Not Ashamed of the Gospel: New Testament Interpretations of the Death of Christ* (Carlisle: Paternoster, 1994), 12. See also William Manson, *Jesus, the Messiah* (London: Hodder and Stoughton, 1943), 169.

79. Acts 5:40; 10:39; Gal. 3:13; Tacitus, *Ann.* 15.44; *b. Sanh.* 43b.

food customs,[80] sorcery,[81] being a "rebellious son,"[82] blasphemy,[83] and false prophecy,[84] it was the royal messianic charge that led to the Roman cross.

Given the historicity of a royal messianic charge underlying the crucifixion, it becomes less problematic to attribute a Jewish messianic meaning to Paul's identification of Jesus as *Christos*. Paul uses the term so frequently that it almost seems like a proper name, not a title.[85] Some scholars think that Paul's use of *Christos* is not particularly "messianic" at all, that Paul never uses *Christos* as a general term and rarely prefaces it with the definite article. In addition, it has been argued that Paul's use of the term never takes a genitive modifier and never takes the form of a predicate of the verb "to be."[86] If these arguments prove decisive, then our earliest evidence for the messianic identification of Jesus would seem to be compromised. But are these arguments compelling?

Matthew Novenson has recently proposed that Paul's use of Χριστός is neither a proper name nor a title but rather an *honorific* that can be used in combination with a proper name or stand in for a proper name.[87] Titles need not be appellatives, that is, they need not only refer to a class as a general term,[88] and Paul does occasionally employ a predicate use of the term.[89] The *relative*

80. Mark 2:24; Luke 13:14; 14:1-6; Mark 7:1-4.

81. Mark 3:22; Matt. 9:34; 10:25; Q 11:20.

82. Deut. 21:18-21; Exod. 20:12; Matt. 11:19 and Q ("glutton and a drunkard"). See also Q 14:26; Mark 3:31-35; 10:29-30; 12:18-27; 13:12; Luke 9:59-60; Q 12:51-53; Matt. 19:10-12.

83. Mark 2:7; Matt. 11:11-18; Luke 19:39; Mark 14:64. *m. Sanh.* 7.4-5;

84. Acts 5:30; Gal. 3:13; Josephus, *Ant.* 18.63; Tacitus, *Ann.* 15.44; Justin, *Dial.* 69.7; *b. Sanh.* 43a; Matt. 27:62-64. See Deut. 13:2-6 and 18:15-22 for the regulations against lawbreakers, deceivers, and imposters.

85. Fredriksen, *From Jesus to Christ*, 56; Martin Hengel, "Christological Titles in Early Christianity," in Charlesworth, ed., *The Messiah*, 425–48, at 444; Larry Hurtado, "Paul's Christology," in *The Cambridge Companion to St. Paul*, ed. James D. G. Dunn (Cambridge: Cambridge University Press, 2003), 185–98, at 191; Kümmel, *Theology of the New Testament According to Its Major Witnesses*, 154; Douglas J. Moo, "The Christology of the Early Pauline Letters," in *Contours of Christology in the New Testament*, ed. Richard N. Longenecker (Grand Rapid: Eerdmans, 2005), 186; Werner R. Kramer, *Christ, Lord, Son of God* (SBT 50; London: SCM, 1966), 67–68, 203–14; James D. G. Dunn, *The Theology of Paul the Apostle* (Grand Rapids: Eerdmans, 1998), 197–99; Magnus Zetterholm, "Paul and the Missing Messiah," in *The Messiah in Early Judaism and Christianity*, ed. Magnus Zetterholm (Minneapolis: Fortress Press, 2007), 33–55.

86. Dahl, "Messiahship of Jesus in Paul." See also Wilhelm Bousset, *Kyrios Christos: Geschichte des Christusglaubens von den Anfängen des Christentums bis Irenaeus* (Göttingen: Vandenhoeck & Ruprecht, 1913); English: *Kyrios Christos: A History of the Belief in Christ from the Beginning of Christianity to Irenaeus*, trans. J. E. Steely (Nashville: Abingdon, 1970);.

87. Matthew Novenson, *Christ Among the Messiahs*, ch. 3, esp. 88–97. See also Earl Richard, *Jesus, One and Many: The Christological Concept of New Testament Authors* (Wilmington, DE: Michael Glazier, 1988).

88. Ibid., 102–4.

scarcity of the definite article in Paul's use of *Christos* has been exaggerated. Paul uses the definite article forty-nine times in seven letters.[90] The problem, then, is not that Paul does not mean "messiah" when he uses the term; rather, the problem is that Paul invests the term with new associations.

Paul is justified by faith "*in* Christ,"[91] "crucified *with* Christ,"[92] "baptized into Christ,"[93] and "clothed with Christ." Christ is the "power" and "wisdom of God."[94] Paul's coworkers are "in Christ Jesus,"[95] and all those "in Christ" are "anointed" by God.[96] Paul's innovative use of the term *Christos* can be understood within the semantic range of meanings given to the term "messiah" in the Second Temple period, but it is precisely this innovation that points to our need to move beyond normative definitions of "the messianic *idea*" and toward the reevaluation of the diversity of Second Temple messianic texts and social movements.[97] The Jewish scriptures provided a complex array of "linguistic resources" with which new forms of "messianic" expressions could take shape and form.[98] Paul's use of *Christos* is consistent with Jewish *messianism*.

Paul's early use of *Christos* also points to the term's prior use, presumably in an Aramaic-speaking milieu.[99] The most plausible explanation of the term's

89. Ibid., 104–8, citing 1 Cor. 10; Gal. 3:16.

90. Ibid., 111–15. See also Dahl, "Messiahship of Jesus in Paul," 15–25; Marinus de Jonge, "The Earliest Christian Use of *Christos*: Some Suggestions," *NTS* 32 (1986): 321–43, at 321–24; Aune, "Christian Prophecy and the Messianic Status," 405.

91. Gal. 2:17. On the prepositional phrase ἐν χριστῷ see A. J. M. Wedderburn, "Some Observations on Paul's Use of the Phrases 'In Christ' and 'With Christ,'" *JSNT* 25 (1985): 83–97, at 88; Adolf Deissmann, *Die neutestamentliche Formel "In Christo Jesu" untersucht* (Marburg: Elwert, 1892); Fritz Neugebauer, *In Christus: Eine Untersuchung zum paulinischen Glaubensverständnis* (Göttingen: Vandenhoeck & Ruprecht, 1961); Michel Bouttier, *En Christ: Étude d'exégèse et de théologie pauliniennes* (Études d'histoire et de la philosophie religieuses 54; Paris: Presses Universitaires de France, 1962). For the interpretation of ἐν χριστῷ as referring to "corporate personality," see Joshua Roy Porter, "The Legal Aspects of the Concept of 'Corporate Personality' in the Old Testament," *VT* 15 (1965): 361–80; John W. Rogerson, "The Hebrew Conception of Corporate Personality: A Re-examination," *JTS* 21 (1970): 1–16; A. J. M. Wedderburn, "The Body of Christ and Related Concepts in 1 Corinthians," *SJT* 2 (1971): 74–96.

92. Gal. 2:19.

93. Gal. 3:27.

94. 1 Cor. 1:24.

95. Rom. 16:3.

96. 1 Cor. 1:21-22.

97. On the "messianic idea" see Moshe Idel, *Messianic Mystics* (New Haven: Yale University Press, 1998), 17; Klausner, *The Messianic Idea*, 385; Scholem, *The Messianic Idea in Judaism*.

98. Novenson, *Christ Among the Messiahs*, 47–65.

99. Adela Yarbro Collins and John J. Collins, *King and Messiah as Son of God: Divine, Human, and Angelic Messianic Figures in Biblical and Related Literature* (Grand Rapids: Eerdmans, 2008), 122.

pervasive presence in the Pauline corpus is that the expression originated as a confession, that is, Ἰησοῦς (ὁ) Χριστός derives from the Aramaic ישוע משיחא.[100] Paul's use of *Christos* "should regularly be read as 'Messiah.'"[101] Suetonius indicates that *Christos* was already in use in Rome during the 40s. The description of "Christians" at Antioch as Χριστιανοί presupposes its use as a name/title at approximately the same time.[102]

Paul seems to have been aware that Jesus did not fulfill the traditional politico-military functions of the Davidic king.[103] He affirms Jesus' Davidic ancestry (ἐκ σπέρματος Δαυὶδ κατὰ σάρκα),[104] and states that *Christos* is the "root of Jesse" (ἡ ῥίζα τοῦ Ἰεσσαί), but he recognizes that a crucified messiah is a "stumbling block" for Jews and "foolishness" for Gentiles.[105] Accordingly, he redefines the term *Christos*. He anticipates an imminent, albeit future fulfillment of these expectations, that is, the παρουσία, and he develops a new model of ritual communion in fellowship with *Christos*. This redefinition and ritualization, once opened to Gentiles, led to hostility between Paul and other Jews who did not accept Jesus as *Christos*, especially when they began to think that Paul was abolishing Jewish law.

100. *Contra* the idea that the term has no clear meaning or is not a clear "messianic" reference, as proposed by Kramer, *Christ, Lord, Son of God*, 203; Dahl, "Messiahship of Jesus in Paul," 15; George MacRae, "Messiah and Gospel," in *Judaism and Their Messiahs*, 171. For further examples see de Jonge, "The Earliest Christian Use of *Christos*: Some Suggestions," 321–22; Fredriksen, *From Jesus to Christ*, 56; Dunn, *Theology of Paul*, 197; Hurtado, "Paul's Christology," 191; Moo, "Christology of the Early Pauline Letters," 186; Zetterholm, "Paul and the Missing Messiah," 37.

101. N. T. Wright, "ΧΡΙΣΤΟΣ as 'Messiah' in Paul: Philemon 6," in idem, *The Climax of the Covenant: Christ and the Law in Pauline Theology* (Minneapolis: Fortress Press, 1992), 41–55, at 41; S. A. Cummins, "Divine Life and Corporate Christology: God, Messiah Jesus, and the Covenant Community in Paul," in *The Messiah in the Old and New Testaments*, ed. Stanley E. Porter (Grand Rapids: Eerdmans, 2007), 190–209; Richard B. Hays, "Christ Prays the Psalms: Paul's Use of an Early Christian Exegetical Convention," in *The Future of Christology*, ed. Abraham J. Malherbe (Minneapolis: Fortress Press, 1993), 122–36, esp. 111–30; J. Ross Wagner, *Heralds of the Good News: Isaiah and Paul 'in Concert' in the Letter to the Romans* (NovT Sup 101; Leiden: Brill, 2002), 308 n. 7.

102. Acts 11:26.

103. Andrew Chester, "The Christ of Paul," in *Redemption and Resistance: The Messianic Hopes of Jews and Christians in Antiquity*, ed. Markus Bockmuehl and James C. Paget (London/New York: T&T Clark, 2007), 109–21, esp. 110. See also Dahl, *The Crucified Messiah*, 46–47. On Paul's downplaying the Davidic ancestry of Jesus see also Martin Hengel, *Between Jesus and Paul: Studies in the Earliest History of Christianity* (Philadelphia: Fortress Press, 1983); idem, *Studies in Early Christology* (Edinburgh: T&T Clark, 1995), 213–14; Kramer, *Christ, Lord, Son of God*; MacRae, "Messiah and Gospel," 169–85. As an honorific, see Novenson, *Christ Among the Messiahs*, ch 3.

104. Rom. 1:3.

105. 1 Cor. 1:23.

Jesus' execution as a political criminal, the *titulus*-inscription "King of the Jews," Paul's repeated use of the term Χριστός, its ubiquitous presence in the New Testament, and the exalted manner in which the earliest Jesus tradition portrays him all point to an early Jewish identification of the historical Jesus as a "messianic" figure.

Jesus did not fulfill popular or politico-military Davidic expectations. He may even have challenged them. So the messianic identification of Jesus has always been regarded as a paradox, a "stumbling block" or "foolishness." Jesus' death by crucifixion, however, is more than a mere "stumbling block" to faith; it is the exact opposite of what most first-century Jews would have expected of a royal messiah. A sudden, violent death at the hands of the Romans or the Jewish religious leadership was just about the last thing most Jews would have expected of a successful messianic candidate. So it is not just that Jesus was executed and apparently defeated as a prospective "king." Jesus did not even resist arrest. In fact, he seems to have maintained a position of *defenselessness* during his trial, apparently trusting in God's providence even to the point of death.[106] Jesus' ministry and voluntary death is thus a riddle in relation to his messianic identity, an historical enigma that continues to puzzle: the idea of a nonviolent messiah.

106. Allison, *Jesus of Nazareth,* 63 n. 233; idem, *Constructing Jesus*, 433.

6

The Christologies of Q

Q does not explicitly identify Jesus as *messiah* or Χριστός.[1] The conspicuous absence of this term, so frequently used by Paul and the Gospels, has sometimes been taken to mean that Q is uninterested in, unaware of, and/or rejects *kerygmatic* traditions that understood Jesus as a messianic figure.[2] Indeed, the dominant paradigm in the study of Q's Christology is that Q shifted from a low Christology in its formative period to a significantly higher Christology in its redaction.[3] This paradigm also reflects the idea that Q represents a distinct community, theology, and Christological profile as well as a complex compositional history.[4] These ideas have generated considerable debate and cogent questions have been raised in response.[5] For example, can the absence

1. This chapter was previously published as "'Blessed is Whoever is Not Offended by Me': The Subversive Appropriation of (Royal) Messianic Ideology in Q 3–7," *NTS* 57, no. 3 (2011): 307–24. A version of this chapter and article was also presented as a paper in the Q Section at the Annual Meeting of the Society of Biblical Literature on November 18, 2006, in Washington DC.

2. Marcus J. Borg, *The Lost Gospel Q* (Berkeley: Ulysses, 1996), 27–28; Burton L. Mack, "The Christ and Jewish Wisdom," in *The Messiah: Developments in Earliest Judaism and Christianity: The First Princeton Symposium on Judaism and Christian Origins*, ed. James H. Charlesworth, et al. (Minneapolis: Fortress Press, 1992), 192–221, at 214; Christopher M. Tuckett, *Q and the History of Early Christianity: Studies on Q* (Peabody, MA: Hendrickson, 1996), 214; Leif E. Vaage, *Galilean Upstarts: Jesus' First Followers According to Q* (Valley Forge, PA: Trinity Press International, 1994), 90–91; Paul Foster, "The Pastoral Purpose of Q's Two-Stage Son of Man Christology," *Biblica* 89 (2008): 81–91, esp. 82.

3. See especially John S. Kloppenborg, *The Formation of Q: Trajectories in Ancient Wisdom Collections* (Philadelphia: Fortress Press, 1987).

4. Heinz Eduard Tödt, *The Son of Man in the Synoptic Tradition*, trans. Dorothea M. Barton (London: SCM, 1963); Dieter Lührmann, *Die Redaktion der Logienquelle* (WMANT 33; Neukirchen-Vluyn: Neukirchener Verlag, 1969); Siegfried Schulz, "Die Gottesherrschaft ist nahe herbeigekommen (Mt 10,7/ Lk 10,9). Der kerygmatische Entwurf der Q-Gemeinde Syrien," in *Das Wort und die Wörter. G. Friedrich FS* (Stuttgart: Kohlhammer, 1973), 57–67; Richard A. Edwards, *A Theology of Q* (Philadelphia: Fortress Press, 1976); Leif E. Vaage, *Galilean Upstarts: Jesus' First Followers According to Q* (Valley Forge, PA: Trinity Press International, 1994).

of the term *messiah* really be regarded as a convincing argument for the community's lack of interest in *kerygmatic* traditions? Could the Q community not have been aware of messianic interpretations of Jesus when Paul—at the very same time, and presumably in contact with the Jerusalem community—uses Χριστός like a proper name? If the earliest version of Q did have a low Christology, regarding Jesus as a prophet, healer, and teacher, then how—and why—did Q come to regard Jesus as the coming "son of man?" This transition seems inexplicable without some kind of conceptual bridge, that is, an exalted view of Jesus, which must then itself be explained.[6]

Q scholarship continues to be challenged by these questions. Indeed, many Q specialists regard Q as a non-messianic text reflecting a non-messianic Jesus movement in Galilee positioned between Jesus' execution as "King of the Jews," the messianic proclamations of Paul and the Jerusalem community, and Q's later incorporation into the explicitly messianic Gospels of Mark, Matthew, and Luke. This is a remarkably anomalous parallel existence for Q and may have as much to do with Q's pivotal role in ideologically motivated reconstructions of Christian origins as it does with disinterested assessments of the historical and literary data. But even granting this scenario, what are we to make of passages in Q that seem literally to cry out for a messianic interpretation?

Even if Q does focus on the kingdom of God, this concept is related to the myth of divine kingship. Jesus is "the One Who Is To Come,"[7] the Son of God,[8] the "Son" of the Father,[9] and the "son of man."[10] The devil offers him "all the kingdoms of the world" and he has the authority to appoint his disciples as eschatological judges.[11] Q contained an implicit Christology.[12] Moreover, the

5. Edward P. Meadors, *Jesus the Messianic Herald of Salvation* (WUNT 2d ser. 72; Tübingen: Mohr Siebeck, 1995); Larry Hurtado, *Lord Jesus Christ: Devotion to Jesus in Earliest Christianity* (Grand Rapids: Eerdmans, 2003), 229–44; James D. G. Dunn, *Jesus Remembered* (Grand Rapids: Eerdmans, 2003), 150–52; Graham N. Stanton, "On the Christology of Q," in *Christ and Spirit in the New Testament*, ed. Barnabas Lindars and Stephen S. Smalley (Cambridge: Cambridge University Press, 1973), 27–42, at 27–28.

6. John S. Kloppenborg, "'Easter Faith' and the Sayings Gospel Q," *Semeia* 49 (1990): 71–99, esp. 83.

7. Q 7:22.

8. Q 3:22; 4:3; 4:9.

9. Q 10:22.

10. Q 6:22; 7:34.

11. Q 4:5; 22:30

12. John S. Kloppenborg Verbin, *Excavating Q: The History and Setting of the Sayings Gospel* (Minneapolis: Fortress Press, 2000), 396, notes that there is "at least implicitly a Christology" in Q. See also B. H. Streeter, *The Four Gospels: A Study of Origins, Treating of the Manuscript Tradition, Sources, Authorship, and Dates* (London: Macmillan, 1924), 291.

title Son of God could represent the Davidic heir to the throne,[13] and both the titles "son of man" and "the One Who Is To Come" could refer to a messianic figure.[14] 4Q521 also illuminates how Q 7:22 would have been seen as an Isaianic list of miracles expected during the messianic age.[15] Finally, if Q contained a baptism account, it would also appear as if Jesus was indeed "anointed" by the Spirit.[16] It is difficult to deny that these passages are consistent with messianic ideas.[17] Yet it is also hard to accept the idea that Q's lack of the term Χριστός is entirely accidental.[18] Perhaps we should consider the possibility that the absence

13. 2 Sam. 7:14; Pss. 2:7, 72:1-7, 89:26; 1 Chron. 17:13, 4QFlor; 4Q246; Mark 1:1, 14:61.

14. 4 Ezra 13:37, 52; *1 En.* 48:2-10, 52:4; Mark 14:61-62; John 12:34; Ps. 118:26; Mark 11:9-10; Luke 19:28-38; John 12:13-15.

15. Joseph A. Fitzmyer, *The Dead Sea Scrolls and Christian Origins* (SDSSRL; Grand Rapids: Eerdmans, 2000), 37; Émile Puech, "Une Apocalypse Messianique (4Q521)," *RevQ*15 (1992): 475–519; idem, *Discoveries in the Judaean Desert XXV: Qumran Grotte 4 XVIII: Textes Hebreux (4Q521–4Q528, 4Q576–4Q579)* (Oxford: Clarendon Press, 1998), 1–38; Robert Eisenman, "A Messianic Vision," *BAR* 17, no. 6 (1991): 65; Robert Eisenman and Michael O. Wise, *The Dead Sea Scrolls Uncovered* (Shaftesbury: Element, 1992), 19–23; James D. Tabor and Michael O. Wise, "4Q521 'On Resurrection' and the Synoptic Gospel Tradition: A Preliminary Study," in *Qumran Questions*, ed. James H. Charlesworth (Sheffield: Sheffield Academic Press, 1995), 161–63; Geza Vermes, "Qumran Forum Miscellanea I," *JJS* 43 (1992): 299–305; Lawrence H. Schiffman, *Reclaiming the Dead Sea Scrolls: The History of Judaism, the Background of Christianity, the Lost Library of Qumran* (Philadelphia: Jewish Publication Society, 1994), 347–50; John J. Collins, "The Works of the Messiah," *DSD* 1 (1994): 98–112.

16. Adolf von Harnack, *The Sayings of Jesus: The Second Source of St. Matthew and St. Luke*, trans. John Richard Wilkinson (NTS 2; London: Williams & Norgate, 1908), 310–14; B. H. Streeter, *The Four Gospels*, 188; Petros Vassiliadis, "The Nature and Extent of the Q Document," *NovT* 20 (1978): 49–73, esp. 73; Athanasius Polag, *Fragmenta Q: Textheft zur Logienquelle* (Neukirchen-Vluyn: Neukirchener Verlag,1979), 30–31; Dieter Zeller, *Kommentar zur Logienquelle* (SKNT 21; Stuttgart: Katholisches Bibelwerk, 1984), 23; Migaku Sato, *Q und Prophetie: Studien zur Gattungs- und Traditionsgeschichte der Quelle Q* (Inaugural dissertation; Evangelisch-Theologische Fakultät, Bern, 1988), 25; Arland Jacobson, *The First Gospel: An Introduction to Q* (Sonoma, CA: Polebridge, 1992), 85–86; James M. Robinson, "The Sayings Gospel Q," in *The Four Gospels: Festschrift Frans Neirynck*, ed. Frans van Segbroeck, et al. (3 vols.; BETL 100; Leuven: Peeters 1992), 1:361–88. See also Heinz Schürmann, *Das Lukasevangelium* (Freiburg: Herder, 1969), 1:197, 218; Paul Hoffmann, *Studien zur Theologie der Logienquelle* (3rd ed.; NA 8. Münster: Aschendorff, 1982 [1972]), 4, 39; Arland D. Jacobson, "Wisdom Christology in Q," Ph. D. dissertation, Claremont Graduate School, 1978, 35–36, 152. For scholars denying the existence of Jesus' baptism in Q see Frans Neirynck, "The Minor Agreements and Q," in *The Gospel behind the Gospels: Current Studies on Q*, ed. Ronald A. Piper (NovTSup 75; Leiden: Brill, 1995), 49–72; Burton L. Mack, *The Lost Gospel: The Book of Q and Christian Origins* (San Francisco: HarperSanFrancisco, 1993); Vaage, *Galilean Upstarts*, 8–9.

17. Meadors, *Jesus the Messianic Herald of Salvation*; idem, "The 'Messianic' Implications of the Q Material," *JBL* 118, no. 2 (1999): 253-77. Rudolf Bultmann, "What the Sayings Source Reveals about the Early Church," in *The Shape of Q: Signal Essays on the Sayings Gospel*, ed. John S. Kloppenborg

of the term in Q *is* significant and requires explanation. Here I would like to propose that the use of the term Χριστός was problematic for the author of Q, who both appropriated and subverted traditional messianic expectations in order to construct a new identity for Jesus.

Like Paul, the author of Q sought to convince others that Jesus was the long-awaited fulfillment of God's promise to Israel. To that end, Q's wisdom traditions were integrated with material that supported Jesus' identification as "the One Who Is To Come" and the "Son of God." This is worked out most clearly in Q 3:2b–7:35, which many Q specialists regard as an integrated unit.[19] Yet the significance of the literary structure of Q 3–7 has not been given sufficient weight in recent discussions of Q's Christology, which is odd, considering that this section focuses on the question of Jesus' identity.[20] This first major section consists of an "aggressive rhetorical strategy whose focus . . . is legitimation, establishing the ethos of the sage, and recruitment" in order to legitimate Jesus as "the One Who Is To Come."[21] Yet if the central purpose of Q 3–7 is the "legitimation and authorization"[22] of Jesus' identity, the beginning of Q seems to be a carefully constructed sequence that both subverts and appropriates traditional messianic ideology. The structure of Q 3–7 frames this subversion:

(Minneapolis: Fortress Press, 1994), 23–34; originally published as "Was lässt die Spruchquelle über die Urgemeinde erkennen," *Oldenburgische Kirchenblatt* 19 (1913): 35–37, 41–44.

18. Hurtado, *Lord Jesus Christ*, 252.

19. T. W. Manson, *The Sayings of Jesus* (London: SCM, 1949), 39–148; Dale C. Allison Jr., *The Jesus Tradition in Q* (Harrisburg: Trinity Press International, 1997); Jacobson, *The First Gospel*, 125, 130; Migaku Sato, *Q und Prophetie: Studien zur Gattungs- und Traditionsgeschichte der Quelle Q* (WUNT 2d ser. 29; Tübingen: Mohr Siebeck, 1988), 35, 389; idem, "The Shape of the Q Source," in *The Shape of Q*, 156–79, esp. 166–67; John Dominic Crossan, *In Fragments: The Aphorisms of Jesus* (San Francisco: Harper and Row, 1983), 156, 342–45; James M. Robinson, "The Sayings Gospel Q," in *The Four Gospels 1992*, 1:361–88, esp. 365–66; Elisabeth Sevenich-Bax, *Israels Konfrontation mit den letzten Boten der Weisheit: Form, Funktion und Interdependenz der Weisheitselemente in der Logienquelle* (MThA 21; Altenberge: Oros, 1993), 267; Alan Kirk, *The Composition of the Sayings Source: Genre, Synchrony, and Wisdom Redaction in Q* (NovTSup 91; Leiden: Brill, 1998), 364–97.

20. Stanton, "On the Christology of Q," 27–42, esp. 29, 35.

21. Kirk, *Composition of the Sayings Source*, 367, 376.

22. Ibid., 390.

Q 3:16b-17	John's prediction of "the One Who Is To Come"
Q 3:21b-22	Jesus is "anointed" by the Spirit
Q 4:1-13	Jesus refuses "all the kingdoms of the world"
Q 6:20-49	Jesus inaugurates the nonviolent kingdom of God
Q 7:22	Jesus confirms that he is "the One Who Is To Come"
Q 7:23	Jesus blesses those not "offended" by him.

The rhetorical power and persuasive force of this structure should not be underestimated. My argument here has six components: (1) John's prediction of "the One Who Is To Come"; (2) a baptismal account in Q; (3) Q's Jesus' rejection of worldly kingdoms; (4) the placement of the Inaugural Sermon within the literary structure of Q 3–7; (5) Jesus' reply to John in Q 7:22; and (6) the isolated macarism of Q 7:23. First, the arrival of "the One Who Is To Come" is announced in Q 3:16b-17, citing Ps. 118:26 (LXX Ps. 117:26a):

> "Blessed is the one who comes in the name of the Lord."
> Εὐλογημένος ὁ ἐρχόμενος ἐν ὀνόματι Κυρίου

John predicts the arrival of a powerful figure who will vindicate the righteous and condemn the wicked. The "One Who Is To Come" is not a "usual messianic title."[23] A number of scholars see John's expectation as complementary to Q's description of the son of man, who is also powerful and will arrive unexpectedly to reward the faithful and punish the wicked. The "One Who Is To Come" is best understood as a reference to an individual human agent. Q affirms Jesus' identity as "the One Who Is To Come," but does so in such a way as to leave Jesus' future role unspecified.[24] Second, although the minor agreements are "notoriously inconclusive," there is good reason to posit a baptismal account in Q.[25] Q begins by introducing John the Baptist, a fitting way to narrate a baptismal account of Jesus, yet in the Temptation narrative Q presupposes that Jesus is the son of God. A bridge is needed, therefore,

23. Dieter Zeller, "Redactional Processes and Changing Settings," in *The Shape of Q*, 116–30, at 123, citing Paul Hoffmann, *Studien zur Theologie der Logienquelle*, 199. Fitzmyer, *The Gospel According to Luke I–IX: Introduction, Translation, and Notes* (AB 28; New York: Doubleday, 1981), 666.

24. Paul Foster, "The Pastoral Purpose of Q's Two-Stage Son of Man Christology," *Biblica* 89 (2008): 81–91, esp. 84, 91, sees the role of ὁ ἐρχόμενος as complementary to that of the "son of man." See Daniel A. Smith, *Post-Mortem Vindication of Jesus in the Sayings Gospel Q* (NTS 338; London: T&T Clark International, 2007).

25. James M. Robinson, *The Sayings Gospel Q: Collected Essays* (Leuven and Dudley, MA: Leuven University Press/Peeters, 2005), 342. Ulrich Luz, *Matthew 1–7: A Commentary*, trans. Wilhelm C. Linss (Minneapolis: Augsburg Fortress Press, 1989), 184.

between John the Baptist's own ministry and Jesus' Temptation in the desert as the son of God.[26] Jesus' "sonship" in Q seems to support an earlier baptismal account. The International Q Project gave the baptism account a grade of {C} for "uncertainty,"[27] but the verbal agreements, as minimal as they are, do point to a version of the account quite similar to Mark's, in which the heavens open and the "Spirit" descends on Jesus as he is declared to be God's Son:[28]

> 'Ιησου . . . βαπτισθε . . . νεῳχθη . . .
> ο . . . οὐρανο καὶ τὸ πνεῦμα . . . ἐπ 'αὐτόν . . . υἱ . . .

If Q included a baptismal account, it is likely that it described Jesus being "baptized" (βαπτισθε), the heavens opening (νεῳχθη . . . ο . . . οὐρανο) and the "Spirit" (τὸ πνεῦμα) descending upon him (ἐπ 'αὐτόν), after which he is declared "son" (υἱός). If so, then Jesus' "anointing" by the Spirit and being declared the "Son of God" suggests that the Spirit serves as the agent of a spiritual anointing paralleling the physical baptism.

Third, in Q 4:5-8, Jesus is tempted by the devil but refuses "all the kingdoms of the world" (πάσας τὰς βασιλείας τοῦ κόσμου), rejecting "political-messianic world rule."[29] Jesus' identity as the "Son of God" (ὁ υἱὸς τοῦ θεοῦ) is not "convertible with political messianism."[30] Nonetheless, the use of the title "Son of God" echoes the designation of Jesus as the "son" in

26. Kloppenborg, *Formation of Q*, 84–85; Robinson, *The Sayings Gospel Q*, 343; Luz, *Matthew 1–7*, 148.

27. *The Sayings Gospel Q in Greek and English*, ed. James M. Robinson, Paul Hoffmann, and John S. Kloppenborg (Minneapolis: Fortress Press, 2002), 78.

28. Matthew and Luke both drop Mark's references to John and the Jordan; both change Mark's aorist indicative use of βαπτίζω to an aorist participial form; both include the name 'Ιησοῦς (whereas Mark has the name earlier); both change Mark's use of the verb σκίζω (σχιζομένους) to the verb ἀνοίγω, although Matthew uses the aorist passive indicative (ἠνεῴχθησαν) while Luke uses the aorist passive infinitive (ἀνεῳχθῆναι); both change Mark's εἰς αὐτόν ("on him") to ἐπ' αὐτόν ("onto him"). Robert L. Webb, "Jesus' Baptism by John: Its Historicity and Significance," in *Key Events in the Life of the Historical Jesus: A Collaborative Exploration of Context and Coherence*, ed. Darrell L. Bock and Robert L. Webb (Tübingen: Mohr Siebeck, 2009), 95–150, at 98.

29. Paul Hoffmann, "Die Versuchungsgeschichte in der Logienquelle," *BZ* n.s. 13 (1969): 207–23, esp. 214; idem, *Studien zur Theologie der Logienquelle*, 74–78, 308–11, 326. See also Iris Bosold, *Pazifismus und prophetische Provokation* (SBS 90; Stuttgart: Katholisches Bibelwerk, 1978), 63. On the other hand, see Jacobson, *The First Gospel*, 89; Ernst Percy, *Die Botschaft Jesu. Eine traditionskritische und exegetische Untersuchung* (LUA, n.s. 1, 49.5; Lund: Gleerup, 1953), 13–18.

30. Kloppenborg, *Formation of Q*, 254; Rudolf Bultmann, *History of the Synoptic Tradition*, trans. John Marsh (Oxford: Blackwell, 1963), 256. Stanton, "On the Christology of Q," 34–35; Luz, *Matthew 1–7: A Commentary*, 185. See also Donald H. Juel, "The Origin of Mark's Christology," in *The Messiah* (1992),

Q 3, so Q 3:21b-22 and Q 4:1-13 function together as a unit.[31] Q 4:1-13 also develops what kind of "Son of God" Jesus is.[32] Jesus' renunciation of worldly power functions both to affirm his identity as the "son of God" and to qualify his identity by rejecting any political expectations associated with this title. Q rejects the idea of Jesus leading a political, worldly kingdom. Q 4:5-8 contains the theme of eschatological reversal, a radical countercultural stance that subverts traditional assumptions.[33] The reversal of expectations is characteristic of Q.[34] Consequently, if the popular expectation was of a warrior-king, the reversal of that expectation would be a rejection of such ideas, which is precisely what we find in Q 4:5-8.

Fourth, the location of the Inaugural Sermon (Q 6:20-49) within Q 3–7 highlights its function as the very heart of Jesus' teaching on love, compassion, and nonviolence. The Sermon's Jesus is not a warrior-king intent on restoring Jewish political independence. As in the Temptation narrative, where Jesus will not be what is expected, here too Jesus demands the reversal of expectations. The traditions from which Q developed subverted traditional "messianic" politico-military assumptions.[35]

Fifth, in Q 7:18-22, John the Baptist sends his disciples to confirm whether or not Jesus is "the One Who Is To Come" (ὁ ἐρχόμενος), echoing the earlier prediction in Q 3.[36] Here Jesus responds to John's inquiry regarding his identity

449–60; Robert G. Hamerton-Kelly, "Sacred Violence and the Messiah: The Markan Passion Narrative as a Redefinition of Messianology," in *The Messiah* (1992), 461–93.

31. Robinson, *The Sayings Gospel Q*, 343.

32. Kloppenborg, *Formation of Q*, 256; David R. Catchpole, *The Quest for Q* (Edinburgh: T&T Clark, 1993), 230–31.

33. Gary T. Meadors, "The 'Poor' in the Beatitudes of Matthew [5:3] and Luke," *GTJ* 6, no. 2 (1985): 305–14.

34. William E. Arnal, *Jesus and the Village Scribes: Galilean Conflicts and the Setting of Q* (Minneapolis: Fortress Press, 2001), 160. See Q 3:8; Q 4:5-8; Q 6:20-23; Q 6:27-28; Q 6:32-34; Q 7:9; Q 7:22; Q 12:2-3; Q 13:30; Q 13:18-19; Q 13:20-21; Q 14:11; Q 14:16-18; Q 14:26; Q 16:18; Q 17:33.

35. See also Donald Juel, "The Origin of Mark's Christology," in *The Messiah* (1992), 449–60; Hamerton-Kelly, "Sacred Violence," 461–93.

36. Martin Dibelius, *Die urchristliche Überlieferung von Johannes dem Täufer* (FRLANT 15; Göttingen: Vandenhoeck & Ruprecht, 1911), 6–8; Josef Ernst, *Johannes der Täufer: Interpretation—Geschichte—Wirkungsgeschichte* (BZNW 53; Berlin: de Gruyter, 1989), 55; Kloppenborg, *Formation of Q*, 115; Tuckett, *Q and the History of Early Christianity*, 126. On Q 7:18-23 being a later addition to an earlier layer of Q see Kloppenborg, *Formation of Q*, 166–70; Wendy Cotter, "'Yes, I Tell You, and More Than a Prophet,': The Function of John in Q," in *Conflict and Invention: Literary, Rhetorical, and Social Studies on the Sayings Gospel Q*, ed. John S. Kloppenborg (Valley Forge, PA: Trinity Press International, 1995), 135–50, esp. 135. On the disconnect between the Baptist's question and Q 7:22 see Tuckett, *Q and the History of Early Christianity*, 126. As tradition see W. D. Davies and Dale C.

by listing a series of miracles he has already performed. Q 7:22 brings together two scriptural traditions: a royal messianic proof-text in Ps. 117:2 and a string of Isaianic prophecies from Isaiah 26, 35, and 61. These scriptural references revolve around Jesus' identity as "the One Who Is To Come." Jesus' reply to John is an indirect claim to be messiah.[37] Both Matthew and Luke interpret Q 7:22 as Jesus' messianic credentials.[38] Yet here Jesus is evasive, neither confirming nor denying his identity, although Q interprets his reply through Isa. 29:18, 35:5, and 61:1. Jesus' reply is not "an explicit messianic claim," but his deeds are "part of the eschatological events in which God acts."[39] Jesus' answer "seems to be a rhetorical signal" since Q does not seem to regard the question as one that "can be answered by a clear yes or no."[40] Jesus' reply does not quite tally with John's expectations: John does not seem to have predicted a miracle-worker. The acceptance of Jesus as "the One Who Is To Come" requires a modification of expectations.

4Q521 provides a list of Isaianic miracles characterizing the messianic age,[41] that is, what God would perform when "his messiah" arrived on the scene:[42]

Allison Jr., *A Critical and Exegetical Commentary on the Gospel According to Saint Matthew* (3 vols.; ICCHSONT; Edinburgh: T&T Clark, 1988–1997), 2: 244–46; James D. G. Dunn, *Jesus and the Spirit: A Study of the Religious and Charismatic Experience of Jesus and the First Christians as Reflected in the New Testament* (London: SCM, 1975), 56–60; Werner G. Kümmel, "Jesu Antwort an Johannes den Täufer: Ein Beispiel zum Methodenproblem in der Jesusforschung," in idem, *Heilsgeschehen und Geschichte: Gesammelte Aufsätze*, ed. Erich Grässer, et al. (2 vols.; MTS 3, 16; Marburg: Elwert, 1965–1978), 2:177–200, esp. 195–200. See also Thomas Hieke, "Q 7, 22: A Compendium of Isaian Eschatology," *ETL* 82, no. 1 (2006): 175–87. James M. Robinson, "Building Blocks in the Social History of Q," in *The Sayings Gospel Q*, 500, proposes that Q 7:22 plays an important role in Q, for it provides a summarizing and organizing principle for the first major section of Q 3–7. Michael Labahn, "The Significance of Signs in Luke 7:22-23 in the Light of Isaiah 61 and the Messianic Apocalypse," in *From Prophecy to Testament: The Function of the Old Testament in the New*, ed. Craig A. Evans (Peabody, MA: Hendrickson, 2004), 146–68, at 153 n. 33, sees Q 7:18-23 as part of the earliest tradition in Q.

37. Stanton, "On the Christology of Q," 32; C. K. Barrett, *The Holy Spirit and the Gospel Tradition* (London: SPCK, 1947), 118; Dieter Lührmann, *Die Redaktion der Logienquelle* (WMANT 33; Neukirchen-Vluyn: Neukirchener, 1969), 26.

38. Stanton, "On the Christology of Q," 32.

39. Labahn, "The Significance of Signs," 158.

40. Ibid., 153; See also Cotter, "Yes, I Tell You," 140–42; James I. H. McDonald, "Questioning and Discernment in Gospel Discourse: Communicative Strategy in Matthew 11:2-19," in *Authenticating the Words of Jesus*, ed. Bruce D. Chilton and Craig A. Evans (NTTS 28, no. 1; Leiden: Brill, 1999), 333–61, at 344.

41. 4Q521 2 ii 1,7-8, 12. For a fuller discussion see Simon J. Joseph, *Jesus, Q, and the Dead Sea Scrolls: A Judaic Approach to Q* (WUNT 2d ser. 333; Tübingen: Mohr Siebeck, 2012), 163–86.

כי השמים והארץ ישמעו למשיחו
כי יכבד את חסידים על כסא מלכות עד
מתיר אסורים פוקח עורים זוקף כפופים
ונכבדות שלוא היו יעשה אדני כאשר דבר
כי ירפא חללים ומתים יחיה ענוים יבשר

The heavens and the earth will listen to his anointed . . .
He will honor the pious on a throne of an eternal kingdom,
liberating the captives, giving sight to the blind,
straightening the bent . . .
And glorious deeds that never were the Lord will perform as he said.
For he will heal the wounded, revive the dead,
and proclaim good news to the poor.

4Q521 contains an explicit reference to a messianic figure, a series of eschatological blessings described in Isaiah, and an explicit reference to the resurrection of the dead. The eschatological blessings bear a striking similarity to those in Q 7:18-22.[43] Jesus instructs the messengers to tell John what they have seen:

the blind see, and the lame walk,
the lepers are cleansed,
and the deaf hear, and the dead are raised,
and the poor have good news preached to them.

τυφλοὶ ἀναβλέπουσιν καὶ χωλοὶ περιπατοῦσιν,
λεπροὶ καθαρίζονται
καὶ κωφοὶ ἀκούουσιν, καὶ νεκροὶ ἐγείρονται
καὶ πτωχοὶ εὐαγγελίζονται

42. Fitzmyer, *The Dead Sea Scrolls and Christian Origins*, 37. For the original publication see Puech, "Une Apocalypse Messianique (4Q521)," 475–519; idem, *Discoveries in the Judaean Desert XXV*, 1–38; Eisenman, "A Messianic Vision," 65; Eisenman and Wise, *The Dead Sea Scrolls Uncovered*, 19–23; Tabor and Wise, "4Q521 'On Resurrection'"; Vermes, "Qumran Forum Miscellanea I," 299–305; Schiffman, *Reclaiming the Dead Sea Scrolls*, 347–50; Collins, "The Works of the Messiah," 98–112.

43. John S. Kloppenborg, "The Sayings Gospel Q and the Quest of the Historical Jesus," *HTR* 89 (1996): 307–44, at 330 n. 101: "The deeds of the Messiah listed in 4Q521 bear an uncanny resemblance to the deeds of Jesus listed in Q 7:22." See also Kloppenborg Verbin, *Excavating Q*, 405 n. 72: "It would appear that a synthesis of Isaian texts was already in circulation by the time of the composition of Q (and certainly, Matthew) and that Q 7:22 reflects this exegetical development."

Jesus seems to be giving John's messengers recognizable signs of his messianic identity through a kind of exegetically coded message.[44] His response to John's inquiry confirms that miraculous healing was a legitimate sign of the messianic advent. Matthew 11:2 confirms this reading, interpreting the events as "the works of the messiah" (τὰ ἔργα τοῦ Χριστοῦ).

Before the publication of 4Q521, Q 7:22 did not seem to reflect "traditional Jewish expectations about the messiah."[45] 4Q521 has characteristics reminiscent of Qumranic sectarian texts,[46] and while there is still some debate about what kind of messiah is present in 4Q521 (that is, royal, apocalyptic, or prophetic), the text is best seen as referring to a singular, royal messianic figure.[47] The

44. Tabor and Wise, "4Q521 'On Resurrection,'" 163.

45. Kloppenborg, *Formation of Q*, 107. Foster, "The Pastoral Purpose," 86: "the catalogue of activities drawn from Isaianic passages do not readily fit into a hitherto known set of Messianic expectations."

46. Émile Puech, "Some Remarks on 4Q246 and 4Q521 and Qumran Messianism," in *The Provo International Conference on the Dead Sea Scrolls: Technological Innovations, New Texts, and Reformulated Issues*, ed. Donald W. Parry and Eugene Ulrich (STDJ 30; Leiden: Brill, 1999), 552; Craig A. Evans, "Qumran's Messiah: How Important Is He?" in *Religion in the Dead Sea Scrolls*, ed. John J. Collins and Robert A. Kugler (Grand Rapids: Eerdmans, 2000), 135–49, esp. 137 n. 17; Eisenman and Wise, *The Dead Sea Scrolls Uncovered*, 19; Tabor and Wise, "4Q521 'On Resurrection' and the Synoptic Gospel Tradition," 162; James H. Charlesworth, "Have the Dead Sea Scrolls Revolutionized Our Understanding of the New Testament?" in *The Dead Sea Scrolls Fifty Years After Their Discovery: Proceedings of the Jerusalem Congress, July 20–25, 1997*, ed. Lawrence H. Schiffman, Emanuel Tov, and James C. VanderKam (Jerusalem: Israel Exploration Society/The Shrine of the Book, Israel Museum, 2000), 116–32, at 129; George J. Brooke, "The Pre-Sectarian Jesus," in *Echoes from the Caves: Qumran and the New Testament*, ed. Florentino García Martínez (STDJ 85; Leiden: Brill, 2009), 46. As non-sectarian see Vermes, "Qumran Forum Miscellanea I," 303–4; Schiffman, *Reclaiming the Dead Sea Scrolls*, 347; Roland Bergmeier, "Beobachtungen zu 4Q521 f2, II, 1-13," *ZDMG* 145 (1995): 38–48, at 44–45. Collins, "The Works of the Messiah," 106, is undecided.

47. Eisenman and Wise, *The Dead Sea Scrolls Uncovered*, 19; Florentino García Martínez, "Messianic Hopes in the Qumran Writings," in *The People of the Dead Sea Scrolls*, ed. Florentino García Martínez and J. Trebolle Barrera (Leiden: Brill, 1995), 159–89, at 169; Puech, "Une apocalypse messianique," 498–99; idem, *DJD* 25:18–19, 37; idem, "Messianism, Resurrection and Eschatology at Qumran and in the New Testament," in *The Community of the Renewed Covenant: The Notre Dame Symposium on the Dead Sea Scrolls*, ed. Eugene Ulrich and James C. VanderKam (Notre Dame, IN: University of Notre Dame Press, 1994), 235–56; Peter Stuhlmacher, *Wie treibt man biblische Theologie* (Neukirchen-Vluyn: Neukirchener Verlag, 1995), 32; Otto Betz and Rainer Riesner, *Jesus, Qumran und der Vatikan, Klarstellungen* (Giessen: Brunnen, 1993), 112. John J. Collins has suggested that the messianic figure of 4Q521 (and so perhaps the Jesus of Q 7:22) represents a "prophetic messiah of the Elijah type rather than of the royal messiah" (Collins, "The Works of the Messiah," 112). See also idem, *The Scepter and the Star*, 117–22. For criticism of Collins's position see Frans Neirynck, "Q 6, 20b-21; 7, 22 and Isaiah 61," in *Scriptures in the Gospels*, ed. Christopher M. Tuckett (BETL 131; Leuven: Leuven University Press, 1997), 27–64, at 58–59 n. 16.

author of Q inherited or had access to traditions in which such deeds were already ascribed to a coming messianic age and/or figure.[48] Q 7:22 "could be a mosaic put together in some other context and just taken over (and perhaps adapted) by Q to its redactional purposes . . . one might find here in the redactional layer of Q already dependence on an erudition shared with Qumran."[49] John J. Collins has also proposed that it is "quite possible that the author of the Sayings source knew 4Q521; at least he drew on a common tradition."[50] While interest in the relationship between 4Q521 and the New Testament was initially brought about through the premature publication of 4Q521 by Robert Eisenman and Michael Wise, who mistakenly proposed that the grammatical subject of line 12 ("raising the dead," "preaching good news to the poor") was the "messiah" mentioned in line 1,[51] it *is* significant that 4Q521 mentions the raising of the dead, an event not found in either Isaiah 61 or Psalm 146. Considering the fact that 4Q521 12 contains an allusion to Isaiah 61, and that Q 7:22 does so as well, the similarity is striking: "both texts juxtapose an allusion to Isa 61,1 with a reference to giving life to the dead."[52] In "the whole of

48. James M. Robinson, "The Sayings Gospel Q," Unpublished Claremont Graduate School Doctoral Seminar Course Notes (REL 484, Fall 1992), 5.

49. Ibid., 5.

50. Collins, "The Works of the Messiah," 107. See also Tabor and Wise, "4Q521 'On Resurrection,'" 161. Klaus Koch, "Heilandserwartungen im Judäa der Zeitenwende," in *Die Schriftrollen von Qumran: Zur aufregenden Geschichte ihrer Erforschung und Deutung*, ed. Shemaryahu Talmon (Regensburg: Pustet, 1998), 107–35, esp. 116; Michael Labahn, "The Significance of Signs in Luke 7:22 in the Light of Isaiah 61 and the Messianic Apocalypse," in *From Prophecy to Testament: The Function of the Old Testament in the New*, ed. Craig A. Evans (Peabody, MA: Hendrickson, 2004), 146-68, at 166. But see also Johannes Zimmermann, *Messianische Texte aus Qumran: Königliche, priesterliche, und prophetische Messiasvorstellungen in den Schriftfunden von Qumran* (WUNT 2d ser. 104; Tübingen: Mohr Siebeck, 1998), 343–89, esp. 343 n. 84. For a more skeptical position see Linda Novakovic, "The Relationship between 4Q521 and Matt 11:2-6/Luke 7:18-23 (Q)," in *Qumran Studies: New Approaches, New Questions*, ed. Michael T. Davis and Brent A. Strawn (Grand Rapids: Eerdmans, 2007), 225–30, at 225; Dale C. Allison Jr., *The Intertextual Jesus: Scripture in Q* (Harrisburg, PA: Trinity Press International, 2000), 112. See also Hans Kvalbein, "Die Wunder der Endzeit—Beobachtungen zu 4Q521 und Mt. 11.5p," *ZNW* 88 (1997): 111–25; idem, "The Wonders of the End-Time: Metaphoric Language in 4Q521 and the Interpretation of Matthew 11.5 par," *JSP* 9, no. 18 (1998): 87–110.

51. See Wise and Tabor, "The Messiah at Qumran," 60–65; Tabor and Wise, "4Q521 'On Resurrection." For critique see Otto Betz and Rainer Riesner, *Jesus, Qumran und der Vatikan: Klarstellungen* (Giessen: Brunnen, 1993), 111–15; Paul Stuhlmacher, *Wie treibt man Biblische Theologie* (BThSt 24; Neukirchen-Vluyn: Neukirchener, 1995), 32; Karl Wilhelm Niebuhr, "Die Werke des eschatologischen Freudenboten (4Q521 und die Jesusüberlieferung)," in *The Scriptures in the Gospels*, ed. Christopher M. Tuckett (BETL 131; Leuven: Leuven University Press, 1997), 637–46; Kvalbein, "Wonders of the End-Time."

Jewish literature between the Bible and the Mishnah, it is only in 4Q521 and the Jesus saying" in Q that Isaiah 61 is expanded with a statement about the raising of the dead.[53] John Kloppenborg notes that "neither the cleansing of lepers . . . nor raising of the dead . . . is mentioned in Psalm 146 or any of the Isaianic texts which seem otherwise to have informed both 4Q521 and Q 7:22."[54] The eschatological blessings described in 4Q521 bear a striking resemblance to those described in Q 7:22.

4Q521 2 ii	Q 7:22
Blind see	Blind see
Lame walk	Lame walk
Lepers cleansed	
Deaf hear	Deaf hear
Dead raised	Dead raised
Poor/Good News	Poor/Good News

The author(s) of Q would have had to *independently* allude to three different Isaiah texts in order to accomplish something similar to what the author of 4Q521 has done. 4Q521 is a missing link in the compositional history of Q, since 4Q521 links language from Isaiah 61 with language from Psalm 146 set in an eschatological context.[55] A "similar exegetical tradition . . . lies behind the Q tradition."[56] For Christopher Tuckett, Isa. 61:1-2 provides "an even closer link" to Q 7:22 than Q 6:20 does.[57] Tuckett proposes that "the language and form" of Q was "significantly influenced . . . by an exegetical tradition in which Isa 61 and Ps 146 had already been allowed to influence and interpret each other."

Jesus' answer to John's query appeals to an Essenic/Qumranic sequence of proof-texts, which implies that John and Jesus both knew what they were. Q 7:22 represents Jesus as fulfilling John the Baptist's and Qumranic/Essenic messianic expectations, although not in the way they may have anticipated.

Sixth, the dissonance between John's expectation and Jesus' reply is expressed in Q 7:23, a beatitude expressing the truth that some could be "offended" by Jesus: "Blessed is whoever is not offended (σκανδαλισθῇ) by

52. Christopher M. Tuckett, "Scripture and Q," in *The Scripture in the Gospels*, 3–26, at 22.

53. George J. Brooke, *The Dead Sea Scrolls and the New Testament* (Minneapolis: Fortress Press, 2005), 262.

54. Kloppenborg Verbin, *Excavating Q*, 123 n.17.

55. Tuckett, "Scripture and Q," esp. 24.

56. Christopher M. Tuckett, "Introduction," *The Scriptures in the Gospels*, ed. Christopher M. Tuckett (BETL 131; Leuven: Leuven University Press, 1997), xiii–xiv.

57. Tuckett, "Scripture and Q," 20, 24.

me."[58] Not only does Q 7:23 serve "an apologetic purpose" in reflecting Q's criticism of "this generation,"[59] it also echoes Paul's own recognition of the "scandal" of the cross. At the same time, Q 7:23 rhetorically secures and legitimizes Jesus' identity as the "Son of God" and "the One Who Is To Come" by declaring those "blessed" who are not offended by him. The saying both criticizes "this generation" of nonbelievers and affirms the blessedness of the faithful. In this light Q 7:23 is comparable with 4Q521's promise of salvation to the pious.[60] The framework of the first major section of Q, and particularly Q 7:18-23,[61] mediates the conflict between John's expectation and Jesus' fulfillment of that role.[62] Q 7:22-23 is a pivotal narrative moment in Q, for it betrays a tension, an admission of scandal, an awareness that Jesus might disappoint some expectations.

The Jesus of Q is not a king defending territory, maintaining an army, or violently expelling his enemies. He is not a priest in the Temple. He shares characteristics with prophetic figures, but if John the Baptist is "more than a prophet," then what does that make Jesus, a figure whom "prophets and kings" have longed to see (Q 10:24)? The author of Q does not use Χριστός as a title for Jesus, but this does not mean that the author of Q was not interested in or rejected messianic ideas. The author avoids the term as a problematic referent but exalts Jesus by advancing a program essentially opposed to traditional messianic ideas that required and presupposed politico-military violence.

Q both affirms and appropriates Jesus as "anointed" while it simultaneously qualifies and subverts traditional or popular messianic associations by reinterpreting them through the lens of eschatological reversal: Jesus is the embodiment of an eschatological reversal of royal messianic expectations. The author of Q drew on motifs consistent with royal messianism but aimed higher, moving on to more exalted referents,[63] giving the title "Son of God" greater significance in Q 10:22, conflating the earthly son of man sayings with sayings

58. Paul uses similar language to describe how Jesus was an "offense" (σκάνδαλον) to Jews (1 Cor. 1:23).

59. Labahn, "The Significance of Signs," 161, cites 7:31; 11:29-32, 51.

60. Ibid., 157.

61. Ibid., citing Ron Cameron, "'What Have You Come Out to See? Characterizations of John and Jesus in the Gospels," *Semeia* 49 (1990): 35–70.

62. Kirk, *The Composition of the Sayings Source*, 380; Sevenich-Bax, *Konfrontation*, 326, Hoffmann, *Studien zur Theologie der Logienquelle*, 214–15, Cotter, "Yes, I tell you, and more than a prophet," 135–50, esp. 140–41; John S. Kloppenborg, "Literary Convention, Self-Evidence and the Social History of the Q People," *Semeia* 55 (1991): 77–102, esp. 93–94; Robinson, "The Sayings Gospel Q," 361–62.

63. Hurtado, *Lord Jesus Christ*, 252.

identifying Jesus with the cosmic figure of Dan. 7:13, and identifying Jesus as "the One Who Is To Come," an eschatological agent of judgment.

We are left, then, with another Christological enigma. The Jesus of Q is "anointed," but he is not a traditional Davidic king. Like Paul, the author of Q is well aware that Jesus "scandalizes" and offends his Jewish contemporaries. But if the Jesus of Q does not fulfill traditional Davidic expectations, then what *kind* of "messiah" is he?

7

The Messianic Secret of the Son of Man

Like Q, the Gospel of Mark seems to be well aware that Jesus did not fulfill or outwardly conform to traditional messianic expectations.[1] For example, in Mark 12:35-37 ("Is the messiah the son of David?") Jesus seems to be "disputing the Davidic origin of the messiah."[2] Was this saying created by the Church? Some have thought so,[3] but Jesus seems to be doing more here than merely disputing Davidic messianism; he appears to be claiming an authority *higher* than Davidic messianism.[4] Mark's Christology is designed to address such concerns by developing two distinctive motifs: the idea of a "messianic secret" and the motif of the suffering "son of man." Mark's Gospel is a narrative "apology for the

1. On Mark's christological focus on the cross see Michael F. Bird, "Jesus is the Christ: Messianic Apologetics in the Gospel of Mark," *RTR* 64 (2005): 1–15; C. Clifton Black, "Christ Crucified in Paul and in Mark: Reflections on an Intracanonical Conversation," in *Theology and Ethics in Paul and His Interpreters. Festschrift V. P. Furnish*, ed. E. H. Lovering and Jerry L. Sumney (Nashville: Abingdon, 1966), 184–206, at 201–6. On Mark's relative lack of interest in Davidic messianism see James G. Crossley, *The Date of Mark's Gospel: Insight from the Law in Earliest Christianity* (London: T&T Clark International, 2004), 76–79, although see Mark 10:48, 11:10, 12:35-37.

2. Walter Wink, *The Human Being: Jesus and the Enigma of the Son of the Man* (Minneapolis: Fortress Press, 2002). See also Eduard Schweizer, *The Good News according to Mark*, trans. Donald H. Madvig (Richmond: John Knox, 1970), 256; Joel Marcus, "The Jewish War and the Sitz im Leben of Mark," *JBL* 111 (1992): 441–62, at 457.

3. Rudolf Bultmann, *The History of the Synoptic Tradition*, trans. John Marsh (Oxford: Blackwell, 1963), 136; Wilhelm Bousset, *Kyrios Christos: A History of the Belief in Christ from the Beginnings of Christianity to Irenaeus* (Nashville: Abingdon, 1970), 43.

4. Vincent Taylor, *The Gospel According to St. Mark: The Greek Text with Introduction, Notes, and Indexes* (Grand Rapids: Baker Book House, 1981), 493; R. T. France, *Jesus and the Old Testament: His Application of Old Testament Passages to Himself and His Mission* (Downers Grove: InterVarsity, 1971), 101; I. Howard Marshall, *The Gospel of Luke: A Commentary on the Greek Text* (NIGTC; Grand Rapids: Eerdmans, 1978), 743–49; William L. Lane, *The Gospel According to Mark* (NICNT; Grand Rapids: Eerdmans, 1974), 435. See also Chrys C. Caragounis, *The Son of Man: Vision and Interpretation* (WUNT 38; Tübingen: Mohr Siebeck, 1986), 222–23.

cross."[5] Both Paul and Mark focus on the cross as the centerpiece of their respective theologies and Christologies.[6] Indeed, the idea that Paul influenced the composition of the Gospel of Mark is the dominant view in Markan studies.[7] The Gospel of Mark represents a Petrine-Pauline compromise.[8]

Since the publication of William Wrede's *Das Messiasgeheimnis in den Evangelien* in 1901, it has generally been thought that the Gospel of Mark is dominated by the theme of a "messianic secret," a theological motif invented or developed by the author to convince readers that, despite appearances, Jesus really was the messiah.[9] Jesus goes out of his way to keep his identity a secret. He directs his disciples *not* to tell anyone about him[10] or about the things they have seen.[11] He forbids others to tell of his cures,[12] and he silences the demons who

5. On Mark as an apology for the cross see Robert H. Gundry, *Mark: A Commentary on His Apology for the Cross* (Grand Rapids: Eerdmans, 1993), 1022–26; Craig A. Evans, *Mark 8:27–16:20*, ed. Ralph P. Martin and Lynn A. Losie (WBC 34b; Nashville: Thomas Nelson, 2002), xciii; Joel F. Williams, "Is Mark's Gospel an Apology for the Cross?" *BBR* 12 (2002): 97–122; Robert H. Gundry, "A Rejoinder to Joel F. Williams' 'Is Mark's Gospel an Apology for the Cross?'" *BBR* 12 (2002): 123–40.

6. Bird, "Mark," 39 n. 29.

7. Michael D. Goulder, "Those Outside (Mk 4:10-12)," *NovT* 33 (1991): 289–302; David Seeley, "Rulership and Service in Mark 10:41-45," *NovT* 35 (1993): 234–50; William Telford, *The Theology of the Gospel of Mark* (Cambridge: Cambridge University Press, 1999), 164–69; Joel Marcus, "Mark—Interpreter of Paul," *NTS* 46 (2000): 473–87; Michael D. Goulder, "Jesus' Resurrection and Christian Origins: A Response to N. T. Wright," *JSHJ* 3 (2005): 187–95; Michael F. Bird, "Mark: Interpreter of Peter and Disciple of Paul," in *Paul and the Gospels: Christologies, Conflicts and Convergences*, ed. Michael F. Bird and Joel Willitts, (LNTS 411; London: T&T Clark, 2011), 30–61, esp. 32. On the possibility that Mark (c. mid-40s C.E.) influenced Paul, see Crossley, *The Date of Mark's Gospel*, 47–55; idem, "Mark, Paul and the Question of Influences," in *Paul and the Gospels*, 10–29; Maurice Casey, *Jesus of Nazareth: An Independent Historian's Account of his Life and Teachings* (London and New York: T&T Clark/Continuum, 2010).

8. Ferdinand Christian Baur, *Das Markusevangelium nach seinem Ursprung und Charakter* (Tübingen: Fues, 1851); David Dungan, "The Purpose and Provenance of the Gospel of Mark According to the 'Two-Gospel' (Griesbach) Hypothesis," in *Colloquy on New Testament Studies: A Time for Reappraisal and Fresh Approaches*, ed. Bruce Corley (Macon: Mercer University Press, 1983), 133–56, at 145, 155–156.

9. William Wrede, *Das Messiasgeheimnis in den Evangelien: Zugleich ein Beitrag zum Verständnis des Markusevangeliums* (3d ed.; Göttingen: Vandenhoeck & Ruprecht, 1901). See also Rudolf Bultmann, *The Theology of the New Testament*, trans. Kendrick Grobel (2 vols.; New York Scribner, 1951–1955), 1:32; Ernst Käsemann, "The Problem of the Historical Jesus," in idem, *Essays on New Testament Themes* (SBT 41; London: SCM, 1964), 15–47, at 43; Günther Bornkamm, *Jesus of Nazareth*, trans. Irene and Fraser McLuskey with James M. Robinson (New York: Harper, 1960), 171–72, 206–10.

10. Mark 8:30.

11. Mark 9:9.

12. Mark 1:43-45; 5:43; 7:36; 8:26.

recognize him.[13] The crowds are told to keep silent.[14] When Peter confesses that Jesus is the messiah, Jesus enjoins his disciples to secrecy.[15] Throughout Mark, Jesus commands his disciples as well as unclean spirits and demons not to reveal his identity or activities.[16] He withdraws from crowds, embarks on secret missions, moves around Galilee unknown and hidden,[17] and instructs his disciples privately in secret mysteries.[18] Wrede concluded that Jesus' messianic identity originated *after* he was believed to have been resurrected.[19] While Wrede was certainly correct in identifying this literary-theological motif, his conclusions overlooked certain historical factors.[20] First, anyone claiming to be a "messiah" in first-century Judea would have been putting both himself and his followers in immediate physical danger. The Romans did not look favorably upon self-proclaimed "kings." Secrecy and discretion would have been necessary on a purely practical level, and do not in and of themselves require literary invention. What Wrede understood to be Mark's theological agenda could also be regarded as an historically plausible and perhaps even socio-political necessity.

Second, Jesus never *denies* a messianic identification; he simply insists it be kept secret. Mark understands this to mean that the time for Jesus' public declaration had not yet arrived, but the question is whether Jesus' secrecy was *merely* a literary device or whether it represents Jesus' actual behavior? The idea that the historical Jesus kept his identity a secret on purpose has been supported by a number of scholars.[21] Some have argued that Mark's "messianic secret" actually reflects Jesus' covert self-disclosure. Wrede acknowledged that

13. Mark 1:23-25, 34; 3:11-12; 5:6; 9:20.

14. Mark 10:47.

15. Mark 8:29.

16. Mark 1:23-25, 34; 1:43-45; 3:11-12; 5:43; 5:6; 7:36; 8:26; 9:20.

17. Mark 7:24; 9:30.

18. Mark 4:10-12; 4:34; 7:17-23; 8:31; 9:28-29, 31, 33-35; 10:33-34; 13:3-37.

19. William Wrede, *The Messianic Secret*, trans. J. C. G. Greig (Cambridge and London: James Clarke, 1971), 67.

20. David Aune, "The Problem of the Messianic Secret," *NovT* 11 (1969): 1–31; Richard N. Longenecker, "The Messianic Secret in the Light of Recent Discoveries," *EQ* 41 (1969): 207–15; James D. G. Dunn, "The Messianic Secret in Mark," *TynBul* 21 (1970): 92–117; Christopher L. Mearns, "Parables, Secrecy and Eschatology in Mark's Gospel," *SJT* 44 (1991): 423–42; James H. Charlesworth, "From Messianology to Christology: Problems and Prospects," in *The Messiah: Developments in Earliest Judaism and Christianity*, ed. James H. Charlesworth (Minneapolis: Fortress Press, 1992), 3–35, at 34; David F. Watson, "The 'Messianic Secret': Demythologizing a Non-existent Markan Theme," *JT* 110 (2006): 33–44; idem, *Honor Among Christians: The Cultural Key to the Messianic Secret* (Minneapolis: Fortress Press, 2010). In this work Watson refers to the "secret" passages as "concealment passages" (p. 3).

there were contradictions between Mark's "messianic secret" and the ministry of Jesus.[22] For example, how can Jesus' commands to silence be reconciled with the public nature of his miracles? Why was Jesus so famous if he constantly tried to keep his identity a secret? And why do the recipients of his blessings ignore his commands?[23] If Jesus was trying to keep his identity a secret, why did he stage a "triumphal entry?" If Jesus' opponents in Jerusalem knew he was referring to them as "wicked husbandmen,"[24] wasn't he identifying himself as God's son? If Jesus believed his exorcisms to be messianic "signs,"[25] why did he attempt to keep his identity a secret? Why did Jesus command those he cured not to reveal his identity if he knew they would only ignore him? Jesus makes highly authoritative claims for himself. He pronounces the forgiveness of sins,[26] calls sinners to repentance,[27] announces himself as "Lord of the Sabbath,"[28] claims power over Satan,[29] and teaches his disciples about the significance of his role.[30] Jesus clearly speaks and behaves in a way that suggests messianic authority.[31]

21. Albert Schweitzer, *The Quest of the Historical Jesus: A Critical Study of its Progress from Reimarus to Wrede*, trans. W. Montgomery (New York: Macmillan, 1910). But see also William Sanday, *The Life of Christ in Recent Research* (Oxford: Clarendon, 1907); Ernst Lohmeyer, *Das Evangelium des Markus* (Göttingen: Vandenhoek & Ruprecht, 1963); Erik Sjöberg, *Der verborgene Menschensohn in den Evangelien* (Lund: Gleerup, 1955). James D. G. Dunn, "The Messianic Secret in Mark," in *The Messianic Secret*, ed. Christopher M. Tuckett (IRT 1; Minneapolis: Fortress Press, 1983), 116–31, at 122; Ragnar Leivestad, *Jesus in His own Perspective: An Examination of His Sayings, Actions, and Eschatological Titles*, trans. David E. Aune (Minneapolis: Augsburg, 1987), 76, 174. See Pss. Sol. 18.5; *4 Ezra* 7.28-29; 12.31-34; 13:26; *2 Bar.* 30:1-2; *Odes Sol.* 41.15. See also Tuckett, ed., *The Messianic Secret*, 1; Ben Witherington III, *The Gospel of Mark: A Socio-Rhetorical Commentary* (Grand Rapids: Eerdmans, 2001), 41; R. T. France, *The Gospel of Mark: A Commentary on the Greek Text* (Grand Rapids: Eerdmans, 2002), 31; Vincent Taylor, *The Gospel According to St. Mark: The Greek Text with Introduction, Notes, and Indexes* (Grand Rapids: Baker Book House, 1981), 377; James H. Charlesworth, "From Jewish Messianology to Christian Christology: Some Caveats and Perspectives," in *Judaisms and their Messiahs at the Turn of the Christian Era*, ed. Jacob Neusner and William Scott (New York: Cambridge University Press, 1987), 225–64, at 252; T. W. Manson, *The Servant-Messiah: A Study of the Public Ministry of Jesus* (Cambridge: Cambridge University Press, 1953), 71–72; Ben Witherington III, *The Christology of Jesus* (Minneapolis: Fortress Press, 1990), 143.

22. Wrede, *The Messianic Secret*, 124–29; Dunn, "Messianic Secret in Mark" (1983), 121.

23. Mark 1:45; 7:36; 7:24.

24. Mark 12:12.

25. Q 7:22.

26. Mark 2:10.

27. Mark 2:17.

28. Mark 2:28.

29. Mark 3:27.

30. Mark 8:31-33; 9:31-32; 10:32-34, 45; 14:22-25.

31. Meadors, *Jesus the Messianic Herald of Salvation*, 322.

The "messianic secret" may not be just a narrative device or artificial theological construct but rather a literary portrayal of Jesus' actual historical personality.[32]

Third, there are many elements in Mark's narrative that neither hide nor obscure Jesus' messianic identity. For example, Mark declares his Gospel to be "the good news of Jesus *Christ*, Son of God."[33] Peter clearly "confesses" that Jesus is the "Christ."[34] Unclean spirits recognize Jesus as the "Son of God.[35]" Mark assumes that "messiah" and "son of man" are equivalent titles.[36] After Jesus enters Jerusalem, a woman *anoints* him.[37] Jesus is mocked as "king" by Roman soldiers.[38] The *titulus* reads "king of the Jews."[39] One explanation for Jesus' secrecy is that he redefined the messianic role in order to avoid its political implications. Many Jews thought that a "messianic" king would lead the Jewish people in war against the Romans,[40] but Jesus did not want to mislead either his own people or the Romans with ideas of a military revolution. Jesus conceived the role differently from the popular expectation and never used the title "messiah" because of its connotations. Jesus' silence need not be interpreted as denial.[41]

Fourth, the idea that the messiah would be hidden until the time of his appearance is well attested in Early Jewish literature.[42] Some thought the

32. Dunn, "The Messianic Secret in Mark" (1983), 128–30.

33. Mark 1:1.

34. Mark 8:29.

35. Mark 3:7-12.

36. Mark 8; 14:53-65.

37. Mark 14:3-9.

38. Mark 15:16-20.

39. Mark 15:26.

40. John P. Meier, "From Elijah-like Prophet to Royal Davidic Messiah," in *Jesus: A Colloquium in the Holy Land*, ed. Doris Donnelly (New York: Continuum, 2001), 45–83, at 63, 71.

41. Wrede seems to have "renounced" his own view of the "messianic secret" in a private letter to Adolf von Harnack shortly before his death. See Martin Hengel, *Studies in Early Christianity* (Edinburgh: T&T Clark, 1995), 17, and also in Martin Hengel and Anna Maria Schwemer, *Jesus und das Judentum*, Vol. 1, *Geschichte des frühen Christentums* (4 vols.; Tübingen: Mohr Siebeck, 2007), 507–10; also Hans Rollmann and Werner Zager, "Unveröffentlichte Briefe William Wredes zur Problematisierung des messianischen Selbstverständnisses Jesu," *Zeitschrift für neuere Theologiegeschichte* 8 (2001): 274–317; Andrew Chester, *Messiah and Exaltation: Jewish Messianic and Visionary Traditions and New Testament Christology* (WUNT 207; Tübingen: Mohr Siebeck, 2007), 309.

42. *Pss. Sol.* 17; *1 En.* 46:1-3; 48:6-7; 62:7; *4 Ezra* 7:28-29; 12:31-34; 13:26, 32, 52; 14:9; *2 Bar.* 30:1-2; *Odes of Sol.* 41:15; Mic. 4:8; Jer. 3:8; *2 Ezra* 12.32; *2 Bar.* 29:3; 39:7; 73:1; *3 En.* 48:10A; Justin, *Dial.* 8, 10; *Midr. Pss* 21.1; *Pesiq. Rab., Piska* 34.2; *Tg. Jon. re Jer.* 30:21; *Midr. Num. Rab.* 11.2; *Midr. Ruth Rab.* 5.6; *Midr. Son Rab.* 2.9.3; *Pesiq. R. Kahana, Piska* 5.8; *Yal. Shimon* 518, 581, 986; *b. Sukk.* 52b. See also J. C. O'Neill, "The Silence of Jesus," *NTS* 15 (1969): 153–67.

messiah would be hard to identify.[43] Others believed he would come from Bethlehem. Still others believed that "when the messiah comes, no one will know where he is from."[44] The *Parables of Enoch* (*1 En.* 37–71) refer to the son of man as "hidden" before his public appearance.[45] *4 Ezra* states that "no one on earth can see my Son or those who are with him except in the time of his day,"[46] when the messiah "will be revealed."[47] *2 Baruch* affirms that there will come a time "when the anointed one shall be revealed."[48] A "theology of hiddenness" was "natural among those discussing the Messiah."[49] Justin Martyr also refers to a Jewish tradition of the messiah being "hidden" before his public ministry.[50]

If the motif of the "hidden messiah" is a literary and theological *component* of Mark's Christology, the literary and theological *center* of Mark is the revelation of Jesus as the messianic son of man.[51] Mark contains fourteen son of man sayings, which can be grouped into three distinct categories: (1) earthly son of man sayings; (2) suffering son of man sayings; and (3) coming son of man sayings.

The phrase "son of man" (ὁ υἱὸς τοῦ ἀνθρώπου), derived from the Hebrew בן אדם and/or the Aramaic בר (א)נש, appears over eighty times in the Gospels,[52] so it seems to have been used as a title for Jesus in Palestinian Jewish Christian circles.[53] Many scholars think that Jesus used the expression.[54] Some have concluded that Jesus referred to the son of man as a figure other

43. J. C. O'Neill, *Who Did Jesus Think He Was?* (BI 11; Leiden: Brill, 1995).

44. John 7:27.

45. *1 En.* 36–71. Erik Sjöberg, *Der Menschensohn im äthiopischen Henochbuch* (Lund: Gleerup, 1946); *Der verborgene Menschensohn in den Evangelien* (Lund: Gleerup, 1955). See *1 En.* 62.6–7.

46. *4 Ezra* 13:52.

47. *4 Ezra* 13:26, 52; *1 En.* 48:6, 62:7.

48. *2 Bar.* 29:3.

49. J. C. G. Greig, "Translator's Introduction," in Wrede, *The Messianic Secret*, xv.

50. Justin Martyr, *Dial.* 8.4; 110.1.

51. Morna D. Hooker, *The Son of Man in Mark: A Study of the Background of the Term "Son of Man" and Its Use in St. Mark's Gospel* (Montreal: McGill University Press, 1967); Gordon D. Kirchhevel, "The 'Son of Man' Passages in Mark," *BTB* 9 (1999): 181–87; Simon Gathercole, "The Son of Man in Mark's Gospel," *ExpT* 115, no. 11 (2004): 366–72; Edward Adams, "The Coming of the Son of Man in Mark's Gospel," *TynBull* 56, no. 2 (2005): 39–61.

52. Mark uses it fourteen times; Matthew thirty times; Luke twenty-five times; John twelve times. It is also attested in all strata of the early Jesus tradition, including Q, Mark, Matthew, Luke, John, and *Thomas*.

53. Delbert Burkett, *The Son of Man Debate: A History and Evaluation* (SNTSMS 107; New York: Cambridge University Press, 1999), 123. Ivan Havener, *Q: The Sayings of Jesus (with a Reconstruction of Q by Athanasius Polag)* (GNS 19; Wilmington, DE: Michael Glazier, 1987), 72–77.

than himself.[55] Others have argued that *none* of the sayings go back to Jesus because the tradition derived from post-Easter reflection on his death and vindication.[56] Since the late 1960s the assumption that "son of man" referred to an apocalyptic title has been challenged by a model in which Jesus used the expression idiomatically and his followers retroactively apocalypticized the expression.[57] Geza Vermes argued that the expression "son of man" was a

54. Jürgen Becker, *Jesus von Nazaret* (Berlin: de Gruyter, 1996), 249–67; David R. Catchpole, "The Angelic Son of Man in Luke 12:8," *NovT* 24 (1982): 255–65; John J. Collins, "The Second Coming," *CS* 34 (1995): 262–74; Adela Yarbro Collins, "Apocalyptic Son of Man Sayings," in *The Future of Early Christianity*, ed. Birger A. Pearson (Minneapolis: Fortress Press, 1991), 220–28; Volker Hampel, *Menschensohn und historischer Jesus* (Neukirchen-Vluyn: Neukirchener Verlag, 1990); Marius Reiser, *Jesus and Judgment* (Minneapolis: Fortress Press, 1997); E. P. Sanders, *The Historical Figure of Jesus* (London: Penguin, 1993), 247–48; Dale C. Allison Jr., *Jesus of Nazareth: Millenarian Prophet* (Minneapolis: Fortress Press, 1998), 115–20; Gerd Theissen and Annette Merz, *The Historical Jesus: A Comprehensive Guide* (Minneapolis: Fortress Press, 1998), 548; Christopher M. Tuckett, "The Son of Man and Daniel 7: Q and Jesus," in *The Sayings Source Q and the Historical Jesus*, ed. Andreas Lindemann (BETL 158; Leuven: Leuven University Press, 2001), 371–94, at 390; Meadors, *Jesus the Messianic Herald of Salvation*, 145; Chrys C. Caragounis, *The Son of Man: Vision and Interpretation* (WUNT 38; Tübingen: Mohr Siebeck, 1986), 165.

55. See Rudolf Bultmann, *The History of the Synoptic Tradition*, trans. John Marsh (Oxford: Blackwell, 1963), 112,122, 128, 151–52; Adela Yarbro Collins, "Jesus as Son of Man," in Adela Yarbro Collins and John J. Collins, *King and Messiah as Son of God: Divine, Human, and Angelic Messianic Figures in Biblical and Related Literature* (Grand Rapids: Eerdmans, 2008), 149–74, at 150–51.

56. Philip Vielhauer, "Gottesreich und Menschensohn in der Verkündigung Jesu," in *Festschrift für Günther Dehn, zum 75. Geburtstag am 18. April 1957* (Neukirchen: Kreis Moers, Verlag der Buchhandlung Erziehungsvereins, 1957), 51–79, 90–91; idem, "Jesus und der Menschensohn," *ZTK* 60 (1963): 133–77; Norman Perrin, "Mark XIV.62: The End Product of a Christian Pesher Tradition?" *NTS* 12 (1966): 150–55; idem, "The Son of Man in Ancient Judaism and Primitive Christianity: A Suggestion," *BR* 11 (1966): 17–28; idem, "The Son of Man in the Synoptic Tradition," *BR* 13 (1968): 3–25; idem, *Rediscovering the Teachings of Jesus* (New York: Harper and Row, 1967), 154–206, esp. 197–98; Helmut Koester, "One Jesus and Four Primitive Gospels," *HTR* 61 (1968): 203–47; idem, *Ancient Christian Gospels: Their History and Development* (Philadelphia: Trinity Press International, 1990), 149–62; Hans Conzelmann, "Present and Future in the Synoptic Tradition," *JTC* 5 (1968): 26–44; Käsemann, "The Problem of the Historical Jesus," 43; James M. Robinson, *A New Quest of the Historical Jesus* (London: SCM, 1961), 100–4; John S. Kloppenborg, *The Formation of Q: Trajectories in Ancient Wisdom Collections* (Philadelphia: Fortress Press, 1987), 322.

57. Arnold Meyer, *Jesu Muttersprache: Das galiläische Aramäisch in seiner Bedeutung für die Erklärung der Reden Jesu und der Evangelien überhaupt* (Freiburg im Breisgau/Leipzig: Mohr Siebeck, 1896); Hans Lietzmann, *Der Menschensohn: Ein Beitrag zur neutestamentlichen Theologie* (Freiburg im Breisgau/Leipzig: Mohr Siebeck, 1896), 38; Paul Fiebig, *Der Menschensohn: Jesu Selbstbezeichnung mit besonderer Berücksichtigung des aramäischen Sprachgebrauches für 'Mensch'* (Tübingen: Mohr Siebeck, 1901). Matthew Black, "Unsolved New Testament Problems: The 'Son of Man' in the Teachings of Jesus," *ET* 60 (1949):

translation of the Aramaic בר נשא or בר נש, the equivalent of the Hebrew בן אדם, which could refer to (1) human beings in the generic sense; (2) some human being; or (3) "I," as a periphrasis.[58] Vermes claimed that he found ten Palestinian Aramaic examples of this phrase in which the speaker refers to himself not as "I," but as "the son of man," in the third person, and that in each case "son of man" is not a title.[59] He suggested that the phrase was used in a generic and/or indefinite sense *and* as a circumlocution for "I," as a way to avoid immodesty. Vermes concluded that the apocalyptic son of man sayings were created by Jesus' followers by connecting Jesus' idiomatic speech to Dan. 7:13. This proposal has subsequently been adopted by a number of scholars, including Barnabas Lindars and Maurice Casey.[60]

Maurice Casey is well known for his many contributions to the son of man problem.[61] He argues that ὁ υἱὸς τοῦ ἀνθρώπου is not "natural Greek" and must be explained as a translation of בר (א)נש(א). For Casey, the expression

32–36, rejected the idea that בר נש referred to the speaker. See also previous discussions by Nathaniel Schmidt, "Was בר נשא a Messianic Title," *JBL* 15 (1896): 36–53; Julius Wellhausen, "Des Menschen Sohn," in idem, *Skizze und Vorarbeiten* (Berlin: Reimer, 1899), 6: 187–215, found a generic sense of בר נשא in Mark 2:10, 28; Luke 12:10, and indefinite in Matt. 11:19. See also Georges Dupont, *Le Fils de l'Homme: essai historique et critique* (Paris: Fischbacher, 1924); Charles Alfred Honoré Guignebert, *Jesus* (New York: Knopf, 1935), 270–79.

58. Geza Vermes, "Appendix E: The Use of בר נשא/בר נש in Jewish Aramaic," in Matthew Black, *An Aramaic Approach to the Gospels and Acts* (3d ed.; Oxford: Clarendon, 1967), 310–30. Barnabas Lindars, *Jesus Son of Man: A Fresh Examination of the Son of Man Sayings in the Gospels in the Light of Recent Research* (Grand Rapids: Eerdmans, 1984), sees it as referring to "I" or "a man like me."

59. Geza Vermes, *Jesus and the World of Judaism* (Philadelphia: Fortress Press, 1984), 90.

60. See also Athanasius Polag, *Die Christologie der Logienquelle* (WMANT 45; Neukirchen-Vluyn: Neukirchener Verlag, 1977); Barnabas Lindars, "Jesus as Advocate: A Contribution to the Christology Debate," *BJRL* 62 (1980): 476–97; idem, "The New Look on the Son of Man," *BJRL* 63 (1981): 437–62; idem, *Jesus Son of Man*; idem, "Response to Richard Bauckham: The Idiomatic Use of *Bar Enasha*," *JSNT* 23 (1985): 35–41; Richard Bauckham, "The Son of Man: 'A Man in My Position' or 'Someone'?" *JSNT* 23 (1985): 23–33; Reginald Fuller, "The Son of Man: A Reconsideration," in *The Living Text: Essays in Honor of Ernest W. Saunders*, ed. Dennis E. Groh and Robert Jewett (Lanham, MD: University Press of America, 1985), 207–17; Christopher L. Mearns, "The Son of Man Trajectory and Eschatological Development," *ExpT* 97 (1985/86): 8–12; Donald J. Goergen, *The Mission and Ministry of Jesus* (Wilmington, DE: Michael Glazier, 1986), 180–202; Rollin Kearns, *Die Entchristologisierung des Menschensohnes. Die Übertragung des Traditionsgefüges um den Menschensohn auf Jesus* (Tübingen: Mohr, 1988); John Dominic Crossan, *The Historical Jesus: The Life of a Mediterranean Jewish Peasant* (New York: Harper Collins, 1991), 238–59; idem, *Jesus: A Revolutionary Biography* (San Francisco: HarperSanFrancisco, 1994), 49–53; Bruce Chilton, "The Son of Man: Human and Heavenly," in *The Four Gospels 1992: Festschrift Frans Neirynck*, ed. Frans Van Segbroeck, et al. (3 vols.; BETL 100; Leuven: Peeters, 1992), 1:203–18; idem, "The Son of Man: Who Was He?" *BR* 12 (1996): 35–39, 45–47.

"son of man" originated as an Aramaic phrase referring to humanity as a whole that was sometimes used idiomatically to apply to the speaker himself in a "modest" way.[62] If Jesus used the expression, he used it to refer to himself while including its generic meaning. Lindars explained the use of the two articles by "the idiomatic use of the definite article in indefinite statements" in which the definite article denotes "a particular but unspecified member or group of members of the class."[63] Richard Bauckham suggested that Jesus used בר (א)נש as "a deliberately ambiguous self-reference."[64] Reginald Fuller proposed a similar theory, arguing that בר נשא was used by Jesus in the sense of "a man" or "a fellow."[65] Others emphasize Jesus' use of the phrase in a generic sense.[66]

The main problem with the idiomatic interpretation, however, is that it can only explain *some* of the many son of man sayings. Most of them cannot be explained by the use of the proposed idiom and must have been later inventions. Idiomatic interpretations of many sayings, even given the semantic range of the proposed idiom, also seem strained. The majority of the sayings reflecting on the betrayal, suffering, atonement, vindication, and return of the son of man are not only titular but have their inspiration, their *Sitz im Leben*, in the passion, death, and resurrection of Jesus.[67] The proposition that בר (א)נש(א) should be

61. P. Maurice Casey, "The Corporate Interpretation of 'One Like a Son of Man' (Dan VII 13) at the Time of Jesus," *NovT* 18 (1976): 167–80; idem, "The Son of Man Problem," *ZNW* 67 (1976): 147–54; idem, "The Use of the Term 'Son of Man' in the Similitudes of Enoch," *JSJ* 7 (1976): 11–29; idem, *Son of Man: The Interpretation and Influence of Daniel 7* (London: SPCK, 1979); idem, "Aramaic Idiom and Son of Man Sayings," *ExpT* 96 (1985): 233–36; idem, "The Jackals and the Son of Man (Matt. 8.20/Luke 9.58)," *JSNT* 23 (1985): 3–22; idem, "General, Generic, and Indefinite: The Use of the Term 'Son of Man' in Aramaic Sources and in the Teaching of Jesus," *JSNT* 29 (1987): 21–56; idem, "Method in Our Madness and Madness in Their Methods: Some Approaches to the Son of Man Problem in Recent Scholarship," *JSNT* 42 (1991): 17–43; idem, "The Use of the Term בר אנשא in the Aramaic Translations of the Hebrew Bible," *JSNT* 54 (1994): 87–118; idem, "Idiom and Translation: Some Aspects of the Son of Man Problem," *NTS* 41 (1995): 164–82; idem, *The Solution to the 'Son of Man' Problem* (London: T&T Clark, 2007).

62. Casey, *The Solution to the 'Son of Man' Problem*, sees Mark 2:27-28; 9:11–13; 10:45; 14:21 and Q 7:34 and Q 12:10 as examples of idiomatic expression.

63. Lindars, "Jesus as Advocate: A Contribution to the Christology Debate," 35.

64. Bauckham, "The Son of Man: 'A Man in My Position' or 'Someone'?"

65. Fuller, "The Son of Man: A Reconsideration."

66. Kearns, *Die Entchristologisierung des Menschensohnes*; Crossan, *The Historical Jesus*, 238–59; idem, *Jesus: A Revolutionary Biography*, 49–53.

67. Robinson, *A New Quest for the Historical Jesus*, 101–3. See also Helmut Koester, *Introduction to the New Testament*, Vol. 2: *History and Literature of Early Christianity* (2 vols.; FF; Philadelphia: Fortress Press, 1982; 2000); 79–89; Vielhauer, "Gottesreich und Menschensohn in der Verkündigung Jesu," 55–91;

understood solely as an idiomatic expression (mis)interpreted to refer to the "one like a son of man" of Dan. 7:13 has rightly been rejected.[68]

There are only two earthly son of man sayings in the Gospel of Mark, and they are both found in chapter two.[69] In Mark 2:10, Jesus announces that "the son of man has authority on earth to forgive sins." While some interpreters see this use of son of man as idiomatic for the generic "man/humanity,"[70] the most obvious sense here is that it is *Jesus* who has the power to pronounce forgiveness: it should be understood as a title.[71] "Forgiveness of sins" is not a characteristic of the son of man figure anywhere else.[72] In Matthew's version the crowds glorify God who has given this power "to *men* (*human beings*) (τοῖς ἀνθρώποις)."[73] Is Matthew's redaction of Mark to be favored as the more

Heinz Schürmann, "Beobachtungen zum Menschensohn-Titel in der Redequelle," in *Jesus und der Menschensohn: Für Anton Vögtle*, ed. Rudolf Pesch, et al. (Freiburg: Herder, 1975), 124–47.

68. I. Howard Marshall, "The Synoptic Son of Man Sayings in Recent Discussion," *NTS* 12 (1966): 327–51; idem, "The Son of Man in Contemporary Debate," *EvQ* 42 (1970): 67–87; George W. E. Nickelsburg, "Son of Man," *ABD* 6:137–50; John J. Collins, "The Heavenly Representative: The 'Son of Man' in the Similitudes of Enoch," in *Ideal Figures in Ancient Judaism: Profiles and Paradigms*, ed. John J. Collins and George W. E. Nickelsburg (Chico: Scholars Press, 1980), 111–33; idem, "The Son of Man in First-Century Judaism," *NTS* 38 (1992): 448–66; Thomas B. Slater, "One Like a Son of Man in First-Century C.E. Judaism," *NTS* 41 (1995): 183–98; A J. B. Higgins, *Jesus and the Son of Man* (Philadelphia: Fortress Press, 1964); idem, "The Son of Man Concept and the Historical Jesus," *SE* 5 (1968): 14–20; idem, *The Son of Man in the Teaching of Jesus* (SNTSMS 39; Cambridge: Cambridge University Press, 1980); George H. P. Thompson, "The Son of Man: The Evidence of the Dead Sea Scrolls," *ExpT* 72 (1960/61): 125; idem, "The Son of Man—Some Further Considerations," *JTS* n.s. 12 (1961): 203–9; Robert Maddox, "The Function of the Son of Man According to the Synoptic Gospels," *NTS* 15 (1968): 45–74; idem, "The Quest for Valid Methods in 'Son of Man' Research," *AusBr* (1971): 36–51; Caragounis, *The Son of Man*; Margaret Barker, *The Lost Prophet: The Book of Enoch and its Influence on Christianity* (Nashville: Abingdon, 1988); James H. Charlesworth, "The Portrayal of the Righteous as an Angel," in *Ideal Figures in Ancient Judaism*, 135–151.

69. Mark 2:10, 28.

70. Nathaniel Schmidt, "Was בר נשא a Messianic Title?" *JBL* 15 (1896): 36–53, esp. 48; Julius Wellhausen, "Des Menschen Sohn," 202–3; T. W. Manson, *The Teaching of Jesus: Studies of its Form and Content* (2d ed.; Cambridge: Cambridge University Press, 1935), 211–35; Jean Héring, *Le royaume de Dieu et sa venue* (2d ed., Neuchâtel: Delachaux & Niestlé, 1959), 108–10; Lewis S. Hay, "The Son of Man in Mark 2:10 and 2:28," *JBL* 89 (1970), 69–75.

71. Heinz Eduard Tödt, *The Son of Man in the Synoptic Tradition*, trans. Dorothea M. Barton (Philadelphia: Westminster, 1965), 126–30; Karl Kertelge, "Die Vollmacht des Menschensoshnes zur Sündenvergebung (Mk 2,10)," in *Orientierung an Jesus: Zur Theologie der Synoptiker. FS Josef Schmid*, ed. Paul Hoffmann, et al. (Freiburg: Herder, 1973), 205–13; Joachim Gnilka, "Das Elend vor dem Menschensohn (Mk 2, 1-12)," in *Jesus und der Menschensohn*, 196–209.

72. Casey, *The Solution*, 163, 167.

"authentic" version? This leaves one with the problematic conclusion that God gave *human beings* the authority to forgive sins.[74] This seems incredible: God has *not* given humanity in general this authority; it is God who forgives. A similar observation can be made for Mark 2:28, where Jesus states that "the son of man is Lord even of the Sabbath." Some scholars see this as idiomatic for "man/humanity."[75] Others regard it, perhaps more plausibly, as titular: *Jesus*, as the son of man, is Lord of the Sabbath.[76]

By far the majority (nine out of fourteen) of Mark's son of man sayings focus on Jesus' suffering and death. Mark attempts to address the same problem that Paul faced: the idea of a crucified messiah. The first suffering son of man saying is part of the first of three passion predictions (Mark 8:31; 9:31; 10:33-34) immediately following Peter's confession that Jesus is the Χριστός (Mark 8:29) and Mark's aside that Jesus "warned them not to tell anyone about him." In Mark 8:31, Jesus predicts his death: "He *then* began to teach them that the son of man *must* (δεῖ) suffer many things and be rejected by the elders, the chief priests and the scribes, and be killed and after three days rise again."

In Mark's narrative, Peter does not understand this kind of messianic role and rebukes Jesus (8:32), prompting Jesus to rebuke Peter in turn as "Satan" (8:33). After the Transfiguration, Jesus again orders his disciples (Peter, James, and John) "to tell no one about what they had seen until after the son of man had risen from the dead" (9:9). Jesus then confirms that the son of man has been "written about," referring to how "he is to go through many sufferings and be treated with contempt" (9:12).

The second prediction elaborates on the fate of the son of man, how he is to be "handed over" (παραδίδοται), but again the disciples "did not understand what he was saying" (9:31-32). Mark uses παραδίδοται several times to describe the son of man's fate, alluding to the Suffering Servant of Isa. 53:6.[77]

73. Matt. 9:8.

74. Casey, *The Solution*, 166–67; Lindars, *Jesus Son of Man*, 45. Wink, *The Human Being*, 80, sees this as Jesus' followers being able to declare others forgiven on God's behalf.

75. Arnold Meyer, *Jesu Muttersprache*, 93; Schmidt, "Was בר נשא a Messianic Title?" 49; Wellhausen, "Des Menschen Sohn," 202–3; Bultmann, *History of the Synoptic Tradition*, 16–17; Manson, *The Teaching of Jesus*, 211–35; Guignebert, *Jesus*, 278; Hay, "The Son of Man in Mark 2:10 and 2:28."

76. Tödt, *The Son of Man in the Synoptic Tradition*, 130–32; Francis Wright Beare, "The Sabbath Was Made for Man?" *JBL* 79 (1960): 130–36, esp.132. But see James M. Robinson, "The Son of Man in the Sayings Gospel Q," in *The Sayings Gospel Q: Collected Essays*, ed. Joseph Verheyden and Christoph Heil (BETL 189; Leuven: Peeters, 2005), 405–26, at 410.

77. The LXX translates ויהוה הפביא בו in MT Isa. 53:6b as καὶ κύριος παρέδωκεν αὐτὸν ("and the Lord handed him over").

> . . . the son of man will be *handed over* (παραδοθήσεται)
> to the chief priests
> and the scribes and they will condemn him to death
> and will *hand him over* (παραδώσουσιν) to the Gentiles;
> they will mock him, and spit upon him,
> and flog him, and kill him.[78]
> For the son of man goes as it is written of him,
> but woe to that one
> by whom the son of man is *handed over* (παραδίδοται).[79]
> . . . the son of man is *handed over* (παραδίδοται)
> into the hands of sinners.[80]

Mark is clearly at pains to inform his readers that although "all things" about the son of man had been "written by the prophets," Jesus' disciples "understood none of these things; this saying was hidden from them, and they did not know the things which were spoken." Why didn't Jesus' disciples "know" about the suffering and death of the son of man if it was so clearly "written about" in the scriptures and Jesus told them about it several times? The disciples' lack of understanding here seems to represent Mark's readers, who need to be instructed in this new revelation: "the son of man came not to be served but to serve, and to give his life a ransom (λύτρον) *for many* (ἀντὶ πολλῶν)."[81] Mark's reference to Jesus' death as a "ransom for many" is indebted to Paul's idea of salvation as well as to Isaiah 53.[82] Both Paul and Mark identify the "handing over" of the son of man (Jesus) with the Suffering Servant of Isaiah 53. By the time of Paul (c. 50 C.E.), Jesus' death had already been associated with that passage in Isaiah:[83]

78. Mark 10:33.

79. Mark 14:21.

80. Mark 14:41.

81. Mark 10:45.

82. Paul prefers ἀπολυτρώσεως, which means release or redemption (of slaves) (Rom. 3:24; 8:23; 1 Cor. 1:30). On the authenticity of Mark 10:45 see Peter Stuhlmacher, "Vicariously Giving His Life for Many, Mark 10:45 (Matt. 20:28)," in idem, *Reconciliation, Law, and Righteousness: Essays in Biblical Theology* (Philadelphia: Fortress Press, 1986), 16–29; Sydney H. T. Page, "Ransom Saying," in *Dictionary of Jesus and the Gospels*, ed. Joel B. Green, Scot McKnight, and I. Howard Marshall (Downers Grove: InterVarsity, 1991), 660–62; Scot McKnight, *Jesus and His Death* (Waco: Baylor University Press, 2005), 159–71.

83. John D. Crossan, *The Birth of Christianity: Discovering What Happened in the Years Immediately After the Execution of Jesus* (San Francisco: HarperSanFrancisco, 1998), 439.

> . . . that the Lord Jesus on the night when he was *handed over* (παρεδίδετο).[84]
> The Lord *handed him over* (παρέδωκεν) *for our sins.*[85]
> He bore the sins of *many* (πολλῶν) and was *handed over* (παρεδόθη).[86]

By the time Mark is writing his Gospel, the identification of Jesus with the Suffering Servant is a tradition that is at least twenty years old. It is the son of man's mission, his very life-purpose, to die "according to the scriptures." The identification of Jesus with the son of man serves several purposes: it redefines his messianic role and associates Jesus/son of man with the Suffering Servant and Pauline atonement theology. Mark combined the motifs of Servant and Son in the baptism account,[87] where the voice from heaven echoes Ps. 2:7 ("You are my son"), Genesis 22 ("Beloved One"), and Isa. 42:1: Jesus as God's Servant, the "one in whom I am well pleased."

Finally, Mark used the son of man motif several times to describe Jesus' return or *parousia* as a heavenly being coming "on the clouds of heaven":

> If anyone is ashamed of me and my words in *this* adulterous
> and sinful *generation* (γενεᾷ ταύτῃ),
> the son of man will be ashamed of them
> when he comes in his Father's glory with the holy angels.[88]
> . . . you will see the son of man
> *coming on clouds* (ἐρχόμενον ἐν νεφέλαις)
> with great power and glory. Then he will send out the angels
> and gather his elect.[89]
> . . . you will see the son of man seated
> at the right hand of power,
> and coming (ἐρχόμενον) with the clouds of the heaven.[90]

The coming son of man sayings indicate that Jesus' work is not over until he returns and dispenses judgment on "this generation," a distinctive phrase that is also found numerous times in Q, as is the theme of "the One Who Is To Come"

84. 1 Cor. 11:23.
85. Isa. 53:6.
86. Isa. 53:12.
87. Mark 1:9–11.
88. Mark 8:38.
89. Mark 13:26.
90. Mark 14:62.

(ὁ ἐρχόμενος).[91] These resemblances to Q strongly suggest that Mark did not invent the son of man tradition; he simply (indirectly) adapted this motif from the early Jesus tradition in Q.

The son of man sayings are a distinctive feature of Q.[92] The phrase appears nine times,[93] and many scholars regard the son of man sayings as belonging to Q's *earliest* traditions.[94] Does an idiomatic use of the phrase lie behind the earliest compositional stages of Q? Two Q sayings have been identified as candidates: Q 7:34 and Q 9:58.[95] In Q 7:34 ("the son of man has come eating and drinking"), Jesus is contrasted with John. This is clearly a reference to *Jesus*. Casey posits an Aramaic use of בר (א)נש(א) as "due to Jesus being in the humiliating situation of being falsely accused of a serious offense,"[96] a reference to Jesus but also to the "reality of the general level of meaning. Lindars sees this not as an *exclusive* self-reference, but as a response to Jesus' preaching that "this generation" is rejecting him, the generic raised "to the level of principle."[97]

Q 9:58 ("the son of man has nowhere to lay his head"), a saying widely regarded as authentic,[98] is a self-reference to Jesus' homeless, wandering lifestyle.[99] People, in general, *do* have homes and beds. Casey sees this saying as

91. Q 3:16b; 7:19; 13:35.

92. Christopher M. Tuckett, *Q and the History of Early Christianity: Studies on Q* (Edinburgh: T&T Clark, 1996), 253, identifies them as the *most* distinctive feature of Q.

93. Q 6:23; Q 7:34; Q 9:58; Q 11:30; Q 12:8; Q 12:10; Q 12:40; Q 17:23–24; Q 17:26–30. For the study of the son of man in Q, see Paul Hoffmann, "The Redaction of Q and the Son of Man: A Preliminary Sketch," in *The Gospel Behind the Gospels*, ed. Ronald A. Piper (NovTSup 75; Leiden: Brill, 1995), 159–98.

94. See Frans Neirynck, "Recent Developments in the Study of Q," in *Logia: Les paroles de Jésus—The Sayings of Jesus*, ed. Joseph Coppens, et al. (BETL 59; Leuven: Peeters, 1982), 29–75; Schürmann, "Beobachtungen zum Menschensohn-Titel."

95. Robinson, *The Sayings Gospel Q*, esp. 304; Leif E. Vaage, "The Son of Man Sayings in Q: Stratigraphical Location and Significance," *Semeia* 55 (1991): 103–29, esp. 123, 126.

96. Casey, *The Solution*, 137.

97. Lindars, *Jesus Son of Man*, 33.

98. Eduard Schweizer, "Der Menschensohn (Zur eschatologischen Erwartung Jesu)," *ZNW* 50 (1959): 185–209, esp. 199; idem, "The Son of Man," *JBL* 79 (1960): 119–29, esp. 121; idem, "The Son of Man Again," *NTS* 9 (1963): 256–61, esp. 258; Frederick H. Borsch, *The Son of Man in Myth and History* (Philadelphia: Westminster, 1967), 325; Leonhard Goppelt, "Zum Problem des Menschensohns: das Verhältnis von Leidens- und Parusieankündigung," in *Mensch und Menschensohn, FS Karl Witte*, ed. Hartmut Sierig (Hamburg: Wittig, 1963), 20–32, esp. 20; Carsten Colpe, "ὁ υἱὸς τοῦ ἀνθρώπου." *TDNT*, VIII, 400–77, at 432; Casey, *Son of Man*, 229; Marshall, "The Synoptic Son of Man Sayings in Recent Discussion," *NTS* 12 (1966): 327–51, esp. 340; Lindars, *Jesus Son of Man*, 29; Black, "Aramaic Barnāshā and the Son of Man," *ET* 95 (1984): 200–6, esp. 205; Mahlon H. Smith, "No Place for a Son of Man," *Forum* 4 (1988): 83–107.

having "a general level of meaning . . . as well as a specific reference to Jesus."[100] Here Jesus "means anyone who shares in the conditions of his own missionary vocation."[101] This is not an exclusively generic use, but an inclusive use, the contrast being not between humans and animals but between Jesus/his group and *other people*.[102] Here ὁ υἱὸς τοῦ ἀνθρώπου could *theoretically* both refer to Jesus and retain its general level of meaning, along with an implicit reference to other people, but it is far more likely to refer only to Jesus.[103]

The problem with the argument that בר נשא/בר נש was an Aramaic expression that meant "me" or "I" is that it is contradicted by passages where this expression is used as a *title* for *Jesus*.[104] Second, none of the texts cited support the claim that the idiom is used to refer to the speaker *exclusively*.[105] The examples refer to an *indefinite* sense, to "a man/any man" or to the generic, but do not show that the phrase could be used to refer *exclusively* to the speaker.[106] Third, a generic and indefinite use of the phrase may be plausible in some cases, but it does not explain *most* of the son of man sayings.[107]

The idiomatic use of בר (א)נש(א) cannot explain the Q tradition, because the identification of Jesus as the son of man is not based on an Aramaic idiom but rather on (post-Easter) reflection on the exaltation of Jesus.[108] The "earthly"

99. Lindars, *Jesus Son of Man*, 30.

100. Casey, *The Solution*, 177.

101. Lindars, *Jesus Son of Man*, 30.

102. Casey posits that translators used ὁ υἱὸς τοῦ ἀνθρώπου whenever בר (א)נש(א) referred to *Jesus*.

103. Casey, *The Solution*, 253–54. He admits that a number of sayings are clearly secondary, redactional, and "inauthentic" (e.g., Matt. 24; Q 21:27, 17:23–24:37, 17:26-27; Q 12:39-40, 42-46).

104. Theissen and Merz, *The Historical Jesus*, 550.

105. See Adela Yarbro Collins, "The Origins of the Designation of Jesus as 'Son of Man,'" *HTR* 80 (1987): 391–407, at 397–98; Joseph A. Fitzmyer, *The Semitic Background of the New Testament* (combined edition of *Essays on the Semitic Background of the New Testament* and *A Wandering Aramean: Collected Aramaic Essays*) (Grand Rapids: Eerdmans, 1997), 153.

106. Burkett, *The Son of Man Debate*, 86–87.

107. Paul Owen and David Shepherd, "Speaking up for Qumran, Dalman and the Son of Man: Was *Bar Enasha* a Common Term for 'Man' in the Time of Jesus?" *JSNT* 81 (2001): 81–122.

108. Vielhauer, "Gottesreich und Menschensohn in der Verkündigung Jesu," 51–79, 90–91; idem, "Jesus und der Menschensohn." *ZTK* 60 (1963): 133–77; Norman Perrin, "Mark XIV.62: The End Product of a Christian Pesher Tradition?" *NTS* 12 (1965–66): 150–55; idem, "The Son of Man in Ancient Judaism and Primitive Christianity: A Suggestion," *BR* 11 (1966): 17–28; idem, "The Son of Man in the Synoptic Tradition," *BR* 13 (1968): 3–25; idem, *Rediscovering the Teachings of Jesus* (New York: Harper & Row, 1967), 154–206, 197–98; Koester, "One Jesus and Four Primitive Gospels." H. J. de Jonge, "The Historical Jesus' View of Himself and of His Mission," in *From Jesus to John: Essays on Jesus and New Testament Christology in Honour of Marinus de Jonge*, ed. Martinus C. de Boer (Sheffield:

son of man sayings date to the *post*-Easter period. The expression is not a holdover from Jesus' Aramaic speech patterns subsequently apocalypticized; it is an apocalyptic title, an identification of Jesus *cast* in the role of the coming son of man, the "One Who Is To Come":

Q 3:16b:	John predicts "the One Who Is To Come."
Q 7:19:	John asks Jesus directly if he is "the One Who Is To Come."
Q 7:22-23:	Jesus confirms that he is "the One Who Is To Come."

John's prediction of "the One Who Is To Come" (ὁ ἐρχόμενος) in Q 3 seems to be an indirect allusion to Dan. 7:13's son of man "coming" (ἤρχετο) with the clouds. The identification of Jesus as the son of man is confirmed in Q 7:34: "the 'son of man' *came* (ἦλθεν), eating and drinking."[109]

Q 11:20 shifts the discursive focus of what has "come" (ἔφθασεν) to the presence of the kingdom.[110] Q then shifts back to its son of man Christology:

> the son of man is *coming* (ἔρχαται) as a robber.[111]
> *I have come* (ἦλθον) to hurl fire on the earth,
> and how I wish it had already blazed up.[112]
> Do you think that *I have come* (ἦλθον) to hurl peace on earth?
> I did not *come* (ἦλθον) to hurl peace, but a sword![113]

JSOT, 1993), 21–37; Tödt, *Der Menschensohn*, 59–61, 105–16, regards Q 17:28-29, Q 6:22-23, Q 7:34, Q 9:58, and Q 12:10 (i.e., both Q's coming and earthly son of man sayings) as secondary creations. John S. Kloppenborg, "The Sayings Gospel Q and the Quest of the Historical Jesus," *HTR* 89, no. 4 (1996), 307–44, at 319: "the coming Son of Man sayings are not the earliest sayings in Q from a compositional point of view and probably not from a tradition-historical perspective either." See also Hoffmann, "QR und der Menschensohn: Eine vorläufige Skizze," in *The Four Gospels 1992: FS Frans Neirynck*, ed. Frans van Segbroeck and Christopher M. Tuckett (3 vols.; BETL 100; Leuven: Peeters, 1992), 421–56, at 453–56; idem, "The Redaction of Q and the Son of Man: A Preliminary Sketch," 190–98; Koester, "The Sayings Gospel Q and the Quest for the Historical Jesus: A Response to John S. Kloppenborg," *HTR* 89, no. 4 (1996): 345–49, at 347: "the sayings about the coming Son of Man and the judgment introduce a new element into this document and are secondary." See also Egon Brandenburger, *Markus 13 und die Apokalyptik* (Göttingen: Vandenhoeck & Ruprecht, 1984). But see Casey, *The Solution*, 29.

109. Q 7:34.

110. Q 17:20-21.

111. Q 12:39.

112. Q 12:49.

113. Q 12:51.

> For *I have come* (ἦλθον) to divide son against father, daughter against her mother, daughter-in-law against her mother-in-law.[114]

These references to Jesus in the first person ("*I* have come") appear to be son of man sayings in which Jesus causes division, separating the "wheat" from the "chaff" as John predicted in Q 3:9, 17. Finally, Q 13:34-35 combines several significant elements: the figure of Wisdom; the Deuteronomistic motif of the rejected prophets; the implication that Jesus is among those who have been killed; the city's leadership's rejection of Jesus; the imminent judgment on (or the destruction of) the Temple; the *parousia* and the so-called "second coming" of "the One Who Is To Come." Q 13:34-35 functions as a striking *inclusio* to Q 3 and Q 7's references to Jesus as "the One Who Is To Come":

> Look! Your House is forsaken! I tell you:
> You will not see me again *until the time comes* when you say:
> "Blessed is *the one who comes* (ὁ ἐρχόμενος) in the name of the Lord!"

What are we to make of Q's present *and* future sayings? The fact that Q 7:34 and Q 9:58 identify Jesus as the *present* son of man; that Q 11:20 and Q 17:21 identify the kingdom as *present* during his ministry; and that Q 7:22-23 indirectly confirms Jesus' acceptance of the title "the One Who Is To Come" indicates that the kingdom, the son of man, and "the One Who Is To Come" are indeed portrayed as interrelated components of Jesus' ministry in Q. At the same time, the kingdom is *coming* (Q 11:2b, Q 13:28), the son of man is *coming*, and "the One Who Is To Come" is *returning* (to Jerusalem).

The identification of Jesus as the "son of man" and "the One Who Is To Come," insofar as he represents a rejected and persecuted group, shifts the discursive focus from Jesus' ministry toward a radically different future expectation of eschatological fulfillment. Since the late 1960s, Q specialists have recognized that a dominant compositional theme in Q is the pronouncement of violent apocalyptic judgment on "this generation."[115] This theme is characteristic of the final redaction of Q.[116] Based on the number and frequency of sayings, as well as the fact that the theme of judgment on "this generation" is found in sayings framing the entire document (from Q 3:7-9 to Q 22:28-30)

114. Q 12:53.

115. Dieter Lührmann, *Die Redaktion der Logienquelle* (Neukirchener-Vluyn: Neukirchener Verlag, 1969); Arland D. Jacobson, *The First Gospel: An Introduction to Q* (Sonoma, CA: Polebridge, 1992); Migaku Sato, *Q und Prophetie: Studien zur Gattungs- und Traditionsgeschichte der Quelle Q* (Tübingen: Mohr Siebeck, 1988); Kloppenborg, *Formation of Q*.

and complements the theme of the rejected prophets (Q 6:23c, Q 11:47-51, Q 13:34-35), these two major themes create a thematic unity to Q. The author(s) of Q perceived that they were met with hostility, unbelief, opposition, rejection, and persecution. This does not mean that the author(s) or Q group actually engaged in *physical* violence with other Jews or that Jesus pronounced eschatological judgment on his wayward disciples or enemies. On the contrary, the rhetorical pronouncement of apocalyptic violence allowed the Jesus people of Q to criticize, condemn, and attack their opponents without ever having to resort to *physical* violence. It is also this rhetorical violence that allows us to reconstruct the social history and social conflict(s) of the Q group.

Burton Mack has suggested that "the history of the Q community can be traced by noting the shifts in its discourse documented in its collection of the sayings of Jesus."[117] The sharp difference in tone between the sapiential orientation of much of Q and the theme of critical judgment may reflect changes in the movement's social orientation. This "sudden shift in tone" must be explained.[118] Changes in social circumstances must have been behind this shift.[119] The Q people experienced "a period of frustration with failed expectations" that occasioned the language and rhetoric of judgment directed at those who opposed the group or created obstacles for them.[120] Mack rightly posits "rejection" as a major factor leading to this sudden shift in tone. The people of "this generation" were like children who refused to play in the marketplace; they rejected the message of John and Jesus (and by extension, the Q group or Q community). The heated "language of divisive conflict" in Q is closely related to "the theme of inclusion versus exclusion, a theme that presupposes the notion of boundaries and borders."[121]

Jewish loyalties to the early Jesus movement seem to have been at odds with some traditional norms of Jewish cultural identity and community belonging. We find hints of this in Q 3:8, where John warns the crowds that Jewish ethnic identity in and of itself was insufficient to avoid the coming judgment. Consequently, the author(s) of Q seem to have *distanced* themselves

116. Q 3:7-9; Q 3:16b-17; Q 10:3; Q 10:10-12; Q 10:13-15; Q 10:14; Q 13:34-35; Q 11:16, 29-30; Q 7:31-35; Q 11:31-32; Q 11:42, 39b, 43-44; Q 11:46b, 52, 47-48; Q 11:49-51; Q 12:39-40; Q 12:42-46; Q 17:23-24; Q 17:26; Q 13:29; Q 13:28; Q 22:28, 30.

117. Burton L. Mack, *The Lost Gospel: The Book of Q and Christian Origins* (San Francisco: HarperSanFrancisco, 1993), 203.

118. Ibid., 131.

119. Ibid., 134.

120. Ibid., 45.

121. Ibid., 136.

from those norms, to *differentiate* themselves from Pharisaic customs,[122] normative family values, and ethnic identity. This differentiation led to social conflict. The Q group perceived and/or experienced rejection and this intergroup conflict became a major factor leading to the final redaction of Q.

The social dynamics responsible for producing the apocalyptic rhetoric of violence in Q were *mutual*: the author(s) of Q criticized and condemned their fellow Jews who had themselves rejected and opposed the message and teachings of John and Jesus. Q represents a poignant moment of mutual hostility in the long history of the Judeo-Christian heritage. After Q was incorporated into the Gospels of Matthew and Luke, Q's apocalyptic rhetoric, which was originally and solely directed at other Jews, became an effective tool in the polemical repertoire of early Christian apologists, and what was once an internal Jewish conflict *within* first-century Judaism was translated into a conflict *between* Jews and Christians.[123] The Jew was constructed as the other, and Q's condemnation of "this generation" was redirected toward the Jewish people as a whole, resulting in a history of prejudice, discrimination, anti-Semitism, and violence.

Q emerged in a specific social context as the expression of a Palestinian Jewish religious renewal movement,[124] and it represents this movement undergoing social strain. The socially subversive message of much of the Q material reflects its perceived rejection by "this generation." This theme of rejection is a predominant characteristic of Q. The motif of the rejection of the prophets sent by Wisdom who suffer rejection and violence is neither Matthean nor Lukan, but rather distinctively representative of Q.[125]

The son of man is a figure who "arouses hostility and rejection." The son of man sayings presuppose the perceived rejection of the Q community. A social

122. Q 11: 42, 39b, 41, 43-44.

123. For Q's Jewish ethnicity see Siegfried Schulz, *Q: Spruchquelle der Evangelisten* (Zürich: Theologischer Verlag, 1972), 57; Hoffmann, *Studien*, 332–33; idem, "QR und der Menschensohn," 455; Robinson, *The Sayings Gospel Q*, 195; John S. Kloppenborg Verbin, *Excavating Q: The History and Setting of the Sayings Gospel* (Edinburgh: T & T Clark, 2000), 256; Tuckett, *Q and the History of Earliest Christianity*, 236, 435 n. 37; William E. Arnal, *Jesus and the Village Scribes: Galilean Conflicts and the Setting of Q* (Minneapolis: Fortress Press, 2001), 202; idem, "The Q Document," in *Jewish Christianity Reconsidered: Rethinking Ancient Groups and Texts*, ed. Matt Jackson-McCabe (Minneapolis: Fortress Press, 2007), 119–54, 317–21, at 129; Markus Cromhout, *Jesus and Identity: Reconstructing Judean Ethnicity in Q* (M/BMC; Eugene, OR: Cascade, 2007); David R. Catchpole, *The Quest for Q* (Edinburgh: T&T Clark, 1993), 279.

124. Gerd Theissen, *Sociology of Early Palestinian Christianity*, trans. John Bowden (Philadelphia: Fortress Press, 1978).

125. Tuckett, *Q and the History of Earliest Christianity*, 38, 219, 252–67.

boundary has been constructed between the community and the rest of Israel. This division of us/them casts Jesus in the role of a judge who will punish nonbelievers. The son of man sayings in Q were transmitted by a follower of Jesus who came to adopt a sectarian stance of judging "this generation" for rejecting the message of the Jesus group.[126] The son of man tradition reflects this redactor's perceived rejection.

As the son of man, Jesus pronounces judgment. The Inaugural Sermon, on the other hand, is not characteristic of the judgment motif. It is difficult not to conclude that we are dealing with two streams of tradition in Q: one in which Jesus teaches the way of the kingdom and a secondary stream in which Jesus, as the son of man, will return as a heavenly judge to punish the wicked. This second stream, based on Dan. 7:13's heavenly "one like a son of man," ultimately came to influence the composition of Q, the Synoptics, and *4 Ezra*, but it originally derived from the Enochic *Book of Parables*.

126. Risto Uro, "Apocalyptic Symbolism and Social Identity in Q," in *Symbols and Strata: Essays on the Sayings Gospel Q* (PFES 65; Helsinki: Finnish Exegetical Society; Göttingen: Vandenhoeck & Ruprecht, 1996), 67–118, esp. 116–18, argues that the introduction of the son of man figure marks a shift in the symbolic universe of Q.

8

The Enochic Son of Man

The Enochic *Book of Parables*,[1] a pre-Christian Jewish text extant only in Ethiopic *Ge'ez*, can be dated around the turn of the era or,[2] at the latest, c. 70 C.E.[3] The consensus of the Enoch Seminar at its 2005 meeting in Camaldoli, Italy, was that the *Parables* can be dated to the end of the first century B.C.E. or the beginning of the first century C.E. This conclusion is based on several arguments. First, the *Parables* appears to be a pre-Christian Jewish text. If a Christian author had composed the *Parables*, Jesus would surely have been identified as the "son of man," whereas it is unlikely that a Jewish author would have used this imagery after Jesus' identification as "son of man" became well known after 60 C.E. This suggests that the *Parables* were composed before 60

1. The *Parables* can be dated to the early first century C.E. See Jonas C. Greenfield and Michael E. Stone, "The Enochic Pentateuch and the Date of the Similitudes," *HTR* 70 (1977): 51–65; David W. Suter, *Tradition and Composition in the Parables of Enoch* (SBLDS 47; Missoula: Scholars Press, 1979), 32; James H. Charlesworth, "From Jewish Messianology to Christian Christology: Some Caveats and Perspectives," in *Judaisms and their Messiahs at the Turn of the Christian Era*, ed. Jacob Neusner and William Scot (New York: Cambridge University Press, 1987), 225–64, at 237; idem, "Messianology in the Biblical Pseudepigrapha," in *Qumran Messianism: Studies on the Messianic Expectations in the Dead Sea Scrolls*, ed. James H. Charlesworth, Herman Lichtenberger, and Gerbern S. Oegema (Tübingen: Mohr Siebeck, 1998), 21–52, at 40; Gillian Bampfylde, "The Similitudes of Enoch: Historical Allusions," *JSJ* 15 (1984): 9–31, at 10; Paolo Sacchi, "Qumran e la datazione del Libro delle Parabole di Enoc," *Henoch* 25 (2003): 149–66; George W. E. Nickelsburg, "Son of Man," *ABD* 6 (1992): 138–49; Gabriele Boccaccini, *Beyond the Essene Hypothesis: The Parting of the Ways between Qumran and Enochic Judaism* (Grand Rapids: Eerdmans, 1998), 144.

2. Greenfield and Stone, "Enochic Pentateuch"; Suter, *Tradition and Composition*, 32.

3. John J. Collins, "The Son of Man in First-Century Judaism," *NTS* 38 (1992): 448–66; Thomas B. Slater, "One Like a Son of Man in First-Century C.E. Judaism," *NTS* 41, no. 2 (1995): 183–98; Paolo Sacchi, *Jewish Apocalyptic and Its History*, trans. William J. Short (JSPSup 20; Sheffield: Sheffield Academic Press, 1990). Michael A. Knibb, "The Date of the Parables of Enoch: A Critical Review," *NTS* 25 (1979): 345–59.

C.E. Second, a possible allusion to the Parthians (*1 En.* 56:5-7) suggests a date sometime after the Parthian invasion into Roman territory in 40 B.C.E. Third, a mention of hot springs that "serve the kings" seems to refer to Herod the Great at Callirhoe.[4] There is no consensus on the provenance, social setting, or group responsible for the *Parables*. The *Parables* were not found at Qumran, although all the other books of Enoch *were* found. Nonetheless, there *are* affinities between the *Parables* and Qumran.[5] The *Book of Parables* is derived from the *Book of the Watchers* and the author(s) of the *Parables* are heirs to the Enochic tradition, as were the authors of the Qumran sectarian texts. The absence of the *Parables* at Qumran need not signify that it was rejected there.[6]

In the *Parables* a heavenly figure with "the appearance of a man,"[7] but "like one of the angels," is identified as the "son of man."[8] He is seated on a "throne of glory" as a "heavenly judge."[9] He is preexistent, "chosen and hidden," and "the Lord of Spirits will reveal him to the holy and righteous."[10] In his preexistence he resembles the figure of Wisdom.[11] He is "the messiah,"[12] the "Elect One." He has been chosen for a special purpose, although he is opposed by (and to) kings and the mighty. The elect and the righteous are, as in Daniel, in close association with the angelic world.[13] The *Parables* conflate royal messianism with Dan. 7:13 by portraying the messiah as a preexistent heavenly figure.[14] There are also indications of influence from Isaiah's "Servant."[15]

4. *1 En.* 67.4-13; Josephus, *Ant.* 17.6.5.171-73; *War* 1.33.5.657-58.

5. Ida Fröhlich, "The Parables of Enoch and Qumran Literature," in *Enoch and the Messiah Son of Man: Revisiting the Book of Parables*, ed. Gabriele Boccaccini (Grand Rapids: Eerdmans, 2007), 343–51.

6. Part of this chapter was previously published as "'Seventh from Adam' (Jude 1:14-15): Re-examining Enoch Traditions and the Christology of Jude," *JTS* 64, no. 2 (2013): 463–81.

7. *1 En.* 46.1. Matthew Black, *The Book of Enoch or 1 Enoch: A New English Edition. With Commentary and Textual Notes* (Leiden: Brill, 1985), 48.

8. *1 En.* 46.2. Black, *Book of Enoch*, 48. The title "son of man" is frequent in the *Parables* (*1 En.* 46.2, 3, 4; 48.2; 62.5, 7, 9, 14; 63.11; 69.26, 27, 29; 70.1; 71.14; 71.17); moreover, he has a "throne of glory" from which he will judge sinners (*1 En.* 62.5; 69.27, 29).

9. *1 En.* 45.3; 51.3; 55.4; 61.8; 62.2, 3, 5; 69.27, 29.

10. *1 En.* 48.3, 6; 62.7; 48.7. Black, *The Book of Enoch*, 49–50.

11. Prov. 8:22-26; *1 En.* 49.1-4; 51.1-3.

12. *1 En.* 48.10; 53.2.

13. John J. Collins, "The Heavenly Representative: The 'Son of Man' in the Similitudes of Enoch," in *Ideal Figures in Ancient Judaism: Profiles and Paradigms*, ed. John J. Collins and George W. E. Nickelsburg (Chico: Scholars Press, 1980), 111–33, at 113.

14. Ibid., 119; Christopher Rowland, *The Open Heaven: A Study of Apocalyptic in Judaism and Early Christianity* (New York: Crossroad, 1982), 95.

Daniel Boyarin suggests that "the Son of Man" was "a known figure already in the discursive world of the Gospels."[16] The key to the transformation of Daniel's simile into a title/name, therefore, "is to be found . . . in the Apocalypse that we know of as the second book of 1 Enoch."[17] He finds evidence of a "Son of Man spirituality as being a widespread form of Jewish belief at the end of the Second Temple period":

> All of the elements of Christology are essentially in place then in the Parables. We have a pre-existent heavenly figure, identified as well with Wisdom, who is the Son of Man. We have an earthly life, a human sage exalted into heaven at the end of an earthly career, enthroned in heaven at the right side of the Ancient of Days as the pre-existing and forever reigning Son of Man.[18]

The relationship between the *Parables* and the early Jesus tradition has recently come under renewed study.[19] Boyarin does not draw the obvious conclusion—that the *Parables* influenced the Gospels' identification of Jesus as the son of man—and he denies that "the Parables of Enoch are a source for or influenced the Gospels in any way."[20] He may protest too much. He argues rather for a "widespread" tradition within which we can observe "the

15. The "Servant" in Isaiah 40–55 (Isa. 42:1-7; 49:1-6; 50:4-9; 52:13–53:12) is called "my Elect" in Isa. 42:1, the one who brings justice to the nations. The "Servant" is also "a light to the nations" (Isa. 42:6; 49:6). It is less clear that these titles signify an individual figure as opposed to a symbolic collective, i.e., "Israel." The Servant sayings are generally seen today as referring to Israel. See Christopher Richard North, *The Suffering Servant in Deutero-Isaiah: An Historical and Critical Study* (London: Oxford University Press, 1948). This individual/collective ambiguity is reminiscent of the "son of man" as a (possibly) corporate figure in Daniel. The *Parables* do not refer to the suffering of the Servant. For the motif of the "Suffering Righteous" vindicated after death see George W. E. Nickelsburg, *Resurrection, Immortality and Eternal Life in Intertestamental Judaism* (HTS 26; Cambridge, MA: Harvard University Press, 1972), 48–58.

16. Daniel Boyarin, "How Enoch Can Teach Us about Jesus," *EC* 2 (2011): 51–76, at 52; idem, *The Jewish Gospels: The Story of the Jewish Christ* (New York: The New Press, 2012); Steven R. Scott, "The Binitarian Nature of the Book of Similitudes," *JSP* 18 (2008): 55–78. But see Larry W. Hurtado, "Summary and Concluding Observations," in *'Who is This Son of Man'? The Latest Scholarship on a Puzzling Expression of the Historical Jesus*, ed. Larry W. Hurtado and P. L. Owen (London: T&T Clark, 2011), 159–77; idem, *Lord Jesus Christ*, 250–51, 290–316.

17. Boyarin, "How Enoch Can Teach Us," 53.

18. Ibid., 74–75.

19. See *Parables of Enoch, Early Judaism, Jesus, and Christian Origins*, ed. Darrell Bock and James H. Charlesworth (JCT 11; London: T&T Clark International, 2013).

20. Boyarin, "How Enoch can Teach Us," 61.

hermeneutical and theological historical process that must have taken place . . . in order for The Son of Man to become the Christological title," but seems to suggest that this relatively "widespread" son of man tradition somehow had no influence on the composition of the Gospels?

The *Parables* provide us with a first-century C.E. text tradition that conflates several major Christological themes associated with Jesus: (Davidic) messianism, the son of man, and Isaiah's Servant. We need not appeal to direct literary dependence to posit the *Parables'* influence on the Jesus tradition; it seems far more difficult to conclude that these are entirely independent developments in first-century Palestinian Judaism.[21]

The *Parables* represent a Jewish tradition contemporary with the Jesus movement that could explain how Jesus' rejection, suffering, exaltation, and return came to be associated with the eschatological figure of the son of man: the *Parables* had *already* associated the messianic son of man with Isaiah's Servant. Jesus' disciples sought out scriptural warrants to explain Jesus' suffering and death, but this would not have occurred until *after* his death. There is no historical reason why we should assume that the *Parables* or the coming (Q) or suffering (Mark) son of man traditions predate Easter.

Q, like the *Parables*, does not refer to the son of man's suffering and death.[22] This seems to be a distinctively Markan innovation in the son of man tradition. What this means is that Q seems to be closer—thematically, chronologically, and geographically—to the *Parables* than Mark. Did the *Parables* influence Q? Since Q and the *Parables* both come from a Palestinian Jewish milieu, the author of Q could well have been familiar with this Enochic tradition, perhaps not with the *text* of the *Parables* but with tendencies to conflate the messianic idea with the Danielic "one like a son of man."[23] Q and the *Parables* both envision the son of man as a figure of apocalyptic judgment.[24] Q also shares the Enochic orientation of the divided kingdom(s) of God and Satan and accepts the view that diseases can be caused by evil spirits requiring exorcism. In Q 6:20-23 the followers of the son of man are described as hated, reviled, and persecuted. This is not unlike the oppression experienced by the righteous

21. Ben Witherington III, *The Christology of Jesus* (Minneapolis: Fortress Press, 1990), 235.

22. The *Parables* use the titles "Righteous One" (38.2); 47.1, 4; 53.6) and the "Elect/Chosen One" (39.6; 40.5; 45.3, 4; 48.6; 49.2, 4; 51.3, 5; 52.6, 9; 53. 6; 55. 4; 61.5, 8, 10, 62.1).

23. Helge S. Kvanvig, "The Son of Man in the Parables of Enoch," in *Enoch and the Messiah Son of Man*, 179–215, esp. 213.

24. Leslie W. Walck, "The Son of Man in the Parables of Enoch and the Gospels," in *Enoch and the Messiah Son of Man*, 299–337, at 314.

and elect in the *Parables*.[25] In Q 9:58 the son of man has nowhere to lay his head. Similarly, in *1 En.* 42.1, "Wisdom could not find a place in which she could dwell."[26] Considering that Jesus is identified with Wisdom in Matthew (whereas he is only Wisdom's messenger in Q),[27] and that the son of man has a special relationship with Wisdom in the *Parables* (*1 En.* 49.3: "in him dwells the spirit of Wisdom"), these similarities are intriguing.[28] The messianic son of man reveals "all the treasures of what is hidden."[29] He has been given "the secrets of Wisdom," which "will go forth from the counsel of his mouth."[30] He is revealed by Wisdom.[31] The spirit of Wisdom dwells within him.[32] As in Q, the son of man is not identified *as* Wisdom, but is closely associated *with* Wisdom.

In Q 10:24 Jesus is a figure whom "prophets and kings" have longed to see. In *1 En.* 62.9 the "son of man" is worshiped by kings. The "day" of the "son of man" is also a striking similarity in both traditions. Q 12:40 describes the son of man as a thief coming at an unexpected hour, which is not unlike the unexpected judgment brought by the son of man (*1 En.* 62.5). Of course, there are also differences between Q and the *Parables*. Q 7:34 has Jesus' opponents describe him as "eating and drinking," a "glutton and a drunkard." No such

25. *1 En.* 46.8; 47.2, 4; 48.7; 62.15. Christopher M. Tuckett, "The Son of Man and Daniel 7: Q and Jesus," in *The Sayings Source Q and the Historical Jesus*, ed. Andreas Lindemann (BETL 158; Leuven: Leuven University Press, 2001), 371–94, at 371–73. For Tuckett the son of man in Q is a "prototype" (p. 373) for the suffering and hostility experienced by the prophets of Israel and his followers, a "paradigmatic figure" and example of what Jesus' followers will experience (p. 374) (see Q 6:22-23; Q 7:35; Q 9:58; Q 4:1-13; Q 14:27; Q 6:40).

26. In Sirach 24, Wisdom is also portrayed as seeking to find a home in Israel.

27. M. Jack Suggs, *Wisdom, Christology and Law in Matthew's Gospel* (Cambridge, MA: Harvard University Press, 1970); James D. G. Dunn, *Christology in the Making* (London: SCM, 1980), 197.

28. Paul Hoffmann, *Studien zur Theologie der Logienquelle* (3rd ed.; NA 8; Münster: Aschendorff, 1982 [1972]), 181; Robert G. Hamerton-Kelly, *Pre-Existence, Wisdom and the Son of Man* (SNTSMS 21; Cambridge: Cambridge University Press, 1973), 29; Ronald A. Piper, *Wisdom in the Q-Tradition: The Aphoristic Sayings of Jesus* (SNTSMS 61; New York: Cambridge University Press, 1989), 167; Arland D. Jacobson, *The First Gospel: An Introduction to Q* (Sonoma: Polebridge, 1992), 136. John S. Kloppenborg, *The Formation of Q: Trajectories in Ancient Christian Wisdom Collections* (SAC; Philadelphia: Fortress Press, 1987), 192, sees this as "far-fetched: Q 9:57-58 says nothing of rejection . . . Instead the saying describes the vagrant existence of the Son of Man." Christopher M. Tuckett, *Q and the History of Early Christianity: Studies on Q* (Edinburgh: T&T Clark, 1996), 181–82, sees clear echoes of the son of man's homelessness as a sign or symbol of rejection. Thus "the idea of rejected Wisdom, who also can find no home in texts such as *1 En* 42, is quite in line with the Q saying here."

29. *1 En.* 46.3; 60.10.

30. *1 En.* 51.3.

31. *1 En.* 48.7.

32. *1 En.* 49.3.

description of the son of man can be found in the *Parables*, although *1 En.* 62.13-15 does refer to feasting under the rule of the son of man. Q 12:10 envisions the possibility of forgiveness for speaking against the son of man, yet the son of man in the *Parables* offers no such forgiveness. Nonetheless, George Nickelsburg argues that Q 12:8–9's judicial function "reflects the *interpretation* of Daniel 7 in the Parables of Enoch rather than simple dependence on Daniel 7."[33] The most striking correspondence between Q and the *Parables* is Q 17:26:

> καθὼς ἐγένετο ἐν ταῖς ἡμέραις Νῶε,
> οὕτως ἔσται ἐν τῇ ἡμέρᾳ τοῦ υἱοῦ τοῦ ἀνθρώπου.
>
> . . . just as it was in the days of Noah,
> so it will be also in the day[s] of the son of man.

Q contains a number of distinctive "eschatological correlatives"[34]: here, for example, between the "days of Noah" and the "days of the son of man," the correlative is the divine judgment which destroyed everything. The explicit references to Noah, the flood, judgment, and destruction are strikingly similar:

> ὡς γὰρ ἦσαν ἐν ταῖς ἡμέραις ἐκείναις τρώγοντες
> καὶ πίνοντες, γαμοῦντες καὶ γαμίζοντες,
> ἄχρι ἧς ἡμέρας εἰσῆλθεν Νῶε εἰς τὴν κιβωτόν
> καὶ ἦλθεν ὁ κατακλυσμὸς καὶ ἦρεω ἅπαντας.
>
> For as in those days, they were eating and drinking,
> marrying and being given in marriage,
> until the day Noah entered the ark,
> and the Flood came and took all of them.

Another "intriguing parallel" is the lightning associated with the coming son of man in Q 17:24 and the comets flashing with the "son of God" figure in 4Q246:

> ὥσπερ γὰρ ἡ ἀστραπὴ ἐξέρχεται
> ἀπὸ ἀνατολῶν καὶ φαίνεται ἕως δυσμῶν,

33. George W. E. Nickelsburg, *1 Enoch: A Commentary on the Book of 1 Enoch* (Hermeneia; Philadelphia: Fortress Press, 2001), 83.

34. See Richard A. Edwards, "The Eschatological Correlative as a *Gattung* in the New Testament," *ZNW* 60 (1969): 9–20; idem, "The Eschatological Correlative," in his *The Sign of Jonah in the Theology of the Evangelists and* Q (SBT 2.18; London: SCM, 1971), 47–58; Daryl Schmidt, "The LXX Gattung 'Prophetic Correlative,'" *JBL* 96 (1977): 517–22.

> οὕτως ἔσται ὁ υἱὸς τοῦ ἀνθρώπου [ἐν τῇ ἡμέρᾳ αὐτοῦ].
>
> For as the lightning streaks out
> from sunrise and flashes as far as sunset,
> so will the son of man be [on his day].

Here the "correlative appears in an eschatological context (and) raises the possibility that Q 17:24 was not a Christian creation *ex nihilo*, but was an adaptation of a current apocalyptic slogan."[35] The son of man will be revealed, which presupposes that the son of man has been hidden, a motif shared by Q, the *Parables*, and Mark. Q 17:26-27, 30, with its connection between Noah's flood and eschatological judgment in relation to the coming son of man, reflects a pattern present in the *Parables* (*1 En.* 65.1–67.3), where Noah and the flood are described after the revelation of the "Elect One" as judge in *1 Enoch* 62. George Nickelsburg has argued that the *Parables* can be dated "no later than the early decades of the first century C.E. on the grounds that Mark, the Q source, and the apostle Paul knew a form of the son of man tradition that we find in the Parables but not in Dan 7." Q 17:26-27 "draws a parallel between the days of the son of man and the days of Noah, which brings us to the Enochic typology . . . the author knew the Parables in a Noachic redactional form."[36] A common *model* of a transcendent judge and redeemer is reflected in the Christian tradition about the son of man.[37] George Nickelsburg and James VanderKam presuppose this model in the Gospel son of man tradition.[38] There is no evidence of direct literary dependence from the *Parables* to Q.[39] But this does *not* mean that the author(s) of Q was unaware of the son of man *tradition* found in the *Parables*. Q's awareness of an Enochic/parabolic son of man tradition indicates that the Q movement found the Enoch tradition authoritative and demonstrates Q's ideological compatibility with the Enochic traditions found in the *Parables*.[40]

35. Kloppenborg, *Formation of Q*, 160.

36. George W. E. Nickelsburg, *Jewish Literature between the Bible and the Mishnah: A Historical and Literary Introduction* (Philadelphia: Fortress Press, 1981), 222; idem, "Discerning the Structure(s) of the Enochic Book of Parables," in *Enoch and the Messiah Son of Man*, 23–47, esp. 47.

37. Nickelsburg, "Son of Man," *ABD*, 138–49.

38. George W. E. Nickelsburg and James C. VanderKam, *1 Enoch: A New Translation* (Minneapolis: Fortress Press, 2004), 6.

39. Walck, "The Son of Man in the Parables of Enoch and the Gospels," 315, 331.

40. For Q's relationship to the *Parables of Enoch* see Nickelsburg, *1 Enoch: A Commentary*, 83; Nickelsburg and VanderKam, *1 Enoch: A New Translation*, 6; Nickelsburg, *Jewish Literature between the*

The *Parables* influenced the early Jesus movement. In Q 12:4-5,[41] a saying located within the larger context of Q's judgment sayings,[42] Jesus tells his disciples:[43]

> καὶ μὴ φοβεῖσθε ἀπὸ τῶν ἀποκτεννόντων τὸ σῶμα,
> τὴν δὲ ψυχὴν μὴ δυναμένων ἀποκτεῖναι
> φοβεῖσθε δὲ . . . τὸν δυνάμενον καὶ ψυχὴν
> καὶ σῶμα ἀπολέσαι ἐν τῇ γεέννῃ
>
> Do not be afraid of those who kill the body
> but cannot kill the soul,
> but fear . . . the one who is able to destroy both the soul
> and body in Gehenna.

There is no consensus on whether Q 12:4-5 is an authentic historical Jesus saying.[44] In its clear differentiation between body and soul it represents a

Bible and the Mishnah, 222; Martin Hengel, *The Son of God: The Origin of Christology and the History of Jewish-Hellenistic Religion* (Philadelphia: Fortress Press, 1976), 75.

41. For bibliography see Dale C. Allison Jr., "Matthew 10:26-31 and the Problem of Evil," *VTQ* 32 (1988): 293–308; Gerhard Dautzenberg, *Sein Leben Bewahren:* ψυχή *in den Herrenworten der Evangelien* (SZANT 14; Munich: Kösel, 1966); Jacques Dupont, "L'après-mort dans l'oeuvre de Luc," *RTL* 3 (1972): 3–21; I. Howard Marshall, "Uncomfortable Words VI: Fear Him Who Can Destroy Both Body and Soul in Hell," *ExpT* 81 (1970): 276–82; Chaim Milikowsky, "Which Gehenna? Retribution and Eschatology in the Synoptic Gospels and in Early Jewish Texts," *NTS* 34 (1988): 238–49; Harry S. Pappas, "The Exhortation to Fearless Confession (Mt 10:26-33)," *GOTR* 25 (1980): 239–48; Günther Schwarz, "Matthäus 10:28: Emendation und Rucküberseztung," *ZNW* 72 (1981): 277–82.

42. See Brian Han Gregg, *The Historical Jesus and the Final Judgment Sayings in Q* (WUNT 2d ser. 207; Tübingen: Mohr Siebeck, 2006), 146–60; idem, "The Historical Jesus and the Final Judgment Sayings in Q," Ph. D. dissertation, University of Notre Dame, 2005, 198–217; Marius Reiser, *Jesus and Judgment: The Eschatological Proclamation in its Jewish Context* (Minneapolis: Fortress Press, 1990); J. Arthur Baird, *The Justice of God in the Teaching of Jesus* (Philadelphia: Westminster, 1963); Jürgen Becker, *Jesus of Nazareth*, trans. J. E. Crouch (New York: de Gruyter, 1998), 49–83.

43. Dale C. Allison Jr., "The Problem of Gehenna," in idem, *Resurrecting Jesus: The Earliest Christian Tradition and Its Interpreters* (New York: T&T Clark, 2005), 83.

44. Dale C. Allison Jr., *Jesus of Nazareth: Millenarian Prophet* (Minneapolis: Fortress Press, 1998), 139; Ulrich Luz, *Das Evangelium nach Matthäus (Mt 8–17)* (EKKNT 1.2; Neukirchen-Vluyn: Neukirchener Verlag, 1990), 124. See also Jacques Schlosser, *Le Règne de Dieu dans les Dits de Jésus* (Études Bibliques; 2 vols.; Paris: Gabalda, 1980), 2: 632–33; idem, "Le logion de Mt 10,28 par. Le 12,4-5," in *The Four Gospels: Festschrift Frans Neirynck*, ed. Frans van Segbroeck et al. (Leuven: Peeters, 1992), 621–31, at 622. There is no compelling reason to conclude that the reference to Gehenna is "authentic." *Contra* Gregg, *The Historical Jesus and the Final Judgment Sayings in Q*, 217.

distinctive kind of (Hellenistic) dualism within first-century Jewish thought.[45] Most scholars agree that Q is referring to God, not the devil, as the one who has the power to decide the fate of the soul.[46] But did Q refer to God "throwing" (ἐυβαλεῖν) or "destroying" (ἀπολέσαι) the soul in(to) Gehenna? According to Luke, God is to be feared because he has the "authority" (ἐξουσίαν) to "throw/cast" (ἐυβαλεῖν) the soul into Gehenna. It is not clear precisely *what* is "thrown" into Gehenna (the "resurrected" body or soul?) and whether this will take place immediately at death or at the last judgment. Chaim Milikowsky argues that Luke foresaw a resurrection only for the righteous and that the wicked were cast into Gehenna immediately after their death.[47] This is why Luke redacted Q: because Matthew defers judgment until the final judgment at the time of the "general resurrection." On the other hand, *2 Clement* 5.4 agrees with Luke's reading.[48]

> μὴ φοβεῖσθε τοὺς ἀποκτέννοντας ὑμᾶς
> καὶ μηδὲν ὑμῖν δυναμένους ποιεῖν,
> ἀλλὰ φοβεῖσθε τὸν μετὰ τὸ ἀποθανεῖν ὑμᾶς
> ἔχοντα ἐξουσίαν ψυχῆς
> καὶ σώματος τοῦ βαλεῖν
> εἰς υέενναν πυρός.
>
> Do not fear those who kill you
> and have the power to do nothing more,
> but fear the one who after your death
> has authority over soul and body to cast them
> into the fires of Gehenna.

There is also a similar construction to Luke's version of Q 12:4-5 in Rev. 2:10, a saying of the risen Jesus:

> *Do not fear* (μηδὲν φοβοῦ) what you are about to suffer. Beware, the devil is about *to throw* (βάλλειν) some of you into prison so that you

45. Dale C. Allison Jr., *The Jesus Tradition in Q* (Harrisburg, PA: Trinity Press International, 1997), 203.

46. Siegfried Schulz, *Q: Spruchquelle der Evangelisten* (Zürich: Theologischer Verlag, 1972), 160; Joseph A. Fitzmyer, *The Gospel According to Luke I–IX: Introduction, Translation, and Notes* (AB 28; New York: Doubleday, 1981), 959; Kloppenborg, *Formation of Q*, 207 n. 150. See also Harry S. Pappas, "'Exhortation to Fearless Confession,'" 242–43; N. T. Wright, *Jesus and the Victory of God*, Vol. 2, *Christian Origins and the Question of God* (Minneapolis: Fortress Press, 1996), 454–55.

47. Milikowsky, "Which Gehenna?"

48. Karl P. Donfried, *The Setting of Second Clement in Early Christianity* (Leiden: Brill, 1974), 79.

> may be tested, and for ten days you will have affliction. Be faithful unto death, and I will give you the crown of life.

Luke may have omitted Q's reference to the soul's destruction because his more Hellenized audience would have found the notion unthinkable or at least unpalatable.[49] A number of Lukan redactional fingerprints also suggest favoring Matt. 10:28 over Luke 12:4-5.[50] Matthew's Q seems preferable: God can "destroy" the soul in Gehenna.[51] Matthew's focus on God's "power" (δυνάμενον) to *destroy* (ἀπόλλυμι) need not be taken literally, as the verb can also mean "ruin" or "loss" and is commonly used to describe the metaphorical or *spiritual* fate of the unfaithful.[52] For example, Jas. 4:12 refers to God as the "lawgiver and judge who is able to save (σῶσαι) and destroy (ἀπολέσαι)." Matthew's version, whether it refers to the soul's ruin, loss, or permanent destruction, is the more difficult reading and may be preferred, implying that Q 12:4-5 challenges the idea of the soul's immortality because it *can* be destroyed (ἀπολέσαι) in Gehenna.

The term Gehenna (γεέννα) originally referred to a place outside Jerusalem called the "Valley of Hinnom" where children were once sacrificed to Molech.[53]

49. See Schulz, Q, 158; Dieter Zeller, *Die Weisheitlichen Mahnsprüche bei den Synoptikern* (FxB 17; Würzburg: Echter Verlag, 1977), 94; Piper, *Wisdom in the Q-Tradition*, 52; Eduard Schweizer, *The Good News According to Luke* (Atlanta: John Knox, 1984), 205; Harry T. Fleddermann, *Q: A Reconstruction and Commentary* (BTS 1; Leuven: Peeters, 2005), 569.

50. *The Critical Edition of Q: A Synopsis including the Gospels of Matthew and Luke, Mark and Thomas with English, German, and French Translations of Q and Thomas* [hereafter *CEQ*], ed. James M. Robinson, Paul Hoffmann, and John S. Kloppenborg (Leuven: Peeters/Minneapolis: Fortress, 2000), 296–99; Schulz, Q, 158–59; Joachim Jeremias, *Die Sprache des Lukasevangeliums: Redaktion und Tradition im Nicht-Markusstoff des dritten Evangeliums* (KKNT; Göttingen: Vandenhoeck & Ruprecht, 1980), 212; Schlosser, "Le Logion," 625; Marshall, "Uncomfortable Words," 277–78; Gerhard Dautzenberg, *Sein Leben bewahren: ψυχή in den Herrenworten der Evangelien* (SANT 14; München: Kösel Verlag, 1966), 138; W. D. Davies and Dale C. Allison Jr., *A Critical and Exegetical Commentary on the Gospel According to Saint Matthew* (3 vols.; ICCHSONT; Edinburgh: T&T Clark, 1988–1997), 2: 206; Fleddermann, Q, 569. Luke's introductory φίλοις is characteristically Lukan (*CEQ*, 296–99; Schulz, Q, 157; *contra* Davies and Allison, *Matthew*, 2: 206 n. 32). Second, μετὰ ταῦτα represents a Lukan addition to Q. Both 5:27 and 10:1 are concrete examples of Lukan additions of this phrase in Markan material (*CEQ*, 296–99; Schulz, Q, 158; Jeremias, *Die Sprache*, 212; Marshall, "Uncomfortable Words," 277; Fleddermann, Q, 569). Third, Luke characteristically uses ἔχω with the infinitive (*CEQ*, 296–99; Jeremias, *Die Sprache*, 212; Marshall, "Uncomfortable Words," 277; Fleddermann, Q, 569). Fourth, Luke's μετὰ τό with the infinitive is uncharacteristic of Matthew (*CEQ*, 296–99). Luke's ὑποδείκνυμι is also Lukan redaction.

51. Dale C. Allison Jr., *The Intertextual Jesus: Scripture in Q* (Harrisburg, PA: Trinity Press International, 2000), 84.

52. Rom. 14:15; 1 Cor. 1:18; *Barn.* 20.1; Herm. *Sim.* 9.26.3.

Its exact location is disputed, but it may have been below the southern wall of ancient Jerusalem, stretching from Mount Zion to the Kidron Valley. Josiah seems to have put an end to the practice, but the valley came to be considered cursed and symbolized the place of fiery judgment of the wicked in Early Jewish apocalyptic literature,[54] perhaps because it was used as a burning garbage dump.[55] It is mentioned as a place of punishment and destruction of the wicked in the Mishnah and the Babylonian Talmud, a location where the wicked go to suffer.[56] The Targums refer to "Gehinnom" in relation to the final judgment and the fate of the wicked, but it is not mentioned in the Apocrypha, Dead Sea Scrolls, Pseudepigrapha, Philo, or Josephus. In the Synoptics, Jesus uses the term eleven times to describe the opposite to life in the kingdom, a place where the body and soul could be destroyed "in unquenchable fire."[57]

The identification of Gehenna as a place of eschatological judgment was thus a well-known motif in Second Temple Judaism and could easily have been added to Q at a redactional stage. The threat of judgment in Q 12:4-5 is quite similar to the explicitly imminent judgment described by John the Baptist:

> The ax already lies at the root of the trees. So every tree not bearing healthy fruit is to be chopped down and thrown on the fire.[58]
> He will clear his threshing floor and gather the wheat into his granary, but the chaff he will burn on a fire that can never be put out.[59]

The introduction of a judgment of eternal fire in Gehenna is consistent with the tenor of apocalyptic judgment in Q as well as Q's indictment of "this generation," symbolized and heralded by the imminent arrival of the son of man. Q 12:4-5 is commonly located within the larger compositional structure of Q 12:2-12, a "son of man" complex:

Q 12:2-3:	Proclaiming What Was Whispered
Q 12:4-5:	Not Fearing the Body's Death

53. Lev. 18:21; 1 Kgs. 11:7; 2 Kgs. 16:3; 21:6; Jos. 15:8, 18:16; Jer. 7:31; 19:4-5; 32:35; 2 Chron. 28:3; Neh. 11:30.

54. *1 En.* 26–27; 54.1-6; 56.1-4; 90.24-27.

55. Although see Lloyd R. Bailey, "Gehenna: The Topography of Hell," *BA* 49 (1986): 189.

56. *Qidd.* 4.14, *Abot* 1.5, 5.19, 20, *Tos. t. Ber.* 6.15; and *b. Roš. Haš.* 16b:7a; *b. Ber.* 28b, respectively.

57. Mark 9:43-48; Matt. 5:22, 29, 30; 10:28; 18:9; 23:15; 23:33; Mark 9:43, 45, 47; Luke 12:5; Jas. 3:6. Mark adds "Gehenna" to the quotation of Isa. (9:44, 46, 48).

58. Q 3:9.

59. Q 3:17.

Q 12:6-7: More Precious than Many Sparrows
Q 12:8-9: Confessing or Denying (the Son of Man)
Q 12:10: Speaking against the Holy Spirit
Q 12:11-12: Hearings before Synagogues

Q 12:4-5 appeals to the authority of the son of man. The dominant theme of *1 Enoch* is an imminent judgment.[60] Note the reference to *a valley of fire*:

> I looked and turned to another part of the earth,
> and saw there *a deep valley with burning fire.*
> And they brought the kings and the mighty,
> and began to cast them into this deep valley.[61]
> . . . the abyss of complete condemnation.[62]
> . . . the "*burning furnace.*[63]

A number of Q specialists hold that Q 12:4-5 is a "sapiential saying."[64] At first sight this seems difficult to believe. After all, Jesus is issuing a prophetic warning about *hell*, which is hardly what immediately comes to mind when one thinks of wisdom literature. Accordingly, it might prove useful to take a closer look at how the discussion of the saying sheds light on the discursive difficulties of our subject. John Kloppenborg, for example, holds that Q 12:2-12, a unit that has undergone secondary expansion, is "untouched or only marginally influenced" by the themes of rejection and judgment.[65] Its implied audience is Jesus' disciples and its tone is "hortatory and instructional," not "polemical or threatening": Q 12:4-6 is "better classified as a sapiential admonition to courage in the face of possible martyrdom."[66] Similarly, Ronald Piper argues that this saying is based on the sapiential theme of God's providential care:[67] Q 12:4-7 "ultimately bases the command not to fear men in an assurance of God's

60. *1 En.* 38.1; 45.2; 45.6; 48.8-9; 51.1.

61. *1 En.* 54.1.

62. *1 En.* 54.5.

63. *1 En.* 56.3.

64. Kloppenborg, *Formation of Q*, 171, 206. See also Heinz Schürmann, "Observations on the Son of Man Title in the Speech Source. Its Occurrence in Closing and Introductory Expressions," in *The Shape of Q: Signal Essays on the Sayings Gospel*, ed. John S. Kloppenborg (Minneapolis: Fortress Press, 1994), 85–87.

65. Kloppenborg, *Formation of Q*, 244.

66. Ibid., 210–11.

67. Piper, *Wisdom in the Q-Tradition*, 51–61, citing Q 11:9-13; Q 12:22-31; Q 6:37-42; Q 6:43-45.

care."[68] The "admonition to fear God" is "a reasonable case . . . for deciding whom to fear."[69] Alan Kirk notes that the pairing of Q 12:4-5 and Q 12:4-7 "joins together what appear to be two heterogeneous, almost thematically antithetical units,"[70] but suggests that these two units belong together because both "motivate the hearer or reader to fear God."[71] Q 12:4-5's admonition to fear God was "necessary in order to counteract the danger of apostasy." The fear of Gehenna encourages "courageous witness" through "threats of sanction,"[72] although this threat "is a sharp prod indeed," even if "the wound is immediately salved with images which assure of God's tender and provident care."[73]

Q 12:4-5 may be *reminiscent* of sapiential literature, but it conforms to the category of "eschatological wisdom" (or sapiential eschatology).[74] Q's exhortation to avoid anxiety in Q 12:22-31 and 12:4-7 is based on a vision of *eschatological* reversal requiring unconditional trust in God.[75] The interpretation of Q 12:4-7 cuts both ways: it is form-critically sapiential but framed within an eschatological context, and the wisdom-argument from providence is redeployed in terms of mission.[76] The motif of the fear of God may be a regular occurrence in wisdom literature,[77] and "exhortations to courage in the face of martyrdom" may be found in a variety of near-contemporary texts such as 4 Maccabees and *1 Enoch* 101,[78] but these are not solely "sapiential" texts. While Q 12:6-7 encourages Jesus' disciples "not to be afraid because God in

68. Ibid., 55.

69. Ibid., 56.

70. Kirk, *The Composition of the Sayings Source*, 207–8.

71. Ibid., 208.

72. Ibid., 205.

73. Ibid., 208.

74. Walter Grundmann, "Weisheit im Horizont des Reiches Gottes. Eine Studie zur Verkündigung Jesu nach der Spruchüberlieferung Q," in *Die Kirche des Anfangs. Für Heinz Schürmann*, ed. Rudolf Schnackenburg, et al. (Freiburg: Herder, 1978), 175–99.

75. Luise Schottroff, "Sheep among Wolves: The Wandering Prophets of the Sayings-Source," in *Jesus and the Hope of the Poor*, ed. Luise Schottroff and Wolfgang Stegemann, trans. Matthew J. O'Connell (Maryknoll, NY: Orbis Books, 1986), 39–43.

76. Schulz, Q, 143, 160–61, identifies Q 12:4-7 as a *prophetische Warnung* to fear God See also Rudolf Bultmann, *History of the Synoptic Tradition*, trans. John Marsh (Oxford: Blackwell, 1963), 119. Richard A. Horsley and Jonathan A. Draper, *Whoever Hears You Hears Me: Prophets, Performance, and Tradition in Q* (Harrisburg, PA: Trinity Press International, 1999), 272, locate Q 12:2-12 in the context of "the possibility of repressive action by the rulers." Dale C. Allison Jr., *The Jesus Tradition in Q* (Valley Forge, PA: Trinity Press International, 1997), 168–75, esp. 165, 170, 175, proposes that Q 12:7 has more to do with God's "sovereignty" (than his immediate care) in future-oriented eschatological terms.

77. Kloppenborg, *Formation of Q*, 209, citing Prov. 3:7; 7:1; 24:21; Eccl. 5:6; 12:13; Sir. 4:8, 21; 7:31.

78. 4 Macc. 13:14-15. See also *1 Enoch* 101.

His providence will care for them," Q 12:4-5 "seem to breathe a rather different atmosphere."[79] The point of the saying is not an absence of fear, but rather "that one *should* 'fear'—but fear God rather than men." This contrasts with Q 12:6-7, which encourages the follower to have no fear by trusting in God. These two sayings seem to have "a different origin."[80] The link connecting Q 12:4-5 with Q 12:6-7 is the verb "to fear," yet the theological thrusts of the two sayings are remarkably different.[81] Q 12:4-5 was coupled with the providential promise of Q 12:6-7 through a similar use of the negative imperative "do *not* fear/do *not* be anxious" (μὴ φοβεῖσθε/μὴ μεριμνᾶτε). The book of Proverbs, an undeniably sapiential wisdom instruction, repeatedly refers to the "fear (φόβος) of the Lord" as the beginning of wisdom, knowledge, and "a fountain of life."[82] Given the repetitious use of the verb "to fear" in the LXX, it is reasonable to associate the "fear of the Lord" with wisdom. In Proverbs, however, the "fear" of the Lord is better understood as respect, reverence, and awe, not *terror*. Q 12:4-5 clearly reads more like a thinly veiled threat of eschatological destruction than a sapiential encouragement. This saying is not sapiential in the sense of worldly wisdom, nor does it reflect the vision of a providential God. Q 12:6-7 is a sapiential form set within the wider context of Q's mission instruction, which is itself located within a social context of a persecuted, rejected mission in which Jesus' identity as the son of man is a defining feature and "this generation" is condemned.

Q 12:4-5 "encourages" Jesus' followers to fear God more than worldly authorities because God's judgment is greater and permanent. Q 12:5 is a *threat*. Q 12:4-5 is part of the darker vision of judgment pronounced on "this generation." Jesus is literally putting the fear of God into his disciples, an idea seemingly incompatible with his confident assertion that God loves *everyone* unconditionally and his imperative *not* to judge.[83]

Q represents a critical moment in the emergence of the Jesus movement when Jesus' teaching on the providential kingdom was being compromised by the movement's rejection, requiring "Jesus" and his verbal authority to be redeployed to serve as encouragement in the face of rejection, as a warning to keep the faith during times of persecution ("hearings before synagogues") and, finally, as an eschatological threat of soul-destruction. Jesus' disciples are privileged potential members of the kingdom, but they are not exempt from

79. Tuckett, *Q and the History of Early Christianity*, 250, 318.

80. Ibid., 316.

81. Ibid., 318.

82. Prov. 14:26-27; 9:10-11; 1:7, respectively.

83. Q 6:27-28, 35c-d; 6:37-38.

judgment if they falter: God can consign them to hell. This is presumably intended to serve as an incentive: serving God is more important than preserving your physical life. The problem, of course, is that the juxtaposition of Q 12:4-5 and Q 12:6-7 sends two very different messages: God loves you so much that he cares for your every need *and* he will destroy you in Gehenna if you do not fear him.[84]

The *Sitz im Leben* of Q 12:2-9 is arguably in the post-Easter period, when the redactor of Q had "access" to the *Book of Parables*, in which judgment and the coming son of man are dominant compositional themes. The coming judgment stands in tension with the "good news" of the present-kingdom tradition with its vision of divine providence. The Inaugural Sermon is not characteristic of the judgment motif typically associated with the "day of the son of man," but rather represents Jesus' instruction.[85] One could attribute this dissonance to Q's (or Jesus'!) theological inconsistency as opposed to a theologically disparate redaction of generically distinct literary materials,[86] but this does not adequately address the antithetical nature of the unit, something that also characterizes much of Q. It is difficult again not to conclude that we are dealing with two streams of tradition in Q: one in which Jesus is the Son of God who teaches the way of the kingdom and a secondary stream in which Jesus is represented as the rejected son of man who will return as a heavenly judge to punish the wicked. The major problem in Q studies, therefore, is not one of generic incompatibility between two "strata" but the failure to recognize the influence of the *Book of Parables*, which bifurcated the tradition into (at least) two different Christological orientations, the first a utopian vision of divine providence, the other casting Jesus in the role of the rejected and avenging son of man.[87] Q represents a confluence of these cultural streams.

Why was the *Book of Parables* useful to the early Jesus movement? First, it provided a contemporary textual precedent and parallel for the heavenly *exaltation* of a human being, and Jesus' exaltation or resurrection would have reminded his disciples of the Enoch tradition and been modeled after it. Second,

84. Robert W. Funk, Roy W. Hoover, and the Jesus Seminar, *The Five Gospels: The Search for the Authentic Words of Jesus: A New Translation and Commentary* (New York: Macmillan, 1993), 173, notes that this saying "teaches fear of God, a tenet of Israelite religious tradition (Deut 6:13)," but argues that "Such admonitions . . . do not comport well with what is otherwise known of Jesus."

85. John S. Kloppenborg, "The Sayings Gospel Q and the Quest of the Historical Jesus," *HTR* 89 (1996): 3007–44, at 336.

86. Dale C. Allison Jr., "The Problem of Audience," in *Resurrecting Jesus*, 48–50.

87. Simon J. Joseph, "'His Wisdom Will Reach All Peoples': 4Q534-36, Q 17:26-27, 30, and *1 En.* 65.1–67.3, 90," *DSD* 19. no. 1 (2012): 71–105.

Jesus' exaltation reversed his worldly rejection and execution and aroused the expectation that he would soon return to inaugurate the eschatological *judgment*, which facilitated the idea that the enemies of Jesus' followers would be punished for rejecting the movement. Third, the *Parables* conflate the Servant motif from Isaiah with the son of man and served to connect the *suffering* of the Servant to Jesus' suffering, death, and, ultimately, his vicarious atonement. Fourth, the *Parables* use the figure of Wisdom as *rejected* by Israel; this, too, was conflated with the rejected son of man in Q. Fifth, the *Parables* appeal to the Davidic *messianic* tradition, and this served to support Jesus' legitimacy as a messianic figure.

The *Book of Parables*, although a secondary development within the larger Enochic corpus, represents a missing link in the origins of early Jewish Christology. The *Parables* conflate a number of messianic templates, themes, and functions: the Davidic messiah, whose traditional function is warrior-king; the Danielic son of man, who is cast as an agent of imminent eschatological judgment; the Servant of Isaiah, whose description is marked by suffering and death; and the figure of Wisdom, who is rejected and returns to her heavenly abode. Considering the economic utility of the *Parables* in explaining the conflicted ministry, religious opposition, political execution, and divine vindication of Jesus, it is not difficult to see why this emergent text would have been exegetically irresistible to the authors(s) and redactors of the early Jesus tradition. It is also not difficult to see how biblical, eschatological, and divine violence were reinscribed into the Jesus tradition at a remarkably early stage in its development.

The *Book of Parables* also seems to have influenced Paul's Christology.[88] James Waddell has recently identified a number of correspondences between the figure in the *Parables* and Paul's Χριστός. He concludes that "The combination of shared elements is so striking as to preclude the possibility that the *Book of the Parables* and the Letters of Paul constituted independent, parallel developments."[89] There is no evidence of direct literary dependency, but Paul seems to be "familiar with the conceptual elements of the Enochic messiah." These elements include "a pre-existent messiah figure who is both human and

88. James A. Waddell, *The Messiah: A Comparative Study of the Enochic Son of Man and the Pauline Kyrios* (JCT 10; London: T&T Clark, 2011), 13, argues that the *Parables* "[are] either not taken seriously as a text reflecting messianic ideology that predates the New Testament, or the evidence in the Parables is minimized in some way that enhances the status or the uniqueness of the evidence in the New Testament."

89. James A. Waddell, "The Messiah in the Parables of Enoch and the Letters of Paul: A Comparative Analysis," Ph. D. dissertation, University of Michigan, 2010, x.

from heaven, who moves between the earthly and heavenly realms, who sits on God's throne, administers God's judgment, executes God's punishment, and reigns over an eternal kingdom, *and* receives worship from humans."[90] The messianic son of man is an agent of *salvation*,[91] judgment,[92] and punishment.[93] Paul's contribution to this developing tradition seems to have been adding the functions of crucifixion, resurrection, and the forgiveness of sins.[94]

There is evidence that the *Parables* influenced the composition of the Gospel of Matthew.[95] The son of man figures in Matthew and the *Parables* share many characteristics: both are heavenly beings.[96] Both have a judicial role.[97] Both have followers called the "righteous" and the "elect."[98] Both figures will provide eternal bliss for the righteous yet no mercy for the condemned.[99] Both are also described as seated on the "throne of his glory," a distinctive phrase that Matthew seems to have taken from the *Parables*.[100] Leslie Walck has recently performed a comparative analysis of the son of man figure in the *Parables* and Matthew and concludes that Matthew knew the *Parables*.[101] Matthew's emphasis

90. Ibid, 8.

91. *1 En.* 48.7.

92. The Chosen One will sit on the heavenly throne on the "day of affliction and tribulation" (*1 En.* 45.2-3; 51.2-3; 55.4; 61.8; 62.1-3). The son of man will sit on the heavenly throne (*1 En.* 62.5; 69.27, 29) and the Chosen One will judge "the things that are secret" (*1 En.* 49.1-4; 61.8-9).

93. *1 En.* 46.4-6; 48.8-9, 10; 62.1-2, 4-5; 69.27, 29.

94. In the *Parables*, Enoch is *transformed* into the messianic son of man (*1 En.* 71.9-12, 14). If Enoch's identification as the preexistent son of man is integral to the original *Parables* (and not a post- and non-Christian Jewish critique of Jesus' role as the son of man), then Jesus' identification as the (new) son of man in Q may be either an identification of Jesus-as-Enoch or a subversive appropriation of the Enoch tradition (a kind of dethroning of Enoch and enthronement of Jesus). In either case Q's adoption of this preexisting Enochic template created theological tensions in the early Jesus tradition.

95. Johannes Theisohn, *Der auserwählte Richter: Untersuchungen zum traditiongeschichtlichen Ort der Menschensohngestalt der Bilderreden des Äthiopischen Henoch* (Göttingen: Vandenhoeck & Ruprecht, 1975), 153, 182; David R. Catchpole, "The Poor on Earth and the Son of Man in Heaven: A Re-appraisal of Matthew XXV. 31-46," *BJRL* 61 (1979): 355–97; Collins, "The Son of Man in First-Century Judaism." For opposition to Matthean dependence see Maurice Casey, *Son of Man: The Interpretation and Influence of Daniel* 7 (London: SPCK, 1979); Douglas R. A. Hare, *The Son of Man Tradition* (Minneapolis: Fortress Press, 1990).

96. *1 En.* 46; 48.2-8; 62–63; 70–71; Matt. 13:36-43; 16:24-28; 19:28; 24:30; 25:31-46.

97. *1 En.* 46; 62–63; 69:26-29; Matt. 13:36-43; 16:27; 19:28; 24:30; 25:31.

98. *1 En.* 48:2-8; 62–63; Matt. 13:36-43; 25:31-46; *1 En.* 48:2-8; 62–63; Matt. 24:30-31.

99. *1 En.* 62:13-16; 71:16-17; Matt. 13:43; 25:34, 46; *1 En.* 62–63; Matt. 13:36-43; 25:31-46. Walck, "The Son of Man in the Parables of Enoch and the Gospels," 330.

100. *1 En.* 62:5; 69:27, 29; Matt. 19:28; 25:31.

on the coming son of man figure is strikingly similar to the *Parables'* view of the son of man as "a future, non-suffering figure."[102]

The letter of Jude also shows "a close familiarity" with and an "evidently high respect for" the *Book of Enoch.*[103] It is time, therefore, to reexamine and reevaluate the cultural contours of the early Jesus tradition in light of recent research in Enochic Judaism. The *Book of Enoch* (*1 En.*) has been described as "the most important text in the corpus of Jewish literature from the Hellenistic and Roman periods."[104] An "appeal to Enochic authority" is explicit in Jude, Barnabas, Irenaeus, Tertullian, Clement of Alexandria, and Origen.[105] Enoch traditions were clearly regarded as authoritative in early Jewish Christianity and were still influential in Jewish Christian circles as late as the fourth century C.E.[106] The authority of *1 Enoch* was ultimately rejected by the Church for a

101. Leslie W. Walck, *The Son of Man in the Parables of Enoch and in Matthew* (JCT 9; Edinburgh: T&T Clark, 2011), 224; idem, "The Son of Man in the Parables of Enoch and the Gospels." See now also Amy E. Richter, *Enoch and the Gospel of Matthew* (PTMS; Eugene, OR: Pickwick, 2012), 2.

102. Walck, *The Son of Man in the Parables of Enoch and in Matthew*, 165, citing Matt. 10:23; 13:41; 16:27, 28; 19:28; 24:30-31; 25:31-32.

103. See Simon J. Joseph, "'Seventh from Adam.'" On Jude as the "most neglected letter in the New Testament" see Richard Bauckham, *Jude and the Relatives of Jesus in the Early Church* (Edinburgh: T&T Clark, 1990), 2; idem, *Jude, 2 Peter* (WBC 50; Waco: Word, 1983); John H. Elliott, *I–II Peter/Jude* (ACNT; Minneapolis: Augsburg, 1982), 161. Bauckham, *Jude, 2 Peter*, 7, 10, argues that Jude shows "a close familiarity with *1 Enoch* (vv 6, 12-16), from which he takes his only formal quotation from a written source (vv 14-15)." See also idem, "A Note on a Problem in the Greek Version of 1 Enoch i. 9," *JTS* 32 (1981): 136–38; Matthew Black, "The Maranatha Invocation and Jude 14, 15 (I Enoch 1:9)," in *Christ and Spirit in the New Testament: In Honour of Charles Francis Digby Moule*, ed. Barnabas Lindars and Steven S. Smalley (Cambridge: Cambridge University Press, 1973); Carroll D. Osburn, "The Christological Use of 1 Enoch i. 9 in Jude 14, 15," *NTS* 23, no. 3 (1977): 334–41; J. Daryl Charles, "Jude's Use of Pseudepigraphical Source-Material as Part of a Literary Strategy," *NTS* 37 (1991): 130–45; Boudewijn Dehandschutter, "Pseudo-Cyprian, Jude and Enoch: Some Notes on 1 Enoch 1:9," in *Tradition and Re-Interpretation in Jewish and Early Christian Literature: Essays in Honour of Jürgen C. H. Lebram*, ed. Jan W. van Henten, et al. (SPB 36; Leiden: Brill, 1986), 114–20; Stephan J. Joubert, "Facing the Past: Transtextual Relationships and Historical Understanding in the Letter of Jude," *BZ*, n. s. 42 (1998): 56–70.

104. Nickelsburg, *1 Enoch: A Commentary*. Boccaccini, *Beyond the Essene Hypothesis*, 12: *1 Enoch* forms "the core of an ancient and distinct variety of second temple Judaism." See also Sacchi, *Jewish Apocalyptic and Its History*.

105. Nickelsburg, *1 Enoch*, 101.

106. Eibert Tigchelaar, "Manna-Eaters and Man-Eaters: Food of Giants and Men in the Pseudo-Clementine Homilies 8," in *The Pseudo-Clementines*, ed. Jan N. Bremmer (SECA 10; Leuven: Peeters, 2010), 92–114, esp. 97; Nickelsburg, *1 Enoch*, 97–98. F. Stanley Jones, "Pseudo-Clementine Literature," in *Encyclopedia of the Dead Sea Scrolls*, ed. Lawrence H. Schiffman and James C. VanderKam (2 vols.;

number of reasons, including its absence from the Hebrew Bible, its use by Manichaeans, and its alternative explanation of evil, but in doing so Christianity also lost part of its ancient Jewish heritage.[107] The discovery of the Dead Sea Scrolls and the publication of the Aramaic Enoch fragments has resulted in "a growing awareness that the Enochic corpus and the kind of apocalypticism that it reflects have influenced the shaping of early Christian theology."[108] Christianity maintained "continuity" with the "Enochic paradigm" of the supernatural origins of evil and an eschatological judgment.[109] A central theme of these compositions is a distinctive conception of evil.[110] The Enochic tradition proposed that the origin of evil was to be found in a group of fallen angels.[111] The Watchers and their demon offspring are responsible for evil, sickness, and disease.[112] Rebellious angels took human sexual partners, transgressed the divine order before the flood, and that their offspring continue to cause disease (15.3-7). *1 Enoch* also describes the Watchers as wrongly revealing heavenly secrets to humanity, resulting in violence, bloodshed, and sexual misconduct.[113]

The Qumran community's evident interest in the Enochic tradition illustrates that Second Temple Judaism developed at least two major theodicial

New York: Oxford University Press, 2000), 718–19; James C. VanderKam, *Enoch: A Man for All Generations* (Columbia, SC: University of South Carolina Press, 1995), 179–80.

107. Nickelsburg, *1 Enoch*, 101–2.

108. Ibid., 123. For the influence of Enochic traditions on Petrine traditions see Kelley Coblentz Bautch, "Peter and the Patriarch: A Confluence of Traditions?" in *With Letters of Light: Studies in the Dead Sea Scrolls, Early Jewish Apocalypticism, Magic, and Mysticism: in Honor of Rachel Elior*, ed. Daphna Arbel and Andrei A. Orlov (Ekstasis 2; Berlin: de Gruyter, 2010), 14–27.

109. Gabriele Boccaccini, "Enochians, Urban Essenes, Qumranites: Three Social Groups, One Intellectual Movement," in *The Early Enoch Literature*, ed. Gabriele Boccaccini and John J. Collins (JSJSup 121; Leiden: Boston, 2007), 301–27, esp. 320–21. On Enochic influence on early Christianity see Nickelsburg, *1 Enoch*, 82–100; H. J. Lawlor, "Early Citations from the Book of Enoch," *JPh* 25 (1897): 164–225; James C. VanderKam, "1 Enoch, Enochic Motifs, and Enoch in Early Christian Literature," in *The Jewish Apocalyptic Heritage in Early Christianity*, ed. James C. VanderKam and William Adler (CRINT 3/4; Minneapolis: Fortress Press, 1996), 32–101.

110. John J. Collins, "The Origin of Evil in Apocalyptic Literature and the Dead Sea Scrolls," in idem, *Seers, Sibyls and Sages in Hellenistic-Roman Judaism* (Leiden: Brill, 1997), 287–99.

111. John J. Collins, "Creation and the Origin of Evil," in *Apocalypticism in the Dead Sea Scrolls* (London: Routledge, 1997), 30–51; Sacchi, *Jewish Apocalyptic*; Nickelsburg, *1 Enoch*, 46.

112. In the Scrolls these demons, the offspring of the Watchers and the "daughters of men" mentioned in *1 En.* 15:11 and Genesis 6, are called "bastards," or "Giants" (Nephilim). See Philip S. Alexander, "The Demonology of the Dead Sea Scrolls," in *The Dead Sea Scrolls After Fifty Years: A Comprehensive Assessment*, ed. Peter W. Flint and James C. VanderKam (Leiden: Brill, 1998), 331–53, at 347.

113. *1 En.* 8.1; 9.6; 10.4-8.

axes–"The Enochic Axis" and "The Axis of Adam and Eve"–which provided two significantly different, even contrasting, explanations for what Michael E. Stone calls "the state of the world."[114] According to the Enochic view, the origin of evil was the result of an angelic rebellion; the traditional view, on the other hand, holds Adam and Eve's disobedience as responsible for the fallen condition of the world, although this latter view—so familiar to the Western world via the Pauline letters and the Augustinian doctrine of "Original Sin"—is strikingly absent at Qumran.[115]

In the Enochic tradition, it is the fallen angels who enslaved humanity "by magical writings" (διὰ μαγικῶν γραφῶν), "teaching them to offer sacrifices and incense and libation."[116] The angels' spirits (πνεύματα) led humanity astray "to sacrifice to demons" (ἐπιθῦειν τοῖς δαιμονίοις). The *Book of the Watchers* accuses Asael of causing human violence by introducing weapons (*1 En.* 8.1-2). Justin expands the list of wicked influences to include "murders" (φόνους) and "wars" (πολέμους). In the Gospels, Jesus engages in conflict with evil powers and heals people of demonic possession in order to counteract the effects of the fallen angels and their offspring. In Matt. 12:29 casting out demons requires *binding* the strong one. In Matt. 16:13-19 Peter is given the power to *bind* and loose in heaven and on earth. Jesus expels demons and challenges Satan during his temptation. These motifs are clearly consistent with Enochic demonology.

Jude 1:6 describes how "the angels (ἀγγέλους) who did not keep their own position, but left their proper dwelling" in heaven have been "kept" in "eternal chains in deepest darkness for the judgment of the great day."[117] Jude uses the Watcher myth similarly to the usage of the author of the *Damascus Document* (CD), which cites the story of the Watchers as "a paradigm of God's judgment of the wicked, applied to sinners in the end time," and in doing so "appeals to the prophetic authority of Enoch."[118] This is the only explicit reference in the New Testament to "angels" that "sinned."[119] Jude then refers to Sodom and Gomorrah, which *also* "indulged in sexual immorality and pursued unnatural

114. Michael E. Stone, *Ancient Judaism: New Visions and Views* (Grand Rapids: Eerdmans, 2011), 51.

115. Ibid., 50–51.

116. Annette Yoshiko Reed, *Fallen Angels and the History of Judaism and Christianity: The Reception of Enochic Literature* (New York: Cambridge University Press, 2005), 164, citing Justin, *2 Apol.* 5.4. For sorcery, spells, and divination see *1 En.* 7.1, 8.3, 9.7. For idolatry and pagan sacrifices see *1 En.* 19.1.

117. The reference to "eternal chains" is found in *1 En.* 13.1; 14.5; 54.3–5; 56.1–4; 88.1; 4QenGiants[a] 8:14, as well as in *2 Apoc. Bar.* 56.13; *Jub.* 5.6, where it also refers to the Watchers.

118. Nickelsburg, *1 Enoch*, 100; VanderKam, *Enoch: A Man For All Generations*, 122.

119. VanderKam and Adler, *The Jewish Apocalyptic Heritage in Early Christianity*, 66.

lust (1:7)." Jude's quotation from *1 Enoch* is "to be seen as Jude's key text in his midrash."[120] According to *1 En.* 1.9, Enoch predicts the "Day of Tribulation":

> Behold, he comes with the myriads of his holy ones,
> to execute judgment on all,
> and to destroy the wicked,
> and to convict all fleshfor all the wicked deeds
> that they have done, and the proud and hard words
> that wicked sinners spoke against him.[121]

In Jude 1:14–15 the simple addition of the word "Lord" (κύριος) transforms the eschatological divine judgment into the *parousia* of the "Lord *Jesus*":

> It was also about these that Enoch (Ἑνὼχ), the seventh from Adam, prophesied, saying, "See, the Lord is coming with ten thousands of his holy ones (ἁγίαις) to execute judgment on all, and to convict all the ungodly of all their deeds of ungodliness that they have committed in such an ungodly way, and of all the harsh things that ungodly sinners have spoken against him."

This quotation from *1 En.* 1.9 does not mean that Jude regarded *1 Enoch* as "canonical Scripture,"[122] but Jude's evidently "high respect" for the Enochic tradition, in conjunction with Q, Matthew, and Paul's possible familiarity with the *Parables*, warrants a closer look at the full Enochic corpus, in particular the *Animal Apocalypse*, one of the oldest works in the *Book of Enoch*, for it is this apocalyptic text that may yet shed the clearest light on the earliest messianic identification of the historical Jesus.

120. Bauckham, *Jude, 2 Peter*, 100.

121. Nickelsburg, *1 Enoch*.

122. Charles, "Jude's Use," 143–44; idem, *Literary Strategy in the Epistle of Jude* (Scranton: University of Scranton Press, 1993).

9

The Enochic Adam

The *Animal Apocalypse* (*1 En.* 85–90), written around the time of the Maccabean revolt (c. 165 B.C.E.),[1] is an extensive allegory representing the history of the world from the creation of Adam to the end-time judgment.[2] The *Animal Apocalypse* (*An. Apol.*) was "originally an independent work."[3] Nonetheless, it shares the basic worldview of other Enoch texts[4] and was probably written in Aramaic in Judea.[5] *An. Apoc.* also has affinities with the Qumran corpus.[6] Patrick Tiller has proposed that it originated within "a

1. Albert I. Baumgarten, *The Flourishing of Jewish Sects in the Maccabean Era: An Interpretation* (JSJSup 55; Leiden: Brill, 1997), 170; John J. Collins, *The Apocalyptic Imagination: An Introduction to Jewish Apocalyptic Literature* (BR; Grand Rapids: Eerdmans, 1998), 53–56, 90; George W. E. Nickelsburg, "Enoch, First Book of," *ABD* 2: 508–16, at 511. George W. E. Nickelsburg and James C. VanderKam, *1 Enoch: A New Commentary Based on the Hermeneia Commentary* (Minneapolis: Fortress Press, 2004), 9–10, date the present form of the work to approximately 164–160 B.C.E., "although the parallel passages in 90:6-19 may indicate an earlier date around 200 B.C.E. " See also Christopher Rowland, *The Open Heaven: A Study of Apocalyptic in Judaism and Early Christianity* (New York: Crossroad, 1982), 252.

2. Parts of this chapter were previously published in the following articles: "'His Wisdom Will Reach All Peoples': "4Q534-36, Q 17:26-27, 30, and *1 En.* 65.1-67.3, 90," *DSD* 19, no. 1 (2012): 71–105; "The Eschatological 'Adam' of the *Animal Apocalypse* (*1 En.* 90) and Paul's 'Last Adam': Excavating a Trajectory in Jewish Christianity," *Henoch* 34, no. 1 (2012): 144–70.

3. Patrick A. Tiller, *A Commentary on the Animal Apocalypse of 1 Enoch* (EJ 4; Atlanta: Scholars Press, 1993), 98–99.

4. Ibid., 83, 118–19.

5. J. T. Milik, ed., *The Books of Enoch: Aramaic Fragments of Qumrân Cave 4* (Oxford: Clarendon Press, 1976). The Qumran Aramaic Enoch fragments include seven manuscripts that contain parts of chs. 1–36, 85–90, and 91–107, represented by fragments of four manuscripts (4QEn^{c} to 4QEn^{f}).

6. Devorah Dimant, "Qumran Sectarian Literature," in *Jewish Writings of the Second Temple Period*, ed. Michael E. Stone (Assen: Van Gorcum, 1984), 483–550, at 544–45; Tiller, *A Commentary on the Animal Apocalypse,* 116. Florentino García Martínez, "Estudios Qumránicos 1975–1985: Panorama Critico (I)," *EstBib* 45 (1987): 125–206, esp. 156, sees the *An. Apoc.* as a "non-sectarian" part of the apocalyptic tradition.

sociological group of students of Enochic traditions,"[7] a group of elite, learned men given to speculations about hidden heavenly tablets, the secrets of creation, and the mysteries of the beginning and end-times. This was not a static tradition, and political and religious loyalties may have changed over time.[8] Consequently, there is still considerable debate on the militant (or pacifistic) orientation of the group[9] as well as the anti- or non-Mosaic character of the Enochic corpus as a whole.[10] A major theme of the *An. Apoc.* is the periodization of history from the first days of creation to the "end of days."[11] Enoch's vision includes the flood, the punishment of the fallen angels, and the history of Israel in symbolic or zoomorphic form until the final judgment. In the *An. Apoc.* the Maccabean revolt is an eschatological inaugurating event. Michael open the books of judgment (90.20), the Watchers are brought forth bound, to be condemned and cast into a fiery abyss (90.24), the "seventy shepherds" are judged and thrown into the abyss (90.25), the "blinded sheep" are thrown into another fiery abyss (90.26), the new Jerusalem is created (90.28-29), and the Gentiles return with those who were destroyed (90.34), uniting all nations (90.33) and ending all violence (90.34), when "there will be One Humanity," the "transformation of all the nations into a single, Adamic race."[12]

Although the *An. Apoc.* is marked by a clear "lack of interest in the Davidic monarchy,"[13] its author looked forward to a glorious redemption: Enoch sees that the end-time will *reverse* the earlier "fallen" state of Israel and humanity: a new "white bull" is born and all of creation is "transformed and they all became white bulls":

7. Tiller, *A Commentary on the Animal Apocalypse*, 124.

8. Ibid., 118.

9. Ibid., 115, 126. Daniel Assefa, *L'Apocalypse des animaux (1 Hen 85–90): une propagande militaire?: Approches narrative, historico-critique, perspectives théologiques* (JSJSup 120; Leiden: Brill, 2007), challenges the idea that the *An. Apoc.* is a militant, pro-Maccabean text and argues that it develops very different ideas and does not endorse violent conflict. Assefa contends that the *An. Apoc.* is pre-Maccabean (but after 198 B.C.E.) and that the "ram" of 90.9b-12, 16 is not Judas Maccabee but a spiritual leader of the group behind the *An. Apoc.* The original work is non-militaristic and the theology and goals of the *An. Apoc.* are radically different from those of the Maccabean revolt.

10. Veronika Bachmann, "The Book of the Watchers (1 Enoch 1-36): An Anti-Mosaic, Non-Mosaic, or Even Pro-Mosaic Writing?" *JHS* 11 (2011): 1–23; eadem, *Die Welt im Ausnahmezustand: eine Untersuchung zu Aussagegehalt und Theologie des Wächterbuches (1 Hen 1–36)* (BZAW 409; Berlin: de Gruyter, 2009).

11. Chapters 85.3–89.9.

12. Tiller, *A Commentary on the Animal Apocalypse*, 20.

13. John J. Collins, "Response: The Apocalyptic Worldview of Daniel," in *Enoch and Qumran Origins*, ed. Gabriele Boccaccini (Grand Rapids: Eerdmans, 2005), 59–66, esp. 62.

And I saw that a white bull was born, with large horns,
and all the beasts of the field and all the birds of the air feared him
and made petition to him all the time.
And I saw till all their species were transformed
and they all became white bulls.[14]

George Nickelsburg sees this imagery as "daring and perhaps without parallel in pre-Christian Jewish literature."[15] *An. Apoc.* 90.37-38 marks the second stage of the restoration and "the beginning of the ideal future, which corresponds to the primordial past." The Enoch tradition looked to the remote Edenic past, not the monarchial age, for its hope of eschatological restoration.[16] The "anthropological restoration of humanity to the primordial conditions enjoyed by Adam" is inaugurated by "a new individual" who represents a "restored Adamic humanity."[17] This figure is a catalyst for the "transformation of all humanity."[18] While some scholars question the universalistic implications of 90.38 ("*all* their species were transformed"), arguing either that the passage refers only to the sheep (Israel),[19] to the Gentiles alone,[20] or that 90.37-38 is a secondary interpolation,[21] there is no manuscript evidence of any such

14. Matthew Black, *The Book of Enoch, or, 1 Enoch: A New English Edition with Commentary and Textual Notes* (SVTP 7; Leiden: Brill, 1985), 82–83; Michael A. Knibb, *The Ethiopic Book of Enoch: A New Edition in the Light of the Aramaic Dead Sea Fragments* (2 vols.; Oxford: Clarendon Press/New York: Oxford University Press, 1978), 216.

15. In Nickelsburg and VanderKam, *1 Enoch: A New Commentary*, 407.

16. Tiller, *A Commentary on the Animal Apocalypse*, 388.

17. Ibid., 383.

18. Ibid., 385.

19. George H. Schodde, *The Book of Enoch: Translated from the Ethiopic, with Introduction and Notes* (Andover: Draper, 1882), 241-242; Maxwell J. Davidson, *Angels at Qumran: A Comparative Study of 1 Enoch 1-36, 72-108 and Sectarian Writings from Qumran* (JSPSS 11; Sheffield: JSOT Press, 1992), 101; Ida Fröhlich, *'Time and Times and Half a Time': Historical Consciousness in the Jewish Literature of the Persian and Hellenistic Eras* (JSPSS 19; Sheffield: Sheffield Academic Press, 1996), 85; Mark Adam Elliott, *The Survivors of Israel: A Reconsideration of the Theology of Pre-Christian Judaism* (Grand Rapids: Eerdmans, 2000), 470-471, 526.

20. Beato Ego, "Vergangenheit im Horizont eschatologischer Hoffnung: Die Tiervision (1 Hen 85-90) als Beispiel apolkalyptischer Geschichtskonzeption," in *Die antike Historiographie und die Anfänge der christlichen Geschichtsschreibung* (ed. Eve-Marie Becker; Berlin: Walter de Gruyter, 2005), 171-195, here 186; David R. Jackson, *Enochic Judaism: Three Defining Paradigm Exemplars* (JSPSS 49; New York: T & T Clark, 2004), 39.

21. See Günter Reese, *Die Geschichte Israels in der Auffassung des frühen Judentums: eine Untersuchung der Tiervision und der Zehnwochenapokalypse des äethiopischen Henochbuches, der Geschichtsdarstellung der Assumptio Mosis und der des 4Esrabuches* (BBB 123; Berlin: Philo, 1999); Karlheinz Müller, *Studien zur*

interpolation. There is indeed a universal salvation of all humanity envisioned here.

There is still an ongoing scholarly discussion as to the *identity* of the eschatological "white bull" of *An. Apoc.* 90. Some associate the figure with Seth,[22] some with Abraham,[23] and some prefer not to attempt a precise identification at all.[24] The Ethiopic text of 90.38 is corrupt at this point. There has also been discussion about whether the appearance of the "white bull" will be followed by that of a "successor" (a "wild ox"),[25] whether there will be "succeeding generations,"[26] and whether the white bull will be transformed into some other animal,[27] especially as it *seems* that the white bull becomes even further transformed into a great beast with black horns.[28]

frühjüdischen Apokalyptik (SBAB11; Stuttgart: Katholisches Bibelwerk, 1991), 164-166. Müller argues that between the direct actions of God in 90.18 and the victories of the armed sheep in 90.19, there is no place for a "messiah," so the unexpected appearance of the white bull in 90.37-38 is secondary redaction. Andreas Bedenbender, *Der Gott der Welt tritt auf den Sinai: Entstehung, Entwicklung und Funktionsweise der frühjüdischen Apokalyptik* (ANTZ 8; Berlin: Institut Kirche und Judentum, 200), 208-211, sees in the eschatological white bull an odd combination of Second Adam and political messiah. Daniel Assefa, "The Enigmatic End of the Animal Apocalypse in the Light of Traditional Ethiopian Commentary," in *Proceedings of the XVth International Conference of Ethiopian Studies* (ed. S. Uhlig; Wiesbaden: Harrassowitz, 2006), 552-560, argues that the *nagar* ("word," "thing") in 90.38b is to be distinguished from the "white bull" of 90.37-38a and that 90.38b may be a secondary interpolation.

22. A. F. J. Klijn, "From Creation to Noah in the Second Dream-Vision of the Ethiopic Enoch, in *Miscellanea Neotestamentica* (NovTSup 46-47; Leiden: Brill, 1977), 1:147-159, here 158. James C. VanderKam, *Enoch: A Man for All Generations* (Columbia, SC: University of South Carolina Press, 1995), 84–85, sees the "white bull" as *possibly* Seth.

23. Nickelsburg and VanderKam, *1 Enoch: A New Commentary*, 407.

24. VanderKam, *Enoch and the Growth*, 168; Nickelsburg, *1 Enoch 1*, 407.

25. Knibb, *The Ethiopic Book of Enoch,* 216, suggests that what we might have here is "a belief in two Messiahs—a priestly leader and a military leader." This is an intriguing idea, considering the dual messianism prevalent at Qumran, but the passage is generally translated so as to identify the white bull with the white ox. Moreover, there is nothing in the text to "indicate either priestly or military activity" by the two animals (Tiller, *A Commentary on the Animal Apocalypse*, 388).

26. Milik, *The Books of Enoch*, 45.

27. Tiller, *A Commentary on the Animal Apocalypse*, 17 n. 5. See also Georg Beer, "Das Buch Enoch," in *Die Apokryphen und Pseudepigraphen des Alten Testaments*, Vol. 2, *Die Pseudepigraphen des Alten Testaments*, ed. Emil Kautzsch (Tübingen: Mohr, 1900), 217–300, at 298: "Die doppelte Verwandlung des Messias, zuerst in einen Büffel, als dann in ein grosses Tier, ist aber überhaupt befremdlich."

28. Nickelsburg's proposal—that the Aramaic word for "leader" was read as if it were Hebrew ("word")—seems like the most likely explanation (*1 Enoch 1*, 403). Barnabas Lindars, "A Bull, a Lamb and a Word: 1 Enoch XC.38," *NTS* 22 (1976): 483-486, here 485-486, suggests that the Greek translator read "lamb/sheep" as "word," and used λόγος, which was then rendered into the Ethiopic *nagar*. Ethiopic tradition differentiates between the white bull of 90.37 and the great beast of 90.38.

While many scholars see the figure simply as the *Davidic* messiah,[29] this identification is not explicitly stated in the text. The white bull is never described as "anointed" nor does he fulfill common or traditional "messianic" functions (military action); moreover, the figure appears *after* the defeat of Israel's enemies, the divine judgment, and the New Jerusalem. We are clearly dealing here with an *alternative* form of Jewish "messianism."[30] The most popular interpretation is that the white bull represents a second Adam.[31] Alternatively, Daniel Olson suggests that the white bull represents "the *true Jacob*, the patriarch of the 'true Israel.'"[32] For Olson, this is the eschatological fulfillment of the Abrahamic covenant (Gen. 22:18; 26:4; 27:14). Olson points out that the *An. Apoc.*'s eschatological white bull is the first to appear since Isaac and argues that it is a fulfillment of the biblical promise that all nations would be blessed through Abraham and his offspring.[33] One problem with this proposal is that the figure of Abraham appears only briefly in *An. Apoc.* 89.10-11 and

29. August Dillmann, *Das Buch Henoch übersetzt und erklärt* (Leipzig: Vogel, 1853), 286-287; Georg Beer, "Das Buch Henoch," in *Die Apokryphen und Pseudepigraphen des Alten Testaments* (ed. Emil Kautzsch; 2 vols.; Tübingen: Mohr, 1900), 217-310, here 2:298; Francois Martin, *Le livre d'Hénoch traduit sur le texte éthiopien* (Paris: Letouzey et Ané, 1906), 235; Charles, *Book of Enoch*, 215-216; Sacchi, *Jewish Apocalyptic*, 159-60; Boccaccini, *Middle Judaism*, 134; Jonathan A. Goldstein, "How the Authors of 1 and 2 Maccabees Treated the 'Messianic' Promises," in *Judaisms and Their Messiahs at the Turn of the Era*, ed. J. Neusner, W. S. Green, and E. S. Frerichs (Cambridge: Cambridge University Press, 1987), 69-96, esp. 72-73. N. T. Wright, *Paul and the Faithfulness of God*, Vol. 4 of *Christian Origins and the Question of God* (2 vols.; Minneapolis: Fortress Press, 2013), 1:122-123, questions whether this is "the Messiah," noting that "Some have doubted it," although he finds this "unnecessarily cautious." He further notes that "the final animal resembles Adam," concluding that this tells "neither for nor against a messianic identification" (123, n. 192).

30. Nickelsburg, *1 Enoch 1*, 406-407.

31. Pedersen, "Zur Erklärung," 419; Milik, *Books of Enoch*, 45; Black, *Book of Enoch*, 20-21, 279-280; García Martínez, *Qumran and Apocalyptic*, 75; André Lacocque, "Allusions to Creation in Daniel 7," in *The Book of Daniel: Composition and Reception* (ed. J. J. Collins and P. W. Flint; VTSup 83; Leiden: Brill, 2001), 114-131, esp. 123, 125, n. 42. Olson's objections are negligible: "One problem with a 'second Adam' typology, however, is that it does not account for certain qualities in the eschatological bull, such as its powerful demeanor and its role as absolute monarch. Another problem is that the original Adam is not a unique figure in the allegory but simply the beginning of an apparently unbroken string of white cattle that extends into the Patriarchal era" (27).

32. Daniel C. Olson, *A New Reading of the Animal Apocalypse of 1 Enoch: "All Nations Shall Be Blessed": With A New Translation and Commentary* (Studia in Veteris Testamenti Pseudepigrapha 24; Leiden: Brill, 2013), 14-15, here 31, suggests a "fourth possibility": that "the *An. Apoc.* is an ambitious theological interpretation of human history through the lens of the Abrahamic covenant, setting forth an *Urzeit wird Endzeit* model that puts Eden-to-Isaac on one end and Jacob-to-Eden (regained) on the other."

Jacob is *never* named. Consequently, Jacob seems a relatively unlikely figure to be featured so prominently in the Enoch tradition—partly because Jacob is the one patriarch who is *not* identified as a white bull and the new "white bull" most plausibly represents an eschatological restoration of the original Adamic humanity.[34] While Olson is surely correct to emphasize the anticipated fulfillment of the biblical promise to Abraham of "universal blessing through his offspring"—and a "new" Jacob would indeed represent a new *Israel*—it seems safer to say that our figure is a non-Davidic redeemer who symbolizes both Israel *and* universal salvation. The white bull restores the *human* condition and is not associated with military violence. The white bull may represent "a synthesis of more than just one biblical image," but the identification of this figure as a new Adam possesses a clear, compelling, and "immediate plausibility."[35] As we will see, there is good reason to think that this identification not only fulfills an *Urzeit/Endzeit* plan of salvation, but was also interpreted along these lines by the Qumran community.

Although the "white bull" is born *after* the last judgment (90.20-27) and the restoration of Israel (90.37), we have seen that literary sequences of judgment-salvation did not deter Second Temple Jews and early Christians from adopting and maintaining semi-realized eschatological worldviews in which end-time hopes were thought to be at least partially fulfilled, in and out of sequence. Certain traditional Davidic prophecies were not fulfilled in Jesus' lifetime; this led to the indefinite postponement of the *parousia* or "second coming." Similarly, our difficulties in determining the temporal nature of the inaugurated kingdom in the Jesus tradition (already/not yet) result from this ambiguity over the *timing* of eschatological events. The fact remains that the *An. Apoc.* anticipates the arrival of a quasi-messianic figure who is instrumental in the eschatological restoration of humanity and will gather both Israel and the

33. Ibid., 31. Olson recognizes that his hypothesis is "admittedly ambitious" yet maintains that the "Enochians" took a special interest in the Abrahamic covenant. At the same time, Olson's proposal is inclusive and does not "invalidate the other interpretations entirely . . . because the 'true Jacob' is an exalted, idealized figure who carries with him something of these other meanings as well').

34. Ibid., 242-243. Olson admits that "the closest parallel to the theological vision of the *An. Apoc.* is in fact found in the writings of the Apostle Paul . . . Two areas where the similarities are particularly striking are (1) Jew-Gentile relations and the future of Israel, and (2) the Messiah conceived as both the seed of Abraham and a new Adam." The difference between Paul and the *Animal Apocalypse* is that "whereas Paul sees in Christ the redemption of a catastrophically fallen Adam, the Enochic allegorist thinks only in terms of a resumption and an expansion of the Adamic inheritance. The sin of Adam and Eve is conspicuously missing from the allegory. The *An. Apoc.* is more at home with a theology that stresses the 'glory of Adam' than with one that stresses the plight of Adam."

35. Ibid., 29, noting that there is "no need to deny the [Adamic] typology altogether."

Gentiless into a New Jerusalem.[36] The white bull later becomes "an eschatological patriarch of a restored race"—a second Adam[37]—appearing at the end of days as a *messianic* figure.[38]

The messianic identification of the Adamic figure must be carefully qualified, for unlike the Davidic messiah, whose primary function seems to be war, the Adamic messiah "is depicted as not doing anything, other than 'becoming' a leader and a large animal with large horns."[39] Furthermore, the Adamic messiah is a new "white *bull*," not a sheep, like David and Solomon. The "white bull" must therefore be more closely related to and identified with the original patriarchs Abraham, Isaac, Shem, Noah, or Adam.[40] If it is reasonable to identify the *Endzeit* figure with the *Urzeit* Adam, then despite the superficial similarities to other patriarchs the "white bull" should probably be seen as "a new Adam" who becomes "the head of a new human race."[41]

The *Animal Apocalypse* provides us with "the most detailed ancient description of the Messianic Age" in Early Judaism.[42] The "new white bull with

36. Put this way, Collins' objection that "there is little role for a messiah" here (*The Scepter and the Star*, 34) loses much of its force while Tiller's conclusion that this figure is "not a messiah but an eschatological patriarch of a restored race" can be affirmed (Tiller, *Commentary*, 388).

37. Black, *The Book of Enoch*, 20–21; Milik, *The Books of Enoch*, 45; Gerbern S. Oegema, *The Anointed and his People: Messianic Expectations from the Maccabees to Bar Kochba* (JSPSup 27; Sheffield: Sheffield Academic Press, 1998), 56; Martin Hengel, *Judaism and Hellenism: Studies in Their Encounter in Palestine During the Early Hellenistic Period* (2 vols.; Philadelphia: Fortress Press, 1974), 344; Helge S. Kvanvig, "The Son of Man in the Parables of Enoch," in *Enoch and the Messiah Son of Man: Revisiting the Book of Parables*, ed. Gabriele Boccaccini (Grand Rapids: Eerdmans, 2007), 179–215, at 194.

38. Ibid., 20–21. Johs Pedersen, "Zur Erklärung der eschatologischen Visionen Henochs," *Islamica* 2 (1926): 416–29, esp. 419, seems to have been the first to suggest that the eschatological white bull represents the messianic second Adam. See also Oegema, *The Anointed and his People*, 68. See also Gabriele Boccaccini, "Finding a Place," in *Enoch and the Messiah Son of Man*, 263–89, esp. 273; Kelley Coblentz Bautch, "Adamic Traditions in the Parables? A Query on 1 Enoch 69:6," in *Enoch and the Messiah Son of Man*, 352–60, esp. 354; Robin Scroggs, *The Last Adam: A Study in Pauline Anthropology* (Philadelphia: Fortress Press, 1966), 23; Richard Laurence, *The Book of Enoch the Prophet* (London: K. Paul, Trench, 1883), xxiiii; George W. E. Nickelsburg, "Salvation Without and With a Messiah: Developing Beliefs in Writings Ascribed to Enoch," in *Judaisms and their Messiahs at the Turn of the Christian Era*, ed. Jacob Neusner, et al. (New York: Cambridge University Press, 1987), 49–68, at 55–56; Baumgarten, *Flourishing*, 171; Barnabas Lindars, *Jesus, Son of Man: A Fresh Examination of the Son of Man Sayings in the Gospels in the Light of Recent Research* (Grand Rapids: Eerdmans, 1983), 14.

39. George W. E. Nickelsburg, in Nickelsburg and VanderKam, *1 Enoch: A Commentary*, 406–7.

40. Ibid.

41. Ibid.

42. Eyal Regev, *Sectarianism in Qumran: A Cross-Cultural Perspective* (RS 45; New York: de Gruyter, 2007), 209. See also Tiller, *A Commentary on the Animal Apocalypse*, 19–20, 365–92.

great horns" represents the messiah, and "all animals are then transformed into white bulls, just like Adam and the early patriarchs, implying a new creation."[43] The new Adam transforms others according to his own likeness.[44] In the end, "all the species representing the diversity of nations and people return to the primordial unity from which they diverged."[45] The white bull is "a symbol for the Messiah,"[46] but he is not a warrior-king defeating Israel's enemies. He possesses transforming power and authority, but he is not a judge, since the messianic figure appears after the judgment,[47] something highly unusual in apocalyptic literature.[48] The bull's function "as 'leader' parallels the role ascribed to David and Solomon,"[49] but there is no longer any need for war. The wild animals have been transformed and "there is no longer enmity in the human race."[50] The eschatological Adam is a "catalyst for the transformation of all humanity."[51] There will be "neither Jew nor Gentile, but one Adamic race."[52] The *An. Apoc.* envisions "a return to the beginning," a "*universal* transformation."[53] The birth of the white bull "catalyzes the transformation of all the species into white bulls, the one species from which all of them came."[54] His function is not to *judge*, nor to engage in *warfare*, nor to *die*, but to *transform*.

43. Ibid., 210.

44. Black, *The Book of Enoch*, 20–21; J. C. O'Neill, *The Point Of It All: Essays on Jesus Christ* (Leiden: Deo Publishing, 2000), 66.

45. Nickelsburg, in Nickelsburg and VanderKam, *1 Enoch: A Commentary*, 406-07.

46. See August Dillmann, *Liber Henoch Aethiopice, ad quinque codicum fidem editus, cum variis lectionibus* (Leipzig: Vogel, 1851), 286; R. H. Charles, *The Book of Enoch: Translated from Dillmann's Ethiopic Text* (London: SPCK, 1917), 215–16; Black, *The Book of Enoch*, 279–80; Jonathan K. Goldstein, "How the Authors of 1 and 2 Maccabees Treated the 'Messianic' Promises," in *Judaisms and Their Messiahs*, 69–96, at 72–73.

47. *1 En.* 90.37-38.

48. Marius Reiser, *Jesus and Judgment: The Eschatological Proclamation in its Jewish Context*, trans. Linda M. Maloney (Minneapolis: Fortress Press, 1997), 145.

49. George W. E. Nickelsburg, in Nickelsburg and VanderKam, *1 Enoch: A Commentary*, 406–7. Charles, *The Book of Enoch*, 215, argued that this figure has "no function" to perform and so cannot be a "prophetic Messiah." This is "only partly true," for although he has no function in *judgment*, he does have "a function as the patriarch of a restored Adamic/Sethite humanity" (Tiller, *A Commentary on the Animal Apocalypse*, 384).

50. Nickelsburg and VanderKam, *1 Enoch: A Commentary*, 406–7. See also Tiller, *A Commentary on the Animal Apocalypse*, 385; Kvanvig, "The Son of Man in the Parables of Enoch," esp. 210. For the distinction between the "national, Davidic" messiah and the "international son of Adam" see Klaus Koch, "Messias und Menschensohn," in *Vor der Wende der Zeiten. Beiträge zur apokalyptischen Literatur* (Gesammelte Aufsätze 2; Neukirchen-Vluyn: Neukirchener Verlag, 1996), 235–66.

51. Nickelsburg and VanderKam, *1 Enoch: A Commentary*, 385.

52. Ibid.

There are significant literary and theological similarities between the Adamic figure of the *An. Apoc.* and the "one like a son of man" in Dan. 7:13.[55] These similarities are so striking that there must have been a literary and historical relationship between the two traditions:

An. Apoc. 90	*Daniel* 7
c. 165 B.C.E.	c. 165 B.C.E.
Judean	Judean
Aramaic	Aramaic
eschatological	eschatological
apocalyptic vision	apocalyptic vision
scene on earth	scene in heaven
Adamic figure	angelic figure
quasi-messianic	quasi-messianic
non-Davidic	non-Davidic
universal salvation	universal salvation

The Danielic "son of man," a text and tradition that was adopted, developed, and transformed in the *Parables*, Q, *4 Ezra*, and the Gospels, seems to have originated in the *Animal Apocalypse*'s figure of a new Adam/humanity.

The biblical figure of Adam (אדם) was created in the "image of God" (בצלמו).[56] "Adam," however, is both an individual literary character in Genesis (אדם) and the symbolic representative of all humankind (האדם), representing the species as a whole.[57] To "be human is to be made in the image of God."[58]

53. Gabriele Boccaccini, *Beyond the Essene Hypothesis: The Parting of the Ways between Qumran and Enochic Judaism* (Grand Rapids: Eerdmans, 1998), 93 (emphasis added). Regev, *Sectarianism in Qumran*, 217.

54. George W. E. Nickelsburg, in Nickelsburg and VanderKam, *1 Enoch: A Commentary*, 407.

55. For the full argument see Simon J. Joseph, "Was Daniel 7:13's 'Son of Man' Modeled After the 'New Adam' of the *Animal Apocalypse* (*1 En.* 90)? A Comparative Study," *JSP* 22, no. 4 (2013): 269–94. See also Klaus Koch, *Vor der Wende der Zeiten: Beiträge zur apokalyptischen Literatur* (Gesammelte Aufsätze 3; Neukirchen-Vluyn: Neukirchener Verlag, 1996), 247-250.

56. Gen. 1:27.

57. Phyllis Bird, "'Male and Female He Created Them': Gen. 1:27b in the Context of the Priestly Account of Creation," *HTR* 74 (1981): 129–59, esp. 159. See also Adela Yarbro Collins, "The Historical-Critical and Feminist Readings of Genesis 1:26-28," in *Hebrew Bible or Old Testament?: Studying the Bible in Judaism and Christianity*, ed. Roger Brooks and John J. Collins (CJA 5; Notre Dame, IN: University of Notre Dame Press, 1990), 197–99; Paul Niskanen, "The Poetics of Adam: The Creation of אדם in the Image of אלהים," *JBL* 128, no. 3 (2009): 417–36.

58. Paul Humbert, "L''imago Dei' dans l'Ancien Testament," in *Études sur le récit du paradis et de la chute dans la Genèse* (Mémoires de l'université de Neuchâtel 14; Neuchâtel: Secrétariat de l'université,

The "image of God" (צלם אלהים) appears to "derive its meaning from a special association with the royal ideology of the ancient Near East."[59] In Egypt "the idea of the king as 'image' of the god is a common one."[60] Mesopotamian texts use a similar expression as a "designation of the king."[61] The king is the image of the god. Adam, having "dominion" or "rule" over creation, parallels the role of the king. Adam is "God's own special representative . . . by design."[62] In Genesis the צלם אלהים is "a royal designation, the precondition or requisite for rule."[63] The *royal* status of Adam/humanity is highlighted in Ps. 8:5-6:

> What is *man* (אנוש) that you are mindful of him,
> and the *son of man* (בן אדם), that you care for him?
> Yet you have made him a little lower than אלהים
> and crowned him with glory and honor.
> You have given him dominion over the works of your hands;
> you have put all things under his feet.

1940), 153–75; Ludwig Koehler, "Die Grundstelle der Imago-Dei-Lehre, Gen. 1:26," *ThZ* 4 (1948): 16–22; Bernhard W. Anderson, "Human Dominion over Nature," *Biblical Studies in Contemporary Thought: The Tenth Anniversary Commemorative Volume of the Trinity College Biblical Institute, 1966–1975*, ed. Miriam Ward (Somerville, MA: Greeno, Hadden, 1975), 27–45; James Barr, "The Image of God in the Book of Genesis: A Study of Terminology," *BJRL* 51 (1968): 11–26; J. Maxwell Miller, "In the 'Image' and 'Likeness' of God," *JBL* 91 (1972): 289–304; Norman Snaith, "The Image of God," *ExpT* 86, no. 1 (1974): 24. See also Karl Barth, *Church Dogmatics*, trans. Harold Knight, G. W. Bromiley, J. K. S. Reid, and R. H. Fuller (Edinburgh: T&T Clark, 1960); Gunnlauger A. Jónsson, *The Image of God: Genesis 1:26-28 in a Century of Old Testament Research*, trans. Lorraine Svensen (ConBT 26; Lund: Almqvist & Wiksell International, 1988); David Cairns, *The Image of God in Man* (New York: Philosophical Library, 1953); Edward Mason Curtis, "Man as the Image of God in Genesis in the Light of Ancient Near Eastern Parallels," Ph. D. dissertation, University of Pennsylvania, 1984; J. Richard Middleton, *The Liberating Image: The* Imago Dei *in Genesis 1* (Grand Rapids: Brazos, 2005); John F. A. Sawyer, "The Meaning of צלם אלהים ('In the Image of God') in Genesis i–xi," *JTS* 25 (1974): 418–26.

59. Johannes Hehn, "Zum Terminus 'Bild Gottes,'" in *Festschrift Eduard Sacahu*, ed. Gotthold Weil (Berlin: Reimar, 1915), 36–52; Gerhard von Rad, *Genesis: A Commentary* (Philadelphia: Westminster, 1961), 58; Hans Wildberger, "Das Abbild Gottes: Gen. 1:26-30," *TZ* 21 (1965): 245–59, 481–501; Werner H. Schmidt, *Die Schöpfungsgeschichte der Priesterschrift* (WMANT 17; 3d ed.; Neukirchen-Vluyn: Neukirchener Verlag, 1973), 137–48.

60. Bird, "'Male and Female He Created Them,'" 140.

61. Ibid., 141.

62. Ibid., 138.

63. Ibid., 140.

Adam/humanity is a royal figure, the "king" of creation.[64] The difference in the Genesis account of creation is a "democratization of Mesopotamian royal ideology," extending the divine image to all humankind, not just to the king.[65]

The biblical figure of Adam is referred to numerous times in the Dead Sea Scrolls.[66] In 4Q504 frg. 8, 4-5, Adam's identity as the "image of glory" is highlighted:

> אדם א[בינו יצרתה בדמות בבוד]כה
> נשמת חיים נ[פתחה באפו ובינה ודעת

> Adam,] our [Fa]ther, you fashioned in the image of [your] glory.
> The breath of life] you [b]lew into his nostril, and insight and knowledge.

In 1QS 4.22-23, CD 3.20, and 1QH 4.15, the "*glory* of Adam" (כבוד אדם) is set in an eschatological context.[67] God will purify the elect "by the Holy Spirit" (ברוח קודש) and sprinkle "the Spirit of Truth like waters of purification" (רוח אמת במי נדה) upon them:

> כיא בם בחר אל לברית עולמים
> ולהם כול כבוד אדם

> . . . for those God has chosen for an eternal covenant
> and all the glory of Adam will be theirs.

Similarly, in CD 3.20 God

> in his wonderful mysteries has built the elect/remnant
> a sure house in Israel" (בית נאמן בישראל)
> [and] those who hold fast to it are destined to live for ever

64. Scroggs, *Last Adam*, 5. On Adam as "king" see Job 2:14; *2 En.* 30:12; *4 Ezra* 6:53; *Apoc. Moses* 24.4. On Adam's kingship as convertible to humankind see Sir. 49:16, 17:1-14; Wis Sol. 9:1-3. Burton L. Mack, *The Christian Myth: Origins, Logic, and Legacy* (New York: Continuum, 2001), 98–99.

65. Middleton, *The Liberating Image*, 204.

66. CD 3.20; 4QpPs37 iii 1-2; Esther G. Chazon, "The Creation and Fall of Adam in the Dead Sea Scrolls," in *The Book of Genesis in Jewish and Oriental Christian Interpretation: A Collection of Essays*, ed. Judith Frishman and Lucas Van Rompay (TEG 5; Louvain: Peeters, 1997), 13–24. *Dibre Hamme'orot*, the *Gen-Exod Paraphrase*, and *Sap. Work A* (frg. 2, 4Q423) cast Adam in a negative light, *Ben Sira* and *Jubilees* in a (relatively) positive light.

67. Oscar Cullmann, *The Christology of the New Testament* (London: SCM, 1963), 141; Scroggs, *The Last Adam*, 26.

and all the glory of Adam (כבוד אדם) will be theirs.

In 4Q171 the "*inheritance* of Adam" (נחלת אדם) will be made available to the community. This inheritance, according to 1QS 4.7-8, is "a crown of glory with majestic raiment in eternal light." 1QS envisions "some kind of metamorphosis"[68] to be inaugurated at the "renewal" (1QS 4.25), a profound transformation of the community, when "all the glory of Adam" (כול כבוד אדם) will be "theirs," that is, when the *original* human design will be restored.[69] 4Q174 identifies the community with the Temple,[70] a "*Temple* of Adam" (מקדש אדם),[71] an "Adamic sanctuary of Eden restored."[72]

68. Geza Vermes, *The Complete Dead Sea Scrolls in English* (New York: Allen Lane/Penguin, 1997), 87.

69. Alex R. G. Deasley, *The Shape of Qumran Theology* (Carlisle: Paternoster, 2000), 291.

70. Bertil Gärtner, *The Temple and the Community in Qumran and the New Testament: A Comparative Study in the Temple Symbolism of the Qumran Texts and the New Testament* (Cambridge: Cambridge University Press, 1965), 30–42; Theodore H. Gaster, *The Dead Sea Scriptures, in English Translation: With Introduction and Notes* (Garden City, NY: Doubleday Anchor, 1976), 446–47; Devorah Dimant, "4QFlorilegium and the Idea of Community as Temple," in *Hellenica et Judaica: Hommage à Valentin Nikiprowetzky*, ed. André Caquot, et al. (Leuven: Peeters, 1986), 165–89; Michael A. Knibb, *The Qumran Community* (New York: Cambridge University Press, 1987), 258–62; Geza Vermes, *The Dead Sea Scrolls in English* (3d ed.; Sheffield: JSOT, 1987), 293–94.

71. See Michael Wise, "4QFlorilegium and the Temple of Adam," *RevQ* 15 (1991): 103–32; published in revised form as "That Which Has Been is That Which Shall Be: 4QFlorilegium and the *mqds 'dm*," in *Thunder and Gemini and Other Essays on the History, Language and Literature of Second Temple Palestine* (JSPSup 15; Sheffield: JSOT Press, 1994), 152–85. See also George J. Brooke, *The Dead Sea Scrolls and the New Testament* (Minneapolis: Fortress Press, 2005), 242–43; idem, *Exegesis at Qumran: 4QFlorilegium in its Jewish Context* (JSOTSup 29; Sheffield: JSOT Press, 1985), 184–93; Dimant, "4Qflorilegium"; Brooke, *Dead Sea Scrolls and the New Testament*, 243.

72. Brooke, *Dead Sea Scrolls and the New Testament*, 245; idem, "Miqdash Adam, Eden and the Qumran Community," in *Gemeinde ohne Tempel—Community without Temple: Zur Substituierung und Transformation des Jerusalemer Tempels und seines Kultes im Alten Testament, antiken Judentum und frühen Christentum*, ed. Beate Ego, et al. (WUNT 118; Tübingen: Mohr Siebeck, 1999), 285–301; Crispin H. T. Fletcher-Louis, *Luke-Acts: Angels, Christology and Soteriology* (WUNT 2d ser. 94; Tübingen: Mohr Siebeck, 1997), 192. The correlation between the cult and Eden in the post-biblical period has been noted. See *Jub.* 3.26-27, 8.19. See also Margaret Barker, *The Gate of Heaven: The History and Symbolism of the Temple in Jerusalem* (London: SPCK, 1991), 57–103; Martha Himmelfarb, "The Temple and the Garden of Eden in Ezekiel, the Book of Watchers, and the Wisdom of Ben Sira," in *Sacred Places and Profane Spaces: Essays in the Geographies of Judaism, Christianity and Islam*, ed. Jamie S. Scott and Paul Simpson-Housely (Westport, CT: Greenwood, 1991), 63–78; eadem, *Ascent to Heaven in Jewish and Christian Apocalypses* (Oxford: Oxford University Press, 1993); Robert Hayward, "The Figure of Adam in Pseudo-Philo's Biblical Antiquities," *JSJ* 23 (1992): 1–20; Sandra R. Shimoff, "Gardens: From Eden to Jerusalem," *JSJ* 26 (1995): 145–55.

The sense of an imminent and profound eschatological mystery is a frequent motif in the Dead Sea Scrolls.[73] The most common expression for God's "mysteries" is "the mystery that is to come" (רז נהיה), referred to several times in the *Book of Mysteries* and *4QInstruction*. 4Q417 2 i 10-11 mentions "the mystery that is to come" as a prerequisite for understanding "the birth time of salvation" (מולדי ישע).[74] In 4Q418 77 the student is advised to study "the mystery that is to come, and understand the *nature* of [m]an" (רז נהיה וקח תולדות [א]דם).[75] Meditating on the רז נהיה will help one to understand "the generations of (hu)mankind" (4Q418 77.2) and "the inheritance of all that lives" (4Q418 2 i 18). The author of 4Q417 2 i envisions humanity as having been made "according to the pattern of the holy ones" (כתבנית קדושים).[76] The idea that the angels were involved in the creation of Adam draws from Gen. 1:26, where God (אלהים) says "let *us* make man in *our* image, in *our* likeness.[77] 4Q418 suggests that humanity was created in the image of the angels.[78] The author of *4QInstruction* seems to anticipate the restoration of the original design of humankind.[79]

73. Carol A. Newsom, *The Self as Symbolic Space: Constructing Identity and Community at Qumran* (STDJ 52; Leiden: Brill, 2004), 75.

74. 4Q416 2 iii 9 encourages the student to study the "origins" of the "mystery" in order to know what is "allotted" to it.

75. *Qumran Cave 4: XXXIV; 4QInstruction (Musar LeMevin)*, ed. John T. Strugnell, Daniel J. Harrington, and Torleif Elgvin (DJD 34; Oxford: Clarendon, 1999), 297. See also Torleif Elgvin, "The Mystery to Come: Early Essene Theology of Revelation," in *Qumran Between the Old and New Testaments*, ed. Frederick H. Cryer and Thomas L. Thompson (Sheffield: Sheffield Academic Press, 1998), 135.

76. The term תבנית conveys the idea of an image, blueprint, pattern, or template. It is used in the Hebrew Bible with "the sense of a blueprint for a construction," notably the blueprint for the Tabernacle in Exod. 25:9, 40. See John J. Collins, "In the Likeness of the Holy Ones: The Creation of Humankind in a Wisdom Text from Qumran," in *The Provo International Conference on the Dead Sea Scrolls: Technological Innovations, New Texts, and Reformulated Issues*, ed. Donald W. Parry and Eugene C. Ulrich (Leiden: Brill, 1999), 610, 612–13. In Deut. 4:16-18, תבנית is an "image" or "likeness." In 4Q403 it is used for the "likeness" of God's glory. In 4Q405 20.ii-22 l.8 the cherubim bless the תבנית or "likeness" of the divine throne. The word תבנית seems to convey "a sense of the numinous" (p. 613), signifying its divine nature. In 1QM 10:4 תבנית אדם refers to the creation of the human form. 1QM specifically mentions "the shape of Adam and of the gene[rations of] his [seed]" (1QM 10.14). See Crispin H. T. Fletcher-Louis, *All the Glory of Adam: Liturgical Anthropology in the Dead Sea Scrolls* (STDJ 42; Leiden: Brill, 2002), 96.

77. ויאמר אלהים נעשה בצלמנו בדמותנו

78. Collins, "In the Likeness of the Holy Ones." See Fletcher-Louis, *All the Glory of Adam*, 114–15; Jarl Fossum, "Gen. 1, 26 and 2,7 in Judaism, Samaritanism, and Gnosticism," *JSJ* 16 (1985): 203–39.

79. Fletcher-Louis, *All the Glory of Adam*, 12; Deasley, *The Shape of Qumran Theology*, 295; *1 En.* 69.11; *2 Bar.* 51.10; 1QS 11.7; 1QH 3.22, 11.12; Mark 12:24.

The attainment of an ideal humanity is a pervasive theme in apocalyptic literature.[80] Early Jewish literature shows great interest in the figure of Adam.[81] Many texts portray Adam as a "being of light" who radiated the original glory of the εἰκὼν or "image" of God.[82] Adam was a king, an angelic being,[83] the "image of God," a divine template of humanity.[84] The eschatological restoration of the "glory of Adam" was highly anticipated.[85] Indeed, the biblical and apocalyptic figure of Adam continued to inspire a wide range of apocalyptic, apocryphal, Jewish Christian, Gnostic Christian, and rabbinical Jewish literary works throughout late antiquity.[86] The idea that the messianic age would inaugurate a

80. Baumgarten, *Flourishing*, 155.

81. Michael E. Stone, *A History of the Literature of Adam and Eve* (SBLEJL 3; Atlanta: Scholars Press, 1992); John R. Levison, *Portraits of Adam in Early Judaism: From Sirach to 2 Baruch* (Sheffield: JSOT Press, 1987); idem, "Adamic Traditions in Early Judaism (Qumran, *1 Enoch*, Sirach, Philo, *Jubilees*, Josephus, *4 Ezra, 2 Baruch*)," paper presented at the Fifth Enoch Seminar, Naples, Italy, June 14–18, 2009; Johannes Tromp, "Adamic Traditions in Early Judaism and Christianity (*Books of Adam and Eve*)," paper presented at the Fifth Enoch Seminar, Naples, Italy, June 14–18, 2009; Alexander Toepel, "Adamic Traditions in Early Christian and Rabbinic Literature (from NT to the *Cave of Treasures*)," paper presented at the Fifth Enoch Seminar, Naples, Italy, June 14–18, 2009; Gary A. Anderson, *The Genesis of Perfection: Adam and Eve in Jewish and Christian Imagination* (Louisville: Westminster John Knox, 2001).

82. Alan Segal, "The Risen Christ and the Angelic Mediator Figures in Light of Qumran," in *Jesus and the Dead Sea Scrolls*, ed. James H. Charlesworth (New York: Doubleday, 1992), 302–28, at 310. Fletcher-Louis, *Luke-Acts: Angels, Christology and Soteriology*, 118. James H. Charlesworth, "The Portrayal of the Righteous as an Angel," in *Ideal Figures in Ancient Judaism: Profiles and Paradigms*, ed. George W. E. Nickelsburg and John J. Collins (SBLSCS 12; Chico: Scholars Press, 1980), 135–51, at 137–39, refers to a number of texts in which Adam is divine or angelic.

83. On Adam as related to the angels see Sir 49:16; *1 En.* 37.1; *2 En.* 33.10, 58.1-2; *Jub.* 2.14; *2 En.* 30.12; *4 Ezra* 6.53-54; *Vit. Ad.* 12.1–17.3; *1 En.* 69.11.

84. In rabbinic literature Adam is a *king*. See Davies, *Paul and Rabbinic Judaism*, 45–46; Scroggs, *Last Adam*, 41–52. On the two streams of tradition see Scroggs, *Last Adam*, 1–15.

85. Alexander Golitzin, "Recovering the 'Glory of Adam': 'Divine Light' Traditions in the Dead Sea Scrolls and the Christian Ascetical Literature of Fourth-Century Syro-Mesopotamia," in *The Dead Sea Scrolls as Background to Postbiblical Judaism and Early Christianity: Papers from an International Conference at St. Andrews in 2001*, ed. James R. Davila (STDJ 46; Leiden: Brill, 2003), 275–308. See also David H. Aaron, "Shedding Light on God's Body in Rabbinic Midrashim: Reflections on the Theory of a Luminous Adam," *HTR* 90 (1997): 299–314; Alon Goshen Gottstein, "The Body as Image of God in Rabbinic Literature," *HTR* 87 (1994): 171–95.

86. Philo interpreted Gen. 1:27 as a reference to the pattern for all humanity (*De Opificio Mundi* 69–71; *Legum Allegoria* I.31-42; 88). The "original" or "heavenly" man is the pre-earthly heavenly perfect "image" of humankind (*De Opificio Mundi* 1.46). In *2 En.*, Adam is an angelic being (30.11), a glorious wise king intended to reign on earth. Adam's lordship over creation, his kingship, and his wisdom were rooted in biblical ideas (Gen. 1:24-30; Sir. 17:1; 49:16; *Jub.* 2.14; *2 Bar.* 14.18). For further references, see Gary Anderson, "Celibacy or Consummation in the Garden?," *HTR* 82 (1989): 121-48. On the

new era of healing, redemption, salvation, and the regeneration of the original divine human design also finds substantial echoes in Pauline thought.[87]

Paul refers to Jesus as both Χριστός and "the last Adam" (ὁ ἔσχατος Ἀδὰμ).[88] Adamic Christology seems to have been "widely current" in the 40s and 50s C.E. [89] Adam speculation also appears to have played a formative role in the "cultic veneration of Christ," facilitating the Jewish worship of someone other than God.[90] The identification of Jesus as Adamic is reflected in 1 Cor. 15, Rom. 5:12-19, and Phil. 2:5-11. The question is whether this identification predates Paul's letters.[91] The Adamic identification of "Christ Jesus" in the

relationship between Adam and the messiah/messianic age, see B. Murmelstein, "Adam, ein Beitrag zur Messiaslehre," *WZKM* 35 (1928): 242-75; 36 (1929): 51-86.

87. Nickelsburg and VanderKam, *1 Enoch: A New Commentary*, 9.

88. Ulrich Wilckens, "Christus, der 'letzte Adam,' und der Menschensohn," in *Jesus und der Menschensohn*, ed. Rudolf Pesch, et al. (Freiburg: Herder, 1975), 387–403; A. J. M. Wedderburn, "Adam and Christ: An Investigation into the Background of 1 Corinthians XV and Romans V:12-21," Ph. D. dissertation; Cambridge University, 1970; idem, "Adam in Paul's Letters to the Romans," *StudBib* 3 (1976): 413-30; W. D. Davies, *Paul and Rabbinic Judaism: Some Rabbinic Elements in Pauline Theology* (New York: Harper & Row, 1967); Jacob Jervell, *Imago Dei: Gen 1,26ff. im Spätjudentum, in der Gnosis und in der paulinischen Briefen* (Göttingen: Vandenhoeck & Ruprecht, 1960); C. K. Barrett, *From First Adam to Last: A Study in Pauline Theology* (New York: Scribner's, 1962); Egon Brandenburger, *Adam und Christus: Exegetisch-religionsgeschichtliche Untersuchung zu Röm. 5.12-21 (I. Kor.15)* (WMANT 17; Neukirchen-Vluyn: Neukirchener Verlag, 1962); Scroggs, *The Last Adam*. On the origins, literary contexts, and social and ethical implications of the Pauline Adamic motif, see now Felipe de Jesús Legarreta-Castillo, *The Figure of Adam in Romans 5 and 1 Corinthians 15: The New Creation and Its Ethical and Social Reconfiguration* (Emerging Scholars; Minneapolis: Fortress Press, 2014); N. T. Wright, "Adam in Pauline Christology," in *SBL Seminar Papers 22* (Chico: Scholars Press, 1983), 359-89; C. Marvin Pate, *Adam Christology as Exegetical & Theological Substructure of 2 Corinthians 4:7—5:21* (WUNT 2/4; Tübingen: Mohr Siebeck, 1984), 162-92.

89. James D. G. Dunn, *Christology in the Making: An Inquiry into the Origins of the Doctrine of the Incarnation* (London: SCM, 1980), 98–128, esp. 114.

90. David Steenburg, "The Worship of Adam and Christ as the Image of God," *JSNT* 39 (1990): 95–109, esp. 95.

91. Dunn, *Christology in the Making*, 111, 114–19. For the hymn's pre-Pauline provenance see Oscar Cullmann, *The Christology of the New Testament* (London: SCM, 1963), 181; Jerome Murphy O'Connor, "Christological Anthropology in Phil. 2:6-11," *RB* 83, no. 1 (1976): 25–50; Davies, *Paul and Rabbinic Judaism*, 41; Morna D. Hooker, "Philippians 2:6-11," in *Jesus und Paulus: Festschrift für W. G. Kümmel*, ed. E. Earle Ellis and Erich Grässer (Göttingen: Vandenhoeck & Ruprecht, 1975), 151–64; Barrett, *From First Adam to Last*, 69–72; Lincoln D. Hurst, "Christ, Adam, and Preexistence Revisited," in *Where Christology Began: Essays on Philippians 2*, ed. Ralph P. Martin and Brian J. Dodd (Louisville: Westminster John Knox, 1998), 84–95. See also James D. G. Dunn, *The Theology of Paul the Apostle* (Grand Rapids: Eerdmans, 1998), 281–88; George Eldon Ladd, *A Theology of the New Testament* (Grand Rapids: Eerdmans, 1974), 460–61; Seyoon Kim, *The Origin of Paul's Gospel* (Tübingen: Mohr Siebeck, 1984),

Philippian hymn has thus become one of the most discussed and debated sites in Pauline Christology:

> Christ Jesus, though he was *in the form of God* (ἐν μορφῇ θεοῦ),
> did not regard equality with God as something to be exploited,
> but emptied himself, taking the form of a slave,
> being born *in human likeness* (ἐν ὁμοιώματι ἀνθρώπων),
> and being found *as a man* (ὡς ἄνθρωπος),
> he humbled himself and became obedient to the point of death—
> even death on a cross. Therefore God also highly exalted him
> and gave him the name that is above every name,
> so that at the name of Jesus every knee should bend,
> in heaven and on earth, and under the earth,
> and every tongue should confess that Jesus Christ is Lord (κύριος),
> to the glory of God the Father (πατρός).

According to James Dunn the figure of Adam "plays a larger role in Paul's theology than is usually realized" and it is "often misunderstood."[92] For Dunn, Phil. 2:5-11 represents "the most coherent and most complete" Adamic Christology in early Christianity.[93] The Philippians hymn "is an attempt to read the life and work of Christ through the grid of Adam theology." The point of the hymn is "the epochal significance of the Christ-event, as determinative for humankind as the 'event' of Adam's creation and fall." It is because Christ "has so completely reversed the catastrophe of Adam . . . that the paradigm is so inviting, and so 'fitting' in the first place." Jesus is described in a manner reminiscent of the creation of Adam in the image, likeness, and "form of God" (ἐν μορφῇ θεοῦ) from Gen. 1:27. The phrase ἐν μορφῇ θεοῦ in verse 6 seems to echo Gen. 1:26. Paul uses the term μορφὴ instead of εἰκών (which the LXX uses to render צלם), but is its meaning so similar as to warrant being called "synonymity?"[94] The linguistic variations between Gen. 1:26-27

265; N. T. Wright, *The Climax of the Covenant: Christ and the Law in Pauline Theology* (Minneapolis: Fortress Press, 1992), 57–58; George Howard, "Phil. 2:6-22 and the Human Christ," *CBQ* 40 (1978): 368–87; Elias Andrews, *The Meaning of Christ for Paul* (New York: Abingdon-Cokesbury, 1946), 158–61; E. Earle Ellis, *Paul's Use of the Old Testament* (Grand Rapids: Baker, 1991 [1957]), 129 n. 6; John A. Ziesler, *Pauline Christianity* (Oxford and New York: Oxford University Press, 1990), 43.

92. Dunn, *Christology in the Making*, 101.

93. Dunn, "Foreword to Second Edition," *Christology in the Making* (Grand Rapids: Eerdmans, 1989), xix.

94. Ralph Martin, *Carmen Christi: Philippians 2:5-11 in Recent Interpretation* (Grand Rapids: Eerdmans, 1983), 102–19, but esp.108, suggests that Phil. 2:6's "in the form of God" can also be taken as "in the

(LXX: κατ' εἰκόνα θεοῦ) and Phil. 2:5-11 may dampen our enthusiasm for an exact semantic correspondence in terms, but the density of parallels between the Christ-figure and Adam require careful consideration. It is not just that Jesus takes the "form" (or "image") of God, but Christ may also be contrasted with Adam in that he did not regard equality with God as something to be exploited, in contrast to Adam's seeking to become like God in Gen. 3:5.[95] Furthermore, Christ's enslavement to corruption and sin (Rom. 8:3; Gal. 4:4), his submission to death (Rom. 5:21-21; 7:7-11; 1 Cor. 15:21-22), and his eschatological glorification (1 Cor. 15:27, 45) are themes highly reminiscent of Adamic tradition. This does not mean that Phil. 2:5-11 solely, consistently, or exclusively refers to Adamic motifs. Dunn carefully qualifies his argument by suggesting that it is the "Adamic *significance* of Christ which the hymn brings out . . . not necessarily a chronological parallel phase by phase."[96] Nonetheless, Dunn is confident that "the most informative and probable background" to Phil. 2:5-11 is an Adamic Christology. Dunn argues that this early Adamic Christology was subsequently obscured, perhaps even eclipsed, by the higher Incarnational Christology characteristic of the Gospel of John. Dunn's approach has been criticized, not least because it is claimed that he overestimates Adam's significance for Paul and presupposes that significance in Phil. 2:5-11 based on prior exegetical study of Romans, where Christ is explicitly compared and contrasted to Adam.[97] Larry Hurtado and Richard Bauckham have both argued vigorously in support of an early veneration of Christ as pre-existent.[98] It seems

image of God." See also Kim, *Origin*, 200–4; Cullmann, *Christology*, 176; Dunn, *Theology*, 284; Barrett, *From First Adam to Last*, 71. Andrew Chester, *Messiah and Exaltation* (WUNT 207; Tübingen: Mohr Siebeck, 2007), 392, argues that the Philippian hymn "is integrally connected with Adam speculation." Dave Steenburg, "The Case Against the Synonymity of Morphē and Eikōn," *JSNT* 34 (1988): 77–86, has argued that μορφὴ and εἰκών may have had some "general conceptual linkage," but there is no evidence that they were ever used interchangeably. Steenburg notes only one instance in which the LXX uses μορφὴ for צלם (Dan. 3:19). But see Adela Y. Collins, in John J. Collins and Adela Yarbro Collins, *King and Messiah as Son of God: Divine, Human, and Angelic Messianic Figures in Biblical and Related Literature* (Grand Rapids: Eerdmans, 2008), 147 n. 95.

95. Hooker, "Philippians 2.6-11," 96–98.

96. Dunn, *Christology in the Making*, xix.

97. For criticism see Charles A. Wanamaker, "Philippians 2:6-11: Son of God or Adamic Christology?" *NTS* 33 (1987): 179–93; L. D. Hurst, "Re-Enter the Pre-existent Christ in Philippians 2.5-11?" *NTS* 32 (1986): 449–57; Brendan T. Byrne, "Christ's Pre-Existence in Pauline Soteriology," *TS* 58, no. 2 (1997): 308–30. It should not need to be stated that Adam is also properly identified as the "Son of God" (Luke 2).

98. Larry Hurtado, *How on Earth Did Jesus Become a God? Historical Questions About Earliest Devotion to Jesus* (Grand Rapids: Eerdmans, 2005), has argued that Jesus was identified as divine through worship at a very early period. Richard Bauckham, *Jesus and the God of Israel: God Crucified and Other Studies on*

that the real point of contention is not simply whether the subject of Phil. 2:5-11 is the human Jesus as opposed to the pre-existent Christ[99] or whether there are Adamic echoes in its representation of Christ Jesus (there certainly are), but rather the more heated question of whether the earliest Christians worshiped Jesus as divine. Dunn seems unequivocal on this point: "Jesus is not the God of Israel. He is not the Father. He is not Yahweh."[100] Early Jewish Christian devotion to and veneration of Jesus did not transgress Jewish monotheism.[101] Moreover, there is no need to choose *between* Incarnation Christology and Adamic Christology.[102] As in Rom. 5:12-21, Christ is both compared and contrasted to Adam in Phil. 2:5-11. The Philippians hymn may not be *limited* to an identification with Adam, but there is no fixed or monolithic Adam tradition in pre-Christian Judaism; rather, there are multiple "portraits of Adam."[103] The eschatological Adam of the *Animal Apocalypse*, the Danielic "son of humanity/Adam/man," the Qumranic "glory of Adam" and "Temple of Adam" all point to diverse expressions of a common soteriological interest: a new humanity. Dunn notes that "a Jesus who makes an Adamic choice is more of a model for Christian behavior (Phil. 2.1-13) than a pre-existent Christ."[104] Yet there is no special need to drive a wedge between a pre-existent messiah and Paul's Adamic Christ: the literary and theological fusion of pre-existence, Jewish messianism, and apocalyptic son of man/Adam traditions had already been made by the author of the Enochic *Book of Parables*.

the New Testament's Theology of Divine Identity (Grand Rapids: Eerdmans, 2008), suggests that "the exalted Jesus is given the divine name, the Tetragrammaton (YHWH)." See also David B. Capes, *Old Testament Yahweh Texts in Paul's Christology* (Tübingen: Mohr, 1992), 157–60. Hooker, "Philippians 2.6-11," 99, suggests that Christ's name being placed "above every other name" may reflect Adam's original place in the creation.

99. Jerome Murphy-O'Connor, "Christological Anthropology in Phil. 2.6-11," *RB* 83 (1976): 25–50; John A. T. Robinson, *The Human Face of God* (London: SCM, 1973), 162–66; Charles H. Talbert, "The Problem of Pre-Existence in Philippians 2:6-11," *JBL* 86 (1967): 141–53; George Howard, "Phil 2:6-11 and the Human Christ"; Stanley K. Stowers, *A Rereading of Romans: Justice, Jews and Gentiles* (New Haven: Yale University Press, 1995), 220.

100. James D. G. Dunn, *Did the First Christians Worship Jesus? The New Testament Evidence* (Louisville: Westminster John Knox, 2010), 142.

101. See James F. McGrath, *The Only True God: Early Christian Monotheism and its Jewish Context* (Urbana: University of Illinois Press, 2009), 52–54, esp. 53.

102. Wright, *Climax of the Covenant*, 59, 90–94, does not find pre-existence in the hymn to exclude an allusion to Adam.

103. See Levison, *Portraits of Adam in Early Judaism*, 160–61.

104. Dunn, *Christology in the Making*, xxxiv n. 23.

Philippians 2:5-11 represents a remarkably early example of high Christological reflection on Jesus' significance as an Adamic figure.

Paul's thought emphasizes Christ's eschatological relevance and correlation to Adam and/or humanity. Paul explicitly identifies Adam as ἄνθρωπος:

> the *first man* (πρῶτος ἄνθρωπος) was from the earth, a man of dust;
> the *second man* (δεύτερος ἄνθρωπος) is from heaven . . .
> just as we have borne the image (εἰκόνα) of the man of dust (χοικοῦ).[105]

In 2 Cor. 4:16, Paul uses ἄνθρωπος to represent human nature or "humanity":

> our outer *man* (ἄνθρωπος) is wasting away,
> our *inner* (*man*) (ἔσω ἡμῶν) is being renewed day by day.

In Rom. 6:6, Paul proclaims that

> we know that our old *humanity* (ἄνθρωπος) was crucified with him
> so that . . . we might no longer be enslaved to sin.[106]

In Eph. 2:15-16, Christ is said to have created

> in himself *one new man/humanity* (ἕνα καινὸν ἄνθρωπον)
> in place of the two (Jew and Gentile).[107]

105. 1 Cor. 15:47-49.

106. In Eph. 3:16-17. Ephesians 4:24 notes how disciples are to "clothe yourselves with the *new self* created according to the likeness of God." 1 Pet. 3:4 states: "let your adornment be *the hidden/inner self*." In the LXX the word ἄνθρωπος, in referring to Adam, is translated with the *definite* article ὁ (Gen. 2:7, 15, 18). In Deut. 8:3 Moses tells Israel that human beings/people (האדם) do not live by bread alone. The LXX translates האדם with ὁ ἄνθρωπος. In Q, Jesus quotes Deut. 8:3, ὁ ἄνθρωπος.

107. In Col. 3:9-10 readers are told that they have "put off" or "stripped off *the old self* (τὸν παλαιὸν ἄνθρωπον) with its practices and have clothed yourselves with the new 'man' according to the image of its creator." Similar ideas can be found in the *Gospel of Mary*, where Mary tells the disciples to put on the "Perfect Man." See Karen L. King, *The Gospel of Mary of Magdala: Jesus and the First Woman Apostle* (Santa Rosa: Polebridge, 2003), 3. See also Esther A. De Boer, *The Gospel of Mary: Beyond a Gnostic and a Biblical Mary Magdalene* (London: Continuum, 2004); eadem, *The Gospel of Mary: Listening to the Beloved Disciple* (London: Continuum, 2006). The *Gospel of Mary* may be echoing Adamic tradition when Mary proclaims that the "son of man" is "within you" (4.34) and that the savior "has prepared us and made us into 'Men'" (5.3).

The semantic range of ἄνθρωπος includes (hu)man, self, humanity, and human nature. There is a generic level of meaning to our humanity that is also represented in the figure and name of "Adam." For Paul our ἄνθρωπος, that is, our humanity, is *Adamic*, and Christ is the bearer of the "image." Adam was a "type" of Christ. Our inner "man/humanity" contains the "image of God" (Christ/Adam), and the faithful are one body, for all dwell "in Christ." Paul's motif of "putting on Christ" in the "baptismal reunification formula" may also be pre-Pauline, with "roots in certain aspects of the Adam legends."[108] If Gal. 3:28 and 1 Cor. 12:13 represent Adamic traditions, this shows a marked interest in a new humanity ἐν τῷ Χριστῷ, which is strikingly similar to the Enochic symbol of the "white bull" transforming others into white bulls.

The corporate idea of being ἐν τῷ Χριστῷ has been much discussed in Pauline scholarship. The most obvious and cogent explanation is that fellowship ἐν τῷ Χριστῷ is derived from an Adamic identification of the messiah.[109] Albert Schweitzer described this as "the preordained union of those who are elect to the Messianic Kingdom with one another and with the Messiah which is called 'the community of the Saints.'"[110] The elect of God are to be united with the messiah. While Paul drew on a number of Jewish models for his messianic portrait of Jesus—including traditional Davidic messianism and Isaiah's (Suffering) Servant as "a light to the nations"—Paul's soteriological system is largely based on, even *depends* on, an Adamic identification of Jesus. For Paul, Jesus' "saving grace" is that he died "for us," "for our sins," restoring the broken Adamic covenant.

Paul uses an Adam-Christ typology in a double parallelism, stating that just as death came through a man (Adam), so resurrection also came through a man (Christ):[111]

> ἐπειδὴ γὰρ δι' ἀνθρώπου θάνατος καὶ δι'ἀνθρώπου ἀνάστασις νεκρῶν.[112]

108. Wayne A. Meeks, *The First Urban Christians: The Social World of the Apostle Paul* (New Haven: Yale University Press, 1983), 88, citing Gal. 3:28, 1 Cor. 12:13, and perhaps Col. 3:11.

109. Davies, *Paul and Rabbinic Judaism*, 324, took the phrase to mean "in Israel." Wedderburn, "Observations," relates it to God's promise to Abraham (Gal. 3:8).

110. Albert Schweitzer, *The Mysticism of Paul the Apostle*, trans. William Montgomery (New York: Macmillan, 1955), 101.

111. Sang-Won (Aaron) Son, *Corporate Elements in Pauline Anthropology: A Study of Selected Terms, Idioms, and Concepts in the Light of Paul's Usage and Background* (AnB 148; Rome: Pontifical Biblical Institute, 2001), 44.

112. 1 Cor. 15:21.

ὥσπερ γὰρ ἐν τῷ Ἀδὰμ πάντες ἀποθνῄσκουσιν οὕτως καὶ ἐν τῷ Χριστῷ πάντες ζῳοποιηθήσονται.[113]

Paul's parallelism contrasts Adam's sin and Jesus' sinlessness, Adam's disobedience and Jesus' obedience, Adam's death and Jesus' resurrection:[114]

Adam	Christ
"transgression" (παράπτωμα)	"grace" (χάρισμα)
"sin" (ἁμαρτία)	"righteousness" (δικαιοσύνη)
"disobedience" (παρακοή)	"obedience" (ὑπακοή)

The resurrection was the divine vindication of the Son.[115] Jesus' death restored the original covenant between God and humanity, resulting in the expansion of Israel to now include Gentiles and transcend ethnic limitations.

Χριστός is a new Ἀδὰμ,[116] the herald of the "new creation,"[117] the "image of God,"[118] who gave "himself for our sins to set us free from the present evil age."[119] He has "disarmed the rulers and authorities … triumphing over them,"[120] setting us free "from the law of sin and of death."[121] God has now called all those "predestined to be conformed to the image of his Son."[122] Paul's idea of salvation is the restoration of humanity according to the "image of God" in which Adam had been created and that Christ perfected.[123] Paul's reference to Jesus as the "*image* of God" (εἰκὼν τοῦ θεοῦ) and his confession that it was God's will "to reveal his Son *in me*" (ἀποκαλύψαι τὸν υἱὸν αὐτοῦ ἐν ἐμοὶ) strongly suggest that Paul is working with Jewish apocalyptic ideas of Adamic messianism.[124] The "image" of God, once identified as *Christ*-messiah, signifies the eschatological restoration of the Adamic "image" for all humanity.

113. 1 Cor. 15:22.

114. Rom. 5:12-21.

115. 1 Cor. 15:21-22. Son, *Corporate Elements in Pauline Anthropology*, 44.

116. 1 Cor. 15:45.

117. 2 Cor. 5:17. For Jesus as the "last Adam" and the perfect man in whom the "image" can be seen, see S. Vernon McCasland, "'The Image of God' According to Paul," *JBL* 69 (1950): 85–100. In Col. 1:14-15, Jesus is "the image of the invisible God, the first-born of every creature."

118. Gal. 4:4; 2 Cor. 4:4; 1 Cor. 11:7.

119. Gal. 1:4.

120. Phil. 2:15.

121. Rom. 8:2.

122. Rom. 8:29.

123. Dunn, *Christology in the Making*, 105–6: salvation is "the fashioning or reshaping of the believer into the image of God" and Jesus is "the indispensable model or pattern for this process."

124. 2 Cor 4:4. Cf. Col 1:15; Gal 1:15-16, respectively.

Christ's renewal of humanity was a "mystery," a "secret" hidden from the ages. A "new creation" and a new humanity were brought into being.[125] Christ received the "glory" intended for Adam that now enables believers to be transformed according to his likeness.[126] Χριστός, unlike Adam, was an obedient servant. Adam was "the first man," Χριστός "the last Adam."[127] The "first man" was "a man of dust," the second, a man "from heaven."[128] Humanity before Χριστός bore the "image of the man of dust."[129] Χριστός is now the "image of the heavenly man":[130]

15:45a	Ἐγένετο ὁ πρῶτος ἄνθρωπος Ἀδὰμ εἰς ψυχὴν ζῶσαν	
15:45b	ὁ ἔσχατος Ἀδὰμ	εἰς πνεῦμα ζῳοποιοῦν.
15:47a	ὁ πρῶτος ἄνθρωπος	ἐκ γῆς χοικός,
15:47b	ὁ δεύτερος ἄνθρωπος	ἐξ οὐρανοῦ
15:49a	καὶ καθὼς ἐφορέσαμεν	τὴν εἰκόνα τοῦ χοικοῦ,
15:49b	φορέσομεν καὶ τὴν εἰκόνα τοῦ ἐπουρανίου.	

For Paul, Χριστός is *superior* to Adam.[131] Adam is only "a *type* of the Coming One."[132] Sin and death came into the world through Adam.[133] Χριστός reversed this condition. Adam's death was due to his disobedience; Χριστός's voluntary death was an act of obedience.[134] It is Χριστός, not Adam, who fulfills God's design for a fallen humanity.[135] Paul's theology is derived from his understanding of the significance of Jesus' resurrection.[136] Through his resurrection Christ received the "glory" intended for Adam since the beginning, which now enables believers to be transformed according to *his* likeness (Phil. 3:21). Paul's Adam-Christ typology has its roots in apocalyptic Jewish speculation on a new creation (καινὴ κτίσις),[137] the messianic age inaugurating

125. Denise Buell, *Why this New Race?: Ethnic Reasoning in Early Christianity* (New York: Columbia University Press, 2005).

126. Phil. 3:21.

127. 1 Cor. 15:45.

128. 1 Cor. 15:47.

129. 1 Cor. 15:49.

130. 1 Cor. 15:45-49.

131. Son, *Corporate Elements in Pauline Anthropology*, 53–54. See also Karl Barth, *A Shorter Commentary on Romans*, trans. David H. van Daalen (London: SCM, 1959), 63.

132. Q identifies Jesus as the "Coming One." The parallelism is striking: for Paul, Adam is a "type" of the "coming one" (Christ); in Q, Jesus *is* the "coming one."

133. Rom. 5:12-19.

134. Dunn, *Christology in the Making*, 110.

135. Scroggs, *Last Adam*, xxii, 100.

136. Ibid., 124.

a new humanity.[138] Jesus represents not the restoration of the Jewish nation but the restoration of the whole *creation*,[139] which is precisely what we find in *An. Apoc.* 90, where messianic expectations are found in conjunction with the appearance of a second Adam.

What was Paul's inspiration for his Adam-Christ typology? Paul is arguably dependent on Genesis for his portrayal of Adam, but the particular concepts he applies to Adam and Christ go well beyond Genesis,[140] which focuses on Adam's fall.[141] Paul views Christ as inaugurating a new creation,[142] but Paul clearly did not invent the concept of a new creation. He *inherited* it from the Jewish apocalyptic tradition, along with the idea that the messianic age would inaugurate the regeneration of humanity. Paul affirmed and transformed the messianic faith of his Jewish Christian colleagues.[143]

137. Davies, *Paul and Rabbinic Judaism*, 36–57; Scroggs, *Last Adam*, 61–74; Wedderburn, "Adam and Christ," 67–73.

138. Menahem Kister, "'In Adam': 1 Cor 15:21-22; 12:27 in their Jewish Setting," in *Flores Florentino: Dead Sea Scrolls and Other Early Jewish Studies in Honour of Florentino García Martínez*, ed. Anthony Hilhorst, Émile Puech, and Elbert Tigchelaar (JSJSup 122; Leiden: Brill, 2007), 685–90, esp. 685, argues that the relationships between Adam and Christ in Paul's letters "have their source in contemporary Judaism, to which Paul gives a peculiar christological twist." 1 Cor. 15:45-49 is "a Christianized version of Jewish ideas, modes of thought, and exegesis" (p. 690). See also idem, "Romans 5:12-21 against the Background of Torah-Theology and Hebrew Usage," *HTR* 100 (2007): 391–424; idem, "'First Adam' and 'Second Adam' in 1 Cor 15:45-49 in the Light of Midrashic Exegesis and Hebrew Usage," *New Testament and Rabbinic Literature: Proceedings of a Symposium held at the K . U. Leuven on January 2006*, ed. Reimund Bieringer (JSJ Sup 136; Leiden: Brill, 2010), 351–65. See also Egon Brandenburger, "Alter und neuer Mensch, erster und letzer Adam-Anthropos," in *Vom alten zum neuen Adam: Urzeitmythos und Heilsgeschichte*, ed. Walter Strolz (Freiburg: Herder, 1986), 205–17.

139. 1 Cor. 15:20-28.

140. Some scholars have located the cultural background of Paul's thought in the myth of the "Primal Man" (*Urmensch*), arguing that this myth influenced the biblical Adam narrative (as in Philo) and, combined with Jewish messianism, produced the son of man tradition. See Richard Reitzenstein, *Hellenistic Mystery-Religions: Their Basic Ideas and Significance*, trans. John E. Seely (3d ed.; Pittsburgh: Pickwick, 1978), 426–96; Wilhelm Bousset, *Kyrios Christos: A History of the Belief in Christ from the Beginnings of Christianity to Irenaeus* (Nashville: Abingdon, 1970), 178, 188–200; Rudolf Bultmann, *The Theology of the New Testament*, trans. Kendrick Grobel (New York: Scribners, 1955), 1: 173–74, 251, 289–90; Brandenburger, *Adam und Christus*; J. M. Creed, "The Heavenly Man," *JTS* 26 (1925): 113–26. See also Benjamin Murmelstein, "Adam, ein Beitrag zur Messiaslehre," *WZKM* 35 (1928): 242–75; *WZKM* 36 (1929): 51–86; Willi Staerk, *Die Erlösererwartung in den Östlichen Religionen: Soter II* (Stuttgart: Kohlhammer, 1938), 7–138.

141. George W. E. Nickelsburg, in Nickelsburg and VanderKam, *1 Enoch: A Commentary*, 102.

142. See Davies, *Paul and Rabbinic Judaism*, 36–37; Scroggs, *Last Adam*, 61–74; Wedderburn, "Adam and Christ," 67–73.

The History-of-Religions School (*Religionsgeschichtliche Schule*) located the cultural background of Paul's thought in ancient Near Eastern speculation on the Primal Man (*Urmensch*), arguing that this myth influenced the biblical narrative and, combined with Jewish messianism, produced the son of man tradition.[144] This thesis has been severely criticized.[145] A wide range of Adamic speculations were conflated with other ideas, for example, the Primal Man, Manichaeism, Mandaeanism, and Zoroastrianism's Gayomart, to construct a "son of man concept," but there is no such ancient myth.[146] The Primal Man is a composite figure produced over long periods of time and space.[147] The sources used to (re)construct this myth are post-Pauline. There is no clear evidence of a pre-Christian Gnostic conception of a Primal Man.[148]

A number of scholars have argued that Paul derived his Christ-Adam typology from Jesus' identification as the son of man.[149] Adamic interpretations

143. Davies, *Paul and Rabbinic Judaism*, 50–51, 52, suggests that "the Church at Corinth must have been familiar with . . . ideas about Adam." He also points out that the Pseudo-Clementine *Homilies* contain a highly exalted portrait of Adam (as Christ) and that it is "also possible that the *Homilies* reflect traditions of controversies in the first century in which Paul was accused of calumniating the first Adam." Davies recognizes that "there was a polemical motive, possibly motives, behind Paul's use of the term, the Second Adam, for Christ."

144. See Reitzenstein, *Hellenistic Mystery-Religions*, 426–96; Bousset, *Kyrios Christos*, 178, 188–200; Bultmann, *Theology of the New Testament*, 1: 173–74, 251, 289–90; Brandenburger, *Adam und Christus*; Creed, "Heavenly Man," 113–26; Murmelstein, "Adam, ein Beitrag zur Messiaslehre," 242–75; Staerk, *Die Erlösererwartung*, 7–138. See also Carl Kraeling, *Anthropos and the Son of Man: A Study in the Religious Syncretism of the Hellenistic Orient* (CUOS 25; New York: AMS, 1927); Sigmund Mowinckel, *He that Cometh*, trans. G. W. Anderson (New York: Abingdon, 1954), 420–37; Cullmann, *Christology*, 139–52.

145. Colpe, *Die religionsgeschichtliche Schule*; Wedderburn, "Adam and Christ."

146. John J. Collins, in Adela Yarbro Collins and John J. Collins, *King and Messiah as Son of God: Divine, Human, and Angelic Messianic Figures in Biblical and Related Literature* (Grand Rapids: Eerdmans, 2008), 76–77; Carsten Colpe, "ὁ υἱὸς τοῦ ἀνθρώπου," *TDNT* 8 (1972): 400–77, esp. 408–15; idem, *Die religionsgeschichtliche Schule*; Ragnar Leivestadt, "Exit the Apocalyptic Son of Man," *NTS* 18 (1972): 243–67; Geza Vermes, *Jesus and the World of Judaism* (Philadelphia: Fortress Press, 1984), 96–98; Norman Perrin, *A Modern Pilgrimage in New Testament Christology* (Philadelphia: Fortress Press, 1974), 26; Lindars, *Jesus, Son of Man*, 3.

147. Colpe, *Die religionsgeschichtliche Schule*, 191; Scroggs, *Last Adam*, ix; Black, "Second Adam," 177.

148. Kim, *Origin*, 177; Black, "The Pauline Doctrine of the Second Adam," 170–79, esp. 171–72.

149. A. E. J. Rawlinson, *The New Testament Doctrine of the Christ* (London: Longmans, 1978), 122–23; T. W. Manson, *The Teaching of Jesus* (Cambridge: Cambridge University Press, 1935), 233–34; Black, "Second Adam," 173; Cullmann, *Christology*, 166–81; Barrett, *From First Adam to Last*, 75–76; Ellis, *Paul's Use*, 96–97; Wedderburn, "Adam and Christ," 86–114. Rawlinson, *The New Testament Doctrine of the Christ*, 122–36; Barrett, *From First Adam to Last*, 75–76; Black, "Second Adam," 172–75, 179; Joachim Jeremias, "Adam," *TDNT* 1: 141–43; Manson, *The Teaching of Jesus*, 234; Vincent Taylor, *The Person of*

of the son of man have an ancient pedigree among the early Church Fathers. The term "Son of Man" was often interpreted to refer to Jesus' *humanity*, and "Son of God" to his divinity.[150] According to Ignatius of Antioch, the phrase "son of man" complemented the expression "Son of God."[151] Tertullian taught that Christ was both the human "Son of Man" born of the Virgin Mary and the divine "Son of God" conceived by the Holy Spirit.[152] The term was understood to refer to Jesus' *humanity*. Athanasius stated that Jesus "appeared as son of a man, not becoming some different (type of man), but a second Adam (δεύτερος Ἀδάμ)."[153] Gregory of Nazianzus wrote that Jesus was called "Son of man . . . because of Adam" (Υἱὸς δὲ ἀνθρώπου, καὶ δὶ τον Ἀδὰμ).[154] Irenaeus also noted that "The Lord professes to be the Son of Man, comprising in himself the first man,"[155] because "He is the one that has recapitulated in himself all races dispersed from the time of Adam, all languages, and the generations of men with Adam."[156]

Christ in New Testament Teaching (London: Macmillan, 1958), 48; Cullmann, *Christology*, 172, 145; Ragnar Leivestad, "Der apokalyptische Menschensohn ein theologisches Phantom," *ASTI* (1968): 49–105, esp. 102–3, argued that Paul's "Second Adam" is a proper interpretation of Jesus' self-expression. James Waddell, "The Messiah in the Parables of Enoch and the Letters of Paul: A Comparative Analysis," Ph. D. Dissertation, University of Michigan, 2010, 234–59, suggests that the absence of the term "son of man" in Paul can be explained "in the context of a first-century Jewish soteriological debate which made reference to the biblical figure of Adam" (p. 235). For Paul's non-use of the son of man tradition see Anton Vögtle, *'Der Menschensohn' und die paulinische Christologie* (Rome: Pontifical Biblical Institute, 1963), 19–218; idem, "Die Adam-Christus-Typologie und 'der Menschensohn,'" *TTZ* 60 (1951): 309–28; idem, "'Der Menschensohn' und die paulinishe Christologie," in *Studiorum Paulinorum Congressus Internationalis Catholicis* (2 vols.; AnB 17/18; Rome: Pontifical Biblical Institute, 1961), 1: 199–218. Similarly, see Joseph A. Fitzmyer, *A Wandering Aramean: Collected Aramaic Essays* (Missoula: Scholars Press, 1979), 144; Kim, *Origin*, 184–85; Margaret E. Thrall, "The Origin of Pauline Christology," in *Apostolic History and the Gospel: Biblical and Historical Essays Presented to F. F. Bruce on his 60th Birthday*, ed. W. Ward Gasque and Ralph P. Martin (Grand Rapids: Eerdmans, 1970), 304–16, at 306–7; Reginald H. Fuller, *The Foundation of New Testament Christology* (New York: Scribners, 1965), 233–34.

150. Wayland Hoyt, *The Teaching of Jesus concerning His Own Person* (New York: American Tract Society, 1909), 87–121; Alfred Plummer, *The Gospel according to St. John* (Cambridge: Cambridge University Press, 1882), 88–89.

151. Ignatius *Eph.* 20.2.

152. Tertullian, *Against Marcion* 4.10.

153. Athanasius, *Contra Apollinarium* 1.8; MPG 26.1105–1108.

154. Gregory of Nazianzus, *Oration* 30, 21.

155. Irenaeus, *Adv. Haer.* 5.21.1.

156. *Adv. Haer.* 3.22.3. See also Hilary, *Commentarius in Matthaeum* 4.12; Augustine, *Enarratio in Psalmum* CXLII.3; Peter Chrysologus, *Sermo* CXL; Cyril of Alexandria, *Adversus Nestorium* I.

Since the Reformation many scholars have regarded the Greek title as a translation of either בן אדם or בר אנש, with Jesus representing a "lowly," "weak," or "suffering" humanity.[157] Another interpretation sees the son of man as the ideal human messiah,[158] or the messiah as a superior or "ideal man."[159] While it may not seem necessary to emphasize the humanity of Jewish messianic expectations, the relationship between the new Adam of the *Animal Apocalypse* and Daniel's "one like a son of man," in conjunction with a possibly *linguistic* relationship between the son of *man* and *Adam* in the *Book of Parables*,[160] indicates that messianic speculation on Adamic/son of man

157. Delbert Burkett, *The Son of Man Debate: A History and Evaluation* (SNTSMS 107; Cambridge: Cambridge University Press, 1999), 13–17. See Edwin Abbott, *'The Son of Man' or Contributions to the Study of the Thoughts of Jesus* (Cambridge: Cambridge University Press, 1910), 82–107. But see also Maurice Casey, *The Solution to the Son of Man Problem* (London: T&T Clark, 2007), 15; Olaf Moe, "Der Menschensohn und der Urmensch," *ST* 14 (1960): 119–29, esp. 124; Juan B. Cortés and Florence M. Gotti, "The Son of Man or The Son of Adam," *Bib* 49 (1968): 457–502, esp. 472; and Joel Marcus, "Son of Man as son of Adam," *RB* 110 (2003): 38–61, 370–86.

158. Augustus Wilhelm Neander, *The Life of Jesus Christ in its Historical Connexion and Historical Development* (London: Bell, 1888), 99.

159. Gottlob Christian Storr, *Doctrinae christianae pars theoretica e sacris litteris repetita* (Stuttgart: Metzler, 1793), 201; Christian Gottlieb Kühnöl, *Commentarius in libros novi testamenti historicos*, Vol. 1: *Evangelium Matthaei* (3d ed.; Leipzig: Barth, 1823), 231; Augustus Tholuck, *Commentar zu dem Evangelio Johannis* (Hamburg: Perthes, 1827), 61–62; Hermann Olshausen, *Biblical Commentary on the New Testament* (New York: Sheldon, Blakeman, 1858), 1: 217–21, 377, 442, 455; Karl von Hase, *Life of Jesus: A Manual for Academic Study* (Boston: Walker, Wise, 1860), 136; idem, *Geschichte Jesu, nach akademischen Vorlesungen* (2d ed.; Leipzig: Breitkopf und Härtel, 1891), 514; Christian Friedrich Böhme, *Versuch das Geheimnis des Menschensohn zu enthüllen* (Neustadt: Orla, 1839), 84–92; Ludwig Friedrich Otto Baumgarten-Crusius, *Theologische Auslegung der johanneischen Schriften*, ed. Ernst Julius Kümmel (2 vols.; Jena: Luden, 1843–45), 1: 77; Carl Wittichen, *Beiträge zur biblischen Theologie 2: Die Idee des Menschen: Zweiter Beitrag zur biblischen Theologie* (Göttingen: Dieterich, 1868), 61–62, 66–69, 97–98, 137–58; idem, *Das Leben Jesu in urkundlicher Darstellung* (Jena: Dufft, 1876), 111, 140–41, 338–39; Wilhelm Mangold, "Über die Bedeutung des Ausdrucks: ὁ υἱὸς τοῦ ἀνθρώπου," in *Theologische Arbeiten aus dem rheinisch-wissenschaftlichen Predigerverein* 3 (1877): 1–25; Wilhelm Brückner, "Jesus 'des Menschen Sohn,'" *JPT* 12 (1886): 254–78; Vincent Henry Stanton, *The Jewish and the Christian Messiah: A Study in the Earliest History of Christianity* (Edinburgh: Clark, 1886), 237–50; Georg Schnedermann, *Jesu Verkündigung und Lehre vom Reiche Gottes in ihrer geschichtlichen Bedeutung* (2 vols.; Leipzig: Deichert, 1893–95), 1: 206–9; Joseph MacRory, "The Son of Man," *ITQ* 10 (1915): 50–63; Roland K. Harrison, "The Son of Man," *EvQ* 23 (1951): 46–50.

160. Helge S. Kvanvig, "The Son of Man in the Parables of Enoch," esp. 193, proposes that the Ethiopic text uses *walda be'si* in the singular for "son of man" (62.5, 69.29, 71.14), which can be translated as 'son of Adam' in Aramaic and refers to Adam as the "primeval" man, implying "an eschatological interpretation of the first man reappearing at the end of time." Klaus Koch, "Questions regarding the So-Called Son of Man in the Parables of Enoch: A Response to Sabino Chialà and Helge Kvanvig," in *Enoch*

messianism was current in the Jewish (Christian) Palestinian circles known to Paul. Can this eschatological Adam ideal also be found in the Jesus tradition in Q?

In the next chapter I will examine three dominant themes and traditions in Q: the eschatological kingdom of God, Jesus' identification as the "Son of God," and the Inaugural Sermon's dominant ethic of love and nonviolence. Since these traditions are widely regarded as reliably authentic historical Jesus tradition they can serve as controls in assessing whether the Christology of Q is comparable to and consistent with the eschatological Adamic messianism of Early Jewish apocalypticism, and whether this tradition, in turn, can be related to the ethical instructions of the historical Jesus.

and the Messiah Son of Man, 228–37, esp. 231, points out that the construction can mean "son of the Adam," perhaps signifying the new Adam, "an early parallel to the praise of Jesus Christ as the second Adam."

PART III

10

The Kingdom, the Son, and the Gospel

I: "Seek His Kingdom"

The kingdom,[1] reign, or rule of God is the central theme of Jesus' ministry.[2] The expression has generally been understood as a reference to the belief that God was the king of Israel and linked to royal ideology and divine kingship.[3]

1. Parts of this chapter previously appeared in the following publications: "'Seek His Kingdom': Q 12,22b-31, God's Providence, and Adamic Wisdom," *Bib* 92, no. 3 (2011): 392–410; "Why Do You Call Me 'Master?'… : Q 6:46, the Inaugural Sermon, and the Demands of Discipleship," *JBL* (2013): 953-969; "'Love Your Enemies': The Adamic Wisdom of Q 6:27-28, 35c-d," *BTB* 43, no. 1 (2013): 29–41.

2. Rudolf Bultmann, *Theology of the New Testament*, trans. Kendrick Grobel (New York: Scribners, 1955), 4; G. R. Beasley-Murray, *Jesus and the Kingdom of God* (Grand Rapids: Eerdmans, 1986); Bruce Chilton, ed., *The Kingdom of God in the Teaching of Jesus* (Philadelphia: Fortress Press, 1984); C. H. Dodd, *The Parables of the Kingdom* (New York: Scribners, 1961); Richard H. Hiers, *The Kingdom of God in the Synoptic Tradition* (Gainesville FL: University of Florida Press, 1970); Klaus Koch, "Offenbaren wird sich das Reich Gottes," *NTS* 25 (1978): 158–65; Helmut Koester, "One Jesus and Four Primitive Gospels," in idem and James M. Robinson, *Trajectories Through Early Christianity* (Philadelphia: Fortress Press, 1971), 158–204; Werner G. Kümmel, *Promise and Fulfillment: The Eschatological Message of Jesus*, trans. Dorothea M. Barton (SBT 23; London: SCM, 1957); George Eldon Ladd, "The Kingdom of God—Reign or Realm?" *JBL* 81 (1962): 230–38; Michael Lattke, "On the Jewish Background of the Synoptic Concept 'The Kingdom of God,'" in Chilton, ed., *The Kingdom of God*, 72–91; Gösta Lündstrom, *The Kingdom of God in the Teaching of Jesus: A History of Interpretation from the Last Decades of the Nineteenth Century to the Present Day*, trans. Joan Bulman (Richmond: John Knox, 1963); Rudolf Otto, *The Kingdom of God and the Son of Man: A Study in the History of Religion* (Grand Rapids: Zondervan, 1938); Norman Perrin, *Jesus and the Language of the Kingdom: Symbol and Metaphor in New Testament Interpretation* (Philadelphia: Fortress Press, 1976); idem, *The Kingdom of God in the Teaching of Jesus* (NTL; London: Westminster, 1963); Rudolf Schnackenburg, *God's Rule and Kingdom*, trans. John Murray (New York: Herder & Herder, 1963); Albert Schweitzer, *The Mystery of the Kingdom of God: The Secret of Jesus' Messiahship and Passion*, trans. Walter Lowrie (1901; repr. New York: Macmillan, 1964); Johannes Weiss, *Jesus' Proclamation of the Kingdom of God*, trans. Richard H. Hiers and David L. Holland (Philadelphia: Fortress Press, 1971).

3. E. P. Sanders, *Jesus and Judaism* (Philadelphia: Fortress Press, 1985), 127.

The idea that God is "king" is widespread in Early Jewish literature, particularly in the Dead Sea Scrolls.[4] New Testament scholars continue to debate whether the kingdom was going to arrive in the future,[5] was already present,[6] or was somehow both.[7] Some passages suggest that Jesus referred to the kingdom as a heavenly realm to be entered at death.[8] Other passages suggest that it will be manifest on earth.[9] Still others refer to it as imminent.[10]

Given the widespread disagreement about the temporal and geographical nature of the kingdom, it is fortunate that we have Q as a control text for evaluating one early stream of kingdom sayings, especially as the kingdom of God is the central theme of Q's ethic, missionary activity, and theology,[11] as well as the focal point and goal of Jesus' disciples' soteriological expectations.[12] The "kingdom" appears twelve times in Q.[13] In ten of the twelve passages, the kingdom is (grammatically) *present*:

4. 1QM 12.7; 6.6; 4Q491 11 ii 17; 4Q252 1 5.3-4; 4Q521; 4Q400 1ii1, 4Q400 1ii3, 4Q401 14i6.

5. Albert Schweitzer, *The Quest of the Historical Jesus: A Critical Study of its Progress from Reimarus to Wrede*, trans. W. Montgomery (London: Adam & Charles Black, 1911).

6. Dodd, *Parables of the Kingdom*, 34–110; T. Francis Glasson, *The Second Advent: The Origin of the New Testament Doctrine* (London: Edgeworth, 1963); John A. T. Robinson, *Jesus and His Coming* (New York: Abingdon, 1958); Ernst Käsemann, *New Testament Questions of Today* (Philadelphia: Fortress Press, 1969), 66–137; G. B. Caird, *Jesus and the Jewish Nation* (Ethel M. Wood Lecture, 9 March 1965; London: Athlone, 1965); idem, *The Language and Imagery of the Bible* (Philadelphia: Westminster, 1980), 243–71; John P. Meier, *A Marginal Jew: Rethinking the Historical Jesus*, Vol. 2: *Mentor, Message and Miracles* (ABRL; New York: Doubleday, 1994), 398–506; N. T. Wright, *Christian Origins and the Question of God*, Vol. 1: *The New Testament and the People of God* (Minneapolis: Fortress Press, 1992), 280–338; idem, *Christian Origins and the Question of God*, Vol. 2: *Jesus and the Victory of God* (Minneapolis: Fortress Press, 1996), 320–68.

7. Kümmel, *Promise and Fulfillment*; Perrin, *The Kingdom of God in the Teaching of Jesus*; idem, *Jesus and the Language of the Kingdom*, 29–34; Ben F. Meyer, "Appointed Deed, Appointed Doer: Jesus and the Scriptures," in *Authenticating the Activities of Jesus*, ed. Bruce Chilton and Craig A. Evans (NTTS 28.2; Leiden: Brill, 1999), 155–76, at 162–63; idem, "Jesus' Scenario of the Future," *DRev* 109 (1991): 1–15.

8. Mark 9:47; 10:17-22; Matt. 7:21.

9. E. P. Sanders, *The Historical Figure of Jesus* (London: Penguin, 1993), 173–78, esp. 174, citing Matt. 6:10; Luke 11:2, 22, 29; Mark 14:25.

10. Mark 1:15; Matt. 10:7; 16:28; Luke 9:27; 10:9; Q 11:2; Q 6:20-23; Q 13:28-29; Matt. 10:23; Mark 9:1; Mark 13:30.

11. John S. Kloppenborg, *The Formation of Q: Trajectories in Ancient Christian Wisdom Collections* (SAC; Philadelphia: Fortress Press, 1987), 241–42; John S. Kloppenborg Verbin, *Excavating Q: The History and Setting of the Sayings Gospel* (Edinburgh: T&T Clark, 2000), 392–94.

12. Q 9:62; 11:2; 12:29-31. Kloppenborg Verbin, *Excavating Q*, 391–92, 394.

13. Q 6:20; Q 7:28; Q 10:5-9; Q 11:2b-4; Q 11:20; Q 11:52; Q 12:31; Q 13:18-19; Q 13:20-21; Q 13:29-28; Q 16:16; Q 17:20-21.

Q 6:20:	the kingdom of God *is* (ἐστὶν) for you
Q 7:28:	the least in the kingdom of God *is* (ἐστιν)
Q 10:9:	the kingdom of God *has* (ἤγγικεν) reached you
Q 11:20:	the kingdom of God *has arrived* (ἔφθασεν)
Q 11:52:	you *shut* (κλείετε) the kingdom of God from people
Q 12:31:	*seek* (ζητεῖτε) his kingdom
Q 13:18–19:	what *is* (ἐστὶν) the kingdom of God like?
Q 13:20–21:	the kingdom of God . . . *is* (ἐστὶν)
Q 16:16:	the kingdom of God *is* violated (βιάζεται)
Q 17:20–21:	the kingdom of God *is* (ἐστιν) within/among you.[14]

The kingdom of God in Q is dawning and present in Jesus' ministry.[15] The "good news" is that the kingdom of God, that is, the *presence of God*, has arrived. The sign of the kingdom's eschatological arrival is God's providential care. According to Q 12:22b, 31, Jesus assures his disciples that God will provide for them:

> Therefore I tell you: Do not be anxious about your life, what you are to eat, nor about your body, with what you are to clothe yourself . . . for all these the nations seek; your Father knows that you need them. But seek (ζητεῖτε) his kingdom and these things will be given to you.

Many scholars affirm Q 12:31 as an authentic saying of Jesus.[16] Nonetheless, the reconstruction of Q 12:22b-31 still requires the identification of Matthean and Lukan redactional traits.[17] Many scholars regard Q 12:25 ("And who of

14. James M. Robinson, "The Study of the Historical Jesus after Nag Hammadi," *Semeia* 44: *The Historical Jesus and the Rejected Gospels* (Atlanta: Scholars Press, 1988), 45–55, notes that the translation of ἐντὸς has often been amended to mean "among you" or "in your midst." Matt. 23:26, uses ἐντὸς to refer to the *inside* (τὸ ἐντὸς) of a cup and dish.

15. The two exceptions are Q 13:29-28 (and many *will* come (ἥξουσιν) [Matt. 8:11-12]) and Q 11:2b-4 (The Lord's Prayer): "may your reign/kingdom (βασιλεία) come."

16. I. Howard Marshall, *The Gospel of Luke: A Commentary on the Greek Text* (NIGTC; Exeter: Paternoster, 1978), 525; Herman Hendrickx, *The Sermon on the Mount: Studies in the Synoptic Gospels* (London: Geoffrey Chapman, 1984), 133; Robert A. Guelich, *The Sermon on the Mount: A Foundation for Understanding* (Waco: Word, 1982), 323, 335; David R. Catchpole, *The Quest for Q* (Edinburgh: T&T Clark, 1993), 39.

17. The reconstruction of Q 12:22b-31 is complicated by the possibility that the *Gospel of Thomas* (*P. Oxy*. 655) contains an earlier reading of this saying. Developing a proposal by Theodore C. Skeat, James M. Robinson and Christoph Heil have argued that Q 12:22b-31 can be traced back to a "pre-Q text" used by Matthew and Luke that closely resembles the reading found in *GThom* 36, as preserved in *P. Oxy.*

you . . . ?") as a "secondary insertion."[18] We can also see Matthew's hand in various places.[19] Matthew adds πρῶτον in order to give priority to the "seeking" of the kingdom.[20] Seeking the kingdom comes first, although Matthew has

655 and Codex Sinaiticus at Matt. 6:28. See T. C. Skeat, "The Lilies of the Field," *ZNW* 37 (1938): 211–14; James M. Robinson, "The Pre-Q Text of the (Ravens and) Lilies: Q 12:22-31 and P. Oxy. 655 (Gos. Thom. 36)," in *Text und Geschichte: Facetten theologischen Arbeitens aus dem Freundes- und Schülerkreis. Dieter Lührmann zum 60. Geburtstag*, ed. Stefan Maser and Egbert Schlarb (MThSt 50; Marburg: N. G. Elwert, 1999), 143–80; idem, "A Written Greek Sayings Cluster Older than Q: A Vestige," *HTR* 92 (1999): 61–77; idem, "Excursus on the Scribal Error in Q 12:27," in *The Critical Edition of Q*, ed. James M. Robinson, Paul Hoffmann, and John S. Kloppenborg (Leuven: Peeters/Minneapolis: Fortress Press, 2000), xcix–ci; James M. Robinson and Christoph Heil, "Zeugnisse eines schriftlichen, griechischen vorkanonischen Textes: Mt 6,18b ℵ, P. Oxy 655 I,1-17 (*EvTh* 36) und Q 12,27," *ZNW* 89 (1998): 30–44; Robinson and Heil, "The Lilies of the Field: Saying 36 of the Gospel of Thomas and Secondary Accretions in Q 12.22b-31," *NTS* 47 (2001): 1–25; Robinson and Heil, "Noch einmal: Der Schreibfehler in Q 12,27," *ZNW* 92 (2001): 113–22. The problem pivots on whether Skeat, Robinson, and Heil's reconstruction of [ο]ὐ ξα[ί]νει ("they do not card") in *P. Oxy*. 655 is to be preferred to [α]ὐξάνει ("they grow").

18. Kloppenborg, *Formation of Q*, 218; Joseph A. Fitzmyer, *The Gospel According to Luke X–XXIV: Introduction, Translation and Notes* (AB 28A; Garden City, NY: Doubleday, 1985), 976; Robert C. Tannehill, *The Sword of his Mouth: Forceful and Imaginative Language in Synoptic Sayings* (SBLSS 1; Philadelphia: Fortress Press, 1975), 60–61; Rudolf Bultmann, *The History of the Synoptic Tradition*, trans. John Marsh (Oxford: Blackwell, 1963), 81; Joachim Jeremias, *The Parables of Jesus* (New York: Scribners, 1963), 71; Hans-Theo Wrege, *Die Überlieferungsgeschichte der Bergpredigt* (Tübingen: Mohr, 1968), 119; Siegfried Schulz, *Q: Spruchquelle der Evangelisten* (Zürich: Theologischer Verlag, 1972), 154; Marshall, *Gospel of Luke*, 527; Ronald A. Piper, *Wisdom in the Q Tradition: The Aphoristic Sayings of Jesus* (SNTSMS 61; Cambridge and New York: Cambridge University Press, 1989), 28–29; W. D. Davies and Dale C. Allison Jr., *A Critical and Exegetical Commentary on the Gospel According to Saint Matthew* (3 vols.; ICC; Edinburgh: T&T Clark, 1988–1997), 1: 651; Paul S. Minear, *Commands of Christ* (Nashville: Abingdon, 1972), 136–37; Dieter Zeller, *Die Weisheitlichen Mahnsprüche bei den Synoptikern* (FB 17; Würzburg: Echter Verlag, 1977), 87; Helmut Merklein, *Die Gottesherrschaft als Handlungsprinzip: Untersuchung zur Ethik Jesu* (Würzburg: Echter Verlag, 1978), 178; Luz, *Matthew 1–7*, 365; Joachim Gnilka, *Das Matthäusevangelium 1. Teil: Kommentar zu Kap. 1,1–13,58* (HThK 1/1; Freiburg: Herder, 1986), 246; Paul Hoffmann, *Tradition und Situation: Studien zur Jesusüberlieferung in der Logienquelle und den synoptischen Evangelien* (NA 28; Münster: Aschendorff 1995), 108. But see Gundry, "Spinning the Lilies," 155–60, esp. 157.

19. Eduard Schweizer, *The Good News According to Matthew* (Atlanta: John Knox, 1975), 164; T. W. Manson, *The Sayings of Jesus*, Vol. 2, *The Mission and Message of Jesus* (New York: E. P. Dutton, 1938), 405; Luz, *Matthew 1–7*, 401; Robert H. Gundry, *Matthew: A Commentary on his Literary and Theological Art* (Grand Rapids: Eerdmans, 1984), 116, 118.

20. Marshall, *The Gospel of Luke*; Gundry, *Matthew*, 118; Georg Strecker, *The Sermon on the Mount: An Exegetical Commentary*, trans. O. C. Dean Jr. (Nashville: Abingdon, 1988), 140; Hendrickx, *Sermon on the Mount*, 146; Davies and Allison, *Matthew*, 1: 651; Catchpole, *Quest for Q*, 37.

softened the blow by allowing for secondary concern over food and clothing despite the fact that "the underlying tradition said precisely the opposite."[21] Seeking (ζητέω) is an active pursuit, a striving after something desired.[22] In sapiential literature seeking for wisdom is a common motif.[23] Yet wisdom is not mentioned in this passage. It is not wisdom that one is to seek, but the kingdom.[24] One is "to give oneself unreservedly to the pursuit of the Kingdom."[25] A number of scholars hold that Q 12:22b-31 is a collection of once-independent sapiential sayings subsequently expanded into its present form.[26] Q 12:31 is sometimes thought to be the "most problematic verse"[27] because it seems to represent an "intrusion" of kingdom-language into an otherwise sapiential collection.[28] Others have argued that Q 12:22b-31 is

21. Catchpole, *Quest for Q*, 37; Göran Agrell, *Work, Toil and Sustenance: An Examination of the View of Work in the New Testament, Taking into Consideration Views found in the Old Testament, Intertestamental, and Early Rabbinic Writings* (Lund: Verbum, 1976), 73; Davies and Allison, *Matthew*, 1: 651; Erich Klostermann, *Matthäusevangelium* (Tübingen: Mohr, 1927), 64; Josef Schmid, *Das Evangelium nach Matthäus: Übersetzt und erklärt* (RNT 1; Regensburg: Pustet, 1956), 143; Jacques Dupont, *Les Béatitudes*, Vol. 3, *Les Évangélistes* (EBib; Paris: Gabalda, 1969–1973), 3: 275–77; Marshall, *Luke*, 530. As "above all else," see Thaddaeus Soiron, *Die Bergpredigt Jesu: Formgeschichtliche, exegetische und theologische Erklärung* (Freiburg: Herder, 1941), 393–94; Harald Riesenfeld, "Vom Schätzesammeln und Sorgen—ein Thema urchristlicher Paränese," in *Neotestamentica et Patristica*, ed. Oscar Cullmann (FSO; Leiden: Brill, 1962), 47–58, at 49; Guelich, *Sermon*, 342.

22. Edward P. Meadors, *Jesus the Messianic Herald of Salvation* (WUNT 2d ser. 72; Tübingen: Mohr Siebeck, 1995), 201–2, citing Heinrich Greeven, "ζητέω," *TDNT* II, 893 n. 5. See 1 Cor. 4:2; Matt. 28:5; John 8:50; Matt. 26:59; Phil. 2:21.

23. Prov. 2:4; 14:6; 15:14; 18:15; Qoh. 7:25; Wis. 6:12; Sir. 4:11-12; 6:27; 51,13.

24. C. F. Evans, *Saint Luke* (London: SCM, 1990), 529; Jürgen Becker, *Jesus of Nazareth*, trans. James E. Crouch (New York: de Gruyter, 1998), 132.

25. Guelich, *Sermon*, 344. Piper, *Wisdom in the Q Tradition*, 31.

26. Bultmann, *History of the Synoptic Tradition*, 88; Zeller, *Die weisheitlichen Mahnsprüche*, 86–87; Kloppenborg, *Formation of Q*, 218; Klostermann, *Matthäusevangelium*, 62; Christopher M. Tuckett, *Q and the History of Early Christianity: Studies on Q* (Peabody, MA: Hendrickson, 1996), 149; Catchpole, *Quest for Q*, 31–35; Hoffmann, *Tradition und Situation*, 62–87, 88–106, 107–34; idem, "Der Q-Text der Sprüche vom Sorgen. Mt 6,25-33 / Lk 12,22-31. Ein Rekonstruktionsversuch," in *Studien zum Matthäusevangelium. Festschrift für Wilhelm Pesch*, ed. Ludger Schenke (Stuttgart: Katholisches Bibelwerk, 1988), 128–55; Robinson, "The Pre-Q Text of the (Ravens and) Lilies," 157; Evans, *Saint Luke*, 535.

27. Kloppenborg, *Formation of Q*, 219.

28. Minear, *Commands of Christ*, 139–40; Zeller, *Die weisheitlichen Mahnsprüche*, 87; Robinson, "The Pre-Q Text," 165; Arland D. Jacobson, *The First Gospel: An Introduction to Q* (Sonoma, CA: Polebridge, 1992), 190; Hoffmann, *Tradition und Situation*, 93, 113.

essentially integral,[29] and that Q 12:31 was the original climax of the collection.[30]

Whether or not Q 12:31 originated as a wisdom statement with an "eschatological background,"[31] with Jesus perhaps making "use of wisdom material,"[32] the reference to the kingdom presupposes "*some kind* of eschatological expectation," even if it may not be "sufficiently intense to overpower the sapiential features of the argument."[33] The kingdom is an eschatological motif.[34] Yet the kingdom is so central to the message of Jesus that it is rather bold to dissociate it from Q 12:22b-31.[35] The ethos of wisdom encouraged in that text is "quite *un*like the wisdom literature's general expectation that human beings will and should work to sustain themselves." The saying is "thoroughly impregnated with a powerful eschatological awareness and expectation."[36] Q 12:22-31 "involves a resounding clash with the wisdom tradition which lavishly praises the worker and severely chides the non-worker." Q "conflicts with the conventional wisdom of a text like Prov. 6:6 with its hard-headed observations about the diligence of the ant."[37] John Kloppenborg designates Q's formative sapiential material as "the radical wisdom of the kingdom of God,"[38] and this is precisely the point: sapiential forms, motifs, and strategies are being deployed to advance an eschatological message. Is Jesus recommending that his disciples not work because the end is coming?[39]

29. Walter Grundmann, *Das Evangelium nach Matthäus* (THKNT 1; Berlin: Evangelische Verlagsanstalt, 1968), 214; Schulz, *Spruchquelle*, 154; Guelich, *Sermon*, 323, 335.

30. Merklein, *Die Gottesherrschaft als Handlungsprinzip*, 177–80; Richard J. Dillon, "Ravens, Lilies, and the Kingdom of God (Matthew 6:25-33/Luke 12:22-31)," *CBQ* 53 (1991): 605–27; esp. 626; Luz, *Matthew 1–7*; Gundry, "Spinning the Lilies," 166.

31. Migaku Sato, "Wisdom Statements in the Sphere of Prophecy," in *The Gospel Behind the Gospels: Current Studies on Q*, ed. Ronald A. Piper (NovTSup 75; Leiden: Brill, 1995), 139–58, at 152.

32. Becker, *Jesus of Nazareth*, 132.

33. Piper, *Wisdom in the Q Tradition*, 33, 31; Kloppenborg, *Formation of Q*, 220; Alan Kirk, *The Composition of the Sayings Source: Genre, Synchrony, and Wisdom Redaction in Q* (NovTSup 91; Leiden: Brill, 1998), 224–26, esp. 226.

34. Marshall, *Gospel of Luke*, 525; Luz, *Matthew 1–7*, 401; Hendrickx, *Sermon on the Mount*, 133.

35. Merklein, *Die Gottesherrschaft*, 177, 180–81; Luz, *Matthew 1–7*, 401–2, 407–8; Gnilka, *Das Mätthausevangelium 1. Teil*, 251; Dillon, "Ravens, Lilies, and the Kingdom of God," 605–27, at 606, 626; Becker, *Jesus of Nazareth*, 131–35.

36. Tuckett, *Q*, 152.

37. David Mealand, "'Paradisial' Elements in the Teaching of Jesus," *Studia Biblica* 2 (1978): 179–84, at 183.

38. Kloppenborg, *Formation of Q*, 242.

Or simply not to *worry* about their needs, because God will supply them?[40] The message seems to be that "'God will provide' without human labor."[41]

The admonition of the collection is clear: trust in God's providence. Yet the introduction of the kingdom at the climax indicates that seeking the kingdom is the critical factor in receiving God's providence. Q 12:31 transforms what *could* be interpreted as a simple sapiential saying into an eschatological imperative. We might even want to question whether the simple assertion of God's providence without qualification, effort, or requirement could be considered traditional wisdom at all. The point here is "devote your life to the Kingdom of God."[42] Q contrasts trust in God with the ways of the "nations," which worry about their needs, and insists that the things we need "come to us as God's gift" when the kingdom is a "constant consideration."[43]

Jesus gives specific *instructions* ("seek") on how to receive God's providence. God loves his sons and daughters and will provide for them, provided that they *seek* to have God "reign" over their lives *and* have total trust that God will do so. The present tense orientation of ζητεῖτε ("seek") indicates that the kingdom is accessible in the present (otherwise we could not seek it). The kingdom is a way of being and can be seen, not as a catastrophic event or as a politico-religious empire, but rather as a symbol-metaphor for God's original intention for human-divine relationship. The kingdom is "something not totally new, but a reinstatement, or a deliverance from the curse which has come over creation."[44] The idea that the kingdom in Q 12:31 can be seen as a "new creation" or "a restoration of creation" is supported by Luke's description of Jesus' kingdom-ministry coinciding with the year of God's grace, the Jubilee,[45] the year in which people need not work but can live on the Lord's blessing. Q 12:22-31 also "shows several structural similarities to Gen. 2–3."[46] In Q "there

39. Catchpole, *Quest for Q*, 34–35; idem, "The Ravens, the Lilies and the Q Hypothesis," *SNTU* A/6-7 (1981–82): 77–87. See also Jeremias, *Parables*, 214–15; M. F. Olsthoorn, *The Jewish Background and the Synoptic Setting of Mt 6,25-33 and Lk 12,22-31* (SBF 10; Jerusalem: Franciscan Printing Press, 1975), 5, 19, 27. See also Julius Schniewind, *Das Evangelium nach Matthäus* (NTD 2; Göttingen: Vandenhoeck & Ruprecht, [1937] 1984).

40. Donald A. Hagner, *Matthew 1–13; 14–28* (2 vols.; WBC 33 A, B; Dallas: Word, 1993), 166–67; Francis Wright Beare, *The Gospel According to Matthew: A Commentary* (Oxford: Blackwell, 1981), 185.

41. C. G. Montefiore, *The Synoptic Gospels, Edited with an Introduction and a Commentary* (2 vols.; London: Macmillan, 1927), 111–12.

42. Schweizer, *The Good News According to Matthew*, 164–66; Leif E. Vaage, *Galilean Upstarts: Jesus' First Followers According to Q* (Valley Forge, PA: Trinity Press International, 1994), 61, 62.

43. John Nolland, *Luke 9:21–18:34* (WBC 35B; Dallas: Word, 1993), 695–96.

44. Agrell, *Work, Toil and Sustenance*, 80–81. *Contra* Becker, *Jesus of Nazareth*, 135.

45. Luke 4:16.

is no compulsion to procure one's own sustenance. The exhortation points in a direction opposite to the curse in Gen 3,17-19,"[47] that humanity will live on what the earth provides with "grief" (λύπη).

God is the one who provides. Disciples are to be "provided for," independently of work, or labor, "as in paradise, according to Gen. 2."[48] Here we have "a connection" between the kingdom and the restoration of Eden.[49] Since "the need to worry about clothing, and the need to work for food *came* after the Fall," Jesus "seems to disregard the emphasis on the fall," and demonstrates "a simple dependence on God characteristic of Paradisial conditions."[50] Jesus' message of God's providence as Father (ἀββά) reverses expectations of worldly wisdom. According to Gen. 3:17-21, God told Adam:

> Cursed is the ground because of you; in toil you shall eat of it all the days of your life; thorns and thistles it shall bring forth for you; and you shall eat the plants of the field. By the sweat of your face you shall eat bread until you return to the ground, for out of it you were taken; you are dust, and to dust you shall return.

Jesus' promise of God's providence in Q 12:22b-31 contradicts the biblical narrative: where Genesis explicitly describes God's displeasure with Adam and his decision that humans will labor for their food, Jesus' message of divine providence reverses the labor, "sweat," and toil, ushering in a new era of human existence, an eschatological reversal of the fallen condition of human life, a new covenant of divine providence.

II: "Why Do You Call Me 'Master?'"

The Inaugural Sermon of Q (6:20-49) is a carefully crafted collection of wisdom instruction.[51] This collection includes Jesus' most characteristic and distinctive ideas on nonviolence, the Golden Rule, unconditional love, compassion, non-

46. Agrell, *Work, Toil, and Sustenance*, 81.

47. Ibid.

48. Ibid., 84.

49. Mealand, "'Paradisial' Elements in the Teaching of Jesus," 179.

50. Ibid., 182.

51. James M. Robinson, "Early Collections of Jesus' Sayings," in *Logia: Les Paroles de Jésus—The Sayings of Jesus*, ed. Joël Delobel (BETL 59; Leuven: Peeters, 1982), 169–75. But see Leif E. Vaage, "Composite Texts and Oral Mythology: The Case of the 'Sermon' in Q (6:20-49)," in *Conflict and Invention: Literary, Rhetorical, and Social Studies on the Sayings Gospel Q*, ed. John S. Kloppenborg (Valley Forge, PA: Trinity Press International, 1995), 75–97.

judgment, and discipleship.[52] There is no great need to analyze each individual saying in detail here. It will suffice to simply draw some conclusions about what the Jesus of Q is intending with this high ethic. Jesus speaks here by his own authority, like a "new Moses,"[53] and "like Moses, rewrites part of the Torah, and experiences a new exodus."[54] There are numerous Mosaic and Deuteronomic allusions in Q.[55] The identification of Jesus as the prophet predicted by Moses is as old as the Gospel of Matthew, and possibly from Q:[56]

> The Lord your God will *raise up* (LXX: ἀναστήσει) for you a prophet (Προφήτην) like me from among your own people. You shall heed such a prophet . . . I will raise up for them a prophet like you from among their own people, and I will put my words in the mouth of the prophet, who will speak to them everything that I command.[57]

In the Temptation narrative Jesus quotes from Deuteronomy three times:

> It is written: "A person is not to live only from bread."[58]
> It is written: "Bow down to the Lord your God, and serve only him."[59]
> It is written: "Do not put to the test the Lord your God."[60]

These allusions present Jesus as a new lawgiver reinterpreting the Torah. This section of Q seems to be a "rewriting" of Leviticus 19.[61] For example, Lev. 19:18 ("love your neighbor") may be echoed in Q 6:27 ("love your enemies"). The

52. Thomas Bergemann, *Q auf dem Prüfstand: Die Zuordnung des Mt/Lk-Stoffes zu Q am Beispiel der Bergpredigt* (FRLANT 158; Göttingen: Vandenhoeck & Ruprecht, 1993).

53. Dale C. Allison Jr., "Q's New Exodus and the Historical Jesus," in *The Sayings Source Q and the Historical Jesus*, ed. Andreas Lindemann (BETL 158; Leuven: Peeters, 2001), 395–428. But see also Howard M. Teeple, *The Mosaic Eschatological Prophet* (JBLMS 10; Philadelphia: Society of Biblical Literature, 1957), 115–21.

54. Allison, "Q's New Exodus and the Historical Jesus," 423.

55. Dennis R. MacDonald, *Two Shipwrecked Gospels: The Logoi of Jesus and Papias's Exposition of Logia about the Lord* (EC 8; Atlanta: Society of Biblical Literature, 2012), 180.

56. Dale C. Allison Jr., *The Intertextual Jesus: Scripture in Q*, (Harrisburg, PA: Trinity Press International, 2000), 72; idem, *The New Moses: A Matthean Typology* (Minneapolis: Fortress Press, 1993).

57. Deut. 18:15-18.

58. Q 4:4/Deut. 8:3.

59. Q 4:8/Deut. 6:13.

60. Q 4:12/Deut. 6:16.

Sermon seems to be an "expansion of or contrast with the holiness code" in terms of mercy, not holiness:[62]

> Be merciful/full of pity, just as God is merciful/full of pity.[63]
> You shall be holy; for I the Lord your God am holy.[64]

Jesus instructs his disciples to be merciful because God is merciful.[65] This instructional theme is elaborated in a variety of distinctive teachings and imperatives:

Q 6:23:	rejoice and be glad (ἀγαλλιᾶσθε).
Q 6:27:	love (ἀγαπᾶτε) your enemies . . .
Q 6:28:	pray (προσεύχεσθε) for those persecuting you
Q 6:29:	offer the other as well . . . the coat as well
Q 6:30:	to the one who asks of you, give (αἰτοῦντί)
Q 6:30:	do not ask back what is yours
Q 6:31:	treat them . . . the way you want people to treat you
Q 6:36:	be full of pity (οἰκτίρμονες)
Q 6:37:	do not pass judgment (κρίνετε)
Q 6:40:	the disciple (μαθητὴς) to be *like* (ὡς) the Teacher.
Q 6:42:	throw the beam out from your own eye
Q 6:46:	do (ποιεῖτε) what I say (λέγω)
Q 6:47:	acting (ποιῶν) on my sayings (λόγους)

The Jesus tradition's numerous proverbs, aphorisms, parables, and beatitudes indicate that a central theme of early Christian discipleship was following the "way" of Jesus.[66] Q is "primarily a call for action, much more than a theological statement."[67] Jesus' high ethical instruction has never been easy to implement, of course, and the medieval Christian solution—to distinguish between "two classes of Christians," those committed to practice and the "mass

61. Allison, "Q's New Exodus and the Historical Jesus," 411; Catchpole, *The Quest for Q*, 101–34; Christopher M. Tuckett, "Scripture in Q," in *The Scriptures in the Gospels*, ed. idem (BETL 131; Leuven: Peeters, 1997), 3–26, at 25; idem, *Q*, 431–34.

62. Allison, "Q's New Exodus and the Historical Jesus," 413.

63. Q 6:36.

64. Lev. 19:1-2.

65. Allison, *Jesus Tradition in Q*, 67–95; idem, "Q's New Exodus and the Historical Jesus," 424.

66. Adolf Jülicher, *Die Gleichnisreden Jesu* (2 vols.; Freiburg: Mohr, 1886).

67. Robinson, *The Sayings Gospel Q*, 187.

of lay Christians"—is "not the original intention of Q, which seems to be oriented almost exclusively to the more rigorous alternative."

Jesus' ideals have been ignored and dismissed as impractical and unrealistic, but these ideals have also been "revived and actualized" again and again in Christendom through martyrdom, asceticism, monasticism, the Franciscans, Tolstoy's pacifism, Gandhi's activism, Martin Luther King Jr.'s nonviolent resistance, and liberation theology.[68] The real challenge to Christianity today, therefore, is "to catch sight of Jesus' ideal and to implement it effectively in our world . . . What is needed is a hermeneutic of practice."[69] This call to *action* is clearly expressed in Q 6:46, where Jesus asks his followers: "Why do you call me 'Master, Master,' but do not *do* what I *say*?" (τί . . . με καλεῖτε κύριε κύριε, καὶ οὐ ποιεῖτε ἅ λέγω;).[70] Q 6:46 serves as the framing conclusion to the Inaugural Sermon, admonishing those who simply pay lip-service to "following Jesus."[71] It is not calling Jesus "Lord" that counts, but "*doing* what he *says*."[72] Accordingly, Q 6:46 is "The hardest saying of Jesus,"[73] Its use of κύριος signifies Jesus' role as "Teacher," as in Q 6:40.[74] Q 6:46 frames the Sermon as an eschatological warning about the consequences of *not* following Jesus' teaching.[75] Jesus suggests that those who fail to practice his teachings (but only call him "Lord, Lord") will not be secure in the future, when the rain pours

68. Robinson, "The Jesus of the Sayings Gospel Q," ed. Jon Ma. Asgeirsson (OPIAC 28; Claremont: Institute for Antiquity and Christianity, 1993), repr. in *Sayings Gospel Q*, 375–88; idem, "Jesus' Theology in the Sayings Gospel Q," 689–709 at 709; also in *Early Christian Voices: In Texts, Traditions, and Symbols*, ed. David H. Warren, Ann Graham Brock, and David W. Pao (Boston: Brill, 2003), 25–43.

69. Robinson, "Jesus of the Sayings Gospel Q," 387–88.

70. The word κύριος is used for Jesus three times in Q (Q 6:46; Q 7:6; Q 9:59). The term is used for God six times (Q 4:8; Q 4:12; Q 10:2; Q 10:21; Q 13:35; Q 16:13), and in parables (with probable reference to God) ten times (Q 12:42, 43, 45, 46; Q 13:25; Q 14:21; Q 19:15, 16, 18, 20). For Luke's version as "more original" see Tuckett, Q, 214–15; Heinz Schürmann, *Das Lukasevangelium* (Freiburg: Herder, 1969), 1: 361; Georg Strecker, *Der Weg der Gerechtigkeit* (FRLANT 82; Göttingen: Vandenhoeck & Ruprecht, 1962), 160; Schulz, *Q*, 428; Guelich, *Sermon on the Mount*, 398; Catchpole, *Quest for Q*, 97; Fleddermann, Q, 306.

71. Kloppenborg, *Formation of Q*, 188: "Q 6:46, 47-48 provides a good example of the warnings which typically conclude these instructions."

72. Robinson, "The Sayings of Jesus in Q," in *Sayings Gospel Q*, 177–92, at 187–89.

73. Robinson, "Theological Autobiography," in *Sayings Gospel Q*, 3–34, at 33–34.

74. James M. Robinson, "The Q Trajectory: Between John and Matthew via Jesus," in *Sayings Gospel Q*, 285–308, at 301; Kloppenborg, *Formation of Q*, 117. But see Fleddermann, Q, 133; Marco Frenschkowski, "Welche biographischen Kenntnisse von Jesus setzt die Logienquelle voraus?: Beobachtungen zur Gattung von Q im Kontext antiker Spruchsammlungen," in *From Quest to Q: Festschrift James M. Robinson*, ed. Jon Ma. Asgeirsson, Kristin de Troyer, and M. W. Meyer (BETL 146; Leuven: Peeters, 2000), 3–42, at 23–24.

down and the "flash floods" come.[76] There are eschatological consequences for not following Jesus' teachings. On the other hand, the saying may have originated as an isolated logion. Bultmann held that the saying derived from Jesus and contains no explicit references to any coming judgment.[77]

The saying is form-critically independent, aphoristic, and not necessarily eschatological, although it is certainly set in an eschatological context. Q 6:46 plays a double function, criticizing those who do not do what Jesus says as well as issuing a warning for such behavior. Hans Dieter Betz suggested that Matthew's version of the saying (Matt. 7:21-23) may be "a direct challenge to Pauline Christianity," a polemic "aimed at those Christian prophets who do not do the works of the law."[78] Q 6:46-47 uses the metaphor of bedrock (πέτραν) to describe the one who faithfully follows Jesus' teachings. Is this an allusion to "Peter and his church" from Matt. 16:18?—"You are Peter (Πέτρος), and on this rock (πέτρᾳ) I will build my church." [79] The Jesus of Q seems to be saying that it is upon *this* "rock," that is, his *teachings*, that a truly solid "house" is built: a person who acts on his sayings is like one who builds a "house" (οἰκίαν) on bedrock (Q 6:48). Is οἰκίαν a covert allusion to the Temple in Jerusalem, the "forsaken house" (οἶκος) of Q 13:34-35? Do Jesus' disciples constitute an alternative Temple?[80] We do not know the original oral or literary context of

75. Tuckett, Q, 71; Dieter Lührmann, *Die Redaktion der Logienquelle* (WMANT 33; Neukirchen-Vluyn: Neukirchener Verlag, 1969), 56.

76. Ibid., 246.

77. Bultmann, *History of the Synoptic Tradition*, 122–23, 135, 163. Hans Dieter Betz, *Essays on the Sermon on the Mount*, trans. Laurence Welborn (Philadelphia: Fortress Press, 1985), 132–33.

78. Betz, *Essays on the Sermon on the Mount*, 20.

79. Ibid., 20–21.

80. Kyu Sam Han, *Jerusalem and the Early Jesus Movement: The Q Community's Attitude Toward the Temple* (JSNTSup 207; Sheffield: Sheffield Academic Press, 2002), sees Q as representative of a "lost allegiance" to the Jerusalem Temple. Robert L. Webb, "Jesus' Baptism by John: Its Historicity and Significance," in *Key Events in the Life of the Historical Jesus: A Collaborative Exploration of Context and Coherence*, ed. Darrell L. Bock and Robert L. Webb (Tübingen: Mohr Siebeck, 2010), 95–150, at 114; Leonhard Goppelt, *Theology of the New Testament*, trans. John E. Alsup (2 vols.; Grand Rapids: Eerdmans, 1981–82), 1: 36; Jürgen Becker, *Johannes der Täufer und Jesus von Nazareth* (BibS[N] 63; Neukirchen-Vluyn: Neukirchener Verlag, 1972), 38–40; Nicholas Perrin, *Jesus the Temple* (Grand Rapids: Baker Academic, 2010), 179; Richard Bauckham, "For What Offence Was James Put to Death?" in *James the Just and Christian Origins*, ed. Bruce D. Chilton and Craig A. Evans (NovTSup 98; Leiden: Brill, 1999), 199–232, at 207; Geza Vermes, *The Dead Sea Scrolls: Qumran in Perspective* (Philadelphia: Fortress Press, 1977), 218; Bertil E. Gärtner, *The Temple and the Community in Qumran and the New Testament: A Comparative Study in the Temple Symbolism of the Qumran Texts and the New Testament* (SNTSMS 1; Cambridge: Cambridge University Press, 1965); Alan R. Kerr, *The Temple of Jesus' Body: The Temple Theme in the Gospel of John* (JSNTSup 220; London: Sheffield, 2002).

Q 6:46.[81] The framer(s) of Q use it in an eschatological-warning context, but it may once have existed as an independent saying related to the Teacher-disciple relationship with Jesus.

Q 6:46 illustrates how a relatively simple aphoristic saying can cut both ways, being sapiential in form but eschatological in context, and possibly in content, thereby precluding any facile assumptions about its origin as an admonition for not following Jesus' wisdom teachings, missionary instructions, or eschatological warnings. We may even go one step further by considering the rhetorical effect of Q 6:46. The Jesus of Q asks his so-called disciples why they are not following his teachings. In the larger context of the Sermon and Q 6:47–49 he is also warning them of the consequences. But while Q 6:46 may not require an eschatological reading, its setting and context in Q do.

The larger question, again, is what *kind* of eschatology is present here and how does it relate to the sapiential form of this particular Q saying within the Sermon? There seem to be several possible readings. The first is that Jesus, as Teacher, is simply rebuking his wayward or half-hearted students for not putting his teachings into practice. In itself this would certainly justify placing the saying within the instructional genre, but that only begs the question: *what* are Jesus' teachings? Are they simply worldly instruction? This hardly seems likely. The motifs of eschatological reversal, kingdom language, and God's providential care in Q suggest far more than mere worldly wisdom; they imply a *transformation* of worldly norms. So even the wisdom forms of the Sermon are arguably eschatological in content. The second possibility is that Jesus is warning his disciples that they will not "enter the kingdom of heaven" unless they do the "will of My Father in heaven."[82] Matthew's redactional signature is apparent here, yet he also seems to be developing further the implied consequences of Q 6:46's placement at the end of the Sermon. Here the threat of eschatological *punishment* is foregrounded, and it is displaced to heaven (or hell), where rewards will be received.

A third possibility is that the Jesus of Q 6:46 is being cast in the role of Teacher of an extraordinary wisdom that can be identified as eschatological in content, with its focus being not only the transformation of the disciple to become "like" the Teacher, but extending to a movement of social renewal.[83]

81. Kloppenborg, *Formation of Q*, 185.

82. Matt. 7:21-23.

83. See especially Richard A. Horsley, "Questions About Redactional Strata and the Social Relations Reflected in Q," in *Society of Biblical Literature 1989 Seminar Papers*, ed. David J. Lull (Atlanta: Scholars Press, 1989), 175–209; idem, "Wisdom Justified," in idem, *Jesus and the Spiral of Violence: Popular Jewish Resistance in Roman Palestine* (San Francisco: Harper and Row, 1987); *Oral Performance, Popular Tradition,*

This third possibility has the merit of bracketing the Matthean and Deuteronomistic judgment redaction that used the saying as an eschatological *threat* while balancing its sapiential and eschatological registers both within its Q context and within the early Jesus movement. The Jesus of Q 6:46 commands assent to and the practice of the ethical ideals of the Inaugural Sermon, ideals that facilitate the transformation of the disciple into a "son of the Father."

III: "Love Your Enemies"

The most distinctive element in the Q Sermon is Jesus' command to "love your enemies."[84] Q 6:27 meets multiple criteria for authenticity: multiple attestation, embarrassment, dissimilarity, coherence, and distinctiveness.[85] It is unlikely "that the early church should invent the saying and thus impose upon themselves such a troublesome requirement."[86] The saying was probably used for "hortatory" purposes,[87] that is, to provide ethical instructions as "eine urchristliche Didache."[88] Yet Q 6:27 also challenges a tradition of stereotyping "others" as "enemies":

> Love your enemies and pray for those persecuting you so that you may become sons of your Father, for he raises his sun on bad and good and rains on the just and unjust.[89]

and Hidden Transcript in Q, ed. Richard A. Horsley (Atlanta: Society of Biblical Literature, 2006); Richard A. Horsley with Jonathan A. Draper, *Whoever Hears You Hears Me: Prophets, Performance, and Tradition in Q* (Harrisburg, PA: Trinity Press International, 1999).

84. R. Conrad Douglas, "'Love Your Enemies': Rhetoric, Tradents, and Ethos," in *Conflict and Invention: Literary, Rhetorical, and Social Studies on the Sayings Gospel Q*, ed. John S. Kloppenborg (Valley Forge, PA: Trinity Press International 1995), 116–31; Ronald A. Piper, "The Language of Violence and the Aphoristic Sayings in Q," in *Conflict and Invention*, 53–72; Paul Hoffmann, "Tradition und Situation: Zur 'Verbindlichkeit' des Gebots der Feindesliebe in der synoptischen Überlieferung und in der gegenwärtigen Friedensdiskussion," in *Ethik im Neuen Testament*, ed. Karl Kertelge (QD 102; Freiburg: Herder, 1984), 50–118, at 61.

85. See also 1 Thess. 5:15; Rom. 12:17; 1 Pet. 3:9.

86. John Piper, *"Love Your Enemies": Jesus' Love Command in the Synoptic Gospels and in the Early Paraenesis: A History of the Tradition and Interpretation of Its Uses* (SNTSMS 38; Cambridge: Cambridge University Press, 1979), 56.

87. Martin Dibelius, *From Tradition to Gospel* (New York: Scribners, 1935), 246.

88. Joachim Jeremias, *Die Bergpredigt* (Stuttgart: Calwer, 1970), 21.

89. Q 6:27. Piper, *"Love Your Enemies"*; William Klassen, "'Love Your Enemies": Some Reflections on the Current Status of Research,' in *The Love of Enemy and Nonretaliation*, ed. Willard M. Swartley (Louisville: Westminster John Knox, 1992) 1–31; idem, "Love Your Enemy: A Study of New Testament

Jesus' call to love enemies undercuts a tradition that had, for centuries, stereotyped other "nations" as enemies.[90] Q's imperative to "love enemies" is a Jewish admonition directed toward Israel ("Gentiles" are "outsiders"), and based on God's love and concern for all. Gentiles may be different, but they are no longer to be *treated* as "enemies."[91] In the Hebrew Bible the enemies of Israel are often regarded as the "enemies" of the God of Israel. God promised Abram that his descendants would possess their enemies' cities.[92] Passover commemorates the defeat of Israel's enemies. Moses defeats the Amalekites and God promises to oppose them forever.[93] Moses kills the Amorites,[94] defeats the Midianites, and slays all the males, taking the women and children captive.[95] God kills the men,

Teaching on Coping with an Enemy," *MQR* 37 (1963): 147–71; idem, "Coals of Fire: Sign of Repentance or Revenge?" *NTS* 9 (1963): 337–50; idem, *Love of Enemies: The Way to Peace* (Philadelphia: Fortress Press, 1984); Douglas, "'Love Your Enemies'"; Piper, "The Language of Violence." On its authenticity see Jürgen Becker, "Feindesliebe-Nächstenliebe-Bruderliebe: Exegetische Beobachtungen als Anfrage an ein ethisches Problemfeld," *ZEE* 25 (1981): 5–18; Heinz-Wolfgang Kuhn, "Das Liebesgebot Jesus als Tora und als Evangelium: Zur Feindesliebe und zur christlichen und jüdischen Auslegung der Bergpredigt," in *Vom Urchristentum zu Jesus. Festschrift Joachim Gnilka*, ed. Hubert Frankemölle and Karl Kertelge (Freiburg: Herder, 1989), 194–230; Simon Legasse, *'Et qui est mon prochain?' Etude sur l'objet de l'agapè dans le Nouveau Testament* (LD 136; Paris: Cerf, 1989); Otto J. F. Seitz, "Love Your Enemies: The Historical Setting of Matthew V. 43f.; Luke VI.27f.," *NTS* 16 (1970): 39–54; W. C. van Unnik, "Die Motivierung der Feindesliebe in Lukas 6:32-35," *NovT* 8 (1966): 284–300; Dieter Lührmann, "Liebet eure Feinde (Lk 6,27-36/Mt 5,39-48)," *ZTK* 69 (1972): 412–38. On its meaning in early Christianity see Ferdinand Kattenbusch, "Über die Feindesliebe im Sinne des Christentums," *TSK* 89 (1916): 1–70. On its political context see Hoffmann, *Studien zur Theologie der Logienquelle*; idem, "Tradition und Situation," 61. For older bibliography see C. H. Dodd, "The Theology of Christian Pacifism," in *The Bases of Christian Pacifism*, ed. Charles E. Raven (London: Council of Christian Pacifist Groups, 1938), 5–15; Michael Waldmann, *Die Feindesliebe in der antiken Welt und im Christentum* (Vienna: Mayer, 1902); Stephan Randlinger, *Die Feindesliebe nach dem natürlichen und positiven Sittengesetz: Eine historisch-ethische Studie* (Paderborn: Schöningh, 1906); Eugen Bach, *Die Feindesliebe nach dem natürlichen Sittengesetz: Eine historisch-ethische Untersuchung* (Kempten: Kösel, 1914).

90. Jacob Neusner, *A Rabbi Talks with Jesus: An Intermillennial Interfaith Exchange* (New York: Doubleday, 1993), 27–28.

91. See also Lev. 19:34, on the "alien" to be loved "as yourself." For Jewish universalism see also Gen. 1:27; 5:1-2; 9:6, for humanity's creation "in the image of God." For the Noachide laws see *t. Avodah Zara* 8.4; *b. Sanh.* 56a; Acts 15:29; Josephus, *Contr. Ap.* 2.15.

92. Gen. 15:17-21; 22:17.

93. Exod. 17:10-13, 14-17.

94. Num. 21:34-35.

95. Num. 31:1-54.

women, and children of Heshbon,[96] destroys the followers of Baalpeor,[97] and promises to fight for Israel if it obeys the covenant.[98]

The Mosaic law contains a complex and problematic legislation of violence.[99] Israel is commanded to "utterly destroy" all those in the land of Canaan.[100] Israel is to pick up the sword and "wipe out their names from under heaven . . . destroy them."[101] The people of Israel are not to "leave alive anything that breathes."[102] They are to drive out the Hittites, Ammonites, Canaanites, and Jebusites from the land.[103] Israel is to be the "sword of the Lord."[104] Salvation is often associated with the defeat of enemies.[105] God instructs Israel to "pursue your enemies, and they will fall by the sword before you."[106]

In the books of the Prophets, Israel's enemies are often characterized as appointed by God in the judgment of Israel, indicating that the authors of these books were capable of creatively adapting the changing fortunes of Israel into new theological narratives that both absolved God for Israel's military defeats and provided hope that God had a master plan that incorporated Israel's suffering as the Lord's "Servant": Israel's "enemies" were sometimes God's instruments. Cyrus the Great was heralded as the Lord's "messiah/anointed,"[107] not because he came from the line of David but because God "appointed" him to liberate the people of Israel. As James Sanders notes, "The disaster of the Assyrian and Babylonian destruction of Israel and Judah had had to be faced,

96. Deut. 2:33–36.

97. Deut. 4:3.

98. Exod 23:22–30.

99. Lev. 20:9, 10, 13, 27; 24:16, 17; 26:14–38; Num. 6:15; 13:12–16; 18:20; 19:18–19; 21:18–21. See also Ra'anan Boustan, *Violence, Scripture, and Textual Practice in Early Judaism and Christianity* (Leiden: Brill, 2010); Eric Seibert, *Disturbing Divine Behavior: Troubling Old Testament Images of God* (Minneapolis: Fortress Press, 2009); Richard Dawkins, *The God Delusion* (New York: Bantam, 1999), 71; Jack Nelson-Pallmeyer, *Jesus Against Christianity: Reclaiming the Missing Jesus* (Harrisburg, PA: Trinity Press International, 2001); David Penchansky, *What Rough Beast? Images of God in the Hebrew Bible* (Louisville: Westminster John Knox, 1999), 82–86; Regina M. Schwartz, *The Curse of Cain: The Violent Legacy of Monotheism* (Chicago: University of Chicago Press, 1997); Phyllis Trible, *Texts of Terror: Literary-Feminist Readings of Biblical Narratives* (Philadelphia: Fortress Press, 1984); Walter Wink, *The Powers That Be: Theology for a New Millennium* (New York: Doubleday, 1998), 84.

100. Deut. 7:1–2; Num. 33:50–56.

101. Deut. 7:17–26.

102. Deut. 20:16.

103. Exod. 3:8, 17; 13:5; 23:23; 33:2; 34:11; Deut. 20:17; Josh. 9:1; 12:8; Judg. 3:5.

104. Lev. 18:24.

105. Exod. 14:30; 15:1–3a, 4a; Ps. 18:45–48a; Isa. 25:9–10.

106. Lev. 26:7–8.

107. Isa. 45:1.

and the Torah and Prophets explained it as God's judgment . . . They also made it clear, however, that the judgment was not only punitive but constructive," that a righteous "remnant" would emerge from this disaster,[108] that suffering would lead to hope.[109] The "prophetic corpus was essentially an argument affirming the uses of adversity" by God.

This brief review of Israel's attitude toward "enemies" is not intended to discount passages that encourage service to enemies or love of one's neighbor,[110] even if the Mosaic commandment to love one's neighbor refers only to fellow Israelites. There are also biblical passages that proscribe hatred and vengeance.[111] Some Jewish sources describe God as "merciful and gracious, slow to anger, and abounding in steadfast love,"[112] a God who is "good to all, and his compassion is over all that he has made," for he loves "all that exists,"[113] a God who does not take "any pleasure in the death of the wicked."[114] Such texts illustrate internal tensions within the biblical tradition and show that some Jews (and Christians) in antiquity were "distressed" by biblical tales of (prophetic) violence.[115] So why did Israel's enemies need to be so brutally and thoroughly wiped out in the exodus narrative? Were they enemies simply because they "occupied" *their* land? Exegetes have suggested that perhaps Israel's traditional enemies were exceptionally wicked and deserving of divine punishment,[116] that the Lord was exceedingly patient and forbearing with their wickedness, that the biblical tradition belongs to another age in which the annihilation of one's enemies was the norm, and/or that the nature of God was "progressively revealed" down through the centuries, culminating in Jesus. As we have seen, these explanations have all been used as viable ways of absolving God from any wrongdoing in his endorsement of acts of violence.

While peace is clearly envisioned as a divine ideal in Early Judaism—the prophets Isaiah and Micah refer to a day when the nations will beat their swords into plowshares and not lift up the sword against other nations or study

108. Jeremiah 34; Ezekiel 36.

109. Hos. 2:14. James A. Sanders, "The Book of Job and the Origins of Judaism," *BTB* 38, no. 2 (2009): 60–70, at 62–63.

110. Exod. 23:4-5; Lev. 19:18. For comparable rabbinic analogies to the Sermon on the Mount see Gerhard Kittel, "Die Bergpredigt und die Ethik des Judentums," *ZSTh* 2 (1924): 555–94.

111. Lev. 19:17-18; Prov. 20:22; 24:17, 29; 25:21-22; Jonah 4:2.

112. Exod. 34:6; Dale C. Allison Jr., "Rejecting Violent Judgment: Luke 9:52-56 and Its Relatives," *JBL* 121 (2002): 459–78, at 470–71.

113. Ps. 145:8-9; Wis. 11:22–12:2.

114. Ezek. 18:23.

115. Allison, "Rejecting Violent Judgment," 478.

116. Deut. 18:12.

war any more—much of the biblical tradition is marked by violence, conflict, and warfare.[117] The Torah "sanctions warfare."[118] The Torah expects Israel to "struggle for God's purpose." It is a "religious duty to resist evil, to struggle for good, to love God, and to fight against those who make themselves into enemies of God. The Torah knows nothing of not resisting evil." Loving enemies is virtually unknown in Early Judaism.[119] There are striking examples of first-century Jewish Palestinian nonviolent resistance to systemic violence,[120] but these, again, did not encourage *loving* one's enemies.[121]

Jesus' imperative to love enemies is based on God's universal love for all. The Sermon itself is an extended exhortation to love, compassion, and nonviolence, its core being "the love command . . . expanded and elaborated in various ways."[122] In Q 6:27, Jesus commands his followers to "love (ἀγαπᾶτε)" their enemies and "pray" (προσεύχεσθε) for those persecuting them. They are to give to all who ask; to treat others the way they want to be treated; to be full of compassion. Some scholars have looked to the social location of Matthew to help elucidate the social setting of this saying. After all, Matthew's Jesus claims to be correcting an older law by antithesis:

> You have heard that it was said, "You shall love your neighbor and hate your enemy," and/but I say to you, love your enemies.[123]

117. Isa. 2:4; Mic. 4:3.

118. Neusner, *A Rabbi Talks with Jesus*, 27–28.

119. Joseph Klausner, *Jesus of Nazareth: His Life, Times, and Teaching*, trans. Herbert Danby (New York: Macmillan, 1925), 392–93, 397. On the dissimilarity of Jesus' command to "love your enemies" from both Judaism and early Christianity, see Tom Holmén, "Hermeneutics of Dissimilarity in the Early Judaism-Jesus-Early Christianity Continuum," in *Jesus in Continuum*, ed. Tom Holmén (WUNT 289; Tübingen: Mohr Siebeck, 2012), 3-42, here 23-27.

120. Josephus, *War* 2.174; 2.197.

121. The Torah calls for kindness and help to the enemy in need (Exod. 23:4-5; Deut. 22:1-4). On the other hand, see Marius Reiser, "Love of Enemies in the Context of Antiquity," *NTS* 47 (2001): 411–27, for the position that Jesus was the first to introduce the idea of love of enemies. See also Gordon Zerbe, *Non-retaliation in early Jewish and New Testament Texts: Ethical Themes in Social Context* (JSPSup 13; Sheffield: JSOT, 1993), 171–72; Luise Schottroff, "Give to Caesar What Belongs to Caesar and to God What Belongs to God: A Theological Response of the Early Christian Church to Its Social and Political Environment," in *The Love of Enemy and Nonretaliation in the New Testament*, ed. Willard Swartley (Louisville: Westminster John Knox, 1992), 223–57, at 232.

122. Kloppenborg, *Formation of Q*, 177.

123. Matt 5:43-44.

The Torah, again, does not advocate *hatred* of enemies.[124] Since the discovery of the Dead Sea Scrolls some scholars have sought to locate the origins of Matthew's antithesis in Qumranic hatred of the "Sons of Darkness."[125] This may be "too daring" and speculative an assumption.[126] The Qumran community is often described in the secondary literature as hateful and misanthropic,[127] but this portrayal requires significant qualifications. Qumran hatred was not a personal or social hatred to be acted out in public, but a rejection of evil in the world.[128] The members were to conceal their opposition to the wicked while accepting their temporary domination through nonviolent resistance.[129] The external "enemies" of the community "are not to be repaid with evil but on the contrary with good."[130] Furthermore, "there was to be no private hatred or revenge . . . enemies were to be repaid with good. Sin was to be hated."[131] The author of 1QS promises that he "will not return evil to anybody, with good will I pursue man."[132]

If it is difficult to find any evidence of indiscriminate hatred of enemies in the Qumran library, it is far more difficult to find it in Josephus, Philo, and Pliny's accounts of the Essenes, for they all claim that the Essenes were characterized by their extraordinary love for others. Josephus tells us that the Essenes were "upright managers of anger and peacemakers" and swore to "keep faith with all men, especially with the powers that be, since no ruler attains his office save by the will of God."[133] Magen Broshi has even suggested that this "Essene teaching of love" influenced Jesus.[134]

124. Although see Ps. 139:19-22.

125. Kurt Schubert, "The Sermon on the Mount and the Qumran Texts," in *The Scrolls and the New Testament*, ed. Krister Stendahl (New York: Harper, 1957), 118–28, 270–73, at 120; Morton Smith, "Mt. 5:43: 'Hate Thine Enemy,'" *HTR* 45 (1952): 71–73; Yigael Yadin, *The Temple Scroll: The Hidden Law of the Dead Sea Sect* (New York: Random House, 1985), 241–42; Hans Bietenhard, "Die Handschriftenfunde vom Toten Meer, (Óirbet Qumran) und die Essener-Frage. Die Funde in der Wüste Juda (Eine Orientierung)," in *ANRW* II 10.1, ed. Hildegard Temporini and Wolfgang Haase (Berlin: de Gruyter, 1982), 704–78, at 753–54.

126. William H. Brownlee, "Jesus and Qumran," in *Jesus and the Historian. Festschrift E. C. Colwell*, ed. F. Thomas Trotter (Philadelphia: Westminster, 1968), 52–81, at 73.

127. Christopher Rowland, *Christian Origins: From Messianic Movement to Christian Religion* (Minneapolis: Augsburg, 1985), 73.

128. 1QS 9.

129. Edmund F. Sutcliffe, "Hatred at Qumran," *RevQ* 7 (1960): 345–56.

130. Ibid., 355.

131. Ibid., 352.

132. 1QS 10.18.

133. Josephus, *War* 2.135; 2.140.

Wherever Jesus derived this distinctive teaching from, Q 6:27-36 clearly commands love of enemies and requires mercy because *God* is loving and merciful.[135] The historical Jesus directly challenges the Jewish biblical tradition of war and violence. Q 6:27-35 introduces a vision of God as loving toward all, undermining traditions in which God is violent and vengeful toward his chosen "enemies."

Jesus' command to love enemies requires a fundamental reevaluation of the Jewish messianic traditions attributed to Jesus. If Early Jewish eschatology envisions a time when "there are no more sinners, and the enemies of Israel have been rooted out or conquered, with the result that the conditions of Paradise are reestablished,"[136] then Jesus' command to love enemies was surely an innovative method for eliminating them and restoring the "paradisial" conditions of universal brotherhood. Similarly, Jesus' inclusive response to "sinners" is also a sign of eschatological fulfillment, not wayward morality. Jesus' enigmatic mission, symbolic gestures, and allusive sayings represent the realization of what Isaiah envisioned as a "new heaven" and a "new earth," the "new creation" being not the end result of a cataclysmic destruction but the invisible renewal of the original divine will and intention for creation.[137]

IV: Sons Of The Father

The Jesus of Q teaches his disciples the way that leads to becoming "sons" of the Father.[138] The Inaugural Sermon sets out a path, a way of transformation that has as its goal to "*become like*" (γένηται ὡς) the Teacher, a son of the Father (Q 6:35c-d).[139] The hermeneutic here is *sonship*. Loving one's enemies is a mark of discipleship and sonship. This is made explicit in Q 6:27, 35c-d, since Q 6:27 is linked to Q 6:35c-d: "*so that* (ὅπως) you may *become* (γένησθε) sons (υἱοὶ) of your Father." Sonship is also a prominent feature in the *Gospel of Thomas*:

134. Magen Broshi, "Hatred: An Essene Religious Principle and its Christian Consequences," in *Bread, Wine, Walls and Scrolls* (JSP Sup 36; Sheffield: Sheffield Academic Press, 2001), 274–83.

135. Dale C. Allison Jr., *The Jesus Tradition in Q* (Valley Forge, PA: Trinity Press International, 1997), 67–95; idem, "Q's New Exodus and the Historical Jesus," 424.

136. Marius Reiser, *Jesus and Judgment: The Eschatological Proclamation in its Jewish Context*, trans. Linda M. Maloney (Minneapolis: Fortress Press, 1997), 152.

137. For the motif of the new creation see *1 En.* 45.4-5; 91.16; *Jub.* 1.29; 4.26; 1QS 4.25; 11QT 29.9; *4 Ezra* 7.25; 2 Pet. 3:13; Rev. 2:1, 5; *Mek. Y.* on Exod 16:25; *b. Sanh.* 92b, 97b.

138. Q 6:35c-d.

139. Piper, *"Love Your Enemies,"* 76.

> "[sons] of the [living] Father ([υἱοί] ἐστε τοῦ πατρὸς τοῦ [ζῶντος]).[140]
> "*sons* of the living Father."
> "you will *become sons* of Man/Humanity."[141]

Jesus is the one "prophets and kings" have longed to see:[142]

> Everything has been entrusted to me by my Father; and no one *knows* (γινώσκει) *the* Son (τὸν υἱὸν) except the Father, nor the Father except *the* Son, and to whomever *the* Son chooses to *reveal* (ἀποκαλύψαι) him.[143]

Q clearly emphasizes its Son of God Christology. The baptismal account in Q 3:22 explicitly identifies Jesus as "Son." The Temptation narrative explicitly identifies Jesus as "the Son of God." Q 4:3 and 4:9 affirm Jesus as the obedient "Son of God" who defies Satan through his obedience to the will and word of God.[144] Jesus' victory over temptation shows that he is "the embodiment of true Israel," the true Son of God.[145] Jesus defeats the devil, reversing the fallen state of humanity described in Genesis. The temptation or "testing" is a

140. *P. Oxy*. 654.

141. L. 106.

142. Q 10:23b-24.

143. Q 10:22. Marinus de Jonge, *Jesus the Servant Messiah* (New Haven: Yale University Press, 1991), 74–75.

144. Craig A. Evans, "Jesus and the Spirit: On the Origin and Ministry of the Second Son of God," in idem and James A. Sanders, *Luke and Scripture: The Function of Sacred Tradition in Luke-Acts* (Minneapolis: Fortress Press, 1993), 26–45, esp. 36–45. In Luke, Jesus' genealogy ends with "son of Adam, son of God" (Luke 3:38), which is immediately followed by the temptation narrative in which Satan calls Jesus "Son of God." William Manson, *The Gospel of Luke* (MNTC; London: Hodder & Stoughton, 1930), 35. Adolf Schlatter, *Das Evangelium des Lukas* (2d ed.; Stuttgart: Calwer, 1960), 218–19, suggested that Luke had in mind an Adam/Jesus typology. Similarly, Joachim Jeremias, "Adam," *TDNT* 1 (1964): 141–43, proposed that the Gospel of Mark's temptation narrative also reflects an Adam typology. More recently the question of an Adam/Jesus typology in Luke has been reopened by Jerome Neyrey, *The Passion according to Luke: A Redaction Study of Luke's Soteriology* (New York: Paulist Press, 1985), 165–84. Neyrey argues that Luke's Adam-typology is found in the genealogy, in the temptation, in the garden, and on the cross: Luke's genealogy links the baptism ("my beloved Son") with the temptation ("Son of God"). For Neyrey the three temptations in the Lukan account mirror Satan's temptations to Adam: the temptation to eat (Gen. 3:6; Luke 4:3), the temptation to obtain dominion (Gen. 3:5; 1:26-30; Luke 4:5-6), and the temptation to defy death (Gen. 3:3, 7; 2:17; Luke 4:9-11) (pp. 173–77). During the crucifixion Jesus is taunted (23:35, 37, 39), mirroring the three times that Satan calls his relationship with God into question, but he conquers death, defeats Satan, and reopens paradise.

145. Allison, *Intertextual Jesus*, 28; Fleddermann, Q, 256.

pivotal narrative moment: it not only functions as an *Adamic* motif in which Jesus emerges as Christus-Adam-Victor, but Jesus' rejection of Satan is also a rejection of "all the kingdoms of this world," and with them the politico-military power often associated with royal Davidic messianism.[146]

The Christology of Q's Sermon is both *inclusive* and exclusive: exclusive in the sense that Jesus is "*the* Son," but inclusive in that sonship is extended to disciples. Jesus' identification as the "Son" *includes* a collective or corporate sense of "sonship." This distinctive Christological feature of Q does not appear to be based on the *Parables'* son of man tradition. The *Parables* describe the preexistent, hidden, and elect son of man as the "messiah,"[147] "a light to the nations,"[148] the object of universal worship[149] and endowed with the spiritual messianic attributes of Isaiah 11,[150] but never call this figure the "Son of God," nor does the identity of the son of man serve a symbolic function as representative of the "*people* of the saints of the Most High" as it does in Daniel. Q's son of man Christology does not explain its Son of God Christology.

The language and vocabulary of "sonship" (υἱός) is used frequently in Early Jewish and Christian sources. A similar form of sonship can be found in the book of Revelation:

> I am the Alpha and the Omega,
> the beginning (ἀρχὴ) and the end . . .
> He who overcomes will inherit . . .
> he will be my son (υἱός).[151]

The tension between Q's apparently exclusive identification of Jesus as *the* Son and its inclusive sonship for Jesus' disciples is also found in Paul's letters, where Jesus is *the* Son and yet all those driven by the Spirit are υἱοὶ θεοῦ, "sons of God."[152] In a famous passage composed c. 55 C.E. [153] Paul elaborates on divine sonship-in-Christ:

146. Simon J. Joseph, "'Blessed is Whoever Is Not Offended By Me': The Subversive Appropriation of (Royal) Messianic Ideology in Q 3–7," *NTS* 57, no. 3 (2011): 307–24.

147. *1 En.* 48.8-10.

148. *1 En.* 48.4.

149. *1 En.* 48.5.

150. *1 En.* 49.3.

151. Rev. 21:6-7.

152. Rom. 8:3, 12-17; Gal. 4:6. See also Eph. 1:5.

153. Scott, *Adoption as Sons of God*; Burke, "Adopted as Sons," 259–87.

> All of you are *sons of God* (υἱοὶ θεοῦ) through faith in Christ Jesus,
> for as many of you as have been baptized into Christ
> have put on Christ . . .
> God sent his *Son* (υἱὸν αὐτοῦ) . . . *so that* (ἵνα) we might receive *sonship* (υἱοθεσίαν). Because you are sons (υἱοί), God has sent the spirit of his Son into our hearts . . . so you are no longer a slave, but a son.[154]

This inclusive sense of sonship is a distinctively Jewish tradition.[155] It is found in eschatological contexts,[156] ethical wisdom contexts,[157] and early Jewish mystical contexts. Rabbinical Jewish tradition recorded that during the life of the Galilean Hasid Hanina ben Dosa a heavenly voice was heard proclaiming that

> The whole universe is sustained on account of my *son* Hanina; but my *son* Hanina is satisfied with one kab of carob from one Sabbath eve to another.[158]

This tradition supports the authenticity of sonship in the Jesus tradition, for it represents "a solidly established Palestinian Jewish belief and terminology." Geza Vermes concludes that "already during his life Jesus was spoken of and addressed by admiring believers as *son of God.* To the legitimate question whether he could also have considered *himself* a *son of God*, the answer must

154. Gal. 3:26–4:6.

155. Moshe Idel, *Ben: Sonship and Jewish Mysticism* (KLJS 5; London/New York: Continuum, 2007). See also Trevor J. Burke, *The Message of Sonship: At Home in God's Household* (Downers Grove: InterVarsity, 2011); Brendan Byrne, *'Sons of God'—'Seed of Abraham': A Study of the Idea of the Sonship of God of All Christians in Paul Against the Jewish Background* (AB 83; Rome: Pontifical Biblical Institute, 1979); Martin Hengel, *The Son of God: The Origin of Christology and the History of Jewish-Hellenistic Religion* (Philadelphia: Fortress Press, 1976); Michael Peppard, *The Son of God in the Roman World: Divine Sonship in its Social World and Political Context* (Oxford and New York: Oxford University Press, 2011); Sinclair B. Ferguson, "The Reformed Doctrine of Sonship," in *Pulpit and People: Essays in Honour of William Still on his 75th Birthday*, ed. Nigel M. de S. Cameron and Sinclair G. Ferguson (Edinburgh: Rutherford House, 1986) 81–88; James M. Scott, *Adoption as Sons of God: An Investigation into the Background of* Huiothesia *in the Pauline Corpus* (WUNT 2d ser. 48; Tübingen: Mohr Siebeck, 1992); Trevor J. Burke, "Adopted as Sons: The Missing Piece in Pauline Soteriology," in *Paul: Jew, Greek and Roman*, ed. Stanley E. Porter (PAST 5; Leiden: Brill, 2008), 259–87; Matthew Vellanickal, *The Divine Sonship of Christians in the Johannine Writings* (AB 72; Rome: Pontifical Biblical Institute, 1977).

156. *Jub.* 1.24; *PsSol.* 17.27, 30; *1 En.* 62.11; *AssMos.* 10.3; *Test Jud.* 24.3.

157. Sir. 4:10; Wis. 2:16-18; *JosAs.* 7.2-6; 13.20; 21.3.

158. *b. Taan.* 24b; *b. Ber.* 17b; *b. Hul.* 86a.

be that he could."[159] In the Hebrew Bible, the title "Son of God" is applied to heavenly or angelic beings,[160] and ancient Jewish traditions of covenantal "sonship" in the Torah:

> Israel is my *son* (בני/υἱὸς).[161]
> You are the *sons* of the Lord your God.[162]
> (Υἱοί ἐστε Κυρίου τοῦ θεοῦ ὑμῶν / בנים אתמ ליהוה אלהיכם)

The theme of sonship is also present in traditional Davidic kingship and messianism:

> I will be his father and he will be *my son* (לבן).[163]
> I will be to him a father, and he shall be to me *a son* (εἰς υἱόν).[164]

The messiah was understood as the "Son of God" in some Jewish circles.[165] 4Q246 seems to interpret Daniel's "son of man" as a messianic figure, providing a missing link in the messianic exegesis of Dan. 7:13. Note the similarities to Luke 1:32-35[166]:

159. Geza Vermes, *Jesus the Jew: A Historian's Reading of the Gospel* (London: Collins, 1973), 209, 211.

160. Gen. 6:2, 4; Deut. 32:8; Pss. 29:1; 89:7; Dan. 3:25. In the Hebrew Bible (MT) the term is found in the plural as בני האלהים (Gen. 6:2, 4; Job 1:6; 2:1; 38:7) to refer to "angelic" beings in the heavenly court or council who report on or oversee human affairs. In Ps. 82:6 this group is addressed: "you are gods, sons of the Most High" In the Qumranic copy of Deuteronomy the phrase "sons of God" occurs two more times in the Song of Moses (Deut. 32:8, 43) and also in the LXX.

161. Exod. 4:22 LXX/MT.

162. Deut. 14:1 LXX/MT. See also Rabbi Akiba on Deut. 14:1: "Beloved are the Israelites, for they are called *sons of God*. Out of an even greater love for them they are told that they are called *sons of God*; as it is written, You are the *sons* of the Lord your *God*" (*m. Ab.* 3:14).

163. 2 Sam. 7:14 (MT).

164. 2 Kgs. 7:14 (LXX).

165. Lawrence H. Schiffman, *Reclaiming the Dead Sea Scrolls: The History of Judaism, the Background of Christianity, the Lost Library at Qumran* (Philadelphia: Jewish Publication Society, 1994), 342. See 2 Sam. 7:14; Ps. 89:26-27; Psalm 2. The expression "Son of God" is linked to the Davidic messiah in 4Q174 and other Qumran texts. See, for example, 1QSa 11–12. See H. Neill Richardson, "Some Notes on 1QSa," *JBL* 76 (1957): 108–22; Joseph A. Fitzmyer, *Essays on the Semitic Background of the New Testament* (London: Chapman, 1971), 153 n. 27; John J. Collins, "The Son of God Text, from Qumran," in Martinus C. De Boer, trans., *From Jesus to John: Essays on Jesus and New Testament Christology in Honour of Marinus de Jonge* (JSNTSup 84; Sheffield: JSOT Press, 1993), 65–82, at 78–79; Hengel, *The Son of God*, 44; Robert Gordis, "The 'Begotten' Messiah in the Qumran Scrolls," *VT* 7 (1957): 191–94; Morton Smith, "'God's Begetting the Messiah' in 1QSa," *NTS* 5 (1958–59): 218–24; Philip Sigal, "Further Reflections on the 'Begotten' Messiah," *HAR* 7 (1983): 221–33.

He shall be called "*Son of God*" (ברא די אל) . . .
Son of the Most High (בר עליון).[167]
He will be great and will be called
the *Son of the Most High* (υἱὸς ὑφίστου) . . .
he will be called *Son of God* (υἱὸς θεοῦ).[168]

Jesus is proclaimed "Son" at his baptism,[169] through his conception by the Holy Spirit,[170] and by his resurrection,[171] and those who have received the Holy Spirit are also "sons of God."[172] The author of John is clearly aware of an *inclusive* fellowship with Christ—the risen Jesus states that he goes to "my Father *and* your Father" (τὸν πατέρα μου καὶ πατέρα ὑμῶν)[173]—even if John's Christology is generally *exclusive*:

For God so loved the world that he *gave* (ἔδωκεν) his *one and only* (μονογενῆ) Son in order that the world might be *saved* (σωθῇ).[174]

Jesus is "the one and *only* Son," as opposed to being the Son who is representative of a universal Adamic sonship. Why does the author of John emphasize Jesus' identification as the "only begotten" Son? Here John protests too much:

I am the way, the truth, and the life.
No one comes to the Father except through me.[175]

John emphasizes Jesus' exclusivity in order to counter rival and competing claims of "sonship" and salvation. For John, Jesus is the *only* Son, the *true*

166. John J. Collins, *The Scepter and the Star: The Messiahs of the Dead Sea Scrolls and Other Ancient Literature* (New York: Doubleday, 1995), 155; Joseph A. Fitzmyer, "The Dead Sea Scrolls and Christian Origins: General Methodological Considerations," in *The Dead Sea Scrolls and Christian Faith: In Celebration of the Jubilee Year of the Discovery of Qumran Cave 1*, ed. James H. Charlesworth and Walter P. Weaver (Harrisburg, PA: Trinity Press International, 1998), 1–19, at 13.

167. 4Q246.

168. Luke 1:32-35.

169. Q 3; Mark 1:11, citing Psalm 2.

170. Luke 1:35; John 1:14.

171. Rom. 1:3-4.

172. Rom. 8:14-17, 29-30; John 1:12-13.

173. John 20:17.

174. John 3:16-17.

175. John 14:6.

Temple (replacing any need for the destroyed Temple), the true "messiah" (as God's Son), and the true Israel (the "firstborn Son" of God). John's response to competing traditions is an emphatic, exclusive, and supersessionistic Christology: Jesus is the exclusive Son of God.[176] This reading is further illustrated by John's use of τέκνα (to refer to the corporate identification with Jesus) instead of υἱός, which is more common in Paul ("he gave the right [ἐξουσίαν] *to become children of God* [τέκνα θεοῦ γενέσθαι])."[177] In John, Jesus is conscious of his preexistence with the Father:[178] he and the Father are "one,"[179] the Son has the power to give life and to judge,[180] and the Son is glorified in death and resurrection.[181] The Johannine Jesus' sonship is preexistent, "before the world existed,"[182] and the purpose of this Gospel is to convince readers to "believe that Jesus is the messiah, the *Son* of God" (ὁ υἱὸς τοῦ θεοῦ).[183] This is high Christology indeed.

The identification of Jesus as "the Son of God" in the New Testament is incontestable. The Gospel of Mark begins with an announcement of the "good news" of "Jesus Christ, *Son of God*" ('Ιησοῦ Χριστοῦ υἱοῦ θεοῦ), without the definite article.[184] A voice from heaven calls Jesus "my Son" (ὁ υἱός μου) at his baptism and transfiguration.[185] At his trial, Jesus himself affirms his messianic identity as "*the Son* of the Blessed One" (ὁ υἱὸς τοῦ εὐλογητοῦ).[186] In Matthew the disciples affirm "you really are *the* Son of God."[187] Peter explicitly conflates his affirmation of Jesus' messianic identity with "*the Son* of the living God" (ὁ χριστὸς ὁ υἱὸς τοῦ θεοῦ τοῦ ζῶντος).[188] Jesus confirms that Peter's confession was revealed to him by "my Father" (ὁ πατήρ μου).[189]

One of the most distinctive characteristics of Jesus' speech is his reference to God as "Father" or *Abba* (אבא)[190] which is partly based on the corporate

176. The term "son" occurs forty-five times in John, mostly in reference to Jesus (see especially 1:34, 49; 3:18; 5:25; 9:35; 10:36; 11:4; 19:7; 20:31).

177. John 1:12.

178. John 8:23, 38–42.

179. John 10:30.

180. John 5:21–26; 6:40; 8:16; 17:2.

181. John 17:1–24.

182. John 17:5, 24.

183. John 20:31.

184. Mark 1:1.

185. Mark 1:11; 9:7.

186. Mark 14:61.

187. Matt. 14:33

188. In Mark 8:30 Peter only recognizes Jesus as the messiah.

189. Matt. 16:15–17.

conceptual apparatus of ancient Judaism.[191] We find evidence for such an attribution not only in Jesus' sayings, but also in rabbinic accounts of the grandson of Honi the Circle-Drawer.[192] This attribution takes on a distinctive significance in the Jesus tradition: "it is in its capacity to be shared that Jesus' consciousness of sonship appears most distinctive . . . This sharing of his sonship with others belonged to his unique mission as the agent of God's eschatological salvation. He was the unique Son through whom the eschatological gift of sonship was bestowed on others."[193] In Mark, Jesus prays to God as "Abba, the Father (Αββα ὁ πατήρ)."[194] As noted above, we find an even earlier tradition of inclusive "sonship" in the letters of Paul:

> For all who are led by the Spirit of God are *sons of God* (υἱοὶ θεοῦ).
> For you did not receive a spirit of slavery to fall back into fear,
> but you have received a spirit of *sonship/adoption* (υἱοθεσίας).
> When we cry, "Abba! Father!" (Αββα ὁ πατήρ) it is that very Spirit bearing witness with our spirit that we are children (τέκνα) of God.[195]
> Because you are *sons* (υἱοί),

190. See also Ben Witherington III, *The Christology of Jesus* (Minneapolis: Fortress Press, 1990), 215; Vermes, *Jesus the Jew*, 210. James D. G. Dunn, *Christology in the Making: An Inquiry into the Origins of the Doctrine of the Incarnation* (London: SCM, 1980), 24–25, argues that Jeremias is incorrect in concluding that Jesus was "unique" in addressing God as *abba*, citing *b. Taan* 23b; *Targ. Ps.* 89.27; *Targ. Mal.* 2.10. However, *b. Taan.* 23b refers to Hanin ha Nehba, the grandson of Honi the Circle Drawer, and Hanin does not address God as *abba*. Similarly, *Targ. Mal.* 2.10 does not address or invoke God as *abba*. In *Targ. Ps.* 89.27, God promises the Davidic king that he will call God "*abba*," but this is a Targum of a common messianic attribution. Witherington, *Christology*, 218, 220, finds "no evidence to dispute Jeremias's claim that *abba* is a unique feature of Jesus' and early Christians' prayer language." See also James Barr, "'Abba, Father' and the Familiarity of Jesus' Speech," *Theology* 91 (1988): 173–79; idem, "Abba Isn't Daddy," *JTS* 39 (1988): 28–47.

191. John Ashton, "Abba," *ABD* 1 (1992): 7–8; Robert Hamerton-Kelly, *God the Father: Theology and Patriarchy in the Teaching of Jesus* (OBT 4; Philadelphia: Fortress Press, 1979); Joachim Jeremias, "Abba," in *The Prayers of Jesus* (Naperville, IL: A. R. Allenson, 1967), 11–65; Jacques Schlosser, *Le Dieu de Jésus: Étude exégétique* (LD 129; Paris: Cerf, 1987), 179–209. Even the Jesus Seminar concluded that "Abba" was authentic in Q 11:4. See Robert W. Funk, Roy Hoover, and the Jesus Seminar, *The Five Gospels* (New York: Macmillan, 1993), 148–50. So too Gerd Lüdemann, *Jesus after Two Thousand Years* (Amherst, MA: Prometheus, 2001), 147.

192. *b. Taan* 23b. See also Wis. 14:3; Sir. 23:1, 4; 51:10; and 3 Macc. 6:3, 8.

193. Richard Bauckham, "The Sonship of the Historical Jesus in Christology," *SJT* 31 (1978): 245–60, at 249, 250.

194. Mark 14:36.

195. Rom. 8:14-15.

> God has sent the Spirit of his *Son* (τοῦ υἱοῦ αὐτοῦ)
> into our hearts, crying, "Abba! Father!" (Αββα ὁ πατήρ).
> So you are no longer a slave but a *son* (υἱός),
> and if a son then also an heir, through God.[196]

In addition to explicit narrative identifications of Jesus as the "Son" in Q (Q 3:22; 4:3; 4:9), Jesus affirms that God is "*your* Father" (πατρὸς ὑμῶν) (Q 6:35c-d): "your Father" (ὁ πατὴρ ὑμῶν) is full of pity and compassion (Q 6:36). The Lord's Prayer itself is such an affirmation (even without Luke 11:2's explicit "*Our* Father"):

> When you pray, say, "[Our] *Father* (πάτερ), may your name be kept holy!"[197]

Jesus instructs his disciples to be free from anxiety:

> Do not be anxious . . . *your Father* (ὁ πατὴρ ὑμῶν) knows that you need.[198]

Jesus repeatedly refers to God as his "Father" in Q:

> I praise you, *Father*, Lord of heaven and earth.
> (ἐξομολογοῦμαι σοι, πάτερ, κύριε τοῦ οὐρανοῦ καὶ τῆς γῆς).[199]
> Everything has been entrusted to me by *my Father* (πατρός μου).[200]

The language of sonship is applied both to Jesus as "the Son," and to disciples. The language and vocabulary of sonship are so pervasive in the early Jesus tradition that it must surely be regarded as authentic.[201] It is a motif found in Q, Paul, the Synoptics, John, the *Gospel of Thomas*, and Jewish Christian gospel traditions. The tradents of the tradition bear witness to a gradual increase in exclusivity from Q, Mark, and Paul toward John and the Apostle's Creed,

196. Gal. 4:6-7.

197. Q 11:2b.

198. Q 12:29-30.

199. Q 10:21.

200. Q 10:22. On Q's Johannine "thunderbolt," see Karl von Hase, *Die Geschichte Jesu* (2d ed.; Leipzig: Breitkopf und Hartel, 1876), 422. Bas M. F. van Iersel, *'Der Sohn' in den synoptischen Jesusworten* (Leiden: Brill, 1964), 146, regards it as the cornerstone of New Testament Christology.

201. Gerd Theissen and Annette Merz, *The Historical Jesus: A Comprehensive Guide*, trans. John Bowden (Minneapolis: Fortress Press, 1998), 527.

yet the seeds of exclusivity were firmly planted in the exalted nature of Jesus' identification as messiah, Adam, and son of man, even if the inclusive aspects of sonship were constituent elements of these traditions.

The historical Jesus' affirmation of an inclusive sonship he shared with his disciples is firmly grounded in his ministry and in ancient Israelite and Jewish traditions. Jesus' call to sonship was not merely an honorific idiom given to the sons/children of Israel but a radical demand that his disciples live up to their divine heritage as "sons of God." This nexus between Jesus' self-reference as the Son, Adamic messianism, and discipleship allows for both an inclusive sonship and Jesus' preeminence as "*the* Son," a preeminence from which increasingly exclusive Christologies drew.[202] Nonetheless, the identification of Jesus as "the Son" not only serves as the Christological center of Q, Paul, and *Thomas*; it also forms the core of Western and Eastern orthodoxy.

The true follower of Jesus practices love of enemies in order to *become* a "son of God."[203] Jesus' call to "love enemies" and aspire toward divine sonship is not a Christian revelation of love and grace to be contrasted with Jewish legalism and hatred, but a radical universal Jewish vision *within* first-century Palestinian Judaism.[204]

The New Testament clearly portrays God as able to take vengeance on his enemies.[205] Consequently, Q 6:27-35c-d reflects a theological dissonance in the early Jesus tradition, between "loving enemies" and the expectation of a violent judgment. This dissonance can best be explained by positing two streams of tradition resulting in two different Christological orientations: one positive, the other negative; one bringing "good news," the other not-so-good news; one exalting Jesus as the Son of God with a utopian vision of divine providence,

202. The conceptual language of Christian divinization, deification, and the *theosis* tradition appealed to texts like 2 Pet. 1:4, which refers to the divine promises through which "you may *become* (γένησθε) participants (κοινωνοὶ) of the divine nature." The early Church Fathers understood salvation as deification through *union* with Christ. This mystical identification with Christ forms the core of Irenaeus's Christology: "For this is why the Word became man . . . so that man, by entering into communion with the Word and thus receiving divine sonship, might *become a son of God*" (*Adv. Haer.* 4.33.4). Similarly, Clement of Alexandria affirmed that "The Logos of God had become man so that you might learn from a man how a man may *become* God" (*Prot.* 1.8.4). Origen notes "From [Christ] there began the union of the divine with the human nature, in order that the human, by *communion* with the divine, might rise to the divine" (*Contra Cels.* 3.28; *Orat.* 27.13).

203. Piper, *"Love Your Enemies,"* 61–62.

204. Wright, *Jesus and the Victory of God*; John Dominic Crossan, *The Birth of Christianity: Discovering What Really Happened in the Years Immediately After the Execution of Jesus* (San Francisco: HarperSanFrancisco, 1998), 287.

205. Rom. 2:8; 12:19; Rev. 20:9, 15; Matt. 13:30.

the other casting Jesus in the role of the rejected and avenging son of man. Q represents a confluence of these two streams.

Q's concurrent identification of Jesus as the Enochic son of man and the Enochic/Adamic Son of God conflates two distinct roles: the end-time judge and the transforming Adamic messiah. Both roles reflect first-century Jewish apocalyptic traditions with strong wisdom components, but they are in certain respects thematically and theologically incompatible. There is a gospel *of* Jesus and a gospel *about* Jesus.[206]

John Kloppenborg has described Q's ethic as "characterized by nonviolence."[207] We could even call Q's Inaugural Sermon a "*gospel* (εὐαγγέλιον) *of nonviolence.*" Martin Hengel speaks of this as the "heart of the proclamation of Jesus, the conscious rejection of violence . . . unequivocally represented in the oldest sayings-tradition of the logia (Q) source."[208] The imperative to "love enemies" is further emphasized by imperatives to pray for enemies, turn the other cheek (Q 6:29), walk the extra mile (Q 6:29-30), and not judge (Q 6:37-38). Other Q sayings further support the central message of the Sermon. Jesus' disciples are "sheep among wolves" (Q 10:3), that is, they are nonviolent and defenseless among those who resort to violence. They are forbidden even to carry a stick or staff for self-defense (Q 10:4). They are to declare "Peace" (εἰρήνη) when they enter the home of a "*son* of peace" (υἱὸς εἰρήνης) who welcomes them, let their "peace" come upon those in the house, and announce the *presence* of the kingdom. The followers of Jesus are to forgive their brothers repeatedly (Q 17:3-4).

Jesus' vision of a providential, loving, and forgiving God is the message and content of the kingdom, the "good news." There are numerous Q sayings that implicitly or explicitly affirm the principle and practice of nonviolence, the "way" of Jesus:

Q 6:23:	rejoice and be glad (ἀγαλλιᾶσθε).
Q 6:27:	love (ἀγαπᾶτε) your enemies . . .
Q 6:28:	pray (προσεύχεσθε) for those persecuting you

206. Michael F. Bird, "Mark: Interpreter of Peter and Disciple of Paul," in *Paul and the Gospels: Christologies, Conflicts and Convergences*, ed. Michael F. Bird and Joel Willitts (LNTS; New York: T&T Clark International, 2011), 30–61, at 44.

207. John S. Kloppenborg, "The Function of Apocalyptic Language in Q," *SBLASP* 25 (1986): 224–35, at 235, citing Q 6:27-28. See also idem, "Symbolic Eschatology and the Apocalypticism of Q," *HTR* 80, no. 3 (1987): 287–306, at 305.

208. Martin Hengel, *Was Jesus a Revolutionist?* trans. William Klassen (Philadelphia: Fortress Press, 1971), 26.

Q 6:29:	offer the other as well . . . the coat as well
Q 6:30:	to the one who asks of you, give (αἰτοῦντί)
Q 6:30:	do not ask back what is yours
Q 6:31:	treat them . . . the way you want people to treat you
Q 6:36:	be full of pity (οἰκτίρμονες)
Q 6:37:	do not pass judgment (κρίνετε)
Q 6:40:	the disciple (μαθητὴς) to be *like* (ὡς) the Teacher.
Q 6:42:	throw the beam out from your own eye
Q 6:46:	do (ποιεῖτε) what I say (λέγω)
Q 6:47:	acting (ποιῶν) on my sayings (λόγους)

These sayings envision a new world in which "conventional values are inverted and turned on their heads."[209] This is Jesus' eschatological reversal and rejection of violence.

According to Luke 2:14, Jesus' birth heralds "peace on earth, good will toward all." The passion narratives do not support a reading of an armed Jesus movement.[210] Two swords were not "enough" to resist arrest or mount a rebellion against Rome. In Matthew's passion narrative Jesus rebukes Peter for drawing a sword:

> For all who take the sword will perish by the sword.[211]
> (πάντες γὰρ οἱ λαβόντες μάχαιραν ἐν μαχαίρῃ ἀπολοῦνται)

Matthew also adds to Mark's allusion to Zech. 9:9–10 to further emphasize the *peaceful* nature of Jesus' entry into Jerusalem:

> Rejoice greatly, O daughter of Zion! Shout aloud, O daughter of Jerusalem! Lo, your king comes to you; *triumphant* and *victorious* is he, *humble* and riding on a donkey, on a colt, the foal of a donkey . . . and he will command *peace* to the nations.[212]

Matthew adds "blessed are the *peacemakers* (εἰρηνοποιοί)" to Q's beatitudes. On the other hand, Matthew also contains parables of eschatological violence that are even more severe and pronounced than those in Q,[213] signifying that despite

209. William E. Arnal, *Jesus and the Village Scribes: Galilean Conflicts and the Setting of Q* (Minneapolis: Fortress Press, 2001), 2. See Q 3:8; Q 4:5–8; Q 6:20–23; Q 6:27–28; Q 6:32–34; Q 7:9; Q 7:22; Q 12:2–3; Q 13:30; Q 13:18–19; Q 13:20–21; Q 14:11; Q 14:16–18; Q 14:26; Q 16:18; Q 17:33.

210. Matt. 26:52; Luke 22:51; John 18:11.

211. Matt. 26:52.

212. Zech. 9:9–10.

the evangelist's best intentions, Matthew ultimately (mis)represented Jesus as eschatologically inconsistent, his instructions intelligible only as an idealized *Interimsethik*.[214] It is Q 6:27, with its uncompromising call to "love enemies," that gives us the *Ipsissima Vox* of Jesus.

Q 6:46 clearly calls for the *practice* of Jesus' teachings. The Jesus of Q still speaks to Jews, to Israel, and, today, to Christians, for a universal and unconditional love for all, including Israel's traditional "enemies." The Jesus of Q continues to call disciples in a world torn by injustice, poverty, crime, separation, war, and violence, a world ever in need of the dangerous, demanding, and subversive message of the early Jesus tradition.

213. Matt. 13:24–30; 13:36–43; 13:47–50; 18:23–35; 21:33–46; 22:1–14; 24:45–51; 25:14–30; 25:31–46.

214. Albert Schweitzer, *Von Reimarus zu Wrede: Eine Geschichte der Leben-Jesu-Forschung* (Tübingen: Mohr Siebeck, 1906); ET: *The Quest of the Historical Jesus: A Critical Study of its Progress from Reimarus to Wrede*, trans. W. Montgomery (London: Adam and Charles Black, 1910).

11

Conclusion

Jesus was born into a world that had seen more than its share of warfare and violence. He need not have been especially endowed with divine insight to realize that violence, hatred, and warfare had not served Israel particularly well. He need not have been a legal expert to have known Genesis 2-3, with its Edenic state of nonviolence, or Isa. 11:6-9, with its vision of nonviolent messianism.[1] Peace is the very essence of the relationship between humanity and God envisioned in Genesis 2-3. Jesus' distinctive stance on nonviolence was eschatologically grounded, biblically mandated, and politically conscious.[2] The meaning of statements such as "those who live by the sword die by the sword," "put away your sword," and "love your enemies" seems fairly self-explanatory. Jesus' "eschatological nostalgia for perfection" challenged the Davidic tradition of political violence and would not have endeared him to those who sought to use military power in their struggle against Rome. Jesus' teachings constitute, in part, a call to return to an idealistic, even Edenic state of nonviolence, harmony, and divine providence.[3] Jesus' nonviolence

1. See also Isa. 2:4; Allison, *Jesus of Nazareth*, 122, refers to Jesus' "eschatological nostalgia for perfection."; John Riches, *Jesus and the Transformation of Judaism* (New York: Seabury, 1982), 87–111. Guy G. Stroumsa, "Introduction: The Paradise Chronotrope," in *Paradise in Antiquity: Jewish and Christian Views*, ed. Markus Bockmuehl and Guy G. Stroumsa (Cambridge: Cambridge University Press, 2010), 1–14, at 1–2, notes that eschatology can be seen as both "nostalgia for an irretrievable loss" and an "unquenchable expectation for regaining it," a "viably transcendent hope for the human condition, the . . . expectation of a world at once restored and new."

2. Jerome F. D. Creach, *Violence in Scripture* (IRUSC; Louisville: Westminster John Knox Press, 2013), 18, notes that Genesis 2-3 "presents a view of God and an expectation for humankind that suggest violence will represent a major disruption of the order God intended." Accordingly, as the Bible unfolds, "violence enters the created order and threatens to overtake it" (23).

3. Sanders, *Jesus and Judaism*, 72. Sanders proposes that "the expectation that Israel would be restored points to the hope for a fundamental renewal, a new creation accomplished by God" (230) and sees Q 16:18 as signifying "a serious decree for a new age and a new order" (234). On the theme of restoration

"scandalized" his contemporaries. But if Jesus was consistent about anything, it seems to have been his commitment to nonviolence. It follows that any tradition that suggests, implicitly or explicitly, that the historical Jesus was an agent of violence could well be deemed inauthentic. Our methodological commitment to Jesus' nonviolence has not only isolated a distinctive interpretation of Q's Inaugural Sermon; it also makes sense of Jesus' messianic vision and *restores* the message of the one who sought to restore what was broken, the "*good* news" (τό εὐαγγέλιον) of the kingdom being the restoration of what was declared by God to be "*very* good" (טוב מאד / καλὰ λίαν) at the beginning of creation.[4] We may not be able to turn back the wheel of history on a world-religion that has openly embraced Just War theory for over fifteen-hundred years, but we can still affirm the living faith, practice, and tradition of Jesus' radical nonviolence,[5] a vision and way of life that challenged age-old assumptions about Israel's "enemies," but promised the renewal of creation itself.

The "Gospel" of Jesus did not endorse the idea that violent warfare would bring about an age of peace because it was itself the eschatological enactment of that very peace. Jesus *demonstrated* – by his own example—his highly idealized kingdom-vision of universal sonship, unconditional love, and divine providence. By doing so he crossed social boundaries, family loyalties, ethnic allegiances, and religious customs. He was not unaware of the fact that he was "scandalizing" his contemporaries and that he would pay the price for that.

The early Jesus tradition could not hold this radical vision in its original form for long. The Jewish Jesus movement's sectarian tensions within Judaism

see *Restoration: Old Testament, Jewish, and Christian Perspectives*, ed. James M. Scott (JSJSup 72; Leiden: Brill, 2001); Joseph, "'Seek His Kingdom,'" 392–410; Mark J. Allman, *Who Would Jesus Kill? War, Peace, and the Christian Tradition* (Winona, MN: Anselm, 2008), 76: "the Gospels see Jesus' life and ministry as ushering in a new age of peace, similar to the one found in Isaiah's oracles." See also Allison, *Resurrecting Jesus*, 149–197.

4. Gen. 1:31.

5. A remarkable development in contemporary Christian theology is the affirmation of the eschatological *restoration* of creation. See J. Richard Middleton, *A New Heaven and a New Earth* (Grand Rapids: Baker Academic, 2013); idem, "A New Heaven and a New Earth: The Case for a Holistic Reading of the Biblical Story of Redemption," *JCTR* 11 (2006): 73–97, esp. 90–91. Acts 3:17-21; Eph. 1:7-10; Col. 1:16-20; 2 Pet. 3:10-13; Rom. 8:19-23 are representative texts. See also Brian J. Walsh and J. Richard Middleton, *The Transforming Vision: Shaping a Christian World View* (Downers Grove: InterVarsity, 1984); Al Wolters, *Creation Regained: Biblical Basics for a Reformational Worldview* (Grand Rapids: Eerdmans, 1985); Steven Bouma-Prediger, *For the Beauty of the Earth: A Christian Vision of Creation Care* (Grand Rapids: Baker Academic, 2001); Wesley Granberg-Michaelson, *A Worldly Spirituality: The Call to Redeem Life on Earth* (San Francisco: Harper & Row, 1984); Paul Marshall, with Lela Gilbert, *Heaven Is Not My Home: Learning to Live in God's Creation* (Nashville: Word, 1998).

were rapidly transferred and translated into Jewish/Christian conflicts. Early Christianity—a universalistic stream of Early apocalyptic Judaism—emerged within yet rapidly moved beyond its apocalyptic Jewish matrix of eschatological speculation on messianic Adam traditions. The letters of Paul—with their explicit identification of Jesus as both *Christos* and the last/second Adam heralding a "new creation"—attest to this Early Jewish apocalyptic influence. This apocalyptic speculation on the eschatological restoration of an ideal Adamic humanity—seen most prominently in the messianic Adam figure of the *Animal Apocalypse* (c. 165 B.C.E.) and developed most innovatively in Daniel 7's "one like a son of man"—established alternative models to the traditional Davidic messianic expectation of a new warrior-king of Israel. The Qumran community and corpus are examples of further creative developments combining Adamic speculation, Danielic imagery, and Davidic models in their messianic imaginations. By the middle of the first century C.E., the *Parables of Enoch* could combine Enochic traditions, Daniel's "son of man," Davidic messianism, and Isaianic Servant motifs into a new synthesis that would come to have an indirect yet traceable effect on the early Jesus tradition in Q, Matthew, and Paul. In particular, Q's two dominant Christological motifs—the Son of God and the son of man/humanity—represent the confluence of these two Enochic streams intersecting in the life, teachings, and community of the historical Jesus. These Christological motifs were then incorporated into the Gospels and woven together in order to construct biographical narratives in which Jesus fulfills all the eschatological functions of Davidic, Danielic, Enochic, Adamic, and Isaianic messianism.

Bibliography

Aaron, David H. "Shedding Light on God's Body in Rabbinic Midrashim: Reflections on the Theory of a Luminous Adam." *Harvard Theological Review* 90 (1997): 299–314.

Abbott, Edwin. '*The Son of Man*' *or Contributions to the Study of the Thoughts of Jesus*. Cambridge: Cambridge University Press, 1910.

Adams, Edward. "The Coming of the Son of Man in Mark's Gospel." *Tyndale Bulletin* 56, no. 1 (2005): 39–61.

Ådna, Jostein. "Jesus and the Temple." In *Handbook for the Study of the Historical Jesus*. 4 vols. Edited by Tom Holmén and Stanley E. Porter. Leiden: Brill, 2011, 2635–75.

Agrell, Göran. *Work, Toil and Sustenance: An Examination of the View of Work in the New Testament, Taking into Consideration Views found in the Old Testament, Intertestamental, and Early Rabbinic Writings*. Translated by Stephen Westerholm. Lund: Verbum, 1976.

Albright, William F. *From the Stone Age to Christianity: Monotheism and the Historical Process*. Baltimore: John Hopkins University Press, 1940.

Aichele, George. "Jesus' Violence." In *Violence, Utopia and the Kingdom of God: Fantasy and Ideology in the Bible*. Edited by George Aichele and Tina Pippin. London: Routledge, 1998, 72–91.

Aichele, George, Peter Miscall, and Richard Walsh. "An Elephant in the Room: Historical-Critical and Postmodern Interpretation of the Bible." *Journal of Biblical Literature* 128.2 (2009): 383-404.

Akers, Keith. *The Lost Religion of Jesus: Simple Living and Nonviolence in Early Christianity*. New York: Lantern, 2000.

Alexander, Philip S. "The Demonology of the Dead Sea Scrolls." In *The Dead Sea Scrolls After Fifty Years: A Comprehensive Assessment*. 2 vols. Edited by Peter W. Flint and James C. VanderKam. Leiden: Brill, 1998, 331–53.

Allison, Dale C. *The End of the Ages Has Come: An Early Interpretation of the Passion and Resurrection of Jesus*. Philadelphia: Fortress Press, 1985.

———. "Matthew 10:26-31 and the Problem of Evil." St. *Vladimir's Theological Quarterly* 32 (1988): 293–308.

———. *The New Moses: A Matthean Typology*. Minneapolis: Fortress Press, 1993.

———. "A Plea for Thoroughgoing Eschatology." *Journal of Biblical Literature* 114 (1994): 651–68.

———. *The Jesus Tradition in Q*. Harrisburg, PA: Trinity Press International, 1997.

———. *Jesus of Nazareth: Millenarian Prophet*. Minneapolis: Fortress Press, 1999.

———. "Q 12:51-53 and Mark 9:11-13 and the Messianic Woes." In *Authenticating the Words of Jesus*. Edited by Bruce D. Chilton and Craig A. Evans. Leiden: Brill, 1999, 289-310.

———. "The Eschatology of Jesus." In *The Encyclopedia of Apocalypticism*. Vol. 1: *The Origins of Apocalypticism in Judaism and Christianity*. Edited by John J. Collins. New York: Continuum, 2000, 267–302.

———. "Q's New Exodus and the Historical Jesus." In *The Sayings Source Q and the Historical Jesus*. Edited by Andreas Lindemann. BETL 158. Leuven: Peeters, 2001, 395–428.

———. "John and Jesus: Continuity and Discontinuity." *Journal for the Study of the Historical Jesus* 1, no. 1 (2002): 6–27.

———. *Resurrecting Jesus: The Earliest Christian Tradition and Its Interpreters*. New York: T & T Clark, 2005.

———. *Constructing Jesus: Memory, Imagination, and History*. Grand Rapids: Baker Academic, 2010.

———. "How to Marginalize the Traditional Criteria of Authenticity." In *Handbook for the Study of the Historical Jesus* (2011), 3–30.

Allman, Mark J. *Who Would Jesus Kill? War, Peace, and the Christian Tradition*. Winona, MN: Anselm, 2008.

Anderson, Bernhard W. "Human Dominion over Nature." In *Biblical Studies in Contemporary Thought*. Edited by Miriam Ward. Somerville, MA: Greeno, Halden, 1975, 27–45.

Anderson, Gary. "Celibacy or Consummation in the Garden?" *Harvard Theological Review* 82 (1989): 121–48.

———. *The Genesis of Perfection: Adam and Eve in Jewish and Christian Imagination*. Louisville: Westminster John Knox, 2001.

Anderson, John. Review of Eric Seibert, *Disturbing Divine Behavior*. *Review of Biblical Literature* March 2011: http://www.bookreviews.org/pdf/7354_8359.pdf">http://www.bookreviews.org/pdf/7354_8359.pdf [accessed 17 February 2014].

Andrews, Elias. *The Meaning of Christ for Paul*. New York: Abingdon-Cokesbury, 1946.

Archer, Gleason L. *New International Encyclopedia of Bible Difficulties*. Grand Rapids: Zondervan, 1982.

Ardrey, Robert. *The Territorial Imperative: A Personal Inquiry into the Origins of Property and Nations*. New York: Atheneum, 1966.

Arendt, Hannah. *On Violence*. New York: Harcourt, Brace, and World, 1969.

Arnal, William E. "Why Q Failed: From Ideological Project to Group Formation." In *Redescribing Christian Origins*. Edited by Ron Cameron and Merrill P. Miller. SBLSS 28. Atlanta: Society of Biblical Literature, 2004, 67–87.

———. *The Symbolic Jesus: Historical Scholarship, Judaism, and the Construction of Contemporary Identity*. London: Equinox, 2005.

———. Review of *The Sayings Source Q and the Historical Jesus*. *Catholic Biblical Quarterly* 69, no. 3 (2007): 627–29.

———. "The Q Document." In *Jewish Christianity Reconsidered: Rethinking Ancient Groups and Texts*. Edited by Matt Jackson-McCabe. Minneapolis: Fortress Press, 2007, 119–54.

Ashton, John. "Abba." *Anchor Bible Dictionary* 1 (1992): 7–8.

Aslan, Reza. *Zealot: The Life and Times of Jesus of Nazareth*. New York: Random House, 2013.

Assefa, Daniel. "The Enigmatic End of the Animal Apocalypse in the Light of Traditional Ethiopian Commentary." In *Proceedings of the XVth International Conference of Ethiopian Studies*. Edited by S. Uhlig. Wiesbaden: Harrassowitz, 2006, 552-560.

———. *L'Apocalypse des animaux (1 Hen 85–90): une propagande militaire? Approches narrative, historico-critique, perspectives théologiques*. JSJSup 120. Leiden: Brill, 2007.

Astell, Ann W., and Sandor Goodhart, eds. *Sacrifice, Scripture, and Substitution: Readings in Ancient Judaism and Christianity*. Notre Dame, IN: University of Notre Dame, 2011.

Attenborough, Richard. *The Words of Gandhi*. New York: Newmarket Press, 1982.

Aune, David E. "Christian Prophecy and the Messianic Status of Jesus." In *The Messiah: Developments in Earliest Judaism and Christianity. The First Princeton Symposium on Judaism and Christian Origins*. Edited by James H. Charlesworth. Minneapolis: Fortress Press, 1992, 404–22.

———. "The Problem of the Messianic Secret." *Novum Testamentum* 11 (1969): 1–31.

Avalos, Hector. *Fighting Words: The Origins of Religious Violence*. Amherst, MA: Prometheus, 2005.

———. "The Letter Killeth: A Plea for Decanonizing Violent Biblical Texts." *Journal of Religion, Conflict, and Peace* 1 (2007): http://religionconflictpeace.org/volume-1-issue-1-fall-2007/letter-killeth">http://religionconflictpeace.org/volume-1-issue-1-fall-2007/letter-killeth [accessed July 15, 2013].

Bach, Eugen. *Die Feindesliebe nach dem natürlichen Sittengesetz: Eine historisch-ethische Untersuchung*. Kempten: Kösel, 1914.

Bachmann, Veronika. *Die Welt im Ausnahmezustand: eine Untersuchung zu Aussagegehalt und Theologie des Wächterbuches (1 Hen 1–36)*. BZAW 409. Berlin: de Gruyter, 2009.

———. "The Book of the Watchers (1 Enoch 1–36): An Anti-Mosaic, Non-Mosaic, or Even Pro-Mosaic Writing?" *Journal of Hebrew Scriptures* 11 (2011): 1–23.

Bailey, Lloyd R. "Gehenna: The Topography of Hell." *Biblical Archaeologist* 49 (1986): 187–91.

Bainton, Roland. *Christian Attitudes Toward War and Peace: A Historical Survey and Critical Re-evaluation*. New York: Abingdon, 1960.

Baird, J. Arthur. *The Justice of God in the Teaching of Jesus*. Philadelphia: Westminster, 1963.

Bammel, Ernst. "The Revolution Theory from Reimarus to Brandon." In *Jesus and the Politics of His Day*. Edited by Ernst Bammel and C. F. D. Moule. Cambridge: Cambridge University Press, 1984, 11–68.

———. "The Poor and the Zealots." In *Jesus and the Politics of His Day*. Edited by E. Bammel and C. F. D. Moule. Cambridge: Cambridge University Press, 1984, 109–28.

———. "The Titulus." In *Jesus and the Politics of His Day*, 353–64.

Bampfylde, Gillian. "The Similitudes of Enoch: Historical Allusions." *Journal for the Study of Judaism in the Persian, Hellenistic, and Roman Periods* 15 (1984): 9–31.

Barker, Margaret. *The Gate of Heaven: The History and Symbolism of the Temple in Jerusalem*. London: SPCK, 1991.

———. *The Lost Prophet: The Book of Enoch and its Influence on Christianity*. Nashville: Abingdon, 1988.

Barr, James. "The Image of God in the Book of Genesis: A Study of Terminology." *Bulletin of the John Rylands University Library of Manchester* 51 (1968): 11–26.

———. "'Abba, Father' and the Familiarity of Jesus' Speech." *Theology* 91 (1988): 173–79.

———. "Abba Isn't Daddy." *Journal of Theological Studies* 39 (1988): 28–47.

Barclay, John M. G. *Jews in the Mediterranean Diaspora: From Alexander to Trajan (323 B.C.E.–117 CE)*. Edinburgh: T & T Clark, 1996.

Bardtke, Hans. "Die Kriegsrolle v. Qumran übersetzt." *Theologische Literaturzeitung* 80 (1955): 401–20.

Barnstone, Willis S. *The Other Bible*. New York: Harper San Francisco, 1984.

Barrett, C. K. *The Holy Spirit and the Gospel Tradition*. London: SPCK, 1947.

———. *From First Adam to Last: A Study in Pauline Theology*. New York: Charles Scribner's Sons, 1962.

———. *Jesus and the Gospel Tradition*. London: SPCK, 1967.

Barth, Karl. *Church Dogmatics*. Translated by Harold Knight, et al. Edinburgh: T & T Clark, 1960.

———. *A Shorter Commentary on Romans*. Translated by David H. van Daalen. London: SCM, 1959.

Bartlett, Anthony. *Cross Purposes: The Violent Grammar of Christian Atonement*. Harrisburg, PA: Trinity Press International, 2001.

Bateman IV, Henry, Gordon Johnston, and Darrell Bock. *Jesus the Messiah: Tracing the Promises, Expectations, and Coming of Israel's King*. Grand Rapids: Kregel, 2012.

Bauckham, Richard. "The Sonship of the Historical Jesus in Christology." *Scottish Journal of Theology* 31 (1978): 245–60.

———. "A Note on a Problem in the Greek Version of 1 Enoch i. 9." *Journal of Theological Studies* 32 (1981): 136–38.

———. *Jude, 2 Peter*. WBC 50. Waco: Word, 1983.

———. "The Son of Man: 'A Man in My Position' or 'Someone'?" *Journal for the Study of the New Testament* 23 (1985): 23–33.

———. *Jude and the Relatives of Jesus in the Early Church*. Edinburgh: T & T Clark, 1990.

———. "For What Offence Was James Put to Death?" In *James the Just and Christian Origins*. Edited by Bruce D. Chilton and Craig A. Evans. NTSup 98. Leiden: Brill, 1999, 199–232.

———. *Jesus and the Eyewitnesses: The Gospels as Eyewitness Testimony*. Grand Rapids: Eerdmans, 2006.

———. *Jesus and the God of Israel: God Crucified and Other Studies on the New Testament's Theology of Divine Identity*. Grand Rapids: Eerdmans, 2008.

Baumgarten, Albert I. *The Flourishing of Jewish Sects in the Maccabean Era: An Interpretation*. JSJSup 55. Leiden: Brill, 1997.

Baumgarten-Crusius, Ludwig Friedrich Otto. *Theologische Auslegung der johanneischen Schriften*. Edited by Ernst J. Kimmel. 2 vols. Jena: Luden, 1843–45.

Bauer, Walter. "Das Gebot der Feindesliebe und die alten Christen." *Zeitschrift für Theologie und Kirche* (1917): 37–54.

Baur, Ferdinand Christian. *Das Markusevangelium nach seinem Ursprung und Charakter*. Tübingen: Fues, 1851.

Beare, Francis Wright *The Gospel According to Matthew: A Commentary*. Oxford: Blackwell, 1981.

———. "The Sabbath Was Made for Man?" *Journal of Biblical Literature* 79 (1960): 130–36.

Beasley-Murray, G. R. *Jesus and the Kingdom of God*. Grand Rapids: Eerdmans, 1986.

Bautch, Kelley Coblentz. "Adamic Traditions in the Parables? A Query on 1 Enoch 69:6." In *Enoch and the Messiah Son of Man: Revisiting the Book of Parables*. Edited by Gabriele Boccaccini. Grand Rapids: Eerdmans, 2007, 352–60.

———. "Peter and the Patriarch: A Confluence of Traditions?" In *With Letters of Light: Studies in the Dead Sea Scrolls, Early Jewish Apocalypticism, Magic, and Mysticism: in Honor of Rachel Elior*. Edited by Daphna Arbel and Andrei A. Orlov. Ekstasis 2. Berlin: de Gruyter, 2010, 14–27.

Beck, Robert R. *Nonviolent Story: Narrative Conflict Resolution in the Gospel of Mark*. Maryknoll, NY: Orbis Books, 1996.

———. *Banished Messiah: Violence and Nonviolence in Matthew's Story of Jesus*. Eugene, OR: Wipf & Stock, 2010.

Becker, Jürgen. *Johannes der Täufer und Jesus von Nazareth*. Biblische Studien 63. Neukirchen-Vluyn: Neukirchener Verlag, 1972.

———. "Feindesliebe-Nächstenliebe-Bruderliebe: Exegetische Beobachtungen als Anfrage an ein ethisches Problemfeld." *Zeitschrift für evangelische Ethik* 25 (1981): 5–18.

———. *Jesus von Nazaret*. Berlin: de Gruyter, 1996.

———. *Jesus of Nazareth*. Translated by James E. Crouch. New York: de Gruyter, 1998.

Bedenbender, Andreas. *Der Gott der Welt tritt auf den Sinai: Entstehung, Entwicklung und Funktionsweise der frühjüdischen Apokalyptik*. ANTZ 8. Berlin: Institut Kirche und Judentum, 2000.

BeDuhn, Jason D. *The First New Testament: Marcion's Scriptural Canon*. Salem: Polebridge, 2013.

Beer, Georg. "Das Buch Enoch." In *Die Apokryphen und Pseudipigraphen des Alten Testaments*. Vol. 2. *Die Pseudepigraphen des Alten Testaments*. Edited by Emil Kautzsch. Tübingen: Mohr, 1900, 217–310.

Bergemann, Thomas. *Q auf dem Prüfstand: Die Zuordnung des Mt/Lk-Stoffes zu Q am Beispiel der Bergpredigt*. FRLANT 158. Göttingen: Vandenhoeck & Ruprecht, 1993.

Bergmeier, Roland. "Beobachtungen zu 4Q521 f2, II, 1–13." *Zeitschrift für deutschen morgenländischen Gesellschaft* 145 (1995): 38–48.

Bergsma, John Sietze. *The Jubilee from Leviticus to Qumran: A History of Interpretation*. VTSup 115. Leiden: Brill, 2007.

Berkowitz, Leonard. *Aggression: Its Causes, Consequences, and Control*. Philadelphia: Temple University Press, 1993.

Bermejo Rubio, Fernando. "The Fiction of the 'Three Quests': An Argument for Dismantling a Dubious Historiographical Paradigm." *Journal for the Study of the Historical Jesus* 7 (2009): 211–53.

Bernat, David A., and Jonathan Klawans, eds. *Religion and Violence: The Biblical Heritage*. Sheffield: Sheffield Phoenix Press, 2007.

Betz, Hans Dieter. *Nachfolge und Nachahmung Jesu Christi im Neuen Testament*. Tübingen: Mohr Siebeck, 1967.

———. *Essays on the Semon on the Mount*. Translated by Laurence Welborn. Philadelphia: Fortress Press, 1985.

Betz, Otto. "Die Frage nach dem messianischen Bewusstsein Jesu." *Novum Testamentum* 6 (1963): 24–37.

———. *Jesus: Der Messias Israels: Aufsätze zur biblischen Theologie*. Tübingen: Mohr Siebeck, 1987.

——— and Rainer Riesner. *Jesus, Qumran und der Vatikan: Klarstellungen*. Giessen: Brunnen, 1993.

Bietenhard, Hans. "Die Handschriftenfunde vom Toten Meer, (Óirbet Qumran) und die Essener-Frage. Die Funde in der Wüste Juda (Eine Orientierung)." In *ANRW* II 19.1. Edited by Hildegard Temporini and Wolfgang Haase. Berlin: de Gruyter, 1982, 704–78.

Bilde, Per. "The Roman Emperor Gaius (Caligula)'s Attempt to Erect his Statue in the Temple of Jerusalem." *Studia Theologica* 32, no. 1 (1978): 67–93.

Bird, Michael F. "Jesus is the Christ: Messianic Apologetics in the Gospel of Mark." *Reformed Theological Review* 64 (2005): 1–15.

———. *Are You the One who is to Come? The Historical Jesus and the Messianic Question*. Grand Rapids: Baker, 2009.

———. "Mark: Interpreter of Peter and Disciple of Paul." In *Paul and the Gospels: Christologies, Conflicts, and Convergences*. LNTS 411. Edited by Michael F. Bird and Joel Willitts. London: T & T Clark, 2011, 30–61.

Bird, Phyllis. "'Male and Female He Created Them': Gen 1:27b in the Context of the Priestly Account of Creation." *Harvard Theological Review* 74 (1981): 129–59.

Bivin, David and Roy B. Blizzard Jr., eds. *Understanding the Difficult Words of Jesus: New Insights from a Hebraic Perspective*. Shippenburg: Destiny Image Publishers, 1994.

Black, C. Clifton. "Christ Crucified in Paul and in Mark: Reflections on an Intracanonical Conversation." In *Theology and Ethics in Paul and His Interpreters. Festschrift V. P. Furnish*. Edited by Eugene H. Lovering and Jerry L. Sumney. Nashville: Abingdon, 1966, 184–206.

Black, Matthew. "Unsolved New Testament Problems: The 'Son of Man' in the Teachings of Jesus." *Expository Times* 60 (1949): 32–36.

———. "The Pauline Doctrine of the Second Adam." *Scottish Journal of Theology* 7 (1954): 170–79.

———. "Uncomfortable Words III. The Violent Word." *Expository Times* 81 (1970): 115-18.

———. "The Maranatha Invocation and Jude 14, 15 (I Enoch 1:9)." In *Christ and Spirit in the New Testament: In Honour of Charles Francis Digby Moule*. Edited by Barnabas Lindars and Stephen S. Smalley. Cambridge: Cambridge University Press, 1973, 189–96.

———. "Aramaic Barnāshā and the Son of Man." *Expository Times* 95 (1984): 200–6.

———. *The Book of Enoch or 1 Enoch: A New English Edition with Commentary and Textual Notes*. SVT 7. Leiden: Brill, 1985.

Blackman, Edwin C. *Marcion and His Influence*. New York: Ams, 1978.

Blasi, Anthony J. *Early Christianity as a Social Movement*. TSR 5. New York: Peter Lang, 1988.

Blosser, Donald W. "Jesus and the Jubilee (Luke 4:16-30): The Year of Jubilee and Its Significance in the Gospel of Luke." PhD diss., St. Andrew's University, 1979.

Blumenthal, David R. *Facing the Abusive God: A Theology of Protest*. Louisville: Westminster John Knox, 1993.

Boccaccini, Gabriele. *Beyond the Essene Hypothesis: The Parting of the Ways between Qumran and Enochic Judaism*. Grand Rapids: Eerdmans, 1998.

———. "Finding a Place." In *Enoch and the Messiah Son of Man* (2007), 263–89.

———. "Enochians, Urban Essenes, Qumranites: Three Social Groups, One Intellectual Movement." In *The Early Enoch Literature*. Edited by Gabriele Boccaccini and John J. Collins. JSJSup 121. Leiden and Boston: Brill, 2007, 301–27.

Bock, Darrell L. *Recovering the Real Lost Gospel: Reclaiming the Gospel as Good News*. Nashville: B & H Academic, 2010.

Bock, Darrell, and James H. Charlesworth, eds. *Parables of Enoch: A Paradigm Shift: Early Judaism, Jesus, and Christian Origins*. Jewish and Christian Texts in Contexts and Related Studies 11. London: T & T Clark International, 2013.

Bockmuehl, Markus. *This Jesus: Martyr, Lord, Messiah*. Edinburgh: T & T Clark, 1994.

———. Review of Dale C. Allison, *Jesus of Nazareth: Millenarian Prophet*. *Journal of Theological Studies* 51, no. 2 (2000): 637–41.

———. and James Carleton Paget, eds. *Redemption and Resistance: The Messianic Hopes of Jews and Christians in Antiquity*. London: T & T Clark, 2007.

Böhme, Christian Friedrich. *Versuch das Geheimnis des Menschensohn zu enthüllen*. Neustadt: Orla, 1839.

Bondurant, Joan V. *Conflict: Violence and Non-Violence*. Chicago: Aldine-Atherton, 1971.

———. *The Conquest of Violence: The Gandhian Philosophy of Conflict*. Princeton: Princeton University Press, 1988.

Booth, Wayne C. *The Company We Keep: An Ethics of Fiction*. Berkeley: University of California Press, 1988.

Borg, Marcus J. *Conflict, Holiness, and Politics in the Teaching of Jesus*. New York: Edwin Mellen, 1984.

———. "A Temperate Case for a Non-Eschatological Jesus." *Forum* 2, no. 3 (1986): 81–103.

———. *Jesus in Contemporary Scholarship*. Valley Forge, PA: Trinity Press International, 1994.

———. "Jesus and Eschatology: A Reassessment." In *Images of Jesus Today*. Edited by James H. Charlesworth and Walter P. Weaver. Valley Forge, PA: Trinity Press International, 1994, 42–67.

———. "Con: Jesus was not an Apocalyptic Prophet." In *The Apocalyptic Jesus: A Debate*. Edited by Robert J. Miller. Santa Rosa: Polebridge, 2001, 31–82.

———. *Jesus: Uncovering the Life, Teachings, and Relevance of a Religious Revolutionary*. New York: HarperSanFrancisco, 2006.

———, consulting ed. *The Lost Gospel Q: The Original Sayings of Jesus*. Edited by Mark Powelson and Rray Riegert. Berkeley: Ulysses, 1999.

Boring, M. Eugene. "Criteria of Authenticity: The Beatitudes as a Test Case." in *Foundations and Facets Forum* 1 (1985): 3–38.

Borman, William. *Gandhi and Nonviolence*. New York: SUNY Press, 1986.

Bornkamm, Günther. *Jesus of Nazareth*. London: Hodder & Stoughton, 1973.

Borsch, Frederick H. *The Son of Man in Myth and History*. Philadelphia: Westminster, 1967.

Bosold, Iris. *Pazifismus und prophetische Provokation*. SBS 90; Stuttgart: Katholisches Bibelwerk, 1978.

Boteach, Rabbi Schmuley. *Kosher Jesus*. Jerusalem: Gefen, 2012.

Bouma-Prediger, Steven. *For the Beauty of the Earth: A Christian Vision of Creation Care*. Grand Rapids: Baker Academic, 2001.

Bousset, Wilhelm. *Kyrios Christos: Geschichte des Christusglaubens von den Anfängen des Christentums bis Irenaeus*. Göttingen: Vandenhoeck & Ruprecht, 1913.

———. *Kyrios Christos: A History of the Belief in Christ from the Beginnings of Christianity to Irenaeus*. Translated by John E. Steely. Nashville: Abingdon, 1970.

——— and Hugo Gressmann. *Die Religion des Judentums im späthellenistischen Zeitalter*. HNT 21. 4th ed. Tübingen: Mohr Siebeck, 1966.

Boustan, Ra'anan. *Violence, Scripture, and Textual Practice in Early Judaism and Christianity*. Leiden: Brill, 2010.

Bouttier, Michel. *En Christ: Étude d'exégèse et de théologie pauliniennes*. Études d'histoire et de la philosophie religieuses 54. Paris: Presses Universitaires de France, 1962.

Boyarin, Daniel. *Border Lines: The Partition of Judaeo-Christianity*. Divinations. Philadelphia: University of Pennsylvania Press, 2004.

———. "How Enoch Can Teach Us about Jesus." *Early Christianity* 2 (2011): 51–76.

———. *The Jewish Gospels: The Story of the Jewish Christ*. New York: New Press, 2012.

Boyd, Gregory A. *The Myth of a Christian Religion: Losing Your Religion for the Beauty of a Revolution*. Grand Rapids: Zondervan, 2009.

Brandenburger, Egon. *Adam und Christus: Exegetisch-religionsgeschichtliche Untersuchung zu Röm. 5.12-21 (I. Kor.15)*. WUNT 17. Neukirchen-Vluyn: Neukirchener Verlag, 1962.

———. *Markus 13 und die Apokalyptik*. Göttingen: Vandehoeck & Ruprecht, 1984.

———. "Alter und neuer Mensch, erster und letzer Adam-Anthropos." In *Vom alten zum neuen Adam: Urzeitmythos und Heilsgeschichte*. Edited by Walter Strolz. Freiburg: Herder, 1986, 205–17.

———. "Gerichtskonzeption im Urchristentum und ihre Voraussetzungen. Eine Problemstudie." *Studien zur Umwelt des Neuen Testaments* 16 (1991): 5–54.

Brandon, S. G. F. *The Fall of Jerusalem and the Christian Church: A Study of the Effects of the Jewish Overthrow of A. D. 70 on Christianity*. London: SPCK, 1951.

———. *Jesus and the Zealots: A Study of the Political Factor in Primitive Christianity*. New York: Scribners, 1967.

———. "Jesus and the Zealots: A Correction." *New Testament Studies* 17 (1971): 453.

———. "Jesus and the Zealots: Aftermath." *Bulletin of the John Rylands Library* 54 (1971): 47-66.

Braun, Willi. "The Schooling of a Galilean Jesus Association (The Sayings Gospel Q)." In *Redescribing Christian Origins* (2004), 43–66.

Bredin, Mark R. "John's Account of Jesus' Demonstration in the Temple: Violent or Nonviolent?" *Biblical Theology Bulletin* 33 (2003): 44–50.

Brett, Mark G. *Decolonizing God: The Bible in the Tides of Empire*. Sheffield: Sheffield Phoenix Press, 2008.

Brock, Peter and Paul Socknat, eds. *Challenge to Mars: Essays on Pacifism from 1918 to 1945*. Toronto: University of Toronto Press, 1999.

Brooke, George J. "4QFlorilegium in the Context of Early Jewish Exegetical Method." PhD diss., Claremont Graduate School, 1978.

———. *Exegesis at Qumran: 4QFlorilegium in its Jewish Context*. JSNTSup 29. Sheffield: JSOT Press, 1985.

———. "Miqdash Adam, Eden and the Qumran Community." In *Gemeinde ohne Tempel—Community without Temple: Zur Substituierung und Transformation des Jerusalemer Tempels und seines Kultes im Alten Testament, antiken Judentum und frühen Christentum*. Edited by Beate Ego, et al. WUNT 118. Tübingen: Mohr Siebeck, 1999, 285–301.

———. *The Dead Sea Scrolls and the New Testament*. Minneapolis: Fortress Press, 2005.

———. "The Pre-Sectarian Jesus." In *Echoes from the Caves: Qumran and the New Testament.* Studies on the Texts of the Desert of Judah 85. Edited by Florentino García Martínez. Leiden: Brill, 2009, 33–48.

Broshi, Magen. "Hatred: An Essene Religious Principle and its Christian Consequences." In *Bread, Wine, Walls and Scrolls.* JSPSup 36. Sheffield: Sheffield Academic Press, 274–83.

Brown, Joanne Carlson, and Rebecca Parker. "For God So Loved the World?" In *Christianity, Patriarchy, and Abuse: A Feminist Critique.* Edited by Joanne Carlson Brown and Carole R. Bohn. New York: Pilgrim Press, 1989, 1–30.

Brown, Raymond E. *The Death of the Messiah: From Gethsemane to the Grave: A Commentary on the Passion Narratives in the Four Gospels.* ABRL. 2 vols. New York: Doubleday, 1994.

Brown, Robert McAfee. *Religion and Violence.* Philadelphia: Westminster, 1987.

Brownlee, William H. "Jesus and Qumran." In *Jesus and the Historian. Festschrift E. C. Colwell.* Edited by F. Thomas Trotter. Philadelphia: Westminster, 1968, 52–81.

Bruce, William Straton. *The Ethics of the Old Testament.* Edinburgh: T & T Clark, 1909.

Brueggemann, Walter. *Divine Presence Amid Violence: Contextualizing the Book of Joshua.* Eugene, OR: Cascade, 2009.

Buell, Denise. *Why this New Race? Ethnic Reasoning in Early Christianity.* New York: Columbia University Press, 2005.

Bultmann, Rudolf. "Was lässt die Spruchquelle über die Urgemeinde erkennen?" *Oldenburgische Kirchenblatt* 19 (1913): 35–37, 41–44.

———. *Die Geschichte der synoptischen Tradition.* FRLANT 29. Göttingen: Vandenhoeck & Ruprecht, 1931. English: *The History of the Synoptic Tradition.* Translated by John Marsh. New York: Harper, 1963.

———. *The Theology of the New Testament.* Translated by Kendrick Grobel. 2 vols. New York: Scribners, 1951–55.

———. "What the Sayings Source Reveals about the Early Church." In *The Shape of Q: Signal Essays on the Sayings Gospel.* Edited by John S. Kloppenborg. Minneapolis: Fortress Press, 1994, 23–34.

Burke, Trevor J. "Adopted as Sons: The Missing Piece in Pauline Soteriology." In *Paul: Jew, Greek and Roman.* Edited by Stanley E. Porter. PS 5. Leiden: Brill, 2008, 259–87.

———. *The Message of Sonship: At Home in God's Household.* Downers Grove: InterVarsity, 2011.

Burkett, Delbert. *The Son of Man Debate: A History and Evaluation*. SNTSMS 107. Cambridge and New York: Cambridge University Press, 1999.

Burridge, Richard A. *What Are the Gospels?: A Comparison with Graeco-Roman Biography*. SNTSMS 70. Cambridge: Cambridge University Press, 1992.

Butler, Trent C. *Luke*. Harper's Bible Commentary. Nashville: Abingdon, 2000.

Byrne, Brendan. *'Sons of God'—'Seed of Abraham': A Study of the Idea of the Sonship of God of All Christians in Paul Against the Jewish Background*. AnBib 83. Rome: Pontifical Biblical Institute, 1979.

———. "Christ's Pre-Existence in Pauline Soteriology." *Theological Studies* 58, no. 2 (1997): 308–30.

Cadoux, Cecil J. *The Historic Mission of Jesus: A Constructive Re-examination of the Eschatological Teaching in the Synoptic Gospels*. London: Lutterworth, 1941.

Caird, George B. *Jesus and the Jewish Nation*. Ethel M. Wood Lecture, 9 March 1965. London: Athlone, 1965.

———. *The Language and Imagery of the Bible*. Philadelphia: Westminster, 1980.

Cairns, David. *The Image of God in Man*. New York: Philosophical Library, 1953.

Calvert, D. G. A. "An Examination of the Criteria for Distinguishing the Authentic Words of Jesus." *New Testament Studies* 18 (1972): 209–19.

Calvin, Jean. *Institutes of the Christian Religion*. Edited by John T. McNeill. Translated by Ford Lewis Battles. 2 vols. LCC 20–21. Philadelphia: Westminster, 1960.

Cámara, Helder. *Spiral of Violence*. London: Sheed and Ward, 1971.

Cameron, Peter Scott. *Violence and the Kingdom: The Interpretation of Matthew 11:12*. ANTJ 5. New York: Peter Lang, 1988.

Cameron, Ron. "'What Have You Come Out to See? Characterizations of John and Jesus in the Gospels." *Semeia* 49 (1990): 35–70.

———. "The Sayings Gospel Q and the Quest for the Historical Jesus: A Response to John S. Kloppenborg." *Harvard Theological Review* 89, no. 4 (1996): 351–54.

———. "The Anatomy of a Discourse: On 'Eschatology' as a Category for Explaining Christian Origins." *Method and Theory in the Study of Religion* 8 (1996): 231–45.

——— and Merrill P. Miller, eds. *Redescribing Christian Origins*. SBLSS 28. Atlanta: Society of Biblical Literature, 2004.

——— and Merrill P. Miller, eds. *Redescribing Paul and the Corinthians*. Early Christianity and its Literature 5. Atlanta: Society of Biblical Literature, 2011.

Cannon, W. W. "Isaiah 61,1-3 an Ebed-Jahweh Poem." *Zeitschrift für die alttestamentliche Wissenschaft* 47 (1929): 284–88.

Capes, David B. *Old Testament Yahweh Texts in Paul's Christology*. Tübingen: Mohr, 1992.

Caragounis, Chrys C. *The Son of Man: Vision and Interpretation*. WUNT 38; Tübingen: Mohr Siebeck, 1986.

Carlson, Jeffrey, and Robert A. Ludwig, eds. *Jesus and Faith: A Conversation on the Work of John Dominic Crossan*. Maryknoll, NY: Orbis Books, 1994.

Carlston, Charles E. "A Positive Criterion of Authenticity." *Biblical Research* 7 (1962): 33–44.

——— and Dennis A. Norlan. "Once More—Statistics and Q." *Harvard Theological Review* 64 (1971): 59–78.

Carson, D. A., ed., *The Scriptures Testify About Me: Jesus and the Gospel in the Old Testament*. Wheaton: Crossway, 2013.

Carter, Warren. "Constructions of Violence and Identity in Matthew's Gospel." In *Violence in the New Testament*. Edited by Shelly Matthews and E. Leigh Gibson. New York: T & T Clark, 2005, 81–108.

Casey, P. Maurice. "The Corporate Interpretation of 'One Like a Son of Man' (Dan VII 13) at the Time of Jesus." *Novum Testamentum* 18 (1976): 167–80.

———. "The Son of Man Problem." *Zeitschrift für die neutestamentliche Wissenschaft und die Kunde der älteren Kirche* 67 (1976): 147–54.

———. "The Use of the Term 'Son of Man' in the Similitudes of Enoch." *Journal for the Study of Judaism* 7 (1976): 11–29.

———. *Son of Man: The Interpretation and Influence of Daniel 7*. London: SPCK, 1979.

———. "Aramaic Idiom and Son of Man Sayings." *Expository Times* 96 (1985): 233–36.

———. "The Jackals and the Son of Man (Matt. 8.20/Luke 9.58)." *Journal for the Study of the New Testament* 23 (1985): 3–22.

———. "General, Generic, and Indefinite: The Use of the Term 'Son of Man' in Aramaic Sources and in the Teaching of Jesus." *Journal for the Study of the New Testament* 29 (1987): 21–56.

———. "Method in Our Madness and Madness in Their Methods: Some Approaches to the Son of Man Problem in Recent Scholarship." *Journal for the Study of the New Testament* 42 (1991): 17–43.

———. "The Use of the Term בר אנש in the Aramaic Translations of the Hebrew Bible." *Journal for the Study of the New Testament* 54 (1994): 87–118.

———. "Idiom and Translation: Some Aspects of the Son of Man Problem." *New Testament Studies* 41 (1995): 164–82.

———. *The Solution to the 'Son of Man' Problem*. London: T & T Clark, 2007.

———. *Jesus of Nazareth: An Independent Historian's Account of his Life and Teachings*. London and New York: T & T Clark/Continuum, 2010.

Cassidy, Richard J. *Christian and Roman Rule in the New Testament*. New York: Crossroad, 2001.

Catchpole, David R. "The Poor on Earth and the Son of Man in Heaven: A Re-appraisal of Matthew XXV. 31-46." *Bulletin of the John Rylands University Library of Manchester* 61 (1979): 355–97.

———. "The Ravens, the Lilies and the Q Hypothesis." *Studien zum Neuen Testament und seiner Umwelt* 6–7 (1981–82): 77–87.

———. "The Angelic Son of Man in Luke 12:8." *Novum Testamentum* 24 (1982): 255–65.

———. "The 'Triumphal' Entry." In *Jesus and the Politics of His Day*. Edited by Ernst Bammel and C. F. D. Moule. Cambridge: Cambridge University Press, 1984, 319–34.

———. "Did Q Exist?" In *The Quest for Q*. Edinburgh: T & T Clark, 1993, 1–59.

Chapman, David W. "Perceptions of Crucifixion Among Jews and Christians in the Ancient World." PhD diss., Cambridge University, 1999.

Chapple, Christopher. *Nonviolence to Animals, Earth, and Self in Asian Traditions*. Albany, NY: SUNY Press, 1993.

Charles, J. Daryl. "Jude's Use of Pseudepigraphical Source-Material as Part of a Literary Strategy." *New Testament Studies* 37 (1991): 130–45.

———. *Literary Strategy in the Epistle of Jude*. Scranton, PA: University of Scranton Press, 1993.

Charles, Robert Henry. *The Book of Enoch or 1 Enoch: Translated from the Editor's Ethiopic Text*. Oxford: Clarendon Press, 1912.

Charlesworth, James H. "Jesus and Jehohanan." *Expository Times* 84 (1973): 147–150.

———. "The Portrayal of the Righteous as an Angel." In *Ideal Figures in Ancient Judaism: Profiles and Paradigms*. Edited by George W. E. Nickelsburg and John J. Collins. SBLSCS 12. Chico, CA: Scholars Press, 1980, 135–51.

———. "From Jewish Messianology to Christian Christology: Some Caveats and Perspectives." In *Judaisms and their Messiahs at the Turn of the Christian Era*.

Edited by Jacob Neusner, William Scott Green, and Ernest S. Frerichs. New York: Cambridge University Press, 1987, 225–64.

———. *Jesus within Judaism: New Light from Exciting Archaeological Discoveries*. New York: Doubleday, 1988.

———. "Messianology in the Biblical Pseudepigrapha." In *Qumran Messianism: Studies on the Messianic Expectations in the Dead Sea Scrolls*. Edited by James H. Charlesworth, Herman Lichtenberger, and Gerbern S. Oegema. Tübingen: Mohr Siebeck, 1998, 21–52.

———. "Have the Dead Sea Scrolls Revolutionized Our Understanding of the New Testament?" In *The Dead Sea Scrolls Fifty Years After Their Discovery: Proceedings of the Jerusalem Congress, July 20–25, 1997*. Edited by Lawrence H. Schiffman, Emanuel Tov, and James C. VanderKam. Jerusalem: Israel Exploration Society/The Shrine of the Book, Israel Museum, 2000, 116–32.

———. "The Historical Jesus: How to Ask Questions and Remain Inquisitive." In *Handbook for the Study of the Historical Jesus* (2011), 104–9.

——— and Joe Zias. "Crucifixion." In *Jesus and the Dead Sea Scrolls*. Edited by James H. Charlesworth. New York: Doubleday, 1992, 273–89.

———, ed. *The Messiah: Developments in Earliest Judaism and Christianity* (1992).

Chazon, Esther G. "The Creation and Fall of Adam in the Dead Sea Scrolls." In *The Book of Genesis in Jewish and Oriental Christian Interpretation: A Collection of Essays*. Edited by Judith Frishman and Lucas Van Rompay. TEG 5. Louvain: Peeters, 1997, 13–24.

Chester, Andrew. *Messiah and Exaltation: Jewish Messianic and Visionary Traditions and New Testament Christology*. WUNT 207. Tübingen: Mohr Siebeck, 2007.

———. "The Christ of Paul." In *Redemption and Resistance: The Messianic Hopes of Jews and Christians in Antiquity*. Edited by Markus N. A. Bockmuehl and James C. Paget. London/New York: T & T Clark, 2007, 109–21.

Childs, Brevard S. *Biblical Theology in Crisis*. Philadelphia: Westminster, 1970.

———. *Old Testament Theology in a Canonical Context*. London: SCM, 1985.

———. *Biblical Theology of the Old and New Testaments: Theological Reflection on the Christian Bible*. London: SCM, 1992.

Chilton, Bruce. "The Son of Man: Human and Heavenly." In *The Four Gospels 1992: Festschrift Frans Neirynck*. Edited by Frans Van Segbroeck, et al. 3 vols. Leuven: Peeters, 1992, 203–18.

———. *The Temple of Jesus: His Sacrificial Program within a Cultural History of Sacrifice*. University Park, PA: Pennsylvania State University, 1992.

———. "The Son of Man: Who Was He?" *Biblical Research* 12 (1996): 35–39, 45–47.

———, ed., *The Kingdom of God in the Teaching of Jesus*. Philadelphia: Fortress Press, 1984.

Clines, David J. A. *What Does Eve Do to Help? And Other Readerly Questions to the Old Testament*. JSOTSup 94. Sheffield: JSOT Press, 1990.

———. *Interested Parties: The Ideology of Writers and Readers of the Hebrew Bible*. JSOTSup 205. Sheffield: Sheffield Academic Press, 1995.

———. *The Bible and the Modern World*. Bible Seminar 51. Sheffield: Sheffield Academic Press, 1997.

Cohn-Sherbok, Dan. *The Jewish Messiah*. Edinburgh: T & T Clark, 1997.

Collins, Adela Yarbro. "The Origins of the Designation of Jesus as 'Son of Man.'" *Harvard Theological Review* 80 (1987): 397–98.

———. "The Historical-Critical and Feminist Readings of Genesis 1:26-28." In *Hebrew Bible or Old Testament? Studying the Bible in Judaism and Christianity*. Edited by Roger Brooks and John J. Collins. CJA 5. Notre Dame, IN: University of Notre Dame Press, 1990, 221–32.

———. "Apocalyptic Son of Man Sayings." In *The Future of Early Christianity*. Edited by Birger A. Pearson. Minneapolis: Fortress Press, 1991, 220–28.

———. *Mark: A Commentary*. Hermeneia. Minneapolis: Fortress Press, 2007.

——— and John J. Collins. *King and Messiah as Son of God: Divine, Human, and Angelic Messianic Figures in Biblical and Related Literature*. Grand Rapids: Eerdmans, 2008.

Collins, John J. "Introduction: Towards the Morphology of a Genre." In *Apocalypse: The Morphology of a Genre*. Edited by John J. Collins. *Semeia* 14. Missoula: Scholars Press, 1979, 1–20.

———. "The Heavenly Representative: The 'Son of Man' in the Similitudes of Enoch." In *Ideal Figures in Ancient Judaism: Profiles and Paradigms*. Edited by John J. Collins and George W. E. Nickelsburg. Chico, CA: Scholars Press, 1980, 111–33.

———. "The Kingdom of God in the Apocrypha and Pseudepigrapha." In *The Kingdom of God in 20th-Century Interpretation*. Edited by Wendell Lee Willis. Peabody, MA: Hendrickson, 1987, 81–95.

———. "The Son of Man in First-Century Judaism." *New Testament Studies* 38 (1992): 448–66.

———. *Daniel: A Commentary on the Book of Daniel*. Hermeneia. Minneapolis: Fortress Press, 1993.

———. "The *Son of God* Text from Qumran." In *From Jesus to John: Essays on Jesus and New Testament Christology*. Edited by Martinus C. De Boer. Sheffield: JSOT Press, 1993, 65–82.

———. "The Works of the Messiah." *Dead Sea Discoveries* 1 (1994): 98–112.

———. *The Scepter and the Star: The Messiahs of the Dead Sea Scrolls and Other Ancient Literature*. New York: Doubleday, 1995.

———. "The Second Coming." *Chicago Studies* 34 (1995): 262–74.

———. "The Origin of Evil in Apocalyptic Literature and the Dead Sea Scrolls." In *Seers, Sibyls and Sages in Hellenistic-Roman Judaism*. JSJSup 54. Leiden: Brill, 1997, 287–99.

———. "Creation and the Origin of Evil." In John J. Collins, *Apocalypticism in the Dead Sea Scrolls*. London: Routledge, 1997, 30–51.

———. *The Apocalyptic Imagination: An Introduction to Jewish Apocalyptic Literature*. Biblical Resource. Grand Rapids: Eerdmans, 1998.

———. "In the Likeness of the Holy Ones: The Creation of Humankind in a Wisdom Text from Qumran." In *The Provo International Conference on the Dead Sea Scrolls: Technological Innovations, New Texts, and Reformulated Issues*. Edited by Donald W. Parry and Eugene Ulrich. STDJ 30. Leiden: Brill, 1999, 609–18.

———. "The Zeal of Phineas: The Bible and the Legitimiation of Violence." *Journal of Biblical Literature* 122 (2003): 3–21.

———. *Does the Bible Justify Violence?* Facets. Minneapolis: Fortress Press, 2004.

———. "Response: The Apocalyptic Worldview of Daniel." In *Enoch and Qumran Origins*. Edited by Gabriele Boccaccini. Grand Rapids: Eerdmans, 2005, 59–66.

Colpe, Carsten. *Die religionsgeschichtliche Schule: Darstellung und Kritik ihres Bildes vom gnostischen Erlösermythus*. Göttingen: Vandenhoeck & Ruprecht, 1961.

———. "ὁ υἱὸς τοῦ ἀνθρώπου." *Theological Dictionary of the New Testament* 8 (1972): 400–77.

Conrad, Edgar W. *Fear Not Warrior: A Study of the 'al tira' Pericopes in the Hebrew Scriptures*. BJS 74. Chico, CA: Scholars Press, 1985.

Conzelmann, Hans. "Jesus Christus." *Religion in Geschichte und Gegenwart*. 3d ed. 7 vols. Vol. 3 (1959) edited by K. Galling. Tübingen: Mohr, 1959, 619–53. See now Conzelmann, *Jesus: The Classic Article from RBB Expanded and Updated*. Translated by J. Raymond Lord. Edited by John Reumann. Philadelphia: Fortress Press, 1973.

———. *The Theology of St. Luke*. Translated by Geoffrey Buswell. New York: Harper, 1960.

———."Present and Future in the Synoptic Tradition." In *God and Christ: Existence and Province*. Edited by Robert T. Funk. *Journal for Theology and the Church* 5. New York: Harper & Row, 1968, 26–44.

Cooney, Robert, and Helen Michalowski. *Power of the People: Active Nonviolence in the United States*. Philadelphia: New Society Press, 1987.

Copan, Paul. *Is God a Moral Monster?: Making Sense of the Old Testament God*. Grand Rapids: Baker Books, 2011.

Cortés, Juan B., and Florence M. Gotti. "The Son of Man or The Son of Adam." *Biblica* 49 (1968): 457–502.

Cotter, Wendy. "'Yes, I Tell You, and More Than a Prophet,': The Function of John in Q." In *Conflict and Invention: Literary, Rhetorical, and Social Studies on the Sayings Gospel Q*. Edited by John S. Kloppenborg. Valley Forge, PA: Trinity Press International, 1995, 135–50.

Cowles, C. S. "The Case for Radical Discontinuity." In C. S. Cowles, Eugene H. Merrill, Daniel L. Gard, and Tremper Longman III, *Show Them No Mercy: 4 Views on God and Canaanite Genocide*. Counterpoints, ed. Stanley N. Gundry. Grand Rapids: Eerdmans, 2003, 13–44.

Craig, William Lane and Joseph E. Gorra. *A Reasonable Response: Answers to Tough Questions on God, Christianity, and the Bible*. Chicago: Moody Publishers, 2013.

Crawford, Barry S. "*Christos* as Nickname." In *Redescribing Christian Origins* (2004), 337–48.

Creach, Jerome F. D. *Violence in Scripture*. Interpretation: Resources for the Use of Scripture in the Church. Louisville: Westminster John Knox Press, 2013.

Creed, J. M. "The Heavenly Man." *Journal of Theological Studies* 26 (1925): 113–26.

Croatto, J. Severino. *Biblical Hermeneutics: Toward a Theory of Reading as the Production of Meaning*. Maryknoll, NY: Orbis Books, 1987.

Cromhout, Markus. *Jesus and Identity: Reconstructing Judean Ethnicity in Q*. Matrix: The Bible in Mediterranean Context. Eugene, OR: Cascade, 2007.

Crook, Zeba A. "Collective Memory Distortion and the Quest for the Historical Jesus." *Journal for the Study of the Historical Jesus* 11 (2013): 53-76.

Cross, Frank Moore. *The Ancient Library of Qumran*. 3d ed. Minneapolis: Fortress Press, 1995.

Crossan, John Dominic. *In Parables: The Challenge of the Historical Jesus*. New York: Harper & Row, 1973.

———. *In Fragments: The Aphorisms of Jesus*. San Francisco: Harper & Row, 1983.

———. *The Historical Jesus: The Life of a Mediterranean Jewish Peasant*. San Francisco: Harper & Row, 1991.

———. *Jesus: A Revolutionary Biography*. San Francisco: HarperSanFrancisco, 1994.

———. *The Birth of Christianity: Discovering What Happened in the Years Immediately After the Execution of Jesus*. San Francisco: HarperSanFrancisco, 1998.

———. "Eschatology, Apocalypticism, and the Historical Jesus." In *Jesus Then and Now: Images of Jesus in History and Christology*. Edited by Marvin W. Meyer and Charles Hughes. Harrisburg, PA: Trinity Press International, 2001, 91–112.

———. *The Essential Jesus: Original Sayings and Earliest Images*. Eugene, OR: Wipf & Stock, 2008.

———. "Context and Text in Historical Jesus Methodology." In *Handbook for the Study of the Historical Jesus* (2011), 159–81.

———, and Jonathan L. Reed. *Excavating Jesus: Beneath the Stones, Behind the Texts*. New York: HarperSanFrancisco, 2001.

Crossley, James G. *The Date of Mark's Gospel: Insights from the Law in Earliest Christianity*. London and New York: T & T Clark/Continuum, 2004.

———. "Writing about the Historical Jesus: Historical Explanations and 'the Big Why Questions,' or Antiquarian Empiricism and Victorian Tomes." *Journal for the Study of the Historical Jesus* 7 (2009): 63–90.

———. "Mark, Paul and the Question of Influences." In *Paul and the Gospels: Christologies, Conflicts, and Convergences*. Edited by Michael F. Bird. LNTS 411. London: T & T Clark, 2011, 10–29.

Culler, Jonathan D. *On Deconstruction: Theory and Criticism after Structuralism*. London: Routledge, 1983.

Cullmann, Oscar. *Christus und die Zeit: Die urchristliche Zeit-und Geschichtsauffassung*. Zollikon-Zürich: Evangelischer Verlag, 1946. English: *Christ and Time: The Primitive Christian Conception of Time and History*. Translated by Floyd V. Filson. Rev. ed. Philadelphia: Westminster, 1964.

———. *The Christology of the New Testament*. London: SCM, 1963.

———. *Jesus and the Revolutionaries*. New York: Harper & Row, 1970.

Cummins, Stephen A. "Divine Life and Corporate Christology: God, Messiah Jesus, and the Covenant Community in Paul." In *The Messiah in the Old and*

New Testaments. Edited by Stanley E. Porter. Grand Rapids: Eerdmans, 2007, 190–209.

Curtis, Edward Mason. "Man as the Image of God in Genesis in the Light of Ancient Near Eastern Parallels." PhD diss., University of Pennsylvania, 1984.

Dahl, Nils A. "Die Messianität Jesus bei Paulus." In *Studia Paulina in honorem Johannis de Zwaan septuagnarii*. Haarlem: Bohn, 1953, 83–95.

———. "The Messiahship of Jesus in Paul." In idem, *The Crucified Messiah: and Other Essays*. Minneapolis: Augsburg, 1974, 37–47.

———. *Jesus the Christ: The Historical Origins of Christological Doctrine*. Minneapolis: Fortress Press, 1991.

———. "Messianic Ideas and the Crucifixion of Jesus." In *The Messiah: Developments in Earliest Judaism and Christianity* (1992), 382–403.

Daly, Robert J. "The New Testament and Early Church." In *Non-Violence, Central to Christian Spirituality: Perspectives from Scripture to the Present*. Edited by Joseph T. Culliton. TST 8. New York: Edwin Mellen, 1982, 34–62.

Dautzenberg, Gerhard. *Sein Leben Bewahren: ψυχή in den Herrenworten der Evangelien*. SANT 14. Munich: Kösel, 1966.

Davidson, Andrew B. *The Theology of the Old Testament*. Edited by Stewart D. F. Salmond. Edinburgh: T & T Clark, 1904.

Davidson, Maxwell J. *Angels at Qumran: A Comparative Study of 1 Enoch 1-36, 72-108 and Sectarian Writings from Qumran*. JSPSup 11. Sheffield: JSOT Press, 1992.

Davies, Eryl W. *The Dissenting Reader: Feminist Approaches to the Hebrew Bible*. Aldershot: Ashgate, 2003.

———. "The Morally Dubious Passages of the Hebrew Bible: An Examination of Some Proposed Solutions." *Currents in Biblical Research* 3, no. 2 (2005): 196–228.

———. *The Immoral Bible: Approaches to Biblical Ethics*. New York: T & T Clark, 2010.

Davies, W. D. *Paul and Rabbinic Judaism: Some Rabbinic Elements in Pauline Theology*. London: SPCK, 1948.

———, and Dale C. Allison Jr. *The Gospel according to Saint Matthew*. 3 vols. ICC. Edinburgh: T & T Clark, 1988–1997.

Dawkins, Richard. *The God Delusion*. New York: Bantam Press, 2006.

Day, John, ed. *King and Messiah in Israel and the Ancient Near East*. JSOTSup 270. Sheffield: Sheffield Academic Press, 1998.

Dehandschutter, Boudewijn. "Pseudo-Cyprian, Jude and Enoch: Some Notes on 1 Enoch 1:9." In *Tradition and Re-Interpretation in Jewish and Early Christian Literature: Essays in Honour of Jürgen C. H. Lebram*. Edited by Jan W. van Henten, et al. SPB 36. Leiden: Brill, 1986, 114–20.

De Boer, Esther A. *The Gospel of Mary: Beyond a Gnostic and a Biblical Mary Magdalene*. London: Continuum, 2004.

———. *The Gospel of Mary: Listening to the Beloved Disciple*. London: Continuum, 2006.

De Heusch, Luc. *Sacrifice in Africa: A Structuralist Approach*. Translated by Linda O'Brien and Alice Morton. Bloomington: Indiana University Press, 1985.

De Jonge, H. J. "The Historical Jesus' View of Himself and of His Mission." In *From Jesus to John: Essays on Jesus and New Testament Christology in Honour of Marinus de Jonge*. Edited by Martinus C. de Boer. Sheffield: JSOT Press, 1993, 21–37.

De Jonge, Marinus. "The Use of the Word 'Anointed' in the Time of Jesus." *Novum Testamentum* 8 (1966): 132–48.

———. "The Earliest Christian Use of *Christos*: Some Suggestions." *New Testament Studies* 32 (1986): 321–43.

———. *Christology in Context: The Earliest Christian Response to Jesus*. Philadelphia: Westminster, 1988.

———. *Jesus the Servant Messiah*. New Haven: Yale University Press, 1991.

———. *God's Final Envoy: Early Christology and Jesus' Own View of His Mission*. SHJ. Grand Rapids: Eerdmans, 1998.

De Pisón, Ramon Martínez. *From Violence to Peace: Dismantling the Manipulation of Religion*. CES 1. Leuven: Peeters, 2013.

De Villiers, Pieter G. R. and Jan Willem, eds. *Coping with Violence in the New Testament*. STR 16. Leiden: Brill, 2012.

Dear, John. *The God of Peace: Toward a Theology of Nonviolence*. Maryknoll, NY: Orbis Books, 1994.

———. *Put Down Your Sword: Answering the Gospel Call to Creative Nonviolence*. Grand Rapids: Eerdmans, 2008.

Deasley, Alex R. G. *The Shape of Qumran Theology*. Carlisle, Cumbria: Paternoster, 2000.

Deissmann, Adolf. *Die neutestamentliche Formel "In Christo Jesu" untersucht*. Marburg: Elwert, 1892.

Delitzsch, Franz. *Biblical Commentary on the Prophecies of Isaiah*. Translated by James Martin. 2 vols. Grand Rapids: Eerdmans, 1950.

Desjardins, Michel. *Peace, Violence and the New Testament.* Sheffield: Sheffield Academic Press, 1997.

Detweiler, Robert, ed. *Reader Response Approaches to Biblical and Secular Texts.* Semeia 31. Decatur, GA: Scholars Press, 1985.

De Vaux, Roland. *Ancient Israel.* 2 vols. New York: McGraw-Hill, 1965.

Dibelius, Martin. *Die urchristliche Überlieferung von Johannes dem Täufer.* FRLANT 15. Göttingen: Vandenhoeck & Ruprecht, 1911.

———. *From Tradition to Gospel.* New York: Scribners, 1935.

Dillmann, August. *Liber Henoch Aethiopice, ad quinque codicum fidem editus, cum variis lectionibus.* Leipzig: Vogel, 1851.

———. *Das Buch Henoch übersetzt und erklärt.* Leipzig: Vogel, 1853.

Dillon, Richard J. "Ravens, Lilies, and the Kingdom of God (Matthew 6:25-33/ Luke 12:22-31)." *Catholic Biblical Quarterly* 53 (1991): 605–27.

Dimant, Devorah. "Qumran Sectarian Literature." In *Jewish Writings of the Second Temple Period.* Edited by Michael E. Stone. Assen: Van Gorcum, 1984, 483–550.

———. "4QFlorilegium and the Idea of Community as Temple." In *Hellenica et Judaica: Hommage à Valentin Nikiprowetzky.* Edited by André Caquot, et al. Leuven: Peeters, 1986, 165–89.

Dinkler, Erich. "Peter's Confession and the Satan Saying: The Problem of Jesus' Messiahship." In *The Future of Our Religious Past: Essays in Honour of Rudolf Bultmann.* Edited by James M. Robinson. New York: Harper & Row, 1971, 169–202.

Dodd, C. H. "The Eschatological Element in the New Testament and Its Permanent Significance." *The Interpreter* 20 (1923): 17–21.

———. "The Theology of Christian Pacifism." In *The Bases of Christian Pacifism.* Edited by Charles E. Raven. London: Council of Christian Pacifist Groups, 1938, 5–15.

———. *The Parables of the Kingdom.* Rev. ed. London: Nisbet, 1961.

———. *The Founder of Christianity.* London: Collins, 1971.

———. *The Authority of the Bible.* Rev. ed. London: Nisbet, 1983.

——— and Gerhard Kittel. "The This-Worldly Kingdom of God in Our Lord's Teaching." *Theology* 14 (1927): 258–62.

Donahue, John R. "A Neglected Factor in the Theology of Mark." *Journal of Biblical Literature* 101 (1982): 563–94.

Donfried, Karl. *The Setting of Second Clement in Early Christianity.* Leiden: Brill, 1974.

Douglas, R. Conrad. "'Love Your Enemies': Rhetoric, Tradents, and Ethos." In *Conflict and Invention* (1995), 116–31.

Duguid, Iain M. *Is Jesus in the Old Testament? Basics of the Faith*. Philipsburg: P & R Publishing, 2013.

Duhaime, Jean. "War Scroll." In *The Dead Sea Scrolls: Hebrew, Aramaic, and Greek Texts with English Translations*. Vol. 2: *Damascus Document, War Scroll, and Related Documents*. Edited by James H. Charlesworth. PTSDSSP 2. Tübingen: Mohr Siebeck, 1995, 80–203.

Dumouchel, Paul, ed. *Violence and Truth: On the Work of René Girard*. Stanford, CA: Stanford University Press, 1988.

Dungan, David. "The Purpose and Provenance of the Gospel of Mark According to the 'Two-Gospel' (Griesbach) Hypothesis." In *Colloquy on New Testament Studies*. Edited by Bruce Corley. Macon: Mercer University Press, 1983, 133–56.

Dunn, James D. G. "The Messianic Secret in Mark." *Tyndale Bulletin* 21 (1970): 92–117.

———. *Unity and Diversity in the New Testament: An Inquiry into the Character of Earliest Christianity*. Philadelphia: Westminster, 1977.

———. *Christology in the Making: An Inquiry into the Origins of the Doctrine of the Incarnation*. London: SCM, 1980.

———. "The Messianic Secret in Mark," In Christopher M. Tuckett, ed., *The Messianic Secret*. IRT 1. Minneapolis: Fortress Press, 1983, 116–31.

———. *Christology in the Making: An Inquiry into the Origins of the Doctrine of the Incarnation*. 2d ed. Grand Rapids: Eerdmans, 1989.

———. "Messianic Ideas and Their Influence on the Jesus of History." In *The Messiah: Developments in Earliest Judaism and Christianity* (1992), 365–81.

———. *The Theology of Paul the Apostle*. Grand Rapids: Eerdmans, 1998.

———. *Jesus Remembered*. Grand Rapids: Eerdmans, 2003.

———. Review of *Redescribing Christian Origins*, *Journal of Biblical Literature* 124, no. 4 (2005): 760–64.

———. *A New Perspective on Jesus: What the Quest for the Historical Jesus Missed*. Grand Rapids: Baker Academic, 2005.

———. *Did the First Christians Worship Jesus? The New Testament Evidence*. Louisville: Westminster John Knox, 2010.

———. "Remembering Jesus: How the Quest of the Historical Jesus Lost Its Way." In *Handbook for the Study of the Historical Jesus* (2011), 183–205.

Dupont, Georges. *Le Fils de l'Homme: essai historique et critique*. Paris: Fischbacher, 1924.

Dupont, Jacques. "L'après-mort dans l'oeuvre de Luc." *Revue théologique de Louvain* 3 (1972): 3–21.

———. *Les Béatitudes*. Vol. 3. *Les Évangélistes*. EtBib. Paris: Gabalda, 1973.

Earl, Douglas S. *The Joshua Delusion: Rethinking Genocide in the Bible*. Eugene, OR: Cascade/Wipf & Stock, 2010.

Eco, Umberto. *The Role of the Reader: Explorations in the Semiotics of Texts*. London: Hutchinson, 1981.

Edwards, Richard A. "The Eschatological Correlative as a *Gattung* in the New Testament." *Zeitschrift für die neutestamentliche Wissenschaft und die Kunde der älteren Kirche* 60 (1969): 9–20.

———. "The Eschatological Correlative." In *The Sign of Jonah in the Theology of the Evangelists and Q*. SBT 2, no. 18. London, 1971, 47–58.

———. *A Theology of Q*. Philadelphia: Fortress Press, 1976.

Ego, Beato. "Vergangenheit im Horizont eschatologischer Hoffnung: Die Tiervision (1 Hen 85-90) als Beispiel apolkalyptischer Geschichtskonzeption." In *Die antike Historiographie und die Anfänge der christlichen Geschichtsschreibung*. Edited by Eve-Marie Becker. Berlin: Walter de Gruyter, 2005, 171-195.

Ehrman, Bart D. *Jesus: Apocalyptic Prophet of the New Millennium*. New York: Oxford University Press, 1999.

______. *Jesus, Interrupted: Revealing the Hidden Contradictions in the Bible (And Why We Don't Know About Them*. New York: HarperOne, 2010.

Eichrodt, Walther. *Theology of the Old Testament*. Translated by J. A. Baker. 2 vols. London: SCM, 1961, 1967.

Eisenman, Robert. "A Messianic Vision." *Biblical Archaeology Review* 17, no. 6 (1991): 65.

———, and Michael O. Wise. *The Dead Sea Scrolls Uncovered*. Shaftesbury: Element, 1992.

Eisler, Robert. ΙΗΣΟΥΣ ΒΑΣΙΛΕΥΣ ΟΥ ΒΑΣΙΛΕΥΣΑΣ*: Die messianische Unabhängigkeitsbewegung vom Auftreten Johannes des Täufers bis zum Untergang Jakobs des Gerechten nach der Neuerschlossenen Eroberung von Jerusalem des Flavius Josephus und den Christlichen Quellen*. 2 vols. Heidelberg: Carl Winters Universitätsbuchhandlung, 1929, 1930.

———. *The Messiah Jesus and John the Baptist*. Translated by Alexander Haggerty Krappe. London: Methuen, 1931.

Elgvin, Torleif. "The Mystery to Come: Early Essene Theology of Revelation." In *Qumran Between the Old and New Testaments*. Edited by Frederick H.

Cryer and Thomas L. Thompson. Sheffield: Sheffield Academic Press, 1998, 113–50.

Ellens, J. Harold, ed. *The Destructive Power of Religion: Violence in Judaism, Christianity and Islam*. 4 vols. Westport, CT: Praeger, 2004.

Eller, Vernard. *War and Peace from Genesis to Revelation*. Scottdale, PA: Herald Press, 1981.

Elliott, John H. *I–II Peter/Jude*. Augsburg Commentary on the New Testament. Minneapolis: Augsburg, 1982.

Elliott, Mark Adam. *The Survivors of Israel: A Reconsideration of the Theology of Pre-Christian Judaism*. Grand Rapids: Eerdmans, 2000.

Ellis, E. Earle. *Paul's Use of the Old Testament*. Grand Rapids: Baker, 1991.

Emerson, Ralph Waldo. *The American Scholar. Self Reliance. Compensation*. New York: American Book Company, 1893.

Emilsen, William W. "Gandhi, Scripture and Non-violence." In *Validating Violence—Violating Faith? Religion, Scripture, and Violence*. Edited by William W. Emilsen and John T. Squires. PACT series. Adelaide: ATF Press, 2008, 127–42.

Enslin, Morton Scott. *Christian Beginnings*. New York: Harper & Brothers, 1938.

Enz, Jacob J. *The Christian and Warfare: The Roots of Pacifism in the Old Testament*. Scottdale, PA: Herald Press, 1972.

Erasmus, Desiderius. *Novum testamentum, cui in hac editione, subjectae sunt singulis paginis adnotationes*. Vol. 6. *Opera omnia*. Lugdini-Batavorum: Vander, 1705.

Ernst, Josef. *Johannes der Täufer: Interpretation—Geschichte—Wirkungsgeschichte*. BZNW 53. Berlin: de Gruyter, 1989.

Evans, Craig A. "Authenticity Criteria in Life of Jesus Research." *Christian Scholar's Review* 19 (1989): 6–31.

———. "Jesus and the Spirit: On the Origin and Ministry of the Second Son of God," in idem and James A. Sanders, *Luke and Scripture: The Function of Sacred Tradition in Luke-Acts*. Minneapolis: Fortress Press, 1993, 26–45.

———. *Jesus and His Contemporaries: Comparative Studies*. AGAJU 25. Leiden: Brill, 1995.

———. "Authenticating the Activities of Jesus." In *Authenticating the Activities of Jesus*. Edited by Bruce D. Chilton and Craig A. Evans. NTTS 28, no. 2. Leiden: Brill, 1999, 3–29.

———. "Qumran's Messiah: How Important Is He?" In *Religion in the Dead Sea Scrolls*. Edited by John J. Collins and Robert A. Kugler. Grand Rapids: Eerdmans, 2000, 135–49.

———. *Mark 8:27—16:20*. WBC. Nashville: Thomas Nelson, 2001.
———. "Jesus' Dissimilarity from Second Temple Judaism and the Early Church." In *Memories of Jesus: A Critical Appraisal of James D. G. Dunn's Jesus Remembered*. Edited by Robert B. Stewart and Gary R. Habermas. Nashville: B & H Academic, 2010, 145–58.
——— and James A. Sanders. *Luke and Scripture: The Function of Sacred Tradition in Luke-Acts*. Minneapolis: Fortress Press, 1993.
Evans, C. F. *Saint Luke*. London, 1990.
Farrer, Austin. "On Dispensing with Q." In *Studies in the Gospels: Essays in Memory of R. H. Lightfoot*. Edited by Dennis E. Nineham. Oxford: Blackwell, 1955, 55–88.
Felson, Richard B., and James T. Tedeschi, eds. *Aggression and Violence: Social Interactionist Perspectives*. Washington, DC: American Psychological Association, 1993.
Ferguson, Sinclair B. "The Reformed Doctrine of Sonship." In *Pulpit and People: Essays in Honour of William Still on his 75th Birthday*. Edited by Nigel M. de S. Cameron and Sinclair B. Ferguson. Edinburgh: Rutherford House, 1986, 81–88.
Fetterley, Judith. *The Resisting Reader: A Feminist Approach to American Fiction*. Bloomington and London: Indiana University Press, 1978.
Fiebig, Paul. *Der Menschensohn: Jesu Selbstbezeichnung mit besonderer Berücksichtigung des aramäischen Sprachgebrauches für 'Mensch.'* Tübingen: Mohr Siebeck, 1901.
Finney, Paul C. "The Rabbi and the Coin Portrait (Mark 12:15b, 16): Rigorism Manqué." *Journal of Biblical Literature* 112 (1993): 629–44.
Firestone, Reuven. *Holy War in Judaism: The Fall and Rise of a Controversial Idea*. New York: Oxford University Press, 2012.
Fish, Stanley E. *Is There a Text in This Class? The Authority of Interpretive Communities*. Cambridge: Harvard University Press, 1980.
Fitzgerald, F. Scott. "The Crack-Up." *Esquire* (2/3/4/1936).
Fitzmyer, Joseph A. "The Oxyrhynchus Logoi of Jesus and the Coptic Gospel According to Thomas." *Theological Studies* 20, no. 4 (1959): 505–60.
———. "The Use of Explicit Old Testament Quotations in Qumran Literature and in the New Testament." *New Testament Studies* 7 (1961): 297–333.
———. "Further Light on Melchizedek from Qumran Cave 11." *Journal of Biblical Literature* 86 (1967): 25–41.
———. "The Priority of Mark and the 'Q' Source in Luke." In *Jesus and Man's Hope*. Pittsburgh: Pittsburgh Theological Seminary, 1970, 131–70.

———. *Essays on the Semitic Background of the New Testament*. London: Chapman, 1971.
———. *The Gospel according to Luke: Introduction, Translation, and Notes*. 2 vols. Anchor Bible 28, 28A. New York: Doubleday, 1983–1985.
———. *The Semitic Background of the New Testament* (combined edition of *Essays on the Semitic Background of the New Testament* and *A Wandering Aramean: Collected Aramaic Essays*). Grand Rapids: Eerdmans, 1997.
———. "The Dead Sea Scrolls and Christian Origins: General Methodological Considerations." In *The Dead Sea Scrolls and Christian Faith: In Celebration of the Jubilee Year of the Discovery of Qumran Cave 1*. Edited by James H. Charlesworth and Walter P. Weaver. Harrisburg, PA: Trinity Press International, 1998, 1–19.
———. *The Dead Sea Scrolls and Christian Origins*. Grand Rapids: Eerdmans, 2000.
———. *The One Who Is To Come*. Grand Rapids: Eerdmans, 2007.
Fleddermann, Harry T. *Q: A Reconstruction and Commentary*. BTS 1. Leuven: Peeters, 2005.
Fletcher-Louis, Crispin H. T. *Luke-Acts: Angels, Christology and Soteriology*. WUNT 2d ser. 94. Tübingen: Mohr Siebeck, 1997.
———. *All the Glory of Adam: Liturgical Anthropology in the Dead Sea Scrolls*. STDJ 42. Leiden: Brill, 2002.
———. "Jewish Apocalyptic and Apocalypticism." In *Handbook for the Study of the Historical Jesus* (2011), 1569–1607.
———. "Jesus and Apocalypticism." In *Handbook for the Study of the Historical Jesus* (2011), 2877–2909.
Flusser, David. "Melchizedek and the Son of Man." *Christian News from Israel* 17 (1966): 23–29.
———. *The Spiritual History of the Dead Sea Sect*. Translated by Carol Glucker. Tel Aviv: MOD, 1989.
Fosdick, Harry Emerson. *A Guide to Understanding the Bible: The Development of Ideas within the Old and New Testaments*. London: Harper & Brothers, 1938.
Fossum, Jarl. "Gen. 1, 26 and 2,7 in Judaism, Samaritanism, and Gnosticism." *Journal for the Study of Judaism* 16 (1985): 203–39.
Foster, Paul. "The Pastoral Purpose of Q's Two-Stage Son of Man Christology." *Biblica* 89 (2008): 81–91.
———. "Memory, Orality, and the Fourth Gospel: Three Dead-Ends in Historical Jesus Research." *Journal for the Study of the Historical Jesus* 10, no. 3 (2012): 191–227.

France, R. T. *Jesus and the Old Testament: His Application of Old Testament Passages to Himself*. Downers Grove: InterVarsity, 1971.

———. *The Gospel of Mark: A Commentary on the Greek Text*. Grand Rapids: Eerdmans, 2002.

Frankemölle, Hubert. "Jesus als deuterojesajanische Freudenbote? Zur Rezeption von Jes 52,7 und 61,1 im Neuen Testament, durch Jesus und in den Targumim." In *Vom Christentum zu Jesus. Festschrift für Joachim Gnilka*. Edited by Hubert Frankemölle and Karl Kertelge. Freiburg: Herder, 1989, 34–67.

Fredriksen, Paula. *From Jesus to Christ: The Origins of the New Testament Images of Christ*. New Haven: Yale University Press, 1988.

———. *Jesus of Nazareth, King of the Jews*. New York: Alfred A. Knopf, 1999.

Frenschkowski, Marco. "Welche biographischen Kenntnisse von Jesus setzt die Logienquelle voraus? Beobachtungen zur Gattung von Q im Kontext antiker Spruchsammlungen." In *From Quest to Q: Festschrift James M. Robinson*. Edited by Jon Ma Asgeirsson, Kristin De Troyer, and Marvin W. Meyer. BETL 146. Leuven: Peeters, 2000, 535–59.

Fretheim, Terence E. "Theological Reflections on the Wrath of God in the Old Testament." *Horizons in Biblical Theology* 24 (2002): 1–26.

———. "God and Violence in the Old Testament." *Word and World* 24 (2004): 18–28.

———. "'I Was Only a Little Angry': Divine Violence in the Prophets." *Interpretation* 58 (2004): 365–75.

——— and Karlfried Froehlich. *The Bible as Word of God: In a Postmodern Age*. Minneapolis: Fortress Press, 1998.

Frey, Jörg. "Die Apokalyptik als Herausforderung der neutestamentlichen Wissenschaft. Zum Problem: Jesus und die Apokalyptik." In *Apokalyptik als Herausforderung neutestamentlicher Theologie*. Edited by Michael Becker and Markus Öhler. WUNT 2d ser. 214. Tübingen: Mohr Siebeck, 2006, 23–94.

Fröhlich, Ida. *'Time and Times and Half a Time': Historical Consciousness in the Jewish Literature of the Persian and Hellenistic Eras*. JSPSup 19. Sheffield: Sheffield Academic Press, 1996.

———. "The Parables of Enoch and Qumran Literature." In *Enoch and the Messiah Son of Man* (2007), 343–51.

Fuller, Reginald H. *The Mission and Achievement of Jesus*. SBT 12. London: SCM, 1954.

———. *The Foundations of New Testament Christology*. New York: Scribners, 1965.

———. "The Criterion of Dissimilarity: The Wrong Tool?" In *Christological Perspectives*. Edited by Robert F. Berkey and Sarah A. Edwards. New York: Pilgrim, 1982, 42–48.

———. "The Son of Man: A Reconsideration." In *The Living Text: Essays in Honor of Ernest W. Saunders*. Edited by Dennis Groh and Robert Jewett. Lanham, MD: University Press of America, 1985, 207–17.

Funk, Robert. *Honest to Jesus: Jesus for a New Millennium*. New York: HarperSanFrancisco, 1996.

———, Roy W. Hoover, and The Jesus Seminar. *The Five Gospels: The Search for the Authentic Words of Jesus*. New York: Maxwell Macmillan International, 1993.

Furnish, Victor P. "War and Peace in the New Testament." *Interpretation* 38 (1984): 369–71.

Gabrielson, Jeremy. *Paul's Non-Violent Gospel: The Theological Politics of Peace in Paul's Life and Letters*. Eugene: Pickwick, 2013.

Gager, John C. *Kingdom and Community: The Social World of Early Christianity*. Englewood Cliffs, NJ: Prentice-Hall, 1975.

Galtrung, Johan. "Violence, Peace and Peace Research." *Journal of Peace Research* 6/3 (1969): 167-91.

———. "Cultural Violence." *Journal of Peace Research* 27/3 (1990): 291-305.

Gandhi, Mohandas K. "Render Unto Caesar," *Young India* (1930): 43.

———. *Nonviolent Resistance*. New York: Schocken, 1961.

García Martínez, Florentino. "Estudios Qumránicos 1975–1985: Panorama Critico (I)." *Estudios biblicos* 45 (1987): 125–206.

———. "Messianism, Resurrection and Eschatology at Qumran and in the New Testament." In *The Community of the Renewed Covenant: The Notre Dame Symposium on the Dead Sea Scrolls*. Edited by Eugene Ulrich and James C. VanderKam. Notre Dame, IN: University of Notre Dame Press, 1994, 235–56.

———. "Messianic Hopes in the Qumran Writings." In *The People of the Dead Sea Scrolls*. Edited by Florentino García Martínez and J. Trebolle Barrera. Leiden: Brill, 1995, 159–89.

Gard, Daniel L. "The Case for Eschatological Continuity." In *Show Them No Mercy* (2003), 111–44.

Gärtner, Bertil E. *The Temple and the Community in Qumran and the New Testament: A Comparative Study in the Temple Symbolism of the Qumran Texts and the New Testament*. SNTSMS 1. Cambridge: Cambridge University Press, 1965.

Gaster, Theodore H. *The Dead Sea Scriptures*. New York: Doubleday/Anchor Books, 1964.

Gathercole, Simon. "The Son of Man in Mark's Gospel." *Expository Times* 115, no. 11 (2004): 366–72.

Giblin, Charles Homer. "The 'Things of God' in the Question Concerning Tribute to Caesar (Lk 20:25; Mk 12:17; Mt 22:21)." *Catholic Biblical Quarterly* 33 (1971): 510–27.

Girard, René. *Things Hidden Since the Foundation of the World*. Stanford, CA: Stanford University Press, 1987.

———. *Violence and the Sacred*. Baltimore: Johns Hopkins University Press, 1977.

Glancy, Jennifer A. "Violence as Sign in the Fourth Gospel." *Biblical Interpretation* 17 (2009): 100-117.

Glasson, Thomas F. *The Second Advent: The Origin of the New Testament Doctrine*. London: Epworth, 1963.

Glock, Charles Y., and Rodney Stark. *Christian Belief and Anti-Semitism*. New York: Harper & Row, 1966.

Gnilka, Joachim. "Das Elend vor dem Menschensohn (Mk 2, 1-12)." In *Jesus und der Menschensohn: Für Anton Vögtle*. Edited by Rudolf Pesch and Rudolf Schnackenburg. Freiburg: Herder, 1975, 196–209.

———. *Das Matthäusevangelium 1. Teil: Kommentar zu Kap. 1,1–13,58*. HTKNT 1/1. Freiburg: Herder, 1986.

———. *Jesus von Nazareth. Botschaft und Geschichte*. HTKNTSup 3. Freiburg: Herder, 1990.

———. *Jesus of Nazareth: Message and History*. Translated by Siegfried S. Schatzmann. Peabody, MA: Hendrickson, 1997.

Goergen, Donald J. *The Mission and Ministry of Jesus*. Wilmington, DE: Michael Glazier, 1986.

Goldstein, Jonathan K. "How the Authors of 1 and 2 Maccabees Treated the 'Messianic' Promises." In *Judaisms and Their Messiahs at the Turn of the Christian Era* (1987), 69–96.

Goldstein, Morris. *Jesus in the Jewish Tradition*. New York: Macmillan, 1950.

Golitzin, Alexander. "Recovering the 'Glory of Adam': 'Divine Light' Traditions in the Dead Sea Scrolls and the Christian Ascetical Literature of Fourth-Century Syro-Mesopotamia." In *The Dead Sea Scrolls as Background to Postbiblical Judaism and Early Christianity: Papers from an International Conference at St. Andrews in 2001*. Edited by James R. Davila. STDJ 46. Leiden: Brill, 2003, 275–308.

Goodacre, Mark S. *Goulder and the Gospels: An Examination of a New Paradigm*. JSNTSup 133. Sheffield: Sheffield University Press, 1996.

———. "A Monopoly on Marcan Priority? Fallacies at the Heart of Q." In *Society of Biblical Literature Seminar Papers 2000*. Atlanta: Society of Biblical Literature, 2000, 538–622.

———. *The Case Against Q: Studies in Markan Priority and the Synoptic Problem*. Harrisburg, PA: Trinity Press International, 2002.

Gopin, Marc. *Holy War, Holy Peace: How Religion Can Bring Peace to the Middle East*. Oxford and New York: Oxford University Press, 2002.

Goppelt, Leonhard. "Zum Problem des Menschensohns: das Verhältnis von Leidens- und Parusieankündigung." In *Mensch und Menschensohn*. Edited by Hartmut Sierig. Hamburg: Wittig, 1963, 20–32.

———. *Theology of the New Testament*. Translated by John E. Alsup. 2 vols. Grand Rapids: Eerdmans, 1981–82.

Gordis, Robert. "The 'Begotten' Messiah in the Qumran Scrolls." *Vetus Testamentum* 7 (1957): 191–94.

Gorringe, Timothy. *God's Just Vengeance: Crime, Violence, and the Rhetoric of Salvation*. Cambridge: Cambridge University Press, 1996.

Goshen-Gottstein, Alon. "The Body as Image of God in Rabbinic Literature." *Harvard Theological Review* 87 (1994): 171–95.

Gottwald, Norman K. "'Holy War' in Deuteronomy: Analysis and Critique." *Review and Expositor* 61 (1964): 296–310.

Goulder, Michael D. "On Putting Q to the Test." *New Testament Studies* 24 (1978): 218–34.

———. "Those Outside (Mk 4:10-12)." *Novum Testamentum* 33 (1991): 289–302.

———. "Is Q a Juggernaut?' *Journal of Biblical Literature* 115 (1996): 667–81.

———. "Jesus' Resurrection and Christian Origins: A Response to N. T. Wright." *Journal for the Study of the Historical Jesus* 3 (2005): 187–95.

Grabbe, Lester L. *Priests, Prophets, Diviners, Sages: A Socio-Historical Study of Religious Specialists in Ancient Israel*. Valley Forge, PA: Trinity Press International, 1995.

———. "Warfare." In *The Encyclopedia of the Dead Sea Scrolls*. Edited by James C. VanderKam and Lawrence H. Schiffman. 2 vols. New York: Oxford University Press, 2000, 2: 963–65.

———. "Introduction and Overview." In *Knowing the End from the Beginning: The Prophetic, the Apocalyptic and their Relationships*. Edited by Lester L. Grabbe and Robert D. Haak. London: T & T Clark, 2003, 2–43.

Granberg-Michaelson, Wesley. *A Worldly Spirituality: The Call to Redeem Life on Earth*. San Francisco: Harper & Row, 1984.

Green, Joel B. *The Death of Jesus*. WUNT 2d ser. 33. Tübingen: Mohr Siebeck, 1988.

Greenfield, Jonas C. and Michael E. Stone. "The Enochic Pentateuch and the Date of the Similitudes." *Harvard Theological Review* 70 (1977): 51–65.

Greenstone, Julius H. *The Messiah Idea in Jewish History*. Philadelphia: Jewish Publication Society, 1906.

Greeven, Heinrich. "ζητέω." *Theological Dictionary of the New Testament*. 10 vols. Edited by Gerhard Kittel, Geoffrey W. Bromiley, and Gerhard Friedrich. Grand Rapids: Eerdmans, 1964–1976, 2: 892–96.

Gregg, Brian Han. "The Historical Jesus and the Final Judgment Sayings in Q." PhD diss., University of Notre Dame, 2005.

———. *The Historical Jesus and the Final Judgment Sayings in Q*. WUNT 2d ser. 207. Tübingen: Mohr Siebeck, 2006.

Grenfell, Bernard P., and Arthur S. Hunt, *New Sayings of Jesus and Fragment of a Lost Gospel from Oxyrhynchus*. London: Egyptian Exploration Fund, 1904.

Grimsrud, Ted. *Embodying the Way of Jesus: Anabaptist Convictions for the Twenty-First Century*. Eugene, OR: Wipf & Stock, 2007.

Gruenwald, Ithamar, Shaul Shaked, and Gedaliahu A. G. Stroumsa, eds. *Messiah and Christos: Studies in the Jewish Origins of Christianity, Presented to David Flusser on the Occasion of his Seventy-Fifth Birthday*. Tübingen: Mohr (Siebeck), 1992.

Grundmann, Walter. *Das Evangelium nach Matthäus*. THKNT 1. Berlin: Evangelische Verlangsanstalt, 1968.

———. "Weisheit im Horizont des Reiches Gottes. Eine Studie zur Verkündigung Jesu nach der Spruchüberlieferung Q." In *Die Kirche des Anfangs. Für Heinz Schürmann*. Edited by Rudolf Schnackenburg, Josef Ernst, and Joachim Wanke. Freiburg: Herder, 1978, 175–99.

Guelich, Robert A. *The Sermon on the Mount: A Foundation for Understanding*. Waco: Word, 1982.

———. "What Is the Gospel?" *Theology, News, and Notes* 51 (2004): 4–7.

Guignebert, Charles Alfred Honoré. *Jesus*. New York: Knopf, 1935.

Gundry, Robert H. *Matthew: A Commentary on his Literary and Theological Art*. Grand Rapids: Eerdmans, 1984.

———. *Mark: A Commentary on His Apology for the Cross*. Grand Rapids: Eerdmans, 1993.

———. "A Rejoinder to Joel F. Williams' 'Is Mark's Gospel an Apology for the Cross?'" *Bulletin for Biblical Research* 12 (2002): 123–40.

———. "Spinning the Lilies and Unraveling the Ravens: An Alternative Reading of Q 12:22b-31 and P. Oxy. 655." In *The Old is Better: New Testament Essays in Support of Traditional Interpretations*. WUNT 178. Tübingen: Mohr Siebeck, 2005, 149–70.

Gundry, Stan. "Introduction." In *Show Them No Mercy* (2003), 7–9.

Guthrie, Nancy. *The Son of David: Seeing Jesus in the Historical Books*. Wheaton: Crossway, 2013.

Gutiérrez, Gustavo. *A Theology of Liberation*. London: SCM, 1974.

Häfner, Gerd. "Das Ende der Kriterien? Jesusforschung angesichts der geschichtstheoretischen Diskussion." In *Historiographie und fiktionales Erählen: Zur Konstruktivität in Geschichtstheorie und Exegese*. BTS 86. Neukirchen-Vluyn: Neukirchener Verlag, 2007, 102–14.

Hagner, Donald A. *Matthew 1–13*. WBC 33A. Dallas: Word, 1993.

Hahn, Ferdinand. *The Titles of Jesus in Christology*. London: Lutterworth, 1969.

———. *Christologische Hoheitstitel: Ihre Geschichte im frühen Christentum*. 5th ed. Göttingen: Vandenhoeck & Ruprecht, 1995.

Hamerton-Kelly, Robert G. *Pre-Existence, Wisdom and the Son of Man*. SNTSMS 21. Cambridge: Cambridge University Press, 1973.

———. *God the Father: Theology and Patriarchy in the Teaching of Jesus*. Philadelphia: Fortress Press, 1979.

———. *Sacred Violence: Paul's Hermeneutic of the Cross*. Minneapolis: Fortress Press, 1992.

———. "Sacred Violence and the Messiah: The Markan Passion Narrative as a Redefinition of Messianology." In *The Messiah: Developments in Earliest Judaism and Christianity* (1992), 461–93.

Hampel, Volker. *Menschensohn und historischer Jesu*. Neukirchen-Vluyn: Neukirchener Verlag, 1990.

Han, Kyu Sam. *Jerusalem and the Early Jesus Movement: The Q Community's Attitude Toward the Temple*. JSNTSup 207. Sheffield: Sheffield Academic Press, 2002.

Hardin, Michael. "'All We Are Saying Is Give Peace A Chance': An Appraisal of Willard Swartley's *Covenant of Peace*." Paper presented to the Colloquium on Violence and Religion, Washington, DC, November 2006.

Hare, Douglas R. A. *The Son of Man Tradition*. Minneapolis: Fortress Press, 1990.

———. "When Did 'Messiah' Become a Proper Name?" *Expository Times* 121 (2009): 70–73.

Harnack, Adolf von. *The Sayings of Jesus: The Second Source of St. Matthew and St. Luke*. Translated by John Richard Wilkinson. CTL 23. NTS 2. London: Williams & Norgate, 1908.

———. *Marcion: Das Evangelium vom fremden Gott*. Darmstadt: Wissenschaftliche Buchgesellschaft, 1996 [1921].

Harrison, Roland K. "The Son of Man." *Evangelical Quarterly* 23 (1951): 46–50.

Harvey, A. E. *Jesus and the Constraints of History*. Philadelphia: Westminster, 1982.

Hauerwas, Stanley. *The Peaceable Kingdom: A Primer in Christian Ethics*. Notre Dame, IN: University of Notre Dame Press, 1983.

Havener, Ivan. *Q: The Sayings of Jesus (with a Reconstruction of Q by Athanasius Polag)*. Good News Studies 19. Wilmington, DE: Michael Glazier, 1987.

Hay, Lewis S. "The Son of Man in Mark 2:10 and 2:28." *Journal of Biblical Literature* 89 (1970): 69–75.

Hays, Richard B. "Christ Prays the Psalms: Paul's Use of an Early Christian Exegetical Convention." In *The Future of Christology*. Edited by Abraham J. Malherbe. Minneapolis: Fortress Press, 1993, 111–30.

———. "The Corrected Jesus." *First Things* 43 (1994): 43–48.

———. *The Moral Vision of the New Testament: Community, Cross, New Creation: A Contemporary Introduction to New Testament Ethics*. San Francisco: HarperSanFrancisco, 1996.

Hayward, Robert. "The Figure of Adam in Pseudo-Philo's Biblical Antiquities." *Journal for the Study of Judaism* 23 (1992): 1–20.

Hecht, Richard D. "Studies on Sacrifice." *Religious Studies Review* 8, no. 3 (1982): 253–59.

Hedley, Douglas. *Sacrifice Imagined: Violence, Atonement, and the Sacred*. New York: Continuum, 2011.

Hehn, Johannes. "Zum Terminus 'Bild Gottes.'" In *Festschrift Eduard Sacahu*. Edited by Gotthold Weil. Berlin: Reimar, 1915, 36–52.

Heil, Christoph. "Die Rezeption von Micah 7,6 in Q und Lukas." *Zeitschrift für die neutestamentliche Wissenschaft* 88 (1997): 211-222.

Heinsius, Daniel. *Sacrarum exercitationum ad novum testamentum*. 2d ed. Lugduni-Batavorum: Ex officinâ Elseviriorum, 1640.

Hellerman, Joseph H. *Jesus and the People of God: Reconfiguring Ethnic Identity*. NTM 21. Sheffield: Sheffield Phoenix Press, 2007.

Hendrickx, Herman. *The Sermon on the Mount: Studies in the Synoptic Gospels*. London: Harper Collins, 1984.

Hengel, Martin. Review of S. G. F. Brandon, *Jesus and the Zealots*. *Journal of Semitic Studies* 14 (1969): 231-40.

——. *Was Jesus a Revolutionist?* Translated by William Klassen. Philadelphia: Fortress Press, 1971.

——. *Victory over Violence*. Translated by David E. Green. Philadelphia: Fortress Press, 1973.

——. *Judaism and Hellenism: Studies in Their Encounter in Palestine During the Early Hellenistic Period*. Translated by John Bowden. Philadelphia: Fortress Press, 1974.

——. *The Son of God: The Origin of Christology and the History of Jewish-Hellenistic Religion*. Translated by John Bowden. Philadelphia: Fortress Press, 1976.

——. *Crucifixion in the Ancient World and the Folly of the Message of the Cross*. Translated by John Bowden. Philadelphia: Fortress Press, 1977.

——. *Between Jesus and Paul: Studies in the Earliest History of Christianity*. Translated by John Bowden. Philadelphia: Fortress Press, 1983.

——. "The Titles of the Gospels and the Gospel of Mark." In *Studies in the Gospel of Mark*. Edited by Martin Hengel. Translated by John Bowden. London: SCM, 1985, 64–84.

——. "Christological Titles in Early Christianity." In *The Messiah: Developments in Earliest Judaism and Christianity* (1992), 425–48.

——. *Studies in Early Christology*. Edinburgh: T & T Clark, 1995.

——. *The Four Gospels and the One Gospel of Jesus Christ: An Investigation of the Collection and Origin of the Canonical Gospels*. Translated by John Bowden. London: SCM, 2000.

—— and Anna Maria Schwemer. *Jesus und das Judentum*. Vol. 1. *Geschichte des frühen Christentums*. 4 vols. Tübingen: Mohr Siebeck, 2007.

Herford, R. Travers. *Christianity in Talmud and Midrash*. London: Williams & Norgate, 1903.

Héring, Jean. *Le royaume de Dieu et sa venue*. 2d ed. Neuchâtel: Delachaux & Niestlé, 1959.

Herschberger, Guy F. *War, Peace, and Nonresistance*. Scottdale, PA: Herald Press, 1969.

Herzog, William R. II. "Dissembling, a Weapon of the Weak: The Case of Christ and Caesar in Mark 12:13-17 and Romans 13:1-7." *Perspectives in Religious Studies* 21 (1994): 339–60.

———. *Prophet and Teacher: An Introduction to the Historical Jesus*. Louisville: Westminster John Knox, 2005.

———. *Jesus, Justice, and the Reign of God*. Louisville: Westminster John Knox, 2000.

Heschel, Susannah. *The Aryan Jesus*. Princeton, NJ: Princeton University Press, 2008.

Hess, Richard S., and M. Daniel Carroll R., eds. *Israel's Messiah in the Bible and the Dead Sea Scrolls*. Grand Rapids: Baker Academic, 2003.

———, and Elmer A. Martens, eds. *War in the Bible and Terrorism in the Twenty-First Century*. Winona Lake: Eisenbrauns, 2008.

Hieke, Thomas. "Q 7, 22: A Compendium of Isaian Eschatology." *Ephemerides theologicae lovanienses* 82, no. 1 (2006): 175–87.

Hiers, Richard H. *The Kingdom of God in the Synoptic Tradition*. Gainesville, FL: University of Florida Press, 1970.

Higgins, A. J. B. *Jesus and the Son of Man*. Philadelphia: Fortress Press, 1964.

———. "The Son of Man Concept and the Historical Jesus." *Studia Evangelica* 5 (1968): 14–20.

———. *The Son of Man in the Teaching of Jesus*. SNTSMS 39. Cambridge: Cambridge University Press, 1980.

Himmelfarb, Martha. "The Temple and the Garden of Eden in Ezekiel, the Book of Watchers, and the Wisdom of Ben Sira." In *Sacred Places and Profane Spaces: Essays in the Geographies of Judaism, Christianity and Islam*. Edited by Jamie S. Scott and Paul Simpson-Housely. Westport, CT: Greenwood, 1991, 63–78.

———. *Ascent to Heaven in Jewish and Christian Apocalypses*. Oxford: Oxford University Press, 1993.

Hobbs, Edward C. "A Quarter Century Without Q." *Perkins School of Theology Journal* 33, no. 4 (1980): 10–19.

Hobbs, T. R. *A Time for War: A Study of Warfare in the Old Testament*. Wilmington, DE: Michael Glazier, 1989.

Hoffmann, Paul. "Die Versuchungsgeschichte in der Logienquelle." *Biblische Zeitschrift* 13 (1969): 207–23.

———. *Studien zur Theologie der Logienquelle*. NA 8. Münster: Aschendorff, 1972.

———. "Tradition und Situation: Zur 'Verbindlichkeit' des Gebots der Feindesliebe in der synoptischen Überlieferung und in der gegenwärtigen Friedendiskussion." In *Ethik im Neuen Testament*. Edited by Karl Kertelge. QD 102. Freiburg: Herder, 1984, 50–118.

——. "The Redaction of Q and the Son of Man: A Preliminary Sketch." In *The Gospel Behind the Gospels*. Edited by Ronald A. Piper. NTSup 75. Leiden: Brill, 1995, 159–98.

———. "QR und der Menschensohn." In *The Four Gospels 1992*, 421–56.

———. *Tradition und Situation: Studien zur Jesusüberlieferung in der Logienquelle und den synoptischen Evangelien*. NA 28. Münster: Aschendorff, 1995.

———. "Der Q-Text der Sprüche vom Sorgen. Mt 6,25-33 / Lk 12,22-31. Ein Rekonstruktionsversuch." In *Studien zum Matthäusevangelium. Festschrift für Wilhelm Pesch*. SBS. Edited by Ludger Schenke. Stuttgart: Katholisches Bibelwerk, 1988, 128–55.

Hoffmeier, James K. and Dennis R. Magary, eds. *Do Historical Matters Matter to Faith?: A Critical Appraisal of Modern and Postmodern Approaches to Scripture*. Wheaton: Crossway, 2012.

Holland, Scott. "The Gospel of Peace and the Violence of God." In *Seeking Cultures of Peace: A Peace Church Conversation*. Edited by Fernando Enns, Scott Holland, and Ann Riggs. Scottdale, PA: Herald Press, 2004, 132–46.

Hollenbach, Paul W. "Recent Historical Jesus Studies and the Social Sciences." *Society of Biblical Literature 1983 Seminar Papers* (22). Edited by Kent H. Richards. Chico, CA: Scholars Press, 1983, 61–78.

Holmén, Tom. "Doubts about Double Dissimilarity: Restructuring the Main Criterion of Jesus-of-History Research." In *Authenticating the Words of Jesus*. Edited by Bruce D. Chilton and Craig A. Evans. NTTS 28, no. 1. Leiden: Brill, 1999, 47–80.

———. "The Jewishness of Jesus in the 'Third Quest,." In *Jesus, Mark and Q: The Teaching of Jesus and its Earliest Records*. JSNTSup 214. Sheffield: Sheffield Academic Press, 2001, 143–62.

———. "Hermeneutics of Dissimilarity in the Early Judaism-Jesus-Early Christianity Continuum." In *Jesus in Continuum*. Edited by Tom Holmén. WUNT 289. Tübingen: Mohr Siebeck, 2012, 3-42.

———, ed. *Jesus from Judaism to Christianity: Continuum Approaches to the Historical Jesus*. London: T & T Clark, 2007.

Holmes, Robert L., ed. *Nonviolence in Theory and Practice*. Belmont, CA: Wadsworth, 1990.

Hooker, Morna D. *The Son of Man in Mark: A Study of the Background of the Term "Son of Man" and Its Use in St. Mark's Gospel*. Montreal: McGill University Press, 1967.

———. "On Using the Wrong Tool." *Theology* 75 (1972): 570–81.

———. "Philippians 2:6-11." In *Jesus und Paulus: Festschrift für W. G. Kümmel*. Edited by E. Earle Ellis and Erich Grässer. Göttingen: Vandenhoeck & Ruprecht, 1975, 151–64.

———. *Not Ashamed of the Gospel: New Testament Interpretation of the Death of Christ*. Carlisle: Paternoster, 1994.

Horbury, William. *Jewish Messianism and the Cult of Christ*. London: SCM, 1998.

———. "'Gospel' in Herodian Judaea." In *The Written Gospel*. Edited by Markus Bockmuehl and Donald Hagner. Cambridge: Cambridge University Press, 2005, 7–30.

Horsley, Richard A. "Ethics and Exegesis: 'Love Your Enemies' and the Doctrine of Non-Violence." *Journal of the American Academy of Religion* 54 (1986): 3–31.

———. *Jesus and the Spiral of Violence: Popular Jewish Resistance in Roman Palestine*. San Francisco: Harper & Row, 1987.

———. "Q and Jesus: Assumptions, Approaches, and Analyses." *Semeia* 55 (1991): 175–209.

———. "'Messianic' Figures and Movements in First-Century Palestine." In *The Messiah: Developments in Earliest Judaism and Christianity* (1992), 276–95.

———. "Response to Walter Wink: Neither Passivity nor Violence: Jesus' 'Third Way.'" In *The Love of Enemy and Nonretaliation in the New Testament*. Edited by Willard M. Swartley. Louisville: Westminster John Knox, 1992, 126–32.

———. "Questions About Redactional Strata and the Social Relations Reflected in Q." In *Society of Biblical Literature 1989 Seminar Papers*. Edited by David J. Lull. Atlanta: Scholars Press, 1989, 175–209.

———. "Wisdom Justified by All Her Children: Examining Allegedly Disparate Traditions in Q." In *Society of Biblical Literature Seminar Papers* 33. Missoula: Scholars Press, 1994, 733–51.

———. *Jesus and Empire: The Kingdom of God and the New World Disorder*. Minneapolis: Fortress Press, 2003.

———. *The Prophet Jesus and the Renewal of Israel: Moving Beyond Diversionary Debate*. Grand Rapids: Eerdmans, 2012.

——— with Jonathan A. Draper. *Whoever Hears You Hears Me: Prophets, Performance, and Tradition in Q*. Harrisburg, PA: Trinity Press International, 1999.

——— and John S. Hanson. *Bandits, Prophets, and Messiahs: Popular Movements in the Time of Jesus*. Minneapolis: Winston, 1985.

———, ed. *Oral Performance, Popular Tradition, and Hidden Transcript in Q.* Atlanta: Society of Biblical Literature, 2006.

Howard, George. "Phil. 2:6-22 and the Human Christ." *Catholic Biblical Quarterly* 40 (1978): 368–87.

Hoyt, Wayland. *The Teaching of Jesus Concerning His Own Person.* New York: American Tract Society, 1909.

Hultgren, Arland. "Eschatology in the New Testament: The Current Debate." In *The Last Things: Biblical and Theological Perspectives on Eschatology*. Edited by Carl E. Braaten and Robert W. Jenson. Grand Rapids: Eerdmans, 2002, 67–89.

Humbert, Paul. "L''imago Dei' dans l'Ancien Testament." In *Études sur le récit du paradis et de la chute dans la Genèse.* Mémoires de l'université de Neuchâtel 14. Neuchâtel: Secrétariat de l'université, 1940, 153–75.

Hurst, Lincoln D. "Re-Enter the Pre-existent Christ in Philippians 2.5-11?" *New Testament Studies* 32 (1986): 449–57.

———. "Christ, Adam, and Preexistence Revisited." In *Where Christology Began: Essays on Philippians 2.* Edited by Ralph P. Martin and Brian J. Dodd. Louisville: Westminster John Knox, 1998, 84–95.

Hurtado, Larry W. *Lord Jesus Christ: Devotion to Jesus in Earliest Christianity.* Grand Rapids: Eerdmans, 2003.

———. "Paul's Christology." In *The Cambridge Companion to St. Paul.* Edited by James D. G. Dunn. Cambridge: Cambridge University Press, 2003, 185–98.

———. *How on Earth Did Jesus Become a God? Historical Questions About Earliest Devotion to Jesus.* Grand Rapids: Eerdmans, 2005.

———. "Summary and Concluding Observations." In *'Who is This Son of Man'? The Latest Scholarship on a Puzzling Expression of the Historical Jesus.* Edited by Larry W. Hurtado and Paul Owen. London: T & T Clark, 2011, 159–77.

Huxley, Aldous. *Do What You Will: Essays by Aldous Huxley.* London: Chatto & Windus, 1929.

Idel, Moshe. *Messianic Mystics.* New Haven: Yale University Press, 1998.

———. *Ben: Sonship and Jewish Mysticism.* Kogod Library of Judaic Studies 5. London/New York: Continuum, 2007.

Ingolfsland, Dennis. "Kloppenborg's Stratification of Q and its Significance for Historical Jesus Studies." *Journal of the Evangelical Theological Society* 46, no. 2 (2003): 217–32.

Iser, Wolfgang. *The Implied Reader: Patterns of Communication in Prose Fiction from Bunyan to Beckett.* Baltimore: Johns Hopkins University Press, 1974.

Jackson, David R. *Enochic Judaism: Three Defining Paradigm Exemplars*. LSTS 49. London and New York: T & T Clark, 2004.

Jacobson, Arland D. "Wisdom Christology in Q." PhD diss., Claremont Graduate School, 1978.

———. *The First Gospel: An Introduction to Q*. Sonoma, CA: Polebridge, 1992.

Janzen, Waldemar. "War in the Old Testament." *Mennonite Quarterly Review* 46 (1972): 155–66.

Jauss, Hans Robert. *Toward an Aesthetic of Reception*. Translated by Timothy Bahti. Minneapolis: University of Minnesota Press, 1982.

Jefferson, Thomas. *The Jefferson Bible: The Life and Morals of Jesus of Nazareth*. Boston: Beacon, 1989.

Jenkins, Philip. *Hidden Gospels: How the Search for Jesus Lost Its Way*. New York: Oxford University Press, 2002.

———. *Laying Down the Sword: Why We Can't Ignore the Bible's Violent Verses*. New York: HarperOne, 2011.

Jeremias, Joachim. *Die Gleichnisse Jesu*. Göttingen: Vandenhoeck & Ruprecht, 1953. English: *The Parables of Jesus*. Translated by S. H. Hooke. New York: Scribners, 1963.

———. "Adam." *Theological Dictionary of the New Testament* 1: 141–43.

———. "Abba." In idem, *The Prayers of Jesus*. London: SCM, 1967, 11–65.

———. *Die Bergpredigt*. Stuttgart: Calwer Verlag, 1970.

———. *Neutestamentliche Theologie: 1. Die Verkündigung Jesu*. Gütersloh: Mohn, 1971. English: *New Testament Theology*. London: SCM, 1971.

———. *Die Sprache des Lukasevangeliums: Redaktion und Tradition im Nicht-Markusstoff des dritten Evangeliums*. KEKNT. Göttingen: Vandenhoeck & Ruprecht, 1980.

Jervell, Jacob. *Imago Dei: Gen 1,26ff. im Spätjudentum, in der Gnosis und in der paulinischen Briefen*. Göttingen: Vandenhoeck & Ruprecht, 1960.

Johnson, Marshall D. *The Purpose of the Biblical Genealogies with Special Reference to the Setting of the Genealogies of Jesus*. 2d ed. SNTSMS 8. Cambridge: Cambridge University Press, 1988.

Jones, F. Stanley. "Pseudo-Clementine Literature." Pages 2:717–19 in *Encyclopedia of the Dead Sea Scrolls* 2: 717–19.

Jones, Gareth L. "Sacred Violence: The Dark Side of God." *Journal of Beliefs and Values* 20 (1999): 184–99.

Jones, Gwilym H. "'Holy War' or 'Yahweh War'?" *Vetus Testamentum* 25 (1965): 642–58.

Jónsson, Gunnlauger A. *The Image of God: Genesis 1:26-28 in a Century of Old Testament Research*. Translated by Lorraine Svensen. Coniectanea neotestamentica 26. Lund: Almqvist & Wiksell International, 1988.

Joseph, Simon J. "'Blessed is Whoever is Not Offended by Me': The Subversive Appropriation of (Royal) Messianic Ideology in Q 3–7." *New Testament Studies* 57, no. 3 (2011): 307–24.

———. "'Seek His Kingdom': Q 12,22b-31, God's Providence, and Adamic Wisdom." *Biblica* 92, no. 3 (2011): 392–410.

———. *Jesus, Q, and the Dead Sea Scrolls: A Judaic Approach to Q*. WUNT 2d ser., 333. Tübingen: Mohr Siebeck, 2012.

———. "'His Wisdom Will Reach All Peoples': 4Q534-36, Q 17:26-27, 30, and *1 En.* 65.1–67.3, 90." *Dead Sea Discoveries* 19, no. 1 (2012): 71–105.

———. "The Eschatological 'Adam' of the *Animal Apocalypse* (*1 En.* 90) and Paul's 'Last Adam': Excavating a Trajectory in Jewish Christianity." *Henoch* 34, no. 1 (2012): 144–70.

———. "Why Do You Call Me 'Master?' . . . : Q 6:46, the Inaugural Sermon, and the Demands of Discipleship." *Journal of Biblical Literature* 132, no. 4 (2013): 955–72.

———. "'Love Your Enemies': The Adamic Wisdom of Q 6:27-28, 35c-d." *Biblical Theology Bulletin* 43, no. 1 (2013): 29–41.

———. "Was Daniel 7:13's 'Son of Man' Modeled After the 'New Adam' of the *Animal Apocalypse* (*1 En.* 90)? A Comparative Study." *Journal for the Study of the Pseudepigrapha* 22, no. 4 (2013): 269–94.

———. "'Seventh from Adam' (Jude 1:14-15): Re-examining Enoch Traditions and the Christology of Jude." *Journal of Theological Studies* 64, no. 2 (2013): 463–81.

Jossa, Giorgio. *Jews or Christians?* WUNT 202. Tübingen: Mohr Siebeck, 2006.

Joubert, Stephan J. "Facing the Past: Transtextual Relationships and Historical Understanding in the Letter of Jude." *Biblische Zeitschrift* 42 (1998): 56–70.

Juel, Donald H. *Messianic Exegesis*. Philadelphia: Fortress Press, 1988.

———. "The Origin of Mark's Christology." In *The Messiah: Developments in Earliest Judaism and Christianity* (1992), 449–60.

Juergensmeyer, Mark. *Terror in the Mind of God: The Global Rise of Religious Violence*. Berkeley/Los Angeles: University of California Press, 2000.

Jülicher, Adolf. *Die Gleichnisreden Jesu*. 2 vols. Freiburg: Mohr, 1886.

Karrer, Martin. *Der Gesalbte. Die Grundlagen des Christustitels*. FRLANT 151. Göttingen: Vandenhoeck & Ruprecht, 1990.

Käsemann, Ernst. "The Problem of the Historical Jesus." In *Essays on New Testament Themes*. SBT 41. London: SCM, 1964, 15–47.

———. *New Testament Questions of Today*. Philadelphia: Fortress Press, 1969.

Kattenbusch, Ferdinand. "Über die Feindesliebe im Sinne des Christentums." *Theologische Studien und Kritiken* 89 (1916): 1–70.

Kearns, Rollin. *Die Entchristologisierung des Menschensohnes*. Tübingen: Mohr, 1988.

Kee, Howard Clark. *What Can We Know about Jesus?* Cambridge and New York: Cambridge University Press, 1990.

Kennard, J. Spencer Jr. *Render to God: A Study of the Tribute Passage*. New York: Oxford, 1950.

Kerr, Alan R. *The Temple of Jesus' Body: The Temple Theme in the Gospel of John*. JSNTSup 220. London: Sheffield, 2002.

Kertelge, Karl. "Die Vollmacht des Menschensoshnes zur Sündenvergebung (Mk 2,10)." In *Orientierung an Jesus: Zur Theologie der Synoptiker. FS Josef Schmid*. Edited by Paul Hoffmann, et al. Freiburg: Herder, 1973, 205–13.

Keith, Chris. "Memory and Authenticity: Jesus Tradition and What Really Happened." *Zeitschrift für die neutestamentliche Wissenschaft* 102.2 (2011): 155-77.

Keith, Chris, and Anthony Le Donne, eds. *Jesus, Criteria, and the Demise of Authenticity: The 2012 Lincoln Christian University Conference*. New York: T & T Clark International, 2012.

Kim, Seyoon. *The Origin of Paul's Gospel*. Tübingen: Mohr, 1984.

Kimball, Charles. *When Religion Becomes Evil*. San Francisco: HarperSanFrancisco, 2002.

King, Karen L. *The Gospel of Mary of Magdala: Jesus and the First Woman Apostle*. Santa Rosa, CA: Polebridge, 2003.

King, Martin Luther Jr. *Strength to Love*. New York: Harper & Row, 1963.

———. *Where Do We Go From Here: Chaos or Community?* New York: Harper & Row, 1967.

———. *A Testament of Hope: The Essential Writings and Speeches of Martin Luther King, Jr.* San Francisco: Harper & Row, 1986.

Kirchhevel, Gordon D. "The 'Son of Man' Passages in Mark." *Biblical Theology Bulletin* 9 (1999): 181–87.

Kirk, Alan. *The Composition of the Sayings Source: Genre, Synchrony, and Wisdom Redaction in Q*. NovTSup 91. Leiden: Brill, 1998.

———. "Memory Theory: Cultural and Cognitive Approaches to the Gospel Tradition." In *Understanding the Social World of the New Testament*. Edited by Dietmar Neufeld and Richard DeMaris. London: Routledge, 2010, 157-167.

———. "Memory Theory and Jesus Research." In *Handbook for the Study of the Historical Jesus* (2011), 809–42.

Kirk, Alan and Tom Thatcher, eds. *Memory, Tradition, and Text: Uses of the Past in Early Christianity*. SS 52. Atlanta: Society of Biblical Literature, 2005.

Kister, Menahem. "'In Adam': 1 Cor 15:21-22; 12:27 in their Jewish Setting." In *Flores Florentino: Dead Sea Scrolls and Other Early Jewish Studies in Honour of Florentino García Martínez*. Edited by Antonius Hilhorst, Émile Puech, and Eibert J. C. Tigchelaar. JSJSup 122. Leiden: Brill, 2007, 685–90.

———. "Romans 5:12-21 against the Background of Torah-Theology and Hebrew Usage." *Harvard Theological Review* 100 (2007): 391-424.

———. "'First Adam' and 'Second Adam' in 1 Cor 15:45-49 in the Light of Midrashic Exegesis and Hebrew Usage." In *New Testament and Rabbinic Literature: Proceedings of a Symposium held at the K . U. Leuven on January 2006*. Edited by Reimund Bieringer. JSJSup 136. Leiden: Brill, 2010, 351-365.

Kittel, Gerhard. "Die Bergpredigt und die Ethik des Judentums." *Zeitschrift für systematische Theologie* 2 (1924): 555–94.

———. "The This-Worldly Kingdom of God in Our Lord's Teaching." *Theology* 14 (1927): 260–62.

Klassen, William. "Love Your Enemy: A Study of New Testament Teaching on Coping with an Enemy." *Mennonite Quarterly Review* 37 (1963): 147–71.

———. "Coals of Fire: Sign of Repentance or Revenge?" *New Testament Studies* 9 (1963): 337–50.

———. "Jesus and the Zealot Option." *Canadian Journal of Theology* 16 (1970): 12-21.

———. *Love of Enemies: The Way to Peace*. Philadelphia: Fortress Press, 1984.

———. "'Love Your Enemies': Some Reflections on the Current Status of Research." In *Love of Enemy and Nonretaliation* (1992), 1–31.

Klausner, Joseph. *Jesus of Nazareth: His Life, Times, and Teaching*. Translated by Herbert Danby. New York: Macmillan, 1925.

———. *The Messianic Idea in Israel from Its Beginning to the Completion of the Mishnah*. New York: Macmillan, 1955.

Klijn, A. F. J. "From Creation to Noah in the Second Dream-Vision of the Ethiopic Enoch." In *Miscellanea Neotestamentica*. NovTSup 46-47. Leiden: Brill, 1977, 1:147-159.

Kloppenborg, John S. "The Function of Apocalyptic Language in Q." In *Society of Biblical Literature1986 Seminar Papers* (25). Atlanta: Scholars Press, 1986, 224–35.

———. "Symbolic Eschatology and the Apocalypticism of Q." *Harvard Theological Review* 80 (1987): 287–306.

———. *The Formation of Q: Trajectories in Ancient Wisdom Collections*. SAC. Philadelphia: Fortress Press, 1987.

———. "'Easter Faith' and the Sayings Gospel Q," *Semeia* 49 (1990): 71–99.

———. "Literary Convention, Self-Evidence and the Social History of the Q People." *Semeia* 55 (1991): 77–102.

———. John S. Kloppenborg, "The Sayings Gospel Q and the Quest of the Historical Jesus." *Harvard Theological Review* 89 (1996): 307–44.

———. *Q, The Earliest Gospel: An Introduction to the Original Stories and Sayings of Jesus*. Louisville: Westminster John Knox, 2008.

———. "Memory, Performance, and the Sayings of Jesus." *Journal for the Study of the Historical Jesus* 10 (2012): 97-132.

Kloppenborg Verbin, John S. *Excavating Q: The History and Setting of the Sayings Gospel*. Edinburgh: T & T Clark, 2000.

———. "Discursive Practices in the Sayings Gospel Q and the Quest of the Historical Jesus." In *The Sayings Source Q and the Historical Jesus* (2001), 149–90.

———. "Goulder and the New Paradigm: A Critical Appreciation of Michael Goulder on the Synoptic Problem." In *The Gospels according to Michael Goulder: A North American Response*. Edited by Chris A. Rollston. Harrisburg, PA: Trinity Press International, 2002, 29–60.

Klostermann, Erich. *Matthäusevangelium*. HNT 2/1. Tübingen: Mohr, 1909.

Knibb, Michael A. *The Ethiopic Book of Enoch: A New Edition in the Light of the Aramaic Dead Sea Fragments*. 2 vols. Oxford: Clarendon Press/New York: Oxford University Press, 1978.

———. "The Date of the Parables of Enoch: A Critical Review." *New Testament Studies* 25 (1979): 345–59.

———. *The Qumran Community*. New York: Cambridge University Press, 1987.

Knight, Douglas A. "Canon and the History of Tradition: A Critique of Brevard S. Childs' Introduction to the Old Testament as Scripture." *Horizons in Biblical Theology* 2 (1980): 127–49.

Knight, Jonathan. *Jesus: An Historical and Theological Investigation*. London: T & T Clark, 2004.

Koch, Klaus. "Offenbaren wird sich das Reich Gottes." *New Testament Studies* 25 (1978): 158–65.

———. *Vor der Wende der Zeiten: Beiträge zur apokalyptischen Literatur*. GA 3. Neukirchen-Vluyn: Neukirchener Verlag, 1996.

———. "Heilandserwartungen im Judäa der Zeitenwende." In *Die Schriftrollen von Qumran: Zur aufregenden Geschichte ihrer Erforschung und Deutung*. Edited by Shemaryahu Talmon. Regensburg: Pustet, 1998, 107–35.

———. "Messias und Menschensohn." In idem, *Vor der Wende der Zeiten. Beiträge zur apokalyptischen Literatur. Gesammelte Aufsätze* 2. Neukirchen-Vluyn: Neukirchener Verlag, 1996, 235–66.

———. "Questions regarding the So-Called Son of Man in the Parables of Enoch: A Response to Sabino Chialà and Helge Kvanvig." In *Enoch and the Messiah Son of Man* (2007), 228–37.

Koehler, Ludwig. "Die Grundstelle der Imago-Dei-Lehre, Gen 1:26." *Theologische Zeitschrift* 4 (1948): 16–22.

Koester, Helmut. "One Jesus and Four Primitive Gospels." *Harvard Theological Review* 61 (1968): 203–47.

———. *Introduction to the New Testament*. 2 vols. Philadelphia: Fortress Press, 1982.

———. *Ancient Christian Gospels: Their History and Development*. Philadelphia: Trinity Press International, 1990.

———. "The Sayings Gospel Q and the Quest for the Historical Jesus: A Response to John S. Kloppenborg." *Harvard Theological Review* 89, no. 4 (1996): 345–49.

———. "Jesus the Victim." *Journal of Biblical Literature* 111 (1992): 10–11.

Kosch, Daniel. "Q und Jesus." *Biblische Zeitschrift* 36 (1992): 30–58.

Kraeling, Carl H. *Anthropos and the Son of Man: A Study in the Religious Syncretism of the Hellenistic Orient*. CUOS 25. New York: AMS Press, 1927.

———. "The Episode of the Roman Standards at Jerualem." *Harvard Theological Review* 35, no. 4 (1942): 263–89.

Kramer, Werner R. *Christ, Lord, Son of God*. SBT 50. London: SCM, 1966.

Kuhn, Heinz-Wolfgang. "Das Liebesgebot Jesus als Tora und als Evangelium: Zur Feindesliebe und zur christlichen und jüdischen Auslegung der Bergpredigt." In *Vom Urchristentum zu Jesus* (1989), 194–230.

Kühnöl, Christian Gottlieb. *Commentarius in libros novi testamenti historicos*. Vol. 1. *Evangelium Matthaei*. 3d ed. Leipzig: Barth, 1823.

Kümmel, Werner Georg. *Promise and Fulfillment: The Eschatological Message of Jesus*. Translated by Dorothea M. Baron. SBT 23. London: SCM, 1957.

———. "Jesu Antwort an Johannes den Täufer: Ein Beispiel zum Methodenproblem in der Jesusforschung." In idem, *Heilsgeschehen und Geschichte: Gesammelte Aufsätze, 1965–1977*. 2 vols. Edited by Erich Grässer and Otto Merk. MThS 16. Marburg: Elwert, 1965–1978, 2: 177–200.

———. *The Theology of the New Testament according to Its Major Witnesses: Jesus-Paul-John*. Translated by John E. Steely. Nashville: Abingdon, 1973.

Kvalbein, Hans. "Die Wunder der Endzeit—Beobachtungen zu 4Q521 und Mt. 11.5p." *Zeitschrift für die neutestamentliche Wissenschaft und die Kunde der älteren Kirche* 88 (1997): 111–25.

———. "The Wonders of the End-Time: Metaphoric Language in 4Q521 and the Interpretation of Matthew 11.5 par." *Journal for the Study of the Pseudepigrapha* 18 (1998): 87–110.

———. "The Son of Man in the Parables of Enoch." In *Enoch and the Messiah Son of Man* (2007), 179–215.

Laato, Antti. *A Star is Rising: The Historical Development of the Old Testament Royal Ideology and the Rise of the Jewish Messianic Expectations*. Atlanta: Scholars Press, 1997.

Labahn, Michael. "The Significance of Signs in Luke 7:22-23 in the Light of Isaiah 61 and the Messianic Apocalypse." In *From Prophecy to Testament: The Function of the Old Testament in the New*. Edited by Craig A. Evans. Peabody, MA: Hendrickson, 2004, 146–68.

Lacocque, André. "Allusions to Creation in Daniel 7." In *The Book of Daniel: Composition and Reception*. Edited by J. J. Collins and P. W. Flint. VTSup 83. Leiden: Brill, 2001, 114-131.

Ladd, George Eldon. "The Kingdom of God—Reign or Realm?" *Journal of Biblical Literature* 81 (1962): 230–38.

———. *A Theology of the New Testament*. Grand Rapids: Eerdmans, 1974.

Lamb, David T. *God Behaving Badly: Is the God of the Old Testament Angry, Sexist and Racist*. Downers Grove: InterVarsity Press, 2011.

Lane, William L. *The Gospel According to Mark*. NICNT. Grand Rapids: Eerdmans, 1974.

Lasserre, Jean. *War and the Gospel*. Translated by Oliver Coburn. Scottdale, PA: Herald Press, 1962.

Lattke, Michael. "On the Jewish Background of the Synoptic Concept 'The Kingdom of God.'" In *The Kingdom of God in the Teaching of Jesus*. Edited by Bruce Chilton. Philadelphia: Fortress Press, 1984, 72–91.

Lauterbach, Jacob Z. *Rabbinic Essays*. Cincinnati: Hebrew Union College, 1951.

Law, David R. *The Historical-Critical Method: A Guide for the Perplexed.* London/New York: Bloomsbury T & T Clark, 2012.

Lawlor, H. J. "Early Citations from the Book of Enoch." *Journal of Philology* 25 (1897): 164–225.

Le Donne, Anthony. *The Historiographical Jesus: Memory, Typology, and the Son of David.* Waco: Baylor University Press, 2009.

———. *Historical Jesus: What Can We Know and How Can We Know It?* Grand Rapids: Eerdmans, 2011.

Lefebure, Leo D. *Revelation, the Religious, and Violence.* Maryknoll, NY: Orbis Books, 2000.

Lefebvre, Jean-François. *Le jubilé biblique: Lv 25—exégèse et théologie.* OBO 194. Göttingen: Vandenhoeck & Ruprecht, 2003.

Legarreta-Castillo, Felipe de Jesús. *The Figure of Adam in Romans 5 and 1 Corinthians 15: The New Creation and Its Ethical and Social Reconfiguration.* ES. Minneapolis: Fortress Press, 2014.

Legasse, Simon. *'Et qui est mon prochain?' Etude sur l'objet de l'agapè dans le Nouveau Testament.* LD 136. Paris: Cerf, 1989.

Leivestadt, Ragnar. "Exit the Apocalyptic Son of Man." *New Testament Studies* 18 (1972): 243–67.

———. "Jesus-Messias-Menschensohn: Die jüdischen Heilandserwartungen zur Zeit der ersten römischen Kaiser und die Frage nach dem messianischen Selbstbewusstsein Jesu." *ANRW* II 25.1 (1982): 220–64.

———. *Jesus in His own Perspective: An Examination of His Sayings, Actions, and Eschatological Titles.* Translated by David E. Aune. Minneapolis: Augsburg, 1987.

Levine, Amy-Jill. *The Misunderstood Jew: The Church and the Scandal of the Jewish Jesus.* New York: Harper San Francisco, 2006.

——— and Marc Zvi Brettler, eds. *The Jewish Annotated New Testament: New Revised Standard Version Bible Translation.* New York: Oxford University Press, 2011.

Levison, John R. *Portraits of Adam in Early Judaism: From Sirach to 2 Baruch.* Sheffield: JSOT Press, 1987.

———. "Adamic Traditions in Early Judaism (Qumran, *1 Enoch*, Sirach, Philo, *Jubilees*, Josephus, *4 Ezra, 2 Baruch*)." Paper presented at the Fifth Enoch Seminar, Naples, Italy, June 14–18, 2009.

Lietzmann, Hans. *Der Menschensohn: Ein Beitrag zur neutestamentlichen Theologie.* Freiburg/Leipzig: Mohr Siebeck, 1896.

Lind, Millard. *Yahweh Is A Warrior.* Scottdale, PA: Herald Press, 1980.

Lindars, Barnabas. "A Bull, a Lamb and a Word: 1 Enoch XC.38." *New Testament Studies* 22 (1976): 483-486.

———. "Jesus as Advocate: A Contribution to the Christology Debate." *Bulletin of the John Rylands University Library of Manchester* 62 (1980): 476–97.

———. "The New Look on the Son of Man." *Bulletin of the John Rylands University Library of Manchester* 63 (1981): 437–62.

———. *Jesus Son of Man: A Fresh Examination of the Son of Man Sayings in the Gospels in the Light of Recent Research*. Grand Rapids: Eerdmans, 1984.

———. "Response to Richard Bauckham: The Idiomatic Use of *Bar Enasha*." *Journal for the Study of the New Testament* 23 (1985): 35–41.

Llewelyn, Stephen. "The *Traditionsgeschichte* of Matt. 11:12-13, Par. Luke 16:16." *Novum Testamentum* 36, no. 4 (1994): 330–49.

Lohmeyer, Ernst. *Das Evangelium des Markus*. Göttingen: Vandenhoek & Ruprecht, 1963.

Longenecker, Richard N. "The Messianic Secret in the Light of Recent Discoveries." *Evangelical Quarterly* 41 (1969): 207–15.

Longman, Tremper III. "The Case for Spiritual Continuity." In *Show Them No Mercy* (2003), 159–90.

Lorenz, Konrad. *On Aggression*. Translated by Marjorie Kerr Wilson. New York: Bantam Books, 1966.

Lucass, Shirley. *The Concept of the Messiah in the Scriptures of Judaism and Christianity*. LSTS 78. London: T & T Clark, 2011.

Lüdemann, Gerd. *The Unholy in Holy Scriptures: The Dark Side of the Bible*. Translated by John Bowden. Louisville: Westminster John Knox, 1997.

———. *Jesus After 2000 Years: What He Really Said and Did*. Translated by John Bowden. London: SCM, 2000.

Lührmann, Dieter. *Die Redaktion der Logienquelle*. WUNT 33. Neukirchen-Vluyn: Neukirchener Verlag, 1969.

———. "Liebet eure Feinde (Lk 6,27-36/Mt 5,39-48)." *Zeitschrift für Theologie und Kirche* 69 (1972): 412–38.

———. "Die Logienquelle und die Frage nach dem historischen Jesu." Paper presented at the fall meeting at the Westar Institute, Edmonton, Alberta, October 24–27, 1991.

Lündstrom, Gösta. *The Kingdom of God in the Teaching of Jesus: A History of Interpretation from the Last Decades of the Nineteenth Century to the Present Day*. Translated by Joan Bulman. Edinburgh: Oliver and Boyd, 1963.

Luz, Ulrich. *Das Evangelium nach Matthäus (Mt 8–17)*. EKK 1.2. Neukirchen-Vluyn: Neukirchener Verlag, 1990. English: *Matthew 1–7: A Commentary*. Translated by Wilhelm C. Linss. Minneapolis: Augsburg Fortress Press, 1989.

Lynch, Joseph H. "The First Crusade: Some Theological and Historical Context." In *Must Christianity Be Violent? Reflections on History, Practice, and Theology*. Edited by Kenneth R. Chase and Alan Jacobs. Grand Rapids: Brazos, 2003, 23–36.

MacDonald, Dennis R. *Two Shipwrecked Gospels: The Logoi of Jesus and Papias's Exposition of Logia about the Lord*. EC 8. Atlanta: Society of Biblical Literature, 2012.

Macgregor, G. H. C. "Does the New Testament Sanction War?" In *A Peace Reader*. Edited by E. Morris Sider and Luke Keefer Jr. Nappanee, IN: Evangel Press, 2002, 49–57.

Maccoby, Hyam. *Revolution in Judaea: Jesus and the Jewish Resistance*. London: Orbach and Chambers, 1973.

Mack, Burton L. "The Kingdom Sayings in Mark." *Forum* 3 (1987): 3–47.

———. *A Myth of Innocence: Mark and Christian Origins*. Philadelphia: Fortress Press, 1988.

———. "The Christ and Jewish Wisdom." In *The Messiah: Developments in Earliest Judaism and Christianity* (1992), 192–221.

———. *The Lost Gospel: The Book of Q & Christian Origins*. San Francisco: HarperSanFrancisco, 1993.

———. *The Christian Myth: Origins, Logic, and Legacy*. New York: Continuum, 2001.

———. "A Jewish Jesus School in Jerusalem." In *Redescribing Christian Origins* (2004), 253–62.

MacRae, George. "Messiah and Gospel." In *Judaisms and Their Messiahs at the Turn of the Christian Era* (1987), 169–85.

MacRory, Joseph. "The Son of Man." *Irish Theological Quarterly* 10 (1915): 50–63.

Maddox, Robert. "The Function of the Son of Man According to the Synoptic Gospels." *New Testament Studies* 15 (1968): 45–74.

———. "The Quest for Valid Methods in 'Son of Man' Research." *Australian Biblical Review* (1971): 36–51.

Maier, Johann. *Jesus von Nazareth in der talmudischen Überlieferung*. EdF 82. Darmstadt: Wissenschaftliche Buchgesellschaft, 1978.

Maier, Paul L. "The Episode of the Golden Shields at Jerusalem." *Harvard Theological Review* 62 (1969): 109–21.

Manson, William. *Christ's View of the Kingdom of God*. London: James Clarke, 1918.

———. *Jesus the Messiah: The Synoptic Tradition of the Revelation of God in Christ*. London: Hodder & Stoughton, 1943.

———. *The Gospel of Luke*. Moffatt New Testament Commentary. London: Hodder & Stoughton, 1930.

Manson, T. W. *The Teaching of Jesus: Studies of its Form and Content*. 2d ed. Cambridge: Cambridge University Press, 1935.

———. *The Sayings of Jesus*. Vol. 2: *The Mission and Message of Jesus: An Exposition of the Gospels in Light of Modern Research*. New York: E. P. Dutton, 1938.

———. *The Servant-Messiah: A Study of the Public Ministry of Jesus*. Cambridge: Cambridge University Press, 1953.

Marcus, Joel. "The Jewish War and the Sitz im Leben of Mark." *Journal of Biblical Literature* 111 (1992): 441–62.

———. "Modern and Ancient Jewish Apocalypticism." *Journal of Religion* 76 (1996): 18–23.

———. "Mark—Interpreter of Paul." *New Testament Studies* 46 (2000): 473–87.

———. "Son of Man as Son of Adam." *Revue Biblique* 110 (2003): 38–61, 370–86.

Marshall, Christopher D. *Beyond Retribution: A New Testament Vision for Justice, Crime, and Punishment*. SPS. Grand Rapids, Eerdmans, 2001.

Marshall, I. Howard. "The Synoptic Son of Man Sayings in Recent Discussion." *New Testament Studies* 12 (1966): 327–51.

———. "Uncomfortable Words: Fear Him Who Can Destroy Both Body and Soul in Hell." *Evangelische Theologie* 81 (1970): 277–78.

———. "The Son of Man in Contemporary Debate." *Evangelical Quarterly* 42 (1970): 67–87.

———. *The Origins of New Testament Christology*. Downers Grove: InterVarsity, 1976.

———. *The Gospel of Luke: A Commentary on the Greek Text*. NIGTC. Exeter: Paternoster, 1978.

———. "New Testament Perspectives on War." *Evangelical Quarterly* 57 (1985): 115–32.

Marshall, Paul, with Lela Gilbert. *Heaven Is Not My Home: Learning to Live in God's Creation*. Nashville: Word, 1998.

Martin, Dale B. *Pedagogy of the Bible: An Analysis and Proposal*. Louisville: Westminster John Knox, 2008.

Martin, Francois. *Le livre d'Hénoch traduit sur le texte éthiopien*. Paris: Letouzey et Ané, 1906.

Martin, Luther H. "History, Historiography, and Christian Origins: The Jerusalem Community." In *Redescribing Christian Origins* (2004), 263–75.

Martin, Ralph. *Carmen Christi: Philippians 2:5-11 in Recent Interpretation*. Grand Rapids: Eerdmans, 1983.

Marty, Martin, and R. Scott Appleby. *The Fundamentalism Project*. 5 vols. Chicago: University of Chicago Press, 1991–1995.

Matson, Mark A. "Luke's Rewriting of the Sermon on the Mount." Pages 623–50 in *Society of Biblical Literature Seminar Papers 2000* (39) Atlanta: Society of Biblical Literature, 2000, 623–50.

Matthews, Shelly, and E. Leigh Gibson. *Violence in the New Testament*. London: T & T Clark International, 2005.

McCasland, S. Vernon. "'The Image of God' According to Paul." *Journal of Biblical Literature* 69 (1950): 85–100.

McCarthy, Emmanuel Charles. *All things flee thee for thou fleest Me: A Cry to the Churches and Their Leaders to Stop Running from the Nonviolent Jesus and His Nonviolent Way*. Wilmington, DE: Center for Christian Nonviolence, 2003.

———. *Christian Just War Theory: The Logic of Deceit*. Wilmington, DE: Center for Christian Nonviolence, 2003.

McCollough, Charles. *The Non-Violent Radical: Seeing and Living the Wisdom of Jesus*. Eugene, OR: Wipf & Stock, 2012.

McDonald, James I. H. "Questioning and Discernment in Gospel Discourse: Communicative Strategy in Matthew 11:2-19." In *Authenticating the Words of Jesus* (1999), 333–61.

McGrath, James F. *The Only True God: Early Christian Monotheism and its Jewish Context*. Urbana: University of Illinois Press, 2009.

McIver, Robert K. *Memory, Jesus, and the Synoptic Gospels*. Atlanta: Society of Biblical Literature, 2011.

McKenzie, John L. *The Civilization of Christianity*. Chicago: Thomas More Press, 1986.

McKnight, Edgar V. *Postmodern Use of the Bible: The Emergence of Reader-Oriented Criticism*. Nashville: Abingdon, 1988.

———, ed. *Reader Perspectives on the New Testament*. *Semeia* 48. Atlanta: Scholars Press, 1989.

McKnight, Scot. *A New Vision for Israel: The Teachings of Jesus in National Context*. Grand Rapids: Eerdmans, 1999.

———. *Jesus and His Death*. Waco: Baylor University Press, 2005.

———. *The King Jesus Gospel: The Original Good News Revisited*. Grand Rapids: Zondervan, 2011.

McLean, Bradley. "The Absence of an Atoning Sacrifice in Paul's Soteriology." *New Testament Studies* 38 (1992): 531–53.

McNicol, Allan J., et al., eds. *Beyond the Q Impasse—Luke's Use of Matthew: A Demonstration by the Research Team of the International Institute for Gospel Studies.* Valley Forge, PA: Trinity Press International, 1996.

Meadors, Edward P. *Jesus the Messianic Herald of Salvation.* WUNT 72. Tübingen: Mohr Siebeck, 1995.

———. "The Messianic Implications of the Q Material." *Journal of Biblical Literature* 118 (1999): 253–77.

Meadors, Gary T. "The 'Poor' in the Beatitudes of Matthew [5:3] and Luke." *Grace Theological Journal* 6, no. 2 (1985): 305–14.

Mealand, David L. "The Dissimilarity Test." *Scottish Journal of Theology* 31 (1978): 41–50.

———. "'Paradisial' Elements in the Teaching of Jesus." In *Studia Biblica II.* Edited by Elizabeth A. Livingstone. JSNTSup 2. Sheffield: JSOT Press, 1980, 179–84.

Mearns, Christopher L. "The Son of Man Trajectory and Eschatological Development." *Expository Times* 97 (1985/86): 8–12.

———. "Parables, Secrecy and Eschatology in Mark's Gospel." *Scottish Journal of Theology* 44 (1991): 423–42.

Meeks, Wayne A. *The First Urban Christians: The Social World of the Apostle Paul*. New Haven: Yale University Press, 1983.

Meier, John P. *A Marginal Jew: Rethinking the Historical Jesus*. Vol. 1: *The Roots of the Problem and the Person*. New York: Doubleday, 1991.

———. *A Marginal Jew: Rethinking the Historical Jesus*. Vol. 2: *Mentor, Message, and Miracles*. New York: Doubleday, 1994.

———. *A Marginal Jew: Rethinking the Historical Jesus*. Vol. 3: *Companions and Competitors*. New Haven: Yale University Press, 2001.

———. "From Elijah-like Prophet to Royal Davidic Messiah." In *Jesus: A Colloquium in the Holy Land*. Edited by Doris Donnelly. New York: Continuum, 2001, 45–83.

Merklein, Helmut. *Die Gottesherrschaft als Handlungsprinzip. Untersuchung zur Ethik Jesu*. FzB. Würzburg: Echter Verlag, 1978.

———. *Jesu Botschaft von der Gottesherrschaft. Eine Skizze*. SBS. 2d ed. Stuttgart: Katholisches Bibelwerk, 1984.

Merrick, J., Stephen M. Garrett, and Stanley N. Gundry, eds. *Five Views on Biblical Inerrancy*. Counterpoints: Bible and Theology. Grand Rapids: Zondervan, 2013.

Merrill, Eugene H. "The Case for Moderate Dicontinuity." In *Show Them No Mercy* (2003), 61–96.

Merton, Thomas. *Faith and Violence: Christian Teaching and Christian Practice*. Notre Dame,IN: University of Notre Dame Press, 1968.

Meyer, Arnold. *Jesu Muttersprache: Das galiläische Aramäisch in seiner Bedeutung für die Erklärung der Reden Jesu und der Evangelien überhaupt*. Freiburg/ Leipzig: Mohr Siebeck, 1896.

Meyer, Ben F. "Jesus' Scenario of the Future," *Downside Review* 109 (1991): 1–15.

———. "Appointed Deeds, Appointed Doer: Jesus and the Scriptures." In *Authenticating the Activities of Jesus* (1999), 162–74.

Michaud, Jean-Paul. "Quelle(s) communauté(s) derrière la Source Q." In *The Sayings Source Q and the Historical Jesus* (2001), 577–606.

———. "Effervescence in Q Studies." *Studien zum Neuen Testament und seiner Umwelt* 30 (2005): 61–103.

———. "De quelques présents débats dans la troisième quête." In *De Jésus à Jésus-Christ. I. Le Jésus de l'histoire*. Paris: Mame-Desclée, 2010, 189–214.

Middleton, J. Richard. *The Liberating Image: The* Imago Dei *in Genesis 1*. Grand Rapids: Brazos, 2005.

———. "A New Heaven and a New Earth: The Case for a Holistic Reading of the Biblical Story of Redemption." *Journal for Christian Theological Research* 11 (2006): 73–97.

———. *A New Heaven and a New Earth*. Grand Rapids: Baker Academic, 2013.

Milbank, John. *Theology and Social Theory: Beyond Secular Reason*. Oxford: Blackwell, 1990.

Milik, Jozef T. "Milkî-Sedeq et Milkî-Reš' dans les anciens écrits juifs et chrétiens." *Journal of Jewish Studies* 23 (1972): 95–112, 124–26.

———, ed. *The Books of Enoch: Aramaic Fragments of Qumrân Cave 4*. Oxford: Clarendon Press, 1976.

Milikowsky, Chaim. "Which Gehenna? Retribution and Eschatology in the Synoptic Gospels and in Early Jewish Texts." *New Testament Studies* 34 (1988): 238–49.

Miller, J. Maxwell. "In the 'Image' and 'Likeness' of God." *Journal of Biblical Literature* 91 (1972): 289–304.

Miller, Merrill P. "The Function of Isa 61:1-2 in 11QMelchizedek." *Journal of Biblical Literature* 88, no. 4 (1969): 467–69.

———. "How Jesus Became Christ: Probing a Thesis." *Continuum* 2, nos. 2–3 (1993): 243–70.

———. "'Beginning from Jerusalem . . .': Re-examining Canon and Consensus." *Journal of Higher Criticism* 2, no. 1 (1995): 3–30.

———. "The Problem of the Origins of a Messianic Conception of Jesus." In *Redescribing Christian Origins* (2004), 301–36.

———. "The Anointed Jesus." In *Redescribing Christian Origins* (2004), 375–416.

Miller, Patrick D. Jr. "God the Warrior: A Problem in Biblical Interpretation and Apologetics." *Interpretation* 19 (1965): 39–46.

———. *The Divine Warrior in Early Israel.* HSM 5. Cambridge, MA: Harvard University Press, 1973.

Miller, Robert. *The Jesus Seminar and Its Critics.* Santa Rosa, CA: Polebridge, 1999.

———, ed. *The Apocalyptic Jesus: A Debate*. Santa Rosa, CA: Polebridge, 2001.

Minear, Paul S. *Commands of Christ*. Nashville: Abingdon, 1972.

Miner, Daniel F. "A Suggested Reading for 11QMelchizedek 17." *Journal for the Study of Judaism* 2 (1971): 144–48.

Mitchell, Hinckley G. T. *The Ethics of the Old Testament*. Chicago: University of Chicago Press, 1912.

Moll, Sebastian. *The Arch-Heretic Marcion.* WUNT 250. Tübingen: Mohr Siebeck, 2010.

Montefiore, Claude G. *The Synoptic Gospels: Edited with an Introduction and a Commentary*. 2 vols. London: Macmillan, 1927.

Moo, Douglas J. "The Christology of the Early Pauline Letters." In *Contours of Christology in the New Testament*. Edited by Richard N. Longenecker. Grand Rapid: Eerdmans, 2005, 169–92.

Moore, Kevin L. "Why Two Swords Were Enough: Israelite Tradition History Behind Luke 22:35-38." PhD diss., University of Denver, 2009.

Moule, C. F. D. *The Origin of Christology*. Cambridge: Cambridge University Press, 1977.

Mowinckel, Sigmund. *He That Cometh.* Translated by G. W. Anderson. Nashville: Abingdon, 1954.

Müller, Karlheinz. *Studien zur frühjüdischen Apokalyptik.* SBAB 11. Stuttgart: Katholisches Bibelwerk, 1991.

Murmelstein, Benjamin. "Adam, ein Beitrag zur Messiaslehre." *Wiener Zeitschrift für die Kunde des Morgenlandes* 35 (1928): 242–75; 36 (1929): 51–86.

Murphy O'Connor, Jerome. "Christological Anthropology in Phil. 2:6-11." *Revue Biblique* (1976): 25–50.

Murray, David. *Jesus on Every Page: 10 Simple Ways to Seek and Find Christ in the Old Testament.* Nashville: Thomas Nelson, 2013.

Myers, Ched. *Binding the Strong Man: A Political Reading of Mark's Story of Jesus.* Maryknoll, NY: Orbis Books, 1990.

Naude, J. A. "חרם."*New International Dictionary of Old Testament Theology and Exegeis.* Edited by Willem A. VanGemeren. 5 vols. Grand Rapids: Zondervan, 1997, 2:275–76.

Neander, Augustus Wilhelm. *The Life of Jesus Christ in its Historical Connexion and Historical Development.* London: Bell, 1888.

Neill, Stephen. *The Difference in Being a Christian.* New York: Association Press, 1955.

Neill, Stephen, and N. T. Wright. *The Interpretation of the New Testament 1861–1986.* 2d ed. Oxford: Oxford University Press, 1988.

Neirynck, Frans. *The Minor Agreements of Matthew and Luke against Mark with a Cumulative List.* BETL 37. Leuven: Leuven University Press, 1974.

———. "Recent Developments in the Study of Q." In *Logia: Les paroles de Jésus—The Sayings of Jesus.* Edited by Jacques Delobel. BETL 59. Leuven: Peeters, 1982, 29–75.

———. "Q: From Source to Gospel." *Ephemerides theologicae lovanienses* 71, no. 4 (1995): 421–30.

———. "The Minor Agreements and Q." In *The Gospel Behind the Gospels* (1995), 49–72.

———. "Q 6.20b-21; 7,22 and Isaiah 61." In *The Scriptures in the Gospels.* BETL 131. Edited by Christopher M. Tuckett. Leuven: Leuven University Press, 1997, 27–64.

Nelson-Pallmeyer, Jack. *Jesus Against Christianity: Reclaiming the Missing Jesus.* Harrisburg, PA: Trinity Press International, 2001.

Neufeld, Thomas R. Yoder. "Resistance and Nonresistance: The Two Legs of a Biblical Peace Stance." *Conrad Grebel Review* 21 (2003): 56-81.

———. *Killing Enmity: Violence and the New Testament*. Grand Rapids: Baker Academic, 2011.

Neugebauer, Fritz. *In Christus: Eine Untersuchung zum paulinischen Glaubensverständnis*. Göttingen: Vandenhoeck & Ruprecht, 1961.

Neusner, Jacob. *Judaism in the Matrix of Christianity*. Philadelphia: Fortress Press, 1986.

———. *A Rabbi Talks with Jesus: An Intermillennial Interfaith Exchange*. New York: Doubleday, 1993.

Neville, David J. *Arguments from Order in Synoptic Source Criticism: A History and Critique*. Macon, GA: Mercer University Press, 1994.

———. "Toward a Teleology of Peace: Contesting Matthew's Violent Eschatology." *Journal for the Study of the New Testament* 30, no. 2 (1997): 131–61.

———. "The Second Testament as a Covenant of Peace." *Biblical Theology Bulletin* 37, no. 1 (2007): 27–35.

———. "Violating Faith via Eschatological Violence: Reviewing Matthew's Eschatology." In *Validating Violence—Violating Faith?* (2008), 95–110.

———. "Justice and Divine Judgment: Scriptural Perspectives for Public Theology." *International Journal of Public Theology* 2, no. 3 (2009): 339–56.

———. "Faithful, True and Violent? Christology and 'Divine Vengeance' in the Revelation to John." In *Compassionate Eschatology: The Future as Friend*. Edited by Ted Grimsrud and Michael Hardin. Eugene, OR: Cascade Books, 2011, 56–84.

———. *A Peaceable Hope: Contesting Violent Eschatology in New Testament Narratives*. Grand Rapids: Baker Academic, 2013.

Newsom, Carol A. *The Self as Symbolic Space: Constructing Identity and Community at Qumran*. STDJ 52. Leiden: Brill, 2004.

Neyrey, Jerome. *The Passion according to Luke: A Redaction Study of Luke's Soteriology*. New York: Paulist Press, 1985.

Nickelsburg, George W. E. *Resurrection, Immortality and Eternal Life in Intertestamental Judaism*. HTS 26. Cambridge, MA: Harvard University Press, 1972.

———. *Jewish Literature between the Bible and the Mishnah: A Historical and Literary Introduction*. Philadelphia: Fortress Press, 1981.

———. "Salvation without and with a Messiah: Developing Beliefs in Writings Ascribed to Enoch." In *Judaisms and their Messiahs at the Turn of the Christian Era* (1987), 49–68.

———. "Son of Man." *Anchor Bible Dictionary* 6 (1992): 137–50.

———. "Enoch, First Book of." *Anchor Bible Dictionary* 2 (1992): 509–12.

———. *1 Enoch: A Commentary on the Book of 1 Enoch*. Hermeneia. Philadelphia: Fortress Press, 2001.

———. "Discerning the Structure(s) of the Enochic Book of Parables." In *Enoch and the Messiah Son of Man* (2007), 23–47.

——— and James C. VanderKam. *1 Enoch: A New Commentary based on the Hermeneia Commentary*. Minneapolis: Fortress Press, 2004.

Rowland, Christopher. *The Open Heaven: A Study of Apocalyptic in Judaism and Early Christianity*. New York: Crossroad, 1982.

Niditch, Susan. *War in the Hebrew Bible: A Study in the Ethics of Violence*. New York: Oxford University Press, 1993.

Niebuhr, Karl Wilhelm. "Die Werke des eschatologischen Freudenboten (4Q521 und die Jesusüberlieferung)." In *The Scriptures in the Gospels* (1997), 637–46.

Niebuhr, Reinhold. *Interpretation of Christian Ethics*. New York: Harper, 1935.

———. *Christianity and Power Politics*. North Haven, CT: Archon, 1969.

———. *An Interpretation of Christian Ethics*. New York: Seabury, 1979.

Nineham, Dennis. *The Use and Abuse of the Bible: A Study of the Bible in an Age of Rapid Cultural Change*. London: Macmillan, 1976.

Niskanen, Paul. "The Poetics of Adam: The Creation of אדם in the Image of אלהים." *Journal of Biblical Literature* 128, no. 3 (2009): 417–36.

Nolland, John. *Luke 9:21–18:34*. WBC 35B. Dallas: Word, 1993.

North, Christopher Richard. *The Suffering Servant in Deutero-Isaiah: An Historical and Critical Study*. London: Oxford, 1948.

North, Robert G. *Sociology of the Biblical Jubilee*. AnBib 4. Rome: Pontifical Biblical Institute, 1954.

Novakovic, Linda. "4Q521: The Works of the Messiah or the Signs of the Messianic Time?" In *Qumran Studies: New Approaches, New Questions*. Edited by Michael T. Davis and Brent A. Strawn. Grand Rapids: Eerdmans, 2007, 208–31.

Novenson, Matthew V. *Christ Among the Messiahs: Christ Language in Paul and Messiah Language in Ancient Judaism*. New York: Oxford University Press, 2012.

Oegema, Gerbern S. "Messianic Expectations in the Qumran Writings: Theses on their Development." In *Qumran Messianism: Studies on the Messianic Expectations in the Dead Sea Scrolls*. Edited by James H. Charlesworth, Hermann Lichtenberger, and Gerbern S. Oegema. Tübingen: Mohr Siebeck, 1998, 53–82.

———. The *The Anointed and His People: Messianic Expectations from the Maccabees to Bar Kochba*. JSPSup 27. Sheffield: Sheffield Academic Press, 1998.

———. "Messiah/Christ." *Encyclopedia of the Historical Jesus*. Edited by Craig A. Evans. New York: Routledge, 2008, 399–404.

Oesterley, William O. E. *The Evolution of the Messianic Idea: A Study in Comparative Religion*. New York: Dutton, 1908.

Olshausen, Hermann. *Biblical Commentary on the New Testament*. New York: Sheldon, Blakeman, 1858.

Olson, Daniel C. *A New Reading of the Animal Apocalypse of 1 Enoch: "All Nations Shall Be Blessed."* SVTP 24. Leiden: Brill, 2013.

Olsthoorn, M. F. *The Jewish Background and the Synoptic Setting of Mt 6,25-33 and Lk 12,22-31*. SBFA 10. Jerusalem: Franciscan Printing Press, 1975.

O'Neill, John C. "The Silence of Jesus." *New Testament Studies* 15 (1969): 153–67.

———. *Who Did Jesus Think He Was?* BI 11. Leiden: Brill, 1995.

———. *The Point Of It All: Essays on Jesus Christ*. Leiden: Deo Publishing, 2000.

Osborn, Robert T. "The Christian Blasphemy: A Non-Jewish Jesus." In *Jews and Christians: Exploring the Past, Present, and Future*. Edited by James H. Charlesworth. New York: Crossroad, 1990, 211–38.

Osburn, Carroll D. "The Christological Use of 1 Enoch i. 9 in Jude 14, 15." *New Testament Studies* (1976–77): 334–41.

Otto, Rudolf. *The Kingdom of God and the Son of Man: A Study in the History of Religion*. Translated by Floyd V. Filson and Bertram Lee Woolf. Grand Rapids: Zondervan, 1938.

Owen, Paul, and David Shepherd. "Speaking up for Qumran, Dalman and the Son of Man: Was *Bar Enasha* a Common Term for 'Man' in the Time of Jesus?" *Journal for the Study of the New Testament* 81 (2001): 81–122.

Page, Sydney H. T. "Ransom Saying." *Dictionary of Jesus and the Gospels*. Edited by Joel B. Green, Scot McKnight, and I. Howard Marshall. Downers Grove: InterVarsity, 1991, 660–62.

Pappas, Harry S. "The 'Exhortation to Fearless Confession'–Mt 10.26-33." *Greek Orthodox Theological Review* 25 (1980): 239–48.

Pate, C. Marvin. *Adam Christology as Exegetical & Theological Substructure of 2 Corinthians 4:7—5:21*. WUNT 2d ser. 4. Tübingen: Mohr Siebeck, 1984.

Patterson, Stephen J. "Fire and Dissension: *Ipsissima Vox Jesu* in Q 12:49, 51-53?" *Forum* 5 (1989): 121–39.

———. *The Gospel of Thomas and Jesus*. Sonoma, CA: Polebridge, 1993.

———. "The End of Apocalypse." *Theology Today* 52 (1995): 29–58.

———. "An Unanswered Question: Apocalyptic Expectation and Jesus' *Basileia* Proclamation." *Journal for the Study of the Historical Jesus* 8, no. 1 (2010): 67–79.

Patton, Carl S. *Sources of the Synoptic Gospels*. New York: Macmillan, 1915.

Pedersen, Johs. "Zur Erklärung der eschatologischen Visionen Henochs." *Islamica* 2 (1926): 416–29.

Penchansky, David. *What Rough Beast? Images of God in the Hebrew Bible* (Louisville: Westminster John Knox, 1999.

Peppard, Michael. *The Son of God in the Roman World: Divine Sonship in its Social World and Political Context*. New York: Oxford University Press, 2011.

Percy, Ernst. *Die Botschaft Jesu. Eine traditionskritische und exegetische Untersuchung*. LUA 1/49.5. Lund: Gleerup, 1953.

Perrin, Nicholas. *Jesus the Temple*. Grand Rapids: Baker Academic, 2010.

Perrin, Norman. *The Kingdom of God in the Teaching of Jesus*. Philadelphia: Westminster, 1963.

———. "Mark XIV.62: The End Product of a Christian Pesher Tradition?" *New Testament Studies* 12 (1966): 150–55.

———. "The Son of Man in Ancient Judaism and Primitive Christianity: A Suggestion." *Biblical Research* 11 (1966): 17–28.

———. *Rediscovering the Teaching of Jesus*. New York: Harper & Row, 1967.

———. "The Son of Man in the Synoptic Tradition." *Biblical Research* 13 (1968): 3–25.

———. *The New Testament: An Introduction: Proclamation and Parenesis, Myth and History*. New York: Harcourt Brace Jovanovich, 1974.

———. *A Modern Pilgrimage in New Testament Christology*. Philadelphia: Fortress Press, 1974.

———. *Jesus and the Language of the Kingdom: Symbol and Metaphor in New Testament Interpretation*. Philadelphia: Fortress Press, 1976.

Pesch, Rudolf. *Das Markusevangelium*. 2 vols. HTKNT. Freiburg: Herder, 1976–77.

Piper, John.*"Love Your Enemies": Jesus' Love Command in the Synoptic Gospels and in the Early Paraenesis: A History of the Tradition and Interpretation of Its Uses*. SNTSMS 38. Cambridge: Cambridge University Press, 1979.

Piper, Ronald A. *Wisdom in the Q-Tradition: The Aphoristic Sayings of Jesus*. SNTSMS 61. Cambridge and New York: Cambridge University Press, 1989.

———. "The Language of Violence and the Aphoristic Sayings in Q." In *Conflict and Invention* (1995), 53–72.

Pitre, Brant. *Jesus, the Tribulation, and the End of the Exile: Restoration Eschatology and the Origin of the Atonement.* Tübingen: Mohr Siebeck; Grand Rapids: Baker Academic, 2005.

Plummer, Alfred. *The Gospel according to St. John.* Cambridge: Cambridge University Press, 1882.

Poirer, John C. and Jeffrey Peterson, eds. *Marcan Priority without Q: Explorations in the Farrer Hypothesis.* LNTS. London/New York: T & T Clark International, 2014.

Pokorný, Petr. *The Genesis of Christology.* Edinburgh: T & T Clark, 1987.

———. "Demoniac and Drunkard: John the Baptist and Jesus According to Q 7:33-34." In *Jesus Research: An International Perspective: The Proceedings of the Biennial Princeton-Prague Symposium on the Current State of Studies on the Historical Jesus.* Edited by James H. Charlesworth and Petr Pokorný. Grand Rapids: Eerdmans, 2009, 170-182.

Polag, Athanasius. *Die Christologie der Logienquelle.* WMANT 45. Neukirchen-Vluyn: Neukirchener Verlag, 1977.

———. *Fragmenta Q: Textheft zur Logienquelle.* Neukirchen-Vluyn: Neukirchener Verlag, 1979.

Polkow, Dennis. "Method and Criteria for Historical Jesus Reseach." In *Society of Biblical Literature 1987 Seminar Papers.* Edited by Kent H. Richards. Atlanta: Scholars Press, 1987, 336–56.

Pomykala, Kenneth E. *The Davidic Dynasty Tradition in Early Judaism: Its History and Significance for Messianism.* EJL 7. Atlanta: Scholars Press, 1995.

Porter, Joshua R. "Legal Aspects of the Concept of 'Corporate Personality' in the Old Testament." *Vetus Testamentum* 15 (1965): 361–80.

Porter, Stanley E. *The Criteria for Authenticity in Historical-Jesus Research: Previous Discussion and New Proposals.* JSNTSup 191. Sheffield: Sheffield Academic Press, 2000.

———. "P. Oxy. 655 and James Robinson's Proposals for Q: Brief Points of Clarification." *Journal of Theological Studies* 52 (2001): 84–92.

Powell, Mark Allan. *Jesus as a Figure in History: How Modern Historians View the Man from Galilee.* Louisville: Westminster John Knox, 1998.

Priest, John F. "The Messiah and the Meal in 1QSa." *Journal of Biblical Literature* 82 (1963): 95–100.

Prior, Michael. *The Bible and Colonialism: A Moral Critique.* Sheffield: Sheffield Academic Press, 1997.

Puech, Émile. "Notes sur le manuscrit de XIMelkîsédeq," *Revue de Qumran* 12 (1987): 483–513.

———. "Une Apocalypse Messianique (4Q521)." *Revue de Qumran* 15 (1992): 475–519.

———. *Qumran Grotte 4 XVIII: Textes Hebreux (4Q521–4Q528, 4Q576–4Q579)*. DJD 25. Oxford: Clarendon Press, 1998.

———. "Some Remarks on 4Q246 and 4Q521 and Qumran Messianism." In *The Provo International Conference on the Dead Sea Scrolls* (1999), 545–65.

Randlinger, Stephan. *Die Feindesliebe nach dem natürlichen und positiven Sittengesetz: Eine historisch-ethische Studie*. Paderborn: Schöningh, 1906.

Rauser, Randal. "Let Nothing that Breathes Remain Alive: On the Problem of Divinely Commanded Genocide." *Philosophia Christi* 11, no. 1 (2009): 27–41.

Rawlinson, Alfred E. J. *The New Testament Doctrine of the Christ*. London: Longmans, 1978.

Reed, Annette Yoshiko. *Fallen Angels and the History of Judaism and Christianity: The Reception of Enochic Literature*. Cambridge and New York: Cambridge University Press, 2005.

Reese, Günter. *Die Geschichte Israels in der Auffassung des frühen Judentums: eine Untersuchung der Tiervision und der Zehnwochenapokalypse des äethiopischen Henochbuches, der Geschichtsdarstellung der Assumptio Mosis und der des 4Esrabuches*. BBB 123. Berlin: Philo, 1999.

Regev, Eyal. *Sectarianism in Qumran: A Cross-Cultural Perspective*. RS 45. New York: de Gruyter, 2007.

Reid, Barbara E. "Violent Endings in Matthew's Parables and Christian Nonviolence." *Catholic Biblical Quarterly* 66 (2004): 237–55.

Reinhold, Wolfgang. *Der Prozess Jesu*. BTS 28. Göttingen: Vandenhoeck & Ruprecht, 2006.

Reiser, Marius. *Jesus and Judgment: The Eschatological Proclamation in Its Jewish Context*. Translated by Linda M. Maloney. Minneapolis: Fortress Press, 1997.

———. "Love of Enemies in the Context of Antiquity." *New Testament Studies* 47 (2001): 411–27.

Reitzenstein, Richard. *Hellenistic Mystery-Religions: Their Basic Ideas and Significance*. Translated by John E. Seely. 3d ed. Pittsburgh: Pickwick, 1978.

Rhoads, David M. *Israel in Revolution 6–74 C. E. A Political History Based on the Writings of Josephus*. Philadelphia: Fortress Press, 1976.

Richard, Earl. *Jesus, One and Many: The Christological Concept of New Testament Authors*. Wilmington, DE: Michael Glazier, 1988.

Richardson, H. Neil. "Some Notes on 1QSa." *Journal of Biblical Literature* 76 (1957): 108–22

Riches, David. "The Phenomenon of Violence." In idem, ed., *The Anthropology of Violence*. Oxford: Blackwell, 1986, 1–7.

Riches, John K. *Jesus and the Transformation of Judaism*. London: Darton, Longman, and Todd, 1980.

———. *Conflicting Mythologies: Identity Formation in the Gospels of Mark and Matthew*. Edinburgh: T & T Clark, 2000.

Richter, Amy E. *Enoch and the Gospel of Matthew*. PTMS 183. Eugene, OR: Pickwick, 2012.

Riesenfeld, Harald. "Vom Schätzesammeln und Sorgen—ein Thema urchristlicher Paränese." In *Neotestamentica et Patristica*. Edited by Oscar Cullmann. Leiden: Brill, 1962, 47–58.

Ringe, Sharon H. "The Jubilee Proclamation in the Ministry and Teachings of Jesus: A Tradition-Critical Study in the Synoptic Gospels and Acts." Ph. D. diss., Union Theological Seminary, 1981.

———. *Jesus, Liberation, and Biblical Jubilee*. Philadelphia: Fortress Press, 1985.

Ringgren, Helmer. *The Faith of Qumran: Theology of the Dead Sea Scrolls*. Translated by Emilie T. Sander. Philadelphia: Fortress Press, 1963.

Robbins, Keith. *The Abolition of War: The Peace Movement in Britain, 1914-1919*. Cardiff: University of Wales Press, 1976.

Roberts, J. J. M. "The Old Testament's Contribution to Messianic Expectations." In *The Messiah: Developments in Earliest Judaism and Christianity* (1992), 39–51.

Robinson, James M. *A New Quest of the Historical Jesus*. London: SCM, 1961.

———. "Early Collections of Jesus' Sayings." In *Logia: Les Paroles de Jésus* (1982), 169–75.

———. "The Study of the Historical Jesus after Nag Hammadi." In *Semeia* 44: *The Historical Jesus and the Rejected Gospels*. Atlanta: Scholars Press, 1988, 45–55.

———. "The Sayings Gospel Q." In *The Four Gospels 1992*, 361–88.

———. "The Sayings Gospel Q." REL 484. Unpublished Instructor's Class Notes. Claremont Graduate School, Fall 1992.

———. "The Jesus of the Sayings Gospel Q." IACOP 28. Claremont: Claremont Graduate School, 1993.

———. "The Pre-Q Text of the (Ravens and) Lilies: Q 12:22-31 and P. Oxy. 655 (Gos. Thom. 36)." In *Text und Geschichte: Facetten theologischen Arbeitens aus dem Freundes- und Schülerkreis. Dieter Lührmann zum 60. Geburtstag*

Edited by Stefan Maser and Egbert Schlarb. MThS 50. Marburg: Elwert, 1999, 143–80.
———. "A Written Greek Sayings Cluster Older than Q: A Vestige." *Harvard Theological Review* 92 (1999): 61–77.
———. "Excursus on the Scribal Error in Q 12:27." In *The Critical Edition of Q*. Edited by James M. Robinson, Paul Hoffmann, and John S. Kloppenborg. Leuven: Peeters/Minneapolis: Fortress Press, 2000, xcix–ci.
———. "The Critical Edition of Q and the Study of Jesus." In *The Sayings Source Q and the Historical Jesus* (2001), 27–52.
———. "Jesus' Theology in the Sayings Gospel Q." In *Early Christian Voices: In Texts, Traditions, and Symbols: Essays in Honor of François Bovon*. Edited by David H. Warren, Ann Graham Brock, and David W. Pao. Boston: Brill, 2003, 25–43.
———. "A Pre-Canonical Greek Reading in Saying 36 of the Gospel of Thomas." In *The Sayings Gospel Q: Collected Essays*. Edited by Joseph Verheyden and Christoph Heil. BETL 189. Leuven: Peeters, 2005, 845–84.
———. *The Gospel of Jesus: In Search of the Original Good News*. New York: HarperSanFrancisco, 2005.
——— and Christoph Heil. "Zeugnisse eines schriftlichen, griechischen vorkanonischen Textes: Mt 6,28b א*, P. Oxy. 655 I, 1-17 (EvTh 36) und Q 12,27." *Zeitschrift für die neutestamentliche Wissenschaft und die Kunde der älteren Kirche* 89 (1998): 30–44.
———. "The Lilies of the Field: Saying 36 of the Gospel of Thomas and Secondary Accretions in Q 12.22b-31." *New Testament Studies* 47 (2001): 1–25.
———. "Noch einmal: Der Schreibfehler in Q 12,27." *Zeitschrift für die neutestamentliche Wissenschaft und die Kunde der älteren Kirche* 92 (2001): 113–22.
———, Paul Hoffmann, and John S. Kloppenborg, eds. *The Sayings Gospel Q in Greek and English*. Minneapolis: Fortress Press, 2002.
Robinson, John A. T. *The Human Face of God*. London: SCM, 1973.
———. *Jesus and His Coming: The Emergence of a Doctrine*. 2d ed. New York: Abingdon, 1979.
Rodd, Cyril. *Glimpses of a Strange Land: Studies in Old Testament Ethics*. Edinburgh: T & T Clark, 2001.
Rodriguez, Rafael. "Authenticating Criteria: The Use and Misuse of a Critical Method." *Journal for the Study of the Historical Jesus* 7 (2009): 152–67.

———. *Structuring Early Christian Memory: Jesus in Tradition, Performance, and Text*. Library of New Testament Studies. London: T & T Clark, 2010.

Rogers, Jack B., and Donald K. McKim. *The Authority and Interpretation of the Bible*. San Francisco: Harper & Row, 1979.

Rogerson, John W. "The Hebrew Conception of Corporate Personality: A Re-examination." *Journal of Theological Studies* 21 (1970): 1–16.

Rohrbaugh, Richard, ed. *The Social Sciences and New Testament Interpretation*. Peabody, MA: Hendrickson, 1996.

Rollmann, Hans, and Werner Zager. "Unveröffentlichte Briefe William Wredes zur Problematisierung des messianischen Selbstverständnisses Jesu." *Zeitschrift für neuere Theologiegeschichte* 8 (2001): 274–317.

Ropes, James Hardy. *The Synoptic Gospels*. Cambridge, MA: Harvard University Press, 1934.

Rost, Leonard. "Zum Buch der Kriege der Söhne des Lichtes gegen die Söhne der Finsternis." *Theologische Literaturzeitung* 80 (1955): 205–8.

Rowland, Christopher C. *The Open Heaven: A Study of Apocalyptic in Judaism and Christianity*. New York: Crossroad, 1982.

———. *Christian Origins*. London: SCM, 1985.

Rowlett, Lori L. *Joshua and the Rhetoric of Violence: A New Historicist Analysis*. JSOTSup 226. Sheffield: Sheffield Academic Press, 1996.

Russell, David S. *The Method and Message of Jewish Apocalyptic: 200 BC–A.D. 100*. Philadelphia: Westminster, 1964.

Sacchi, Paolo. *Jewish Apocalyptic and Its History*. Translated by William J. Short. JSPSup 20. Sheffield: Sheffield Academic Press, 1997.

———. "Qumran e la datazione del Libro delle Parabole di Enoc." *Henoch* 25 (2003): 149–66.

Saldarini, Anthony J. *Pharisees, Scribes and Sadducees in Palestinian Society*. Wilmington, DE: Michael Glazier, 1988.

Salomonsen, Børge. "Some Remarks on the Zealots with Special Regard to the Term 'Qannaim' in Rabbinic Literature." *New Testament Studies* 13 (1966): 164–76.

Sanday, William. *The Life of Christ in Recent Research*. Oxford: Clarendon, 1907.

Sanders, E. P. *Jesus and Judaism*. Philadelphia: Fortress Press, 1985.

———. *Judaism: Practice and Belief, 63 B.C.E.–66 CE*. London: SCM, 1992.

———. *The Historical Figure of Jesus*. London: Penguin, 1993.

——— and Margaret Davies. *Studying the Synoptic Gospels*. London: SCM, 1989.

Sanders, Jack T. "The Criterion of Coherence and the Randomness of Charisma: Poring Through Some Aporias in the Jesus Tradition." *New Testament Studies* (1998): 1–25.

Sanders, James A. "The Old Testament in 11QMelchizedek." *Janescu* 5 (1973): 373–82.

———. "From Isaiah 61 to Luke 4." In *Christianity, Judaism and Other Greco-Roman Cults: Studies for Morton Smith at Sixty*. Edited by Jacob Neusner. 2 vols. Leiden: Brill, 1975, 1:75–106.

———. "Isaiah in Luke." In *Interpreting the Prophets*. Edited by James L. Mays and Paul J. Achtemeier. Philadelphia: Fortress Press, 1987, 75–85.

———. "Sins, Debts, and Jubilee Release." In *Luke and Scripture* (1993), 84–92.

———. "The Book of Job and the Origins of Judaism." *Biblical Theology Bulletin* 38, no. 2 (2009): 60–70.

Sandmel, Samuel. *We Jews and Jesus*. New York: Oxford University Press, 1965.

Sato, Migaku. *Q und Prophetie: Studien zur Gattungs- und Traditionsgeschichte der Quelle Q*. WUNT 2d ser. 29. Tübingen: Mohr Siebeck, 1988.

———. "The Shape of the Q Source." Pages 156–79 in *The Shape of Q* (1994), 156–79.

———. "Wisdom Statements in the Sphere of Prophecy." In *The Gospel Behind the Gospels* (1995), 139–58.

Sawyer, John F. A. "The Meaning of צלם אלהים ('In the Image of God') in Genesis i–xi." *Journal of Theological Studies* 25 (1974): 418–26.

Schäfer, Peter. *Jesus in the Talmud*. Princeton: Princeton University Press, 2007.

Schiffman, Lawrence H. *The Eschatological Community of the Dead Sea Scrolls: A Study of the Rule of the Congregation*. SBLMS 38. Atlanta: Scholars Press, 1989.

———. "Messianic Figures and Ideas in the Qumran Scrolls." In *The Messiah: Developments in Earliest Judaism and Christianity* (1992), 116–99.

———. *Reclaiming the Dead Sea Scrolls: The History of Judaism, the Background of Christianity, the Lost Library of Qumran*. Philadelphia: Jewish Publication Society, 1994.

Schipper, Jeremy. *Disability and Isaiah's Suffering Servant*. Biblical Refigurations. New York: Oxford University Press, 2011.

Schlabach, Theron F. and Richard T. Hughes. *Proclaim Peace: Christian Pacifism from Unexpected Quarters*. Urbana: University of Illinois, 1997.

Schlatter, Adolf. *Das Evangelium des Lukas*. 2d ed. Stuttgart: Calwer, 1960.

———. *Der Evangelist Matthäus. Seine Sprache, sein Ziel, seine Selbständigkeit*. 7th ed. Stuttgart: Calwer, 1982.

———. *The History of the Christ: The Foundation of New Testament Theology.* Grand Rapids: Baker Academic, 1997.

Schlosser, Jacques. *Le Règne de Dieu dans les Dits de Jésus.* ÉtB. 2 vols. Paris: Gabalda, 1980.

———. *Le Dieu de Jésus.* LD 129. Paris: Cerf, 1987.

———. "Le logion de Mt 10,28 par. Le 12,4-5." In *The Four Gospels 1992*, 621–31.

Schmid, Josef. *Das Neue Testament übersetzt und kurz erklärt.* Vol. 1. *Das Evangelium nach Matthäus.* RNT1. Regensburg: Pustet, 1956.

Schmidt, Daryl. "The LXX Gattung 'Prophetic Correlative.'" *Journal of Biblical Literature* 96 (1977): 517–22.

Schmidt, Nathaniel. "Was בר נשא a Messianic Title?" *Journal of Biblical Literature* 15 (1896): 36–53.

Schmidt, Werner H. *Die Schöpfungsgeschichte der Priesterschrift.* WMANT 17. 3d ed. Neukirchen-Vluyn: Neukirchener Verlag, 1973.

Schnackenburg, Rudolf. *God's Rule and Kingdom.* Translated by John Murray. New York: Herder & Herder, 1968.

Schnedermann, Georg. *Jesu Verkündigung und Lehre vom Reiche Gottes in ihrer geschichtlichen Bedeutung.* 2 vols. Leipzig: Deichert, 1893–1895.

Schniewind, Julius. *Das Evangelium nach Matthäus.* NTD 2. Göttingen: Vandenhoeck & Ruprecht, 1984.

Schochet, Jacob Immanuel. *Mashiach: The Principle of Mashiach and the Messianic Era in Jewish Law and Tradition.* New York: S. I. E., 1992.

Schodde, George H. *The Book of Enoch: Translated from the Ethiopic, with Introduction and Notes.* Andover: Draper, 1882.

Schoeps, Hans Joachim. "Von der Imitatio Dei zur Nachfolge Christi." In *Aus Frühchristlicher Zeit: religionsgeschichtliche Untersuchungen.* Tübingen: Mohr, 1950, 286–301.

Scholem, Gershom. *The Messianic Idea in Judaism and Other Essays on Jewish Spirituality.* New York: Schocken, 1971.

Schottroff, Luise. "Non-Violence and the Love of One's Enemies." In *Essays on the Love Command.* Philadelphia: Fortress Press, 1978, 9–39.

———. "Sheep among Wolves: The Wandering Prophets of the Sayings-Source." In *Jesus and the Hope of the Poor.* Edited by Luise Schottroff and Wolfgang Stegemann. Translated by Matthew J. O'Connell. Maryknoll, NY: Orbis Books, 1986, 39–43.

———. "Give to Caesar What Belongs to Caesar and to God What Belongs to God: A Theological Response of the Early Christian Church to Its Social and Political Environment." In *Love of Enemy and Nonretaliation*. Edited by Willard M. Swartley. Louisville: Westminster John Knox, 1992, 223–57.

Schrage, Wolfgang. *The Ethics of the New Testament*. Philadephia: Fortress Press, 1988.

Schröter, Jens. "The Historical Jesus and the Sayings Tradition: Comments on Current Research." *Neotestamentica* 30 (1996): 151–68.

———. *Erinnerung an Jesu Worte. Studien zur Rezeption der Logienüberlieferung in Markus, Q und Thomas*. WMANT 76. Neukirchen-Vluyn: Neukirchener Verlag, 1997.

———. "Markus, Q und der historische Jesus: Methodologische und exegetische Erwägungen zu den Anfängen der Rezeption der Verkündigung Jesu." *Zeitschrift für die Neutestamentliche Wissenschaft und die Kunde der älteren Kirche* 89 (1998): 173–200.

———. "Vorsynoptische Überlieferung auf P. Oxy. 655? Kritische Bemerkungen zu einer erneuerten These." *Zeitschrift für die Neutestamentliche Wissenschaft und die Kunde der älteren Kirche* 90 (1999): 265–72.

———. "Verschrieben? Klärende Bemerkungen zu einem vermeintlichen Schreibfehler in Q und tatsächlichen Irrtümern." *Zeitschrift für die Neutestamentliche Wissenschaft und die Kunde der älteren Kirche* 92 (2001): 283–89.

———. "Rezeptionsprozesse in der Jesusüberlieferung: Überlegungen zum historischen Charakter der neutestamentlichen Wissenschaft am Beispiel der Sorgensprüche." *New Testament Studies* 47 (2001): 442–68.

———. "Die Frage nach dem historischen Jesus und der Charakter historischer Erkenntnis." In *The Sayings Source Q and the Historical Jesus*. Edited by A. Lindemann. Leuven: Leuven University Press, 2001, 207-254.

Schubert, Kurt. "The Sermon on the Mount and the Qumran Texts." In *The Scrolls and the New Testament*. Edited by Krister Stendahl. New York: Harper, 1957, 118–28.

Schulz, Anselm. *Nachfolgen und Nachahmen*. Munich: Loesel, 1967.

Schulz, Siegfried. *Q: Spruchquelle der Evangelisten*. Zürich: Theologischer Verlag, 1972.

———. "Die Gottesherrschaft ist nahe herbeigekommen (Mt 10,7/Lk 10,9). Der kerygmatische Entwurf der Q-Gemeinde Syrien." In *Das Wort und die Wörter. Festschrift Gerhard Friedrich zum 65sten Geburtstag*. Edited by Horst R. Balz and Siegfried Schulz. Stuttgart: Kohlhammer, 1973, 57–67.

Schüssler Fiorenza, Elisabeth. "The Ethics of Biblical Interpretation: Decentering Biblical Scholarship." *Journal of Biblical Literature* 107 (1988): 3-17.

———. *Rhetoric and Ethic: The Politics of Biblical Studies*. Minneapolis: Fortress Press, 1999.

———. "Critical Feminist Historical-Jesus Research." In *Handbook for the Study of the Historical Jesus* (2011), 509–48.

Scroggs, Robin. *The Last Adam: A Study in Pauline Anthropology*. Philadelphia: Fortress Press, 1966.

Schürmann, Heinz. "Beobachtungen zum Menschensohn-Titel in der Redequelle." In *Jesus und der Menschensohn* (1975), 124–47.

———. *Das Lukasevangelium Erster Teil. (Kommentar zu Kap. 1,1–9,50)*. HTKNT 3. 3d ed. Freiburg: Herder, 1984.

———. "Observations on the Son of Man Title in the Speech Source. Its Occurrence in Closing and Introductory Expressions." In *The Shape of Q* (1994), 74–97.

Schwager, Raymund. *Must There Be Scapegoats? Violence and Redemption in the Bible*. San Francisco: Harper & Row, 1987.

Schwartz, Barry. "Christian Origins: Historical Truth and Social Memory." In *Memory, Tradition, and Text: Uses of the Past in Early Christianity*. Edited by Alan Kirk and Tom Thatcher. Leiden: Brill, 2005, 43-56.

Schwartz, Daniel R. "Josephus and Philo on Pontius Pilate." *The Jerusalem Cathedra* 3 (1983): 26–45.

Schwartz, Regina. *The Curse of Cain: The Violent Legacy of Monotheism*. Chicago: University of Chicago Press, 1997.

Schwarz, Günther. "Matthäus 10:28: Emendation und Ruckübersetzung." *Zeitschrift für die Neutestamentliche Wissenschaft und die Kunde der älteren Kirche* 72 (1981): 277–82.

Schweitzer, Albert. *Von Reimarus zu Wrede: Eine Geschichte der Leben-Jesu-Forschung*. Tübingen: Mohr Siebeck, 1906. English: *The Quest for the Historical Jesus: A Critical Study of its Progress from Reimarus to Wrede*. Translated by William Montgomery. London: Adam and Charles Black, 1910.

———. *The Mysticism of Paul the Apostle*. Translated by William Montgomery. New York: Macmillan, 1955.

———. *The Mystery of the Kingdom of God: The Secret of Jesus' Messiahship and Passion*. Translated by Walter Lowrie. New York: Macmillan, 1964.

Schweizer, Eduard. "Der Menschensohn (Zur eschatologischen Erwartung Jesu)." *Zeitschrift für die Neutestamentliche Wissenschaft und die Kunde der älteren Kirche* 50 (1959): 185–209.

———. "The Son of Man." *Journal of Biblical Literature* 79 (1960): 119–29.

———. *Lordship and Discipleship*. SBT 28. Naperville, IL: Allenson, 1960.

———. "The Son of Man Again." *New Testament Studies* 9 (1963): 256–61.

———. *The Good News according to Mark*. Translated by Donald H. Madvig. Richmond: John Knox, 1970.

———. *Jesus*. Translated by David E. Green. Atlanta: John Knox, 1971.

———. *The Good News According to Matthew*. Translated by David E. Green. Atlanta: John Knox, 1975.

———. *The Good News According to Luke*. Translated by David E. Green. Atlanta: John Knox, 1984.

Scott, E. F. "The Place of Apocalyptical Conceptions in the Mind of Jesus." *Journal of Biblical Literature* 41 (1922): 137–42.

Scott, James M. *Adoption as Sons of God: An Investigation into the Background of* Huiothesia *in the Pauline Corpus*. WUNT 2d ser. 48. Tübingen: Mohr Siebeck, 1992.

———, ed. *Restoration: Old Testament, Jewish, and Christian Perspectives*. JSJSup 72. Leiden: Brill, 2001.

Scott, James. "Historical Development of the Messianic Idea." *The Old Testament Student* 7 (1888): 176–80.

Scott, Steven R. "The Binitarian Nature of the Book of Similitudes." *Journal for the Study of the Pseudepigrapha* 18 (2008): 55–78.

Seeley, David. "Rulership and Service in Mark 10:41-45." *Novum Testamentum* 35 (1993): 234–50.

Seibert, Eric A. *Disturbing Divine Behavior: Troubling Old Testament Images of God*. Minneapolis: Fortress Press, 2009.

———. *The Violence of Scripture: Overcoming the Old Testament's Troubling Legacy*. Minneapolis: Fortress Press, 2012.

Segal, Alan. "The Risen Christ and the Angelic Mediator Figures in Light of Qumran." In *Jesus and the Dead Sea Scrolls* (1992), 302–28.

Segovia, Fernando F. *Decolonizing Biblical Studies: A View from the Margins*. Maryknoll: Orbis Books, 2000.

Seitz, O. J. F. "Love Your Enemies." *New Testament Studies* 16 (1969): 43–52.

———. "Love Your Enemies: The Historical Setting of Matthew V. 43f.; Luke VI.27f." *New Testament Studies* 16 (1970): 39–54.

Sevenich-Bax, Elisabeth. *Israels Konfrontation mit den letzten Boten der Weisheit: Form, Funktion und Interdependenz der Weisheitselemente in der Logienquelle.* MThA 21. Altenberge: Oros, 1993.

Sharman, Henry Burton. *The Teaching of Jesus about the Future According to the Synoptic Gospels.* Chicago: University of Chicago Press, 1909.

Sharp, Gene. *The Politics of Nonviolent Action.* Vol. 1: *Power and Struggle.* Boston: Porter Sargent, 1973.

———. *The Politics of Nonviolent Action.* Vol. 3: *The Pole Dynamics of Nonviolent Action.* Boston: Porter Sargent Publishers, 1973.

Sherwood, Yvonne and Jonneke Bekkenkamp, eds. *Sanctified Aggression: Legacies of Biblical and Post-Biblical Vocabularies of Violence.* London/New York: T & T Clark, 2003.

Shimoff, Sandra R. "Gardens: From Eden to Jerusalem." *Journal for the Study of Judaism* 26 (1995): 145–55.

Sigal, Philip. "Further Reflections on the 'Begotten' Messiah." *Hebrew Annual Review* 7 (1983): 221–33.

Sjöberg, Eric. *Der Menschensohn im äthopischen Henochbuch.* Lund: Gleerup, 1946.

———. *Der verborgene Menschensohn in den Evangelien.* Lund: Gleerup, 1955.

Skeat, Theodore C. "The Lilies of the Field." *Zeitschrift für die Neutestamentliche Wissenschaft und die Kunde der älteren Kirche* 37 (1938): 211–14.

Slater, Thomas B. "One Like a Son of Man in First-Century C.E. Judaism." *New Testament Studies* 41 (1995): 183–98.

Sloan, Robert B. Jr. *The Favorable Year of the Lord: A Study of Jubilary Theology in the Gospel of Luke.* Austin: Schola, 1977.

Smallwood, E. Mary. *The Jews Under Roman Rule from Pompey to Diocletian.* Leiden: Brill, 1981.

Smend, Rudolf. *Yahweh War and Tribal Confederation: Reflections upon Israel's Earliest History.* Translated by Max Gray Rogers. Nashville: Abingdon, 1970.

Smith, Daniel A. *The Post-Mortem Vindication of Jesus in the Sayings Gospel Q.* LNTS 338. London: T & T Clark International, 2007.

Smith, Dennis E. "What Do We Really Know about the Jerusalem Church? Christian Origins in Jerusalm according to Acts and Paul." In *Redescribing Christian Origins* (2004), 237–52.

Smith, J. M. Powis. *The Moral Life of the Hebrews.* Chicago: University of Chicago Press, 1923.

Smith, Jonathan Z. "The Social Description of Early Christianity." *Religious Studies Review* 1 (1975): 19–25.

Smith, Mahlon H. "No Place for a Son of Man." *Forum* 4 (1988): 83–107.

———. "Israel's Prodigal Son: Reflections on Reimaging Jesus." In *Profiles of Jesus*. Edited by Roy W. Hoover. Santa Rosa, CA: Polebridge, 2002, 87–113.

Smith, Morton. "Mt. 5:43: 'Hate Thine Enemy.'" *Harvard Theological Review* 45 (1952): 71–73.

———. "'God's Begetting the Messiah' in 1QSa." *New Testament Studies* 5 (1958–1959): 218–24.

———. "What is Implied by the Variety of Messianic Figures?" *Journal of Biblical Literature* 78 (1959): 66–72.

Snaith, Norman. "The Image of God." *Expository Times* 86, no. 1 (1974): 24.

Sobrino, Jon. *Jesus the Liberator: A Historical-Theological View*. Maryknoll, NY: Orbis Books, 1993.

Soiron, Thaddäus. *Die Bergpredigt Jesu: Formgeschichtliche, exegetische und theologische Erklärung*. Freiburg: Herder, 1941.

Son, Sang-Won (Aaron). *Corporate Elements in Pauline Anthropology: A Study of Selected Terms, Idioms, and Concepts in the Light of Paul's Usage and Background*. AnBib 148. Rome: Pontifical Biblical Institute, 2001.

Sparks, Kenton L. *God's Word in Human Words: An Evangelical Appropriation of Critical Biblical Scholarship*. Grand Rapids: Baker Academic, 2008.

———. *Sacred Word, Broken Word: Biblical Authority and the Dark Side of Scripture*. Grand Rapids: Eerdmans, 2012.

Spong, John Shelby. *The Sins of Scripture: Exposing the Bible's Texts of Hate to Reveal the God of Love*. New York: HarperOne, 2006.

Sprinkle, Preston. *Fight: A Christian Case for Non-Violence*. Colorado Springs: David C. Cook, 2013.

Staerk, Willi. *Die Erlösererwartung in den Östlichen Religionen: Soter II*. Stuttgart: Kohlhammer, 1938.

Stanley, Christopher D. "Words of Life: Scripture and Non-violence in Judaism, Christianity and Islam." In *Religion, Scripture, and Violence*. Edited by John T. Squires and William W. Emilsen. Melbourne: Australian Theological Forum, 2008, 39–56.

———. "Words of Death: Scripture and Violence in Judaism, Christianity and Islam." In *Religion, Scripture, and Violence* (2008), 17–37.

Stanton, Graham N. "On the Christology of Q." In *Christ and Spirit in the New Testament* (1973), 27–42.

———. *Gospel Truth? New Light on Jesus and the Gospels*. Valley Forge, PA: Trinity Press International, 1995.

———. "The Fourfold Gospel." *New Testament Studies* 43 (1997): 317–46.

Stanton, Vincent Henry. *The Jewish and the Christian Messiah: A Study in the Earliest History of Christianity*. Edinburgh: T & T Clark, 1886.

Starcky, Jean. "Les quatres étapes du messianisme à Qumran." *Revue Biblique* 70 (1963): 481–505.

Stark, Thom. *The Human Faces of God: What Scripture Reveals When It Gets God Wrong (and Why Inerrancy Tries To Hide It)*. Eugene: Wipf and Stock, 2010.

Steenburg, David. "The Case Against the Synonymity of Morphē and Eikōn." *Journal for the Study of the New Testament* 34 (1988): 77–86.

———. "The Worship of Adam and Christ as the Image of God." *Journal for the Study of the New Testament* 39 (1990): 95–109.

Stegemann, Ekkehard, ed., *Messias-Vorstellungen bei Juden und Christen*. Stuttgart: Kohlhammer, 1993.

Stein, Robert. *Jesus the Messiah*. Downers Grove: InterVarsity, 1996.

Steinmüller, Franz. *Die Feindesliebe nach dem natürlichen und positiven Sittengesetz*. Regensburg: Manz, 1903.

Stephens, Walter. *Demon Lovers: Witchcraft, Sex, and the Crisis of Belief*. Chicago: University of Chicago Press, 2002.

Stern, Jessica. *Terror in the Name of God: Why Religious Militants Kill*. New York: Harper Collins, 2003.

Stern, Philip D. *The Biblical Óerem: A Window on Israel's Religious Experience*. BJS 211. Atlanta: Scholars Press, 1991

Stewart, Robert B., ed. *The Message of Jesus: John Dominic Crossan and Ben Witherington III in Dialogue*. Minneapolis: Fortress Press, 2013.

Stolz, Fritz. *Jahwes und Israels Krieg: Kriegstheorien und Kriegserfahrungen im Glaube des alten Israel*. ATANT 60. Zürich: Theologischer Verlag, 1972.

Stone, Michael E. *A History of the Literature of Adam and Eve*. SBLEJL 3. Atlanta: Scholars Press, 1992.

———. *Ancient Judaism: New Visions and Views*. Grand Rapids: Eerdmans, 2011.

Stoner, John K. "The Two Swords Passage: A Command or a Question? Nonviolence in Luke 22." In *Within the Perfection of Christ*. Edited by Terry L. Brensinger and E. Morris Sider. Nappanee, IN: Evangel Press, 1990, 67–80.

Storr, Gottlob Christian. *Doctrinae christianae pars theoretica e sacris literis repetita*. Stuttgart: Mezler, 1793.

Stowers, Stanley K. *A Rereading of Romans: Justice, Jews and Gentiles*. New Haven: Yale University Press, 1995.

Strack, Hermann. *Jesus, die Häretiker und die Christen nach den altesten jüdischen Angaben*. Leipzig: Hinrischs, 1910.

Strecker, Georg. *Der Weg der Gerechtigkeit*. FRLANT 82. Göttingen: Vandenhoeck & Ruprecht, 1962.

———. *The Sermon on the Mount: An Exegetical Commentary*. Translated by O. C. Dean, Jr. Nashville: Abingdon, 1988.

———, ed. *Minor Agreements: Symposium Göttingen 1991*. Göttingen: Vandenhoeck & Ruprecht, 1993.

Streeter, B. H. *The Four Gospels: A Study of Origins, Treating of the Manuscript Tradition, Sources, Authorship, and Dates*. London: Macmillan, 1924.

Strenski, Ivan. *Religion in Relation: Method, Application, and Moral Location*. Columbia, SC: University of South Carolina Press, 1993.

Stroumsa, Guy G. "Introduction: The Paradise Chronotrope." In *Paradise in Antiquity: Jewish and Christian Views*. Edited by Markus Bockmuehl and Guy S. Stroumsa. Cambridge: Cambridge University Press, 2010, 1–14.

Strugnell, John T., Daniel Harrington, and Torleif Elgvin, eds. *Qumran Cave 4: XXXIV; 4QInstruction (Musar LeMevin)*. DJD 34. Oxford: Clarendon Press, 1999.

Stuhlmacher, Peter. *Das paulinische Evangelium*. Christianisme et philosophie. Göttingen: Vandenhoeck & Ruprecht, 1968.

———. "Vicariously Giving His Life for Many, Mark 10:45 (Matt. 20:28)." In idem, *Reconciliation, Law, and Righteousness: Essays in Biblical Theology*. Philadelphia: Fortress Press, 1986, 16–29.

———. *Jesus of Nazareth, Christ of Faith*. Translated by Siegfried S. Schatzmann. Peabody, MA: Hendrickson, 1988.

———. "The Theme: The Gospel and the Gospels." In *The Gospel and the Gospels*. Edited by Peter Stuhlmacher. Translated by John Vriend. Grand Rapids: Eerdmans, 1991, 1–25.

———. *Wie treibt man Biblische Theologie*. BThSt 24. Neukirchen-Vluyn: Neukirchener Verlag, 1995.

Suggs, M. Jack. *Wisdom, Christology and Law in Matthew's Gospel*. Cambridge, MA: Harvard University Press, 1970.

Sullivan, Clayton. *Rethinking Realized Eschatology*. Macon, GA: Mercer University Press, 1988.

Sutcliffe, Edmund F. "Hatred at Qumran." *Revue de Qumran* 7 (1960): 345–56.

Suter, David W. *Tradition and Composition in the Parables of Enoch*. SBLDS 47. Missoula: Scholars Press, 1979.

Swartley, Willard M. "Politics and Peace (*Eirēnē*) in Luke's Gospel." In *Political Issues in Luke-Acts*. Edited by Richard J. Cassidy and Philip J. Scharper. Maryknoll: Orbis Books, 1983, 26–29.

———. *Covenant of Peace: The Missing Peace in New Testament Theology and Ethics*. Grand Rapids: Eerdmans, 2006.

Tabor, James D., and Michael O. Wise. "4Q521 'On Resurrection' and the Synoptic Gospel Tradition: A Preliminary Study." In *Qumran Questions*. Edited by James H. Charlesworth. Sheffield: Sheffield Academic Press, 1995, 151–63.

Talbert, Charles H. "The Problem of Pre-Existence in Philippians 2:6-11." *Journal of Biblical Literature* 86 (1967): 141–53.

———, ed. *Reimarus: Fragments*. Translated by Ralph S. Fraser. Philadelphia: Fortress Press, 1970.

Talmon, Shemaryahu. "The Concepts of *Mashiah* and Messianism in Early Judaism." In *The Messiah: Developments in Earliest Judaism and Christianity* (1992), 79–115.

Tannehill, Robert C. *The Sword of his Mouth: Forceful and Imaginative Language in Synoptic Sayings*. Philadelphia: Fortress Press, 1975.

Taylor, Vincent. *The Person of Christ in New Testament Teaching*. London: Macmillan, 1958.

———. *The Gospel According to St. Mark*. London: Macmillan, 1966.

Teeple, Howard M. *The Mosaic Eschatological Prophet*. SBLMS 10. Philadelphia: Society of Biblical Literature, 1957.

Telford, William. *The Theology of the Gospel of Mark*. Cambridge: Cambridge University Press, 1999.

Thatcher, Adrian. *The Savage Text: The Use and Abuse of the Bible*. Chichester: Wiley-Blackwell, 2008.

Theisohn, Johannes. *Der auserwählte Richter: Untersuchungen zum traditionsgeschichtlichen Ort der Menschensohngestalt der Bilderreden des Äthiopischen Henoch*. Göttingen: Vandenhoeck & Ruprecht, 1975.

Theissen, Gerd. *Sociology of Early Palestinian Christianity*. Translated by John Bowden. Philadelphia: Fortress Press, 1978.

———. "Gewaltverzicht und Feindeliebe (Mt 5,38-48/Lk 6,27-38) und deren sozialgeschichtlicher Hintergrund." In idem, *Studien zur Soziologie des Urchristentums*. WUNT 19. 3d ed. Tübingen: Mohr Siebeck, 1989, 160–97.

——— and Dagmar Winter. *The Quest for the Plausible Jesus: The Question of Criteria*. Translated by M. Eugene Boring. Louisville: Westminster John Knox, 2002.

——— and Annette Merz. *Der historische Jesus*. Göttingen: Vandenhoeck & Ruprecht, 1996. English: *The Historical Jesus: A Comprehensive Guide*. Translated by John Bowden. Minneapolis: Fortress Press, 1998.

——— and Annette Merz. "The Delay of the Parousia as a Test Case for the Criterion of Coherence." *Louvain Studies* 32 (2007): 49–66.

Thiselton, Anthony C. *New Horizons in Hermeneutics: The Theory and Practice of Transforming Biblical Reading*. Grand Rapids: Zondervan, 1992.

Tholuck, Augustus. *Commentar zu dem Evangelio Johannis*. Hamburg: Perthes, 1827.

Thomas, Heath A., Jeremy Evans, and Paul Copan, eds. *Holy War in the Bible: Christian Morality and an Old Testament Problem*. Downer's Grove: InterVarsity, 2013.

Thompson, George H. P. "The Son of Man: The Evidence of the Dead Sea Scrolls." *Expository Times* 72 (1961): 125.

———. "The Son of Man—Some Further Considerations." *Journal of Theological Studies* 12 (1961): 203–9.

Thompson, Thomas L. and Thomas S. Verenna. *'Is This Not The Carpenter?' The Question of the Historicity of the Figure of Jesus*. Copenhagen International Seminar. Durham: Acumen Publishing, 2013.

Thomson, Jeremy. "Jesus and the Two Swords: Did Jesus Endorse Violence?" *Anabaptism Today* 33 (2003): 10–16.

Thoreau, Henry David. *Civil Disobedience.* New York: Holt, Rinehart, & Winston, 1970.

Thrall, Margaret E. "The Origin of Pauline Christology." In *Apostolic History and the Gospel: Biblical and Historical Essays Presented to F. F. Bruce on his 60th Birthday*. Edited by W. Ward Gasque and Ralph P. Martin. Grand Rapids: Eerdmans, 1970, 304–16.

Tigchelaar, Eibert. "Manna-Eaters and Man-Eaters: Food of Giants and Men in the Pseudo-Clementine Homilies 8." In *The Pseudo-Clementines*. Edited by Jan N. Bremmer. SECA 10. Leuven: Peeters, 2010, 92–114.

Tiller, Patrick A. *A Commentary on the Animal Apocalypse of 1 Enoch*. Atlanta: Scholars Press, 1993.

Tinsley, Ernest J. *The Imitation of God in Christ*. Philadelphia: Westminster, 1960.

Tödt, Heinz Eduard. *Der Menschensohn in der synoptischen Überlieferung*. Gütersloh: Gütersloher Verlaghaus Mohn, 1959. English: *The Son of Man in the Synoptic Tradition*. Translated by Dorothea M. Barton. Philadelphia: Westminster, 1965.

Toepel, Alexander. "Adamic Traditions in Early Christian and Rabbinic Literature (from NT to the *Cave of Treasures*)." Paper presented at the Fifth Enoch Seminar, Naples, Italy, June 14–18, 2009.

Trible, Phyllis. *Texts of Terror: Literary-Feminist Readings of Biblical Narratives*. Philadelphia: Fortress Press, 1984.

Trocmé, André. *Jesus and the Nonviolent Revolution*. New York: Plough, 2011.

Tromp, Johannes. "Adamic Traditions in Early Judaism and Christianity (*Books of Adam and Eve*)." Paper presented at the Fifth Enoch Seminar, Naples, Italy, June 14–18, 2009.

Tuckett, Christopher M. *Q and the History of Early Christianity: Studies on Q*. Peabody, MA: Hendrickson, 1996.

———. "Scripture and Q." Pages 3–26 in *The Scriptures in the Gospels* (1997), 3–26.

———. "The Son of Man and Daniel 7: Q and Jesus." In *The Sayings Source Q and the Historical Jesus* (2001), 371–94.

———. *Christology and the New Testament: Jesus and his Earliest Followers*. Louisville: Westminster John Knox, 2001.

———. Review of Mark Goodacre, *The Case Against Q*. *Novum Testamentum* 46, no. 4 (2004): 401–3.

———, ed. *The Messianic Secret*. IRT 1. Minneapolis: Fortress Press, 1983.

Uro, Risto. "Apocalyptic Symbolism and Social Identity in Q." In *Symbols and Strata: Essays on the Sayings Gospel Q*. PFES 65. Helsinki: Finnish Exegetical Society; Göttingen: Vandenhoeck & Ruprecht, 1996, 67–118.

Vaage, Leif E. "The Son of Man Sayings in Q: Stratigraphical Location and Significance." *Semeia* 55 (1991): 103–29.

———. *Galilean Upstarts: Jesus' First Followers According to Q*. Valley Forge, PA: Trinity Press International, 1994.

———. "Composite Texts and Oral Mythology: The Case of the 'Sermon' in Q (6:20-49)." In *Conflict and Invention* (1995), 75–97.

Valzelli, Luigi. *Psychobiology of Aggression and Violence*. New York: Raven, 1981.

Van der Woude, Adam S. "Melchisedek als himmlische Erlösergestalt in den neugefundenen eschatologischen Midraschim aus Qumran Höhle XI." *Oudtestamentische Studien* 14 (1965): 354–73.

———. "11QMelchizedek and the New Testament." *New Testament Studies* 12 (1966): 301–26.

Van Iersel, Bas M. F. *'Der Sohn' in den synoptischen Jesusworten*. Leiden: Brill, 1964.

Van Seters, John. "A Response to G. Aichele, P. Miscall and R. Walsh, An Elephant in the Room: Historical-Criticism and the Postmodern Interpretation of the Bible." *Journal of Hebrew Scriptures* 9.26 (2009): 2-13.

Van Unnik, W. C. "Die Motivierung der Feindesliebe in Lukas 6:32-35." *Novum Testamentum* 8 (1966): 284–300.

VanderKam, James C. *Enoch: A Man For All Generations*. Columbia, SC: University of South Carolina Press, 1995.

———. "1 Enoch, Enochic Motifs, and Enoch in Early Christian Literature." In *The Jewish Apocalyptic Heritage in Early Christianity*. Edited by James C. VanderKam and William Adler. CRINT 3: Jewish Traditions in Early Christian Literature 4. Minneapolis: Fortress Press, 1996, 32–101.

———. "Sabbatical Chronologies in the Dead Sea Scrolls and Related Literature." In *The Dead Sea Scrolls in Their Historical Context*. Edited by Timothy H. Lim. Edinburgh: T & T Clark, 2000, 159–78.

Vassiliadis, Petros. "The Nature and Extent of the Q Document." *Novum Testamentum* 20 (1978): 49–73.

———. ΛΟΓΟΙ ΙΗΣΟΥ*: Studies in Q*. Atlanta: Scholars Press, 1999.

Vellanickal, Matthew. *The Divine Sonship of Christians in the Johannine Writings*. AnBib 72. Rome: Pontifical Biblical Institute, 1977.

Vermes, Géza. *Discovery in the Judean Desert*. New York: Desclée, 1956.

———. "Appendix E: The Use of בר נשא/בר נש in Jewish Aramaic." In Matthew Black, *An Aramaic Approach to the Gospels and Acts*. 3d ed. Oxford: Clarendon Press, 1967, 310–30.

———. *The Religion of Jesus the Jew*. London: SCM, 1973.

———. *The Dead Sea Scrolls: Qumran in Perspective*. Philadelphia: Fortress Press, 1977.

———. *Jesus and the World of Judaism*. Philadelphia: Fortress Press, 1984.

———. *The Dead Sea Scrolls in English*. 3d ed. Sheffield: JSOT, 1987.

———. "Qumran Forum Miscellanea I." *Journal of Jewish Studies* 43 (1992): 299–305.

———. *The Complete Dead Sea Scrolls in English*. New York: Penguin, 1997.

Vielhauer, Philip. "Gottesreich und Menschensohn in der Verkündigung Jesu." In *Festschrift für Günther Dehn, zum 75. Geburtstag am 18. April 1957*.

Neukirchen: Kreis Moers, Verlag der Buchhandlung Erziehungsvereins, 1957, 51–79.

———. "Jesus und der Menschensohn." *Zeitschrift für Theologie und Kirche* 60 (1963): 133–77.

——— and Georg Strecker. "Apocalyptic in Early Christianity." In *New Testament Apocrypha: Writings Relating to the Apostles, Apocalypses, and Related Subjects*. Edited by Edgar Hennecke, Wilhelm Schneemelcher, and R. McLean Wilson. Translated by A. J. B. Higgins, et al. 2 vols. Louisville; Westminster John Knox, 1992, 2: 568–602.

Vögtle, Anton. "Die Adam-Christus-Typologie und 'der Menschensohn.'" *Trierer theologische Zeitschrift* 60 (1951): 309–28.

———. "'Der Menschensohn' und die paulinishe Christologie." In *Studiorum Paulinorum Congressus Internationals Catholicis*. AnBib 17/18. Rome, 1961, 199–218.

———. *'Der Menschensohn' und die paulinische Christologie*. Rome: Pontifical Bible Institute, 1963.

Volf, Miroslav. *Exclusion and Embrace: A Theological Explanation of Identity, Otherness, and Reconciliation*. Nashville: Abingdon, 1996.

Von Rad, Gerhard. *Holy War in Ancient Israel*. Translated by Marva J. Dawn. Grand Rapids: Eerdmans, 1991.

———. "Deuteronomy and the Holy War." In idem, *Studies in Deuteronomy*. Translated by Davis Stalker. London: SCM, 1953, 45–59.

———. *Genesis: A Commentary*. Philadelphia: Westminster, 1961.

Von Hase, Karl A. *Life of Jesus: A Manual for Academic Study*. Translated by James Freeman Clark. Boston: Walker, Wise, 1860.

———. *Geschichte Jesu*. 2d ed. Leipzig: Breitkopf & Härtel, 1876.

———. *Geschichte Jesu: nach akademischen Vorlesungen*. 2d ed. Leipzig: Breitkopf & Härtel, 1891.

Waddell, James A. "The Messiah in the Parables of Enoch and the Letters of Paul: A Comparative Analysis." PhD disss, University of Michigan, 2010.

———. *The Messiah: A Comparative Study of the Enochic Son of Man and the Pauline Kyrios*. JCT 10. London: T & T Clark, 2011.

Wagner, J. Ross. *Heralds of the Good News: Isaiah and Paul 'in Concert' in the Letter to the Romans*. NTSup 101. Leiden: Brill, 2002.

Walck, Leslie W. "The Son of Man in the Parables of Enoch and the Gospels." In *Enoch and the Messiah Son of Man* (2007), 299–337.

———. *The Son of Man in the Parables of Enoch and in Matthew*. JCT 9. Edinburgh: T & T Clark, 2011.

Waldmann Michael. *Die Feindesliebe in der antiken Welt und im Christentum*. Vienna: Mayer, 1902.

Walsh, Brian J., and J. Richard Middleton. *The Transforming Vision: Shaping a Christian World View*. Downers Grove: InterVarsity, 1984.

Wanamaker, Charles A. "Philippians 2:6-11: Son of God or Adamic Christology?" *New Testament Studies* 33 (1987): 179–93.

Warrior, Robert Allen. "A Native American Perspective: Canaanites, Cowboys, and Indians." In *Voices from the Margin: Interpreting the Bible in the Third World*. Edited by R. S. Sugirtharajah. Maryknoll, NY: Orbis Books, 1995, 289–92.

Watson, David F. "The 'Messianic Secret': Demythologizing a Non-existent Markan Theme." *Journal of Theology* 110 (2006): 33–44.

———. *Honor Among Christians: The Cultural Key to the Messianic Secret*. Minneapolis: Fortress Press, 2010.

Watson, Francis. "Q as Hypothesis: A Study in Methodology." *New Testament Studies* 55 (2009): 397-415.

———. *Gospel Writing: A Canonical Perspective*. Grand Rapids: Eerdmans, 2013.

Weaver, J. Denny. *The Nonviolent Atonement*. Grand Rapids: Eerdmans, 2001.

———. "Narrative *Christus Victor*: The Answer to Anselmian Atonement Violence." In *Atonement and Violence: A Theological Conversation*. Edited by John Sanders. Nashville: Abingdon, 2006, 1–32.

———. *The Nonviolent God*. Grand Rapids: Eerdmans, 2013.

Webb, Robert L. "Jesus' Baptism by John: Its Historicity and Significance." In *Key Events in the Life of the Historical Jesus: A Collaborative Exploration of Context and Coherence*. Edited by Darrell L. Bock and Robert L. Webb. Tübingen: Mohr Siebeck, 2010, 95–150.

Wedderburn, Alexander J. M. "Adam and Christ: An Investigation into the Background of 1 Corinthians XV and Romans V:12-21." PhD diss., Cambridge University, 1970.

———. "The Body of Christ and Related Concepts in 1 Corinthians." *Scottish Journal of Theology* 2 (1971): 74–96.

———. "Adam in Paul's Letters to the Romans." In *Studia Biblica* 3. Edited by E. A. Livingstone. Sheffield: JSOT, 1978, 413-430.

———. "Some Observations on Paul's Use of the Phrases 'In Christ' and 'With Christ.'" *Journal for the Study of the New Testament* 25 (1985): 83–97.

———. *Jesus and the Historians*. WUNT 269. Tübingen: Mohr Siebeck, 2010.

Wegenast, Klaus. *Das Verständnis der Tradition bei Paulus und in den Deuteropaulinen.* WMANT 8. Neukirchen-Vluyn: Neukirchener Verlag, 1962.

Weippert, Manfred. "Heiliger Krieg in Israel und Assyrien: Kritische Anmerkungen zu Gerhard von Rads Konzept des Heiligen Krieges im alten Israel." *Zeitschrift für die alttestamentliche Wissenschaft* 84 (1972): 460–93.

Weiss, Johannes. *Earliest Christianity: A History of the Period A. D. 30–150.* Translated by Frederick C. Grant. Harper Torchbooks. New York: Harper, 1959.

———. *Jesus' Proclamation of the Kingdom of God.* Translated and edited by Richard H. Hiers and David Larrimore Holland. Chico, CA: Scholars Press, 1985.

Wellhausen, Julius. *Prolegomena to the History of Israel.* Translated by J. Sutherland Black and Allan Menzies. Edinburgh: A & C Black, 1885.

———. "Des Menschen Sohn." In idem, *Skizze und Vorarbeiten.* Berlin: Reimer, 1899, 6: 187–215.

Wilckens, Ulrich. "Christus, der 'letzte Adam,' und der Menschensohn." In *Jesus und der Menschensohn* (1975), 387–403.

Wildberger, Hans. "Das Abbild Gottes: Gen. 1:26-30." *Theologische Zeitschrift* 21 (1965): 245–59, 481–501.

Willard, Dallas. *The Divine Conspiracy: Rediscovering Our Hidden Life in God.* San Francisco: HarperSanFrancisco, 1998.

———. *The Great Omission: Reclaiming Jesus's Essential Teachings on Discipleship.* San Francisco: HarperSanFrancisco, 2006.

Williams, James G. *The Bible, Violence, and the Sacred: Liberation from the Myth of Sanctioned Violence.* San Francisco: HarperSanFrancisco, 1991.

Williams, Joel F. "Is Mark's Gospel an Apology for the Cross?" *Bulletin for Biblical Research* 12 (2002): 97–122.

Williams, Michael J. *How to Read the Bible Through the Jesus Lens: A Guide to Christ-Focused Reading of Scripture.* Grand Rapids: Zondervan, 2012.

Wills, Garry. *What the Gospels Meant.* New York: Penguin, 2008.

Wills, Lawrence M. *The Quest for the Historical Gospel: Mark, John and the Origins of the Gospel Genre.* London: Routledge, 1997.

Wilson, Robert Smith. *Marcion.* London: James Clarke, 1933.

Wink, Walter. "Jesus and Revolution: Reflections on S. G. F. Brandon's *Jesus and the Zealots.*" *Union Seminary Quarterly Review* 25 (1969): 37-59.

———. *Naming the Powers: The Language of Power in the New Testament.* Philadelphia: Fortress Press, 1984.

———. *Unmasking the Powers: The Invisible Forces that Determine Human Existence*. Philadelphia: Fortress Press, 1986.

———. *Engaging the Powers: Discernment and Resistance in a World of Domination.* Minneapolis: Fortress Press, 1992.

———. "Counterresponse to Richard Horsley." In *The Love of Enemy and Nonretaliation in the New Testament.* Edited by Willard M. Swartley. Louisville: Westminster John Knox, 1992, 133–36.

———. *The Powers That Be: Theology for a New Millennium.* New York: Doubleday, 1998.

———. *The Human Being: Jesus and the Enigma of the Son of Man.* Minneapolis: Fortress Press, 2002.

———. *Jesus and Nonviolence: A Third Way*. Minneapolis: Fortress Press, 2003.

Winn, Albert Curry. *Ain't Gonna Study War No More: Biblical Ambiguity and the Abolition of War*. Louisville: Westminster John Knox, 1993.

Winter, Dagmar. "Saving the Quest for Authenticity from the Criterion of Dissimilarity: History and Plausibility." In *Jesus, Criteria, and the Demise of Authenticity* (2012), 113–31.

Wise, Michael. "4QFlorilegium and the Temple of Adam." *Revue de Qumran* 15 (1991): 103–32.

———. "That Which Has Been is That Which Shall Be: 4QFlorilegium and the *mqds 'dm*." In *Thunder and Gemini and Other Essays on the History, Language and Literature of Second Temple Palestine*. JSPSup 15. Sheffield: JSOT, 1994, 152–85.

Witherington, Ben III. *The Christology of Jesus*. Minneapolis: Fortress Press, 1990.

———. *Jesus, Paul, and the End of the World: A Comparative Study in New Testament Eschatology*. Downers Grove: InterVarsity, 1992.

———. *The Jesus Quest: The Third Search for the Jew of Nazareth*. Downers Grove: InterVarsity, 1995.

———. *The Gospel of Mark: A Socio-Rhetorical Commentary*. Grand Rapids: Eerdmans, 2001.

Wittichen, Carl. *Beiträge zur biblischen Theologie*. Part 2: *Die Idee des Menschen: Zweiter Beitrag zur biblischen Theologie*. Göttingen: Dieterich, 1868.

———. *Das Leben Jesu in urkundlicher Darstellung*. Jena: Dufft, 1876.

Wolters, Al. *Creation Regained: Biblical Basics for a Reformational Worldview*. Grand Rapids: Eerdmans, 1985.

Worthen, Molly. *Apostles of Reason: The Crisis of Authority in American Evangelicalism*. New York: Oxford University Press, 2013.

Wrede, William. *Das Messiasgeheimnis in den Evangelien: Zugleich ein Beitrag zum Verständnis des Markusevangeliums*. 3d ed. Göttingen: Vandenhoeck & Ruprecht, 1901. English: *The Messianic Secret*. Translated by J. C. G. Greig. Cambridge: James Clark, 1971.

Wrege, Hans-Theo. *Die Überlieferungsgeschichte der Bergpredigt*. Tübingen: Mohr, 1968.

Wright, Christopher J. H. *Living as the People of God: The Relevance of Old Testament Ethics*. Leicester: InterVarsity, 1983.

———. *Walking in the Ways of the Lord: The Ethical Authority of the Old Testament*. Leicester: Apollos, 1995.

———. *Old Testament Ethics for the People of God*. Leicester: InterVarsity, 2004.

———. *The God I Don't Understand: Reflections on Tough Questions of Faith*. Grand Rapids: Zondervan, 2008.

Wright, N. T. "Adam in Pauline Christology." In *Society of Biblical Literature Seminar Papers 22*. Chico: Scholars Press, 1983, 359-89.

———. *The Climax of the Covenant: Christ and the Law in Pauline Theology*. Minneapolis: Fortress Press, 1992.

———. *The New Testament and the People of God*. Vol. 1: *Christian Origins and the Question of God*. Minneapolis: Fortress Press, 1992.

———. *The New Testament and the People of God*. Vol. 2: *Jesus and the Victory of God*. Minneapolis: Fortress Press, 1996.

———. *The New Testament and the People of God*. Vol 4: *Paul and the Faithfulness of God*. 2 Vols. Minneapolis: Fortress Press, 2013.

Yadin, Yigael. "A Note on Melchizedek and Qumran." *Israel Exploration Journal* 15 (1965): 152–54.

———. *The Temple Scroll: The Hidden Law of the Dead Sea Sect*. New York: Random House, 1985.

Yoder, John Howard. *The Politics of Jesus: Vicit Agnus Noster*. Grand Rapids: Eerdmans, 1972.

———. *The Original Revolution: Essays on Christian Pacifism*. Scottdale, PA: Herald Press, 1972.

———. *Nevertheless: The Varieties and Shortcomings of Religious Pacifism*. Scottdale, PA: Herald Press, 1992.

———. *The War of the Lamb: The Ethics of Nonviolence and Peacemaking*. Grand Rapids: Brazos Press, 2009.

———. *Nonviolence: A Brief History: The Warsaw Lectures*. Edited by Paul Henry Martens, Matthew Porter, and Myles Werntz. Waco: Baylor University Press, 2010.

Younger, K. Lawson. *Ancient Conquest Accounts: A Study in Ancient Near Eastern and Biblical History Writing*. Sheffield: JSOT Press, 1990.

Zehnder, Markus and Hallvard Hagelia, eds. *Encountering Violence in the Bible*. BMW. Sheffield: Sheffield Phoenix Press, 2013.

Zeller, Dieter. *Die weisheitlichen Mahnsprüche be den Synoptikern*. FzB 17. Würzburg: Echter Verlag, 1977.

———. *Kommentar zur Logienquelle*. SKNT 21. Stuttgart: Katholisches Bibelwerk, 1984.

———. "Redactional Processes and Changing Settings in the Q-Material." In *The Shape of Q* (1994), 116–30.

Zerbe, Gordon. *Non-retaliation in early Jewish and New Testament Texts: Ethical Themes in Social Context*. JSPSup 13. Sheffield: JSOT Press, 1993.

Zetterholm, Magnus. "Paul and the Missing Messiah." In *The Messiah in Early Judaism and Christianity*. Edited by Magnus Zetterholm. Minneapolis: Fortress Press, 2007, 33–55.

Zias, Joseph, and Eliezer Sekeles. "The Crucified Man from Giv'at ha-Mivtar." *Israel Exploration Journal* 35 (1985): 22–27.

Ziesler, J. A. *Pauline Christianity*. New York: Oxford University Press, 1990.

Zimmermann, Johannes. *Messianische Texte aus Qumran: Königliche, priesterliche, und prophetische Messiasvorstellungen in den Schriftfunden von Qumran*. WUNT 2d ser. 104. Tübingen: Mohr Siebeck, 1998.

Zuckerman, Phil. *Strife in the Sanctuary: Religious Schism in a Jewish Community*. Walnut Creek, CA: AltaMira, 1999.

Zugibe, Frederick T. "Two Questions about Crucifixion." *Bible Review* 5 (1989): 35–43.

Index of Names

Aaron, David H., 180n85
Abbott, Edwin, 192n157
Adams, Edward, 130n51
Adler, William, 163n109, 164n119
Ådna, Jostein, 38n84
Agrell, Göran, 201n21, 203n44, 204n46
Aichele, George, 7n21, 23n1
Akers, Keith, 25n8,
Albright, William F., 59n73
Alexander, Philip S., 163n112
Allison Jr., Dale C., 3n2, 4n7, 4n8, 5n12, 6n16, 7n22, 26n13, 26n15, n16, 27n17, 27n22, 71n1, 81n66, n67, n68, n70, 82n74, 82n76, 83n80, n81, 87n101, n102, 88n109, n113, 95n15, 110n106, 114n19, 117n36, 121n50, 131n54, 152n41, n43, n44, 153n45, 154n50, n51, 157n76, 159n86, 200n18, n20, 201n21, 205n53, n54, n56, 206n61, n62, n65, 213n112, n115, 216n135, 217n145, 229n1, 230n3
Allman, Mark J., 230n3
Anderson, Bernhard W., 176n58
Anderson, Gary A., 180n81, n86
Anderson, G. W., 98n25
Anderson, John, 69n153
Andrews, Elias, 181n91
Appleby, R. Scott, 52n5
Arbel, Daphna, 163n108
Archer, Gleason L., 64n115
Ardrey, Robert, 52n3
Arendt, Hannah, 25n8
Arnal, William E., 6n17, 11n49, 12n54, 117n34, 143n123, 227n209
Arnaud, Émile, 25n11
Ashton, John, 223n191
Aslan, Reza, 23n1, 26n14, 31n45, 34n60, 35n61
Assefa, Daniel, 168n9, 170n21
Astell, Ann W., 54n18
Attenborough, Richard, 25n9
Aune, David E., 93n1, 98n26, 108n90, 127n20, 128n21
Avalos, Hector, 52n11, 58n68

Bach, Eugen, 211n89
Bachmann, Veronika, 168n10
Bailey, Lloyd R., 155n55
Bainton, Roland, 64n121
Baird, J. Arthur, 152n42
Baker, J. A., 59n73
Bammel, Ernst, 23n1, 24n3, 37n81, 106n75
Bampfylde, Gillian, 145n1
Bardtke Hans, 87n104
Barker, Margaret, 134n68, 178n72
Barnstone, Willis S., 87n106
Barr, James, 176n58, 223n190
Barrera, J. Trebolle, 120n47
Barrett, C. K., 118n37, 181n88, n91, 183n94, 190n149
Bartlett, Anthony, 53n12
Barth, Karl, 176n58, 188n131
Bateman IV, Herbert, 67n132
Bauckham, Richard, 6n16, 132n60, 133n64, 162n103, 165n120, 183n98, 208n80, 223n193
Bauer, Walter, 39n87
Baumgarten, Albert I., 104n61, 167n1, 180n80
Baumgarten-Crusius, Ludwig Friedrich Otto, 192n159
Baur, Ferdinand Christian, 126n8

Bautch, Kelley Coblentz, 163n108, 173n38
Beare, Francis Wright, 135n76, 203n40
Beasley-Murray, G. R., 197n2
Beck, Robert R., 46n142, 46n143, 47
Becker, Jürgen, 94n10, 106n71, 131n54, 152n42, 201n24, 202n32, n35, n44, 211n89
Becker, Michael, 88n111
Bedenbender, Andreas, 170n21
BeDuhn, Jason D., 66n130
Beer, Georg, 170n27, 171n29
Bekkenkamp, Jonneke, 51n2
Bergemann, Thomas, 205n52
Bergmeier, Roland, 120n46
Bergsma, John Sietze, 20n107, 21n111, n112
Berkey, Robert F., 5n9
Berkowitz, Leonard, 52n3
Bernat, David A., 51n1, 58n67
Betz, Hans Dieter, 208n77, n78
Betz, Otto, 95n15, 96n16, 120n47, 121n51
Bietenhard, Hans, 215n125
Bilde, Per, 42n112
Bird, Michael F., 94n9, 125n1, 126n5, n7, 226n206
Bird, Phyllis, 175n57, 176n60
Black, C. Clifton, 125n1
Black, Matthew, 26n13, 131n57, 132n58, 138n98, 146n7, n8, 162n103, 169n14, 171n31, 173n37, 174n44, n46, 190n147, n148, n149
Blackman, Edwin C., 56n51
Blosser, Donald W., 21n113
Blumenthal, David R., 55n26
Boccaccini, Gabriele, 145n1, 146n5, 163n109, 168n13, 173n37, n38, 175n53
Bock, Darrell, 17n85, n86, 67n132, 116n28, 147n19
Bockmuehl, Markus, 18n100, 88n109, 95n15, 96n16, 98n25, 109n103
Böhme, Christian Friedrich, 192n159
Bohn, C. R., 42n109
Bondurant, Joan V., 25n8
Booth, Wayne C., 61n88
Borg, Marcus J., 4n5, 8n30, 41n101, 70, 71n1, 94n10, 111n2
Boring, M. Eugene, 4n7, 5n10, 39n86
Borman, William, 25n9
Bornkamm, Günther, 95n13, 126n9
Borsch, Frederick H., 138n98
Bosold, Iris, 116n29
Boteach, Schmuley, 23n1
Bouma-Prediger, Steven, 230n5
Bousset, Wilhelm, 74n27, 107n86, 125n3, 189n140, 190n144
Boustan, Ra'anan, 51n2, 212n99
Bouttier, Michel, 108n91
Bowden, John, 7n22, 57n54, 72n3
Boyarin, Daniel, 98n24, 147n16, n17, n20
Boyd, Gregory A., 33n50
Braaten, Carl E., 71n1
Brandenburger, Egon, 140n108, 181n88, 189n138, n140, 190n144
Brandon, S. G. F., 23n1, 24n3, 34n60, 35n66, 36n70, n71, n75, 37n76, 37n78
Braun, Willi, 12n54
Bredin, Mark R., 38n82
Bremmer, Jan N., 162n106
Brensinger, T. L., 28n27
Brett, Mark G., 51n2
Brettler, Marc Zvi, 31n43
Brock, Peter, 25n11
Brooke, George J., 120n46, 122n53, 178n71, n72
Bowden, John, 143n124
Brooks, Roger, 175n57
Broshi, Magen, 216n134
Brown, Joan Carlson, 42n109
Brown, Raymond E., 9n37, 37n76, 95n13, n14, 106n71
Brown, Robert MacAfee, 24n7, 44n124

Brownlee, William H., 215n126
Bruce, W. S., 59n71
Brückner, Wilhelm, 192n159
Brueggemann, Walter, 58n67
Buell, Denis, 188n125
Bultmann, Rudolf, 22n117, 27n19, 30n34, 37n80, n81, 113n17, 116n30, 125n3, 126n9, 131n55, 135n75, 157n76, 189n140, 190n144, 197n2, 200n17, 201n26, 208n77
Burke, Trevor J., 218n153, 219n155
Burkett, Delbert, 130n53, 139n106, 192n157
Burridge, Richard A., 17n93
Buswell, Geoffrey, 29n28
Butler, T. C., 27n23
Byrne, Brendan T., 183n97, 219n155

Cadoux, Cecil J., 95n15
Caird, George B., 87n101, 197n6
Cairns, David, 176n58
Calvert, D. G. A., 4n7
Cámara, Helder, 42n110
Cameron, Peter Scott, 31n45
Cameron, Ron, 8n25, 12n52, 13n58, 13n62, n64, n65, n67, 14n69, n73, 82n75, 94n11, 123n61
Capes, David B., 184n98
Caragounis, Chrys C., 125n4, 131n54, 134n68
Carlson, Jeffrey, 11n43
Carlston, Charles E., 5n14, 8n31
Carroll, M. Daniel, 98n25
Carson, D. A., 67n132
Carter, Warren, 46n142
Casey, P. Maurice, 126n7, 133n61, n62, 134n72, 135n74, 138n96, n98, 139n100, n102, n103, 140n108, 161n95, 192n157
Cassidy, Richard J., 48n158
Castelli, Elizabeth A., 19n103, 34n59
Catchpole, David R., 8n31, 10n40, 37n81, 106n75, 117n32, 131n54, 143n123, 161n95, 199n16, 200n20, 201n21, n26, 203n39, 206n61, 207n70
Chapman, David W., 105n69
Chapple, Christopher, 25n10
Charles, J. Daryl, 165n122
Charles, R. H., 171n29, 174n46
Charlesworth, James H., 5n9, 19n104, 41n100, 71n1, 72n6, 87n104, 94n10, 98n26, 99n29, 102n51, 104n60, n61, 105n69, 111n2, 120n46, 127n20, 128n21, 134n68, 145n1, 147n19, 180n82
Chase, Kenneth R., 56n51
Chazon, Esther G., 177n66
Chester, Andrew, 94n11, 96n15, 109n103, 129n41, 183n94
Childs, Brevard, 60n83
Chilton, Bruce D., 3n1, 21n112, 26n13, n15, 53n17, 93n1, 118n40, 132n60, 197n2
Clements, Ronald E., 63n108
Clines, D. J. A., 65n128
Coburn, Oliver, 29n29
Cohn-Sherbok, Dan, 98n25
Collins, Adela Yarbro, 106n75, 108n99, 131n54, n55, 139n105, 175n57, 183n94, 190n146
Collins, John J., 19n104, 57n55, n56, n59, 58, 71n1, 82n76, 87n105, 98n25, n27, 99n30, 100n39, 102n50, 103n56, 104n61, n62, 106n71, 108n99, 113n15, 119n42, 120n46, n47, 121n50, 131n54, n55, 134n68, 145n3, 146n13, 161n95, 163n109, n110, n111, 167n1, 168n13, 171n31, 173n36, 175n57, 179n76, n78, 183n94, 190n146, 220n165, 221n166
Colpe, Carsten, 138n98, 190n145, n146, 190n147
Conrad, Edgar W., 62n93

Conzelmann, Hans, 29n28, 74n18, 83n79, 131n56
Cooney, Robert, 25n9
Copan, Paul, 56n52, 58n68
Corley, Bruce, 126n8
Cortés, Juan B., 192n158
Cotter, Wendy, 117n36, 118n40, 123n62
Cowles, C. S., 62n89, 63n104, 64n117, 65n122, 69n151
Craig, William Lane, 56n52
Crawford, Barry, 13n61
Creach, Jerome F. D., 50n164, 56n52, 69n153, 70n153, 229n2
Creed, J. M., 189n140, 190n144
Cromhout, Markus, 143n123
Crook, Zeba A., 6n18
Cross, Frank Moore, 103n56
Crossan, John Dominic, 11n43, 27n17, 39n91, 41n100, 47n151, n153, 69n150, 77n42, 81n69, 82n77, 83n78, 88n113, 114n19, 132n60, 133n66, 136n83, 225n204
Crossley, James G., 125n1, 126n7
Culler, Jonathan D., 61n88
Culliton, Joseph T., 44n122
Cullmann, Oscar, 23n1, 94n10, 177n67, 181n91, 183n94, 190n144, n149
Cummins, S. A., 109n101
Curtis, Edward Mason, 176n58

Dahl, Nils A., 94n11, 95n13, n14, 98n26, 99n37, 105n70, 106n71, n72, n76, 107n86, 108n90, 109n100, n103
Daly, Robert J., 43n122
Dautzenberg, Gerhard, 152n41, 154n50
Davidson, A. B., 59n71
Davidson, Maxwell J., 169n19
Davies, Eryl W., 58, 59n69, n73, 60n77, 61n84, n85, n87, n88
Davies, Margaret, 4n8, 5n10, 9n32
Davies, W. D., 95n15, 117n36, 154n50, 180n84, 181n88, n91, 186n109, 189n137, n142, 190n143, 200n18, n20, 201n21
Davis, Michael T., 121n50
Dawkins, Richard, 57n53, 212n99
Dawn, Marva J., 63n108
Day, John, 98n25
De Boer, Esther A., 185n107
De Boer, Martinus C., 94n10, 97n21, 139n108
De Jonge, H. J., 94n10, 139n108
De Jonge, Marinus, 94n10, n11, 95n15, 97n21, n22, n23, 104n60, 108n90, 109n100, 139n108, 217n143
De Pisón, Ramon Martínez, 67n133
De Vaux, Roland, 62n93
De Villiers, Pieter G. R., 48n154
Dear, John, 25n9
Deasley, Alex R. G., 178n69, 179n78
Dehandschutter, Boudewijn, 162n103
Deissmann, Adolf, 108n91
Desjardins, Michel, 24n6, 70n154
Dibelius, Martin, 27n21, 117n36, 210n87
Dillmann, August, 171n29, 174n46
Dillon, Richard J., 202n30, 202n35
Dimant, Devorah, 167n6, 178n70, n71
Dinkler, Erich, 95n14
Dodd, C. H., 59n72, 76n39, 87n101, 95n14, 197n2, 198n6, 211n89
Donahue, John R., 30n34
Donfried, Karl P., 153n48
Donnelly, D., 96n16
Douglas, R. Conrad, 210n84, 211n89
Draper, Jonathan A., 157n76, 210n83
Duguid, Iain M., 67n132
Duhaime, Jean, 87n104
Dumouchel, Paul, 53n17
Dungan, David, 126n8
Dunn, James D. G., 4n7, 5n15, 6n16, 14n72, 26n13, 39n86, 76, 76n36, 80n64, 93n1, 94n11, 95n13, 96n16, 100n40, 106n71, 107n85, 112n5, 118n36, 127n20, 128n21, n22,

129n32, 149n27, 181n89, n91, n92, n93, 183n94, n96, 184n100, n104, 187n123, 188n134, 223n190
Dupont, Georges, 132n57
Dupont, Jacques, 152n41, 201n21

Earl, Douglas S., 58n67
Eco, Umberto, 61n88
Edwards, Richard A., 111n4, 150n34
Edwards, Sarah A., 5n9
Ego, Beato, 169n20
Ehrman, Bart D., 27n17, 71n1, 76n35
Eichrodt, Walther, 59n73
Eisenman, Robert, 19n104, 113n15, 119n42, 120n46, n47
Eisler, Robert, 23n1
Elgvin, Torleif, 179n75
Ellens, J. Harold, 23n1, 52n10
Eller, Vernard, 52n2
Elliott, John H., 162n103
Elliott, Mark Adam, 169n19
Ellis, E. Earle, 181n91, 190n149
Emerson, Ralph Waldo, 84, 85n91
Emilsen, William W., 47n154, 54n19, n20, n24
Enns, Fernando, 49n160
Enslin, Morton S., 9n32
Enz, Jacob J., 51n2
Ernst, Josef, 117n36
Evans, Craig A., 3n1, 5n9, 17n92, 21n112, 26n13, n15, 34n59, 39n86, 93n1, 95n15, 102n51, 118n40, 120n46, 126n5, 217n144
Evans, Craig F., 201n24, n26
Evans, Jeremy, 58n68

Farrer, Austin, 8n31
Felson, Richard B., 52n3
Ferguson, Sinclair B., 219n155
Fetterley, Judith, 61n88
Fiebig, Paul, 131n57
Filson, Floyd V., 76n39
Finney, Paul C., 30n34
Fiorenza, Elisabeth Schüssler, 7n20, 65n128, 82n77
Fish, Stanley E., 61n88
Fitzgerald, F. Scott, 84n90
Fitzmyer, Joseph A., 8n31, 19n104, 20n108, 78n51, 95n14, 98n26, n27, 103n56, n57, 104n60, 106n71, 113n15, 115n23, 119n42, 139n105, 153n46, 191n149, 200n17, 220n165, 221n166
Fleddermann, Harry T., 8n31, 154n49, 154n50, 207n70, n74, 217n145
Fletcher-Louis, Crispin H. T., 82n76, 178n72, 179n76, n78, n79, 180n82
Flint, Peter W., 163n112, 171n31
Flusser, David, 20n108, 103n52
Fosdick, Harry Emerson, 59n71
Foster, Paul, 6n16, 6n18, 111n2, 115n24, 120n45
France, R. T., 96n16, 125n4, 128n21
Frankemölle, Hubert, 18n100
Fraser, R. S., 23n1
Fredriksen, Paula, 31n41, 39n89, 76n38, 94n11, 95n13, 107n85, 109n100
Frenschkowski, Marco, 207n74
Frerichs, Ernest S., 94n11, 171n29
Fretheim, Terence E., 49n160, 64n115, 69n152
Frey, Jörg, 88n111
Fröhlich, Ida, 146n5, 169n19
Froehlich, Karlfried, 69n152
Fuller, Reginald H., 5n9, 94n10, 132n60, 133n65, 191n149
Funk, Robert T., 5n14, 27n20, 74n19, 83n79, 94n10, 159n84, 223n191
Furnish, Victor P., 23n1

Gabrielson, Jeremy, 48n155
Galtrung, Johan, 24n7
Gandhi, Mahatma K., 25n9, 31n44
García Martínez, Florentino, 120n47, 167n6, 171n31
Gard, Daniel L., 62n90, n93, n94, n95, n96, n97, 65

Gärtner, Bertil, 178n70, 208n80
Gaster, Theodore H., 178n70
Gathercole, Simon, 130n51
Giblin, Charles Homer, 30n34
Gibson, E. Leigh, 70n154
Gilbert, Lela, 230n5
Girard, René, 44n125, 52, 53n12, n13, n16, 63
Glancy, Jennifer A., 23n1
Glasson, T. Francis, 198n6
Glock, Charles Y., 52n4
Glucker, Carol, 103n52
Gnilka, Joachim, 18n100, 74n18, 106n75, 134n71, 200n18, 202n35
Goergen, Donald J., 132n60
Goldstein, Jonathan A., 171n29
Goldstein, Morris, 3n4
Golitzin, Alexander, 180n85
Goodacre, Mark S., 8n31, 9n32, 10n40
Goodhart, Sandor, 54n18
Gopin, Marc, 52n10
Goppelt, Leonhard, 138n98, 208n80
Gordis, Robert, 103n54, n56, 220n165
Gorra, Joseph E., 56n52
Gorringe, Timothy, 52n7
Gotti, Florence M., 192n157
Gottstein, Alon Goshen, 180n85
Gottwald, Norman K., 63n108
Goulder, Michael D., 8n31, 9n32, 9n38, 126n7
Grabbe, Lester L., 75n31, 82n76, 87n104
Granberg-Michaelson, Wesley, 230n5
Green, Joel B., 106n78, 136n82
Green, William Scott, 94n11, 171n29
Greenfield, Jonas C., 145n1, n2
Greenstone, Julius H., 99n31
Greeven, Heinrich, 201n22
Gregg, Brian Han, 75n28, 152n42, n44
Greig, J. C. G., 94n10, 127n19, 130n49
Gressmann, Hugo, 74n27
Grimsrud, Ted, 45n135, 69n150
Grobel, Kendrick, 22n117
Groh, Dennis E., 132n60
Gruenwald, Ithamar, 104n62
Grundmann, Walter, 157n74, 202n29
Guelich, Robert A., 22n116, 199n16, 201n25, 202n29, 207n70
Guignebert, Charles Alfred Honoré, 132n57, 135n75
Gundry, Robert H., 34n59, 126n5, 200n18, n19, n20, 202n30
Gundry, Stan, 62n89
Guthrie, Nancy, 67n132
Guthrie, Shirley C., 94n10
Gutiérrez, Gustavo, 60n80

Haak, Robert D., 82n76
Habermas, Gary R., 5n9
Häfner, Gerd, 6n16
Hagelia, Hallvard, 51n2
Hagner, Donald, 18n100, 203n40
Hahn, Ferdinand, 105n70, 106n75
Hall, Charles A. M., 94n10
Hamerton-Kelly, Robert, 53n16, 117n30, n35, 149n28, 223n191
Hampel, Volker, 131n54
Han, Kyu Sam, 208n80
Hanson, John S., 98n25
Hardin, Michael, 45n135, 49n163
Hare, Douglas R. A., 93n1, 94n11, 161n95
Harrington, Daniel J., 179n75
Harris, Sam, 57
Harrison, Roland K., 192n159
Harvey, A. E., 94n11
Hauerwas, Stanley, 22n115
Havener, Ivan, 130n53
Hay, Lewis S., 134n70, 135n75
Hays, Richard B., 5n9, 23n1, 28n27, 56n52, 109n101
Hayward, Robert, 178n72
Hecht, Richard D., 53n17
Hedley, Douglas, 54n18
Hehn, Johannes, 176n59
Heil, Christoph, 26n13, 135n76, 199n17, 200n17

Hendrickx, Herman, 199n16, 200n20, 202n34
Hengel, Martin, 16n83, 36n76, 44n122, 93n1, 95n14, n15, 103n56, 105n69, 106n71, 107n85, 109n103, 129n41, 152n40, 173n37, 219n155, 220n165, 226n208
Hennecke, Edgar, 81n71
Héring, Jean, 134n70
Herschberger, Guy F., 28n27, 56n50
Herzog, William R., 30n34, 75n32, n33
Heschel, Susannah, 5n10
Hess, Richard S., 58n67, 98n25
Heusch, Luc de, 53n17
Hieke, Thomas, 118n36
Hiers, Richard H., 95n15, 197n2
Higgins, A. J. B., 134n68
Himmelfarb, Martha, 178n72
Hitchens, Christopher, 57
Hobbs, Edward C., 9n32
Hobbs, T. R., 62n93
Hoffmann, Paul, 113n16, 115n23, 116n27, n29, 123n62, 138n93, 140n108, 143n123, 149n28, 154n50, 200n18, 201n26, n28, 210n84, 211n89
Holland, D. Larrimore, 95n15
Holland, Scott, 49n160
Holmén, Tom, 3n3, 4n7, 5n9, 38n84, 82n76, 214n119
Holmes, R. L., 25n9
Hooker, Morna D., 5n9, 106n78, 130n51, 181n91, 184n98
Hoover, Roy W., 4n5, 30n34, 74n19, 94n10, 159n84, 223n191
Horbury, William, 18n100, 98n25, n26
Horsley, Richard A., 7n22, 30n34, 31n38, 42n111, 43n117, n118, 44n123, 45n131, 98n25, 104n60, 157n76, 209n83, 210n83
Howard, George, 181n91, 184n99
Hoyt, Wayland, 191n150
Hughes, Charles, 47n151
Hughes, Richard T., 25n11
Hultgren, Arland, 71n1
Humbert, Paul, 175n58
Hurst, Lincoln D., 181n91, 183n97
Hurtado, Larry, 94n11, 107n85, 109n100, 112n5, 114n18, 123n63, 147n16, 183n98
Huxley, Aldous, 84n90

Ingolfsland, Dennis, 7n23
Idel, Moshe, 108n97, 219n155
Iser, Wolfgang, 61n88

Jackson, David R., 169n20
Jackson-McCabe, Matt, 143n123
Jacobs, Alan, 56n51
Jacobson, Arland, 16n80, 113n16, 114n19, 116n29, 141n115, 149n28, 201n28
Janzen, Waldemar, 51n2
Jauss, Hans Robert, 61n88
Jenkins, Philip, 16n79, 67n133
Jenson, Robert W., 71n1
Jefferson, Thomas, 56n51
Jeremias, Joachim, 95n15, 154n50, 190n149, 200n17, 203n39, 210n88, 217n144, 223n191
Jervell, Jacob, 181n88
Jewett, Robert, 132n60
Johnston, Gordon, 67n132
Jones, F. Stanley, 162n106
Jones, Gareth Lloyd, 51n2
Jones, Gwilym H., 63n106, n108
Jónsson, Gunnlauger, A., 176n58
Joseph, Simon J., 9n39, 15n77, n78, 111n1, 118n41, 146n6, 159n87, 162n103, 167n2, 175n55, 197n1, 218n146, 230n3
Jossa, Giorgio, 96n15
Joubert, Stephan J., 162n103
Juel, Donald H., 106n78, 116n30, 117n35
Juergensmeyer, Mark, 52n9
Jülicher, Adolf, 206n66

Karrer, Martin, 104n60
Käsemann, Ernst, 5n10, 83n79, 126n9, 198n6
Kattenbusch, Ferdinand, 211n89
Kearns, Rollin, 132n60, 133n66
Kee, Howard Clark, 95n15
Keefer, Luke L., 23n1
Keith, Chris, 4n7, 39n86
Kennard Jr., J. Spencer, 30n34
Kerr, Alan R., 208n80
Kertelge, Karl, 134n71
Kim, Seyoon, 181n91, 183n94, 190n148, 191n149
Kimball, Charles, 52n10
King, Karen L., 185n107
King Jr., Martin Luther, 25n9
Kirchhevel, Gordon D., 130n51
Kirk, Alan, 6n16, 114n19, n21, 123n62, 157n70
Kister, Menahem, 189n138
Kittel, Gerhard, 76n39, 213n110
Klassen, William, 36n76, 210n89
Klausner, Joseph, 4n4, 98n25, 99n31, 108n97, 214n119
Klawans, Jonathan, 51n1, 58n67
Klijn, A. F. J., 170n22
Kloppenborg, John S., 7n22, 7n24, 8n25, 8n27, 9n38, 10n40, 11n44, 12, 15, 16n80, 77n43, 88n113, 111n3, 112n6, 113n17, 116n26, n27, n30, 117n32, n36, 119n43, 120n45, 123n62, 131n56, 140n108, 141n115, 149n28, 151n35, 153n46, 154n50, 156n64, n65, 157n77, 159n85, 198n11, 200n17, 201n26, n27, 202n38, 207n71, n74, 209n81, 214n122, 226n207
Kloppenborg Verbin, John S., 8n31, 10n40, 112n12, 119n43, 122n54, 143n123, 198n11, n12
Klostermann, Erich, 201n21, n26
Knibb, Michael A., 145n3, 169n14, 170n25, 178n70
Knight, Jonathan, 96n15
Koch, Klaus, 121n50, 174n50, 175n55, 192n160, 197n2
Koehler, Ludwig, 176n58
Koester, Helmut, 8n25, 16n82, 22n117, 82n73, 131n56, 133n67, 139n108, 140n108, 197n2
Kosch, Daniel, 7n22
Kraeling, Carl H., 42n112, 190n144
Kramer, Werner R., 107n85, 109n100, n103
Kugler, Robert A., 120n46
Kuhn, Heinz-Wolfgang, 211n89
Kühnöl, Christian Gottlieb, 192n159
Kümmel, Ernst Julius, 192n159
Kümmel, Werner Georg, 94n11, 107n85, 118n36, 197n2, 198n7
Kvalbein, Hans, 121n50, n51
Kvanvig, Helge S., 148n23, 173n37, 174n50, 192n160

Laato, Antti, 98n25
Labahn, Michael, 118n36, n39, 121n50, 123n59
Lacocque, André, 171n31
Ladd, George Eldon, 76n40, 181n91, 197n2
Lamb, David T., 56n52
Lane, William L., 125n4
Lasserre, Jean, 29n29
Lattke, Michael, 197n2
Laurence, Richard, 173n38
Lauterbach, Jacob Z., 3n4
Law, David R., 6n19
Lawlor, H. J., 163n109
Le Donne, Anthony, 4n7, 6n16, 39n86, 84n89
Lefebvre, Jean-Francois, 20n107
Lefebure, Leo D., 53n12
Legarreta-Castillo, Felipe de Jesús, 181n88
Legasse, Simon, 211n89
Leivestad, Ragnar, 93n1, 128n21, 191n149

Levine, Amy-Jill, 31n43, 100n41
Levison, John R., 180n81, 184n103
Lichtenberger, Herman, 145n1
Lietzmann, Hans, 131n57
Lind, Millard, 49n160, 52n2
Lindars, Barnabas, 112n5, 132n58, n60, 133n63, 135n74, 138n97, n98, 139n99, n101, 162n103, 170n28, 173n38, 190n146
Lindemann, Andreas, 6n17, 7n22, 149n25
Llewelyn, Stephen, 31n45
Lohmeyer, Ernst, 128n21
Longman III, Tremper, 63n100, n102, n105, 65n125
Longenecker, Richard N., 127n20
Lorenz, Konrad, 52n3
Losie, Lynn A., 126n5
Lovering, E. H., 125n1
Lucass, Shirley, 99n31
Lüdemann, Gerd, 27n19, 57n54, 75n32, 106n71, 223n191
Ludwig, Robert A., 11n43
Lührmann, Dieter, 7n22, 111n4, 118n37, 141n115, 208n75, 211n89
Lündstrom, Gösta, 197n2
Luz, Ulrich, 115n25, 116n26, n30, 152n44, 200n18, 202n30, n34, n35
Lynch, Joseph H., 56n51

Maccoby, Hyam, 23n1
MacDonald, Dennis R., 205n55
Macgregor, G. H. C., 23n1
Mack, Burton L., 11n42, 12n55, 13, 14n68, 19n103, 94n10, 95n12, 111n2, 113n16, 142n117, 177n64
MacRae, George, 94n11, 109n100, n103
MacRory, Joseph, 192n159
Maddox, Robert, 134n68
Maier, Johann, 3n4
Maier, Paul L., 42n112
Maloney, Linda M., 174n48
Mangold, Wilhelm, 192n159
Manson, T. W., 95n15, 96n16, 114n19, 128n21, 134n70, 135n75, 190n149, 200n18
Manson, William, 76n39, 95n15, 106n78, 217n144
Marcus, Joel, 83n81, 125n2, 126n7, 192n157
Marshall, Christopher D., 49n161, 79n55
Marshall, I. Howard, 23n1, 28n27, 78n51, 125n4, 134n68, 136n82, 138n98, 152n41, 154n50, 199n16, 200n17, n20, 201n21, 202n34
Marshall, Paul, 230n5
Martens, Elmer A., 58n67
Martens, Paul H., 21n115, 24n8
Martin, Dale B., 6n19, 34n59
Martin, Francois, 171n29
Martin, Luther H., 12n55
Martin, Ralph P., 126n5, 182n94
Marty, Martin, 52n5
Matson, Mark A., 9n32, 9n36
Matthews, Shelly, 70n154
McCasland, S. Vernon, 187n117
McCarthy, Emmanuel Charles, 40n94, 83n81
McCollough, Charles, 25n8
McDonald, James I. H., 118n40
McGrath, James F., 184n101
McKenzie, John L., 40n93
McKim, Donald K., 69n150
McKnight, Scot, 17n88, 96n15, 136n82
McLean, Bradley, 53n12
McL. Wilson, Robert, 81n71
McNicol, Allan J., 9n32
Meadors, Edward P., 93n1, 112n5, 113n17, 128n31, 131n54, 201n22
Meadors, Gary T., 117n33
Mealand, David L., 5n9, 202n37, 204n49
Mearns, Christopher L., 127n20, 132n60
Meeks, Wayne A., 186n108

Meier, John P., 4n5, 4n8, 5n13, 26n13, 27n17, 41n108, 75n32, 96n16, 129n40, 197n6
Merklein, Helmut, 200n18, 202n30, n35
Merrill, Eugene, 63n106, 64n110, n116, 65
Merton, Thomas, 25n8
Merz, Annette 3n3, 5n14, 7n22, 72n3, n6, 73n14, 77n49, 93n1, 96n15, 106n71, 131n54, 139n104, 224n201
Meyer, Arnold, 131n57, 135n75
Meyer, Ben F., 27n17, 93n1, 198n7
Meyer, Marvin W., 47n151
Meyers, Ched, 33n51
Michalowski, Helen, 25n9
Michaud, Jean-Paul, 16n81
Middleton, J. Richard, 176n58, 177n65, 230n5
Milbank, John, 45n133
Milik, J. T., 20n108, 167n5, 170n26, 171n31, 173n37
Milikowsky, Chaim, 152n41, 153n47
Miller, Merrill P., 12n52, n53, 12n57, 13n59, n61, n67, 14n73, 20n108, 94n11
Miller Jr., Patrick D., 51n2, 62n92
Miller, Robert J., 4n5, 71n1, 76n37, 81n69
Miller, J. Maxwell, 176n58
Minear, Paul S., 120n18, 201n28
Miner, Daniel F., 20n108
Miscall, Peter, 7n21
Mitchell, H. G., 59n71
Moe, Olaf, 192n157
Moll, Sebastian, 66n130, n131
Montefiore, C. G., 203n41
Montgomery, William, 88n110, 94n10
Moo, Douglas J., 107n85, 109n100
Moore, Kevin L., 29n30,
Moule, C. F. D., 23n1, 37n81, 95n15, 106n75
Mowinckel, Sigmund, 98n25, n26, 99n31, 100n38, 190n144
Müller, Karlheinz, 169n21
Murmelstein, B., 181n86, 189n140, 190n144
Murray, David, 67n132

Nadler, Allan, 34n59
Naude, J. A., 57n58
Neander, Augustus Wilhelm, 192n158
Neill, Stephen, 3n2
Neirynck, Frans, 9n33, 16n81, 113n16, 120n47, 138n94
Nelson-Pallmeyer, Jack, 69n151, 212n99
Neville, David J., 45n132, n134, 45n136, 46n141, 47n154, 88n113
Neufeld, Thomas R. Yoder, 38n85, 78n55, 83n82
Neugebauer, Fritz, 108n91
Neusner, Jacob, 4n4, 94n11, 98n25, 104n60, n61, n62, 128n21, 145n1, 171n29, 211n90, 214n118
Newsom, Carol A., 179n73
Neyrey, Jerome, 217n144
Nickelsburg, George W. E., 134n68, 145n1, 146n13, 147n15, 150n33, 151n36, n37, n38, n39, 162n104, n105, n106, 163n107, 164n118, 165n121, 167n1, 169n15, 170n23, n24, n28, 171n30, 173n38, n39, 174n45, n49, n50, n51, 175n54, 181n87, 189n141
Niditch, Susan, 57n55
Niebuhr, Karl Wilhelm, 121n51
Niebuhr, Reinhold, 24n8
Nineham, Dennis E., 8n31, 59n76
Niskanen, Paul, 175n57
Nolland, John, 203n43
Norlan, Dennis A., 8n31
North, Christopher Richard, 147n15
North, Robert G., 20n107
Novakovic, Linda, 121n50
Novenson, Matthew V., 99n31, 107n87, 108n98, 109n103

O'Connor, Jerome Murphy, 181n91, 184n99
O'Neill, J. C., 129n42, 130n43, 174n44
Oegema, Gerbern S., 94n10, 98n25, 103n57, n58, 104n60, 145n1, 173n37, n38
Oesterley, W. O. E., 99n31
Öhler, Markus, 88n111
Olshausen, Hermann, 192n159
Olson, Daniel C., 171n31, n32, n33, n34
Orlov, Andrei A., 163n108
Osborn, R. T., 5n9,
Osburn, Carroll D., 162n103
Otto, Rudolf, 76n39, 197n2
Owen, Paul L., 139n107, 147n16

Page, Sydney H. T., 136n82
Paget, James Carleton, 98n25, 109n103
Pappas, Harry S., 152n41, 153n46
Parker, Rebecca 42n109
Parrish, John, 14n72
Parry, Donald W., 120n46
Pate, C. Marvin, 181n88
Patterson, Stephen J., 26n12, n13, 71n1, 76n41, 84n83
Pearson, Birger A., 131n54
Pedersen, Johs, 171n31, 173n38
Penchanksy, David, 51n2, 212n99
Peppard, Michael, 219n155
Percy, Ernst, 116n29
Perrin, Nicholas, 208n80
Perrin, Norman, 5n10, 26n15, 27n21, 131n56, 139n108, 190n146, 197n2, 198n7
Pesch, Rudolf, 106n71
Peterson, Jeffrey, 10n41
Piper, John, 210n86, n89, 211n89, 216n139, 225n203
Piper, Ronald A., 113n16, 138n93, 149n28, 154n49, 156n67, 200n17, 201n25, 210n84
Pippin, Tina, 23n1
Pitre, Brant, 80n64
Plummer, Alfred, 191n150
Poirer, John C., 10n41
Pokorný, Petr, 72n6, 96n16
Polag, Athanasius, 113n16, 130n53, 132n60
Polkow, Dennis 4n8, 5n14
Pomykala, Kenneth, 98n25, 104n60
Porter, Joshua Roy, 108n91
Porter, Matthew, 21n115, 24n8
Porter, Stanley E., 3n2, 4n7, 38n84, 82n76, 109n101
Powelson, Mark, 8n30
Priest, John F., 103n54
Prior, Michael, 65n128
Prothero, Stephen, 34n59
Puech, Émile, 19n104, 20n108, 113n15, 119n42, 120n46, n47

Randlinger, Stephan, 211n89
Rauser, Randal, 51n2
Rawlinson, A. E. J., 190n149
Reed, Jonathan L., 47n151
Reed, Annette Yoshiko, 164n116
Reese, Günter, 169n21
Regev, Eyal, 173n42, 175n53
Reid, Barbara, 46n142
Reinhold, Wolfgang, 106n75
Reiser, Marius, 73, 74n17, n23, n27, 75n29, 78n52, n54, 131n54, 152n42, 174n48, 214n121, 216n136
Reitzenstein, Richard, 189n140, 190n144
Rhoads, David M., 42n112, 43n121
Richard, Earl, 107n87
Richards, Kent H., 4n8
Richardson, N. Neil, 103n54, 220n165
Riches, David, 52n3
Riches, John K., 47n152, 77n50, 229n1
Riesenfeld, Harald, 201n21
Riegert, Ray, 8n30
Riesner, Rainer, 120n47, 121n51
Riggs, Ann, 49n160
Ringe, Sharon H., 21n113
Ringgren, Helmer, 87n106

Robbins, Keith, 25n11
Roberts, J. J. M., 99n29
Robinson, James M., 7n22, 8n26, 8n29, 16n80, 19n103, n104, 95n14, 113n16, 114n19, 115n25, 116n26, n27, 117n31, 118n36, 121n48, 123n62, 131n56, 133n67, 135n76, 138n95, 143n123, 154n50, 199n14, n17, 200n17, 201n26, n28, 204n51, 206n67, 207n68, n69, n72, n73, n74
Robinson, John A. T., 184n99, 198n6
Rodd, Cyril, 59n76
Rodriguez, Rafael, 4n6, n7, 6n16
Rogers, Jack B., 69n150
Rogers, Max Gray, 62n93
Rogerson, John W., 108n91
Rollmann, Hans, 129n41
Ropes, J. H., 9n32
Rost, Leonard, 87n104
Rowland, Christopher C., 82n76, 146n14, 167n1, 215n127
Rowlett, Lori L., 58n67
Rubio, Fernando Bermejo, 3n2
Russell, David S., 75n27

Sacchi, Paolo, 145n1, n3, 163n111, 171n29
Salomonsen, Børge, 37n78
Sanday, William, 128n21
Sander, Emilie T., 87n106
Sanders, E. P., 3n1, 4n8, 5n9, 5n10, 9n32, 39n88, 79n56, 80n65, 85n92, 88n112, 94n10, 96n17, 104n61, 131n54, 197n3, 198n9, 229n3
Sanders, James A., 17n92, 20n105, 20n108, 21n115, 213n109, 217n144
Sanders, Jack T., 5n14
Sanders, John, 65n127
Sandmel, Samuel, 93n2, 94n8
Sato, Migaku, 113n16, 114n19, 141n115, 202n31
Sawyer, John F. A., 176n58
Schäfer, Peter, 3n4
Scharper, Philip J., 48n158
Schatzmann, Siegfried S., 106n75
Schiffman, Lawrence H., 19n104, 87n104, 103n54, n56, n58, 113n15, 119n42, 120n46, 162n106, 220n165
Schipper, Jeremy, 29n30
Schlabach, Theron F., 25n11
Schlatter, Adolf, 78n51, 95n15, 217n144
Schlosser, Jacques, 152n44, 154n50, 223n191
Schmid, Josef, 201n21
Schmidt, Daryl, 150n34
Schmidt, Nathaniel, 132n57, 134n70, 135n75
Schmidt, Werner H., 176n59
Schnackenburg, Rudolf, 157n74, 197n2
Schnedermann, Georg, 192n159
Schneemelcher, Wilhelm, 81n71
Schniewind, Julius, 203n39
Schochet, Jacob Immanuel, 93n2
Schodde, George H., 169n19
Scholem, Gershom, 99n31, 108n97
Schottroff, Luise 44n122, 49n162, 157n75, 214n121
Schubert, Kurt, 215n125
Schulz, Siegfried, 78n51, 111n4, 143n123, 153n46, 154n49, n50, 157n76, 200n17, 202n29, 207n70
Schürmann, Heinz, 78n51, 113n16, 134n67, 138n94, 156n64, 207n70
Schrage, Wolfgang, 44n122
Scroggs, Robin, 173n38, 177n64, n67, 180n84, 181n88, 188n135, 189n137, n142, 190n147
Schröter, Jens, 4n8, 6n16, 6n17, 7n22
Schwager, Raymund, 53n12
Schwartz, Daniel R., 42n112
Schwartz, Regina M., 51n2, 52n8, 212n99
Schwarz, Günther, 152n41
Schweitzer, Albert, 88n110, 94n10, 95n15, 128n21, 186n110, 197n2, 198n5, 228n214

Schweizer, Eduard, 125n2, 138n98, 154n49, 200n18, 203n42
Schwemer, Anna Maria, 129n41
Scott, E. F., 76n39
Scott, James M., 99n31, 218n153, 219n155
Scott, Steven R., 147n16
Seeley, David, 126n7
Segal, Alan, 180n82
Segovia, Fernando F., 7n20
Seibert, Eric, 51n2, 56n49, 64n115, n116, 68n147, 69n151, n153, 70n153, 85n93, 212n99
Seitz, Otto J. F., 43n122, 211n89
Sekeles, Eliezer, 105n69
Sevenich-Baz, Elisabeth, 114n19, 123n62
Sharman, Henry Burton, 76n39
Sharp, Eugene, 25n9
Shepherd, David, 139n107
Sherwood, Yvonne, 51n2
Shimoff, Sandra R., 178n72
Short, William J., 145n3
Sider, E. Morris, 23n1, 28n27
Sigal, Philip, 103n54, n56, 220n165
Sjöberg, Erik, 128n21, 130n45
Skeat, Theodore C., 199n17, 200n17
Slater, Thomas B., 145n3
Sloan, Robert B., 21n113
Smalley, Stephen S., 112n5, 162n103
Smallwood, E. Mary, 42n112
Smart, Ninian, 53n17
Smend, Rudolf, 62n93
Smith, Daniel A., 115n24
Smith, Dennis E., 12n55
Smith, J. M. P., 59n71
Smith, Mahlon H., 4n5, 138n98
Smith, Morton, 103n56, 104n61, 215n125, 220n165
Snaith, Norman, 176n58
Socknat, Paul, 25n11
Soiron, Thaddaeus, 201n21
Son, Sang-Won, 186n111, 187n115, 188n131
Sparks, Kenton, 56n50
Spong, John Shelby, 68n139
Sprinkle, Preston, 39n86
Squires, John T., 47n154, 54n19, n20
Staerk, Willi, 189n140, 190n144
Stalker, Davis, 63n108
Stanley, Christopher D., 54n22, n23
Stanton, Graham N., 16n83, 93n1, 112n5, 114n20, 116n30, 118n37, n38
Stanton, Vincent Henry, 192n159
Starcky, Jean, 102n49
Stark, Rodney, 52n4
Steenburg, David, 181n90, 183n94
Stegemann, Ekkehard, 104n62
Stegemann, Wolfgang, 157n75
Stein, Robert, 95n15
Stephens, Walter, 52n7
Stern, Jessica, 52n10
Stern, Philip D., 57n58
Stewart, Robert B., 5n9, 69n150
Stolz, Fritz, 62n93
Stone, Michael E., 145n1, n2, 164n114, 180n81
Stoner, John K., 28n27
Storr, Gottlob Christian, 192n159
Stowers, Stanley K., 184n99
Strack, Hermann, 3n4
Strecker, Georg, 9n33, 81n71, 207n70
Steely, John E., 94n11
Strawn, Brent A., 121n50
Strecker, Georg, 200n20
Streeter, B. H., 9n35, 112n12, 113n16
Strenski, Ivan, 53n17
Stroumsa, Guy G., 229n1
Strugnell, John T., 179n75
Stuhlmacher, Peter, 18n95, 18n100, 95n15, 96n16, 120n47, 121n51, 136n82
Suggs, M. Jack, 149n27
Sugirtharajah, R. S., 60n82

Sullivan, Clayton, 76n39
Sumney, Jerry L., 125n1
Sutcliffe, Edmund F., 215n129
Suter, David W., 145n1
Swartley, Willard M., 29n29, 45n130, n131, 48n155, 49n159, n161, n162

Tabor, James D., 19n104, 113n15, 119n42, 120n45, n46, 121n50, n51
Talbert, Charles H., 23n1, 184n99
Talmon, Shermaryahu, 102n51, 103n56
Tannehill, Robert C., 200n17
Taussig, Hal, 19n103
Taylor, Vincent, 96n16, 125n4, 128n21, 190n149
Tedeschi, James T., 52n3
Teeple, Howard M., 205n53
Teichmann, Jenny, 25n11
Telford, William, 126n7
Thatcher, Adrian, 51n2
Theisohn, Johannes, 161n95
Theissen, Gerd, 3n3, 5n10, 5n14, 7n22, 39n86, 41n102, 44n129, 72n3, n6, 73n14, 77n49, 93n1, 96n15, 106n71, 131n54, 139n104, 143n124, 224n201
Thiselton, Anthony C., 60n80
Tholuck, Augustus, 192n159
Thomas, Heath A., 58n68
Thompson, George H. P., 134n68
Thomson, Jeremy, 28n27
Thoreau, Henry David, 25n9
Thrall, Margaret E., 191n149
Tigchelaar, Eibert, 162n106
Tiller, Patrick A., 167n3, n6, n7, 168n12, 169n16, 170n25, n27, 173n36, n42, 174n49, n50
Tödt, Heinz Eduard, 111n4, 134n71, 135n76, 140n108
Toepel, Alexander, 180n81
Trible, Phyllis, 51n2, 212n99
Tromp, Johannes, 180n81
Tuckett, Christopher M., 8n28, 8n31, 9n37, 19n101, n102, 95n14, 96n16, 111n2, 117n36, 122n52, n55, n56, n57, 128n21, 131n54, 138n92, 143n123, 143n125, 149n25, n28, 158n79, 201n26, 202n36, 206n61, 207n70, 208n75

Ulrich, Eugene, 120n46, n47
Uro, Risto, 144n126

Vaage, Leif E., 111n2, n4, 113n16, 138n95, 203n42, 204n51
Van der Woude, Adam S., 20n108
Van Henten, Jan Willem, 48n154, 162n103
Van Iersel, Bas M. F., 224n200
Van Seters, John, 7n21
Van Unnik, W. C., 211n89
VanderKam, James C., 20n107, 87n104, 120n47, 151n38, n39, 162n106, 163n109, n112, 164n118, n119, 167n1, 169n15, 170n22, n23, n24, 174n45, n49, n50, n51, 175n54, 181n87, 189n141
Vassiliadis, Petros, 8n31, 113n16
Vellanickal, Matthew, 219n155
Veryheyden, Joseph, 135n76
Vermes, Geza, 19n104, 87n104, 95n13, 103n55, n57, 113n15, 119n42, 120n46, 132n58, n59, 178n68, n70, 190n146, 208n80, 220n159
Vielhauer, Philip, 81n71, 88n108, 131n56, 133n67, 139n108
Vögtle, Anton, 191n149
Volf, Miroslav, 49n160
Von Harnack, Adolf, 66n130, 113n16, 129n41
Von Hase, Karl, 192n159, 224n200
Von Rad, Gerhard, 63n108, 176n59

Waddell, James A., 160n88, n89, 191n149
Wagner, J. Ross, 109n101
Walck, Leslie W., 148n24, 161n99, 162n101, n102

Waldmann, Michael, 211n89
Walsh, Brian J., 230n5
Walsh, Richard, 7n21
Wanamaker, Charles A., 183n97
Warrior, Robert Allen, 60n82
Watson, David F., 127n20
Watson, Francis, 10n41
Weaver, J. Denny, 41n101, 42n109, 65n127
Weaver, Walter P., 71n1
Webb, Robert L., 116n28, 208n80
Wedderburn, Alexander J. M., 6n16, 108n91, 181n88, 186n109, 189n137, n142, 190n145, n149
Wegenast, Klaus, 17n84
Weippert, Manfred, 63n106
Weiss, Johannes, 95n15, 197n2
Wellhausen, Julius, 59n72, 132n57, 134n70, 135n75
Werntz, Myles, 21n115, 24n8
Wilckens, Ulrich, 181n88
Wildberger, Hans, 176n59
Williams, James G., 53n12
Williams, Joel F., 126n5
Williams, Michael J., 67n132
Wills, Garry, 17n93
Wills, Lawrence M., 16n83
Wilson, M. K., 52n3
Wilson, Robert Smith, 56n51
Wink, Walter, 36n76, 44n125, n126, n127, 45n131, 51n2, 125n2, 135n74, 212n99
Winn, Albert Curry, 24n6
Winter, Dagmar, 5n10, 39n86, 41n102
Wise, Michael O., 19n104, 113n15, 119n42, 120n45, n46, n47, 121n50, n51, 178n71
Witherington III, Ben, 4n5, 39n88, 69n150, 71n1, 75, 76n34, n37, 95n15, 96n19, 128n21, 148n21, 223n190
Wittichen, Carl, 192n159
Wolters, Al, 230n5
Woolf, Bertram L., 76n39
Wrede, William, 94n10, 126n9, 127n19, 128n22, 129n41
Wrege, Hans-Theo, 200n17
Wright, Christopher J. H., 57n52, 61n86
Wright, N. T., 3n2,3n3, 5n9, 26n13, 27n17, 41n103, 42, 70, 71n1, 80n62, 87n101, 95n15, 97, 106n71, 109n101, 153n46, 171n29, 181n88, 182n91, 184n102, 198n6, 225n204

Yadin, Yigael, 20n108, 215n125
Yoder, John Howard, 21n115, 24n8, 33n55, 40n92
Younger, K. Lawson, 57n55

Zager, Werner, 129n41
Zehnder, Markus, 51n2
Zeller, Dieter, 113n16, 115n23, 154n49, 200n18, 201n26, 201n28
Zerbe, Gordon, 214n121
Zetterholm, Magnus, 98n25, 107n85, 109n100
Zias, Joseph, 105n69
Ziesler, John A., 181n91
Zimmermann, Johannes, 121n50
Zuckerman, Phil, 52n6
Zugibe, Frederick T., 105n69

Index of Ancient Sources

Hebrew Bible/Old Testament

Genesis
1-3......229
1:24-30......180n86
1:26......179, 182
1:26-27......33, 182
1:26-28......175n57
1:26-30......217n144
1:27......175n56, 180n86, 182, 211n91
1:27b......175n57
1:31......230n4
2......204
2-3......203
2:7......185n106
2:15......185n106
2:17......217n144
2:18......185n106
3:5......183, 217n144
3:6......217n144
3:7......217n144
3:17-19......204
3:17-21......204
4:3-5......55n37
5:1-2......211n91
6:2......220n160
6:4......220n160
6:5-7......55n25
7:21-23......55n25
9:6......211n91
12:10-20......55n33
12:17......55n25
15:9......55n25
15:17-21......211n92
18:21......155n53
19:24......55n25
20:1-18......55n33
22......137
22:17......211n92
22:18......171
26:4......171
27:1-29......55n34
27:14......171
49:10......99n36, 100n42, 103

Exodus
2:11-15......55n35
3:8......212n103
3:17......212n103
4:22......220n161
4:24-26......55n25
12:12......55n25
12:29......55n38
13:5......212n103
14......55n39
14-17......211n93
14:4-28......55n25
14:30......212n105
15:1-3a......212n105
15:3......55n46
15:4a......212n105
17:10-13......211n93
20:12......107n82
21:15......55n25, n28
21:17......55n25, n28
22:23......55n25
23:4-5......213n110, 214n121
23:22-30......212n98
23:23......212n103
25:9......179n76
25:40......179n76
31:14......55n25
32:27-28......55n25
33:2......212n103
34:6......213n112
34:11......212n103
35:2-3......55n25

Leviticus
4:3......99n28, n29
4:5......99n28, n29
4:16......99n28, n29
6:15......99n29
16:15......99n28
18:22......55n29
18:24......212n104
19:1-2......206n64
19:17-18......213n111
19:18......205, 213n110
19:34......211n91
20:9......212n99
20:9-10......55n25
20:10......212n99
20:11......55n29
20:12......55n29
20:13......55n25, n29, 212n99
20:15-16......55n29
20:27......55n25, 212n99
24:14......55n31
24:16......212n99
24:16-17......55n25
24:17......212n99
25......20
25:10......20n106
26:5......94n7
26:7-8......212n106
26:14-28......212n99

Numbers
3:4......55n25
6:15......212n99
11:1-2......55n25
13:12-16......212n99
14:12......55n25
14:36-37......55n25
15:32-36......55n25, n32
16:31-33......55n25
18:20......212n99
19:18-19......212n99
21:14......55n46
21:18-21......212n99
21:34-35......55n25, 211n94
24:17......99n36, 100n43
25:1-5......55n25
25:6-9......55n25
27:1-11......60n81
31:1-54......55n25, 211n95
33:50-56......212n100

Deuteronomy
2:33-36......55n25, 212n96
4:3......55n25, 212n96
4:16-18......179n76
6:13......205n59
6:15......55n25
6:16......205n60
7:1-2......55n25, 212n100
7:17-25......212n101
8:3......185n106, 205n58
13:2-6......107n84
13:6-11......55n30
13:12-16......55n25
13:12-18......64n109
14:1......220n162
15......20, 20n106
18:12......213n116
18:15-18......205n57
18:15-22......107n84
18:20......55n25
19:18-19......55n25
20:1-20......64n109
20:16......212n102
20:17......212n103
21:18-21......55n25, 107n82
22:1-4......214n121
32:8......220n160
32:43......220n160

Joshua
6-11......56, 58
6:1-27......62n109
6:21......56n48
8:1-29......62n109
9:1......212n103
10-11......62n109

10:40......56n48
12:8......212n103
15:8......155n53
18:16......155n53

Judges
3:5......212n103
8:30......55n26

1 Samuel
2:10......99n29
2:30......78n53
2:35......99n29
12:3......99n29
12:5......99n29
15:1-23......62n109
16:16......99n29
18:17......55n46
24:6......99n28
24:7......99n29
24:10......99n28
24:11......99n29
24:16......99n29
24:23......99n29
25:28......55n46
26:16......99n28
30:26......55n46

2 Samuel
1:14......99n28, n29
1:16......99n28, n29
5:13......55n26
7:11-16......99n32, 103n56
7:13-14......100n44
7:14......113n13, 220n163, n165
11......55n36
19:22......99n29
22:51......99n29
23:1......99n29

1 Kings
11:3......55n26
11:7......155n53
19:16......99n28

2 Kings
7:14......220n164
16:3......155n53
21:6......155n53

1 Chronicles
16:22......99n29
17:13......113n13

2 Chronicles
6:42......99n29
24:20......78n53
28:3......155n53

Ezra
6:14......102n47

Nehemiah
11:30......155n53

Job
1:6......220n160
2:1......220n160
2:14......177n64
38:7......220n160

Psalms
2......99, 220n165, 221n169
2:2......99n29, 103n56
2:7......99n33, 103n56, 113n13, 137
8:5-6......176
18:45-48a......212n105
18:51......99n29
20:7......99n29
24:1......32n49
28:8......99n29
29:1......220n160
72......99
72:1-7......113n13
72:2-14......99n36
82:6......220n160
84:10......99n29
89:7......220n160

89:20-38......99n32
89:26......113n13
89:26-27......220n165
89:39......99n29
89:52......99n29
105:15......99n28, n29
110......99
110:4......99n34
117:2......118
118:26......113n14, 115
132:10......99n29
132:17......99n29
139:19-22......215n124
145:8-9......213n113
146......121

Proverbs
1:7......158n82
2:4......201n23
3:7......157n77
6:6......202
7:1......157n77
8......60n81
8:22-26......146n11
9:10-11......158n82
14:6......201n23
14:26-27......158n82
15:14......201n23
18:15......201n23
20:22......213n111
24:17......213n111
24:19......213n111
24:21......157n77
25:21-22......213n111
31:10-31......60n81

Ecclesiastes
5:6......157n77
7:25......201n23

Song of Songs......60n81

Isaiah
1:16-17......60n80
2:4......93n6, 214n117, 229n1
9:13-17......55n44
10:34-11:5......99n36
11......218
11:1-4......100
11:6-9......93n6, 100, 229
11:10......101n45
11:11-12......93n3
11:12......101n46
11:16......93n3
13:13......74n26
24:1-6......55n44
25:8......93n5
25:9-10......212n105
26......118
29:18......19
30:27-28......55n43
34:2-3......55n46
34:8......74n26
35:5......118
35:5-6......19, 93n4
40-55......147n15
40:9......18n99
42:1......137, 147n15
42:1-7......147n15
42:6......147n15
44:29......102n47
45:1......31n39, 100, 212n107
45:7......55n45
45:13......101n47
49:1-6......147n15
49:6......147n15
50:4-9......147n15
52:7......18, 18n99, 21, 21n112
52:13-53:12......147n15
53:6......135n77, 137n85
53:12......29, 137n86
60:21......93n4
61......118, 121, 122
61:1......18, 18n99, 19, 20n109, 121
61:1-2......21, 21n112, 122
61:1-12......99n28
63:1-6......55n46

65-66......74
65:25......93n6

Jeremiah
3:8......129n42
4:10......55n42
7:31......155n53
19:4-5......155n53
32:35......155n53
34......213n108
46:10......74n26
50:20......93n4

Lamentations
4:20......99n29

Ezekiel
7:19......74n26
7:27......78n53
18:23......213n114
34:12......74n26
36......213n108
37:23......93n4

Daniel
3:25......220n160
7......175, 231
7:13......124, 132, 134, 140, 146, 220
9:25-26......21n112, 99n29, 102
9:26......102

Hosea
2:14......213n109
2:20......93n6

Joel
2:2......74n26
3:1......99n28
4:18......94n7

Amos
3:6......55n45
5:10-12......60n80

Jonah
4:2......213n111

Micah
1:2-3......55n41
4:3......93n6, 214n117
4:8......129n42
7:5-6......23n2, 26

Habakkuk
3:13......99n29

Zephaniah
1:15......74n26
1:18......74n26
2:2......74n26
2:3......74n26
3:13......93n4
13:2......93n4

Zechariah
1:16......102n47
9:9-10......227n212
9:10......93n6

Malachi
3:2......74n26
3:7......78n53
3:19......93n4

New Testament
Q
3......77, 221n169
3-7......19, 114
3:2b-7:35......114
3:7-9......141, 142
3:8......86, 117n34, 142, 227n209
3:9......141, 155n58
3:12......77n45
3:16b......77n46, 138n91, 140
3:16b-17......115, 142
3:17......141, 155n59
3:21b-22......115, 117
3:22......111n8, 217, 224

4......34n58, 47
4:1-13......115, 117, 149n25
4:3......111n8, 217, 224
4:4......205n58
4:5......111n11
4:5-8......116, 117n34, 227n209
4:8......205n59, 207n70
4:9......111n8, 217, 224
4:12......205n60, 207n70
6:20......198n13, 199
6:20-49......15, 86, 115, 117, 204
6:20-23......117n34, 148, 198n10, 227n209
6:20......21, 86
6:22......111n10
6:22-23......140n108, 149n25
6:23......138n93, 206, 226
6:23c......142
6:27......70, 86, 205, 206, 210n89, 214, 216, 226, 228
6:27-28......44, 86n96, 117n34, 158n83, 226n207, 227n209
6:27-35......216
6:27-35c-d......225
6:27-36......216
6:28......86, 206, 226
6:29......226, 227
6:29-30......226
6:30......206, 227
6:31......86, 206, 227
6:32-34......86, 117n34, 227n209
6:35c-d......72n5, 85, 86n96, 158n83, 216n138, 224
6:36......86, 206n63, 224, 227
6:37......77, 206, 227
6:37-42......156n67
6:37-38......158n83, 226
6:40......149n25, 206, 207, 227
6:42......206, 227
6:43-45......156n67
6:46......206, 207, 207n70, 208, 209, 210, 227, 228
6:46-47......208
6:47......206, 227
6:47-49......209
6:48......208
7:6......207n70
7:9......117n34, 227n209
7:18-22......117, 119
7:18-23......117n36, 123
7:19......138n91, 140
7:22......18n97, 19, 21, 86, 111n7, 113, 115, 117n34, 118, 119n43, 120, 121, 122......128, 227n209
7:22-23......73n13, 123, 140, 141
7:23......115, 122, 123
7:28......198n13, 199
7:31......123n59
7:31-35......142n116
7:33-34......72n6
7:34......111n10, 133n62, 138n93, 140n108, n109, 141, 149
7:35......149n25
9:58......138n93, 140n108, 141, 149n25
9:59......207n70
9:62......198n12
10:1-12......29
10:2......207n70
10:3......143n116, 226
10:4......226
10:5-6......27n18
10:5-9......198n13
10:9......199
10:10-12......143n116
10:12......72n4
10:13......72n4
10:13-15......143n116
10:14......72n4, 143n116
10:15......72n4
10:21......207n70, 224n199
10:22......111n9, 123, 217n143, 224n199
10:23b-24......217n142
10:24......123, 149
11:2......198n10, n11, 224
11:2b......141, 224n197

11:2b-4......198n13, n15
11:4......21n114
11:9-13......156n67
11:16......142n116
11:20......107n81, 140, 141, 198n13, 199
11:29......72n4
11:29-30......142n116, 224n198
11:29-32......123n59
11:30......138n93
11:31-32......142n116
11:32......72n4
11:39b......142n116, 143n122
11:42......142n116, 143n122
11:43-44......142n116, 143n122
11:46b......142n116
11:47-51......142
11:49-51......71n2, 142n116
11:50-51......72n4
11:51......123n59
11:52......142n116, 198n13, 199
12:2-3......117n34, 155, 227n209
12:2-9......159
12:2-12......156
12:4-5......152, 153, 154, 155, 156, 157, 158, 159
12:4-6......156
12:4-7......156, 157
12:5......158
12:6-7......156, 158, 159
12:8......138n93
12:8-9......86n100, 150, 156
12:10......133n62, 138n93, 140n108, 150, 156
12:11-12......156
12:22-31......83, 156n67, 157, 202, 203
12:22b......199
12:22b-31......199n17, 201, 202, 204
12:25......199
12:27......200n17
12:29-31......198n12
12:31......198n13, 199, 201, 202, 203
12:39......140n111
12:39-40......139n103, 142n116
12:40......71n2, 138n93, 149
12:42......207n70
12:42-46......138n103, 142n116
12:43......207n70
12:45......207n70
12:46......207n70
12:49......26n12, 140n112
12:51......23n2, 26, 35, 140n113
12:51-53......26n12, n14, n15, 107n82
12:53......141n114
13:18-19......117n34, 198n13, 199, 227n209
13:20-21......117n34, 198n13, 199, 227n209
13:25......207n70
13:28......72n4, 141
13:28-29......198n10, n13, n15
13:29......142n116
13:30......117n34, 227n209
13:34-35......72n4, 141, 142n116, 208
13:35......138n91, 207n70
14:11......117n34, 227n209
14:16-18......86, 117n34, 227n209
14:21......86, 207n70
14:23......86
14:26......107n82, 117n34, 227n209
14:27......149n25
15:4-5a......86
15:7......86
15:8-10......86
16:13......207n70
16:16......27, 27n22, 31n45, 88n112, 198n13, 199
16:18......117n34, 227n209
17:3-4......86, 226
17:20-21......140n110, 198n13, 199
17:21......84, 141
17:23-24......138n93, 142n116
17:23-24:37......139n103
17:24......150, 151
17:26......72n3, n4, 142n116, 150
17:26-27......71n2, 139n103, 151

17:26-30......138n93
17:28-29......140n108
17:30......151
17:33......117n34, 227n209
17:34......21
19:15......207n70
19:16......207n70
19:18......207n70
19:20......207n70
21:27......139n103
22:28......142n116
22:28-30......72n4, 141
22:30......111n11, 142n116

Matthew
4:23......18n98
5:22......155n57
5:29......155n57
5:20......155n57
5:38-48......43, 45n129
5:39......44
5:43-44......214n123
6:10......198n9
6:24......33n54
6:28......200n17
7:21......198n8
7:21-23......208
8:11-12......199n15
8:28-34......41n108
9:8......135n73
9:25......18n98
9:34......107n81
10:4......24n5
10:5-14......29
10:7......198n10
10:23......71n2, 162n102, 198n10
10:25......107n81
10:28......154, 155n57
10:34......26, 26n12, n14, 35
10:36......26
11:2......120
11:11-18......107n83
11:12-13......31n45
11:19......107n82
12:29......164
13:24-30......228n213
13:30......225n205
13:36-43......161n96, n97, n98, n99, 228n213
13:40-43......62n95
13:41......162n102
13:43......161n99
13:47-50......228n213
16:13-19......164
16:15-17......222n189
16:18......208
16:24-28......161n96
16:27......161n97, 162n102
16:28......162n102, 198n10
17:24-27......31n42
18:9......155n57
18:23-35......228n213
19:10-12......107n82
19:28......161n96, n97, n100, 162n102
20:1-15......86n98
21:1-11......37n79
21:12-13......38n82
21:18-22......41n108
21:33-46......228n213
22:1-14......228n213
22:15-22......30n36
22:21......30n34
23:15......155n57
23:26......199n14
23:33......155n57
24:14......18n98
24:30......161n96, n97
24:30-31......161n98, 162n102
24:45-51......228n213
25:13......71n2
25:14-30......228n213
25:31......161n97, n100
25:31-32......162n102
25:31-45......161n96
25:31-46......161n98, n99, 228n213
25:34......161n99
25:36......161n99

25:41......62n95
26:52......29n31, 45, 227n210, n211
27:62-64......107n84

Mark
1:1......18n94, 113n13, 129n33, 222n184, n185
1:4......77n48
1:9-11......137n87
1:11......221n169
1:14......18n96
1:15......198n10
1:23-25......127n13, n16
1:34......127n13, n16
1:43-45......126n12, 127n16
1:45......128n23
2:7......107n83
2:10......128n26, 134n69
2:17......128n27
2:24......30n35, 107n80
2:26......30n35
2:27-28......133n62
2:28......128n28, 134n69, 135
3:4......30n35
3:7-12......129n35
3:11-12......127n13, n16
3:17......24n4
3:18......24n5
3:22......107n81
3:27......128n29
3:31-35......107n82
4:10-12......127n18
4:34......127n18
5:1-20......41n108
5:6......127n13, n16
5:43......126n12, 127n16
6:7-13......29
6:18, 30n35
7:1-4......107n80
7:17-23......127n18
7:24......107n17, 128n23
7:35......126n12
7:36......127n16, 128n23
8......129n36
8:26......126n12, 127n16
8:29......127n15, 129n34, 135
8:30......126n10, 222n188
8:31......127n18, 135
8:31-33......128n30
8:32......135
8:33......135
8:38......137n88
9:1......71n2, 198n10
9:7......222n185
9:9......126n11, 135
9:11-13......26n15, 133n62
9:20......127n13, n16
9:28-29......127n18
9:30......127n17
9:31......127n18, 135
9:31-32......128n30, 135
9:33-35......127n18
9:43......155n57
9:44......155n57
9:45......155n57
9:46......155n57
9:47......155n57, 198n8
9:48......155n57
9:43-48......155n57
10:2......30n35
10:17-22......198n8
10:29-30......107n82
10:32-34......128n30
10:33......136n78
10:33-34......127n18, 135
10:45......133n62, 136n81, n82
10:47......127n14
10:48......125n1
11:1-10......37n79
11:9-10......113n14
11:10......125n1
11:12-14......41n108
11:15-17......38n82
11:20-25......41n108
12:12......128n24
12:17......30n34
12:13-18......30n36

12:18-27......107n82
12:24......179n79
12:35-37......125n1
13:3-37......127n18
13:12......107n82
13:26......137n89
13:30......71n2, 76, 76n37, 198n10
13:32......76n37
14:3-9......129n37
14:21......133n62, 136n79
14:22-25......128n30
14:25......198n9
14:33......222n187
14:36......223n194
14:41......136n80
14:53-65......129n36
14:61......113n13, 222n186
14:61-62......113n14
14:62......137n90
14:64......107n83
15:2......106n73
15:7......45n128
15:9......106n74
15:12......106n74
15:16-20......129n38
15:26......32n48, 105n70, 129n39

Luke
1:32-35......220, 221n168
1:35......221n170
1:79......48
2:14......27n18, 48, 227
4......18n99, 21
4:3......217n144
4:5-6......217n144
4:9-11......217n144
4:18......18n97
6:15......24n5, 41n108
6:27-38......45n129
7:50......48
8:26-39......41n108
9:27......198n10
9:59-60......107n82
10:5-6......48
10:9......198n10
10:30-35......86n99
11:2......198n9
11:22......198n9
11:29......198n9
12:5......155n57
12:12-15......37n79
13:1......43n115
13:14......107n80
14:1-6......107n80
15:11-32......86n97
16:13......33n54
18:7-8......71n2
19:42......27n18
19:28-38......113n14
19:28-40......37n79
19:38......48
19:39......107n83
19:42......48
19:45-46......38n82
20:20-26......30n36
20:25......30n34
21:34-36......71n2
22:35-38......26n15, 28n24
22:36......29n31
22:49......28n25
22:51......29n32, 227n210
22:52......28n26
23:1-4......31n46
23:2......33n56
23:19......45n128
23:25......45n128
23:35......217n144
23:37......217n144
23:39......217n144
24:36......27n18, 48

John
1:12......222n177
1:12-13......221n172
1:14......221n170
1:34......222n176
1:49......222n176
2:13......38n83

2:14-15......38n82
3:16-17......221n174
3:18......222n176
5:21-26......222n180
5:25......222n176
6:40......222n180
7:27......130n44
8:16......222n180
8:23......222n178
8:38-42......222n178
9:35......222n176
10:30......222n179
10:36......222n176
11:4......222n176
12:13-15......113n14
12:31......33n53
12:34......113n14
14:6......221n175
14:30......33n53
16:11......33n53
17:1-24......222n181
17:2......222n180
17:5......222n182
17:24......222n182
18:11......29n31, 227n210
18:36......29n33, 33n52, n57
19:7......222n176
20:17......221n173
20:19......27n18
20:21......27n18
20:26......27n18
20:31......222n176, n183

Acts
1:13......41n108
3:17-21......230n5
5:30......107n84
5:37......32n47
5:40......106n79
5:42......22n116
8:4-5......22n116
8:35......22n116
10:39......106n79
11:20......22n116
11:26......109n102
15:29......211n91
17:18......22n116
19:40......45n128
23:10......45n128

Romans
1:1-4......22n116
1:3......109n104
1:3-4......221n171
1:4......106n77
1:11-17......22n116
2:8......225n205
3:24......136n82
5:12-19......181, 188n133
5:21-21......183, 184, 187n114
6:6......185
7:7-11......183
8:2......187n121
8:3......183, 218n152
8:12-17......218n152
8:14-15......223n195
8:14-17......221n172
8:19-23......230n5
8:23......136n82
8:29......187n122
8:29-30......221n172
10:8-17......22n116
12:17......210n85
12:19......225n205
13:1......31n38
14:15......154n52
15:19-20......22n116
16:3......108n95

1 Corinthians
1:18......154n52
1:21-22......108n96
1:23......109n105, 123n58
1:24......108n94
1:30......137n82
10......108n89
11:7......187n118
11:23......137n84

12:13......186n108
15......17, 181
15:1-2......16n83
15:6......12n57
15:20-28......189n139
15:21......186n112
15:21-22......183, 187n115
15:22......187n113
15:27......183
15:45......183, 187n116, 188n127
15:45-49......188n130
15:45a......188
15:45b......188
15:47a......188
15:47b......188
15:47-49......185n105
15:49......188n129
15:49a......188
15:49b......188
16:22......99n28

2 Corinthians
4:4......33n53, 187n118, n124
4:4-6......22n116
4:16......185
5:17......187n117
11:4......22n116

Galatians
1:4......187n119
1:7......22n116
1:22......12n56
1:15-16......187n124
1:16......22n116
2:7-9......22n116
2:17......108n91
2:19......108n92
3:5......183
3:8......186n109
3:13......106n79, 107n84
3:16......108n89
3:26-4:6......219n154
3:27......108n93
3:28......186n108
4:4......183, 187n118
4:6......218n152
4:6-7......224n196

Ephesians
1:5......218n152
1:7-10......230n5
2:2......33n53
2:15-16......185
3:8......22n116
3:16-17......185n106
4:24......185n106
6:1......45n128

Philippians
1:15-18......22n116
2:1-13......184
2:5-11......181, 182, 183, 184, 185
2:6......182n94
2:15......187n120
3:21......188n126

Colossians
1:15......187n124
1:16-20......230n5
3:9-10......185n107
3:11......186n108

1 Thessalonians
5:15......210n85

2 Thessalonians
2:13-14......22n116

2 Timothy
2:8......22n116

James
3:6......155n57
4:12......154

1 Peter
2:13-14......31n38

3:4……185n106
3:9……210n85

2 Peter
1:4……225n202
3:10-13……230n5
3:13……216n137
4:7……62
4:10……62
4:13……62

1 John
5:18-19……33n53

Jude
1:6……164
1:7……165
1:14-15……146n6, 165

Revelation
2:1……216n137
2:5……216n137
2:10……153
19:11-15……65n126
20:9……225n205
20:15……225n205
21:6-7……218n151

Apocrypha
2 Esdras
12.32……129n42

1 Maccabees
1:29-30……102n48

3 Maccabees
6:3……223n192
6:8……223n192

4 Maccabees
13:14-15……158n78

Sirach
4:8……157n77
4:10……219n157
4:11-12……201n23
6:27……201n23
7:31……157n77
17:1……180n86
17:1-14……177n64
21……157n77
23:1……223n192
23:4……223n192
24……149n26
28:2……78n53
49:16……177n64, 180n83, n86
51……201n23
51:10……223n192

Wisdom of Solomon
2.16-18……219n157
6:12……201n23
9:1-3……177n64
11:22-12:2……213n113
14:3……223n192

Old Testament Pseudepigrapha
Apocalypse of Moses
24.4……177n64

Assumption of Moses
10.3……219n156

2 Baruch
14:18……180n86
29:3……129n42, 130n48
29:5……87n107
30:1-2……128n21, 129n42
36-37……87n107
39:7……129n42
51.10……179n79
56.13……164n117
73:1……129n42

1 Enoch
1.9……165
7.1……164n116

8.1......163n113
8.1-2......164
8.3......164n116
9.6......163n113
9.7......164n116
10.4-8......163n113
13.1......164n117
14.5......164n117
15.3-6......163
15.11......163n112
19.1......164n116
26-27......155n54
37-71......130n45
37.1......180n83
38.1......156n60
38.2......148n22
39.6......148n22
40.5......148n22
42.1......149
45.2......156n60
45.2-3......161n92
45.3......146n9, 148n22
45.4......148n22
45.4-5......216n137
45.6......156n60
46......161n96, n97
46.1......146n7
46.2......146n7
46.3......146n7
46.4......146n7
46.1-3......129n42
46.3......149n29
46.4-6......161n93
46.8......149n25
47.1......148n22
47.2......149n25
47.4......148n22, 149n25
48.2......146n7
48.2-8......161n96, n98
48.2-10......113n14
48.3......146n10
48.4......218n148
48.5......218n149
48.6......130n47, 146n10, 148n22
48.6-7......129n42
48.7......146n10, 149n25, n31, 161n91
48.8-9......156n60, 161n93
48.8-10......218n147
48.10......161n93
48.10......146n12
49.1-4......146n11, 161n92
49.2......148n22
49.3......149n32, 218n150
49.4......148n22
51.1......156n60
51.1-3......146n11
51.2-3......161n92
51.3......146n9, 148n22, 149n30
51.5......148n22
52:4......113n14
52.6......148n22
52.9......148n22
53.2......146n12
53.6......148n22
54.1......156n61
54.1-6......155n54
54.3-5......164n117
54.5......156n62
55.4......146n9, 148n22, 161n92
56.1-4......155n54, 164n117
56.3......156n63
56.5-7......146
60.10......149n29
61.5......148n22
61.8......146n9, 148n22, 161n92
61.8-9......161n92
61.10......148n22
62-63......161n96, n97, n98, n99
62......151
62.1......148n22
62.1-2......161n93
62.1-3......161n92
62.2......146n9
62.3......146n9
62.4-5......161n93

62.5......146n8, n9, 149, 161n92, n100, 192n160
62.6-7......130n45
62.7......129n42, 130n47, 146n8, n10
62.9......146n8, 149
62.11......219n156
62.13-15......150
62.13-16......161n99
62.14......146n8
62.15......149n25
63.11......146n8
65.1-67.3......151
67.4-13......146n4
69.11......179n79, 180n83
69.26......146n8
69.26-29......161n97
69.27......146n8, n9, 161n92, n93, n100
69.29......146n8, n9, 161n92, n93, n100, 192n160
70-71......161n96
70.1......146n8
71.9-12......161n94
71.14......146n8, 161n94, 192n160
71.16-17......161n99
71.17......146n8
85-90......167
85.3-89.9......168n11
88.1......164n117
89.10-11......171
90......170, 175, 189
90.9b-12......168n9
90.16......168n9
90.18......170n21
90.19......170n21
90.20......168
90.20-27......172
90.24......168
90.24-27......155n54
90.25......168
90.26......168
90.28-29......168
90.33......168
90.34......168
90.37......170n28, 172
90.37-38......169, 170n21
90.37-38a......170n21, 174n47
90.38......169, 170n28
90.38b......170n21
91.6-7......27n22
91.11......27n22
91.16......216n137
101......157

2 Enoch
30:11......180n86
30:12......177n64, 180n83
33:10......180n83
58.1-2......180n83

3 Enoch
48:10a......129n42

4 Ezra
6:53......177n64
6:53-54......180n83
7.25......216n137
7.28-29......128n21, 129n42
12.31-34......128n21, 129n42
13:26......128n21, 129n42, 130n47
13:32......129n42
13:37......113n14
13:52......113n14, 129n42, 130n46, n47
14:9......129n42

Jubilees
1.24......219n156
1.29......216n137
2.14......180n83, n86
3.26-27......178n72
4.26......216n137
5.6......164n117
8.19......178n72

Joseph and Aseneth
7.2-6......219n157
13.20......219n157

21.3......219n157

Odes of Solomon
41.15......128n21, 129n42

Psalms of Solomon
17......129n42
17:21-32......104n59
17.27......219n156
17.30......219n156
18:5......128n21

Testament of Judah
24.3......219n156

Dead Sea Scrolls
1QS
4.7-8......178
4.22-23......177
4.25......178, 216n137
9......215n128
9.11......101
10.18......215n132
11.7......179n79

1QSa
11-12......103, 220n165

1QM
6.6......198n4
10.4......179n77
10.14......179n77
12.7......198n4

1QH
3.22......179n79
4.15......177
11.12......179n79

1QHa
10.22-22......27n22

4Q521
2 ii 8......12, 19n104, 20, 21

CD
3.20......177n66

4QEn[c]......167n5

4QEn[f]......167n5

4Q405
20 ii-22 1.8......179n76

4Q416
2 iii 9......179n74

4Q417
2 i 10-11......179

4Q418
77......179
77.2......179
2 i 18......179

4QpPs37
111 1-2......177n66

4QFlor......113n13

4Q171......178
2.14-15......27n22
2.18-19......27n22

4Q174......178, 220n165

4Q246......113n13, 150, 220, 221n167

4Q252 (4QPatrBles)
5.3-4......198n4
5.1-7......103

4QEnGiants[a]
8.14......164n117

4Q400
1 ii 1......198n4

1 ii 3......198n4

4Q401
1 4 i 6......198n4

4Q491
11 ii 17......198n4

4Q504
frg. 8, 4-5......177

4Q521
113......120, 121, 122, 198n4
2 ii 1......7-8, 12, 118n41

11QMelch.
2.4......20n110
2.6......20n110
2.9......20n110
2.13......20n110
2.18......103n58
2.18-19......20n112

11QT
29.9......216n137

Philo
De opificio mundi
1.46......180n86
69-71......180n86

Legum allegoriae
1.31-42......180n86

Legatio ad Gaium
29-43......43n116
38.299-305......42n114

Josephus
War
1.33.5.657-58......146n4
2.56......104n63
2.57......104n63
2.60......104n63
2.117-118......32n47
2.135......215n133
2.139-140......31n40
2.140......215n133
2.169......45n129
2.169-174......42n113
2.174......214n120
2.175-177......43n115
2.184-203......43n116
2.197......214n120
2.261-62......104n63
2.433-34......105n65
4.507-534......105n64
5.11.1......105n69
5.447-449......35n60
6.312......105n67
7.29-31......105n64
7.36......105n64
7.153-54......105n64

Jewish Antiquities
17.6.5.171-73......146n4
17.271-72......104n63
17.273......104n63
17.278-85......104n63
18.116-119......77n47
18.4-10......32n47
18.35......45n129
18.55-59......42n113
18.60-62......43n115
18.63......107n84
18.261-309......43n116
20.97-98......104n63
20.169-71......104n63

Contra Apion
2.15......211n91

Rabbinical Literature
Abot
1.5......155n56
5.19......155n56
5.20......155n56

Ber. Rabba
48.11......93n5
98:9......93n3

b. Ber.
17b......219n158
28b......155n56

b. Gittin
56b......3n4
57a......3n4

b. Hul.
86a......219n158

b. Ros. Has.
16b:7a......155n56

b. Sanh.
43a......3n4, 107n84
43b......106n79
56a......211n91
92b......216n137
97b......216n137
107b......3n4

b. Sukk.
52b......129n42

b. Taan.
23b......223n190, n192
24b......219n158

Eliyahu Rabba
4......93n4

Lev. Rabba
17:4......94n7

Mek. Y. on Exod
16:25......216n137

m. Ab.
3:14......220n162

m. Sanh.
7.4-5......107n83

Midrash Hagadol on Gen.
49:11......93n3

Midr. Pss
21.1......129n42

Midr. Num. Rab.
11.2......129n42

Midr. Ruth Rab.
5.6......129n42

Midr. Son Rab.
2.9.3......129n42

Pesiq. Rabati
33.4......93n4

Pesiq. deR. Kahana
8......94n7

Pesiq. R. Kahana, Piska
5.8......129n42
34.2......129n42

Qidd.
4.14......155n56

Qohelet Rabbah
1:8(3) 3n4

Sukkah
52a......93n4

t. Avodah Zara
8.4......211n91

Targ. Ps. 89.27……223n190

Targ. Mal. 2.10……223n190

Tg. Jon. re Jer. 30.21……129n42

Toledot Yeshu……3n4

Tosefta Hullin
2:22f……3n4

Tos. t. Ber.
6.15……155n56

Yal. Shimoni
1.133……93n4

Yal. Shimon
518……129n42
581……129n42
986……129n42

y. Ta'an
4.8……105n66
4.17……105n66

Apostolic Fathers
Barn.
20.1……154n52

2 Clem.
5.4……153

Ignatius, *Eph.*
20.2……191n151

Tertullian, *Against Marcion*
1.6……66n130
1.15.5……66n130
2.12.1……66n130
4.10……191n152

Tertullian, *On Idolatry*
19……39n87

Tertullian, *On the Crown*
11……39n87

Athanasius, *Contra Apollinarium*
1.8……191n153

Gregory of Nazianzus, *Oration*
30……191n154

Irenaeus, *Adv. Haer.*
1.27.2……66n130
3.12.12……66n130
3.22.3……191n156
4.33.4……225n202
5.21.1……191n155

Herm. Sim.
9.26.3……154n52

Hilary, *Commentarius in Matthaeum*
4.12……191n156

Augustine, *Enarratio in Psalmum*
CXLII.3……191n156

Peter Chrysologus, *Sermo*
CXL……191n156

Cyril of Alexandria, *Adversus Nestorium*
1……191n156

Justin, *Apol.*
1.17……30n37
26.5……66n130
58.1……66n130

Justin, *2 Apol.*
5.4……164n116

Justin, *Dial. Trypho*
8……129n42
8.4……130n50

10......129n42
69.7......107n84
110......39n87
110.1......130n50

Hippolytus, *Ref.*
7.29-31......66n130

Origen, *Contra Cels.*
3.28......225n202
8.73......39n87

Origen, *Orat.*
27.13......225n202

Origen, *Homilies on Joshua*
15.3......56n51

Origen, *De Principiis*
2.5......66n130
4.1.8......56n51

Clement of Alexandria, *Protrepticus*
1.8.4......225n202
10-11......39n87

Clement of Alexandria, *Stromata*
2.39.1......66n130

Epiphanius, *Pan.*
42.3.1-2......66n130

Nag Hammadi Codices

Gos. Mary
4.34......185n107
5.3......185n107

Gos. Thom.
100......30n36
106......217n141
111......71n2

P. Oxy. 655......199n17

P. Oxy. 654......217n140

P. Egerton
2......30n36

Classical and Ancient Authors

Tacitus, *Historiae*
5.9.2......43n116
5.13......105n68

Tacitus, *Ann.*
15.44......106n79, 107n84

Seutonius, *Domitian*
10.1......35n60

Seutonius, *Vesp.*
4.5......105n68

Quintillian, *Institutio Oratoria*
9.2.65......35n60

Paulus, *Sententiae*
5.22.1......35n60

Livy, *Ab urbe condita*
30.43.13......35n60